Happy
Summer
Reading
Mary!

DeWitt
&
Silverenia
June, 2011

D1601228

Terms of Inclusion

Terms of Inclusion

Black Intellectuals in
Twentieth-Century Brazil

PAULINA L. ALBERTO

The University of North Carolina Press Chapel Hill

© 2011 The University of North Carolina Press

All rights reserved

Set in Minion Pro and Chaparral

by IBT

Manufactured in the United States of America

The paper in this book meets the guidelines for permanence and durability
of the Committee on Production Guidelines for Book Longevity of the Council
on Library Resources.

The University of North Carolina Press has been a member of the Green Press
Initiative since 2003.

Library of Congress Cataloging-in-Publication Data

Alberto, Paulina L.

   Terms of inclusion : Black intellectuals in twentieth-century Brazil /
Paulina L. Alberto.

      p. cm.

   Includes bibliographical references and index.

   ISBN 978-0-8078-3437-4 (cloth : alk. paper) — ISBN 978-0-8078-7171-3
(pbk. : alk. paper)

   1. Blacks—Brazil—Intellectual life—20th century.   2. Blacks—Social
conditions—20th century.   3. Brazil—Intellectual life—20th century.
4. Brazil—Social conditions—20th century.   5. Brazil—Race relations—
History—20th century.   I. Title.

   F2659.N4A368 2011

   305.5'5208996081—dc22   2010045627

cloth   15 14 13 12 11   5 4 3 2 1
paper   15 14 13 12 11   5 4 3 2 1

A mis padres, con mucho amor

CONTENTS

ILLUSTRATIONS

ACKNOWLEDGMENTS

For funding my research at several stages, I am grateful to the Social Science Research Council, the Josephine de Kármán Foundation, the Department of History of the University of Pennsylvania, and, at the University of Michigan, the Department of History, the Rackham Graduate School, and the Eisenberg Institute for Historical Studies.

During my many years in the University of Pennsylvania's Department of History, I incurred more debts than I can state here. I would like to begin by thanking the outstanding professors who inspired me, as an undergraduate, to become a scholar and a teacher: John Richetti, Peter Stallybrass, Sumathi Ramaswamy, Lynn Hunt, and, above all, Lynn Lees. In graduate school, Nancy Farriss and Ann Farnsworth-Alvear reintroduced me to Latin America, while Lee Cassanelli, Drew Faust, and Sheldon Hackney enriched my understanding of history beyond that region. Steve Feierman taught me that doing history meant striving to understand why people made particular choices in particular circumstances. I am grateful, finally, to the members of my wonderful committee (from Penn and beyond)—Ann Farnsworth-Alvear, Jeremy Adelman, Barbara Savage, and Barbara Weinstein—for their generosity, guidance, and invaluable critiques at an earlier stage of this project. With fond nostalgia, I thank the group of friends and colleagues that made my graduate student years so fun and intellectually exciting: Yanna Yannakakis, Aidan Downey, Lorrin Thomas, Abby McGowan, Deirdre Brill, Gabriela Ramos, Shefali Chandra, Fran Ryan, Jennifer Sessions, Butch Ware, and Eve Buckley, my traveling companion and roommate in Brazil.

I would like to extend warm thanks to Jeremy Adelman, both for taking me on as one of his students and for introducing me to the wonderful community of Latin Americanists at Princeton University (and by extension, their partners), many of whom have become dear friends and admired colleagues: Eduardo Elena, Ashli White, José Antonio Lucero, María Elena García, Meri Clark, Katie Holt, Todd Stevens, Alejandro Hope, and, not least, the man who would become my husband, Jesse Hoffnung-Garskof.

One of the great pleasures of writing this book has been the contact it afforded me with scholars in Brazil. For their warm welcome to Brazil, and their generous advice and guidance at various stages of this project, I would like to thank João Reis, Jeferson Bacelar, Maria Inês Côrtes de Oliveira, Livio Sansone, Angela Lühning, Ricardo Benzaquen de Araújo, Silvia Lara, Hebe Mattos, Flávio Gomes, Tânia Salgado Pimenta, Christiane Santos, Lise Sedrez, Sátiro Nunes, Álvaro Nascimento, John Monteiro, Maria Helena Machado, and Sidney Chalhoub. Special thanks go to Keila Grinberg and Flávio Limoncic, whose immense knowledge, good cheer, and familial hospitality made Rio feel like home. Elisa Larkin Nascimento, José Maria Nunes Pereira, and Alberto da Costa e Silva generously shared their experiences with me in interviews. Carolina Queiróz and Quincas Rodrigues provided valuable research help after I returned to the United States. Mariana and Maurinete Lima in São Paulo and Elder Santos and Gloria de Morais in Bahia introduced me to their neighborhoods and cities and became good friends. Finally, though they are too many to list individually here, I would like to express my enormous appreciation of all the staff people in the many archives, libraries, and foundations I visited, for their willingness to help a young foreign researcher.

Early on in the project, Jeff Lesser told me that there was not a friendlier, more supportive group of people in U.S. academia than Brazilianists. He was right. From the earliest moments of this project, I have benefited enormously from the encouragement, critiques, and advice of this outstanding community. Warm thanks to Jeff Lesser, Barbara Weinstein, Jerry Dávila, George Reid Andrews, Christopher Dunn, Bryan McCann, Jeffrey Needell, Roderick Barman, John French, James Green, Michael Mitchell, Anani Dzidzienyo, Peter Beattie, Erica Windler, Victoria Langland, Scott Ickes, and Marc Hertzman, a model of friendly collegiality. I am also grateful to Nancy Appelbaum and John Mack Faragher, who, though not Brazilianists, played an important role in the development of my manuscript.

I cannot imagine what this book would have looked like without the input of my brilliant and dedicated colleagues here at the University of Michigan. Working with them has been a transformative experience. For their feedback on portions or entire drafts of this work, I would like to thank Rebecca Scott, Paul Johnson, Richard Turits, Mary Kelley, Penny von Eschen, Kevin Gaines, John Carson, Matthew Countryman, Geoff Eley, Gina Morantz-Sanchez, Phil Deloria, Damon Salesa, Matthew Briones, Hannah Rosen, Tiya Miles, Julius Scott, Jean Hébrard, Sarita See, José Amador, Javier Sanjinés, Leslie Pincus, Rebekah Pite, Laura Halperín, Eugene Cassidy, and Emma Amador. Sueann Caulfield, my dear friend, wise mentor, admired colleague, and trusty running partner soldiered through several drafts of this book, each time providing me with fresh critical insight and enthusiastic support.

Jesse Hoffnung-Garskof has read, edited, and enlivened more versions of this work than I care to remember. I look forward to many opportunities to pay both of them back in kind over the next few years. I am thankful also for the support and friendship of colleagues Sonya Rose, Michele Mitchell, David William Cohen, Lawrence LaFountain-Stokes, Cristina Moreiras-Menor, Gareth Williams, Farina Mir, Peggy McCracken, Ivonne del Valle, Dario Gaggio, Gustavo Verdesio, and Kate Jenckes.

Many thanks to Elaine Maisner, my editor at UNC Press, for seeing the project's potential at an early stage, participating actively in its development (few editors, I imagine, travel to an author's home institution to sit through a five-hour manuscript workshop), and helping to bring it smoothly to completion. Three anonymous reviewers for the press gave me generous feedback and invaluable critiques; I am greatly indebted to them. Thanks, too, to Juan Hernández, Andrew Spears, Bob Lynch, Ekjyot Saini, and Shannon Rolston for their assistance with research and manuscript preparation, and especially to Liliana LaValle, for her crucial help at the eleventh hour.

For sustaining me with their friendship during my years of writing, across long distances, I would like to thank my dear old friends Julieta Pereira, Teresa Ko, Kira Kingren, and Dave Kovel, and, here in Ann Arbor, newer friends Sueann Caulfield, Bebete Martins, Tiya Miles, Joe Gone, Rebekah Pite, Shirli Gilbert, Eliza Parker, Damon and Jenny Salesa, Anne MacDougald, Caitlin Klein, Verónica Miranda, and Heather Halabu. Thanks to Lori Hollander for her multifaceted wisdom. For their love and support, academic and otherwise, I am grateful to Michele Hoffnung (role model and tireless advocate), Johnny Faragher, Bert Garskof, Ellen Lieberman, Josh and Deb Garskof, Sarah and Brian Aucoin, and Robert Garskof and Sharon Montesi. My nephews Artie, Oscar, Jeremy, Sam, and Gabriel, as well as my niece Emily, are sources of pure joy. These families have made the United States truly feel like home.

For introducing me to Brazil and teaching me to love it from an early age, I thank my dear aunt Zulma Alberto and my late uncle Samuel Skiarski; my cousins Fernando and Adriana Skiarski were my first (and my favorite) Portuguese teachers. For reminding me who I am and showing me what I can aspire to be, I thank my amazing sisters, Mariana and Cristina. For encouraging me to travel and pursue my interests, even when it meant leaving them far away, I thank my loving parents, Néstor and Ana Alberto, to whom I dedicate this book.

Finally, for leading me to Jesse—my love and best friend—and for sending me Lalo—*mi chiquitín, pedacito de mi alma*—I thank my lucky stars.

ABBREVIATIONS AND ACRONYMS

ACN	Associação Cultural do Negro / Black People's Cultural Association
ANB	Associação do Negro Brasileiro / Association of Black Brazilians
ANL	Aliança Nacional Libertadora / National Liberation Alliance
CEAA	Centro de Estudos Afro-Asiáticos / Center for Afro-Asian Studies
CEAO	Centro de Estudos Afro-Orientais / Center for Afro-Oriental Studies
CECAN	Centro de Cultura e Arte Negra / Center for Black Culture and Art
CFC	Conselho Federal de Cultura / Federal Council of Culture
CNCS	Clube Negro de Cultura Social / Black Club for Social Culture
DGIE	Departamento Geral de Investigações Especiais / General Department of Special Investigations
DOPS	Departamento Autônomo de Ordem Política e Social / Autonomous Department of Political and Social Order
FESTAC	World Black and African Festival of Arts and Culture
FHC	Federação dos Homens de Cor / Federation of Men of Color
FRELIMO	Frente de Libertação de Mozambique / Liberation Front of Mozambique
FUNARTE	Fundação Nacional de Artes / National Foundation for the Arts
IBEAA	Instituto Brasileiro de Estudos Afro-Asiáticos / Brazilian Institute for Afro-Asian Studies
IBGE	Instituto Brasileiro de Geografia e Estatística / Brazilian Geographical and Statistical Institute
IPCN	Instituto de Pesquisas das Culturas Negras / Institute for Research in Black Cultures
MAM	Museu de Arte Moderna / Museum of Modern Art
MNU	Movimento Negro Unificado / Unified Black Movement

MNUCDR	Movimento Negro Unificado contra a Discriminação Racial / Unified Black Movement against Racial Discrimination
MPB	*música popular brasileira* / Brazilian popular music
PSD	Partido Social Democrático / Social Democratic Party
PTB	Partido Trabalhista Brasileiro / Brazilian Labor Party
SINBA, *SINBA*	Sociedade de Intercâmbio Brasil-África / Society for Brazilian-African Exchange
TEN	Teatro Experimental do Negro / Black Experimental Theater
UDN	União Democrática Nacional / National Democratic Union
UFRJ	Universidade Federal do Rio de Janeiro / Federal University of Rio de Janeiro
UHC	União dos Homens de Cor / Union of Men of Color
UNESCO	United Nations Educational, Scientific, and Cultural Organization

Terms of Inclusion

Brazil

On these sad shoulders,
Now broken, and older,
Was made the Canaan
Of this cruel Brazilian nation
That will not call me brother.

—Lino Guedes, "For the Love
of God," *Urucungo*, 1936

Introduction

Until 1888, when Brazil became the last society in the Americas to abolish slavery, the slave system was as extensive there as it had been anywhere in the new world. Slavery was not just the center of Brazil's brutal economic engine; it was a way of life, the foundation of a deeply hierarchical society marked by pervasive distinctions of color and class. The stigmas of race and servility associated with African slavery extended beyond those in bondage, shaping the lives of a large population of free people of color as well. After abolition, freedom and citizenship were similarly conditioned by racial and class inequities that survived and evolved in the absence of slavery. Brazilians of African descent made up roughly half the country's population in the century after abolition, but they accounted for the vast majority of the nation's poor and dispossessed. Yet throughout this period, many Brazilians, of different racial and class backgrounds, congratulated themselves on the limited social damage that slavery had wrought among them. Centuries of slavery had seemingly not produced a rigid line between "blacks" and "whites." Nor had they bequeathed Brazil a legacy of racial violence and institutionalized discrimination, as in the United States. Instead, many believed, a softer form of slavery had made Brazil into an exceptional postemancipation society, a place where members of a racially mixed and culturally hybrid population coexisted in harmony. Over the course of the twentieth century, regimes authoritarian and democratic made the idea of Brazilian racial harmony into an official ideology.

This book asks what people of color thought about both the racial inequalities and the discourses of racial harmony so central to Brazilian public life in the twentieth century. It does so by considering the words and actions of black intellectuals—a group of men and a few women of some education and public standing, who proudly claimed their African racial or cultural heritage and who aspired to represent other Brazilians of color in national discussions about race and national identity since the early 1900s. It traces the emergence

3

of their writings and organizations in the rich political and cultural life that evolved, with local variations, among people of color in the cities of São Paulo, Rio de Janeiro, and Salvador da Bahia. In recovering their work, the book that follows provides an intellectual and cultural history of the idea of racial harmony in twentieth-century Brazil, told through the life stories and the ideological and political struggles of a small but influential group of black men and women.

Toward the end of the twentieth century, most black thinkers and many other students of black Brazilian politics argued that ideologies of racial harmony had effectively prevented even politically committed black Brazilians from challenging or indeed fully grasping the deep racial inequalities and pervasive racism they encountered in the century after abolition. For this reason, most histories of black thought and politics highlight the moment in the 1970s and 1980s when members of an emerging Black Movement denounced national ideologies of racial harmony, labeling them a pernicious "myth" that hid Brazil's glaring racism from its victims and undermined any attempt at collective race-based action. The story of that rebellion is often told, by black and other thinkers, as the true or definitive moment of racial activism, the long-delayed awakening of consciousness, when a few Brazilians of color finally lifted the veil from their eyes after nearly a century of false freedom and failed political initiatives.

Yet as powerful as this moment was, it should not obscure the equally compelling history of earlier generations of black thinkers who, since the first decades of the century, played a vital role in constructing and contesting Brazilian ideologies of racial harmony. Even as they labored under intense pressure to endorse these ideologies and to remain silent about racial inequality, black thinkers in São Paulo, Rio de Janeiro, and Salvador da Bahia found ways to publicly condemn discrimination and to demand their fuller inclusion as Brazilian citizens. At times, they did so by relying on the sort of open and direct denunciations of racism typically associated with the Black Movement of the late twentieth century. But they also often passionately endorsed national ideologies of racial harmony, recasting them as shared ideals of racial inclusiveness and demanding that these ideals be substantiated in reality. This book seeks to make sense of these different moments of black political thought and action in their particular times and places, while framing them as part of the same century-long struggle by black thinkers to imbue Brazilian ideologies of racial harmony with antiracist meaning.

Telling the history of twentieth-century Brazilian racial thought from the perspective of black intellectuals ultimately helps to uncover a new history of racial ideologies in Brazil. Although the subjects of this study were not representative of the population on whose behalf they claimed to speak—at no point in the twentieth century did a majority of African-descended Brazilians identify as "black" or join explicitly race-based causes—their views resonate closely with what scholars are finding to have been broadly held popular attitudes toward Brazilian ideas of racial harmony. In the long century after abolition, poor or working-class Brazilians of color, far from being blinded by dominant racial ideologies, combined enthusiasm for the ideal of a racially inclusive nation with lucid criticism of the ways racial inequality affected them and the people around them.[1] The writings of black intellectuals display this same conceptual agility regarding the idea of racial harmony and the experience of persistent racial injustice. This book adds their eloquent critiques to an emerging picture of how ideologies of Brazilian racial harmony were both constructed and contested from below.

This history of black thought also reveals that "racial democracy," the phrase most commonly used to refer to Brazilian ideas of racial harmony, was in fact but one historically specific iteration of much longer debates over the terms on which, and through which, African-descended people would be included as citizens in postabolition Brazil. These debates, moreover, took on one set of meanings in the city of São Paulo, which had a regional identity defined largely by whiteness and European immigration, another set of meanings in Rio, in which even white leaders often celebrated racial and cultural mixture, and still another in Salvador, with its African-descended majority. When black thinkers spoke of the role of race in Brazil's national essence, more often than not they were actually commenting on the social tensions and transformations under way in the particular neighborhoods, cities, and regions of Brazil that they inhabited. The history of Brazilian ideas of racial inclusiveness, then, is really the story of how black (and white) thinkers in different parts of Brazil sought to make their temporally and geographically specific visions of interracial relations appear both national and timeless.

Origins of the Idea of Brazilian
Racial Harmony: Colony and Empire

How and when did Brazil—a nation built on the enslaved labor of indigenous and African people, and currently one of the most unequal societies in the world—develop a reputation as a racial paradise? And how did the question of race in a society with a complex history of native conquest, European immigration, and African slavery come to be understood principally in terms of relations between whites and blacks? To answer these questions, we must momentarily step back to a time well before the beginning of our story.

The territory that would become Brazil had a large indigenous population when the Portuguese arrived in 1500, estimated at between 1 and 7 million people.[2] As elsewhere in Latin America, colonists attempted to recruit indigenous people as a labor force. But unlike the large hierarchical polities of Mesoamerica and the Andes, the indigenous societies of Brazil were difficult to control centrally. Native Brazilians were hunters and gatherers, scattered along the Atlantic coastline and across the continent's vast interior, speaking more than one hundred different languages. Indians' ability to escape from coastal plantations, their sharp demographic decline from exposure to European diseases, and the Crown's opposition to their enslavement led Portuguese colonists over the course of the sixteenth century to turn increasingly to African slaves.[3]

By the mid-eighteenth century, Indians and Africans occupied distinct legal categories and social positions. In the 1750s, the Crown instituted a series of reforms aimed at bringing indigenous populations more firmly under the protection of the colonial state and speeding their assimilation. Portugal reissued prohibitions on the enslavement of indigenous people (a practice that continued illegally in some areas), ended religious orders' tutelage of indigenous settlements, and declared Indians to be free vassals of the king. New laws also abolished legal distinctions between Indians and whites, absolving Indians of the stigma of "impure blood" and openly encouraging the marriage and intermixture of Portuguese men (by far the majority of colonists) with indigenous women.[4]

These reforms pointedly did not extend to Africans and their descendants, who by then bore the overwhelming weight of the colony's labor needs. As if to highlight this distinction, a 1755 decree designed to protect Indians from "infamy" prohibited the "unjustifiable and scandalous practice of calling them *negros*," a "vile and base term."[5] Although many slaves found ways to secure their freedom, colonial authorities imposed strictures against people with African ancestry, often without regard for their legal status as slave or free. Blacks (*negros* or *pretos*) as well as mulattoes (*pardos*) were prohibited from carrying certain kinds of weapons, wearing refined clothing, and occupying government or religious posts.[6] In contrast with its policy encouraging the intermarriage of whites and indigenous women, the Crown frowned on Portuguese settlers' partnerships with African and African-descended women. This practice, however, existed widely nonetheless, both in the form of permanent unions and, more commonly, of temporary, violent, or highly unequal sexual encounters.[7]

Despite laws and attitudes that stigmatized them, Africans became increasingly visible as contributors to the development of the colony's wealthiest and most influential regions, including the three cities that are the focus of this book. In the sixteenth and seventeenth centuries, the work of enslaved Africans in sugar production brought dazzling wealth to the city of Salvador da Bahia, Brazil's colonial capital. In the early eighteenth century, the rapid growth of gold and diamond mining in the inland mountains of Minas Gerais (southwest of Salvador), created a new demand for slave labor. Soon, the southeastern coastal city of Rio de Janeiro surpassed Salvador as the most important slave-trading port, and in 1763, Rio replaced Salvador as the colony's capital. The southward shift of slavery and wealth continued in the late eighteenth and early nineteenth centuries, when planters began to rely on slave labor to cultivate extensive and enormously lucrative coffee plantations in the states of Rio de Janeiro and São Paulo.[8]

In 1822 planters, politicians, merchants, and even the Portuguese royal family plotted a cautious course toward Brazilian independence. Hoping to avoid a revolutionary conflict that might disturb the steady expansion of slave labor or inspire widespread slave revolt, members of the Brazilian elite installed Pedro I, son of the Portuguese king João VI, as the head of an independent Brazilian empire.[9] For the next few decades, Brazil's slave-based export economy thrived. But by 1850, responding to external diplomatic pressures as well as to internal concerns over the dangers of an increasingly Africanized population, a young emperor Pedro II and his parliament finally ended the slave trade to Brazil. An internal slave trade that drew slaves away from the declining sugar industry of the Northeast temporarily provided new labor for the booming coffee plantations of the Southeast. But it soon became evident that, without the transatlantic trade, slavery in Brazil was doomed. Facing regional labor shortages and widespread slave uprisings and desertions, many slaveholders began to manumit their slaves in the hopes of keeping them on as workers and dependents. With abolitionist pressure and slave resistance mounting, Pedro II and his parliament passed a series of laws in the 1860s and 1870s aimed at phasing out slavery, and in 1888, Pedro's daughter, Princess Isabel, signed the law definitively abolishing slavery in Brazil.[10]

The erosion of African slavery beginning in the mid-nineteenth century served as the backdrop for some of the earliest literary and artistic expressions of the idea of Brazil's racial harmony. Yet it was Indians, not blacks, whom Brazilian artists, novelists, and historians initially placed at the center of emerging narratives of mixture or peaceful coexistence. Indians—particularly the extinct Tupí—became symbols of a noble but malleable racial "other" who gradually retreated, assimilated, or vanished in the face of European superiority.[11] Such tales of disappearing Indians emerged even as the Brazilian government concentrated "domesticated" Indians in state-controlled settlements and waged war against the "feral" Indians at the Empire's frontiers, whom they saw as impediments to civilization. The imperial government also colluded in the expropriation of indigenous lands (against the explicit protections of the law), and turned a blind eye to labor practices exploiting the newly landless.[12] Meanwhile, the Constitution of 1824 made no mention of the existence of Indians in Brazil. And although the first national census of 1872 counted *caboclos* (mixed indigenous-Europeans) as a color group along with whites, *pretos* (blacks), and *pardos* (mixed African-Europeans), it did not count "pure" indigenous people.[13]

These early accounts of racial harmony thus elevated stylized and historical Indians in the national imaginary precisely at a time when real Indians were erased from an urban, modernizing national landscape—one increasingly dominated by seemingly far more threatening Africans.[14] By the 1870s, facing the imminent collapse of slavery, Brazilian thinkers began directly to apply those narratives of peaceful assimilation to Africans and their descendants. In this, they were aided by contemporary travelers to Brazil, who in their writings often remarked positively on the large free population of color (which, by the 1870s, outnumbered slaves three to one) and on the upward mobility and respectful treatment enjoyed by some of its members. Though this was by no measure the experience of the majority of free people of color, it appeared to outsiders (and several Brazilians) to provide evidence of the mildness of Brazil's racial system in a broader American context. Observers also pointed to the fact that people of different colors mixed widely in Brazil, a situation that to them signaled the relative absence of racial prejudice and helped attenuate the association between color and servile status. As Brazil's abolitionist campaign gained momentum in the 1870s and 1880s, these sorts of accounts helped defenders of Brazilian slavery to portray it as kinder, gentler, and more benevolent than elsewhere in the Americas, especially the United States.[15]

Just as some Brazilians used ideas about Brazil's mild slavery and flexible racial system in attempts to preserve slavery, others marshaled similar ideas in favor of abolition and the fuller integration of African-descended people. The (white) abolitionist Joaquim Nabuco, for instance, contended that former slaves would indeed be able to contribute fruitfully to a liberal, modern society, because "slavery, to our good fortune, never embittered the slave's spirit toward the master, at least collectively, nor did it create between the races that mutual hate which naturally exists between oppressors and oppressed." He added that "color in Brazil is not, as in the United States, a social prejudice against whose persistence no character, talent, or merit can prevail."[16] Nabuco was a committed abolitionist, but his attitudes toward Brazil's African-descended population were hardly devoid of racial prejudice. For Nabuco, as for many other abolitionists, ending slavery would improve the nation by assimilating and civilizing those who, when maintained as a distinct, degraded, and culturally foreign group, threatened the health of the national organism. Like indigenist artists and writers at midcentury, many abolitionists in this period began to view assimilation through intermixture both as evidence of the absence of racial prejudice, and as a solution to an embarrassing history of racial oppression.[17]

The ideas that served defenders and opponents of slavery alike in these years also at times proved useful to Brazilians of color in their struggles for freedom. In the 1860s and 1870s, as a new generation of magistrates came to believe in Brazil's relatively benevolent form of slavery, many slaves, helped by activists and lawyers like Luiz Gama, the son of a Portuguese father and an African mother, made this idea the center of successful suits to demand better conditions and respectful treatment, or to secure their freedom.[18] Ideas of racial inclusiveness also proved useful to free Brazilians of color who sought full civil rights and public respect. Journalist and abolitionist José do Patrocínio, a mulatto, publicly lauded Portuguese colonizers for having "assimilated" rather than "destroyed" Brazil's "savage" races, thereby preparing Brazilians to "resist the devastating invasion of race prejudice." His paean to racial assimilation, phrased in terms of the peaceful "fusion" of Portuguese and Indians in the colonial period, underwrote demands for the fuller integration of *pretos* and *pardos* into what he hoped might become a colorblind Brazilian society in his own time.[19]

Shifting Terms of Racial Inclusion in the Century after Abolition

In the colonial and imperial periods, evolving ideologies of Brazilian racial harmony served a variety of political and ideological projects, from the reactionary to the relatively progressive. This dynamic set the stage for the ways black thinkers would engage with these ideologies over the course of the twentieth century. Black thinkers' positions with respect to ideas of racial inclusiveness were not a measure of the strength of these men and women's racial consciousness. Rather, their changing positions reflected the relative weight of repressive and liberatory elements within these ideologies at any given point, as well as the particular opportunities and limitations created by the changing panorama of local, national, and international politics.

After the abolition of slavery and in the early years of the First Republic (1889–1930), nationalist views of Brazil as a place of exceptional racial harmony intensified, particularly in reaction to ideas about the innate superiority of white or "Aryan" races then circulating in the Atlantic world. According to leading scientists in Europe and the United States, places like Brazil—where people of unmixed European origin were a small minority—stood no chance of ever creating a racially fit citizenry. Brazil was biologically doomed to backwardness and barbarism. Members of the Brazilian elite, many of whom identified as white despite varying measures of African ancestry, adopted some aspects of these ideologies of scientific racism (namely, the idea of European racial superiority) but rejected others. Their principal innovation was the idea that through continued racial mixture, Brazil would gradually "whiten," cleansing itself of the stigma of blackness. Even as this ideology of "whitening" envisioned the disappearance of nonwhite people, particularly those of African descent, it simultaneously cast Brazilians' willingness to intermix as evidence of their unique openness and enlightenment in racial matters. By the 1920s, many Brazilian thinkers, in step with their counterparts across Latin America, portrayed their own nation as proudly *mestiço* or mixed, in pointed contrast with the then legally segregated United States.[20]

Black intellectuals in this period seized on the progressive potentials of ideologies that equated racial mixture with social inclusion. They expressed hope that these newer ideas might help move Brazilian society away from the unyielding certainties of doctrinaire scientific racism, which cast people of color as outsiders to the national community, and toward newer conceptions of national identity that made it possible to imagine people of color as full Brazilians. In the 1920s, for instance, black thinkers in São Paulo and Rio de Janeiro hailed the importance of racial mixture in the formation of Brazil's population; highlighted African inflections in Brazilians' language, music, and temperament; and celebrated the role of black women—and their sons— in shaping a Brazilian family marked by interracial fraternity.

By the 1930s, under a nationalist regime, white and black intellectuals helped to turn the idea of Brazil as a proud, racially and culturally mixed nation into the focal point of new definitions of national identity. Most famously, beginning in the early 1930s, white sociologist Gilberto Freyre

wrote broadly influential histories of family life in the colonial sugar plantations of his native Northeast. His work focused on the close personal and
sexual relations that developed first between Portuguese colonizers and indigenous women, and later, between masters and African slaves. However, rather
than celebrate the eventual erasure of Africans and Indians in the process of
mixture with Europeans, as had proponents of whitening, Freyre lauded the
unique combination of peoples and cultures that resulted.[21] He emphasized
the role of Africans as co-colonists, and made the relations between Africans
and Europeans in particular—indeed, the Africanness of Brazilian culture—
into the centerpiece of a broader argument about the abiding ideal and reality
of harmony among Brazil's racial groups.

Under the presidency of Getúlio Vargas (1930–45), the state deployed the
ideas Freyre helped to popularize in its attempts to unify the nation across
class, racial, and regional divides. Reversing Republican elites' aspirations for
a whitened, Europeanized Brazil, Vargas's nationalist politics and cultural
policies championed black and brown Brazilians as essential members of the
nation and elevated elements of African-inflected popular culture—those from
Rio in particular—as symbols of a racially mixed and harmonious national
identity. Black thinkers across Brazil in this period seized the opportunity to
be considered full nationals, demanding compensation for their real and symbolic exclusion under earlier regimes while proposing their own, regionally
specific interpretations of what it meant to be a black or African Brazilian.

As African culture moved toward the center of official and popular formulations of national identity in this period, indigenous people faded further from the public view. As premodern "others," distant in temporal and
geographic terms from Brazil's political and intellectual centers, indigenous people increasingly became the province of anthropologists. People of
African descent, for their part, gradually became the subject of sociological
and historical investigations as vital (if problematic) members of a dynamic
capitalist society.[22] Official population counts from the 1940s onward, which
collapsed the category *caboclo* under *pardo* (making people of partial indigenous descent indistinguishable from those of partial African descent) and
only intermittently included the category *indígena*, illustrate this further nar-
rowing of definitions of race to a black-white spectrum.[23]

After World War II, reflecting the ascendancy of democracy in Brazil and
much of the West, black and white intellectuals newly began to describe
their society's unique freedom from racial tensions not in an earlier language of harmony or fraternity, but in the language of democracy.[24] Abdias
do Nascimento, a black thinker whose racial activism over the course of the

century spanned the realms of writing, art, acting, academic research, and formal politics, captured the sentiment of many contemporary black thinkers when he declared in 1950 that Brazil's historically "widespread miscegenation" was yielding "a well-delineated doctrine of *racial democracy*, that will serve as a lesson and model to other nations of complex ethnic formation."[25] At the same time that he lauded the inclusive potential of Brazil's "racial democracy," however, Nascimento, like many of his colleagues, used the building blocks of a democratic public sphere—including the press, the theater, academic congresses, and political parties—to point out the enormous work that remained to be done to eradicate racism and its effects from Brazil. Nascimento and his colleagues in Rio, São Paulo, and Salvador also jealously guarded their rights to assert their racial or cultural difference, as blacks or Africans, in the face of increasingly dominant proclamations of racelessness and cultural fusion. For black thinkers across Brazil in this period, then, racial democracy was to be celebrated not as a reality but as a new consensus about what Brazil could rightfully become in an era of redemocratization and expanded participation.

This was not, however, the perspective that immediately prevailed in Brazil and abroad. In a world reeling from the horrors of Germany's state-sponsored racism, Brazil's image as a nation well on its way to peaceful and egalitarian interracial relations acquired international prominence. In the early 1950s, inspired by this reputation, the United Nations Educational, Scientific, and Cultural Organization sent a cadre of social scientists from Europe and the United States to accompany Brazilian scholars in investigating "race relations" in several cities. Their findings qualified, but by no means overturned, Brazil's reputation as a racial democracy. Investigators recognized Brazil's dramatic inequalities and their correlation with color, but they attributed them primarily to class rather than racial discrimination. Absent a system akin to Jim Crow or apartheid, racial disparities would disappear, social scientists predicted, as Brazil completed the transition from a slave society to a capitalist class society.[26]

Though disappointing to many black thinkers, this conclusion was not entirely fanciful. Legal segregation by race or color was absent from the Republic's first constitution (1891) and from subsequent twentieth-century legal codes. Over the course of the century, many Brazilians engaged in behaviors—such as marrying across what would elsewhere be considered racial lines and living in racially mixed neighborhoods—that appeared to many to signal the absence of the sort of extreme racial discrimination associated with the United States or South Africa. Also absent were clear or rigid racial categories. Over the course of the twentieth century, Brazil's population became officially "lighter," with census returns showing a transfer of people from the category "black" to those of "brown" and "white." This suggests a relatively flexible system of color classification within and across generations, and the absence, among many Brazilians, of a sense of belonging definitively to one or another fixed community of racial descent.[27]

Yet the fact that census returns throughout the century reveal Brazilians' broad-based tendency to privilege white or intermediate color categories over blackness also betrays the ongoing importance of whiteness, even a relatively inclusive form of whiteness, as a marker of social status in Brazil.[28] Scholars over the past half century have convincingly demonstrated the ways that color and racial distinctions map onto class status in Brazil, heavily influencing, if not entirely determining, opportunities for social mobility and access to resources. As sociologist Edward Telles argues, "greater race mixture and fluid race relations are not of much consolation to the majority of Brazil's nonwhites," who are more than three times as likely as whites to be poor or illiterate, and who earn, on average, half as much as their white counterparts.[29] Historians, sociologists, and anthropologists have documented the existence of racially discriminatory attitudes and practices at all levels of society over the course of the twentieth century—from color preferences for marriage to police harassment of dark-complexioned Brazilians to restrictions in employment or university admissions.[30] This scholarship, following on the criticisms of black thinkers like Nascimento since midcentury, has helped cast severe doubt on celebrations of Brazil's "racial democracy."

Myth or Reality?

It was not until after the military coup of 1964 that black thinkers definitively abandoned the hopeful tone of earlier years in favor of open attacks on racial democracy as a tool of ideological domination. As in earlier years, their choice of political strategies responded in part to currents of thought coming from abroad. Leftist youth movements from Paris to Prague, the fight for civil rights in the United States, and African liberation struggles provided inspiration to a new generation of university-educated Brazilians of color who joined Brazil's growing black movement. Yet the decisive factor in black thinkers' change of strategy came from within Brazil. Successive military governments in the 1960s and 1970s transformed the idea of racial democracy into an empty phrase, or worse, a smokescreen that imperfectly hid the state's repression of politics built around public claims to blackness. It was in this particularly dark moment of national politics, when ideas of racial inclusiveness appeared no longer to provide a workable common ground and when new ideas of racial and political self-determination beckoned, that black thinkers and activists took the oppositional ideological stance for which they are best known today.

As in earlier decades, Abdias do Nascimento was at the forefront of these transformations. In 1977 he traveled to Lagos, Nigeria, to protest what he saw as the complete disjuncture between the images of racial harmony his government attempted to project abroad and the censorship of meaningful discussions of race that had, by the late 1960s, forced Nascimento and other outspoken thinkers like him into exile. Earlier in 1977, Brazil's Foreign Ministry had sent a showy delegation of diplomats and intellectuals, along with twelve visual artists, four dance and music groups, three films, and an array of historical portraits and paintings, to represent Brazil at the Second World Black and African Festival of Arts and Culture (FESTAC II) in Lagos. The official publication on Brazil's participation in the festival celebrated the nation's peaceful incorporation of African traits and peoples, which the delegation displayed primarily through cultural manifestations like samba music or Afro-Brazilian religions.[31] Appointing himself an unofficial Brazilian delegate to the FESTAC, Nascimento circulated an English-language position paper defiantly titled "'Racial Democracy' in Brazil: Myth or Reality?," which captured the essence of the critique black intellectuals were then developing back home. Nascimento denounced Brazil as a country just as plagued by racial divisions as the United States and South Africa—the nations that, for much of the century, had served as foils for proclamations of Brazil's progressive race relations. Brazil, according to Nascimento, was a nation internally colonized, in which "whites control the means of the dissemination of information; the educational apparatus; they formulate the concepts, the weapons, and the values of the country." With symbolic weapons like discourses of racial and cultural harmony, Nascimento implied, white elites concealed a much uglier reality. "The reality of Afro-Brazilians involves bearing a discrimination so effective that, even [in regions] where they make up the majority of the population, they exist as economic, cultural, and political minorities." This reality persisted because Brazil's much-celebrated racial mixture, and its official embrace of African cultural traits, had achieved its "unstated objective of . . . deny[ing] blacks the possibility of self-definition by removing any means of racial identification."[32]

Nascimento's high-profile attack hit its mark. Brazil's ambassador in Lagos, Geraldo de Heráclito Lima, drafted a rebuttal for publication in Nigeria's newspapers that, though never published, shows what racial democracy had come to mean in the hands of the military dictatorship and its officials.

> The Brazilian Embassy is confident that no Nigerian will be fooled [by Nascimento's allegations], since Brazil is known throughout the world, and described by thousands of political and social scientists, as a country capable of building a multiracial society, where 110 million people of different ancestries stand as a living lesson for other countries in which such a feat has not, until now, been possible. *In two hundred years, no one has yet heard speak of racial problems or conflicts in Brazil.* Brazil presents, in this respect, its great contribution to the world, as the most genuine, spontaneous, and significant example for any country truly interested in learning to practice racial tolerance.[33]

In the 1950s Nascimento himself had declared Brazil a "lesson" to other multiracial societies. If he had changed his mind by the late 1970s, it was because at that historical moment, "racial democracy" no longer embodied a collective aspiration. It had become a preemptive, nonnegotiable declaration about Brazilian reality, intended to muzzle those who contemplated disturbing the alleged silence of two hundred years.

In the 1970s Nascimento and other activists successfully framed the discussion about Brazil's racial ideologies around the question explored in his position paper: Was racial democracy—as it related to relations between blacks and whites—myth or reality? For Nascimento, the question was purely rhetorical. By pointing to the reality of discrimination Brazilians of color suffered in social, economic, and cultural terms, Nascimento intended to demonstrate beyond doubt that Brazilian ideologies of racial mixture and inclusiveness were debilitating myths. From the 1970s through the 1990s, scholars from Brazil and especially the United States joined Nascimento in the attempt to discredit and dismantle the idea of Brazil's "racial democracy." Their work documented pervasive racial inequality and discrimination in a variety of social settings (not so dissimilar, they noted, from the situation in the United States) and argued that dominant ideas of racial mixture and harmony hindered the development of a strong racial consciousness and effective race-based movements among Brazilians of African descent.[34]

This body of revisionist scholarship advanced the cause of antiracism in Brazil by supporting black activists' claims that Brazil was far from free of racial inequality. Yet beginning in the 1990s, a group of scholars (most of them based in Brazil) objected that revisionist works implicitly or explicitly held Brazil to a standard derived from the experience of the United States, where collective identities and social movements based on "blackness" underwrote a powerful and visible civil rights movement. For these scholars, Brazil's racial ideologies were not simply falsehoods, nor were Brazilians' various mixed-race identities and cross-racial movements to be dismissed as compromised or insufficient in contrast with those of the United States. Instead, they argued, both Brazil's racial ideologies and the kinds of political responses they incited reflected a local understanding of race that must be approached on its own terms.[35] They criticized the literature debunking the myth of racial democracy for presenting Brazilians of color as passive dupes of national ideologies of racelessness. In response, other scholars criticized them for overly idealizing Brazilian race relations, or for portraying Brazilians of color who adopt "black" identities as helpless victims of imperialist standards of racial consciousness.[36]

At the beginning of the twenty-first century, a new crop of scholarship is answering Nascimento's question of whether racial democracy is myth or reality in a slightly different way, claiming that it is both. When the issue of the purported absence of race and racism in Brazil is framed narrowly as a choice between reality and myth, there can be no doubt that "racial democracy" is, in strict terms, an untruth. Yet there is evidently much more to the "myth" than this. First, as scholars of Brazil and other Latin American nations have shown, there is "a material and social base" to the myth.[37] Ideas of racelessness have allowed, at different times, for the rise of organizations, institutions, and patterns of social interactions that cut across race and class lines, mitigating (without overturning) enduring structures of inequality.[38] Moreover, to read the "myth" as mere delusion—to treat the ideas about race to which the majority of Brazilians subscribe as mirages obscuring an underlying concrete reality of race—presupposes that people could experience something as socially constructed as "race" without the mediation of ideas and structuring principles. Ideas of racial harmony, scholars have begun to argue, are and have been a myth in a broader anthropological sense—a discourse that guided discussions of what it meant to be a Brazilian and shaped individual and collective choices in ways that often appeared to advance that ideal. This explains their great power, and their persistence even today in the minds of white and nonwhite Brazilians alike.[39]

In many parts of Latin America, where national laws theoretically ensured the equality and full citizenship rights of people of color but allowed discrimination and disdain in practice, politically active people of color frequently identified the symbolic dimensions of citizenship—such as ideologies of racial harmony—as crucial tools in the struggle for full legal, social, and political rights. Scholars of Cuba, for instance, have shown how ideologies of racial brotherhood emerging from national independence wars in which blacks and whites fought side by side constrained white racists' ability to curtail the political participation of Afro-Cubans in subsequent decades.[40] Some scholars have used the concept of "belonging" to capture this "thicker" conception of citizenship that combines legal, social, and political rights with representation in the realms of race, culture, religion, and national identities and histories.[41] It is this broader conception of citizenship that black Brazilian intellectuals and activists invoked for most of the twentieth century in their writings and actions. They used dominant ideas of racial inclusiveness to place an African racial or cultural heritage at the center of images of the Brazilian nation and to assert their own belonging as African-descended Brazilians within it.

In the early 1980s, at the height of black intellectuals' denunciation of the "myth" of racial democracy, Abdias do Nascimento berated himself for his earlier "excessively conciliatory" descriptions of Brazil as a place marked by racial harmony.[42] In the final decades of the century, most black activists and many sympathetic scholars followed his lead in reading an earlier generation of black thinkers' hopeful engagement with ideologies of racial inclusiveness as evidence of capitulation to debilitating, elite-controlled myths of racial harmony. As this book shows, however, Nascimento and his colleagues were no less impassioned critics of racism in their midcentury endorsement of a racially harmonious ideal than they were in denouncing its hypocrisy a quarter of a century later. Their changing position with respect to dominant ideologies does not betray a contradiction in their thought or political sympathies, nor does it suggest an awakening to a higher level of racial consciousness. Rather, it reveals the different strategies black thinkers and activists adopted to demand full belonging in the nation at different historical moments. Nascimento's personal transformation is emblematic of the broader changes in black thought and politics over the course of the twentieth century, as the possibilities for inclusion and equality appeared to flow, crest, and then recede.

Settings and Sources

To tell the story of these transformations in black thought, this book moves among the cities of São Paulo, Rio de Janeiro, and Salvador da Bahia between the early 1900s and the mid-1980s. These three cities were the sites of important, at times nationally visible, race-based movements. Certainly, black intellectual discourses in all three cities converged in important respects. All represented Brazil as racially mixed, and none advocated a separatist politics. They all shared the aim of identifying strongly with an African racial heritage (blackness), an African cultural heritage, and in some cases, a combination of both. They all believed in the legitimacy of and need for autonomous black political, cultural, and intellectual organizations. Yet they also diverged profoundly in the kind of mixture they imagined should characterize the Brazilian nation overall.

São Paulo began as a distant outpost of settlement in the colonial period, but it grew in size and importance during the nineteenth century as a result of the lucrative coffee crops of the state's interior. The arrival of several million migrants—from other parts of Brazil as well as from Europe, Asia, and the Middle East—in the decades following abolition made São Paulo Brazil's most rapidly growing city in the early twentieth century, as well as an industrial powerhouse, a center of cultural and artistic innovation, and to many, a model for what a modern, Europeanized Brazil might become. In São Paulo, where the population of African descent was small by national standards and where European immigration created a white majority, people of color felt the effects of race-based discrimination exceptionally strongly in employment, housing, and public establishments. This book opens by telling the story of how a group of upwardly mobile men of color in that city came to see themselves, over the course of the first decades of the twentieth century, as *negro* thinkers or intellectuals, active on behalf of their race. It charts the emergence of a black press in that city, a source that provides the documentary backbone for this book. Through their early-twentieth-century press, black activists in São Paulo largely represented Brazil as a multiracial nation comprising individuals from separate white and black races—a discourse of coexistence rather than fusion. Most did not construct the two races as different culturally but only socially and politically. These writers' *negro* identity, in other words, came not from a cultural identification with an African heritage, but from the sense of being a small, denigrated minority in an immigrant city. This binary way of seeing Brazilian race relations continued to characterize São Paulo's activism for the rest of the century. And it was this vision, as much as any foreign racial politics, that shaped the position of the Movimento Negro of the 1970s.

Rio de Janeiro in the early decades of the century was a city with less European immigration than São Paulo and a greater population of African descent (itself made up of a majority of *pardos*). No significant black press developed in Rio until the 1940s, but leaders of black organizations in that city were able, on select occasions, to insert their views on race into the mainstream press. In conjunction with prominent white intellectuals, thinkers of color in Rio de Janeiro in the 1920s imagined a new Brazilian race and culture born of fusion. This view of a mixed Brazilian race became the official and popular one adopted as the basis of a Brazilian national identity after the 1930s. It continued to inform black activism in Rio de Janeiro until the 1970s, when the racial and political tensions of the military dictatorship led activists there to adopt a binary vision of race closer to São Paulo's—to highly controversial effects.

The northeastern city of Salvador da Bahia, a major port of entry for African slaves in the colonial period, had a population in which *pretos* and *pardos* together constituted the majority. In Bahia, race was neither the principal vector of discrimination nor the guiding principle around which people of color sought to organize. Instead, as early-twentieth-century Bahian elites attempted to stamp out African cultures and religions from their city, leaders of the most prestigious houses of worship of the Afro-Brazilian religion Candomblé responded by preserving and promoting cultural practices defined as "purely" African. As a result of these religious leaders' efforts and their interactions with Brazilian and foreign academics, Bahia gained prominence on the national stage from the 1930s onward as the cradle of Brazil's most authentic African cultural traditions. This represented yet another variation on the discourse of mixture—one that insisted on the indissolubility of the African traits that contributed to Brazilian culture. As in Rio de Janeiro, by the 1970s a new generation of cultural and political activists in Bahia produced variations of this African identity that engaged with ideas of blackness emerging from other cities but preserved earlier activists' concern with the purity and primacy of Bahia's African culture.

Terms of Inclusion weaves together these regional subplots, seeking to tell a broader national story about the changing terms through and on which black thinkers demanded their inclusion throughout the century. However, readers should not expect an even treatment of all three places over time nor a strictly comparative approach. This book is about a relatively rare category of people: those who identified as black racial or cultural activists in a nation in which such identities were uncommon. Consequently, the kind, availability, and richness of written sources allowing insight into black thought in each of the three cities heavily shape the story I tell. The city of São Paulo, in which thinkers of color produced the most copious written documents throughout the century (a collection of newspapers written by and for people of African descent, known as the *imprensa negra* or black press) receives the most consistent attention throughout the book. Where the black press is largely absent, as in Rio de Janeiro in the early twentieth century or Bahia for much of the century, I attempt to get access to the voices of black intellectuals indirectly, through sources like São Paulo's black press, documents black intellectuals coproduced with mainstream thinkers like journalists or academics, or government documents about black thinkers and movements. By the 1940s Rio de Janeiro developed a small but consistent black press, allowing me to follow the activities of many black intellectuals there for the rest of the century. Bahia, where the black intellectuals whose stories I tell left only indirect records of their thoughts and actions for much of the century, receives relatively briefer treatment. But it plays an important role as both a model and a foil for ideas about black identities produced by black (and white) intellectuals in other cities throughout the century. Within these constraints, I have chosen to focus my narrative around episodes that illustrate the distinct ways in which black intellectuals from different cities responded to the changing opportunities and limitations provided by national politics over the course of the century.

Beyond Racial Democracy

What can the words and deeds of a small, rather exceptional group of black intellectuals tell us about ideas of race in Brazil? Those who have studied this political and intellectual elite in the past have highlighted the problems it faced, and continues to face, in obtaining support from a broader population of color for exclusively race-based movements in a nation in which most African-descended people do not identify as black.[43] And indeed, throughout the century, this small group of educated, upwardly mobile people of color probably felt the role of race and racism in halting their advancement much more sharply than did Brazilians for whom hunger, poverty, illiteracy, unemployment, and geographic marginalization provided more immediate and lasting obstacles than racial discrimination. If black intellectuals throughout the century denounced their unequal access to government jobs or universities, or wrote of the exclusion of blackness or Africanness from national identity, this reflected at least a realistic aspiration to those positions in the first case, and the learning and resources to articulate such matters in print in the second. And indeed, in many ways, the terms on which most black intellectuals argued for their own inclusion into Brazilian identity—as literate, urbane, Catholic men making no claims to cultural distinction, or alternatively, as female leaders of Afro-Brazilian religions emphasizing their congregation's ritual "purity" and prestige—marked them as a privileged leadership and simultaneously outlined the terms of exclusion for a wider swath of the population.[44] Women, the poor, and African-descended people who recognized neither their racial nor their cultural African descent were often implicitly or explicitly left out of these thinkers' definitions of belonging. So were indigenous people, who—in part through the active participation of black intellectuals in national discussions about race and race relations—gradually fell out of such discussions over the course of the century.

These black intellectuals, through their actions, nonetheless made themselves central to the history of race and racial ideologies in twentieth century Brazil. Despite their apparent relative privilege, their stories can help us understand how and why a society like Brazil, where few people identified as *preto* or *negro*, could have produced a vocal minority of people who not only identified as such but worked to make blackness or Africanness fundamental to Brazilian identity. Moreover, the issues of representation and symbolic politics around which black intellectuals structured their public interventions were vital dimensions of experience for broader segments of the population as well. Instances of discrimination against upwardly mobile people of color helped to set the parameters for citizenship, also affecting those who had less and sparking broader movements to contest these structures of prejudice.[45] By the late twentieth century, the critiques made by a growing group of black activists and intellectuals gave rise to projects—such as present-day state and federal affirmative action campaigns—that are reshaping Brazilian society as a whole.

Above all, telling the history of racial thought in Brazil from the perspective of this relatively small group of people of color affords new insights into the history of racial ideologies in Brazil—a history formerly told mainly using evidence about a few white intellectuals.[46] *Racial democracy*, as an idea and a term, has become such a commonplace in scholarship on Brazil that we tend to overlook not just its internal complications and unexpected uses, but more significantly, its historical origins and changing meanings. This, in turn, contributes to its apparent omnipresence and unassailability. Yet as a few scholars are beginning to argue, there was no singular idea of racial democracy in twentieth-century Brazil.[47] At different moments, in different regions of the country, different groups of Brazilians, including people of color, proposed and contested multiple meanings of what is generally collapsed under the single term *racial democracy*. The limited usefulness and indeed the anachronism of this term, when it is imagined as a single, coherent concept throughout time and space, become clear when we pay attention to the language black thinkers used when articulating their ideas of race and national belonging.

A Note on Terminology

Attention to racial terminology, like careful analysis of ideas of racial interactions, is a crucial step toward rendering the complexity and plurality of ideas of belonging in modern Brazil.[48] In using the term *black* to describe intellectuals of varying measures of African ancestry, I am choosing to follow (in translation) the usage of the protagonists of this history, who used the terms *preto* or, increasingly over the course of the century, *negro* to describe themselves, their organizations and publications, and other Brazilians of African descent. Though the Portuguese words *negro* and *preto* both translate into English as "black," they have different connotations. For much of the nineteenth and twentieth centuries, *negro* was considered a particularly derogatory term for people of African descent; the more polite word, used in official documents, was *preto*, which literally means the color black. When activists in the early twentieth century began to refer to themselves as *negros*, they were reclaiming a derogatory term as an emblem of racial unity, in contrast to identifications based on color, like *preto* or especially *pardo* (which literally means "grey" or "brown"). To make this distinction clear in my text, I leave the terms *preto* or *pardo* in the original Portuguese. I also use "black" when paraphrasing writers' own uses of *negro* in any given text. When referring to Brazil's population of African descent more generally, I use "Brazilians of color," "people of color," "Brazilians of African descent," "*pretos* and *pardos*," or "blacks and mulattos" interchangeably. I have made the choice to use these somewhat awkward terms over "Afro-Brazilians," which, though common in the works of many U.S. Brazilianists, was not a term used by black thinkers for most of the century, and, to my ear, is undesirably evocative of a particular anthropological or folkloric perspective on African culture in Brazil from the early twentieth century.

1. Foreigners
São Paulo, 1900–1925

As the twentieth century opened, a small group of men of color in the city and state of São Paulo had cause to be optimistic about their future. Slavery was no more, and the laws of the new Republic (1889–1930) formally declared all literate adult men full and equal citizens of the nation. As a relatively privileged group within São Paulo's small black and brown population, a select "class of color" in one of the nation's wealthiest and most rapidly modernizing states, these men far exceeded those basic requirements for citizenship. They were literate, cultured, and modestly well employed. In their social clubs and newsletters, they initially expressed hopes that displays of respectability, learning, and patriotism would help them overcome the lingering racial prejudice that still barred even middle-class men of color from certain jobs and public spaces.

Yet from their stations of relative privilege in cities like São Paulo and neighboring Campinas, the men of the class of color were also uniquely positioned to glimpse the ways in which contemporary ideologies of whitening, together with state-sponsored European immigration, exacerbated racial exclusions in practice and threatened to reinscribe them in the law. In the early twentieth century, São Paulo was the state where local elites most vigorously, and most successfully, implemented the national goal of replacing former slave laborers with whiter immigrants. By the early 1920s, newspapers by and for the class of color in the cities of São Paulo and nearby Campinas reported with alarm that while white immigrants were welcomed with open arms as desirable citizens, people of color, increasingly losing the competition for employment, housing, and equal treatment, were becoming foreigners in their native lands.

In the first decades of the twentieth century, then, the state and city of São Paulo were places where members of a small elite of color, privileged by national standards, witnessed and experienced a particularly sharp form of racial discrimination as their cities swelled with whiter immigrants. This specific experience of racial exclusion, which writers of color described as foreignness, shaped the strategies these Paulistano (from the city of São Paulo) and Paulista (from the state of São Paulo) writers pursued as they struggled to assert their belonging as Brazilians in the first quarter of the century.[1] It was the feeling of becoming outsiders to the national community that drove many dark-skinned writers to rely on ideas of racial fusion and harmony to repudiate the racism that supported their state's policies of mass immigration. In the hands of writers of color, ideas of racial fusion helped portray people of African descent as central contributors to a Brazilian race and nation, while ideas of racial harmony helped cast immigrants (and racist Brazilians) as the true outsiders in a country that, these writers contended, made interracial respect a basic condition for citizenship.

Fears of being labeled foreigners also led this early generation of Paulista thinkers of color toward nativism, and, in most cases, away from potential ties of solidarity with blacks in Africa or elsewhere in the diaspora. Above all, the experience of being a beleaguered racial minority at the margins of rapidly whitening cities changed these men's perceptions of themselves, defining the contours of what it meant to be a black thinker in that time and place. By the mid-1920s, indignant members of São Paulo's class of color would come to see and present themselves less as an isolated elite and more as leaders of a broader black (*preto* or *negro*) racial community, using their writing to publicly demand inclusion and combat old and new forms of racism.

"Still dreaming of our complete emancipation"

As early as 1903, Benedito Florencio and Francisco José de Oliveira, men of color and editors of a small newspaper from Campinas titled *O Baluarte* (*The Bulwark*), eloquently captured the project of what would come to be known as São Paulo's "black press." They vowed that their newspaper would defend people of color from "pessimistic" attitudes that kept them "still dream[ing] of our complete emancipation."[2] In what sense had Brazilians of color not been completely emancipated by 1903? And, in any case, what meaning did "emancipation" have for writers for newspapers like *O Baluarte*, many—perhaps most—of whom had never been slaves themselves?[3]

In 1888 the monarchy abolished slavery, and in 1891 the first constitution of the new Republic declared all Brazilians equal citizens regardless of color or race and removed property requirements for voting. Yet despite the constitution's race-neutral language, the founders of the First Republic encoded a series of class and racial exclusions in Brazil's legal and political institutions. The constitution restricted the vote to literate men, while the government provided public education only to a select few. As a result, all women and illiterate men of any color were excluded from active citizenship. People of color almost all fell into at least one of those two categories. Nor did the few Brazilians with the right to vote exercise a clear influence over political life in the Republic, which had a one-party system designed to share power among members of a regional elite—primarily planters and cattle ranchers from the states of São Paulo, Minas Gerais, and Rio de Janeiro. Limits on suffrage, extensive political corruption, violence, and coercion further constrained popular participation in national politics. The Republic, as George Reid Andrews has argued, embraced democracy and racial equality as ideals but denied them in practice.[4]

Emancipation was therefore incomplete in spirit, in the sense that most Brazilians of color continued to occupy low social and economic positions, and to be excluded from their nation's formal political life, as the new century began. More pointedly, emancipation was incomplete for many *libertos*, or former slaves, who after abolition sought to diminish their dependence on plantation labor. Some migrated to major cities, where they found precarious employment as domestic servants, shoe shiners, deliverymen, messengers, street vendors, dish washers, and the like. Many, however, ended up returning to work on or near the plantations on which they had toiled as slaves, joining the already substantial ranks of free but dependent rural workers. They struggled to mark their status as free people by negotiating new terms with their employers, and they won some concessions, primarily related to wages and to the conditions under which they would and would not work. Yet planters and other employers during the Republic did not endure such bargaining with their laborers for long. Searching for alternatives to the *libertos*, whom they saw as excessively demanding and intractable or lazy and untrustworthy, Brazilian planters increasingly turned to what they hoped would be responsible, competent, and malleable immigrant workers from Europe.[5] In the last year before abolition, the number of immigrants to Brazil more than doubled, exceeding one hundred thousand for the first time. Newcomers from places like Italy, Portugal, and Spain continued to pour into Brazil by the tens and hundreds of thousands yearly well into the 1920s.[6] Emancipation, then, was also incomplete in the sense that, in many parts of Brazil, planters and politicians devoted their energies to securing new sources of labor from abroad rather than negotiating the terms of free labor with former slaves.

The editors of *O Baluarte* may well have had these dynamics in mind when they pronounced emancipation to be still incomplete in 1903. Though they were better-off men of modest professional achievements—Florencio was a journalist, and Oliveira was a schoolteacher and ex-seminarian—both appear to have shared a concern for the fate of Brazilians of color who had not been able to escape a life of poorly remunerated manual labor. Alongside his efforts in *O Baluarte*, Florencio wrote social commentary for *O Diário do Povo*, a major Campinas daily with working-class sympathies, and Oliveira acted as head of the Irmandade de São Benedito, a lay brotherhood composed primarily of poor people of color. He was also the founder and director of a well-regarded Catholic school (linked to the brotherhood) that educated children of color alongside those of Campinas's wealthier white families.[7] Yet beyond such sympathies, what kept these men "still dream[ing] of . . . complete emancipation" alongside poorer black and brown Brazilians was, as they put it, the salience of elite thinkers who "pontificated, with the authority of dogma, the intellectual degradation of the race and the moral annihilation of the class [of color]." Emancipation, in this sense, was incomplete for Florencio and Oliveira as long as the racist "dogmas" that had sustained slavery continued to cast doubt on the fitness for citizenship of all people of color, regardless of whether they met the necessary legal, civic, and cultural standards.

In the early twentieth century, several strands of racist thought combined to portray people of color as intellectually degraded and morally annihilated. Ideologies of vagrancy, carried over from the nineteenth century, portrayed people of color as irresponsible *vadios* or bums, incapable of working without extreme coercion. These ideologies caricatured men of color in particular as weak, sickly, effeminate, dishonorable, and unable to provide for their families.[8] When combined with long-standing ideas about Brazil as a place supposedly free of racial discrimination, where anyone willing to work could improve his or her lot, the ideology of *vadiagem* heaped blame on black and brown Brazilians themselves for their low social status and unemployment.[9] Several currents of "scientific" racism emerging from Europe, proclaiming the innate and incontestable superiority of whiter over darker races, also gained widespread following among members of Brazil's economic and political elite in the late nineteenth century, further fueling the turn to immigrant labor.[10]

Yet even as Brazilian intellectuals accepted many of the basic premises of scientific racism, they rejected those that ruled out Brazil's chances of becoming a modern, civilized nation. In 1896, for instance, French anthropologist Georges Vacher de Lapouge predicted that Brazil, with its large African and indigenous population and its extensive racial mixture, was doomed to become an "immense black state, unless as is more probable, it reverts entirely to barbarism."[11] In the face of such gloomy pronouncements, based on the notion that racial mixture necessarily led to degeneration, several turn-of-the-century Brazilian thinkers optimistically countered that the process of intermixture produced offspring of intermediate, rather than inferior, qualities. Since white "blood" and European culture were superior, these thinkers argued, those traits would prevail over time, "whitening" and improving the race. Racial mixture, aided by an influx of new white "blood" (in the form of state-sponsored European immigrants) and by the low reproduction and high mortality rates of people of color (caused by miserable living conditions), would gradually help Brazil overcome the "problem" of its mixed-race population.[12] By 1920, in a lengthy preface to the national census, Francisco José de Oliveira Vianna, a leading proponent of whitening, triumphantly announced the "negative growth" of African-descended populations and praised the fecundity of mulattoes and whites. Brazilians, he boasted, had defied the dire forecasts of Lapouge and his ilk and had earned, "without a doubt and without the least irreverence, the right to smile."[13]

The idea that Brazil could "whiten" itself through mass immigration gained many converts among members of the Brazilian elite in the early twentieth century. It not only offered a solution to the problem of Brazilians' being too dark, but it also promised a constant source of labor for a growing agricultural economy no longer based on slavery. Moreover, the "whitening ideal" resonated with long-standing myths about Brazil's harmonious race relations. Ostensibly friendly relations between members of different races, especially sexual encounters among them, could be celebrated both as a mark of the nation's racial tolerance, and as the great hope for whitened nationhood. Brazil's purported racial harmony (an image developed in explicit contrast with the United States since at least the late nineteenth century) became the cornerstone of nationalist discourses of Brazilian uniqueness during the Republic, especially in the years after World War I.[14] With theories of whitening, then, architects of Brazil's national identity ingeniously transformed dismal predictions of national decay into celebrations of national greatness, even as they confirmed the basic tenets of scientific racism. These theories, which Florencio and Oliveira denounced as obstacles to the complete emancipation of black and brown Brazilians, transformed Brazil in the late nineteenth and early twentieth centuries. As a result of immigration, differential mortality rates, and changing measures of who could count as "white" (a relatively flexible category that traditionally encompassed some upwardly mobile people of color and came to include certain immigrants of non-European descent),

Brazil's population (as reflected in national censuses) shifted from a nonwhite to a white majority over the course of the First Republic.[15]

The state of São Paulo and its largest urban center, the city of São Paulo, became the sites par excellence of this national transformation. In the four decades after abolition, planters used the considerable revenues from the region's coffee exports to sponsor almost 2 million European immigrants, providing direct subsidies to nearly half of them. They arrived in an increasingly multiethnic city and state, taking their place alongside nonsponsored immigrants from Europe as well as from Asia and the Middle East.[16] Even taking into account this ethnic diversity, São Paulo was noticeably "whitened" as a result of these immigration policies. Between 1880 and 1920, the population of the city of São Paulo grew from 35,000 to 579,033.[17] Over the course of a slightly longer period (1872–1940), the city's population counted as *preto* (black) or *pardo* (of mixed African and European ancestry) together fell to 8 percent from 37 percent.[18] And despite a nationalist rhetoric praising racial mixture, in the state of São Paulo as a whole in those years, it was the mixed or *pardo* census category that shrank most rapidly relative to others. Paulistas categorized as *branco* or white became an overwhelming majority, the category *preto* became a visible minority encompassing almost all people of African descent, and a new category of *amarelos* (yellows) emerged on the margins. White immigration, rather than creating a city with a significant mixed-race population (like the national capital, Rio de Janeiro, for which the 1940 census found 11 and 17 percent in the *preto* and *pardo* categories, respectively) shaped a city and state in which distinctions between people of European and African descent became increasingly dichotomous, defined primarily around the poles of a small *preto* minority and a *branco* majority.[19] During the Republic, São Paulo's elites successfully presented their state's large population of European immigrants, its small population of African descent, its rapid urbanization and industrialization, and its cultural and artistic vanguardism as the model for a modern and white Brazil, unfettered by the racial legacies of slavery.[20]

Even as the *preto* and *pardo* populations of the city of São Paulo shrank in relative terms, however, they grew absolutely. Many rural migrants from the state of São Paulo or neighboring states like Minas Gerais, newly freed or from families that had been free before abolition, arrived in São Paulo City around the turn of the century. Between 1890 and 1920, the population of color in the city more than quadrupled, growing from 10,842 to 52,112.[21] Yet the very characteristics that made the state and major cities of São Paulo icons of a modernizing, whitened nation also made them particularly hostile places for people of color, places with some of the most developed color prejudice in Brazil. In the first two decades of the twentieth century, as revenues from coffee helped transform São Paulo into the nation's largest and most dynamic industrial economy, people of color seeking jobs in the state's expanding factories found themselves shut out of a largely white and immigrant work-force.[22] As sociologist Carlos Hasenbalg has written of São Paulo, "Nowhere in Brazil were white immigrants so clearly the winners and blacks the losers of economic development and prosperity." This situation "increased the vis-ibility of racial discrimination as a cause of the unequal position of blacks" in the state.[23]

Perhaps because of these particular circumstances, the state of São Paulo was home to an unusual degree of intellectual production by self-identified *pretos* in the years of the Republic. In the state capital and in prosperous nearby cities like Campinas, a small group of literate men of color who found gainful (if precarious) employment in the service sector or in local govern-ment began to set up literary clubs and neighborhood social associations. Some even began to publish small newspapers, like Florencio and Oliveira's *Baluarte*, which was the organ of Campinas's Centro Literário dos Homens de Cor (Literary Center of Men of Color). Newspapers by and for people of color had existed in other Brazilian cities and towns at least since the late nineteenth century, but nowhere else had there been so many papers with the circulation, variety, and frequency of the black press of the cities of São Paulo and Campinas in the early 1900s.[24] The emergence of a prolific black press in this time and place reflects the particular combination of opportunity and constraint experienced by Paulistas of color. On one hand, São Paulo's prosperous, modernizing cities held out the promise of self-improvement for educated men of color, expanding their ambitions and providing the mate-rial conditions with which some of them could sustain a small but active press. On the other hand, the more they accomplished, and the higher they rose into the lower ranks of their city's middle class, the more sharply these men experienced the specifically racial nature of their exclusion. As men who had achieved literacy despite the paucity of educational opportunities, they were not subject to the formal exclusions from citizenship that applied to most people of color. Yet they still faced racism and discrimination in a variety of forms. They were formally or informally barred from a range of jobs, were denied entrance to certain public establishments or leisure spaces, and faced discriminatory attitudes in a range of personal interactions with white Paulistas. These experiences of discrimination, exacerbated by their status as a small racial minority in their city and state, vividly reminded these upwardly mobile *pretos* of the broader ideologies of racial inferiority that marked people of color as unfit for citizenship.

These were the contours of the ways men like Florencio and Oliveira experienced racism in the São Paulo of the Old Republic. Against this backdrop, a generation of men of the class of color used their newspapers to challenge publicly the combination of old and new racial logics that excluded them from full membership in the national community. They celebrated nationalist sentiments that, they hoped, might guarantee them fuller membership in that community. Critical of the tendency of lighter-skinned people of color to attempt to confirm their individual higher status by avoiding race-based associations and publications, and in keeping with the shrinking importance of intermediate color categories in São Paulo, these writers shunned terms like *pardo* or *mulato*. Instead, they identified with the darker color category *preto* or, by the mid-1920s, the racial term *negro*. In the period between 1900 and 1925, this subset of São Paulo's educated and modestly well-off men of color used their newspapers to assert their leadership over, and to speak on behalf of, what they successively called a "class of color," "the men of color," "*preto* men," and, by the middle of the 1920s, "the *negro* race."

The Class of Color

Who made up the small middle class of color of São Paulo and Campinas during the Republic? One man of color later described to sociologist Florestan Fernandes the relatively humble jobs that only tenuously separated this group from the ranks of the working poor: "'There were lawyers and doctors who had Negroes [*sic*] to take care of the office.' To be a private chauffeur, a low-ranking civil servant (janitor, office boy, or clerk as well as to do pick-and-shovel work or be a garbage man), or a police investigator was really something."[25] Whatever social or economic status such jobs bestowed on members of these middling sectors was fragile, constantly threatened by instability and poor pay (particularly in relation to whites in comparable jobs).[26] The people who joined race-based recreational and literary associations in São Paulo and Campinas appear to have come from a still smaller upper echelon of these middling sectors and might more accurately be called a middle class of color. They were teachers in public schools; clerks and low-level officials in the federal, state, or municipal government; or low- to middle-ranking officers in the army or police forces—in short, the sorts of positions Fernandes (paraphrasing his informant) described as "really something," and which, he specified, could only be obtained through connections with a powerful white patron.[27]

It is difficult to judge how many men of color achieved this employment status. A 1923 survey of just over five thousand male military draftees in São Paulo State identified 18 percent of the sample as *pretos* and *pardos*, and about 10 percent of those men (a total of 101) as business employees, civil servants, professionals, and students (the majority were agricultural workers, followed by factory workers).[28] If these percentages were extrapolated to the contemporary urban population of São Paulo, it would suggest as many as several thousand men in this category. Yet it is in no way certain that this small sample was representative of the population of the state, or of São Paulo City.

Whatever their numbers, members of the upper sector of the middling classes of color based their distinctions from working-class or poor people of color not solely on their occupations but also on their desire and ability to conduct themselves according to the values of the Brazilian bourgeoisie. In particular, they were among the minority of *pretos* and *pardos* who had managed to earn educations in the Republic's restricted system of public schools. Through their cultural achievements, leisure activities, religious practices (they were Catholics), and self-presentation, these men and women sought to distinguish themselves from what they saw as the dissolute lower classes, whose members lived in overcrowded tenements (*cortiços*), frequented rowdy *botequins* or bars, and practiced African-derived religions like Macumba or Candomblé. Countless photographs of association members and of writers and readers in São Paulo's black press depict young men of color impeccably coiffed, smartly dressed in suits or military uniforms, bespeaking through their personal appearance the polish, prosperity, and social position they had attained.[29] Yet while literate manhood allowed men of the class of color to vote and hold privileged jobs, their performances of respectability did not earn them unfettered entrance into São Paulo's white middle class. Though not condoned by the law, de facto discrimination was common in many businesses and institutions in early-twentieth-century São Paulo, as in other parts of Brazil. Even two or three decades after abolition, many high-ranking civil or military jobs (like São Paulo's Civil Guard), restaurants, hotels, parks, sports teams, and recreational clubs remained closed to people of color.[30] In response, relatively high-status men of color in cities like Campinas and São Paulo formed their own spaces of leisure and sociability. Their literary clubs and recreational societies bore names that emphasized class and polish more than color: "Centro Smart" and "Elite da Liberdade."[31] When these men called themselves the "class of color" in their early publications, as we will see, they used the word *class* to reference a narrow category of social distinction, not a broad category of shared racial circumstance.

Railroad worker reading newspaper, surrounded by young baggage carriers, at the Estação da Luz in downtown São Paulo. Circa 1910. Vincenzo Pastore, Instituto Moreira Salles Collection.

Although there were dozens of associations for the "class of color," only a few, perhaps the wealthiest among them, left behind a record of their activities and concerns in the form of club newsletters. One contemporary editor called these newsletters "small newspapers [*pequenos jornais*]," and the adjective *small* characterizes the publications in many respects.[32] They averaged about four pages in length and appeared only biweekly or monthly. The papers were also "small" in circulation. Editors published relatively few copies of each issue (since the papers were aimed almost exclusively at members of the clubs and associations) and distributed them primarily through subscriptions or at club meetings and parties.[33] Like the middle class of color itself, the papers had a precarious financial existence. Editors often pleaded with readers to donate money and time to the struggling newspapers. Chronically understaffed as well as underfunded, many of these early papers managed to put out only a handful of issues before folding.[34] Moreover, only a fraction of them have been preserved.[35] Florencio and Oliveira's *Baluarte*, which began circulation in 1903 as the newsletter of Campinas's Centro Literário dos Homens de Cor, offers the best glimpse of the very early years of these societies. Most of the surviving association newsletters, however, circulated between 1916 and 1923, a period of apparent proliferation of clubs and newsletters. After 1923 newsletters published by recreational societies largely gave way to independent newspapers.[36]

The small papers that emerged from the class of color's social clubs served as an "additional press."[37] They sought to complement rather than replace mainstream newspapers, dedicating their few pages specifically to issues affecting the class of color. Editors primarily conveyed information about club and neighborhood activities (dances, meetings, beauty contests, or soccer matches), important events in the lives of individuals (birthdays, deaths, graduations, promotions, marriages), and gossip on members' misbehavior and mischief. But increasingly throughout the second half of the 1910s, even the most lighthearted papers came to include editorials or opinion pieces through which writers addressed their readers on weightier matters affecting people of color. These editorials appear to reflect, in written form, an oral tradition of rhetoric and exhortation within the societies. Many of the men who became editorialists in the newspapers held official positions as *oradores* in their associations.[38] These "orators" commonly gave patriotic or motivational speeches to fellow members, and the papers transcribed the tenor of these speeches. As Frederico Baptista de Souza, himself an orator of the Centro Smart and a frequent contributor to the early black press in São Paulo, explained, society newsletters helped to immortalize the words of deceased great leaders whose advice had once "resonated in all of the clubs and in all of our homes."[39] Editorialists also gave voice to their own concerns in the early press, ranging from discussions of club governance to lofty disquisitions on the values of civic spirit or education. But almost all addressed a central question: the role of the associations in promoting the uplift and performing the respectability of the class of color.

"Men of worth"

Frederico Baptista de Souza was a particularly active member of São Paulo's literary and recreational societies, and a zealous guardian of the respectability of the class of color. He acted as president of the esteemed Gremio Recreativo Kosmos (Kosmos Recreational Club), contributed essays to numerous black papers, and eventually directed the newspaper *O Elite* (*The Elite*), organ of the social club Elite da Liberdade (Elite of Freedom). In 1919, Souza addressed members of various recreational societies in an editorial for *O Alfinete* (*The Pin*), named for its proclivity to "prick" members with criticism. He urged members to devote less of their energy and money to parties and dances and more to the creation of institutions, like libraries and mutual aid funds, that would contribute to members' cultural and financial progress. For Souza, as for the other writers who issued similar stern admonitions, the public behavior of people of color was not just a matter of personal or group improvement. It was a central weapon in the battle against the prejudice of their whiter conationals, whom Souza, and other leaders like him, understood to be watching and judging the class of color at every turn. "We must show that it is not just the One-Steps, Ragtime, and *Picadinhos* [a popular dance] that we know how to cultivate, but that we also feel love and goodwill toward instructive things, good books of literature, poetry, and morals."[40]

"Showing" white Brazilians the good education, financial stability, and morality of the class of color, one of his contemporaries later remembered, was Souza's fondest mission. Under Souza's leadership, the Kosmos Recreational Club "under no circumstances accepted people of dubious morals." Souza also allegedly once sold his own house to ensure Kosmos's financial viability rather than opening the club's membership to a broader, less select segment of society.[41] On another occasion he resigned in anger from Kosmos following accusations by the club's landlady that the club was behind in its rent on its headquarters. "I judged it my duty," he wrote in *A Liberdade*, "to save the honor of that club which, composed of men of color, has always shined in the fulfillment of its moral and social duties, something that not even the landlady herself can deny."[42]

A. J. VEIGA DOS SANTOS   F. BAPTISTA DE SOUZA

Arlindo J. Veiga dos Santos, contributor to *O Clarim d'Alvorada* and future founder of the Frente Negra Brasileira, and Frederico Baptista de Souza, active member and contributor to multiple black Paulistano associations and newspapers. From *O Clarim d'Alvorada*, 15 January 1927. Acervo da Fundação Biblioteca Nacional, Brazil.

Souza's concern with how whites perceived members of the class of color probably reflected the importance, for men like him, of daily interactions with whites of higher status. Souza worked as a clerk at São Paulo's law school; other men of the class of color similarly found themselves in constant professional contact with white Brazilians. Deocleciano Nascimento, editor of *O Menelik* (1915), began his career as a foundry worker and eventually became an accountant. Augusto Oliveira, editor of *O Alfinete* (1919), was a brigadier in the Força Pública, São Paulo's armed guard, and later became a paralegal. Jayme de Aguiar, cofounder of *O Clarim d'Alvorada* (*The Clarion of Dawn*, 1924), worked in the police's fingerprinting lab with "poets and law students." Other editors held day jobs as cooks in large institutions, as workers in electric and telephone companies, or as public employees.[43] In their jobs, these men continually negotiated assumptions about their own characters that reflected broader prejudices against people of color. It was common, for instance, for skilled people of color seeking employment in the early decades of the century to undergo a "trial period" in which they were expected to prove their abilities and moral character to potential employers.[44] Outside work, too, the men of the class of color had to perform for the powerful white patrons on whom many depended for favors, employment, or financial support. These interactions were conditioned by the patron's general opinions about the reliability of men of color. One man identified as "J" (almost certainly José Correia Leite, cofounder of *O Clarim d'Alvorada*) recounted to sociologist Florestan Fernandes his experience approaching his white father (who did not legally recognize him) to request money for the publication of his newspaper. "J" recalled his humiliation as his father, in the process of considering his request, tried to check his breath for alcohol.[45] These fraught day-to-day relationships with whiter conationals help explain why so many articles in the early black press evince a consciousness of being watched and judged. Whether in *O Baluarte*'s call for the men of the class of color to "give a lesson in civic virtue [*civismo*]" or *O Menelik*'s promise to "show the world our knowledge," the early newsletters echoed Souza's sense of urgency in correcting misbehavior and "showing" a broader Brazilian audience the worth of the class of color.[46]

In the first two and a half decades of the century, writers of color eager to disprove the negative racial attitudes of whites outlined a political strategy that largely avoided direct confrontation over racial issues. The editors of the newspaper *O Menelik*, for instance, aimed to "conquer the friendship" of a broader white audience by "piously expuls[ing] from the columns of *O Menelik* the word 'combat.' We will never seek to combat, even though there might be cause."[47] Similarly, an article titled "Race Prejudice" in a 1918 issue of *O Alfinete* advised readers to "see[k] to capture the friendship and consideration of those who think differently than us" by "stay[ing] quiet, and, by means of our example—in the practice of all that might reveal a spirit of goodness, of affection, of sweetness, of perseverance and of abnegation—we will be able to speak louder and better than through words."[48] By opting to fight racism through exemplary behavior rather than words of confrontation, and by choosing to appeal to whites' "friendship" and better sentiments even in the face of stinging discrimination, writers of color were not capitulating to conformist or assimilationist pressures. They were combating racism as they experienced it in the Republic—not in legal form, but as a set of "dogmas" about racial and cultural inferiority that conditioned their interpersonal relationships with white colleagues, family members, or patrons.

Even as they shunned words of confrontation, therefore, these men placed the ability to wield "words" at the center of the project of setting an example. Literacy and culture were the proxies that excluded most men of color from full citizenship in Brazil. So the educated, relatively well-off men of the class of color placed literacy and culture—and particularly writing—at the forefront of their fight against racism and their claims to equality. Writing became a crucial political act, most obviously as a vehicle for communicating and organizing political strategies in a Republic in which access to a national public sphere was severely restricted. But writing was also political for its very capacity to enact men of color's fitness for citizenship, to challenge prevailing ideas of their intellectual degradation. Not infrequently, the cult of writing itself became writers' topic, as in a paean to "The [Written] Word," which declared this "the most beautiful, the most expressive, the most difficult of all the other arts."[49] Even when they were not directly celebrating the written word, writers' use of formal, exceedingly refined linguistic conventions communicated great pride in their hard-earned learning. Sharing the preoccupations of other men of letters of their era, members of one newspaper frequently insulted those of another for their incorrect or pedestrian grammar, revealing the importance they placed on formal literary merit, and not just content, as bases for their individual authority.[50] Alongside society news, these papers gave pride of place to literature—poems, short prose pieces known as *crônicas*, and excerpts from novellas or short stories, often with patriotic themes. Through literary production often unrelated to racial themes, writers and editors of these newspapers—men like Deocleciano Nascimento, the editor of *O Menelik* and a published poet—tried to show that they far exceeded the basic requirements for citizenship.[51] They were not simply literate, but lettered.[52]

To whom were such performances directed? These newspapers circulated primarily among the class of color and were aimed most pointedly at that audience. Yet the memoirs of writers and editors, as well as evidence in the newspapers themselves, suggest that white readers paid attention to the papers with enough frequency, if not regularity, to justify writers' sense that they were on display for a broader segment of society. José Correia Leite, who in 1924 cofounded *O Clarim d'Alvorada*, recalled later in his life that a few "curious" or "learned" whites sent their servants to buy black papers.[53] Moreover, until 1923, all of the newspapers of the class of color were sent out to commercial printers for composition and production. Being overseen by typesetters and copy editors from outside their community almost certainly made writers and editors of color conscious of *how* they wrote and might have even limited their sense of *what* they could write. Finally, throughout the 1920s, editors of the newspapers of the class of color frequently sent select issues of their papers to editors of mainstream dailies.[54] Their attempts to gain the attention of mainstream newspapers is not surprising at a time when journalism rather than books provided the primary outlet for intellectual production on social questions.[55]

Because the mainstream public sphere in Republican Brazil was restricted to men, as was the right to active citizenship, it is not surprising that the newspapers of the class of color sought to demonstrate fitness for citizenship in gendered terms. Most noticeably, these papers largely excluded women as writers. They were an overwhelmingly male space, with almost all male editors and contributors. In this sense, the newspapers appear to have intensified a gender imbalance visible in the clubs and associations, where despite a mixed membership, men occupied most, if not all, positions of leadership.[56] But they also seemingly imagined an audience that was predominantly male. Many papers directed themselves not to the "class of color" but, more narrowly, to the "men of the class of color" or the "class of the men of color." The editors of *O Baluarte*, for their part, tethered the broader project of racial advancement specifically to the "class of the men of color," hoping their paper would "teach them to be citizens in the strictest sense of the word!"[57] Women appeared in these papers as muses of poetry, as subjects of love letters, photos, or stories, or as contestants in beauty contests, but they almost never appeared as writers, readers, or direct beneficiaries of the project of expanded citizenship.[58]

Although their maleness and literacy allowed writers of color to escape the principal formal exclusions of the Republican legal system, their pigment linked them, through the workings of prejudice, to the much larger population of color. Since the early 1900s, writers of color like Benedito Florencio and Francisco Oliveira had decried that racial prejudice made it impossible even for worthy men of color to feel fully free. The writers and editors in the early black press thus came to see their project as a performance not simply of their own superior culture but also of their leadership in uplifting a broader community of color. "It is our duty," wrote the editors of *O Baluarte*, "to defend the black race [*raça negra*], taking charge of its civic education, its moral equilibrium, and its social independence."[59] The self-appointed leaders of the class of color therefore often sharply criticized their community, blaming members of the class of color (and often, a wider population of less fortunate *pretos* and *pardos*) for not taking better advantage of the opportunities that the Republic afforded them. In this vein, Augusto Oliveira, editor of *O Alfinete*, wrote in 1918 of the "lamentable state of men of color in Brazil, oppressed from one side by the slaveholding mentality that has not yet fully disappeared from our social milieu and, on the other, by the nefarious ignorance in which this element of the Brazilian race wallows." Though Oliveira bemoaned the situation of people of color in Brazil, he nonetheless expressed hope that the "slaveholding mentality" would eventually disappear and that people of color might eventually overcome their limitations by taking full advantage of their rights. Sounding what was perhaps the most common note in the early black press, Oliveira urged men of color to pursue an education, which would make them "a much more important factor in the greatness and prosperity of our dear motherland."[60] Elsewhere, writers exhorted readers to improve their work ethic, civic consciousness, or hygiene so as to "present themselves in society in a dignified and decent way, giving an example of good manners, the finest and most delicate characteristic of civilized men."[61] Though they sometimes addressed these pleas to a wide swath of the population of color, most frequently writers limited themselves to the task of preparing only the class of color, the members of their own organizations, for exemplary behavior. As one writer put it, associations were "miniature versions of the nation," and members' actions and self-presentation, the building blocks of citizenship for the class of color.[62]

If membership in recreational societies constituted one level of a geographically layered sense of national belonging for men of the class of color, membership as Paulistas, or natives of the state of São Paulo, constituted another. The newspaper *O Bandeirante* (organ of the Bandeirantes Recreational Society) reflected the aspiration, among many writers in São Paulo's black press, to claim an identity as full and unmarked Paulistas. The paper took its name from what was becoming, in the 1910s and 1920s, the foremost icon of São Paulo's regionalism. In the colonial period, when São Paulo was a rough outpost of Portuguese settlement, European-descended *bandeirantes* (literally, flag bearers) helped build the local economy by leading prospecting and Indian slave-raiding expeditions into the hinterlands. Though considered key protagonists of brutal Portuguese colonialism by writers in the "Black Legend" tradition, in the early decades of the twentieth century, *bandeirantes* came to be celebrated as precursors to São Paulo's European, entrepreneurial, modern civilization.[63] That a black social club and newspaper in São Paulo would take on this name, with all of its whitening pretensions and evocations of violence against natives and Africans, reveals members' desire to be seen as protagonists in São Paulo's emergent regional leadership of the nation. This gesture, echoed in several articles, suggests that the men of the class of color of São Paulo, like Paulistas more generally, saw themselves as marching ahead of the nation in the role of standard-bearers of modernity, their urbane clubs and newspapers standing as examples for all Brazilians of color.[64]

In their exhortative editorials, male writers made it clear that gender norms were central to performances of fitness for citizenship, as both Paulistas and Brazilians. As in other areas of their behavior, leaders of the class of color based their ideals of proper masculinity and womanhood on those of contemporary Brazilian bourgeois society.[65] But as with values like education and patriotism, ideas about gender, and about male and female honor in particular, had special meaning for people of color seeking to dispel ideas of their "moral annihilation." In a newspaper editorial from 1918, J. d'Alencastro, literary director of *O Bandeirante*, declared that people of color would only be able to live as equals with whites if they "sought, by every means, to elevate the character of our men, obligate our children, brothers, and friends to frequent schools, [and] inculcate in the spirit of our daughters, sisters, or wives the exact understanding of honor and appreciation for themselves." He emphasized that "constituting a legal and legitimate family, and creating men of worth" was the basis for "the uplift of our class as we understand it!"[66] In this vein, the gossip columns of newspapers like *A Liberdade* and *O Alfinete* were full of denunciations of young women engaging in behavior (public kissing, "licentious" dances like the *maxixe*) considered improper and unbecoming to ladies of their standing.[67] Protecting women's honor, however, was about policing not just their sexual propriety but also their appearance in public. In his editorial, d'Alencastro expressed additional concern about the undue exposure of women and children of color to the world of work and of the street, both because he saw the presence of worn-down, ragged women and children of color on the streets of São Paulo as a stain on the image of the class of color as a whole and because, in his view, the inability of black and brown men to provide for, and protect, stable patriarchal families recalled the days of slavery.[68] Providing for their families through what d'Alencastro called "honorable work" and protecting the honor of their women were thus particular points of pride and essential attributes of respectability for men of color aspiring to become men of worth and hoping to dispel the images of weakness, effeminacy, and laziness associated with long-standing ideologies of vagrancy.

Fraternity

Just as the metaphor of the legitimate, honorable family provided writers in the black press with the moral guidelines for their behavior as individuals, as members of clubs and as a class of color, so too did ideas of family frame their understandings of citizenship. Writers repeatedly seized on the notion of fraternity to assert their belonging in the national community. Specifically, like *friendship*, they used *fraternity* to describe ideal relations between people of color and whites. In one kind of usage, *fraternity*, along with *liberty* and *equality*, reflected the extensive influence of French revolutionary ideas in the rhetoric of Brazilian republicanism. For several writers, the triad of "Liberty, Equality, and Fraternity" spoke eloquently of the condition of people of color since the rise of the Republic. An article by Conde in *A Liberdade*, for instance, praised the 14 July (the day of the storming of the Bastille in France) as a date that, with its connotations of liberty, should "run parallel and shoulder to shoulder with 13 May [1888], the date that emancipated a race [i.e., when slavery was abolished in Brazil]."[69] In this vein, some writers used *fraternidade* specifically to stand for the end of slavery and the advent of a society in which men of color would be treated as brothers by whites.[70] More frequently black writers, like many of their whiter conationals, linked French revolutionary ideas to the founding of the Brazilian Republic in 1889. The "advent of the Republic," Benedito Florencio wrote in 1903, was "the golden key that closed an extraordinary cycle of our political evolution," a date "ennobled by the highest conceptions of the spirit of liberty and human fraternity!"[71]

But if writers' enthusiasm for fraternity stemmed from an attempt to appropriate a range of useful ideologies from French Republicanism, many also used it to celebrate a specifically Brazilian situation: their nation's purported racial harmony. The clearest example of this usage appears in J. d'Alencastro's "A Grave Error!" (1918), the same long editorial piece that exhorted men of color to become "men of worth." In one of the first explicit discussions of race relations in the black press, d'Alencastro rebuked people of color who believed that the project of "uplifting the class" required a contentious "separation of the races" in the style of the United States. The situation in that country, marked by "lynchings and prejudice," "rancor, persecution, and war to the death" against people of color, was fundamentally different from Brazilian realities, d'Alencastro insisted. Throughout his piece, d'Alencastro characterized as brotherhood the racial harmony he saw as Brazil's unique national patrimony. Brazil was a place where "*pretos* and whites [were] made brothers [*irmanados*] by their same love for this land." "Let us," he continued, "solidify the fraternity that makes us indistinguishable from whites born under the gold and green flag," for "to promote the separation of races is to provoke hatred and possible fratricidal struggles!"[72]

It is significant that the article that most forcefully made the case for honorable, exemplary masculine behavior in the early black press was also the one that most ardently advocated a gentlemanly, brotherly code of conduct (in contrast to "fratricidal struggles") as the class of color's path to racial inclusion. Though few men of color wrote as openly about race relations as d'Alencastro in this period, his celebration of the ideal of racial fraternity—and his refusal to talk about the ways Brazilians failed to live up to it—echoed the black press's broader strategy of fighting racism through example rather than confrontation in the first two decades of the century. Few were the statements, like that of *O Alfinete* editor Augusto Oliveira, that "the equality and fraternization of peoples, guaranteed by the Revolution of '89 in France and which the Republic implanted as a symbol of our democracy is, in relation to *negros*, a fiction and a lie."[73] Even then, Oliveira appears to have made the principle and practice of fraternity the test of a nation's true commitment to equality. In a subsequent article, he wrote that while the U.S. Constitution "theoretically" guaranteed blacks in the United States "all the same rights and freedoms as whites," its failure to substantiate those ideals in everyday relations made that nation "the land of equality and liberty, *though not of fraternity.*"[74] Oliveira's ability to criticize the shortcomings of racial fraternity in Brazil makes his embrace of the ideal all the more poignant.

That writers like d'Alencastro or Oliveira would endorse the ideal of racial fraternity might strike us as perplexing, given what we know about the ways Brazilian elites in the Empire and Republic used ideas of racial harmony to support racist projects, like whitening, that aimed to erase Brazil's black population. Yet the rhetoric of racial fraternity was not always or uniformly a smokescreen for racist schemes; at times, it could provide a line of defense against overt forms of discrimination. Consider the congressional debates of 1921 regarding plans by the Brazilian American Colonization Syndicate to promote the mass migration of black North Americans to Brazil, a land many of the would-be migrants considered free of racial prejudice. Debates over whether and how to discourage these "undesirables" quickly reached the Foreign Ministry and the Congress, for the idea of large groups of black American immigrants settling in Brazil did not sit well with those who hoped for a gradual whitening of the population through European immigration and intermixture.[75] In July 1921, two congressional deputies, Andrade Bezerra (of the northeastern state of Pernambuco) and Cincinnato Braga (of São Paulo), put before the lower house of Congress a bill that would prohibit the entrance "of human individuals of the black races." Although the Constitution of 1891 already banned "Africans" from entering Brazil, a 1907 federal decree had done away with geographic origin restrictions in order to allow the immigration of Japanese workers.[76] The new bill proposed to institute a specifically racial ban in order to keep out U.S. citizens of African descent, who despite being acceptable in geographic terms as North Americans were racially undesirable for their "African" racial origins. Proponents of the bill did not specify whether they feared U.S. black immigrants for their presumed racial identities and politics (which, many Brazilians believed, threatened their nation's racial harmony and mixture) or whether they saw them as posing a setback to the eugenic processes of whitening. They simply cited the migrants' "undesirability" and their own "desire to defend the real interests of our fatherland [*pátria*]."

Opponents of the proposed immigration ban immediately took over the debate, arguing that it was beneath Congress's dignity even to consider the matter. Joaquim Osório, the representative from Rio Grande do Sul, led this opposition, opening with the argument that the bill was incompatible with the Golden Law, which abolished slavery and "celebrated the fraternity of men." Another delegate argued that the bill was an attack on the principles of brotherhood central to the Catholic faith, which saw the sons of Ham "also as God's sons." Above all, opponents argued, the bill was incompatible with the ideals of fraternity inherent in the Brazilian Republic. "The Republic makes brothers of all men, makes them equal before the law; the Republic has no racial prejudice, or exclusivist sentiments; and does not distinguish among whites, *negros*, or *pardos*." Along with legal equality and freedom from slavery, the Republican ideal of fraternity made legal racial discrimination of the sort the bill proposed anathema in Brazil.

As these debates took place in Congress, the Brazilian Foreign Ministry quietly rendered them moot by instructing its consulates in the United States to deny visas to African Americans seeking to travel to Brazil. It is certainly possible, as some scholars have argued, that it was the bill's redundancy in light of extralegal prohibitions of black immigration, together with many representatives' preference for less overt forms of racism, that led to the bill's eventual failure.[77] Yet the bill elicited real debate. Indeed, though it eventually failed to pass, frustrated supporters helped resuscitate a similar version two years later (which would also fail to pass). This suggests that opposition based on avowed antiracism and at least rhetorical commitment to racial fraternity had the power to constrain those who would implement overtly discriminatory policies. And while definitions of racial fraternity among the bill's opponents almost certainly diverged from those of contemporary writers of color, the terms through which representatives like Osório registered their distaste for the bill—their emphasis on racial fraternity as the essence of Brazilians' moral character—left an example for the antiracist uses of *fraternity* that would dominate the black press for the rest of the decade.

In particular, for opponents of the bill, *fraternity* expressed the sentimental particularities of Brazilians in their relations with people of different races. Osório framed the bill as repellent to "Brazilian sentiments, which do not distinguish or condemn men by the color of their skin." Congressman Álvaro Baptista explained that "even if we did not have . . . the law" to expressly disavow the bill, "we would have the protest of our sentiments." Sentiment could, of course, be discriminatory, yet these men implied that in the Brazilian nation it was necessarily antiracist. Citing the "dignity" of the "raça negra," Osório and his colleagues João Cabral and Álvaro Baptista entreated their fellow congressmen to remember the role Africans and their descendants played and continued to play in the formation of the Brazilian nation and race. Baptista, in prescient reference to what would become one of the most popular icons of racial fraternity among groups of black and white thinkers toward the end of the decade, reminded his audience that "the women of that race served as nursemaids even, perhaps, to the majority of these congressmen!" Congressman Gilberto Amado, a noted antiracist intellectual, similarly called Brazil "the son of *negros.*" Throughout the discussion, opponents of the bill defined fraternity as a feeling of familial intimacy and a sentiment of human dignity that made up a particular kind of Brazilian sensibility, especially in contrast to the open racism of the United States. Even those who favored racial restrictions on immigration perceived the power of sentiment to turn the debates. In his attempts to defend his bill, Bezerra condemned "this purely sentimental tendency with which we face the vital problems of this nation." Yet sentiment won the day, and sealed the bill's failure, at least in the short term.[78]

The open use of *fraternity* and sentiment to discredit openly racist policies helps explain the appeal of these concepts for writers seeking to defend the class of color. In a political system where equality had little meaning, but where arguments invoking sentiment might hold the line against racist legislation, the metaphor of fraternity, with its implied mutual obligations of familial love and respect, provided the men of the class of color with a strategic weapon in their battle against racial exclusion. The use of *fraternity* in the 1921 debates about immigration can also help us to understand some writers of color when they went so far as to embrace the ideologies of racial fusion associated with ideals of racial fraternity. The congressmen who opposed the 1921 bill presented racial fusion and intimacy as cultural and sentimental, rather than strictly biological, formulations. It seems likely that this was the interpretation a writer like J. d'Alencastro favored when he called (somewhat unusually) for people of color "not to perpetuate our race but to infiltrate ourselves into the bosom of the privileged, white race," or when he described the "intimate communion" that existed among *preto* and white children in Brazil's classrooms.[79] There is no literal sexual or biological meaning for *bosom* and *intimacy* here; rather, d'Alencastro appears to be using those sentimental metaphors to talk about the social commingling and cultural integration he and his colleagues at *O Bandeirante* repeatedly championed.[80] Dominant discourses of interracial intimacy and fusion, in this sense, could serve as metaphors for the erasure of race as a category of social distinction (not just for the erasure of blacks themselves) and as a way of demanding that people of color be treated as full, unmarked Brazilians.

In the early years of São Paulo's black press (until 1922), while the papers still consisted mostly of society news and literary production, d'Alencastro's writings were remarkably (if unusually) clear expressions of an emerging approach to racial politics. Given the tension between confronting the limits of their freedoms outright or celebrating the possibilities for inclusion, most writers placed their bets on the latter. As a whole, their writings suggest the view that a pact with representatives of relatively progressive visions of racial fraternity would benefit people of color more than racial separation or confrontation. This strategy fit well with the other project these newspapers espoused, namely, that of disproving the lingering remnants of racist "dogmas" through example and uplift. In the black press of the 1910s and early 1920s, several writers thus contributed to the ideas about racial fusion and harmony then taking hold in certain elite circles. They saw these principles, like many other aspects of the Republican order, as alternatives to older, blatantly racist social and political arrangements, and as opportunities—recently earned and still imperfectly implemented, but potentially powerful—to enact their belonging as rightful Brazilians.

"What wounds our souls"

Racial fraternity would become an even more important ideological resource for writers in São Paulo's black press over the course of the 1920s. Yet after 1923 writers increasingly paired celebrations of Brazil's ideals of racial fraternity with denunciations of its shortcomings in practice. A key context for this shift was the emergence of new kinds of newspapers by and for people of color. In July 1923 a group of men of color in Campinas, including Benedito Florencio (formerly of *O Baluarte*) and two poets, Lino Guedes and Gervásio de Moraes, founded a new newspaper: *O Getulino*. Even in its first few issues, *O Getulino* (a nickname for *preto* abolitionist lawyer Luiz Gama) captures the transformations that would affect the form and content of the black press, as well as the attitudes of the men who wrote in it, in subsequent years.[81] In contrast to previous papers, *O Getulino* was independent of associations and clubs, and, as its first issue proudly proclaimed, the paper had "oficinas próprias"—its own typesetting equipment.[82] Coeditors Guedes and Moraes composed and printed about fifteen hundred copies of *O Getulino* weekly for three years with few interruptions, a significant advance in frequency and consistency over earlier journals. Veterans of the *Diário do Povo*, a major Campinas daily with working-class sympathies, Florencio and Guedes carried over their experiences with issue-oriented social critique to their new paper. Whereas editorials had appeared only sporadically in the club newspapers, *O Getulino* devoted the better portion of its pages to editorials and readers' letters on issues affecting people of color in Campinas. They relegated poems, *crônicas*, and society gossip to a secondary position. Benedito Florencio, who had sharpened his editorial pen in a popular satire column for the *Diário do Povo*, and who as early as 1903 had diagnosed the incomplete emancipation of men of color in *O Baluarte*, brought to *O Getulino* a particularly clear sense of his role as an opinion leader for his race, contributing lengthy pieces on a range of subjects in almost every issue.[83]

  O Getulino reconfigured and expanded the scope of the black press in other ways as well. Its topics and audience were no longer circumscribed by a small group of neighborhood associations. It had correspondents and subscribers in São Paulo as well as contributors from Rio de Janeiro. Its editors and writers increasingly commented on articles in mainstream newspapers covering issues affecting people of color in those cities and elsewhere in Brazil. Without links to any specific social club, moreover, writers in *O Getulino* exercised their leadership almost exclusively through the practices of writing, publishing, and reading. Their independence from social clubs also presupposed a new audience of readers marked primarily by their self-identification as people invested in the paper's mission: the "defense of the interests of *preto* men." *O Getulino*'s shift in terminology—its writers used *preto* in the masthead and increasingly turned to *negro* in the text of the articles themselves—reflects writers' increased attention to the ways racial prejudice defined them and their readership not just as men accidentally marked by "color" but as members of a broader racial group with common interests and a common destiny. Its contributors thus no longer wrote to members of a club or an elite class of color. Instead, they imagined themselves, their audience, and their constituency, as members of a global "black race." In Florencio's words, writers "read copiously and studied day and night the problems of the black [*negra*] race in the world."[84] Drawing from mainstream Brazilian and international publications, *O Getulino* commented frequently on issues like the treatment of black troops in Europe following World War I, growing racial radicalism in the United States (particularly the rise of Garveyism), and, occasionally, on events in Africa itself.[85]

  Despite early signs of their shifting view of racial community, however, in the first few issues of *O Getulino* editors continued to express optimism

AO GETULINO

Lino Guedes
Redactor-chefe

Gervasio de Moraes
Redactor-secretario

Ao nosso caro confrade "O GETULINO", que se publica na bel a
qidade campineira, orgam defensor dos nossos interesses, hoje, por occasião
do seu 1.º anniversario, prestamos esta simples homenagem, porem sincera.

Lino Guedes and Gervásio de Moraes, poets and editors of Campinas's *O Getulino*. From an homage to that paper on the occasion of its first anniversary, in *O Clarim d'Alvorada*, 25 January 1925. Acervo da Fundação Biblioteca Nacional, Brazil.

about the Republic's legal order, urging readers to integrate into Brazilian society by following dominant cultural codes and avoiding confrontation. In *O Getulino*'s second issue, for instance, editor Gervásio de Moraes called on the youth of his race to take advantage of their good fortune as citizens of Republican Brazil, where they enjoyed "liberty" and a range of "rights granted them by their fatherland." Foremost among these for Moraes, as for other writers before him, was "the right to educate ourselves so that we may glory in the conquests of Civilization!"[86] Several articles expressed disapproval of *pretos* who undertook separatist racial organizing in a small all-*preto* neighborhood in Campinas, which the editors decried as an example of "terrible and condemnable self-segregation."[87] When *A Protectora*, the organ of Campinas's Association for the Protection of *Preto* Brazilians, published an essay about job discrimination, asking "where, among our youth, do we see a contractor, a doctor, a lawyer, or a priest who carries in his veins the purest *negro* blood and hails from Campinas?," *O Getulino*'s editors responded that the paper's implication of systematic discrimination was "absurd" and "venomous." They supported this opinion through a lengthy and somewhat arbitrary calculation, stating that the earliest date that a descendant of slaves could possibly have attained the rank of doctor through the Brazilian educational system was 1924. As the year was still 1923, they roundly dismissed their rival's argument that racism was responsible for the absence of *preto* doctors.[88] It should be noted, however, that neither side considered citing light-skinned *pardo* doctors or lawyers as evidence for their positions. Rather, true to their commitment to identifying as *pretos*, writers on both sides implicitly agreed that the absence of professionals of the "purest *negro* blood" was the issue—if one O Getulino wished overall to minimize.

Then, in 1923, Robert Abbott, owner and publisher of the U.S. black newspaper *The Chicago Defender*, visited Brazil to revive the possibility of mass settlement by African Americans. Not surprisingly, Abbott's colonization plan, similar to the ones that had led to a proposed immigration ban in 1921, caused an upheaval in Brazil's political circles and newspapers. As in 1921, most editorialists and politicians had little enthusiasm for the prospect of large-scale black immigration from the United States. But by 1923 some opponents of black immigration made their case using the very terms that had helped defeat their cause in 1921: ideas of Brazilian racial fraternity and harmony. An editorial in Rio's *O Paiz*, for instance, explained that "no Brazilian has a prejudice based on color and we are, without a doubt, the promised land for those who do not have light skin." It was precisely the nation's status as a racial "promised land" that made the mass migration of "black North Americans" so unpalatable. Black Americans were not undesirable because they were black, the editorial implied—they were undesirable because of the *way* they were black, because segregation had turned them into a distinct social group with oppositional politics. If they were to arrive in Brazil, they would "establish here exactly the conflicts that we do not have."[89]

The editors of *O Getulino* closely followed Abbott's visit and the debates it sparked in Brazilian public life. Initially, their responses to the Abbott controversy stayed close to the political formulations of the earlier black press, seeking to avoid direct conflict, encourage sentimental ties with white conationals, and express hope in the power of nationalist views of racial mixture to keep public discourse (at least technically) antiracist. With an eye on the growing context of U.S. racial radicalism in the 1920s, particularly Marcus Garvey's International Negro Conference of 1920, *Getulino's* Benedito Florencio, unlike most white commentators, did not hesitate to specify the nature of the threat posed by "black North American immigration": it "harms the solution of the black problem in Brazil and threatens the racial harmony and peace of the nation." By the "solution of the black problem in Brazil," Florencio meant the "peaceful" race relations resulting from activism that was integrationist rather than separatist and the "harmony" resulting from "the mathematical process of the gradual disappearance of the black race in

Brazil."[90] Like d'Alencastro before him, Florencio here trod a fine but perceptible line between championing the disappearance of actual black people and advocating, as he did simultaneously in other writings, for the erasure of race as a fixed category of difference.[91]

Yet the immigration debates that reemerged in the Brazilian Congress in October 1923 as a result of Abbott's visit would soon dramatically shift the tenor of Florencio's largely optimistic articles, and of *O Getulino* more generally. They would crystallize writers' transformation from leaders of middle-class associations of color to ardent "defenders" of a broader group of "*preto* men." The catalyst in this process was a new bill introduced by Fidelis Reis, a federal deputy from Minas Gerais, aimed at meeting Brazil's labor needs by encouraging the immigration of whites while banning immigrants of the "black race" and limiting those of the "yellow race." Fidelis Reis, who had supported the failed attempts to pass similar legislation two years earlier, sought to avoid the "vehement opposition" faced by his colleagues Andrade Bezerra and Cincinnato Braga in previous years. Where those men had been timid in explaining their rationale for a racial bar, Reis and his supporters drew explicitly on the Brazilian variant of scientific racism to outline the threat such immigration would pose to the whitening project. At times, these arguments masqueraded as a defense of Brazilian racial harmony in exactly the ways critics of the "myth" of racial democracy would later denounce as cynical. Expressing a wish to balance Brazil's continued need for immigrant laborers against the overriding concern to protect "the racial fusion that is taking place under our skies," Reis (and his supporters) phrased their concerns about the impact of African and Asian immigrants in unbridled eugenicist terms. Not only would migrants of color be culturally "unassimilable," creating "cysts" in the "national organism," but, Reis avowed, Brazilians' "Hellenic conception of beauty would never harmonize with the features resulting from this sort of racial fusion."[92]

In a subsequent congressional session, Reis read aloud letters from leading intellectuals and politicians stating their opinions on the proposal. In their missives of support, Oliveira Vianna, the lawyer-historian and leading theoretician of "whitening" ideologies, and Afrânio Peixoto, a prominent medical professor, echoed Reis as they proclaimed the degeneracy and undesirability of the *mestiço* or mixed-race person. Vianna predicted that immigrants of color would bring down the quality of Brazil's experiment with racial mixture, "augment[ing] the shapeless mass of inferior *mestiçagem* that so greatly retards our progress." Peixoto, for his part, argued that "as a rule, racial mixture is an unhappy [condition]. . . . Many of our national woes stem from it." Yet he hoped that, in time, this process would yield a lighter population: "We might take three hundred years to change our souls and lighten our skin, and, if not as whites, at least thus disguised, we will lose our *mestiço* character." Faced with the urgency of defending this delicate project against any further setbacks, Peixoto begged leave to speak frankly: "It is precisely at this moment that [North] America intends to rid herself of her body of 15 million *negros* and send them to Brazil. How many centuries will it take to purify this human residue? Will we have enough albumin to refine all this dross? How much more time until we redeem [the sons of] Ham? Was Liberia not enough for them; have they now discovered Brazil?"[93] The editors of Rio's *O Jornal* similarly refused to hold their tongues in the face of such a threat, condemning the role of sentiment in thwarting previous attempts. "Enough of inept sentimentalism; let us not be afraid of words, and say things as they are." It was bad enough that black Brazilians were "indolent," "ignorant," and "hard and slow to absorb, impeding our ethnic unity and depreciating our racial mixture with their inferior contributions." But "of all the disadvantages of African immigration, only one has not manifested itself here: racial struggle." This would be the contribution of U.S. blacks, if allowed to enter Brazil.[94]

Even as it revealed the unapologetic popularity of eugenic schemes for whitening among some politicians and intellectuals in Brazil, Reis's bill earned the opposition of others. Jurist Clóvis Bevilacqua, a leading architect of the Civil Code of 1916, opposed the bill on the grounds that it contravened "human sentiments of fraternity and benevolence."[95] As in 1921, the bill failed to pass, yet the support it commanded among leading thinkers, politicians, and journalists, and the terms in which it was justified, sent shock waves through the black press.

News of the Reis bill and of debates surrounding it first appeared in *O Getulino* through the contributions of the jurist, lawyer, and public intellectual Evaristo de Moraes. Moraes, a (light-skinned) man of color, was an outspoken critic of racism, a self-proclaimed *negro*, and a defender of Brazilian ideals of racial fraternity.[96] During Congress's consideration of the Reis bill, Moraes, who resided in the national capital, Rio de Janeiro, closely followed the lower house's daily proceedings. In his reportage on these events, published directly in *O Getulino*, Moraes made it clear that what was so disquieting about the bill was that, despite targeting Asians as well, "one perceive[d] that the attack [was] primarily against *negros*." Moreover, Moraes worried, it was "immediately evident" that these attacks relied on the doctrinaire scientific racism of "heralds of the superiority of a particular branch of the white race," like the notorious Count Joseph Arthur de Gobineau and Georges Vacher de Lapouge (both of whom Fidelis Reis cited on the floor of Congress).

Moraes's essays in response to the bill and its supporting arguments provided the first and clearest exposition of scientific racism and whitening ideologies—and their legal, intellectual, and moral illegitimacy—in the black press of the early twentieth century and likely acted as a primer on those subjects for the writers of color who subsequently tackled them.[97]

Evaristo de Moraes adopted several strategies in refuting the racial theories behind Reis's bill. First, he cautioned that applying Gobineau's ideas of Aryan superiority to Brazil was "inconvenient," since it was well known that the French author of *Essay on the Inequality of Human Races* (1855) did not consider Southern Europeans (like the Portuguese) to be Aryans at all but rather an inferior race resulting from mixture with Africans and Moors. Second, Moraes admonished that "there does not currently exist any civilized people exempt from race mixture." Civilization and modernity *depended* on racial mixture. A lawyer of mixed ancestry, Evaristo de Moraes would have been particularly pleased to assert this as refutation of the theories of the "lunatic Gobineau" that *mestiços* were "inadaptable" to learning and the law. Finally, like d'Alencastro and Florencio, Moraes strategically posited an inclusive, optimistic version of racial and cultural fusion as the dominant (and rightful) consensus among Brazilians. "It seems incredible that in the year 1923, and *in Brazil*, someone would still remember to draw on Gobineau and Lapouge, who have been revealed to be completely foreign to the conditions of the ethnic fusion that has occurred among us and who, suffused with prejudices, were unable to foresee our civilization's progress." Fidelis Reis's negative view of racial fusion was thus an outdated aberration, "a veritable affront to the Brazilian nation." In the face of the stark reappearance of older eugenic projects, Moraes defended nationalist celebrations of racial fusion all the more passionately.[98]

These immigration debates, and Moraes's coverage of them, were apparently a turning point for men of color like Theophilo Camargo, who in late 1923 took over as editor of *O Elite* (journal of the Dramatic, Recreational, and Literary Society Elite da Liberdade). Details of Camargo's life are scarce, but they show that while still a young man, he rose to become an army sergeant from his humble beginnings as a tailor. Along the way, Camargo obtained the necessary education to publish in several of the newspapers that made up São Paulo's black press.[99] Before the 1923 immigration debates, Camargo appears to have been unusually enthusiastic, even among writers in the black press, about the Republic and the opportunities for upward mobility it had provided him as a lettered man of color. Indeed, only a year earlier, Camargo had engaged in a virulent polemic in the Kosmos Recreational Club (of which he was a member) and in the newspaper *O Kosmos*, during which he accused his adversaries of being insufficiently committed to the Republic and rather viciously corrected their grammar—the currency of civilization and citizenship for the class of color in the Republic. He was eventually expelled from the Kosmos club for his outbursts.[100] Yet in the wake of Moraes's response to the Reis bill in *O Getulino*, Camargo and others who had celebrated the Republic for its principles of fraternity and its opportunities for mobility, or who had advised men of color to follow a course of quiet obedience and sacrifice, began to transform their association newspapers into spaces for open debate about racism and race science. Camargo helped turn *O Elite*, which might otherwise have emerged as a fairly cautious organ of a middle-class club, into a new platform from which to deal with national politics and their effects on people of color.[101] Like Moraes's articles in *O Getulino*, Camargo's writings in *O Elite* explicitly addressed theories of eugenics, ethnology, and "blood," introducing a racial vocabulary previously uncommon in São Paulo's black press.

In his first two issues at the helm of *O Elite*, Camargo published irate articles on the subject of the Reis bill, both of which were republished shortly thereafter by *O Getulino*. Camargo argued that it was shameful that Brazil would refuse hospitality to North American *negros* persecuted by racism. But, zeroing in on the same passages as Evaristo de Moraes, he worried more that the racism in the congressional debates spoke ominously of *negro* Brazilians themselves. Granted, Fidelis Reis had based his proposed ban on the idea that Brazilian blacks were superior to black North Americans: "our *preto* Africans ... fought alongside us in the harshest struggles of the formation of our nation, worked, suffered, and with all their dedication helped us to create the Brazil we see before us today." Tied to narratives about their position in Brazil that black writers held dear, such arguments had not, until then, roused a negative response from the black press. But despite "our Africans" being better than North Americans', Reis added that "it would have been preferable had we not had them at all."[102] This was the heart of the matter, as far as Camargo was concerned. "What wounds our soul like a red-hot iron is, without doubt, the manner in which a certain Congressman [Fidelis Reis] justified this bill, which will appear in the annals of Congress for all eternity. Yes, for all eternity it will be made manifest that *negro* blood is a disorder in the formation of our nation's ethnological character."[103] For Camargo, this turn of events represented a betrayal of the antiracist understanding that journalists of color had been attempting to build with progressive white allies—embracing fraternity, avoiding conflict, extolling uplift and exemplary behavior, displaying their "dedication and sacrifice," and even chiming in to condemn U.S. blacks for their radical separatism. What "wounded his soul" about the proposed immigration restriction was his realization that, far from disappearing with the memory of slavery or being slowly overcome by an ideology of racial harmony, racial prejudice was making its way back into the nation's legal record, where it would remain forever inscribed. Though the Reis bill did not become law, for Camargo, as for Moraes, the terms in which it had been discussed and recorded crossed a line, severed a fraternal pact. Moreover, Camargo worried, if the imputation of inferior racial quality was an argument for barring foreign blacks from Brazilian soil, might it not someday also become an argument for eliminating black Brazilians? "What terrifies us most, what makes us walk in uncertain steps toward the future is the thought that, sooner or later, they will expel us as well!"[104]

In the space of little more than a year between late 1922 and early 1924, Camargo's interventions in São Paulo's black press shifted from passionately defending the Republic and its guarantees to voicing fears of forced exile because of an unfortunate historical tie to Africa. The creation of O Getulino, the publication of Moraes's reports on the Reis bill, and Camargo's dismayed interventions in O Elite all point to a profound intellectual and political transformation that began around the immigration debates of 1923 and became clearly visible across an increasingly issue-oriented press in the following years. From this moment onward, writers in the black press clung ever tighter to racial fraternity as an ideal of national belonging, but they no longer held their tongues about the racism that kept it from becoming reality. In late 1924 Archimimo de Camargo, also of O Getulino, wrote an article calling the usual contrast between U.S. racial violence and a Brazilian racial paradise "pure deception." At least in the United States, he argued, the animosity was "frank, loyal, and sincere"—negros there knew who their enemies were. In Brazil, however, they were treated with hypocritical politeness by people who actually despised them. Echoing the scientific language of Evaristo de Moraes, Camargo called for "a decisive death to prejudice" on the grounds that all "human organisms . . . even of different kinds" were equal.[105] Gervásio de Moraes, who in his first enthusiastic articles for O Getulino had congratulated Brazilian youth on their good fortune and opportunities as citizens of the Republic, by December 1924 excoriated the "iron-clad prejudice" that "strangled" people of color at every turn.[106]

"Foreigners in the land of their birth"

Among the most eloquent of these new critics of Brazilian racism was Getulino's Benedito Florencio. Although only a year earlier Florencio had condemned black immigration as a threat to Brazil's traditions of racial harmony and fusion, in late 1924 he began a series of articles alerting readers to the expansion and intensification of racial prejudice in São Paulo. Florencio was spurred into action, he explained, by a letter to the editor in the São Paulo daily *A Gazeta*. The letter was by one Bernardo Vianna, who, in Florencio's words, "just for being *preto* cannot find a job anywhere!" "He goes to the factories but is refused service; many times they do not even let him speak with the managers. He looks for job advertisements in the newspapers, runs quickly to wherever workers might be needed, but even if he arrives before any other candidate, he is shunted aside and rejected for being of color." Over the course of several long and angry editorials, written "from the trenches of my faith in the race," Florencio denounced this "mute and odious war" against the "*preto* men" of the city and state of São Paulo.[107] In 1924 Florencio, who since 1903 had placed his hopes in Republican principles of fraternity to complete the emancipation of men of color, posed the question, "Are we equal before the law?" and answered, "Theory says yes, but practice says no!"[108] Although no new discriminatory legal measures had been passed in the two intervening decades, increasing discrimination against *pretos* by private citizens (on the job market or as customers in private businesses) had come to "constitut[e] a grave threat to our tranquility and to the stability of our rights." Florencio expressed the gap between the legal theory of equality and everyday practices of racism as a violation of those other Brazilian values of familial sentiment and fraternity. Across the state of São Paulo, Florencio claimed, *pretos* were "being rudely and effectively expelled from the familial conviviality of our society."[109]

In the struggle to achieve true equality, Florencio and others therefore defined the realm of sentiment, and particularly familial metaphors, as their major battleground. Legal liberty and equality were important, but they only became meaningful realities when combined with sentiments of respect, dignity, and full acceptance of the citizenship rights of people of color. Yet these sentiments, attitudes, and relationships among private citizens could not be legislated into reality. The seeming naturalness of family metaphors, especially fraternity, thus helped Florencio and others to argue for people of color's rightful belonging in the nation. "We are Brazilians, legitimate sons of this colossal country . . . , cradle of a heroic people whose greatness was cemented with the blood of our grandfathers, with the sweat of our elders." Theophilo Camargo of *O Elite* similarly celebrated the *negros* who had "built this agricultural Brazil with their arms, made this intellectual Brazil with the blood of their wives, who breastfed, with so much tenderness, the great figures who today take pleasure in becoming our most bitter enemies." *O Getulino* editor Gervásio de Moraes upheld the ideal of fraternity in the face of racial oppression, urging *negros* to continue in their struggles, "smiling toward a fraternal future where one day, there should flicker a flame symbolizing the undistinguishable confraternization of the races."[110]

It is significant that Florencio attributed his new perspective on racism in São Paulo to an article in the mainstream newspaper *A Gazeta*. If Moraes's erudite rebuttal of the European racist theories behind the Reis bill appears to have provided the language with which black writers in São Paulo began to discuss Brazilian racial theories in the mid-1920s, reporting in *A Gazeta* markedly influenced their writing about immigration and labor discrimination in São Paulo in that same period. In September 1924, another *Gazeta* article, titled "Ill Fate for *Pretos*! Cannot Find Employment Anywhere," caught the attention of several writers in the black press, who continued on the lookout for allies in their antiracist project. It is telling of their changing mood that, rather than focusing on white intellectuals who lauded Brazilian ideals of racial fraternity, these writers of color seized on work by a journalist who explicitly attacked the failures of Brazilian antiracism, confirming and granting legitimacy to their own emerging complaints. The article, partially reprinted in *O Getulino*, told the story of Joaquim Brandão Costa, a man who "writes and reads fluently and is trained for many tasks, but who, only because he is *preto*, cannot find an occupation, search as he might." Sympathizing with the predicament of men like Joaquim Costa, the *Gazeta* writer broke step with the usual laudatory contrasts between Brazil and the United States. He cautioned his readers that Brazil was steering dangerously close to the discriminatory practices of Jim Crow, "where *pretos* live separately, so great is the hatred that whites have for them." It was Brazilians, he argued, who were now "systematically . . . expelling [*pretos*] from their midst," especially in areas of commerce, industry, or civil service. Even on the city's streets, the journalist noted, people of color were seldom seen. Little by little, the *Gazeta* author ominously concluded, "our countrymen [of color] are meeting an ill fate—becoming foreigners in the land of their birth!"[111]

The cautionary tale of Joaquim Costa, a man who was well qualified for a range of jobs but was rejected simply because of his color, made a deep impression on writers in the increasingly assertive black press. As men who were not just skilled or literate but lettered, men who had done everything in their power to meet the standards of Brazilian propriety and fulfill the cultural conditions for citizenship only to find themselves still treated like outsiders and impugned by theories of scientific racism, Costa's story indeed appeared to foreshadow the "ill fate" of second-class citizenship that could soon befall *pretos* as a race.[112] Even deeper was the impression left by the *Gazeta* author's use of the word *foreigners* to describe this feared condition of second-class citizenship. The idea that *pretos* were "foreigners" connected the abstract racial theories and attitudes evidenced in immigration debates with writers' everyday experiences of racial discrimination in a city marked by European immigration. It suggested a direct link between African origin and exclusion from citizenship, one that Gervásio de Moraes eloquently captured in 1927: "To be *negro* ... is almost to be an undesirable foreigner, exiled from far-off lands for having committed a national crime!"[113] In the São Paulo of the 1920s, however, most foreigners, especially those of European origin, were not "undesirable"—at least not nearly as undesirable as black nationals. The concern that Brazilian blacks were treated as foreigners while European foreigners were being welcomed as citizens would become one of the most resonant themes in the black press, now increasingly political in its frame, for the remainder of the decade. After 1924 black writers would seek to define the categories "native" and "foreign" to their own advantage by addressing two major concerns: their relationships with European immigrants and their relationship with Africa.

"The foreign facet of the problem"

Before the mid-1920s, to the extent that black writers talked about immigrants at all, they had generally looked on them sympathetically, at times even defending them from the xenophobia of many Brazilians. In a few instances, writers in the black press portrayed people of color and immigrants as equally disoriented but deserving newcomers to São Paulo's cities. Others argued that immigrants should serve as models of political and social organization for people of color, as they struggled to improve themselves and create institutions of mutual support. A few writers even reasoned that while it would be easy to blame immigrants for unemployment among people of color, the true culprits were the poor work ethic and lack of education of black and brown Brazilians themselves.[114] Yet by 1924, as men like Benedito Florencio and Theophilo Camargo began to write about racial discrimination in São Paulo in the wake of controversy over the Reis bill, they also shifted the ways that they wrote about immigrants. A big part of the problem, they argued, was the excessively hospitable way Brazilian employers and officials treated white immigrants—a hospitality that threw into relief the ill treatment of *preto* Brazilians. *O Getulino* and its peer publications were, by the mid-1920s, peppered with accounts of the experiences of people of color like Joaquim Costa and Bernardo Vianna, who were unable to find jobs because of their race. The papers also ran frequent denunciations of the too easy taking, by prized white foreigners, of the few service jobs still available to educated *pretos* in the urban economies of São Paulo or Campinas.[115] Working out the ways that *pretos* were becoming "foreigners," *Getulino*'s Euclydes Oliveira noted with bitter irony that employers commonly used the word *nationals* not as a mark of belonging in the nation, but as a derisive synonym for black, undesirable workers.[116] It was a short step from criticizing racist white employers to identifying immigrants themselves as the problem. By September 1924 Florencio published an exposé on immigrant racism that announced a "sensational revelation": "Even foreigners want to turn us into undesirable guests!"[117]

The early life of black writer and activist José Correia Leite provides a window onto some of the local social dynamics that fueled the increasing sense of outrage toward immigrants in São Paulo's black press by the mid-1920s. Leite was born in the city of São Paulo in 1900. His white professional father did not officially recognize him, and his mother, a black domestic worker, had trouble supporting him and his sister. Leite spent much of his youth in the custody of strangers, working odd jobs. He earned only a patchy primary education by performing small services, like sweeping out the schoolyard, in exchange for lessons. As a young adolescent, following a pattern not uncommon for *preto* and *pardo* children at the time, Leite took a job as a live-in worker and caretaker for a family of Italians in his heavily immigrant neighborhood. Leite later recounted that his weak ties with his own family limited his contact with people of color, and, along with his light complexion, facilitated his assimilation into an immigrant subculture of Italian language, food, opera, dances, and other social relations. He claimed that he became so thoroughly involved in this subculture that his non-Italian friends perceived him to speak with a marked Italian accent. This might have been exaggeration—after all, Leite told this story as part of a self-portrait that emphasized his status as an outsider to the group of relatively well-off, formally educated *pretos* who made up much of São Paulo's elite of color. Perhaps, as Leite himself admitted, some of what passed for an "Italianized" form of speaking could actually have been his uneducated Portuguese.[118]

For Leite, this very closeness with white Italians eventually led to his self-definition as a *negro* (a term he used both in his later interviews and in his early writings). Leite was witness to the racial insults Italians frequently hurled at Brazilians of color, whom they called "tizune" or "tiçule,"

Italianized renditions of the Portuguese *tição*, or charcoal.[119] Italians also associated *negros* with a global history of subordination. In order to "be above us," Leite explained, many Italians told people of color that slavery had ended thanks to the king of Italy.[120] Italians, according to Leite, also often called people of color "meneliques," a reference to Menelik II, a legendary Ethiopian king against whom Italian troops had fought (and lost) fierce battles in the late nineteenth century.[121] Leite never made it clear what this insult meant to Italians in São Paulo. It seems likely that it was a way of calling Brazilians of color Ethiopians, of linking them with an African heritage that they saw as hostile, primitive, and barbaric.[122] But Menelik had famously beaten back Italian colonial ambitions in the Battle of Adwa in 1896, so perhaps the epithet also carried a grudging respect.

Leite had been spared some of these epithets as a child, being considered "*negro* but not too much" by his Italian host family and friends. But as he grew into adolescence, members of the Italian community began to object to his presence at dances and social gatherings, or to his dating Italian women. This, he recalled, led him to conclude that he was "wasting time . . . with these Italians."[123] By his early twenties, Leite reconnected with some of the black friends of his boyhood. One friend in particular, Jayme de Aguiar, steered Leite away from the Italians and introduced him to the social organizations of the class of color, with its own dances and leisure activities. He also taught Leite correct Portuguese grammar and encouraged his growing interest in activism and journalism. This was in the early to mid-1920s, just as the associations and newspapers of the class of color were beginning to articulate a new critique of Brazilian racism. In 1924 Aguiar and Leite founded a newspaper of their own, *O Clarim d'Alvorada*, which like its predecessor *O Getulino* was an independent newspaper for *negros* in the city, not a club newsletter for the class of color. While Leite was critical of immigrant racism, he took the Italian-language immigrant press (familiar from his boyhood) as a model for his own paper. "The black man," he reasoned, "was, in a certain way, also a minority like the Italians, the Germans, the Spanish."[124] Though *pretos* and *pardos* were not immigrants, they were all relative newcomers to Brazilian citizenry, and many were recent arrivals to São Paulo. What they shared with immigrants was a sense of being outside the mainstream of Brazilian society, of needing to claim fuller rights as a group. In this sense, immigrant meeting halls, ethnic associations, and newsletters provided a point of comparison, even a set of models, for the black community. In *O Clarim*, Leite and others repeatedly called for people of color to imitate immigrants in constructing a common identity out of their shared condition, and a politics out of their common identity.[125]

O CLARIM D'ALVORADA

ORGAM LITERARIO, NOTICIOSO E HUMORISTICO

Direcção: JIM DE ARAGUARY & LEITE

ANNO IV — SÃO PAULO, 15 DE JANEIRO DE 1927 — NUM. 28

Anno Velho e Novo!

A noite esta magnifica. Diante de mim não muito longe vejo uma linda creança moresa, que com um suave sorriso a brincar-lhe nos labios, pede gentilmente ao velho tremulo e cançado que se {retire.}

Adeus, ó velho de barbas brancas e rosto enrugado. Os homens esperam anciosamente o teu ultimo suspiro. Vae-te.

Foste bom ou mau? Querido ou amaldiçoado? Deixas boas ou más recordações?

Tu roubaste o avô ao neto, o neto ao avô; o pae ao filho, o filho ao pae; o irmão ao irmão; o amigo ao amigo. Tu despedaçaste cadeias de amor delacceraste corações enamorados... Velho fatal, parte!

Mas em compensação, espalhaste tambem pelo mundo muitas alegrias. Encheste berços vasios, uniste corações apaixonados, dedes-nos novos amigos e encheste-nos de alegria o coração e a alma. Vae, pobre velho parte e leva comtigo dôres e alegria, risos e prantos, tristezas e esperanças.

E tu ó linda creança vem! Ouves? Um grande barulho annuncia a tua chegada; os homens saudam-te com gritos de alegria dizendo: — «Bom Anno!»

Vém, ó linda creança a tua vida é brece. Hoje és festejado e ahançoado; mas daqui a doze mezes o que acontecerá?

Vém, ó creança! Eu te saudo e te pego; auxilia os pobres

JAYME DE AGUIAR.

JOSÉ CORRÊIA LEITE.

Apezar dos pezares...

Muito agradecido...

Jayme de Aguiar and José Correia Leite, coeditors of *O Clarim d'Alvorada*, on the cover of the issue of 15 January 1927. Acervo da Fundação Biblioteca Nacional, Brazil.

Although Leite was unusual among black writers for having lived with a family of Italian immigrants, his admiration for the successful organization of immigrant communities together with his experience of racism and rejection by some Italians reflected the broader patterns of day-to-day contact and rivalry with immigrants that shaped representations of that group in the 1920s black press. Several of the city's oldest black settlements, like Leite's neighborhood of Bexiga, were also places where less wealthy Italian immigrants owned homes, often renting out their basement apartments to families of color.[126] In these neighborhoods, people of color frequently interacted (and clashed) with immigrants as neighbors, tenants, or customers. It seems likely, for instance, that the landlady who accused Frederico Baptista de Souza's Kosmos Club of reneging on its rent was Italian.[127] Black newspapers in this period also newly began to report on the sorts of immigrant taunts and insults Leite later described. *O Getulino*, for instance, ran an indignant article by B. H. Ferreira denouncing a piece in *Il Pasquino*, an Italo-Brazilian newspaper, that had allegedly "ridiculed" a beauty contest recently sponsored by *O Getulino*. According to Ferreira, the writer for *Il Pasquino* had complained of a "certain smell" lingering in the dance hall in which *O Getulino* had held its beauty pageant and dance (and in which, it appears, a group of Italians had subsequently staged their own festivities). Seeking to return the insult "to the filthy source whence it came," Ferreira wrote that the odd smell the Italian writer had perceived among blacks must have been the smell of perfume, "which is why it seemed so peculiar to him, as he is always accompanied by the smell of *formaggio*."[128]

By the end of 1924 writers who had only begun to describe the problem of Brazilian racism a few months earlier increasingly reserved their harshest prose not for immigration policies or racist Brazilians, but for immigrants themselves. Benedito Florencio, for instance, argued that though many white Brazilians of a former slave-owning class were the source of "the most ferocious prejudice," this constituted "the least worrisome part of the problem, since it poses hardly any threat to the stability of our sacred rights as free men." The old *fazendeiros* (landowning slaveholders) would soon die off, and their children and grandchildren "will see in the black man not a lost or 'illegally usurped' piece of property but instead a Brazilian citizen." The imminent threat to blacks' rights and freedom lay elsewhere, in the "foreign facet of the problem." "There exists a kind of prejudice that is absolutely intolerable and barbaric in its origin, and that is the [prejudice] that certain foreigners are practicing against the poor Brazilian black man." "For foreigners," Florencio continued, "mere guests here in our land, to have the criminal petulance to persecute us—that is truly barbaric, it surpasses the limits of stupidity, and deserves to be fought, if necessary even by iron and fire!" Florencio warned that if things continued as they were, people of color would soon face the same restrictions on the use of public spaces as their counterparts in the United States. Unless black people stood up to the "affronters," "our fate tomorrow will be that of true social outcasts."[129] This attitude was broadly reflective of writing in the black press of the mid-1920s. Together with elites' racial preference for white immigrants, many writers argued, these newcomers' own racism would shape the fault lines of Brazilian citizenship in ways that would turn people of color into pariahs.

As they increasingly identified foreigners as the source of the worst kind of racism in Brazil, writers in São Paulo's black press sought to deploy ideas of racial fraternity and fusion as weapons against their new adversaries. B. H. Ferreira, in his polemic with *Il Pasquino*, informed his immigrant interlocutors that *pretos* were "citizens," "in their own land, in their house," to whom "the constitution of their nation granted liberty and equality!" In Brazil, moreover, racial fraternity was a national standard that immigrants were obligated to honor. *Pretos* were "not treated with hostility" by white Brazilians—indeed, Ferreira strategically argued, whites were often allies in the struggle against racism. "Small-minded racial prejudice is almost extinct in this great country, and it is noteworthy that the greatest, most talented Brazilians were the first to combat such a nefarious sentiment, and they did so with enough ardor to extinguish slavery—a foreign invention—in order to equalize *negro* and white Brazilians."[130] Building on Evaristo de Moraes's earlier denunciation of scientific racism as foreign and inimical to Brazilian traditions of racial harmony, Ferreira turned accusations of unfitness for citizenship against racist foreigners themselves. To foreigners who persisted in the un-Brazilian practice of racial discrimination, Benedito Florencio offered his own suggestion: "The only thing to do will be [for immigrants] to look for other lands, transport yourselves to other countries where there exist no specimens of black people, of those imbecilic, backward, and inferior people who can be found here on so large a scale. Leave us here, at peace and ignorant; move to the great civilized cities, for there even exists an aphorism providing wise advice to those who are uncomfortable."[131] Florencio did not spell out the aphorism, but his colleague B. H. Ferreira did: "'Those who are uncomfortable are the ones who should leave.' And, as we well know, there are steamboats leaving Brazilian ports every day."[132]

In these arguments with racist immigrants, writers of color frequently reached for the language of nativism, which at the time was spreading across Brazil. By the mid-1920s many native workers, both white and black, shared their dislike of the Republic's immigration policies with a growing number of politicians and employers, who despite their own earlier hopes to whiten the nation, found European immigrants' penchant for labor radicalism, or, in many cases, their unwillingness to assimilate, to be less than ideal. In São Paulo, so heavily populated by migrants, xenophobia ran high among sectors of both the elite and the working classes, providing people of color traction in the negotiation of their belonging as native-born Brazilians.[133] Nativist attitudes—particularly in the hands of racially progressive white allies—could aid writers like Florencio or Ferreira in their attempts to portray Brazilian identity as essentially fraternal and racism as a distasteful foreign practice. José Inácio Lacerda Werneck, a prominent white writer from Campinas who had once worked at the *Diário do Povo* (the same newspaper for which Benedito Florencio and Lino Guedes wrote before *O Getulino*), was one such ally. At one of *O Getulino*'s social events, Lacerda Werneck explained that black and white Brazilians were "brothers" by virtue of the mixture between Portuguese and African settlers, as well as by the "sentiments of the founders of the Republic, which, in its infancy, received the beneficial influx of equality and fraternity." Though the immigrants may have had jus soli (rights deriving from birth on Brazilian soil) on their side in the struggle for Brazilian citizenship, blacks had jus sanguinis—the right to citizenship through blood or descent. "Neo-Brazilians," Lacerda Werneck continued in a nativist argument that verged on xenophobia, were set apart by their foreign blood, language, and culture (and, he surmised, by having only a base material interest in Brazil). They were also set apart by their failure to abide by the Brazilian sentiments of racial friendship and brotherhood. "Damn all Brazilians," he inveighed, "who dare to consider the black man a being outside of the national communion of our fatherland! . . . Let us always prefer to lose the friendship of a thousand foreigners, than for a black man to lose the friendship of a white man [and vice versa]."[134] In this formulation, racism, as practiced by Brazilians native and foreign, was as foreign to, and as unassimilable by, the national spirit as the undesirable immigrants themselves.

Many writers in São Paulo's black press echoed Lacerda Werneck's nativist idea that true Brazilians were those who not merely had been born on Brazilian soil but also had commingled their "blood" with that of other Brazilians for generations. To these writers, the idea of racial fusion—which in the hands of some white proponents had eugenicist overtones—provided yet another opportunity to assert the belonging of people of color at the expense of immigrants. One contributor to *O Getulino* who signed "U. C." argued, over the course of two editorials titled "Racial Fusion," that Brazil lacked the "homogeneity" of a nation, something that could only be achieved through "aggregation and fusion into a single race." In a clever inversion of standard whitening ideologies, U. C. presented massive white immigration as a torrential flood that "weakened" and diluted the incipient national race. Euclydes Oliveira of *O Getulino*, for his part, argued that Brazil's racial fusion had eliminated all "distinction among races." Yet it was precisely because distinct races did not exist that antiblack racism reflected stupidity or "ignorance of the most rudimentary principles of ethnography" and threatened to "dismember" the unified "raça Brasileira."[135] In both of these examples, writers implicitly portrayed people of African descent as essential components of a unified, racially mixed Brazilian identity, while singling out immigrants—their genetic material, foreign culture, and racism—as threats to the national body.

José Correia Leite's newspaper, *O Clarim d'Alvorada*, issued nativist views in a more humorous but equally biting tone. A regular column in the early editions of *O Clarim* featured a pompous fictional Italian immigrant, "*Professore Dottore* Juó P. Carreta." No doubt written by Leite, the column mocked the speech patterns of Italian immigrants (the "Professor Doctor's" heavily Italianized Portuguese was sprinkled with expressions like *Madonna* and *Mamma mia*). Professor Carreta's first appearance, titled "Naziunale" (an Italo-Portuguese rendition of the word "*nacional*" or "national"), poked fun at immigrants' aspirations to Brazilian nationality. "I really like Brazil and the Brazilians. But I become indignant when I hear it said that I am not a national. And why not, if my wife is a pretty little *mulata* who speaks Portuguese correctly?" Leite had the "Professor Doctor" attempt to give further proof of his belonging in Brazil, adding that he had "tons of money," and that his children studied at the "commercial [school] with [the children of] Matarazzo [a prominent Italo-Brazilian industrialist]." "And so why am I not a national?" Leite had him conclude, leaving the question open for his readers to supply the evident answer: No amount of money, learning, or social connections could turn this bumbling foreigner into a true Paulistano and Brazilian.[136]

The column demonstrated, by contrast, black writers' and readers' proficiency in the culture and language of their city, state, and nation. Indeed, Leite's comical column echoed (and might have been based on) the poems of social commentator Juó Bananére (the Italianized pseudonym of Alexandre Ribeiro Marcondes Machado), which appeared in prominent São Paulo newspapers in the early twentieth century. These were written in the voice of an Italian immigrant eager to prove his literary prowess and his identity as a Paulistano through sonnets dedicated to the people and places of the city, yet whose Portuguese grammar and orthography were irrepressibly, and comically, Italian.[137] Leite's humor, and its goal of demonstrating blacks' aptitude for urbane citizenship through contrast with inept outsiders, was also reminiscent of earlier articles in the black press that mocked the language and experiences of *caipiras*, or hicks from the interior, as people who arrived in the city woefully unprepared for modern life.[138]

The fact that writers in the mid-1920s black press responded to immigrants' racial slurs with accusations of foreignness shows the extent to which, for journalists of color, these were the same order of insult. Trading accusations of racial inferiority and foreignness was part of a single conversation about Brazil's future—what kind of nation it would be, and what place, if any, each group would occupy within it. In a whitened, racially exclusivist Brazil that continued to welcome immigrants as ideal citizens, Brazilians of color would indeed be condemned to the position of "foreigners"—outsiders or second-class citizens. In the mixed, racially inclusive Brazil that black writers imagined, foreign immigrants and racist Brazilians would become the outsiders. The stakes were high, for these were mutually exclusive visions of the nation.

In the mid-1920s, currents of nativism and anti-immigrant stereotypes aided black writers in their attempts to portray racism as a violation of the Brazilian national spirit, and to reaffirm their own status as national insiders. But making nativism a key part of their claims to belonging meant that many activists began in the mid-1920s to envision the categories of *preto* and *negro* in ways that rejected any foreign ethnic or cultural ties. As writers argued that Italian Brazilians were not really Brazilian, in other words, they had little stomach for the idea that they themselves were African Brazilians. In the black press of the mid-1920s, Leite's call to imitate immigrants, especially in the use they often made of their ethnic difference to negotiate a place in the nation, was drowned out by a much stronger tendency to reject ties to Africa.

"Africa is for the Africans"

In the first two decades of the black press, writers generally did not see ties with Africa or an African diaspora outside Brazil as either a significant threat or a significant resource. Before 1924, only one author, J. d'Alencastro, found it necessary to vigorously distance himself from Africa. In the course of his 1918 editorial exhorting men of color to demonstrate their good morals and to embrace Brazilian standards of racial fraternity, he proclaimed, "We are not Africans, we are Brazilians!"[139] He found few allies in this cause, however, as most writers in the 1900s and 1910s were far more focused on affirmatively demonstrating their mastery of Brazilian political, social, and cultural norms than they were on rejecting ties with Africans. It was also rare for writers in the early press to see Africa as a useable resource for their project of racial advancement. In only a few instances did authors seek to depict their ancestral place of origin in a positive light, as a place of civilization and dignity. The poet Deocleciano Nascimento, editor of *O Menelik* and author of a poetry collection titled *Ethiopian Muse*, was a pioneer in reminding his contemporaries of color of their ties to a proud African past. In the first issue of *O Menelik* (1915), he wrote that the paper's title sought to honor "a name which has been, but should not be, forgotten among men of color."[140] This homage to an African anticolonial hero contrasted with most contemporary histories of Africa, which, filtered through the distorted lens of European colonialism, tended to present Africans as uncivilized or in need of tutelage and therefore offered little help in arguing that black Brazilians should be full citizens. Perhaps Nascimento sought to reclaim the "great king of the black race" from the slurs of immigrant neighbors. Or he may simply have reveled in reminding his audience of Menelik's historic humiliation of Italy.

After 1924, however, as *preto* authors began to incorporate nativism into their political repertoire, rejections of Africa like d'Alencastro's increasingly reverberated throughout the black press. Eager to counteract the ideas and practices that cast them as foreigners in their native land, and dedicated in turn to tarring actual foreigners as undesirable, many writers in the black press sought vehemently to distance themselves from any suggestion of an African connection. This tendency was already visible in the articles Theophilo Camargo wrote in dismayed response to debates over the 1923 Fidelis Reis bill. Just as those debates made it clear that many Brazilian legislators and thinkers saw African Americans as Africans first, and Americans second,[141] they also suggested, in their repeated references to "our Africans," that black and brown Brazilians were more African than Brazilian. In response to this characterization, Camargo reaffirmed *preto* Brazilians' love for their Brazilian fatherland, a place for which they had fought and suffered. Were they ever to be expelled, "our beloved, idolized *pátria* will remain only in our memories, just as, in olden days, the African jungles remained in the memories of our forebears."[142] The implication was clear: Our ancestors were from Africa, but we are from Brazil.

For Camargo, leaving Brazil (as some African Americans evidently wished to leave the United States, for places like Brazil or Africa) would be a most grievous exile. Several of his colleagues agreed. Not long after his contribution, some authors began to write in a belittling tone of pan-African politics, particularly singling out Marcus Garvey's "Back to Africa" movement. In a letter to Benedito Florencio in December 1924, a writer signing his name as Claudio Guerra entreated his correspondent to admit publicly to the "absurdity" of importing Garveyist ideologies to Brazil. A "Back to Africa" movement, Guerra conceded, was "extremely natural" for blacks in the United States, where discrimination denied them citizenship and made them into true outsiders. "Let them go to Africa, kick out the owners of the place, learn the native languages or impose their own, [let them] wear a loincloth or else convince the natives to wear a suit. . . . In short, let them do whatever they want to or can." Yet for Brazilians of color to embrace flamboyantly "black nationalist" movements like Garveyism would amount to a betrayal of the opportunities for advancement that their comparatively tolerant nation gave them. More than that, Guerra implied, defecting to a "Back to Africa" movement meant effectively renouncing one's claims to citizenship in Brazil. "Africa is for the Africans, my black brother [*meu nego*]." "[Africa] was for your great-grandfather, whose bones have turned to dust. . . . Africa is for anyone who wants it, except for us, that is, for blacks who were born in Brazil, who in Brazil were raised and multiplied."[143]

At the same time that some writers in the black press eagerly distanced themselves from Africa, they also rejected any solidarity with diasporic calls to militancy, especially those coming from the United States. One writer asked, "Are the blacks of the world preparing to make war on whites? If this is not an imminent danger, it is at least an aspiration, and could well become a reality." Another mocked the idea that "blacks, who only yesterday were slaves, now wish to become lords by founding in Liberia an independent republic. They have already adopted a doctrine, which is a parody of Monroe's: Africa for the Africans." A third writer suggested to dissatisfied people of color that they follow Benedito Florencio's advice to racist immigrants: "'It is the uncomfortable ones who should leave'—we are in our own home."[144] The same logic that writers hoped would preserve their status as true Brazilians in the competition with immigrants, then, also set the parameters for the "right" kind of black Brazilian citizen—namely, one who was prepared to make no claims to a different ethnicity in return for full belonging in a nation strategically defined as racially inclusive. The marriage between nativism and racial fraternity that prevailed in the Paulista black press of the mid-1920s thus proposed a mutual understanding between whites who were personally friendly with and publicly tolerant of blacks (and willing to reject the racism of foreign whites), and blacks who made no gestures toward either ethnic difference or racial organizing (and who were willing to reject the "racism" of foreign blacks).

Despite this general trend, *O Getulino* carried on its commitment to inform readers of developments involving the *raça negra* across the globe.[145] But even this exception shows the difficulties writers in the black press faced when they sought to support claims to full citizenship through ties to Africa and the diaspora. Sources of information on Africa and the diaspora were scarce and, more important, primarily produced by European colonial powers (or the United States). The supposed primitivism of Africa, expressed in the fields of anthropology, history, natural history, journalism, fiction, and film was, after all, one of the tools that European imperialists and white supremacists in the Americas used to strip African-descended people of their humanity and citizenship. It should come as no surprise, then, that with little chance of revising popular notions about Africa, acutely aware of its negative implications for their politics of integration, and faced with open rhetoric in Congress that painted Brazilians of African descent as foreign to the national body, many writers of color in the mid-1920s fervently attempted to emphasize all distance, and deny any political affiliation, between Africans and Brazilians of color. The supposed racial hatreds of people of color in other parts of the Americas likewise encouraged these writers to emphasize all distance, and deny any political affiliation, between themselves and other Americans of African ancestry.

IN DECEMBER 1924, *O Getulino* published its last known issue from Campinas, leaving José Correia Leite and Jayme de Aguiar's *O Clarim d'Alvorada* as the foremost paper for and by *negros* in São Paulo State. Benedito Florencio, Lino Guedes, and Gervásio de Moraes all moved to the city of São Paulo, where all but Florencio (due to frail health) became active contributors to *O Clarim*. The reasons for their move are not clear, although historians have suggested that one of the outcomes of worsening race relations in Campinas was the slow decline of black associational life in that city. *O Getulino* had become the last bastion of black activism in Campinas by the mid-1920s.[146] In relocating to the state capital, *Getulino*'s writers passed the torch of editorial activism to *O Clarim* and helped to consolidate the city of São Paulo, for the rest of the decade and perhaps the century, as the main urban center for black journalism in the nation.

Together, *O Getulino* and *O Clarim* are important markers of the black press's transformations between the late 1910s and the mid-1920s. In the breadth, depth, and complexity of its coverage of issues affecting people of color, and in its bold new sense that it spoke for people of color across the nation, the black press changed dramatically from its early years to the mid-1920s. In the process, writers of color in Campinas and São Paulo shifted from presenting themselves as community leaders, poets, and occasional commentators to what one writer aptly called "modern thinkers" in the vanguard of racial activism.[147] Writers at *O Getulino* and *O Clarim* saw themselves by the mid-1920s as carrying on the tasks of previous activists of color like abolitionists Luiz Gama and José do Patrocínio, but suited to new conditions of racial and political thought—they were "new fighters for the complete emancipation of our class," in the words of one appreciative reader.[148] They became activist intellectuals, using the pen to fight injustices and using their learning—in ethnography, history, law, and politics—to dispel ideas about their foreignness and to argue for their symbolic inclusion. They came to see themselves no longer as an elite of color but as part of a broader *preto* or *negro* racial group, on whose behalf they delegated themselves as speakers. When Lino Guedes and Gervásio de Moraes attempted to relaunch *O Getulino* in São Paulo on the anniversary of the abolition of slavery in 1926, their new masthead no longer advertised a local newspaper aimed at defending the "interests of the men of color" of Campinas. Its editors instead called it an "organ for the defense of the interests of the *preto* men of Brazil."[149]

In his first exposé of employment discrimination in São Paulo, Euclydes Oliveira had turned to history to underscore blacks' native status and to express his outrage at their exclusion from the job market: "*Negros* stepped on these shores with the first explorers, . . . raised roofs, worked the land, watered it with the sweat of their brow, and made it bear fruit, and they have loved and love this fatherland that is theirs!"[150] In the early black press, such proclamations had been directed only at readers from the "class of color" and a few white patrons. In the second half of the 1920s, however, increasingly activist writers self-identifying as *pretos* or *negros* would seek to use their newspapers' new stature to attempt to engage broader national audiences in discussions of this crucial topic: the history of Brazilian racial formation and its implications for contemporary definitions of national identity and citizenship. In July 1925, *O Clarim*'s editors published the following iconic history of Brazilian *negros*:

> African *negros*, imported in Brazil since the first days of its discovery, have always shown themselves worthy of consideration, for their affective sentiments, their stoic resignation, their courage, and their hardworking nature. We owe them immense gratitude. They were the most useful, disinterested colonizers of our land, who made it fertile with their labor. They had great love for their instincts of independence, the proof of which is the formation of the maroon colony [*quilombo*] of Palmares. They sacrificed themselves, nonetheless, for their masters, who were not always benevolent but who were, in any case, less barbarian than those of other countries, especially the United States. *Negra* women were generally the wet-nurses of the children of white men, and [these children] treated them with extraordinary devotion and tenderness. In wars, *negros* fought like heroes.[151]

Black men and women's rights to citizenship, then, were based on Brazilians' debt of gratitude for a history of sacrifice, and for the power of people of color to inspire feelings of "tenderness" and affective sentiment among their lighter-skinned conationals. This complex ideology of belonging, formulated in symbolic terms, mirrored writers' perception that, in their immigrant cities, racial exclusion implied the unwarranted "foreignness" of African-descended Brazilians. With its deployment of sentiment to demand symbolic inclusion and reparation, this ideology of historical and cultural belonging would set the tone for the activism of the rest of the decade.

2. Fraternity
Rio de Janeiro and São Paulo, 1925–1929

Beginning in the early years of the century, writers in São Paulo's black press invoked Brazil's traditions of racial fraternity in an attempt to constitute an alternate public consciousness. This consciousness would oppose scientific racism, whitening ideologies, racist immigration policies, and the racism of immigrants themselves. São Paulo's black journalists used fraternity, in other words, as a bulwark against attitudes that threatened to turn black Brazilians into foreigners in their native land.

Until the mid-1920s, this strategy was confined to the pages of the black press, with its rather narrow readership. In the second half of the 1920s, men of color in São Paulo and Rio de Janeiro seized an opportunity to air their interpretations of racial fraternity on a much broader public stage. In 1926 a group of white men in the national capital, Rio de Janeiro, launched a campaign to build a monument to the iconic Mãe Preta or "Black Mother," representing the African or African-descended wet-nurses who, throughout Brazil's colonial and imperial periods, breastfed and cared for the children of white planters, and of the privileged in general. The project, which promoted the Mãe Preta as the mother of all Brazilians and portrayed black and white men as brothers, earned the enthusiastic support of several black individuals and organizations in both Rio de Janeiro and São Paulo. The mainstream newspapers of those cities, as well as São Paulo's black press, captured the words of these men of color as they joined voices with white allies to place the Mãe Preta, and the ideas of racial fraternity she embodied, at the forefront of new definitions of Brazilian identity.

A series of transformations in national politics and racial thought made it possible for this group of black and white men in mid-1920s Brazil to define citizenship as cross-racial fraternity. The last years of the Republic were a time of heightened social and political instability. Rising nationalism in response to labor unrest by immigrants and to the long shadow of North American imperial expansion made symbols of national tradition, and, particularly, of stable patriarchal social relations from an idealized past, appealing to Brazilians of various class and racial backgrounds. Nationalism also shaped the ways Brazilian thinkers and politicians began to read racial mixture, imagining it no longer simply as racial whitening or cultural Europeanization but instead as the very essence of Brazilianness—what made their nation unique. These changes would help erode an older national consensus based on explicitly racist ideas about black inferiority and pave the way for a growing minority to champion the sorts of ideas of racial fraternity previously put forth by, among others, São Paulo's black writers.

It is significant that the idea to honor the Mãe Preta as the mother of a mixed national race and culture gathered momentum first in Rio de Janeiro, and only later, after considerable transformations, in São Paulo. African-descended Brazilians made up a larger and more visible part of the population in Rio than in São Paulo and were comparatively better integrated into the city's public life and popular culture. Even in the wake of turn-of-the-century urban reforms that had sought to make the city more European, white proponents of the Mãe Preta statue in Rio de Janeiro, echoing and expanding on nationalist reformulations of national identity, publicly proclaimed Africans to be essential contributors to Brazil. In this context, a group of black community leaders in Rio embraced the Mãe Preta and the ideals of racial integration for which she stood. Yet as a counterweight to white men's often self-serving definitions of racial fraternity, which lauded white Brazilians' racial tolerance and praised black Brazilians' passivity, the men who backed the Mãe Preta campaign in Rio used her symbolism to highlight the historical debts and ongoing injustices that made racial fraternity a still unfulfilled ideal.

A similarly successful elite-led, multiracial campaign lauding racial mixture would be difficult to imagine in the São Paulo of the 1920s, where local thinkers and politicians emphasized a white and immigrant regional identity, and where members of a small and marginalized minority of color increasingly self-identified as black. For this reason, when the Mãe Preta campaign did take hold in São Paulo in the late 1920s, it was a significantly different project from the one that Rio's white newspapermen originally proposed in 1926. In São Paulo, it was not white journalists, thinkers, and politicians but writers in the black press who led the charge for national homage to the Mãe Preta. In their hands, the figure of the Mãe Preta underwent a shift in emphasis, reflecting São Paulo's sharpening white/black divide. Especially by the end of the decade, most Paulistano black writers cast the Mãe Preta as the mother of a distinct and proud black race and used her to highlight the achievements of racially black, yet culturally Brazilian (and pointedly not African) men and women. Only in a handful of cases did writers and editors in São Paulo's black press adopt the emerging strain of cultural nationalism that celebrated racial and ethnic mixture. When they did, they, like black monument supporters in Rio, made it clear that the Mãe Preta stood for specifically black or African contributions to a hybrid Brazilian identity.[1]

These alternate approaches to defining Brazil's racial fraternity contained the seeds of political styles that would diverge sharply as the century wore on, and would, in the eyes of later activists and scholars, come to appear almost as opposites. In the Mãe Preta campaigns of the late 1920s, however, both the idea of distinct black and white races, commonly associated with the late-twentieth-century black movement, and the ideal of *mestiçagem*, which black activists since the 1970s have denounced as a tool of elite domination, made up the political strategies of black thinkers and community leaders. Both were means to the same goal: asserting the belonging of Brazilians of color in a racially and culturally inclusive nation, while preserving their right to a distinct identity as blacks or as descendants of Africa. Together, these ideas helped men of color in Rio and São Paulo find inclusive spaces, and denounce persistent racism, in a rapidly changing political and ideological landscape.

A True Expression of the Brazilian Soul

If the national imperative to whiten Brazil's population through immigration had its greatest effects in the state and especially the city of São Paulo, the idea that the Brazilian project of European-style modernization could be accomplished and displayed through the reorganization of urban space reached its apogee in the national capital, Rio de Janeiro. In the first years of the new century, Rio's mayor, Francisco Pereira Passos, led a major project of urban renewal inspired by Baron Georges Eugène Haussmann's much admired transformation of Paris in the 1860s. Just as Haussmann had replaced Paris's dark, winding medieval alleyways and crumbling buildings with wide boulevards, manicured public plazas, and magnificent palaces, Pereira Passos and his team of planners aimed to transform Rio de Janeiro into a splendid, airy city no longer plagued by cramped streets, dilapidated colonial buildings, and overflowing tenements.

Race was an important subtext of these projects for urban renewal. Rio's downtown was home to a large and visible population of poor and working-class people of African descent. Health reformers and politicians had long regarded these multiracial neighborhoods, particularly their overcrowded tenements, as foci of disease and centers of moral corruption. They were stains on the city through which Brazil presented its face to the world—eyesores for foreign visitors and deterrents for potential investors and immigrants. The demolition of Rio's downtown neighborhoods forced many poor residents of color out of the center city and cleared the way for reformers to rebuild Rio as "the Marvelous City [*a Cidade Maravilhosa*]" of wide avenues, plazas, and monuments—itself a monument to the nation's prosperity, civilization, and whiteness.[2]

In 1926 Cândido de Campos, the white editor of the mainstream Rio newspaper *A Notícia*, nonetheless began a campaign to reinscribe a black presence in the whitened, Europeanized landscape of Rio de Janeiro. Campos appealed to his readership to "glorify the black race [*raça negra*] by erecting a monument to the *Mãe Preta*" in the nation's capital city. For Campos, building a statue commemorating the black nursemaids of yore was the logical next step in the process of building and beautification that had transformed his city in previous years. Monuments, Campos reflected, "expressed the truth of [a people's] soul, revealing it in its intimate structure and affirming, in the eyes of foreigners, its particular individuality." Brazilians had already displayed their civic spirit through multiple monuments to their founding fathers. And since the early 1920s, Campos reminded his readers, Rio de Janeiro had begun construction of a massive statue of Christ the Redeemer—the nation's spiritual father—on the Corcovado, a stunning rocky peak overlooking Rio's harbor. Now it was time for Rio's citizens to build a monument to the Mãe Preta, a figure who acted as mother to black and white Brazilians, and who "most vividly captures the significance of the black race in our destiny."[3] Campos's editorial sparked a promonument campaign that quickly gained the support of a small but visible group of intellectuals, politicians, doctors, lawyers, members of recreational and civic associations, and journalists like himself, primarily from Rio but also from many other corners of Brazil.[4]

What do we make of such an enthusiastic response, by prominent white men, to a proposed monument of a black woman in a city recently transformed to resemble Europe? In part, we might read it as a reflection of the success that city planners had in eliminating blackness from the center city in earlier years. No longer as anxious about the presence of poor *pretos* and *pardos* downtown as a previous generation of elite Cariocas (as natives of the city of Rio de Janeiro are known), Campos and his supporters could set about creating monuments that selectively honored people of color. And, as we will see, the ways many of Campos's supporters (and a few of his detractors) interpreted the Mãe Preta and "the significance of the black race in our destiny" limited the terms on which people of color might be included as Brazilian citizens, reinscribing older hierarchies of race, class, and gender. But the Mãe Preta monument campaign also reflects the beginnings of an important shift in how elite Brazilians thought about race in the 1920s, making it newly possible to imagine people of African descent as integral members of the nation.

One measure of the ways ideas about race were shifting in this period is the fact that Campos's project to monumentalize the Mãe Preta elicited scores of letters of support and, it appears, only one or two of opposition. Those exceptions, however, remind us how novel Campos's proposal was in a nation until so recently—and, among some, still—committed to ideologies of whitening.[5] Two years after Campos's initial appeal, for instance, Couto Esher, writing in São Paulo's *Diário Nacional*, rejected the idea of a monument to the Mãe Preta (still not built in 1928) on the grounds that "a few black slaves who suckled the children of their masters did not contribute anything toward the formation of our race and our nationality." A monument to a black woman in the nation's capital, he argued, would undermine the "struggle we Brazilians have undertaken to convince foreigners that we are neither *negros* nor *mulatos*" and would therefore "degrad[e] us in the eyes of the nation and the world."[6] The monument to the Mãe Preta, in other words, would communicate to foreigners that Rio, so meticulously rebuilt, was nevertheless the capital of a black nation. Nor was the symbol of the wet-nurse itself free of controversy. To many sanitation officials, *preto* wet-nurses were vectors of infection, capable of transmitting diseases and even undesirable racial and cultural traits to their white charges. By the 1920s the use of African-descended wet-nurses had waned significantly among members of Brazil's urban elite.[7]

Campos's proposal to "glorify the black race"[8] through a monument to a wet-nurse was thus threatening enough to elicit opposition in some quarters. But what earned his proposal so many supporters was that most did not interpret the monument primarily as an homage to blacks themselves, and even less to wet-nurses. Rather, his supporters saw the monument as a tribute to Brazil's unique climate of racial understanding, framed in terms of the sentimental bonds of brotherhood. The monument, Campos wrote, would embody "one of [the Brazilian soul's] most moving and heartfelt and, therefore, most characteristic sentiments: love and gratitude toward the suffering race brought from Africa."[9] In one of the earliest public expressions of support for Campos's initiative, in April 1926, Washington Luís, president-elect of Brazil, called the monument "one more demonstration of fraternity, . . . a sentiment that unites all men as brothers, without any kind of distinction, [which] will be the accomplishment of the South American people."[10] The monument, in other words, was a tribute to the increasingly popular ideal of racial fraternity and, above all, to the conviction among many Brazilians that, as Washington Luís put it, "Brazil is the country destined to make this fraternity real."[11]

Yet the ideal of racial fraternity that white monument supporters envisioned fulfilling through their homage to the Mãe Preta was one that required no radical social transformations. On the contrary, their choice of the wet-nurse, an icon of nostalgia for the slave past, suggests these men's fondness for older social arrangements in the face of recent rapid changes in Brazilian society. To many monument supporters, it was the Mãe Preta's subservient place in a traditional, patriarchal Brazilian household that made her a comforting symbol in the face of an uncertain destiny. Campos himself called the Mãe Preta "a symbol of the Brazilian family . . . and of a past that is already evaporating into delicious legend."[12] Although the practice of hiring black wet-nurses waned after abolition, some of Brazil's most powerful white men in the 1920s (like many of the monument's supporters) were old enough to have been raised by them.[13] Paeans to the Mãe Preta in the mainstream press thus reveal a highly personal nostalgia for a fading black figure who was at once submissive toward and intimate with white Brazilians—a "guardian angel that slavery placed in Brazilian homes as a self-sacrificing servant."[14]

This image of the Mãe Preta expressed nostalgia not just for the subservience of blacks in the traditional patriarchal Brazilian family, but for that multiracial, hierarchical family itself as the cornerstone of a disappearing social order. The post–World War I period was one of rapid economic, social, and cultural changes. Economic fluctuations resulting from the war, as well as the wartime cessation of exports to Brazil, encouraged further industrialization in major southeastern cities like Rio de Janeiro and São Paulo. New industrial jobs and an invigorated urban economy, in turn, helped accelerate demographic trends already under way, like rural to urban migration and an urban population boom. The emergence of foreign-influenced mass culture—movies, sports clubs, jazz bands—along with changing gender norms—most notably, the emergence of the working, sexually liberated "modern woman"—signaled to many contemporaries the dissolution of traditional values and morals.[15] Indeed, contemporary police publications, which singled out shifting gender norms as the primary index of Brazil's impending social degeneration, reserved particular venom for women of color—particularly, black maids or nursemaids—who succumbed to the vices of "modern" women in public, thereby betraying their position of trust in the bosom of white, wealthy, honorable Brazilian families.[16] The idealized Mãe Preta's subservient and "angelic" nature provided a tonic for these social woes. As a writer for *O Paiz* put it, she "contributed her treasures of love, goodness, affect, and dedication so that we might have the noble, the pure, the perfect Brazilian home, today sadly shaken in its most intimate structure by the corrosive and destructive invasion of a cosmopolitanism of customs, which is the most flagrant negation of the old patriarchal virtues of our familial institution."[17]

For some white supporters, the symbol of the Mãe Preta also stood as a reassuring reminder of a time before the arrival of immigrant workers and their class-based radicalism. The end of the previous decade had witnessed a sharp increase in worker unrest, largely by the European immigrants a previous generation of Brazilian leaders had so eagerly courted. By the second half of the 1920s the increasing militancy of the labor movement, along with many immigrant communities' apparent resistance to assimilation, convinced numerous politicians, planters, and businessmen that national workers were preferable to foreign ones.[18] The symbol of the Mãe Preta, rooted in the traditions of a colonial and imperial past that predated the arrival of recent waves of foreigners, was an ideal vessel for these nativist feelings. As a portrait of relations between white masters and black slaves, the image of the Mãe Preta included these two groups—living in unquestioned hierarchy—as founders of the nation, while excluding immigrants from that tableau. Indeed, in white writers' articles supporting the Mãe Preta, the few mentions of foreigners and their mores were not flattering. Novelist and commentator Benjamin Costallat, in his ode to the Mãe Preta for the *Jornal do Brasil*, lamented, on behalf of "our poor children," that these homegrown wet-nurses were being edged out by interlopers with foreign names: "the 'frauleins,' the 'nurses,' the *governantes* [governesses]." Here, as in other instances, the distaste for foreign labor combined with a nationalist defense of Brazilian culture.[19]

For writers who feared a disintegrating social order, then, the Mãe Preta provided a reassuring vision of a stable, patriarchal Brazilian society free of foreign agitators and cultural penetrations, in which women remained in the domestic sphere and people of color and the poor knew their place in the social hierarchy. Indeed, in a patriarchal society that increasingly eschewed scientific racism and congratulated itself on its racial tolerance, acceptable and apparently "natural" gender and sexual hierarchies could become proxies marking the "black race" as a whole as female, sentimental, and subjugated. In this vein, writers who eulogized the Mãe Preta sought to display their anti-racist credentials by decrying her enslavement, but they almost as frequently recalled their own relationships with wet-nurses in terms that made plain their sense of access and entitlement, as white men, to black women's bodies. One enthusiastic monument supporter, for instance, self-described as "white," boasted of having "sucked from [his Mãe Preta's] ebony breasts the liquor of life."[20] The Mãe Preta's gender, moreover, set the tone for the ways monument supporters envisioned the outcome of the racial mixture they celebrated. When writer Antonio Torres submitted that a monument to the "black race" would be better served by "a Herculean black man, endowed with muscles à la Michelangelo, Bernini, or Rodin" than by the excessively "sentimental" image of the Mãe Preta, Campos politely but firmly rejected his suggestion. The black race he sought to glorify was precisely *not* virile, endowed with reason, vigorous, and potentially threatening, but rather womanly, sentimental, historically distant, and above all, passive.[21] Campos, after all, had selected to honor the image of a black woman who was carefully circumscribed in space (the domestic sphere) and time (a rosy past). He had pointedly not chosen to glorify the many *pretas* who struggled for daily survival as laundresses or peddlers in the streets of contemporary Rio, visible reminders of persistent class and racial inequality. And he had chosen the historical, subservient image of the enslaved black nursemaid over that other, increasingly popular, female figure symbolizing Brazil's racially mixed identity: the *mulata*. For whereas the figure of the alluring, lascivious *mulata* carried potentially subversive meanings about the power of nonwhites over their supposed social betters, the hints of interracial sexual relations that surrounded the Mãe Preta symbolically reinforced white male elite control over people of color.[22] Just as patriarchal ideas aimed to confine women to the domestic sphere by placing them on pedestals as domestic "angels," the project to place the "angelic" Mãe Preta on a pedestal of marble as a symbol of Brazil's racial mixture immobilized the "black race," relegating it to the past, underlining its servility, and heralding its eventual disappearance as a distinct entity.

Until that time, these articles suggested, the monument to the Mãe Preta would provide a model for politically quiescent black citizenship. Nearly every one of *A Notícia*'s scores of supportive articles characterized the Mãe Preta in terms that stressed her quiet consent to her lowly station: she was "suffering," "martyrized," "docile," "altruistic," "stoical," "dedicated," "resigned," and a "slave to her love for the white child." Cândido de Campos came closest to articulating the parallel between the Mãe Preta's idealized demeanor and the desired behavior of contemporary black Brazilians: she represented the "greatness of heart with which [blacks] transformed our moral lapses, which they could have thrown in our face, into infinite dedication, into gentle and humble goodness toward us."[23] Evidently, these writers hoped that their contemporaries of color would deal with the legacies of slavery in much the same way that the idealized Mãe Preta dealt with its realities: by suffering quietly and expressing gratitude for their privileged position at the heart of the Brazilian family. The proposed monument thus entailed a pact. It would place a black woman at the symbolic center of the Brazilian nation, but in exchange for this act of tolerance and largesse, its promoters expected from Brazilians of color gratitude, forgiveness, and conformity. The monument would provide full and final restitution for slavery's evils, definitively proving, as Campos put it, that Brazil was a society "devoid of racial prejudice."[24] This vision of racial fraternity as a fait accompli left little room for pressing claims against ongoing discrimination.

But if many of these white writers' nostalgia for a bygone patriarchal slave society expressed a desire to resist the social transformations around them, their embrace of fraternity simultaneously captured an incipient shift in elite thinking about race, non-European cultures, and national identity that heralded more inclusive ideas about who made up the Brazilian people. In Brazil, as elsewhere in Latin America, the ravages of World War I instilled new doubt among thinkers as to the wisdom of a previous generation's imitation of European racial, cultural, and aesthetic ideals. If Europeans had so brutally massacred one another in the greatest conflagration in modern history, what was their much touted "civilization" worth? Perhaps, many Latin American intellectuals began to argue, their own people and cultures—for all of their once maligned mixture—had the elements to create a more vigorous, virtuous, and peaceful civilization than the corrupt and decadent ones of Europe. Beginning even earlier, the rise of the United States as a power with imperial ambitions in the Americas and beyond had also helped stir nationalist pride in many of the region's thinkers. Uruguayan author José Enrique Rodó's essay *Ariel* (1900), for instance, earned wide acclaim among early-twentieth-century Latin American thinkers for its proud opposition of a spiritual, peaceful, and learned Latin America to a materialist, bullying, and morally bankrupt North America. In the previous decade, Cuban thinker and revolutionary José Martí contrasted a racially divided United States with a racially fraternal Cuba (and by extension, Latin America).[25]

In the context of this emerging cultural nationalism, an array of Latin American intellectuals began to rethink the relationship between their racially diverse populations and national identity. In Mexico, José Vasconcelos looked to the mixture of whites, blacks, Indians, and Asians to form the "cosmic race" that would transcend all others and bring the nation into modernity.[26]

In Cuba, Fernando Ortiz, the once pessimistic author of seminal works on the racial and psychological inferiority of blacks, embraced race mixture and *transculturación* as the foundation of Cuba's national identity.[27] None of these thinkers abandoned the principle of the superiority of whites in the national mixture. But rather than seeing blacks, Indians, mulattos, and mestizos as impediments to modernity and progress, they upheld racial and cultural hybridity as the essence of their nations' unique identities and as the source of an alternative modernity rooted in non-European elements.[28]

In Brazil, these sentiments gained their fullest expression with the Semana de Arte Moderna (Modern Art Week) held in São Paulo in 1922. Timed to coincide with the centennial of Brazil's independence from Portugal, the event was intended as a declaration of cultural independence from Europe. Intellectuals like Oswald de Andrade, Mário de Andrade, and artist Tarsila do Amaral proposed new "modernist" views of national culture that rejected European racial theories and binary paradigms (like civilization vs. barbarism, or modernity vs. primitivism), and emphasized the generative power of the periphery's (in their case, Brazil's) cultural mixture. In the process, they dramatically challenged established myths of national identity. Most famously, Oswald de Andrade's "Cannibalist Manifesto" retold the story of the encounter between Brazil's natives and the Portuguese as an explicit allegory for how Brazilian artists should relate to Europe. In Andrade's account, native Brazilians did not passively accept the blessings of European civilization. Instead, drawing on early colonial accounts of ritual cannibalism among Brazil's indigenous *Tupí* people, Andrade portrayed modern Brazilian culture as the outcome of a native ability to cannibalize and digest foreign influences (especially the European and the African) to produce a new, authentically Brazilian identity.[29]

Just as intellectuals in São Paulo began to rethink encounters with indigenous Brazilians as a source of differentiation from European cultural models, thinkers in Rio de Janeiro and elsewhere began to revise the way they thought about the problem of *mestiçagem* as it referred to people of African descent. Rather than seeing racial and cultural mixture as last-ditch measures to heal a society afflicted with a population that was too dark, some thinkers, like anthropologist Edgard Roquette-Pinto, came to see mixture as the source of a vigorous hybrid national identity, and as the very essence of Brazilianness.[30] The Mãe Preta monument campaign shows that this shift took place not just in the highest academic circles but also in the more accessible public sphere of journalism. The proposed monument, *A Notícia* editor Cândido de Campos argued, recognized the fact that the victims of slavery had become "one of the most dynamic elements of our racial and spiritual formation." Specifically, Campos saw the Mãe Preta as a reminder of the "superior sentiments" that were the most notable black contribution to Brazilian national identity. In article after article, supporters of the monument agreed with this characterization, casting the Mãe Preta as the ideal embodiment of the "affective race."[31] The idea of the superiority of the "affective" or black race stemmed from the later writings of Auguste Comte, the father of orthodox positivism whose early thought had been fundamental to Brazilian intellectuals and politicians in the founding years of the Republic. Though in his early writings Comte had embraced doctrinaire racist ideas about the inferiority of Africans, in the 1840s and 1850s he reformulated his ideas to privilege sentiment over reason, women over men, and Africans over Europeans. Sentiments like familial love, altruism, and humanitarianism, he argued in the works that became most influential to nationalist Brazilian thinkers in the early twentieth century, were the glue that held societies together.[32] For many supporters of the Mãe Preta monument (several of whom directly or indirectly cited Comte), Brazilians had the "black race" and particularly the Mãe Preta to thank for their sensitive national character, their collective generosity of soul. These characteristics stood in explicit contrast to the racism, individualism, and materialism of the United States, where, as one writer noted, "an extreme caste spirit reigns."[33]

As these writers, along with many other Latin American intellectuals, began to revise doctrines of European racial and cultural superiority, they posited the Mãe Preta as an icon of a proudly mixed national race. Contributors to *A Notícia* praised the Mãe Preta as an emblem of fraternity, both in the sentimental sense of "coming truly to love those who suffered the bitterness of our yoke" and in the biological sense of the "fusion of bloods from which we, as a people, were born," the centuries-long "transfusion of blood" that fed Brazilians' "racial plasma."[34] With the exception of one writer who called for a monument to an indigenous mother,[35] most writers who supported the Mãe Preta as a symbol of Brazil's "fusion" or "transfusion" of blood imagined this amalgamation to have taken place principally among peoples of African and European descent. Implicitly, proponents of the monument appear to have agreed with Antonio Torres, who explained in his editorial that the Indian, unlike the fighting, laborious African, "preferred to disappear, thereby proving his inferiority as a race."[36] Even as it erased indigenous people, however, the Mãe Preta campaign's positive recognition of the presence of black "blood" in the creation of a Brazilian race marked a significant interpretive shift away from ideologies of whitening.

For several writers, the "transfusion of blood" (or of other bodily fluids, like breast milk) for which the Mãe Preta stood was a metaphor not just for biological mixture but also for a transfer of character or cultural traits. A writer for Rio's *A Vanguarda*, for instance, explained that through the Mãe Preta, the "black race . . . molded the energy of the Brazilian soul, lovingly transfusing from its own veins to those of the dominant white race all the vigor of its ruby-red blood in the extraordinarily pure milk of the wet-nurses."[37] On the one hand, this use of transfusion—which denotes blood passed directly from vein to vein rather than from parent to child through sexual reproduction—suggests that the Mãe Preta was not biologically related to the white Brazilian family described by the statue's proponents. Similarly, as a surrogate mother, the Mãe Preta shared her milk with children who were not her biological offspring. In this sense, discussions of the transfer of cultural traits through asexual and disembodied "transfusions" of milk and blood partly effaced Brazil's history of racial mixture, even as they purported to celebrate it.[38] On the other hand, these uses of transfusion show enthusiasts of the Mãe Preta relying on the language of biology to celebrate the contributions of Africans to a Brazilian culture that they, as whites, proudly called their own. This too stood in contrast to traditional ideologies of whitening, in which proponents hoped interracial sexual mixture might facilitate the propagation of European cultural and racial traits among the general populace.

Those intellectuals who participated in this shift away from whitening ideologies and toward a proud embrace of Brazil's African heritage—for many resisted it—connected it to ever more vigorous pronouncements that Brazil was a nation uniquely free of racial hatred. Both the "racial and spiritual" contributions of Africans, Campos argued, "placed [Brazilians], in the world, in a unique position in relation to the black race." It was black Brazilians' racial and cultural influence that, "exerting [itself] upon the profound chemistry of our sentiments, has rid us of racial prejudice to an extent unseen among other peoples of the planet."[39] In a few instances, discussions of the Mãe Preta lent themselves to outright rejections of scientific racist verdicts of black inferiority. In his contribution, for instance, Simão de Laboreiro, a prominent Portuguese intellectual residing in Rio, refuted, one by one, a range of theories about the origins of racial difference—from biblical stories about the tribe of Ham to scientific theories about the influence of climate or the significance of cranial size. Instead, he provided a radical historical interpretation of the origins of racism: there were no superior or inferior races but rather "races debased by the domination of others," a situation reflecting an "unjust" political order. All races, Laboreiro concluded, sounding the familiar note of

Christian fraternity, were "children of the same God." Laboreiro's analysis of the Mãe Preta as a symbol of racial fraternity strongly resonated with the interpretations black writers in São Paulo had begun to put forth in the 1920s, particularly in its treatment of the relationship between law and sentiment. The monument, he argued, would supplement an already existing legal equality for people of color with a sentimental component—feelings of respect, gratitude, and equality—without which legal provisions had no meaning.[40]

Although celebrations of submissive black women, cultural mixture, and the supposed sentimental superiority of the black race were laden with much of the racist baggage they purported to leave behind, they nevertheless constituted a significant change in the terms through which a visible and growing group of white intellectuals sought to symbolically include black people in the nation. This was a change black thinkers had been promoting for at least two decades, and they eagerly seized the opportunities it provided to make their demands heard.

"Worthy of the veneration of the *povo*"

In Rio de Janeiro, an array of self-identified *pretos* (including members of black lay brotherhoods or civic associations, workers, journalists, intellectuals, and popular orators) conveyed their enthusiasm for the Mãe Preta monument to Cândido de Campos almost immediately, and he happily republished their opinions (often in his own words). Though their expressions of support for the Mãe Preta echoed the themes and language of white writers, in the hands of people of color, ideas about race mixture, tolerance, and homage to the "black race" took on significantly different political overtones. Even filtered through Campos's pen, black supporters' words clearly communicate their attempts to invert the emphasis in elites' interpretations of the monument. Where Cândido de Campos and others saw the Mãe Preta proposal as a tribute principally intended to glorify Brazil's racial mixture and only peripherally to honor the "black race," black supporters struggled to make the "black race" and its contributions to Brazil the central aspect of the proposed celebration.

One of the most visible black supporters of the Mãe Preta monument in Rio, not surprisingly, was the famous *negro* lawyer and scholar Evaristo de Moraes, who had so eloquently condemned Congress's proposed race-based immigration bans in São Paulo's black press several years earlier. A strong believer in the power of national discourses of racial fraternity to shape laws, politics, and society in antiracist ways, Moraes published two enthusiastic articles in *A Notícia* in support of Campos's project. In his first article, Moraes hailed the Mãe Preta monument as a long-awaited antidote to Brazilian intellectuals' "almost total forgetting of [blacks'] leading role in the formation of Brazilian nationality."[41] He then went on to retell Brazilian history, placing people of color at its center. The Mãe Preta, Moraes wrote, concurring with other disciples of the later Comte, was indeed an ideal symbol of the "affective race." Yet *affection* was by no means a synonym for *passivity*. The "enslaved race," he reasoned, "communicated affection to the Brazilian people through its blood and its behavior, . . . [helping Brazilians] to adopt the humanitarian ideal and ensure their victory over economic utilitarianism." In other words, Brazil owed to the black race the very traits that students of Comte, as well as many other nationalists, identified as the source of their nation's humaneness and of its superiority over the brutal materialism of the United States.[42] For Moraes, the affectionate nature blacks had bequeathed the Brazilian people was behind many of the transformative moments in Brazilian history—above all, the peaceful abolition of slavery. The "black race" had thus been the agent of "its own liberation."[43]

Though Evaristo de Moraes was perhaps the most prominent of all the people of color to express public support for the Mãe Preta monument, he was not the first. This distinction went to a committee of four men of color who visited *A Notícia*'s offices on 6 April 1926, the day immediately after Campos's initial call for the monument. Campos described three of them—David Paulino Coelho, Liberato José Rodrigues, and José Olympio dos Santos—as "workers, rough and simple men." In calling them "rough," Campos must have been referring to what he perceived as the men's lack of formal education, for the accompanying photograph shows them neatly dressed in starched white shirts, ties, and crisp blazers. Leading the committee was Vicente Ferreira, an enigmatic figure of black activism from 1910s and 1920s Rio de Janeiro (and later, São Paulo) about whom historians know relatively little. Campos described him as the "well-known popular orator, so modest, yet so honorable in the humility of his existence."[44]

Ferreira was indeed an intriguing combination of grandeur and humility. He was, as Campos indicated, well known in Rio de Janeiro for his frequent fiery public speeches in city squares, in front of government buildings or churches, at the tombs of great historical figures, and (as his visit to *A Notícia* shows) on the premises of major newspapers, where he occasionally secured broader coverage of his views.[45] Ferreira appears to have believed in his right to address himself to people of any racial or class background. He spoke (not without some resistance by white mourners) at the funeral of the prominent poet Olavo

Bilac in 1918; in front of the Palácio do Catete (the presidential palace in Rio) on whether or not Brazil should enter World War I; and to coffee warehouse workers and stevedores of the "Resistência," a labor organization made up mostly of black and mulatto men. It was thanks to a letter by Ferreira, eliciting Washington Luís's opinion on the monument campaign, that *A Notícia* had the privilege of publishing the president-elect's prominent contribution on the subject. The title of "professor" that always accompanied Ferreira's name (as it did in Campos's article) probably reflected the mixed reactions that this assertiveness elicited among his audience—respect from some, mocking derision from others. For Ferreira was a self-taught man who could read, but not write. He dictated his letters and articles and gave unscripted speeches. He lived precariously, sleeping at guesthouses when he could afford it and otherwise surviving through the hospitality of friends. He was, as the Paulistano activist José Correia Leite later described him, "gaunt" and wore "tattered clothing" "but [had] a certain presence that commanded respect."[46]

Vicente Ferreira led his committee of four to the offices of *A Notícia* to convey what Campos loosely paraphrased as "words of gratitude and fondness—a cry of the soul, vibrant in its joy, warm, pulsing with affection."[47] Campos's portrayal of these black men in the racialized language of "affection" should make us skeptical of his fidelity to those men's actual words. But there is no doubt (as the article's photos attest) that Ferreira and the others had appeared in person—bearing a bouquet of flowers—to express their enthusiastic endorsement of the monument. What might Ferreira have praised in the monument? José Correia Leite later described Ferreira as a man who "was always . . . stirring up trouble on behalf of the black race." He remembered that Ferreira described himself as a staunch nationalist and Republican and that he "lived in the midst of intellectuals," constantly attending public lectures on political and philosophical matters. One of the intellectuals Ferreira greatly admired, Leite recalled, was Raimundo Teixeira Mendes, a leading light of Comtean positivism in Rio. Ferreira also, according to Leite, once became so enthusiastic at the end of a public lecture at Rio's Law School against Gobineau's Aryanist theories and in favor of Brazil's "superior *mestiço* race" that he stood up to deliver his own impromptu speech "on behalf of the black race."[48] Though we may never know exactly on what terms Ferreira supported the Mãe Preta monument in 1926, it is likely that he favored its homage to the black race, its resonance with late Comtean images of the superiority of the "sentimental" race, and its nationalist rejection of doctrinaire scientific racism.[49]

Rio de Janeiro's Federação dos Homens de Cor (FHC, or Federation of Men of Color) also professed its support to *A Notícia*. Little is known of this group, but from its name and occasional references to it in the Paulista black press, it appears that it was a social and mutual aid organization established, like an earlier group of the same name in São Paulo, to defend the interests of people of color in areas like education and employment.[50] Jayme Baptista de Camargo, the FHC's president, explained the group's support for the monument in terms that clearly outline the federation's goals and values: "This Center, which has always accompanied with lively interest all civic movements that affect either our *pátria* or Humanity, and which had even, some time ago, aired the idea of erecting a monument to the Black Race, cannot abstain from applauding, in a rapture of enthusiasm, the lofty suggestion that your brilliant evening paper *A Notícia* launched for the glorification of that race." The monument was a "just acknowledgement" of a history of black civic virtue and active participation in nation building, a conception of belonging similar to the one expressed in the histories contemporaneously published by São Paulo's *Clarim*. The monument would honor "the group of slaves, exiled from African soil, from their free *pátria*, brought in chains to the inhospitable shores of America, where little by little, with unheard-of sacrifice, unspeakable suffering, they saw the rise of prosperous cities, where white children [*filhos*] were suckled by the 'Mãe Preta.'"[51] Not only was there no mention, in Camargo's letter, of racial mixture, but his account of the nature of the debt whites owed to black men and women was the sharpest in all of *A Notícia*'s promonument articles. With his letter, Camargo included copies of the FHC's newspaper, *A Federação*, so that Campos might republish some of their previous articles advocating for a statue to the black race. Unfortunately for scholars interested in the history of black journalism in Rio, Campos ignored this request.[52]

The FHC was seemingly unique as a black organization in publishing an independent newspaper in 1920s Rio, for no scholarly accounts mention a black press in the national capital at that time. Indeed, nearly all accounts of black political activism in Brazil leave early-twentieth-century Rio out of their narratives, precisely because the formal and explicitly "black" organizations of the sort that emerged in São Paulo (which these histories have typically traced) were largely absent from the national capital at this time. Accounting for this situation—without casting Cariocas of color as politically passive or less racially conscious than their Paulista counterparts—requires thinking again about the particular circumstances that gave rise to, and then transformed, a vibrant black press in São Paulo in the 1910s and 1920s.[53] Sociologist Florestan Fernandes has argued that the small size of the community of color in São Paulo, along with strong racial prejudice, immigrant competition, and the related paucity of opportunities for upward mobility for both *pretos* and *pardos* in that city, were precisely the elements that helped create an elite—composed of both *pretos* and *pardos*—whose members identified as *negro* and shaped their political activism explicitly around the issue of race. These circumstances made São Paulo unique in the quantity and strength of its specifically race-based publications and organizations in the early twentieth century.[54]

Although literate Cariocas of color contended with the same general national ideologies of race as did their counterparts in São Paulo in the 1920s, they did not share the particular experience of becoming an ever smaller discriminated minority in a city sharply divided between white and black. *Pretos* and *pardos* together constituted just over 37 percent of Rio's population at the advent of the Republic, with *pardos* making up the larger of the two groups (25%). The next census to count color (1940) shows that even after the urban reforms that sought to whiten the center city, and after decades of European immigration, *pretos* and *pardos* still made up a significant portion of Rio's population—almost 29 percent.[55] Moreover, since the nineteenth century, some of the city's people of color, particularly lighter-skinned *pardos*, had access to a range of social and political institutions that were controlled by, but not limited to, white compatriots. Several important figures of Carioca, and indeed national, public life were men of color. A few, like abolitionist journalist José do Patrocínio and, later, lawyer Evaristo de Moraes, occupied prominent positions as opinion-makers in Rio's society while preserving their public identities as men of color. In the 1910s and 1920s a small but influential group of writers of color—themselves men who rose from humble beginnings to become professional journalists—covered yearly carnival festivities for Rio's mainstream newspapers, celebrating and defending from police repression the African-derived cultural practices of Rio's poor black and brown population.[56] Many other upwardly mobile men of color, however, like the famous mulatto novelist Machado de Assis, quietly disavowed their African heritage.[57] In either case, in contrast to São Paulo, men of color with intellectual or political aspirations in Rio appear to have had alternatives to independent race-based organizing and publishing. And though no studies exist comparing racial discrimination in the two cities in the first half of the century, personal accounts from working people of color who lived in both places suggest that in Rio, greater avenues for integration into mainstream society existed for people of color of more modest backgrounds as well.[58]

This should not be taken to mean that Rio lacked traditions of activism among people of African descent. At least since the turn of the century, blacks and mulattos had been constant and visible participants in the city's elite and popular politics. In particular, historians of Rio de Janeiro have uncovered evidence of widespread participation by people of color in cross-class and cross-racial popular movements and uprisings, like a series of revolts against the sanitation and urbanization campaigns of the early 1900s, uprisings against racism and physical cruelty in the navy, or strikes and walkouts by black laborers (particularly the stevedores and coffee warehouse workers of Rio's port zone), to name just a few.[59] Participation in these broad-based movements rather than in specifically race-based organizations, moreover, did not mean staying silent about racial oppression. Stevedores and warehouse workers in one majority *preto* union with Portuguese leadership, for instance, fought in the 1910s to ensure better conditions, pay, and leadership opportunities for its members—what one activist called "a new 13th of May," in reference to the date of the abolition of slavery.[60] Like their São Paulo counterparts, people of color in Rio engaged in intense and sometimes deadly disputes with their (mostly Portuguese) immigrant neighbors over a range of issues inflected by race—gaming, hiring, living conditions, or competition over women. But they also participated in class-based protests and organizations alongside immigrants.[61]

In the cultural realm, people of African descent in Rio were central participants in the creation of samba and carnival, which, by the late 1920s, were becoming widely accepted elements of Carioca (and eventually national) popular culture. In their form and content, these performances often undermined established hierarchies of race, class, and gender.[62] No comparable process was under way in São Paulo, where white elites largely continued to emphasize their city's European cultural heritage, and where most members of a tiny black middle class concerned with decency and propriety struggled to distance themselves from any "foreign" African cultural markers. Perhaps for this reason, in the 1920s, São Paulo's black press remained almost silent about Afro-Brazilian cultural productions, like samba, then gaining favor among elites in Rio. In the few instances in which samba did appear in these newspapers, writers presented it nostalgically as a "traditional" song and dance form of their slave ancestors, implicitly or explicitly lamenting its contemporary devolution into what one author dismissed as "savage samba," an "epilectic convulsion." These articles, written in the second half of the 1920s, bemoaned the transformations under way in samba precisely at the time when musicians in Rio were developing the sounds that would define samba's "Golden Age," and when black musicians and community leaders founded Rio's first samba schools.[63] It is possible that these incursions by Rio's community of color into their city's and nation's public sphere clashed with the values of São Paulo's journalists of color. In particular, it is worth contrasting the sense of buttoned-down, grave decorum conveyed in photographs of male writers and readers of São Paulo's black press in this period with the flashy image of the *malandro*, the transgressive, womanizing hustler persona defiantly embraced by some men of color, often musicians or performers, in Rio de Janeiro. Presenting oneself as a *malandro*—for all its apparent celebration of a roguish avoidance of work and of other social constraints—might itself be understood as a form of activism, a strategic performance staged by some Cariocas of color in response to the same sorts of exclusionary ideologies (racism, vagrancy, and so forth) that plagued upwardly mobile men of color in São Paulo.[64] Yet it was a response specific to Rio de Janeiro, where entrepreneurial, talented performers of color could, with great effort, carve out spaces for their art in the public life and cultural institutions of their city.

The result of these particular local conditions in Rio de Janeiro were relatively few organizations like the FHC (significantly, a transplant from São Paulo) and almost no independent black newspapers.[65] As a result, the responses of Cariocas of color to the Mãe Preta proposal—when they made it into print at all—appeared primarily in mainstream newspapers and came from organizations different from the social clubs through which São Paulo's class of color typically made its forays into public life. For instance, the Irmandade de Nossa Senhora do Rosário e São Benedito dos Homens Pretos, a black lay brotherhood, was the group (of any racial background) that made the largest impact in *A Notícia*'s coverage of public support for the Mãe Preta monument.[66] Black lay brotherhoods had been integral to the culture of Brazilian cities since the colonial period, projecting, to outside observers, an appearance of conformity to Catholic doctrine and authority even as they became spaces for the development of race-based identities and the maintenance of African-derived religious practices.[67] On 3 May 1926 the brotherhood held a mass to give thanks to Cândido de Campos, followed by a "solemn session" in which members expressed their "heartfelt solidarity and decided support" for the proposed monument.[68] People of various class and racial backgrounds filled the mass, including Cândido de Campos (the guest of honor), *negro* lawyer and public intellectual Evaristo de Moraes, Jayme Baptista de Camargo (leader of Rio's FHC), orator Vicente Ferreira, and representatives of another of Rio's black brotherhoods, the Irmandade de São

Sebastião e Santa Ephigenia do Homem Preto. Also present were members of a local black theater troupe, the Companhia Negra de Revistas, which at the time crowned its popular revue *Tudo Preto* (*All Black*) with a final act titled "Apotheosis of the Mãe Preta"—a choice that suggests the broad resonance of the symbol of the Mãe Preta among Rio's population, elite and nonelite alike.[69] In Rio, unlike São Paulo, not only could professionals of color publish directly in mainstream newspapers, but nonelite *preto* religious brotherhoods with a long history of official sanction could organize multiracial public events, and ensure enthusiastic, front-page illustrated coverage in major papers like *A Notícia*.[70]

In exchange for their greater integration in their city's public life, black organizations in Rio, like the Rosário brotherhood, appear in this case to have operated with less independence than the more marginalized black associations of São Paulo, whose members would a few years later direct their own campaign in favor of the Mãe Preta in the black press. Without newspapers of their own, and in keeping with a long-standing practice of reaching out to powerful white patrons, members of the Rosário brotherhood relied on Campos and other members of a white elite to participate in their celebrations and republish their ideas about the Mãe Preta. Yet this did not wholly limit the brotherhood's attempts to reshape the message of the Mãe Preta statue. Congratulatory letters to Campos from Olympio de Castro, a lawyer and the vicar of the brotherhood of Nossa Senhora do Rosário, drew liberally on the ideas and language circulated by white monument supporters, whom he called "worthy of the veneration of the *povo* [the people, particularly the humbler classes]." Underneath this endorsement, however, Castro's letters and speeches redeployed ideas about Brazilian racial fraternity to make strikingly pointed demands. He referred to the monument as a *"prova* ["proof," but also "test"] of the sentiments of the Brazilian people." Like other supporters of color, Castro made it clear in the speech following his mass that the monument was primarily an act of just restitution to the "black race" and its contributions to Brazilian history.[71] But he went further. In one of his letters of support to Campos, Castro echoed his São Paulo counterparts on the necessary relationship between legal equality and antiracist sentiment. Though the "black race had been integrated into the *pátria* by law, through full rights of citizenship, there remained one great work still to be accomplished—the work of redemption, that is, the extinction of prejudice, which is also a cruel fetter."[72] The dramatic claim that Brazil was *not yet* free of racism thus found its way into newspaper coverage that generally presented the Mãe Preta as a confirmation of Brazil's unique racial harmony.

"Today is the day of the Mãe Negra"

In São Paulo, writers responded to the proposal for the monument from an increasingly active set of separate, explicitly black, and primarily male social institutions. Alongside the (by then) well-established black press, a new activist association had emerged in São Paulo in 1926—the Centro Cívico Palmares (Palmares Civic Center). Named after the legendary fugitive slave community that thrived in northeastern Brazil for most of the seventeenth century, an unequivocal symbol of black resistance to slavery, the Centro Cívico Palmares brought together old and new figures in São Paulo's black politics. José Correia Leite and Jayme de Aguiar, coeditors of *Clarim*, joined the center, as did their new colleagues Gervásio de Moraes, Lino Guedes, and Benedito Florencio, all formerly of Campinas's *Getulino*. The renowned black orator Alberto Orlando was also among the center's estimated 100 to 150 members, as were Arlindo Veiga dos Santos, a Latin teacher and secretary at the Faculdade de Filosofia e Letras, and his brother Isaltino Veiga dos Santos.[73] The center originally had cultural objectives—principally, creating a library of black history and literature. But it soon became an association for the "defense of blacks and their rights."[74] The center began to offer secondary school courses for members wishing to continue their education, as well as a theater group and a medical clinic. Its members were also involved in racial advocacy, as when, in August 1928, they protested racial discrimination in São Paulo's state police force, the Civil Guard.[75]

Members of São Paulo's black institutions and newspapers enthusiastically supported Campos's idea for the monument when it was first proposed in 1926. Although São Paulo's black activists had less access to the mainstream public sphere than did their Rio counterparts, they had their own press in which their opinions were, by 1926, no longer directly mediated by relationships with white editors or technicians. Though on the surface, their interpretations of the Mãe Preta often echoed those of her elite white champions in Rio, Paulistano black writers turned dominant readings of her motherhood to their own political purposes.

Writers in São Paulo's black press reconfigured the dominant theme of the mainstream Rio campaign—nostalgia for the Mãe Preta's tender and submissive motherhood—to promote the inclusion of blacks into national identity. This strategy took several forms. Some writers (displaying their fervent Catholicism) drew on her iconographic resemblance to the image of the Madonna, a symbol of maternal love central to the Western tradition. *Clarim*, for instance, reprinted a poem by white author Saul de Navarro that described the Mãe Preta's motherhood through the attributes of saintliness, echoing descriptions of the Virgin Mary—her "martyrdom" and "Christian capacity for sacrifice," as well as the extreme "purity" of her milk, which carried the virtues of "goodness" and "pardon."[76] That a black woman could take on the role of the Brazilian Madonna confirmed the belonging of black people more generally in a Catholic Brazil. Other writers echoed white Cariocas' nostalgia for the love of black caretakers and expressed sympathy with the white child who lost his wet-nurse. The usually combative *Getulino*, for instance, ran a piece lamenting that black wet-nurses, "who had a predominant and salient role in the daily life of past times," had become "an entity whose influence today fades and vanishes with the changes of daily life and customs."[77] *Clarim*'s coeditor, Jayme de Aguiar, demanded respect for "one whom our greatest writers tirelessly remember in their beautiful and truly Brazilian stories and romances—the *mucamas*, those doting mothers, who even today, once in a while, seek out their [white] child to remember times gone by."[78] In their efforts to construct a national narrative that recognized the presence of black men and women, several of São Paulo's black journalists set aside the disturbing aspects of the Mãe Preta's role in favor of more conciliatory ones.

That black thinkers in an increasingly activist press would choose to write nostalgically about the Mãe Preta might strike us as peculiar, or worse, as evidence of their capitulation to dominant attempts to sugarcoat the history of slavery. Yet this strategy allowed black male writers to affirm their belonging in a (male) citizenry among which there existed a shared memory of the Mãe Preta's tenderness. By invoking this memory, black writers, as literate Brazilian men, positioned themselves alongside the great authors and statesmen who expressed love for their "black mothers" in countless poems, essays, and articles. Similarly, black newspapers frequently published articles (some written by black journalists, some by white contributors) that waxed poetic about the Mãe Preta's "opulent," "swollen," or "rounded" breasts.[79] In so doing, black writers and editors relied on the sentimentalized maternal breast of black women—a resource they evidently felt was theirs to share—as the basis for a proposed fraternal bond among men of different colors and classes. The sexualized imagery that accompanied celebrations of the Mãe Preta's breasts also hinted at a more adult kind of relationship between black women and their male partners, who in these accounts could be imagined as either black or white. By republishing and in some cases penning these eulogies to the Mãe Preta's bosom, then, black writers reaffirmed bonds of masculinity with their white counterparts by alluding to shared experiences of intimacy with black women not just as infants, but also as adults.

For much of 1926 the Mãe Preta monument proposal continued to feature prominently in Rio's *A Notícia*. Letters of support from local governments, historical societies, businesses, and individuals from around Brazil continued to flow in, while newspapers across Brazil opened subscription campaigns to help raise money for the purpose. Cândido de Campos created a monument commission, headed by noted Brazilian writer H. M. Coelho Neto, to oversee the project.[80] In Rio's municipal government and in the national congress, representatives lauded the Mãe Preta in long, romantic speeches and pledged funds for the monument's construction.[81] Despite this nostalgic goodwill, however, the project eventually lost impetus in Rio de Janeiro, and the proposed monument was never built in that city.[82] But in São Paulo, black writers who had lent their support to the monument were not ready to let go of the Mãe Preta's powerful symbolism, nor of the visibility she brought to emerging formulations of citizenship as racial fraternity.[83]

The man who would lead the effort to tie the Mãe Preta to the increasingly political space around the Centro Palmares was journalist and editor José Correia Leite. In February 1928 Leite, with his friend and coeditor Jayme de Aguiar, embarked their newspaper, *O Clarim d'Alvorada*, on its "second phase," hoping to shift its focus from an earlier ideology of racial uplift to a new program of "action," "combat," and "struggle."[84] In one editorial from this second phase, which outlined the obstacles between black Brazilians and full citizenship, Leite foreshadowed the attributes that would make the Mãe Preta such a compelling symbol for black activism for the remainder of the decade: "Once the *negro* ceased to be that formidable productive machine, he was abandoned on the road to progress. . . . Soon thereafter, the *negro* was replaced by the immigrant; the poor soul was left disoriented, bedazzled by his voter's registration card and his title of Brazilian citizen, but he was not taught how to read or write; [he was] classified by high sociologists as a descendant of an inferior race." Building on the diagnoses of Paulista black writers since the early years of the century, Leite noted that citizenship for black Brazilians remained incomplete, a mere "title," in the face of scientific racism, immigration, and restricted access to education. In response, Leite urged the "*negro* family" to "unite," to "acquire our collective patrimony" and "explore our glorious nationalism."[85] In part, this call for black Brazilians to develop a nationalism specific to their shared historical inheritance as *negros* appears to reflect a new stage in Leite's evolving self-perception as a light-skinned mulatto raised by white Italians who, through his political commitments, now claimed proud belonging in a "*negro* family." But his use of *negro* also reflected the most recent stage in the shifting racial self-conception of writers in the Paulista black press more broadly. Over the course of the 1920s, writers generally moved from using the term *homens de cor*, which allowed for a range of colored identities, to *preto*, a defiant identification with dark skin, and increasingly, in the second half of the decade, to *negro*, which eschewed color categories and proudly placed all people of African ancestry within a unified, distinct racial community.[86] Leite's editorial suggested that tending to the "collective patrimony" and "glorious nationalism" of this "*negro* family" was a project for black intellectuals like himself. It required not just basic literacy but an educated intellect capable of contradicting the theories of "high sociologists" or rendering tribute to black historical figures. These were the weapons that would help black people—currently "abandoned," "disoriented," and "bedazzled"—achieve their rightful symbolic position in the nation.

The idea of making the Mãe Preta the central symbol of this new project came to Leite through Vicente Ferreira, the "gaunt," sometimes "tattered," yet always imposing black popular orator from Rio de Janeiro. Ferreira, one of the principal black supporters of the Mãe Preta statue in Rio, moved to São Paulo in 1927, sensing, as José Correia Leite later described it, that he would have a "broader field" for his racial politics and oratory in São Paulo, a city with multiple black social and political institutions. In a speech to the Centro Cívico Palmares in 1928, Ferreira argued for the need to revive the campaign to honor the Mãe Preta. With the monument proposal bogged down in bureaucratic inaction in Rio, Ferreira proposed an inexpensive and elegant alternative: declaring 28 September the "Day of the Mãe Preta," an official holiday.[87] The date referred to the passage of the Law of the Free Womb in 1871, which stipulated that all children born to slave mothers would subsequently be free. Ferreira's idea struck a chord with Leite, who at the time was searching for a grand gesture that would help keep *Clarim* going in his coeditor's absence (Jayme de Aguiar had taken a leave to get married).[88] In the issue of 28 September 1928—the first for which he, a self-described "semiliterate man," was solely responsible—Leite launched the campaign for the holiday. It was a public relations success. For the next few years, *Clarim* and other newspapers in São Paulo's black press succeeded in popularizing the idea of a commemorative day for the Mãe Preta among black thinkers and writers, as well as white journalists and politicians, in their state and beyond.

In promoting his idea for the "Day of the Mãe Preta," Leite, like Cândido de Campos before him, appealed to the Brazilian press as a whole. His edition of 28 September, which Leite distributed among the offices of São Paulo's major newspapers, called for the press to follow up its historic role as Brazil's "conscience" in the abolitionist campaign by supporting the holiday for the Mãe Preta.[89] This appeal to the mainstream print media marked an important shift for São Paulo's black press. Despite constant efforts to reach a wider audience, these papers' main readership had always consisted primarily of members of black organizations. But for a brief time following the September 1928 issue, mainstream newspapers from surrounding cities and states paid overwhelmingly positive attention to *Clarim*. Responding to Leite's call, "some newspapers of the mainstream press published, on their front pages, 'Today is the day of the Mãe Negra.'" Others, Leite recalled, reported this news in internal pages.[90] By choosing a project that had originated among white writers in Rio, and by directing his appeal for a Mãe Preta holiday to members of the national press, Leite created a moment of national attention, of crossover, for his small black newspaper. In the state legislature of São Paulo, representatives pledged money for the effort. They promised to enforce observance of the holiday in all government departments and required schools to arrange lectures on the date's historical significance. Leite's project also won the approval of President Washington Luís (who had expressed support for the monument proposal in *A Notícia*) and of the president of São Paulo State, Júlio Prestes.[91]

This attention was extremely important to Leite, who later recalled that with the September 1928 issue, *Clarim* "embarked on its course to become a medium for struggles, for denunciations, for claiming [our] rights. It became a different sort of newspaper, unlike previous or contemporary ones."[92] It is telling that Leite dated the transformation of *Clarim* into an activist paper to the campaign for the Mãe Preta holiday, for the paper had been engaged in racial activism from its very inception: calling for unity among São Paulo's many black organizations, criticizing racism in Brazil, and by 1928, turning more openly to social protest. But with the Mãe Preta campaign *Clarim* ceased to speak exclusively to audiences of color. Its writers found a way to inject discussions of race, citizenship, and the place of African-descended people in Brazilian identity into a national forum through their own words. It was the coming together of black intellectuals and the white press in discussion over a shared icon of Brazil's past that, for Leite, constituted real political activity.

In his efforts to appeal to a broader white audience, Leite was careful to adopt the celebratory rhetoric about Brazilian racial fraternity produced by Campos and his supporters. A holiday for the Mãe Preta, Leite remarked, "will, we are sure, earn the sympathies of all Brazilians. It is the best way to prove to the world our politics of human fraternity, and to declare our gratitude to those humble contributors to our progress."[93] Yet unlike white monument supporters, Leite and his colleagues did not see the Mãe Preta primarily as a celebration of the racial tolerance of white Brazilians. Rather, they deployed that symbol in their project to define the "cultural patrimony" and "glorious nationalism" of a distinct racial community of *negros*, and to highlight these virtues on the national stage. Toward this goal, they built on the ways black writers and activists in both São Paulo and Rio had interpreted the monument in 1926, as a symbol of the contributions of the black race.

In particular, Leite and his allies were less than enthusiastic about white Carioca writers' presentation of the Mãe Preta as a symbol of racial fusion. Though white monument supporters' formulations of fusion moved away from an explicit project of whitening, they did not abandon the notion of white superiority, and in some cases, they continued to suggest the eventual disappearance of a distinctive black racial identity in Brazil. Nor had these formulations fully displaced earlier ideologies of whitening among elite Brazilians. The idea that Brazil was the product of racial fusion also stood in tension with Leite's project of commemorating the historical contributions of the "black race" in order to improve the status of its present-day members. That political program depended on the presumption that the "black race" was, and continued to be, a distinct entity within the Brazilian population. Thus, in their support for Leite's idea to create a holiday for the Mãe Preta, most writers in São Paulo's black press firmly rejected the value that white proponents of the monument had placed on the blurring of racial groups and, above all, on the disappearance of a distinct black race.

The "mother of Brazilians," Black and White

Most writers who supported Leite's campaign in 1928 and 1929 saw the Mãe Preta as mother to two distinct but equally Brazilian races, black and white, whose members had worked side by side to build Brazil's greatness. In part this interpretation continued an earlier trend in São Paulo's black press to "blacken" the population of color and to portray that city, and indeed Brazil as a whole, as places divided exclusively between the binary poles of black and white—a trend vividly illustrated by a *Clarim* article from the late 1920s that referred to whites as members of the "raça oposta," or opposite race.[94] But writers' interpretation of the Mãe Preta as a mother of two distinct races also reflected recent turns in the city's black politics. By 1929 the Centro Cívico Palmares had begun to decline due to internal disagreements and the leadership's autocratic tendencies.[95] In the wake of the center's demise, José Correia Leite intensified his use of *Clarim* as a platform to call for the confederation of all black organizations in the state of São Paulo. In February 1929, a year into *Clarim*'s new phase of "combat" and "struggle," Leite called for a Congress of Black Youth, through which "the blacks of S. Paulo [would] form a unified front and work with loyalty toward the unification of the class."[96] Other prominent writers and activists, like Latin professor and former Centro Palmares member Arlindo Veiga dos Santos, joined Leite in his intensified calls for *negros* to unite politically around their racial identity.[97]

The series of articles by men like Leite and Santos calling for a Congress of Black Youth in 1929 captures the black press's increasingly critical tone toward the history of slavery and racism in Brazil, and its progressively bolder demands for redress. In one of his appeals to "black youth," for instance, Leite urged them to fight the "ghost of captivity," the "hideous shadow that tarred the institutions of this *pátria* and built the fortune of our high and mighty aristocracy."[98] In this context, writers still upheld the Mãe Preta as a symbol of the sentiments of justice and humanity presumably shared by Brazilians of all racial backgrounds, but they made her a vehicle for ever sharper denunciations of the shortcomings of those ideals. They also differed from white supporters of the monument in making her stand for the concrete contributions of, and debts owed to, the "black race."

Perhaps the most striking example of how the Mãe Preta could be deployed to affirm the historical and contemporary presence of a productive but aggrieved black race was the drawing Leite chose to put on the front page of *Clarim* when he announced his campaign in September 1928. The drawing portrayed a young black woman holding a white infant in her arms. Their faces form the centerpiece of a composition that plays on the themes of black and white, and the stark contrast between them. The woman's dark head is crowned by a billowing white cloud and offset by the brightness of the child's impeccable white pinafore. The shoulder of the young woman's dress has fallen loosely around the crook of her bent elbow, exposing the top of her dark bosom, on which the child places his hand in a gesture of possession. Below and behind the young woman, almost entirely obscured by shadows save for the whiteness of his clothing, stands a small black boy, presumably the wet-nurse's own son.

This drawing of a slave nursemaid with her white charge fits in a genre of wet-nurse images common to Brazil and other Atlantic slave societies. Foreign artists traveling in Brazil, struck by the prevalence of black wet-nurses and their vital role in slaveholding households, frequently depicted these women holding or suckling their white charges.[99] Images of African-descended women posing with their current or former charges continued

The illustration on the cover of *O Clarim d'Alvorada* of September 1928 showed the Mãe Preta with both her white and black children. Courtesy of Princeton University Library.

into the age of photography, providing some of Brazil's earliest examples of portraiture, and affirming the wet-nurse's iconic status in Brazilian visual art.[100] The particular drawing Leite chose for the cover of his paper in 1928, in fact, appears to be based on a nineteenth-century oil painting that hangs in Brazil's Imperial Museum, until recently thought to depict the young emperor Dom Pedro II in the arms of his (unnamed) black nursemaid.[101] This original portrait, however, like nearly all depictions of the Mãe Preta in Brazilian art, does not include the mother's own black son.

Clarim's decision to reference familiar iconography in its own front-page illustration was consistent with the black press's frequent citations of literary and folkloric representations of the Mãe Preta. Both the older oil painting and the newer drawing highlighted Pedro II, a towering figure of Brazilian history, who especially after 1922 (the centennial of Brazilian independence and the date that Pedro II and his wife were reburied in Brazil) was remembered in increasingly positive terms as a model ruler.[102] The allusion to the popular emperor thus helped associate the figure of the Mãe Preta with the heroes

"Nursemaid with Child in Her Arms" (artist unknown; early to mid-1800s). Like most nursemaid iconography, this oil painting, on which *O Clarim*'s 1928 drawing appears to be based, depicts only the Mãe Preta and her white child. Museu Imperial/IBRAM/MINC.

of Brazilian history. Yet by adding the figure of the wet-nurse's black son to their portrait, *Clarim*'s editors dramatically unsettled traditional wet-nurse iconography, as well as white interpretations of the Mãe Preta. In *Clarim*'s expanded drawing (quite possibly commissioned by the paper's editors, like many of their illustrations), the black mother who holds the white child close to her chest is simultaneously turning her back on her own child. This image set the tone for a commemoration of the Mãe Preta that, while celebrating the fraternity between the wet-nurse's black and white sons, also spotlighted the remembered grievances if not of the enslaved woman herself, then of the sons that she bore.

Several writers confirmed this message, reading the symbol of the Mãe Preta as an explicit condemnation of slavery and its consequences for black families. The Black Mother "fed and caressed, on her black breast, the whites who stole from blacks the very drop of milk that represented the vitality, the primordial element of their existence."[103] "Our grandmothers," David Rodolpho de Castro of *Progresso* lamented, "were never able to breastfeed, let alone raise their sons [*filhos*], for they were forced (under pain of the whip) to deny their rounded breasts to the fruits of their love. . . . This prohibition had a sad end: mothers would abandon their sons for those of the masters, who as adults would repay such dedication with the lash." The love white children shared with the Mãe Preta, so amply celebrated in the monument campaign, came at a price for the children born of her womb. Black sons did not experience the "pleasure of receiving maternal caresses," nor the luxury of suckling from the Mother's "rounded breasts"; all they received was "bean broth, corn meal mush, and water." Unlike more common celebrations of the Mãe Preta's expansive maternal love, Castro's stressed the unnatural burden of dual motherhood, and the resentment this generated in the abandoned child: "A mother of another's sons, who remains in perpetual abandonment of her legitimate sons, is like a flower without its scent."[104]

These writers' use of the Mãe Preta as a symbol of abandoned black sons helped make her an emblem of a wronged race imagined principally as masculine. This is not surprising, given that nearly all writers in São Paulo's black press were male, and that they were keenly aware of maleness as a prerequisite for citizenship. An extremely rare inclusion of female perspectives in one issue of *Clarim*, however, gives us insight into what the Mãe Preta could mean for women when they were given the chance to speak publicly on the subject. On 28 September 1929 the small Paulista town of Botucatu held its own celebration of the Mãe Preta, organized by their *Clarim* representative (a woman named Alexandrina Ferreira) and hosted by the Guarany Recreational Society. After a series of speeches by town worthies, organizers yielded the floor to a group of young women who delivered their own speeches and poems in praise of the Mãe Preta. The article does not make clear the women's racial identities, but their speeches, ending in phrases like "Long live the Mãe Preta! Long live the *raça Negra*!," suggest that they were likely *negras* themselves.[105] For these women, the Mãe Preta's sufferings as a mother—perhaps even more than her sons' suffering—was a metaphor for the horrors of slavery more broadly. For Diva de Campos, the Mãe Preta's martyrdom made her the emblem of a race "from which was stolen the right to live." For Yolanda de Camargo, the Mãe Preta was the "mother of Brazilians, who shared her blood with the little white masters [*sinhozinhos*], often sacrificing her own sons." For this writer, the sharing of blood was not a metaphor for cultural transfusion (as it was for many white Mãe Preta supporters) but rather a symbol of a physical sacrifice even more taxing than shared breast milk.[106] These women's readings stand in contrast to many contemporary male black writers' interpretations of the Mãe Preta, which often switched quickly from the theme of motherhood to the theme of male slaves' physical contributions to nation building. The Mãe Preta, in several male writers' formulations, symbolized a "strong and virile" black race, "which contributed the most toward the formation of our nationality."[107] Remembering physical labor in primarily male terms did little to acknowledge the Mãe Preta's own painful labors of childbirth and childrearing, or the fact that women were also among the Brazilian slaves who labored from sunup to sundown in Brazil's fields.

Yet if reminders of the productivity of enslaved black men had been important for people of color who supported the monument project in Rio, they were particularly important to black writers in late 1920s São Paulo, who deployed them in response to decades of employment discrimination in favor of allegedly harder-working European immigrants. Since the mid-1920s, writers in São Paulo's black press had complained of the ease with which immigrants had replaced people of color as workers and even citizens, turning them into "foreigners" in their native lands. By the late 1920s their indignant denunciations grew even stronger. In 1929 one of São Paulo's Italian immigrant newspapers, *O Fanfulla*, published an article complaining about the number of people of color on São Paulo's streets. The writer, clearly intending to give offense through the comparison, claimed that São Paulo was slowly coming to resemble the city of Salvador da Bahia in the darkness of its denizens' complexions. Black writers learned of the insult when São Paulo's *Diário Nacional* reprinted a section of *Fanfulla*'s article in October 1929.[108] This sparked a barrage of angry retorts in the pages of *Clarim*, such as Luis de Sousa's, which pointedly reminded foreigners that blacks were "descendants of the race that most contributed toward the greatness of Brazil, since its first moments." The incident convinced Sousa even more of the need to convene a Congress of Black Youth: "We must at all costs hold our meeting, to show the foreigners that PRETOS IN BRAZIL ARE BRAZILIAN!!"[109]

In his writings calling for a Congress of Black Youth, *Clarim* contributor Arlindo Veiga dos Santos best exemplifies the strains of militant nativism and nationalism—at times bordering on xenophobia—that were developing among some black thinkers and activists in late 1920s São Paulo. Santos held conservative views about religion (he was a fervent Catholic), government (he was a monarchist), and society (he was a strong believer in a patriarchal Brazilian family). That his intense antiracism revolved around both extreme nationalism and a belief in the fixity of a "black race" fits with these conservative leanings. Santos formulated some of the sharpest criticisms of antiblack racism in his time and frequently linked racism to immigrants. "Brazil," he wrote, paraphrasing Miguel Pereira and Belisário Penna, two leaders of the early-twentieth-century campaign to sanitize and modernize Brazilian cities, "is a vast hospital." But it was not, as sanitation campaigners had argued, degenerate racial types and their purported genetic and medical ills that made Brazil sick. Brazil, rather, suffered from "the worst sort of illness, which is racial prejudice; in other words, the sick mentality of our leaders, who allow an entire People to perish, because they must be replaced, because they are mixed, because they are black and should be white, at all costs, even at the expense of the destruction of Brazil by the wave of international immigrant Aryanism." Though he criticized the "pro-Aryan" or "proforeign" leanings of some Brazilian leaders, Santos strategically presented Brazilian traditions as essentially racially tolerant: "The children of foreigners, in order to achieve absolute nationalization, must enter loyally into the rhythm of [our country's] racial solidarity."[110] By law, the children of immigrants in this period automatically received status as nationals—this was the jus soli that had been the subject of nativist discontent in O Getulino in the early 1920s.[111] Santos's warning to immigrants seeking "absolute nationalization" shows that he identified an extralegal condition for Brazilian citizenship—loyalty to and full acceptance of "racial solidarity" as the *spirit* of true Brazilianness.

Writers who used the Mãe Preta as an emblem of black contributions to Brazilian nationality since its "first moments" echoed these growing feelings of nativism. In so doing, they made common cause with a rising tide of anti-immigrant sentiment among members of São Paulo's elite. In 1927 São Paulo State finally ended its policy of subsidized European immigration, and by 1928, the year Leite launched his Mãe Preta holiday campaign, the influx of migrants to São Paulo from other parts of Brazil (which included many people of color) overtook that of international immigrants for the first time in decades.[112] One of the factors facilitating this turn toward national laborers and against immigrants among a segment of the Paulista elite was the rise of fascism in Europe since the early 1920s and its evident appeal to many Italian immigrants in São Paulo.[113] When São Paulo's *Diário Nacional* reprinted the Italian-language *Fanfulla*'s insult to black Brazilians, for instance, the article's author cast racist immigrants as perpetrators of a broader "fascist attack" on Brazil, aimed at transforming Brazil into a "colony of Italy." From an intensely nationalistic position, the unnamed author reminded his readers that "it was not the foreigner who cleared forests and planted our coffee; it was the *preto*," and concluded with an explicit disavowal of the objectives of decades of pro-European immigration policy: "The European immigrant, for us, was nothing more than a substitute for the *negro*."[114] Articles celebrating the strong (male) black laborer in São Paulo's mainstream press by the late 1920s resonate with this incipient defense, among some of the state's intellectuals and employers, of "national" workers—a word that once had such a negative, racialized connotation. At the time that it launched its Mãe Preta campaign, *Clarim*, for instance, proudly reprinted an article from the mainstream *Correio Paulistano* lionizing the "magnificent black man, whose blood," suffusing Brazil's coffee crop, created the nation's "formidable wealth."[115]

The idea of the Mãe Preta as the mother of two races, espoused by the majority of writers in São Paulo's late 1920s black press, thus had three basic elements. First, it affirmed the sentimental bonds between the races (symbolized by the white child at the black mother's breast), thus helping writers to assert the fundamental Brazilianness of racial fraternity, and to position racists as outsiders. Second, it established black writers' bonds of commonality and co-citizenship with white intellectuals, as men with intimate feelings toward the same object. Yet while white intellectuals in Rio had been content to recall only the tenderness of their own memories of the Mãe Preta, imagining a process of racial fusion through her shared milk, black writers in São Paulo noticeably inserted the figure of the abandoned black child into an iconography traditionally restricted to the black mother and her white charge. In so doing, they transformed the threesome of black mother, white baby, and black child into a monument to the pain of slavery and the grievances of the black race. Drawing a distinction between the race that had emerged from her womb and the race that had suckled at her breast allowed black writers to emphasize a third meaning for the Mãe Preta, tied to the question of competition with immigrant workers. The image of the Mãe Preta recalled blacks' solidly Brazilian history primarily by positioning them as native sons and contrasting them to the parasitical, racist foreigners who were sons of neither her breast nor her womb. Although the idea of a distinct black race stood in tension with emerging celebrations of Brazilian racial fusion among white and some black champions of the Mãe Preta in Rio, it made sense in São Paulo, given prevailing attitudes that drew sharp distinctions between whites and nonwhites. The nativist defense of blacks associated with this binary view, moreover, dovetailed with the attitudes of some white Paulistas who, in the late 1920s, began to prefer the memory of patriarchal labor relations with black Brazilians to the labor radicalism of the immigrants they had once taken such pains to import.

The Mother of Brazil's "triumphant mestiço race"

Despite the ascendancy of this vision of distinct black and white races in the Paulistano black press of the late 1920s, a visible minority of writers in this period proposed that the Mãe Preta be remembered as the mother of one

Brazilian race born of fusion. This view, which built on earlier (also minoritarian) celebrations of racial fusion in the black press of the 1910s and early 1920s, posited the Mãe Preta as "the mother of Brazil—mother of Brazil, we say, because she symbolizes, in a sublime manner, all the courage of a race present during the first moments of the formation of . . . this triumphant, *mestiço* race."[116] In a defense of the Mãe Preta statue against the attacks of white opponents like Couto Esher, who feared that the statue would prove to outsiders that Brazil was a black nation, a *Clarim* writer who signed simply "Raul" argued that the Mãe Preta stood, in a way, for the virtues of racial impurity. Race mixture, Raul contended, was an essential part of not only Brazilian reality but also that of any civilized society: "whoever might be embarrassed [by Brazil's mixed race] should ship out to some uncivilized region, where there exist no crossings of any kind."[117]

While it is useful to analyze this defense of racial fusion in distinction to the more prevalent idea of two races, these interpretations should not be read as corresponding to two clear, opposing factions. Leite, a defender in many circumstances of the "two race" model, was almost certainly the author of the unsigned editorial defending the Mãe Preta as a symbol of Brazil's "triumphant, *mestiço* race." Raul's defense of race mixture ran under the headline, "Yes, there are *negros* in Brazil." These positions were not fixed but could often coexist in the minds of individual writers who saw different kinds of political opportunity in the idea of cultural fusion and in the project of independent black organizing. Indeed, the prevalence of pseudonyms among the writers who promoted the "one race" view makes it difficult to know exactly who they were. Pseudonyms, especially ones made up of single names like "Raul," were relatively common in the black press. It is possible that "Raul" was the given name of an infrequent contributor to *Clarim*, or, more likely, that it was one of many pseudonyms used by the paper's regular writers.[118] Raul's proud use of the term *negro* to describe Brazil's people of color suggests he was *negro* himself. Yet in at least one case, as we will see, a supporter of the "mestiço" interpretation of the Mãe Preta was almost certainly a white writer, signing with a pen name. If the view of the Mãe Preta as the mother to one race was espoused partially or perhaps primarily by white contributors to these papers, this explains its minority position in a black press increasingly committed to racial distinctiveness. Still, black editors endorsed these views by republishing them, without clarifying the authors' racial identities or distinguishing among white- and black-authored perspectives.

Despite the difficulties of pinning down the identities and political sympathies of writers who portrayed the Mãe Preta as mother to a single Brazilian race, one issue clearly distinguished them from those who espoused the "two race" view: their attitudes toward Africa. Black thinkers like Arlindo Veiga dos Santos tied their racial activism to nationalist and nativist sentiments, continuing an earlier trend of seeking to distinguish *pretos* or *negros*, who were Brazilian, from Africans, who were foreign. Writers who favored the idea of racial fusion, however, tended to see Africa more positively and associated the Mãe Preta with it. A writer who called himself "Ivan," defending the monument proposal in *Getulino* in 1926, described the Mãe Preta as the prototypical slave woman who bore the suffering of her people, from capture and transportation in Africa through the Middle Passage: "Exiled from Africa by the merciless tyranny of a race that . . . imagined itself privileged, black women wrote with their blood the history of their martyrdom; they sang in moans the epic of their infamous disgrace!" Yet they bore it all, "writing the pages of their groaning history . . . with the resigned impassivity of the desert sands of their homeland."[119] Another article, signed by "Helios," explained that the Mãe Preta paid tribute not to the "black race" as such but to the "*raça africana*, symbolized by the Mãe Preta."[120]

"Helios," according to historian Miriam Ferrara, was the pen name of Paulo Menotti del Picchia, a white Paulista poet and a leading modernist intellectual.[121] Ivan's identity remains unclear; it is possible, though by no means certain, that he too was white. Yet if the editors of *Clarim* and *Getulino* prominently published the works of white collaborators in their pages, this was because it suited their political and intellectual projects. Like writers who saw the Mãe Preta as an emblem of two distinct races, these authors highlighted the contributions of Brazilians of color to the nation. Their celebration of the Mãe Preta's African origins portrayed Brazilians of African descent—like European and indigenous Brazilians—as hailing from a revered ancient civilization that had contributed, through processes of racial and cultural fusion, to shaping Brazilian nationality. "Unconsciously," Ivan wrote, the Mães Pretas "insinuated themselves into the fabric of our race, into the formation of our customs, into the making of our generations of yesterday and today!" As he listed the Africanisms that the Mãe Preta had bequeathed a Brazilian race, Ivan prefigured Gilberto Freyre's theories about African influences on modern Brazilian culture. "Our language is full of expressions that are modifications of their dialect, transformations of terms of endearment, the first heard by our infantile ears. . . . Brazilian music was forged in the mournful melody of the *jongos* they intoned, in their cult to the divine flower of *saudade*! The spirit of the Brazilian people still quakes under the influx of superstitions derived from the delicateness of the African soul and from the submission to fetishism."[122] This celebration of cultural mixture recognized the particular ways that distinct groups had participated in the creation of a unified Brazilian race and culture, allowing for Brazilians of different ancestries to take pride in these contributions.

Presenting the Mãe Preta as a symbol of African cultural contributions was a different political project than presenting her as a symbol of black men's labor. Both views of fraternity, in their own ways, identified a representational realm as the most important space in which to argue for black Brazilians' belonging in the nation. Yet the idea of two Brazilian races responded to one face of the emerging nationalism of the 1920s, namely, the growing rejection of foreign influences, especially of immigrant workers themselves. Black intellectuals who defended the integrity of the "black race" in this context drew on nativist nationalism, and placed racism toward the top of both white and black nativists' list of grievances against foreigners. The proponents of cultural fusion, for their part, took up the nationalism of Brazil's modernists—indeed some, like "Helios" (Paulo Menotti del Picchia) *were* modernists—asserting the uniqueness of Brazil by celebrating the vitality that non-European cultural and aesthetic values lent to national culture. In this intellectual tradition, the trope of racial mixture—embodied in the Mãe Preta—opened up opportunities to proclaim the racial and cultural Brazilianness of African-descended people.

The reassessment of Africa in Brazilian modernism and in the emerging national ideal of cultural fusion provided black writers with an opportunity to deploy information about Africa and the African diaspora in ways that black nativism did not. During the years of the Mãe Preta celebrations, some writers in São Paulo's black press sought to vindicate a continent they considered to have been wronged by the prejudice of observers from the United States and Europe. A *Clarim* writer who took the pseudonym "Booker," for instance, defended the "black continent" as "the sacred land of our grandfathers, so unjustly considered an immense jungle full of beasts and imbecilic blacks."[123] *Clarim* also published an article by a traveler who, having heard much about Liberia as a "republic of cannibals," went there to see for himself. He described instead a promising, peaceful, self-governing country "in the independent history of which the word 'war' does not appear." This was not the case, he clarified, in the African colonies "blessed with the 'civilization' of the great powers," where "revolutions proliferate."[124] By the decade's end, the influences of Brazilian modernist thinkers and artists, of a European vanguard's interest in all things African, and of pan-Africanist movements made themselves felt in papers like *Clarim* and *Progresso*, intensifying an earlier, more tentative interest in Africa and the diaspora.[125] As in an earlier period, "August Ethiopia" continued to capture the imagination of black writers as an ancestral place of origin. They referenced the mythical lineage of newcomer Ras Tafari (later Haile Selassie), reputed to descend directly from the legendary Queen of Sheba and King Solomon. Above all, black writers presented Ethiopia as an icon of black resistance to European imperialism, as well as a successful example of modern (and Christian) black self-government under historic leaders like Menelik or new ones like Ras Tafari.[126]

Thus positive images of Africa, legitimized by the emerging modernist idea of a shared African past common to all Brazilians, could be refashioned to suit some of the goals of black activism, like Leite's aspiration to delineate blacks' "glorious nationalism" and "collective patrimony." Interpretations of the Mãe Preta as mother to a single shared race, whether penned by black or white authors, outlined new possibilities for the inclusion of black Brazilians in a nation proudly portrayed by an intellectual vanguard as partly African in origin. And though the emphasis on *mestiçagem* in these articles preempted black claims for symbolic belonging *as blacks*, they made African ethnic and cultural specificity the bargaining chip that black Brazilians brought to the negotiating table of Brazilian nationality.

The idea of the Mãe Preta as a symbol of an ethnically distinct African past that subsequently dissolved into a mixed Brazilian nationality appears, for a few black writers, to have accompanied a more tolerant view of immigrants. Even as writers like Arlindo Veiga dos Santos intensified their anti-immigrant rhetoric in the late 1920s, others, like José Correia Leite, became increasingly convinced of the need for blacks to emulate immigrants in their strategies of ethnic integration. In 1929, for instance, Leite wrote that following the immigrant example was crucial for independent black organizing. Immigrants, he noted, "establish beneficent societies, newspapers, clubs, etc. They are unified, and so live perfectly protected by the strength of their unified class; and they are always powerful by virtue of their efficient work. And us?!! It is true that we are not foreigners, but we still have much to accomplish in order to succeed, in view of our great lack of cohesion."[127] Around the same time *O Progresso*, edited by Lino Guedes and Argentino Celso Wanderley, reported on the Syrio-Lebanese community's construction of a monument to showcase its integration into the Brazilian nation. The Syrio-Lebanese community had managed to secure a coveted spot for the monument in downtown São Paulo, had commissioned a world-famous sculptor of nationalist art to create the monument, and had chosen to donate the monument on the date of Brazilian independence, marking their patriotism.[128] Like Leite, *Progresso*'s reporters saw in these immigrants a model for black organizing, and like him, they admired the efforts made by immigrants to improve their status in Brazil. Drawing on the ideal of citizenship as brotherhood, the writer for *Progresso* described the inauguration of the monument as a "charming civic celebration of fraternization between Brazilians and Syrio-Lebanese."[129]

In the late 1920s *Progresso*'s editors were active proponents of two statues to black historical figures: one to abolitionist Luiz Gama (to be built in São Paulo) and the other to the Mãe Preta (in Rio de Janeiro).[130] It is evident from their coverage of the Syrio-Lebanese monument that it successfully achieved some of the goals that *Progresso*'s writers imagined for the monuments they hoped someday to build.[131] Above all, the Syrio-Lebanese community's model appears to have confirmed for these black thinkers the potential benefits of celebrating one's deep ethnic origins—in a civilization of mythic proportions—as a resource for achieving fuller belonging as Brazilians. The article in *Progresso* included a picture of the Syrio-Lebanese monument, depicting its complex symbolic representations of the group's racial and ethnic integration into Brazilian society. The base of the monument shows ancient "Syrians'" contributions to world civilization (the Phoenicians' pioneering role in navigation and discovery, and the development of the alphabet), and modern Syrians' contributions to Brazilian prosperity through commerce. At the top of the monument, a female figure representing the Brazilian Republic embraces a Syrian maiden who offers a gift to a Brazilian Indian. The reliefs tell a story in which Syrians drew on their deep, distinctive past to issue what historian Jeff Lesser calls "a clear statement of a hyphenated identity" as desirable "ethnic" Brazilians.[132]

A year after *Progresso*'s publication of the article and picture of the Syrio-Lebanese monument, *Clarim* ran an essay with a picture of a mockup of their preferred version of the still unbuilt Mãe Preta monument. The version *Clarim*'s editors endorsed, by Brazilian sculptor Yolando Mallozzi, was in many respects similar to the Syrio-Lebanese monument, especially in its use of female figures to represent Brazil's different ethnic groups. In the picture of the mockup, an African woman stands tall at the very top of the monument, holding a young baby in her arms, while two other figures (apparently a European and an indigenous woman) sit at her feet. Around the base of the monument, carvings (difficult to see in the reproduced photo but, according to Leite's memory, depicting scenes of black participation in Brazilian history) line the monument's base, as in the Syrio-Lebanese case.[133] Most striking, however, are the similarities in the accompanying essay's symbolic treatment of the relationship of each ethnic group to Brazilian society. The author, Helios (Menotti del Picchia) described the proposed monument to the Mãe Preta in terms of the contributions of African peoples to Brazilian national identity. "Upon three columns is the racial monument of our nationality to be erected: upon the light porphyrian column of the Latin race, upon the bronze column of the Indian race, and upon the vigorous and black column of onyx, carved in the land of Ham, under the African sun, and brought over in the Dantesque holds of the slave ships." Helios went on to add that the "black column," or the Mãe Preta herself, would represent the sacrifices of different African ethnic groups: "the pain of the *cabinda*, the tears of the *benguela*, the homesickness [*banzo*] of the *congo*." The monument to the Mãe Preta would be a monument to the "African Race," whose women went on to nurture the "heroic generation of creators of this new world."[134] Helios's description of Mallozzi's proposed monument to the Mãe Preta—like the Syrio-Lebanese monument several black writers so admired—linked blacks to an ancestral ethnic homeland while affirming that Africans, via the Mãe Preta, had been instrumental to the creation of the younger, "new world" of Brazil. Thus, even as nativists like Arlindo Veiga dos Santos increasingly built their claims to Brazilian belonging on the rejection of all things foreign, others, defining Brazilian culture as dependent on elements from beyond its own boundaries, began to find value in an African past and to propose imitation of and even friendship toward immigrants in Brazil.

The ultimate fate of the proposed Mãe Preta monument suggests that Leite was sadly correct in his assertion that the black community had much to envy immigrants in their organization, unity, and political self-representation. Whereas the Syrio-Lebanese community succeeded in building their monument in the early 1920s, a monument to the Mãe Preta would not be built until the 1950s, and even then, it would not communicate the sorts of messages black intellectuals in São Paulo and Rio de Janeiro had originally envisioned.[135] São Paulo's Syrio-Lebanese community was able, in the early twentieth century, to mobilize the considerable resources of some of its members—as well as images of the group as talented merchants descended from an ancient civilization of explorers and traders—to portray their desirability as new Brazilians. Black intellectuals in São Paulo and Rio de Janeiro, as representatives of a far less cohesive, much less prosperous group, lacked the resources and institutional bases from which to mount a comparably successful public relations campaign. Moreover, they worked against the weight of centuries-long racial and cultural stereotypes about Africans and their descendants that, despite incipient changes in racial attitudes among a sector of the Brazilian elite, and despite their own labors, made it difficult to bring the project to fruition. Perhaps, too, the enthusiasm of the visible and well-connected white men who had initially backed the monument spent itself in self-congratulatory prose about Brazil's racial tolerance well before they managed to cast the homage to the Mãe Preta in bronze. Yet this prose too became a durable legacy, one that black thinkers would take up in the following decade.

THE WRITINGS GENERATED by campaigns to create a monument and then a holiday for the Mãe Preta among a group of black and white Brazilians in the second half of the 1920s reflected shifting discussions of Brazil's multiracial society and the parameters of citizenship within it. By presenting Brazil as a place where black and white men were made brothers by their shared relationship with a symbolic black mother, a group of black and white intellectuals pushed forward a nascent view of a racially inclusive Brazil that challenged earlier visions of a white or whitened Brazil. Among many white champions of the Mãe Preta, however, the discourse of racial fraternity was rooted in nostalgia for the slaveholding past, emphasizing white generosity and reinscribing older hierarchies of race, class, and gender onto a shifting social landscape. Black thinkers and activists in both Rio and São Paulo, for their part, worked to reformulate their white colleagues' interpretations of the Mãe Preta, using the symbol instead to argue for their belonging as Brazilians—whether as members of a distinct black race or as members of a *mestiço* race forged in part through the unique contributions of Africans. Their concern with striking a balance between demanding inclusion and asserting racial or ethnic difference would continue to resonate in the writings and speeches of black activists for the rest of the century.

Black thinkers' writings about the Mãe Preta between 1926 and 1929 suggest very complex associations between racial identities and racial politics. Since the 1970s, as we have seen, many scholars and activists have tended to celebrate a biracial view of race as real and liberating while dismissing a *mestiço* view of race as evidence of an anemic or compromised racial consciousness. Opponents of this view have retorted that binary racial identifications were illegitimate importations from the United States, and that only a view that acknowledged Brazil's extensive experience of race mixture could be authentically national. The campaigns to honor the Mãe Preta in the late 1920s black press show that both views of race—a biracial one and a *mestiço* one—emerged relatively early in the century as proposed paths to blacks' symbolic inclusion in the nation. Both views were equally "Brazilian," in that both emerged from local and national dynamics and concerns, and neither perspective was more intrinsically or immediately liberating than the other. In articulating both of these views, black thinkers and writers in the late 1920s sought to engage with the shifting grounds of nationalism—nativist and modernist—among potential white allies. In both cases, they also turned the mainstream ideas of fraternity, nostalgia, nativism, and *mestiçagem* to their own purposes—especially toward explicit discussions of the limits of Brazilian antiracism.

During the 1920s these different strands never resolved themselves into clear factions but rather coexisted peacefully in a many-voiced campaign to celebrate the Mãe Preta. In the early 1930s, however, the two men most closely associated with each of these two visions—the conservative national-ist and nativist Arlindo Veiga dos Santos and the left-leaning international-ist and pan-Africanist José Correia Leite—would clash over the direction of black politics in Brazil. The view of the Mãe Preta as the symbol of a solidly Brazilian black identity that excluded immigrants, the majority view in the black press of the 1920s, would become enshrined in formal black politics in the early 1930s—specifically, in the Frente Negra Brasileira (Brazilian Black Front), led by (among others) Arlindo Veiga dos Santos. A version of the minority perspective celebrating racial and cultural fusion and stressing Brazil's African origins, however, ultimately became more visible in Brazilian public life. With Getúlio Vargas's rise to power in 1930, this second perspec-tive, in an iteration closer to the arguments that white proponents of the Mãe Preta monument had put forth in Rio de Janeiro in 1926 than to the interpre-tations of black writers, became the centerpiece of official images of national identity. Ideologies of *mestiçagem* in the 1930s and 1940s became increasingly associated with the city of Rio itself—a city with significant white, *preto*, and *pardo* populations and a vibrant, hybrid Afro-Brazilian culture. In this con-text, intellectuals and activists of color outside of Rio would face the chal-lenge of enunciating their own, regionally specific views of black or African identity within and against a spreading national ideology of *mestiçagem*.

3. Nationals
Salvador da Bahia and São Paulo, 1930–1945

During the First Republic, the whitening ideologies that valued European immigrants above black workers had turned the word *nacional* into a derisive euphemism for *pretos* and *pardos*. To be a "national" in the Republic, as writers in São Paulo's black press ruefully pointed out time and again, was essentially to be a second-class citizen, or in their terms, a foreigner in one's own land. This situation changed dramatically after November 1930, when a bloodless coup by Getúlio Vargas put an end to the Republic and inaugurated a fifteen-year nationalist regime.

Like other nationalist leaders taking power across Latin America in this period, Vargas vowed to do away with the political and economic structures and sharp social divisions of an earlier oligarchic regime. In Brazil, this meant that the nation would no longer be run by alternating groups of landholders from the agricultural powerhouses of São Paulo and Minas Gerais. It would be centralized in the national capital of Rio de Janeiro and would (in theory) respond to the collective will of an expanded electorate. The Republic's model of export-led growth, unable to prevail against the effects of the international financial crisis of 1929, would be replaced by an industrial economy. In place of class struggle, Vargas would rule over the nation with a firm but fair hand, tending to the needs of the disadvantaged as a "father of the poor."[1] And instead of a citizenry divided by race, ethnicity, and language, Vargas would promote *brasilidade*, or Brazilianness—a sentiment that combined patriotism, nationalism, and a racially and culturally integrated national identity. "A country," he proclaimed in a speech on May Day 1938, "is not just the conglomeration of individuals in a territory; it is, principally, a unity of race, a unity of language, a unity of national thinking."[2]

In this spirit of nationalist unification, Vargas reversed many of the policies that had made black intellectuals feel like outsiders in the Republic. He curtailed immigration from Europe and passed laws to ensure that native-born Brazilians would be fairly represented in the workforce. Vargas also made many of the ideas about black belonging expressed in the Mãe Preta campaigns of the late 1920s, and espoused by black thinkers since the early 1900s, into an ideology of state. Africans and their descendants, Vargas's speeches and cultural policies announced, were essential members of the Brazilian community—more so, in fact, than many European newcomers who still resisted full assimilation. The politics of *brasilidade*, meted out with an increasingly authoritarian hand after the mid-1930s, thus fulfilled two of the projects dearest to black thinkers in previous decades: casting doubt on the belonging of foreign immigrants, and affirming the place of black and brown Brazilians in a nation imagined as racially inclusive.[3] In this context, black thinkers shifted the terms on which they argued for their belonging. Leaving behind sentimental appeals to fraternity, they found new meaning, and new pride, in boldly affirming their standing as "nationals."

This status, however, came at a price. The Vargas regime's definition of a *mestiço* national race and culture drew primarily on the rich popular culture of Rio de Janeiro, and made that city's particular mix of African and European influences stand for all of Brazil's. Outside the national capital, black thinkers struggled to take advantage of the cultural politics that included them as "nationals" while resisting the homogenizing tendencies this term necessarily implied. In Salvador da Bahia, a majority black and brown city with a deep African cultural heritage, leading practitioners of the Afro-Brazilian religion Candomblé developed, in tandem with regionalist intellectuals, a countervailing view of "pure" and unmixed African traits based on ongoing ties to Africa. It was these authentic, uncorrupted African traditions, they argued, that should be recognized as the cornerstone of a multiethnic Brazilian identity. In São Paulo, a city with a large white majority, a *preto* minority, and even fewer recognized *pardos*, where literate and economically stable *pretos* organized independent political journals and clubs around a distinctly black identity, black activists and journalists took the political opportunities opened by Vargas's regime to found the institution that became the nation's first black political party, the Frente Negra Brasileira, or Brazilian Black Front. The Frente's politics of belonging, which stressed the idea of a separate, culturally unmarked *negro* race, resonated with a broader rejection among black Paulistano thinkers of precisely the sorts of culturally African identities emerging in Bahia. For black thinkers in Bahia and São Paulo, then, the already familiar challenge of seizing the inclusive potential of ideas of mixture without forfeiting racial or ethnic distinctiveness took on a particular regionalist cast under Vargas's nationalist regime. They struggled to defend the particularity of their local visions of blackness or *mestiçagem* not just against the national ones coming out of Rio de Janeiro but also against each other's.

The Shadow and Birthmark of the *Negro*

The most prominent exponent of what would become the official view of Brazilian racial identity in the 1930s was Gilberto Freyre, a young white scholar from the northeastern state of Pernambuco. Freyre's intellectual biography illustrates how international intellectual trends, northeastern Brazilian regionalism, and the particular discourses about *mestiçagem* coming out of Rio de Janeiro in the 1920s converged to reshape ideas of national identity in this period. After obtaining his bachelor's degree at Baylor University in Texas in 1920, Freyre went on to pursue graduate studies at Columbia University, where he was greatly influenced by the theories of anthropologist Franz Boas.[4] Boas, who conducted work on immigrants to the United States, rejected the notion of race as determinant of conduct and character, emphasizing instead the influence of culture and environment.[5] This view of the formative power of culture rather than race, together with older notions of Brazilian racial harmony, shaped Freyre's perspective on Brazilian national identity.

In *Casa-grande e senzala* (1933), released to great acclaim just three years after Vargas came to power, Freyre portrayed the social and sexual relations among people of European, indigenous, and African origins in the sugar plantations of his native Northeast as the source of Brazil's unique character. Contrasting Brazil with the United States, Freyre argued that it was precisely these intimate connections among Brazil's three founding ethnic groups— particularly between Africans and Europeans—that had given rise to a *mestiço* nation relatively free of the scourge of racism. Moreover, to the extent that people of color occupied lower social positions in the past and present, Freyre argued, culture and historical circumstances, not innate racial traits, were to blame. For Freyre, the sort of racism that plagued the United States was unthinkable in Brazil, where "every Brazilian, even the light-skinned, fair-haired one, carries in his soul and his body the shadow, or at least the birthmark, of the Indian and the *negro*."[6] Tellingly, the inclusion of "the Indian" in Brazilians' spiritual and physical makeup came as an afterthought—in the first edition of *Casa-grande*, Freyre only mentioned the *negro*, reflecting the growing trend among Brazilian intellectuals of conceiving of mixture principally in terms of relations among Africans and Europeans.[7]

In many ways, Freyre's discourse celebrating Brazil's racial and cultural hybridity recapitulated the paternalistic logic of the white proponents of the Mãe Preta statue in the previous decade. *Casa-grande e senzala* (later translated into English as *The Masters and the Slaves*) spoke of Brazil's racial mixture and harmony in terms that recalled the nostalgic, patriarchal view of society embraced by many elite Cariocas in the face of increasing social unrest during the final years of the Republic. Freyre's idealization of a colonial and imperial past, in which class, gender, and racial hierarchies were respected as the bases of society, was likewise a response to the modernizing policies of Vargas's regime, and to the loss of privilege they entailed for members of a traditional agrarian elite, like Freyre himself.[8] As it did for writers in *A Notícia*, the concept of cross-racial fraternity played a central role for Freyre in *Casa-grande*. He detailed, for instance, the fraternal (though extremely unequal) bonds among the children of masters and the children of slaves who played together in and around Brazil's "big houses." He made African wet-nurses central characters in his story, crediting these Mães Pretas with cementing early bonds of brotherhood between Brazil's black and white children. Finally, Freyre posited sexual intimacy between European men and indigenous and African women, which he described as "fraternization among the victors and the vanquished," as a model for cultural fusion and social integration in a nation newly proud of its *negro* birthmark.[9]

Though Freyre was perhaps the most prominent regionalist intellectual then celebrating the Northeast as the cradle of an African-inflected Brazilian identity, he was not the only one. In the 1930s, in dialogue with new trends in Brazilian and international thought about race, other thinkers and artists began to sing the praises of the African-derived cultures of the states of Bahia, Pernambuco, and Recife. This "black cycle"[10] in northeastern cultural production, which included the anthropological treatises of men like Gilberto Freyre and Arthur Ramos, the novels of Jorge Amado, and the music of Dorival Caymmi, cast the region's African foods, music, or religious practices as the essence of Brazilianness. Many of these regionalist writers and performers singled out Salvador and the state of Bahia, in particular, as the source and unique repository of Brazil's African traditions. Ruth Landes, a U.S. anthropologist working in Bahia in the late 1930s, noted this emergent trend: "What the Negroes do in Bahia is [considered] 'typical' of Brazil. . . . Out of Bahia come forms and symbols for national chauvinism to cling to."[11]

Freyre's theories of Brazil's cultural fusion drew primarily on the world of the sugar plantations of his native Northeast, but the African-inflected popular culture of Rio de Janeiro—and in particular the Mãe Preta monument campaign—seems also to have influenced his thought at an early stage. In 1926, in the midst of *A Notícia*'s campaign for a monument to the Mãe Preta, twenty-six-year-old Gilberto Freyre visited Rio de Janeiro for the first time. One night, a group of fellow intellectuals took Freyre to see the black theater troupe Companhia Negra de Revistas and their show *Tudo Preto* (*All Black*)— which ended with an "Apotheosis of the Mãe Preta." This experience, particularly the revue's musical accompaniment (led by the famous black samba musician Pixinguinha), made a deep impression on Freyre. In an article he published later that year titled "On the Valorization of Things Black," Freyre recounted his introduction to samba by these black musicians as a transformative moment: "As we listened, [we] could feel the great Brazil that is growing half-hidden by the phony and ridiculous official Brazil where mulattos emulate Greeks." Freyre, it appears, not only succumbed to the charms of Rio's African-inflected popular culture but also imbibed many locals' emerging views of that culture as the basis for a more authentic national identity, distinct from those of Europe and the United States. "In Rio," Freyre pronounced approvingly, "there is a movement to assert the value of things black"[12]—a movement that gained momentum with the Mãe Preta campaign of the 1920s but which in the following decade would find its greatest champion in Freyre himself.

Casa-grande e senzala was an immense success when it was published in 1933, largely because it captured, in a style at once erudite and earthy, ideas about national culture that had been circulating among different sectors of Brazil's population for at least a decade.[13] *Casa-grande* and Freyre's subsequent writings helped crystallize the transition, begun by black and white Brazilian intellectuals in the 1920s, from a paradigm of "whitening" to one that celebrated cultural hybridity, racial mixture, and racial harmony as uniquely Brazilian traits. Though Freyre's work was in many ways a reaction against the changes taking place under Vargas's regime, the ideas of a mixed national identity that he helped to popularize dovetailed with the regime's ongoing project of promoting a national culture capable of overarching the country's class, racial, and regional divisions. In his first decade of rule, Vargas made the ideas that Freyre popularized into the ideological core of his regime's cultural policy. Vargas and his advisors converted select symbols of Brazil's mixed Afro-European heritage, like samba and carnival, into icons of Brazil's unique, racially inclusive national identity. Through increased state control of cultural sites ranging from commercial radio stations to carnival parades, the regime helped to raise samba—originally the music of Rio de Janeiro's African-descended underclass—to the status of a national rhythm. In the hands of nationalist promoters, samba stood for Brazil's easy and unconstrained racial and social relations. Both official and popular proponents of samba held up its purportedly unimpeded flow between the white(r), wealthier neighborhoods of Rio and the darker, poorer *morros* and favelas as evidence of the city's (and by extension the nation's) hybrid and tolerant culture.[14]

Yet just as Freyre's work celebrated mixture within a firmly paternalistic framework, Vargas's projects to endorse a mixed national identity reveal the hierarchies that nonetheless structured his attempts at class, regional, and racial integration. The commercialization of samba under Vargas, for instance, tended to benefit middle-class white entrepreneurs and artists more than their collaborators in the favelas. Furthermore, though Vargas's institutionalization of Rio's carnival in the 1930s invited the residents of Rio's favelas (descendants of the people who, in earlier decades, had been cleared from the center of a whitened and sanitized city) back downtown in the form of carnival groups, it did so on the condition that they perform prescribed roles in a controlled nationalist ritual. Finally, the regime's nationalization of samba in the 1930s and 1940s echoed precisely the self-congratulatory, assimilationist aspects of elite celebrations of the Mãe Preta that many black thinkers had criticized in the previous decade. In this period, proregime sambas that exalted the Brazilian nation proclaimed the absence of racism as a reality rather than an ideal. And like Freyre's celebration of African "contributions" to Brazilian identity, the nationalization of samba emphasized the peaceful mixture and dilution of African musical roots rather than highlighting their distinctiveness. Africanness and blackness, "civilized" by white agents, were celebrated not on their own terms but for enriching Brazil's European cultural matrix and softening its social relations, helping to elevate Brazil above the economically and politically powerful but morally and culturally bankrupt nations of the North Atlantic.[15] As scholars of immigration, education, sanitation, and cultural policy in the Vargas years have made clear, officials and intellectuals allied with the regime continued to imagine the desired outcome of Brazil's racial and cultural mixture in terms of the phenotypical and social attributes of whiteness.[16] If Africanness, as Freyre famously claimed in *Casa-grande*, was the cultural heritage of every Brazilian regardless of ancestry, it was also to be carefully controlled and circumscribed—within a few discrete areas of cultural life (like music, carnival, or religion), a particular space or region (the favelas of Rio or the state of Bahia), or the past (as in the works of Freyre and other prominent anthropologists).

The nationalization of samba also reveals the tensions between regional and national identities under a centralizing regime. During his first years in power, Vargas struggled to centralize a deeply federal nation, subduing a series of regional revolts and ensuring the states' submission by placing loyal political bosses in charge. In 1932, for instance, dissenters in the state of São Paulo staged an armed uprising against Vargas (whose Revolution of 1930 had pre-empted the elected candidate, a Paulista, from taking power) and demanded that he return the nation to a constitutional order. Vargas responded with relatively restrained, but ultimately victorious, military force.[17] His cultural policies echoed those attempts to subordinate the country to the federal government in Rio de Janeiro and to make that city the undisputed center of national life. The elevation of samba to national icon, after all, was the elevation of the music of Rio de Janeiro and of that city's particular racial dynamics to the status of national model.

Vargas, who also saw the Northeast as a bastion of popular support, acknowledged in his cultural policy an African-inflected regional identity emerging from the Northeast and particularly from Bahia. He did so, however, in ways that strengthened his project to subsume all regional identities to the creation of an overarching national one, rooted in Rio de Janeiro. As part of the federal state's increasing regulation of carnival celebrations throughout the 1930s, for instance, Vargas's government stipulated that all carnival groups' parades should contain, among other things, a wing of Bahianas.[18] In a national context, *Bahianas* referred to the Afro-Bahian women who sold food on the streets of the city of Salvador. Bahianas, then becoming icons of Bahian regional identity in songs, novels, and anthropological literature, were known for their elaborate white dresses and headpieces (echoing the fashions of earlier centuries) and for their reputed links with Afro-Bahian religions. In the context of Rio de Janeiro, however, *Bahianas* referred to the women (African-descended migrants from the state of Bahia) who in the early 1900s had been instrumental in the birth of samba by hosting musical gatherings in their homes.[19] In part, then, Vargas's recognition of these women and his requirement that all carnival parades include a wing of Bahianas signals the increased salience of a regional Bahian Africanness in celebrations of a mixed national identity. But it also underscores Vargas's Rio-centered approach to defining national culture: not only were these carnival Bahianas usually black Cariocas dressed in folkloric regional attire, attending a celebration purportedly national in scope but local in practice, but their presence was a tribute less to Bahia than to an episode in Carioca cultural history.

Africans

However limited in scope and fidelity, the consecration of an African-inflected Bahian culture on the national stage of Rio's carnival symbolized the sorts of changes under way in Brazilian ideologies of race and culture in the 1930s. Local and national elites had long regarded Salvador da Bahia's "African" character—the demographic and cultural product of centuries of slave importations from Africa—as the city's greatest handicap. "African," however, meant different things to different people at different times. In the colonial period, traders and planters applied the term *africano* (and also *preto*) to the slaves who arrived in Bahia, generically signaling the place of their birth, their color, and their unfree legal status.[20] This stood in contrast to the practices of slaves themselves, who organized their loyalties, work, religious devotion, and associational lives around the much more specific category of *nação* (literally, "nation"), like those of Angola, Jeje, or Nagô. *Nação* is frequently glossed as "ethnicity," though with the caveat that *nações* did not simply (or even primarily) reflect slaves' place of birth or lineage. Rather, they were collective identifications mediated by, and reconstructed in light of, factors that included slaves' port of embarkation, their broader language group, and personal affiliations developed in the course of the Middle Passage or in the process of integration into Bahian society.[21]

Slaveholders and administrative officials in colonial Bahia and elsewhere in Brazil encouraged the formation of these distinct ethnic identifications among slaves, hoping that rivalries among the *nações* would keep slaves as a group from rising up against the small white minority that ruled them. And indeed, these divisions—along with distinctions between slave versus free, mulatto versus *preto*, and Brazilian- versus African-born—structured the participation of members of the population of color in the series of uprisings that shook Bahia in the late eighteenth and early nineteenth centuries. In 1835, most famously, a group of Malê or Muslim slaves in Salvador, recently arrived from Africa and steeped in that continent's wars of Islamic expansion, staged the largest urban slave revolt in the Americas. As historian João José Reis has shown, the revolt was supported by many African-born slaves and some freedpeople, particularly those of the Nagô nation (the Brazilian term for the Yoruba people of present-day Nigeria and Benin). But it garnered much less support among *crioulos* or Brazilian-born slaves, who had found their own ways of coping with slavery. Although authorities eventually contained the revolt, its careful and competent organization—through scraps of paper written in Arabic—reminded white Bahians of the dangers of foreign Africans and their subversive cultural practices.[22]

In the wake of the anti-African backlash that followed the 1835 uprising, the category of "African" took on new meanings, no longer simply denoting a person's place of birth or servile status. For members of Salvador's ruling classes, *African*, in explicit tension with *creole* or *Brazilian*, also came to connote foreign, unassimilated, and dangerous people and cultural practices.[23] Many African-born people, however, as well as many Brazilian-born Bahians of diverse African origins, increasingly claimed the term *African* for themselves. As the century progressed, they used its implications of a separate, alternative cultural identity to unite descendants of different *nações* around a common heritage proudly distinct from European cultural standards. In the 1890s, for instance, carnival groups made up of mostly Brazilian-born people of color named themselves the "African Embassy," "African Revelers," "Sons of Africa," or "African Knights." Some of these groups, like the African Embassy, sought to present Africa as the seat of a noble and opulent civilization, invoking (like their Paulista counterparts a few decades later) famous African leaders including the Ethiopian king, Menelik. Other groups, like the African Revelers, took as their theme the defense of persecuted Afro-Brazilian religions, featuring parades with *batuques* (ritual drumming) and other elements of what local elites dismissed as "uncultured Africa." Despite their varied approaches, however, none of these carnival groups was able to override elite Bahians' distrust of African culture as foreign, separate, potentially dangerous, and primitive. The central organizing committee for Salvador's carnival banned them all in 1905.[24]

Scholars have argued that the combination of strong ethnic affiliations among Salvador's African-descended population and the heavy persecution of African culture by local elites, particularly in the nineteenth and early twentieth centuries, focused the politics of self-determination and resistance among people of color in that city on the defense of African cultural practices.[25] In particular, Candomblé—an African-derived religion devoted to the cult of divinized ancestors known as *orixás*—provided a crucial organizing force for the preservation of alternative African cultural and ritual practices. Since at least the early nineteenth century, Candomblé ritual communities and their physical grounds, known either as candomblés or *terreiros*, functioned as "refuges," culturally and often physically separate from mainstream society, in which free, freed, and (to a lesser extent) enslaved people of color could find protection, community, solace, and meaningful engagement with an African cultural and ritual world. Relying on a principle of spiritual kinship, senior priests and priestesses in the *terreiros* became spiritual fathers (*babalorixás* in Yoruba and *pais de santo* in Portuguese) or mothers (*iyalorixás* in Yoruba and *mães de santo* in Portuguese) to their initiates, who then became each other's siblings. *Pais* and *mães de santo* ministered not only to followers' religious needs but also to their need for physical healing, spaces of leisure, and social support, such as help with employment or protection from the police (or, in the case of runaway slaves before 1888, from masters and their agents). They also gave their members a strong spiritual identification with a particular African *nação* or ethnic group, one that was often independent of ancestry.[26]

In the 1930s, U.S. anthropologist Ruth Landes reported that in the Candomblé community, to be called "a son of Africans" was among the highest compliments one could receive. Unlike black thinkers in São Paulo, who in this period increasingly embraced the term *negro* as a proud marker of a racially separate but culturally unmarked identity, many Bahians of color read the term as an insult linking them to slave status and preferred instead to be identified by their distinct African heritage.[27] This contrast highlights the continuing role of ethnicity, rather than race, as the primary factor shaping the identities of African-descended Bahians into the twentieth century—a contrast partly explained by Bahia's distinct social and demographic patterns.[28] In São Paulo, people of color were a small minority in a city swelling with white immigrants. In Rio de Janeiro, despite a larger population of *pretos* and *pardos*, people of color were still a minority. In postabolition Salvador, by contrast, those categorized as *pretos* and *pardos* together made up the majority of the city's population, remaining relatively stable at 61 to 65 percent between 1890 and 1940. Moreover, unlike São Paulo, where censuses identified most people of African descent as *pretos* (suggesting an emphasis on racial descent rather than color), Salvador had a significant *pardo* category—larger even than Rio's. Between 1890 and 1940, while *pretos* remained steady at 26.3 percent of Salvador's population, the number of people identified as *pardos* grew from 35.1 to 38.4 percent.

The preponderance of people of color in the city, some scholars have argued, made Bahian society somewhat more open to the upward mobility of people of color than cities in the South—a flexibility partly confirmed by the public recognition of a large *pardo* category. This supposed flexibility should not be overstated, however; people of color were and still are far from being proportionately represented in Salvador's positions of power. And, as scholars have pointed out, the existence of a large *pardo* category reveals the emphasis Bahians placed on color gradations, even if they did not necessarily see *pretos* and *pardos* as members of a single and immutable "race." But in postabolition Salvador, where no mass immigration existed to push *pretos* and *pardos* out of the workforce, there was more equality among people of color and whites engaged in manual labor than elsewhere in the country (though, as elsewhere, *pretos* had less access to white-collar employment).[29] Many lighter-skinned *pardos* were able to enter the "world of whites," winning jobs with relatively higher status and pay. Without the sharper color line that prevailed in São Paulo, then, most people of color in Bahia (like some of their counterparts in Rio) did not see the adoption of racial identities like *negro* or *preto* as a necessary or useful strategy for combating discrimination or securing social advancement.[30]

In Salvador, a greater obstacle to social advancement than race or blackness was the open embrace of the African ethnicities and cultural practices city elites had long since identified as dangerous. In the early years of the twentieth century, members of Salvador's elite, like their southern counterparts, fought to extirpate expressions of African culture from their city's public life. Reformers, backed by medical doctors, the press, and the police, targeted "Africanisms" in food and language, in public celebrations like carnival, and in popular religious practices. To these reformers, Bahia's large African-descended population and its visible African culture, along with the absence of large-scale European immigration, placed their city and state shamefully far behind the modernizing, whitening Southeast, compounding the loss of stature that had begun with the transfer of the national capital from Salvador to Rio de Janeiro in the late eighteenth century. Indeed, southern newspapers in this period, building on long-standing references to Bahia as *a preta velha*, the old black woman, commonly caricatured the state as a "fat [Afro-]Bahiana, wearing a turban and making *angu* [an Afro-Brazilian dish]."[31] In Salvador itself, journalists and politicians fretted that the city showed foreigners "aspects of the Coast of Africa, of savage tribes without government," and generally lamented the African presence as a "sore" on their state's public face.[32]

Of all the African cultural practices that concerned Bahian reformers during the Republic, Candomblé was the most worrisome. Despite assurances of freedom of religion in the Constitution of 1891, from the early years of the century through the late 1920s Bahian police patrolled and repressed the city's many *terreiros*. Newspaper coverage of police raids in this period depicted Candomblé as immoral and dangerous through sensationalized (and often invented) descriptions of violent animal sacrifices, black magic rituals, or orgies among male and female priests and followers.[33] The work of white medical doctor and criminologist Raymundo Nina Rodrigues, a turn-of-the-century authority on Afro-Brazilian cultural practices, contributed to this perspective. Though Nina Rodrigues did not support violently raiding the candomblés, he held Africans to be racially inferior and saw their religions as evidence that Africans were incapable of anything but the most primitive forms of spirituality. He linked these religions, and African cultural practices more broadly, with psychological deviance, cultural and racial degeneracy, and criminality. Nina Rodrigues's research established him as a founder of Afro-Bahian anthropology. But his work, shaped by the racism and cultural fears of his day, ultimately presented African cultural practices as dangerous foreign influences which, if not carefully monitored and controlled, threatened to undermine Bahia's (and eventually Brazil's) tenuous veneer of European civilization.[34]

The Revolution of 1930 did not immediately change the precarious situation of the candomblés. Bahian police, acting on tips from crusading journalists and private citizens, continued to break up ceremonies and arrest spiritual leaders as dangerous charlatans well into the 1930s.[35] But in the wake of shifting conceptions of national identity, a group of northeastern intellectuals began to look at Candomblé, and at Bahia's African traditions more broadly, with new eyes. Alongside Gilberto Freyre, other scholars in the 1930s and 1940s began to portray Bahia's African culture not as something shameful but as a positive factor in Brazilian civilization, and indeed, a unique regional trait from which a broader Brazilian identity had arisen. Reaching back to regionalist gestures made earlier in the century by Nina Rodrigues himself, leaders of a new generation of anthropologists, like Arthur Ramos, asserted the superiority of the Nagô (Yoruba) people, the largest ethnic group in Bahia—"tall, robust, courageous, and hard-working, better-tempered than the others and noted for [their] intelligence"—over the "physically weaker," "quarrelsome" Bantu slaves who initially made up the slave population of Rio de Janeiro and other southern regions. In particular, Ramos put forth Bahia's candomblés as the sites par excellence of the preservation of the noblest, "best," and "purest" Yoruba traditions, while reserving disdain for the "polluted," "diluted," "artificial," and commercialized Bantu-based macumbas of Rio.[36]

By the 1930s anthropologists like Freyre and Ramos thus no longer presented Bahia as having fallen from the grace of a distinguished colonial past. Instead, they portrayed Bahia in particular and the Northeast in general as bastions of tradition (African and otherwise), essential repositories of Brazil's true nationality in a time of rapid modernization.[37] As early as 1926, Gilberto Freyre, in his *Regionalist Manifesto*, called the Northeast the place where "values that had once been seen as merely subnational or even exotic"—particularly African values—"are in the process of being transformed into Brazilian values."[38] These views were not confined to the world of academia. In Bahia, the celebration of African folklore (especially food, music, and clothing) as local and regional characteristics gradually worked its way into public consciousness by the final years of the Republic and the early years of the Vargas regime, slowly displacing earlier concerns with "de-Africanization."[39] In 1929, for instance, Salvador's *Diário de Notícias* wrote proudly of Bahia as "the cradle of our adolescent Brazil, . . . a place so deeply intertwined with the black race, particularly in its culinary delicacies."[40] If the Brazilian South was to be admired for its progress and whiteness, it was, in the context of the new cultural nationalism, equally to be reproached for "denationalizing" itself with excessive European and other foreign cultural influences. By the late 1920s, and particularly after the Revolution of 1930, some elite Bahians could portray their capital city, state, or region as a bulwark of *brasilidade*—a steward of Brazil's colonial cultures and traditions, and a tonic for the Republic's noxious Europhilia.[41] Their arguments found confirmation in Brazilians' enthusiastic embrace of works by northeastern intellectuals, particularly Freyre's *Casa-grande*, as the bibles of a new, partially Africanized national identity.

It was not just white intellectuals who worked actively to present Bahia as the repository of uncorrupted and noble African traditions but also, and perhaps primarily, a group of African-descended practitioners of Candomblé. Indeed, Ramos's and other intellectuals' fascination with African and particularly Yoruba traits in 1930s Bahia reflected transformations within Bahia's leading candomblés themselves. Until the mid- to late nineteenth century, African-born people had dominated the candomblés' leadership, building their religious practices and institutions from memories of their experiences across the Atlantic. By the turn of the twentieth century, however, as African-born Bahians became scarce, Brazilian-born leaders of several Bahian candomblés began to look directly to Africa in their search for new sources of what they considered authentic religious knowledge.[42]

Avenues of contact with Africa and Africans became a valuable commodity in this context. Though greatly reduced from previous centuries, a few regular shipping routes still existed between Bahia and Africa's western coast in the first decades of the twentieth century. Over the course of the 1800s, some Bahian freed slaves and their families had made the return voyage to West

Africa, founding communities of Brazilian returnees in coastal cities like Lagos (in present-day Nigeria) or Whydah (in present-day Benin).[43] Many returnee merchants along the Bight of Benin still made a living, until the 1930s, trading African textiles and ritual objects for Bahian goods like dried meat, tobacco, or cane alcohol.[44] In the first decades of the twentieth century, direct or indirect contact with the returnees not only provided practitioners of Bahian Candomblé with necessary items for their religious practice (hawked by their purveyors as "authentically African") or with information about specific rituals. It also introduced them to an emerging local vision of the splendors of Yoruba culture. In the late nineteenth and early twentieth centuries, the Brazilian returnees of Lagos were key actors in a cultural renaissance that exalted Yoruba ethnicity in the face of the increased infiltration of British colonial power. Promoters of this cultural nationalism sought to recover a dignified Yoruba history and "traditional religion," taking pride in Yoruba names, dress styles, and even discourses of Yoruba racial purity. The Brazilian returnees of Lagos, many of them fluent in Yoruba, English, and Portuguese, were in a unique position to communicate these ideas to traders or religious visitors from Bahia.[45]

The ideas about the integrity, purity, and superiority of a Yoruba race and culture that Bahian travelers of the late nineteenth and early twentieth centuries gleaned from their visits to places like Lagos also contributed to a renaissance of sorts among what would become Bahia's leading candomblés. In the first decades of the twentieth century, a handful of *terreiros* whose leaders claimed deep roots in Bahian Candomblé began a process of re-Africanization, during which fidelity to "pure" African, and particularly Yoruba, ritual practices became the gauge of each house's authenticity and prestige. Between 1911 and 1938, Mãe Aninha (Eugenia Anna dos Santos), the founder and leader of one of these *terreiros*, the Ilê Axé Opô Afonjá, became particularly successful in using transatlantic routes of commercial and intellectual exchange to raise the profile of her house as one that adhered strictly to purportedly unadulterated African traditions. She enlisted several transatlantic travelers, like the Bahian-born, Lagos-educated diviner Martiniano do Bomfim, to bring back information on rites and practices from their travels to Africa.[46] Following the implementation of one of Martiniano's Nigerian-inspired innovations, Aninha boasted, "My temple is pure Nagô, like Engenho Velho [the original Nagô candomblé from nineteenth-century Salvador] . . . But I have revived much of the African tradition which even Engenho Velho has forgotten."[47] These transatlantic contacts and the appearance of orthodoxy they conferred not only increased the symbolic currency of Aninha's candomblé in a highly competitive spiritual marketplace; they also provided economic benefits.[48] Aninha frequently traded with Brazilian returnee merchants in Africa to obtain the ritual objects necessary for what she presented as an authentically African, liturgically correct practice. Revenue from her sale of African products at Salvador's downtown market allowed her to support her *terreiro*, even providing the funds with which she had initially purchased the land on which it stood.[49]

By the 1930s, the Candomblé houses that had taken the lead in the process of re-Africanization—including Aninha's Ilê Axé Opô Afonjá as well as Gantois, Engenho Velho, and Alaketu—emerged as the most powerful and prestigious of the Bahian candomblés, standards of liturgical authority for many others in the Yoruba tradition.[50] This enhanced status resulted in no small part from an informational feedback cycle between the leaders of these candomblés and the scholars who studied them. In the quest to find the purest African traditions for her candomblé, for instance, Aninha avidly read the works of scholars (like Raymundo Nina Rodrigues, Arthur Ramos, Edison Carneiro, and others) who celebrated the preservation of pure Yoruba ritual practices.[51] Yet it was precisely religious thinkers like Aninha and Martiniano do Bomfim who had shaped anthropologists' fascination with Yoruba purity in the first place. Martiniano, who had imbibed ideas about the nobility of Yoruba culture during his sojourns in Lagos, had been one of Nina Rodrigues's main informants in the late nineteenth and early twentieth centuries, and continued to work with subsequent generations of scholars. Aninha and other Candomblé leaders who maintained regular ties to Africa similarly collaborated with scholars whose interest in pure African survivals both reflected and reinforced spiritual leaders' own parameters of prestige.[52]

As channels for academic production expanded in the 1930s and 1940s, northeastern intellectuals' perspectives on Candomblé as a legitimate religion worthy of study reached new audiences. In Brazil, scholars like Ramos and his disciples found employment in the anthropology departments of the federal universities founded under Vargas, and major presses published and circulated their works. The supposedly pure African traditions of Salvador's most prestigious candomblés, endorsed and amplified by the writings of local anthropologists, in turn gave the city new stature in an emerging international field of African and Afro-American studies. Anthropologist Melville Herskovits, a pioneer in the field of Afro-American anthropology, visited Salvador and its leading candomblés in the early 1940s, making it a key case study in his work on African "survivals" or "retentions" in the New World.[53] Other U.S. anthropologists and sociologists, like Ruth Landes and Donald

Pierson, were also drawn by Bahia's reputation in the 1930s and 1940s as one of the most authentically African sites in the New World. Pierson observed that "the connection between Africa and Bahia is perhaps more intimate and has been maintained over a longer period of time than any similar connection elsewhere in the New World."[54] The work of these foreign scholars, together with that of locals, helped to circulate influential Candomblé leaders' own visions of the power and prestige of Bahia's "pure" African culture across national and international academic circles, contributing to an image of legitimacy and respectability for the religion in their city and state and, to some extent, on a national stage.

This growing academic endorsement played an important part in easing state and police repression of Candomblé. In 1934 and 1937, respectively, Gilberto Freyre and anthropologist Edison Carneiro staged the first and second Afro-Brazilian Congresses in Recife and Salvador. Aimed at increasing the acceptance of Afro-Brazilian culture and especially religion among regional and national audiences, the congresses brought together academics and a range of people from Recife's and Salvador's African-descended population—primarily Candomblé practitioners who presented papers, attended events, or sold food at the gatherings. Bahia's congress of 1937 saw particularly high involvement by Candomblé practitioners, with forty local groups participating, and in some cases, holding related events in their own *terreiros*. Their greatest accomplishment during the congress was the creation of a Union of Afro-Brazilian Sects to defend the freedom of religious practice, and to help establish norms of "purity" and "authenticity" among candomblés themselves. Aninha's Ilê Axé Opô Afonjá played a leading role in the union's formation, and her colleague Martiniano do Bomfim became its president. Adherence to the rituals established by the Opô Afonjá and other leading candomblés in the Yoruba tradition, in this sense, became the standard of orthodoxy through which legitimate *terreiros* could be distinguished from inauthentic and potentially criminal practitioners of witchcraft and "black magic."[55] The creation of the union, together with a petition directed to local authorities, helped to end persecution of Afro-Brazilian religions in Bahia. More broadly, as organizer Edison Carneiro remembered, the radio and newspaper publicity surrounding the congress—which included broadcasts of Candomblé music and interviews with priests and priestesses—"contributed to creating an environment of greater tolerance toward those much maligned religions of people of color."[56]

Candomblé leaders were as active in constructing the images of legitimacy and respectability that academics helped publicize as they had been in constructing images of their religion's Yoruba purity. Since the nineteenth century, priests and priestesses had adopted the practice of conferring the honorary title of *ogan* on powerful Africans whose wealth could help sustain the community in times of need. In the first decades of the twentieth century, as police raids intensified, leaders of the most visible candomblés (who were by then almost all female) began to confer that ceremonial title on powerful white members of mainstream society (all male) who not only could provide financial support but also could use their social influence to protect the *terreiro*. Politicians, artists, and academics became *ogãs* in the major Candomblé houses in the first decades of the century.[57] Such ties of goodwill with powerful figures from mainstream society also created new avenues for female leaders of the most prestigious *terreiros* to engage in public displays of respectability in response to a host of negative associations surrounding black women. Not only had anti-Candomblé articles in Salvador's early-twentieth-century mainstream press portrayed female priestesses and initiates as morally and sexually dissolute, but black women in Bahia's public spaces had come under particular attack throughout the early 1900s as members of the city's privileged classes sought to "de-Africanize" their streets. Reformers typically identified the city's African-descended women—whom they saw as beggars, prostitutes, or vendors of unhygienic Afro-Bahian street food—as major threats to a respectable, patriarchal, sanitized social order. Female street vendors in particular came under suspicion for their links to Candomblé—many advertised their wares in Yoruba. Often these women were young initiates who used income from their sales to pay for ritual obligations. Seeking to cast black women, and particularly Candomblé women, in a more positive light, priestesses like Mãe Aninha publicly emphasized their role as "mothers" of their congregations, taking advantage of the authority that contemporary conceptions of female honor conferred on motherhood, family, domesticity, and self-sacrifice. Most of the famous Candomblé priestesses in the 1930s and 1940s did not marry, for reasons that may have included a desire to protect their own and their *terreiros*' financial independence, or to preserve their reputations as spiritual leaders.[58]

To an extent, then, Bahian Candomblé leaders' active engagement with Brazilian and foreign anthropologists in the 1930s and 1940s allowed them to spread their regional vision of cultural self-determination as "Africans" into national public life. Taking advantage of contemporary transformations in national identity that placed new value on African traits, these religious thinkers made inroads into an academic public sphere which helped legitimate cultural practices that had, until recently, been energetically persecuted by the law. Through their collaborations with local and foreign scholars, they helped spread a vision in which distinctly Yoruba traits—not diluted and mixed, as in dominant ideas of *mestiçagem*, but pure and untainted—could be held up as the true essence of a Bahian, and by extension Brazilian, identity. This vision of an exalted Yoruba culture, moreover, encoded ideas about the regional superiority of the Afro-Brazilian cultures of the Northeast over the allegedly less noble (and in any case, corrupted and watered-down) Bantu-derived religions of Rio de Janeiro. Finally, while the celebration of Yoruba purity among the leading Nagô candomblés was not typically an explicitly racial discourse (though Martiniano do Bomfim reportedly exalted African racial purity alongside Yoruba cultural purity), it was in many ways an alternative definition of blackness. Celebrating a "clean," "aristocratic" Yoruba heritage conferred dignity on a group of people who identified strongly with their African ancestry in the face of racial and cultural discrimination against the "black religions."[59]

It was this vision of an Africanized Bahia that organizers of Rio's carnival in the 1930s and 1940s helped popularize when they made the Bahianas mandatory elements in every carnival group's parade. The figure of the Bahiana, with her white colonial-era dresses and headpieces, her iconic presence at Bahian street corners selling Afro-Bahian foods, and her strong association with Candomblé, no longer seemed (as she had to Republican elites) a carrier of physically and morally contagious African traits. Instead, she came to stand specifically for Bahia's African cultural treasures, and more broadly, for Brazil's newly valorized African traditions. Rio's carnival organizers may have cast Bahianas as a regional subplot within an event that increasingly celebrated the centrality of a Rio-based view of cultural and racial *mestiçagem*. And for many in the national capital, Bahianas might have symbolized a primordial Africa (and its archaic Brazilian home, Bahia) from which a more modern, *mestiço* Brazil had subsequently emerged. But as rising icons of an Afro-Bahia, the Bahianas also bore the outlines of the pure, unmixed Africanness that Candomblé leaders had produced together with a new generation of regionalist anthropologists, even as hybridity and mixture became the rage in discourses of national identity.

"God, fatherland, race, and family"

Like northeastern regionalists, many members of São Paulo's political and intellectual elite resisted Vargas's attempts to identify national culture with the culture of Rio de Janeiro. As Barbara Weinstein has shown, the

Paulistas who led a constitutionalist revolt against Vargas's central government in 1932 were fiercely opposed not just to his politics but also to his cultural vision for the nation. The rebels vehemently rejected images of a *mestiço* national identity, with some going so far as to call the Vargas regime a "dictanegra," or black dictatorship, for its courtship of nonwhite Brazilians. They championed a regionalist ideal of Paulista whiteness, which they traced back to São Paulo's colonial history as a frontier region. Drawing on a long-standing local motif, Paulista insurgents argued that the intrepid *bandeirantes* who had explored the state's interior, together with São Paulo's legions of European immigrants, had forged a modern, prosperous, enterprising people—the pioneers of a new Brazil. Paulistas put forth this image of regional superiority in their conflict with the centralizing government in Rio, but also in explicit contrast to what they saw as the stagnant and tradition-bound Northeast, from which the regime drew crucial support as well as much of its African symbolism.[60]

Among black Paulistano intellectuals, however, Vargas's new cultural politics of *brasilidade* generally received a warmer welcome. In 1931, *O Progresso*, the same black newspaper that in the late 1920s had expressed admiration for the Syrio-Lebanese monument to ethnic integration, published an article hailing samba as Brazil's "national hymn" and praising its once maligned African influences. Samba's rhythms contained "all the heat and languor of the tropics," its delightful melodies "full of the lascivious and disorganized jungle." Above all, samba, with its unabashed embrace of "barbarity," represented a new Brazilian philosophy—one of "horror toward the artificiality of European civilization, too quickly assimilated [by Brazilians]."[61] Like Freyre who, following his night of bohemian fun in Rio, discovered that a true, black and mulatto Brazil was hiding under a European veneer, this writer for one of São Paulo's leading black papers celebrated samba precisely for its African primitivism and its rejection of European cultural values. He was not alone. Since the late 1920s, several writers in *O Progresso* had embraced ideas about Brazil's cultural and racial hybridity (a minority vision in São Paulo's black press), celebrating this heritage as part of the artistic and cultural production of people of African descent worldwide. *Progresso* writers punctuated their coverage of economic and political events in Africa and the diaspora with cultural articles about jazz, modernist musicians like Heitor Villa-Lobos, or the dizzying international successes of black cabaret star Josephine Baker.[62] Having spent much of the late 1920s developing precisely the sort of vision of national identity that would take root under Vargas, these writers happily celebrated samba as Brazil's hybrid national rhythm.

But it was the nativism informing Vargas's cultural policies that generated greatest enthusiasm among São Paulo's thinkers of color. Throughout the 1920s, writers in the black press had argued that they should be recognized as "nationals" in contrast to immigrants. They therefore took satisfaction from new laws under Vargas that preferred national workers to foreigners and that cracked down on immigrant enclaves. Early on in his tenure as president, Vargas instituted new immigration restrictions, as well as a labor nationalization law stipulating that two-thirds of employees in industrial firms be Brazilian-born. In 1938 Vargas identified unassimilated immigrant colonies in the South of Brazil as potential threats to national security and integrity, especially in light of their close ties with totalitarian politics in countries (like Germany or Italy) then preparing for war. He warned the nation of the need to "defend ourselves against the infiltration of elements that could transform into foci of ideological or racial dissent within our borders." To "Brazilianize" these citizens, Vargas outlawed foreign-language schools, clubs, and newspapers.[63] The tides were turning, with once prized immigrants identified as interloping foreigners, and people of color—once treated like "foreigners in the land of their birth"—placed at the forefront of new definitions of *brasilidade*.

Especially in its early years, Vargas's regime also seemed to provide an institutional opening for black Paulistano politics. In the months following Vargas's rise to power, São Paulo's leading black newspapers, *O Clarim* and *O Progresso*, expressed elation at the changing political climate. In particular, they voiced hopes that the new government would finally provide the city's black thinkers and activists the opportunity to create a broad political organization.[64] This dream became a reality in September 1931. After months of intense work among leaders of the city's black social and political groups, former Palmares Center president and *Clarim* contributor Arlindo Veiga dos Santos read the statutes of a new organization, the Frente Negra Brasileira, or Brazilian Black Front, to an audience of more than one thousand Paulistanos of color.[65] Consistent with the definitions of belonging developed in the black newspapers of the 1910s and 1920s, the Frente Negra's statutes proclaimed the organization to be a "political and social union of Black Nationals [*Gente Negra Nacional*], aimed at affirming their historical rights in light of their material and moral activity in the past, and reclaiming their social and political rights in the present."[66] This use of the word *national* to describe black Brazilians echoes the ways that many black writers in the 1920s, and particularly Arlindo Veiga dos Santos himself, had deployed nativism and the historical contributions of the "black race" to claim precedence over the foreigners who predominated in São Paulo's working class. It also reflects the encouragement that this sort of politics received from the Vargas government, which through its labor, immigration, and cultural policies had helped to rehabilitate the term *national* and turn it into the leading political precept of the times. Under the new regime, black Brazilians in the Frente—as *nationals*—could finally, realistically, hope to obtain recognition in the present for their ancestors' past contributions to their nation, thereby approximating the sort of symbolic belonging to which so many thinkers of color had aspired throughout the 1910s and 1920s.

The Frente's activism drew on the practices developed in the earlier black social clubs of São Paulo, especially the Centro Cívico Palmares. As with earlier clubs, Frente leaders sought to promote racial unity and consciousness through journalism. At first, the Frente addressed itself to black audiences through *O Progresso*, but after 1933 its leaders relied on their own newspaper, *A Voz da Raça* (*The Voice of the Race*). In Sunday meetings called *domingueiras*, famed black orators like Vicente Ferreira, Alberto Orlando, and Arlindo Veiga dos Santos conveyed messages of racial pride and uplift before turning the meetings over to activities designed to promote sociability and community building. Young people flocked to these weekly meetings to socialize, court members of the opposite sex, play in the Frente's jazz band, or enjoy the leisurely exchange of ideas. Beyond these gatherings, the Frente also provided a range of social services to its members—from a hair salon and a dental office to economic and financial advice, labor advocacy, an elementary school, and adult literacy courses. Though implemented on a modest scale, as membership dues and members' own volunteer efforts permitted, these services seem to have filled a need for many young and working-class Paulistas of color at a time of national economic hardship. Frente Negra chapters spread into São Paulo's interior and across the states of Minas Gerais, Espírito Santo, Rio Grande do Sul, and Bahia. Estimates (made by leaders) of six thousand members in the main São Paulo branch and up to one hundred thousand nationwide were probably exaggerated. But given that previous black social and political associations had memberships that rarely surpassed the very low hundreds, the Frente's membership, almost certainly in the thousands, signals an organization of unprecedented reach.[67]

The Frente's success in attracting members also reflects changes in national politics. Vargas's government encouraged certain kinds of working-class mobilization and, at least initially, was open to the Frente's model of political action along racial lines. The Frente's 1931 statutes captured this opportunity, promising to give the "Black Brazilian People" a greater say in local and national politics by working to elect black representatives. In 1933 the organization made its first foray into national politics by running Arlindo Veiga dos Santos as an independent candidate for the Constituent Assembly.[68] Though this initiative failed, it generated momentum for those who wished to see the Frente involved in electoral politics, a project that would culminate in the Frente's registration as a political party in 1936. More important, perhaps, under the new regime the Frente Negra could exert political influence through nonelectoral channels as well. Vargas's early government was corporatist, granting representatives of institutionally recognized social groups— like workers or industrialists—a measure of political influence through direct ties to the president. Members of the organized women's suffrage movement, for instance, obtained the vote for women in 1932 by appealing personally to Vargas.[69] The Frente's leadership likewise presented itself as the legitimate institutional representative of a distinct group in the Brazilian body politic— black Brazilians—in order to press its claims with the state. Most notably, in 1932, a delegation of Frente members visited Vargas in Rio de Janeiro to request his help in integrating São Paulo's informally segregated Civil Guard (something the Palmares Civic Center had attempted earlier, without success). Vargas assented, ordering that the guard begin immediate recruitment of black officers. The Frente used similar techniques with local officials, appealing to São Paulo's chief of police to end racially discriminatory practices in city businesses, with some success.[70]

In the months following the Frente's foundation, however, enthusiasm gave way to doubts and internal strife. Almost immediately, dissent emerged over who would lead the new organization. Amid much contention, Arlindo Veiga dos Santos became president and his brother Isaltino secretary-general. Though Leite and his group at *O Clarim* had misgivings about the Santos brothers' authoritarian tendencies as Frente leaders, they cautiously backed them, fearing that too much internal squabbling might destroy the Frente just as it had doomed its predecessor, the Palmares Civic Center.[71] This fragile alliance, however, came to an end in early 1932, following an incident involving the alleged seduction by Isaltino Veiga dos Santos (who was married) of a young black woman during an official visit to a small town in Minas Gerais. The young woman's outraged family, receiving no responses from the Frente, appealed directly to Leite to obtain a public apology. Leite presented the family's grievance to the Frente, calling for Isaltino's resignation.[72] Isaltino refused to step down, and Arlindo refused to depose him, instead dismissing Leite and his group as "Judases of the Race" for making the issue public. In response, Leite and his colleagues at *O Clarim* began to publish a newspaper titled *A Chibata* (*The Whip*) specifically to criticize the Santos brothers and call for new leadership of the Frente. *A Chibata*'s first issue (in February 1932) was full of satirical articles portraying Isaltino as "cynical, hypocritical, and vain," reminding him of the "respect due to black women," and reprimanding Arlindo for failing to punish his brother.[73] Their second issue demanded, more pointedly, that Arlindo stop using "an association maintained by the money of the race" as a "cover for his brother's lack of moral manliness."[74]

A Chibata, however, only lasted for two issues, for just as Leite and his colleagues were preparing the type plates for the third issue, the Santos brothers had Leite's home workshop sacked. The attack took place one evening in March 1932, while Leite and his family stood by. According to Leite and other witnesses, a group of drunken men armed with heavy sticks smashed and overturned furniture and typewriters, threw bookcases out of windows, shattered dishes, and physically intimidated Leite and two of the household's women. The men stopped short of destroying Leite's typesetting machine, which was out of sight in a small room.[75] The incident had repercussions beyond the black community; in the following days, for instance, São Paulo's *Diário Nacional* ran a front-page article on the attack, along with a picture of Leite's destroyed workshop.[76]

Divisions within the Frente, however, did not simply reflect individual struggles over power, or even concerns with the honor and respectability of São Paulo's (and Brazil's) foremost black organization. Increasingly, divisions between the Santos brothers and Leite's group—all formerly colleagues at *O Clarim*—reflected the deepening schisms of national politics. The political strategies of Arlindo Veiga dos Santos and José Correia Leite had already begun to diverge in the late 1920s, with the former, a nativist conservative, penning some of *Clarim*'s sharpest anti-immigrant rhetoric, and the latter, a left-leaning internationalist, expressing admiration for immigrant organizations and their strategies for ethnic inclusion. This division deepened in the context of the political polarization of the early 1930s, as São Paulo's black activists increasingly split their allegiances between socialism and the emerging Brazilian fascist movement known as Integralism. In the early 1930s Arlindo Veiga dos Santos expressed strong Integralist sympathies and became the leader of a deeply conservative Catholic and monarchist movement known as *patrianovismo*.[77] Leite, in contrast, became increasingly committed to socialism and international movements like pan-Africanism. In *A Chibata* and *O Clarim* he began to criticize not just Santos's "absolutist" leadership style but also his political ideology (which Leite characterized as backward-looking) and his use of the Frente as a platform for these "political maneuvers."[78] Though in 1932 Santos had not yet begun publishing the newspaper that would most clearly convey his own conservative ideology, his smashing of Leite's workshop early that year announced many of the political ideals and tactics he would shortly thereafter advocate in writing: factionalism, violence, and disdain for democracy and freedom of the press. (A year later, in an early issue of the Frente's newspaper, Santos threatened violent retribution against his opponents, warning that "against the free press we will freely use the stick.")[79] Santos tolerated no political disagreements within his ranks. Over the course of 1932, in the context of São Paulo's failed military uprising against Getúlio Vargas, the Frente Negra's leadership officially declared its neutrality in the conflict and allowed members to act according to their consciences.[80] Yet former members recalled that Santos and others in the Frente's leadership, which supported Vargas, expelled from the organization *frentenegrinos* sympathetic to the São Paulo movement. Among those who left the Frente willingly or by force in this period were orators Vicente Ferreira and Alberto Orlando and lawyer Joaquim Guaraná de Santana. Santana went on to create the Legião Negra (Black Legion), battalions of black soldiers who fought on São Paulo's side in the constitutionalist uprising.[81]

In consolidating his own power over the organization, Santos sought to push the Frente Negra toward the political right. He developed and disseminated his ideology in front-page editorials of the Frente Negra's official newspaper, *A Voz da Raça*. *A Voz*, published weekly from March 1933 to November 1937, built on the structure of the Paulista black newspapers of the second half of the 1920s. It dedicated prime space to editorials on racial issues and Frente activities and reserved secondary space for society pages, fiction or poetry, and advertising. *A Voz* was the first black newspaper to reach mass distribution levels—one to five thousand copies of each issue circulated weekly among the Frente's chapters in São Paulo and across Brazil.[82] Though Arlindo Veiga dos Santos would step down as president of the Frente in 1934, his editorials set the tone for much of the newspaper's subsequent ideological production and for the Frente's projection of its ideology to members nationwide.

Santos and other prominent writers in *A Voz da Raça* condemned democracy and portrayed liberal ideologies as "exotic" importations that had contributed to disinheriting black Brazilians.[83] In particular, they blamed Republican projects of "whitening" through the promotion of European immigration for blacks' marginalization and used *A Voz* to call for immigration restrictions. Building on the nativism he had begun to articulate in the late 1920s, Santos, in an article detailing his political platform, demanded the suspension of immigration for twenty years so that the black and mixed populations of

Brazil—newly valorized under Vargas's regime—could "assimilate all of the newcomers nationally and racially."[84] In marked contrast to white opponents of black immigration to Brazil in the early 1920s, Santos feared the threat that white newcomers posed to Brazil's *mestiço* essence. The theme of blacks' disinheritance during the Republic in favor of "Aryan" immigrants ran powerfully through his and other *frentenegrinos'* writings, showing that resentment toward foreigners, and toward having been made to feel like foreigners, was still raw among many Paulistanos of color in the early 1930s. As Arlindo's brother Isaltino Veiga dos Santos saw it, the Frente's reason for being was to work "in favor of the black Brazilian, who has always been an outsider in his own land and a mere THING in society."[85]

A Voz da Raça also published frequent tirades against communism, which Arlindo dos Santos referred to on several occasions as a "worldwide Judeo-cosmopolitan bolshevist revolution," one of several "dastardly" plots orchestrated by "foreign or semiforeign slime."[86] His choice of words expressed not only his anti-Semitism (a common trait among conservative nationalists) but also his deep rejection of the supposedly cosmopolitan in favor of the rigidly national. Just as racism was an unholy import by "foreign slime," so was labor radicalism. In opposition to communism, Santos championed "organico-syndicalism," a corporatist-authoritarian state that resembled European fascism as well as the evolving Vargas regime.[87] As a fervent monarchist, Santos advocated a strong, father-like leader who would rule the different social groups under his command like the limbs and organs of a national body. He looked back fondly on the colonial period, when Portuguese monarchs had enacted "an organic conception of the State, not yet afraid of free corporations within it." This idea of independent "corporations" protected by a strong state was essential to Santos's racial politics. "We did not have [then], as today," he wrote, "the antinatural monism that desires the DISAPPEARANCE of blacks. . . . The natural truths within our Social and Political Unity were recognized."[88] In a corporatist nation, blacks would be recognized as distinct but "natural" and integral parts of the body politic.[89]

For Santos, the ideal example of the rightful relationship between *negros* as a corporate group and the state was the black brigades that fought in Brazil's seventeenth-century wars against the Dutch, particularly their leader, the "exalted" Henrique Dias.[90] Dias was the Brazilian-born son of freed Africans who organized and led a detachment of free Africans to repel Dutch troops in the Northeast, and whom colonial officials accepted as a legitimate general. The essays of Santos and others frequently portrayed blacks as loyal soldiers guarding the nation against external threats, and the example of Henrique

Dias and his black troops helping to repel a foreign invasion provided a fitting precedent.[91] Frente leaders also frequently reminded members that they should be prepared to use violence in the joint project of integrating blacks and defending the nation. In this vein, *A Voz* urged members to join the Frente's militia or "civic-military phalanx."[92] Militaristic metaphors of authority, discipline, righteous violence, and respectful subordination not only structured black Brazilians' relationship to the nation but described the power hierarchy of the Frente Negra itself. Power resided almost completely in the president and the Grand Council, whose members received military titles like "major" and "colonel"; dues collectors were called "corporals."

An organization that imagined citizens and members as soldiers, and whose hymn urged "Black People" to "raise up their manly brows," clearly understood ideals of political participation and citizenship to be gendered male.[93] It is perhaps surprising, therefore, that women made up more than half of the Frente's membership, and were among its hardest-working supporters, according to Francisco Lucrécio, secretary-general of the Frente after 1934. Black women were drawn to the Frente, Lucrécio believed, for the help it provided them in obtaining and keeping the jobs that, in many cases, supported entire families.[94] Yet it seems that despite their participation in numbers far greater than those in previous black organizations, women's roles in the Frente remained limited, constrained as in earlier years by ideas about "properly" domestic and feminine spaces. *Frentenegrinas'* most visible participation was as "Black Roses," an auxiliary created to host fund-raising parties for the Frente and as teachers in the Frente's elementary-school classes.[95] In November 1937 *A Voz da Raça* inaugurated a section dedicated specifically to women. This first appearance of the "Feminine Section" (also its last, since the newspaper ceased publication thereafter) did not promise great changes in the roles envisioned for *frentenegrinas*—it consisted mainly of several pieces of romantic prose, along with some "beauty tips."[96]

What Arlindo dos Santos proposed for the Frente was a politics of black recognition blended with the emerging political ideals of fascism, especially its Brazilian variant, Integralism. Editorials in *A Voz* expressed admiration for the authoritarian regimes of Italy and Germany, and frequently praised Hitler, whom some writers saw as rightfully defending his race against degeneration and infiltration by outsiders. "Hitler is right!" Santos proclaimed in an editorial titled "The Affirmation of the Race." The Brazilian government, he argued, ought to have "affirmed our Luso-indigenous-black race, rather than making our national home into an international orgy." By courting immigrants and emulating Europe, the leaders of the Republic had "denied our Black People, making them stand . . . at the margins of national life, yielding their place to the opportunist newcomers." In another article Santos reasoned, "Hitler affirms the German race. We affirm the Brazilian Race, especially its strongest element: THE BLACK BRAZILIAN."[97] Writing in the early to mid-1930s, well before the Nazis would carry their racial vision to its most murderous consequences, the Frente's leadership defended Hitler's "racism," by which they meant pride in one's national race. The enemies Santos and others attacked were "antiracist" governments, like the Republic, which had betrayed Brazil's native races in its concern with "the so-called GENERAL ARY-ANIZATION of the Brazilian nation."[98]

The Santos brothers' use of A Voz as an almost personal political mouth-piece in its early years—and the uniformity of opinion they appear to have required of other editorialists in their paper—conceals nuances of political views that must certainly have existed among the leadership and broader membership. Historian Kim Butler argues that the Frente's official ideology only represented the viewpoint of its rather idiosyncratic leadership, standing at odds with the political ideas of most of São Paulo's black activists. Indeed, in its seven years of existence, the Frente underwent six major factional dis-putes, four of which had the effect of creating rival associations (at least two of them, the Black Legion and the Socialist Black Front, firmly on the left). As for the largely working-class membership, Butler contends, most joined more for the Frente's social services than out of adherence to its political ideas. The memories of former Frente member Aristides Barbosa confirm this view. He recalled that many young members were attracted by the group's "appear-ance of grandeur" rather than by its specific political visions.[99] Moreover, as political scientist Michael Mitchell points out, though São Paulo's Frente Negra chapter was by far the most nationally prominent of the organiza-tion's branches, the particular political ideologies and alliances of different branches varied widely. For instance, in the neighboring port city of Santos, where traditions of labor activism among black port workers ran deep, the local Frente Negra frequently allied itself with the Socialist Party.[100]

Many defectors from the Frente Negra, and still more Brazilians of color who had never joined explicitly black social and political organizations, saw the attractions of the Left in this period. The Brazilian Communist Party, intermittently outlawed since the early decades of the century, attempted in 1935 to bring together other proworker, antifascist groups to create the Aliança Nacional Libertadora (ANL, or National Liberation Alliance). The ANL sought to battle foreign imperialism, champion workers' rights, demand land reform, and to a lesser extent, challenge xenophobia and anti-Semitism, while calling for racial equality and celebrating instances of black revolt.[101] Across Brazil, the ANL attracted working-class members in urban and rural areas. Many of these were people of color who chose to pursue their rights to racial and economic equality not through explicitly racial movements like those that gave rise to São Paulo's black press (which were, in any case, largely directed toward an anticommunist, privileged sector of the population of color), but rather through class-based organizations.[102] The ANL and other leftist movements were not a viable opposition force for long. In 1935, citing a series of attempted uprisings by the Brazilian Communist Party (whose dangers the administration intentionally exaggerated), Vargas declared a state of siege that suspended the constitution and granted emergency powers to the executive. The ANL, lacking widespread mass support, and internally divided, fell victim to Vargas's intensified anticommunist campaigns. The Integralists, though also closely watched by Vargas's secret police, fared better in this increasingly authoritarian climate.

Given the Vargas government's early persecution of communism, its flirtation with European fascism, and its relative openness to the political demands of the Frente Negra's leadership, it is no surprise, as one Frente Negra member later remembered, that an ambitious but vulnerable black organization would have cast its lot with the right-leaning nationalism increasingly earning the state's favor.[103] It is crucial to recognize, however, that the Frente's ideology and rhetoric, as voiced primarily by Santos and a handful of other writers in A Voz, contained ideas about race, history, and national belonging that were in fact a continuation of the majority view emerging in the black press of 1910s and 1920s São Paulo.

Writers associated with the Frente Negra resembled writers in the black press of the preceding decades in two main ways. First, they generally espoused the view that black belonging was earned through a history of vigorous participation in nation building. In essay after essay, writers in A Voz portrayed blacks as integral contributors to the *pátria* or fatherland, past and present—as slaves who tilled the country's fields or as soldiers who defended the nation against foreign invasion. Their preferred heroes were all homegrown, like abolitionists José do Patrocínio and Luiz Gama, soldier Henrique Dias, or Zumbi, warrior-king of the maroon community of Palmares.[104]

Second, and most prominent, the Frente's leadership attempted to balance the politically inclusive potentials of new nationalist discourses of racial mixture with a desire to preserve blacks' racial distinctiveness and group unity. On the one hand, the notion of *mestiçagem* could be useful in contesting visions of Brazil, or São Paulo, as exclusively white. In one article, for instance, Arlindo dos Santos urged Frente members to work in the "unitarian and racist spirit of the Bandeiras of yore, which . . . were made up almost exclusively of *mestiços* of all kinds."[105] Reconfiguring *bandeirantes'* brutal slave-raiding expeditions as the early precursors of contemporary nationalist ideas of racial pride, Santos suggested that the participation of mixed-race people in the life of their state took historical priority over the more recent, foreign ideals of whiteness put forth by state elites, particularly during the revolt of 1932. On the other hand, while writers in *A Voz* saw official views of a "mestiço" Brazilian race as preferable to earlier ideas of whitened nationhood, they nonetheless took pains to emphasize that Brazil was made up of distinct communities of black, white, and indigenous people. All three races, in this view, had legitimate claims to Brazilianness as distinct entities.[106] They were highly suspicious of mixture as an individual or collective category of racial self-definition, especially when mixture seemed to stand in for whitening. In a poem titled "The Mulatto," Arlindo dos Santos dramatized his disdain for people of color who embraced intermediate racial categories instead of *negro*: "Mulattos, in order to be good / Must keep their kinky hair / Or they are fakes / . . . they are neither black nor white."[107] The Frente Negra's official racial vocabulary—its proud and insistent repetition of the term *negro* as the proper category of racial identification for people of African descent—finalized the transition from Paulista activists' earlier use of color categories like *preto* or *de cor* to a unified black racial category imagined as a fixed community of descent.[108] As the Frente's motto, "God, fatherland, race, and family," made clear, race was the second-tier corporatist entity (immediately above the family) to which people of color belonged, and through which they would intervene in national life.

In this context, we might read Santos's early call (1933) for "a fraternal Brazil, devoid of petty prejudices, in which the Black brother and the White brother stand arm in arm" as auguring a continuation of the "two races" politics of fraternity developed by black Paulista writers since the turn of the century.[109] As they came to reject the Republic and its political underpinnings, however, the leaders of the Frente Negra soon discarded racial fraternity, particularly in its sentimental forms, in favor of other metaphors that would better capture their ideals of interracial social and political relations.[110] The figure of the Mãe Preta, in this context, nearly disappeared from *A Voz*, except in a very few rare instances, as when Arlindo dos Santos used her as an image not of racial fraternity but of the suffering of a race forced to yield its jobs, its well-being, and its nation to "thieving" foreigners.[111] The Mãe Preta had made sense as a symbol of black politics during the Republic, when a weak central government allowed black writers to imagine fraternity as an interpersonal dynamic independent of the state, through which they, as black men, could claim brotherhood directly with their white conationals. Under a centralizing regime in which Vargas portrayed himself as a "father" of the nation, however, writers affiliated with the Frente Negra described political belonging in terms of family metaphors that were not primarily horizontal, but vertical. The Mãe Preta, with her sentimentalized message of cross-racial fraternity, was replaced by military figures, benevolent kings, and metaphors of soldierly discipline and hierarchy, suggesting that Frente writers newly understood citizenship as a filial and martial relationship between loyal *negro* sons and soldiers, on the one hand, and the state, on the other.

This shift in the style and content of familial metaphors of belonging among Paulistano black activists reflected not just the Frente's ideology but also the broader political atmosphere of early 1930s São Paulo, where ideals of soldiering and military violence as paths to citizenship held wide appeal. Only Leite's *Clarim* continued to promote the idea for a monument and a holiday for the Mãe Preta during this period; Leite later recalled that the projects gradually faded from public view because they were incompatible with the transformed national climate.[112] Lawyer Joaquim Guaraná de Santana also invoked the ideal of the black mother when he left the Frente Negra to form the Black Legion in 1932, making her a rallying point in his foundational "Manifesto" to the "descendants of the *raça negra* in Brazil." Tellingly, however, he reconfigured her as the Mãe *Negra*, a word that in the context of São Paulo's contemporary racial politics carried a stronger racial identification than the adjective *preta*, preferred in 1920s celebrations of the wet-nurse, which only described her color. *Negros*, Santana proclaimed, were "the builders of the economic greatness of our fatherland, who with our blood have redeemed it of all oppression." The "milk of the Mãe Negra," Santana continued, had imbued her children with "great love for Brazil," making them "some of the greatest soldiers of this crusade [the 1932 constitutionalist uprising]." The Mãe Negra, Santana seemed to suggest, was mother only to the black race, and as such she was no longer a sentimental symbol of national conciliation. Instead, she was a symbol of black soldiers' military heroism and of black Paulistas' rightful belonging as patriotic sons of their state and nation.[113]

Though the Frente's leadership moved away from metaphors of racial fraternity, Santos's repeated calls to celebrate the "fiercely nationalistic conscience of all black countrymen" and to discourage "any sort of alliance with foreign blacks" show them to have continued the trend, common to most black Paulistano thinkers in the 1920s, of disavowing any ties with Africa or diasporic Africans.[114] Francisco Lucrécio, a member and leader of the Frente Negra, remembered, "We exchanged some correspondence with Angola, we knew about Marcus Garvey's movement, but we did not agree. We always affirmed our identities as Brazilians and positioned ourselves thus, with the logic that our ancestors, from Zumbi of Palmares to the black abolitionists, worked, sacrificed themselves, and battled in Brazil. . . . We did not wish to lose our identity as Brazilians. So we followed the line of our ancestors."[115] As a result, apart from an early mention of correspondence with a sympathetic black newspaper in Lourenço Marques (as Maputo, capital of Mozambique, was known during colonial times), and the occasional opinion column signed with the pseudonym "Menelik" (no doubt the work of the former editor of O Menelik, Deocleciano do Nascimento, by this point a convert to the Frente Negra's brand of nationalism), no positive references to Africa appear in A Voz.[116] The militant racialism of the Frente Negra was a defense not of Africans but of black Brazilians.

Leite and other left-leaning black activists who split with the Frente Negra differed on this point. Leite's Clarim started off the 1930s with increased pan-Africanist fervor. Beginning in January 1930, Leite dedicated a full page of his newspaper to international news concerning blacks, paying particular attention to the activities of Marcus Garvey and his "Back to Africa" movement. Aside from conveying information on events in the United States, Ethiopia, Haiti, and other parts of Africa and the diaspora, including special contributions from African and African American writers, this international page frequently ran articles from Garvey's publication The Negro World, transcribed and translated by a collaborator from Bahia, Mário Vasconcelos.[117] In late 1930 the title of Garvey's famous publication, rendered in Portuguese as "O mundo negro," became the title of Leite's black internationalist page.[118] By mid-1931 Garvey's ideas and those of Clarim's editors became increasingly blurred: articles transcribed from The Negro World were no longer clearly labeled as such, and Garveyist slogans like "Blacks of the Old and New worlds, unite!" or "African Fundamentalism" floated in large bold typeface across Clarim's pages, unconnected to any given piece.[119] Other publications, like Cultura (the organ of a politically independent black social and athletic organization Leite founded in 1934), as well as O Clarim (a short-lived offshoot of O Clarim d'Alvorada after 1933) and Tribuna Negra (a collaboration with members of the former Black Legion), all included several internationally focused articles reminiscent of "O mundo negro." In particular, Mussolini's aggression toward the "Black Empire" of Ethiopia in 1935 received indignant attention from these black internationalists besieged, in their home city, by fascist Italian immigrants and by ultranationalist, quasi-fascist *frentenegrinos*.[120]

Yet while writers for *O Clarim d'Alvorada* and members of the Frente Negra differed sharply in their views on Africa and pan-African politics, both factions, comprised of middle-class black Paulistanos, rejected certain kinds of African culture in Brazil itself. In his writings, for instance, Arlindo dos Santos at times used words related to Afro-Brazilian culture, especially religion, as a vocabulary of political denigration. The term *macumbeiros* (a derisive name for practitioners of Afro-Brazilian religions), appears as a euphemism for political traitors and fakers; *batuque*, the term for Afro-Brazilian ritual drumming, was used to characterize the excess and decadence of the Republic; and defenders of democracy appeared as "primitives."[121] *A Voz da Raça*, despite its tactical endorsement of national ideas of racial mixture, did not celebrate the African imprint on Brazilian culture in the fashion of the aesthetic modernism of the 1920s or of Freyre's *Casa-grande*. Instead, its articles directly or indirectly enforced a notion of black Brazilian identity in which Christianity and respectability went hand in hand. A writer by the name of Castelo Alves, for instance, declared, "We are good Catholics, we like religious festivals and encourage all respect for religious rituals, but we cannot abstain from protesting the terrible habit of certain party-makers in performing *samba* and *batuque* in front of churches." Not only did these practices "drag victims into a culture of the most infamous habits," like alcoholism, but they more generally undermined the public respectability of hardworking blacks, like those in the Frente. "We must put an end to the *bombo* and *pandeiro* [the drum and tambourine used in Afro-Brazilian music], because they are a war cry against *frentenegrinos*!"[122]

These uses of Afro-Brazilian culture as markers of social or political barbarism reflected the ideas of not just the Frente Negra leadership but São Paulo's black activists more broadly. The Paulistanos of color who frequented São Paulo's black social and political associations were mostly staunch Catholics who saw their religion as central to what qualified them as true, unmarked Brazilians. Therefore, as Leite remembered when asked about Afro-Brazilian ritual practices, he and other politically active blacks were not only "uninterested in those things," but saw them as antithetical to the goals of their racial politics—a "sort of backward move in the process of obtaining social progress for blacks."[123] In its own way, the pan-Africanism that Leite espoused ran parallel to the ideals of the Frente Negra in its commitment to hierarchies of culture and civilization. Marcus Garvey and Ras Tafari were modern, rational, political black men, not superstitious primitives.

The rejection of Afro-Brazilian religions by vocal members of São Paulo's black community had a regionalist cast as well. Candomblé and other Afro-Brazilian religious forms had persisted and even flourished clandestinely in other parts of the country, like Rio de Janeiro and especially Salvador da Bahia, which in the 1930s was gaining positive visibility for its preservation of African culture and religion. Yet until the early 1940s, São Paulo's police strictly repressed Afro-Brazilian religions, pushing those practices even further to the margins of society. As sociologist Reginaldo Prandi notes, until the 1970s Candomblé in particular was seen by most Paulistas as "a curiosity . . . , imagined as a holdover of an Africanness that was maintained in Bahia."[124] Elite Paulistas, in their rejection of Vargas's "dictanegra," explicitly contrasted the regional identity of São Paulo as modern and white against the backwardness and Africanness of the Northeast. In this context, black thinkers, even as they sought to retell the history of São Paulo to emphasize its *mestiço* origins, implicitly profiled themselves as modern intellectuals from an industrializing, vanguardist city, against what they saw as the backward practices of African-descended people in other parts of the nation. Therefore, both the Frente Negra's subtle but palpable rejection of Afro-Brazilian culture *and* opponents like Leite's embrace of a contemporary, political pan-Africanism portrayed São Paulo's black politics as essentially modern, while excluding certain kinds of African manifestations deemed "primitive" and rejecting the reevaluation of African culture rooted in the Northeast and in the national capital.

For much of the 1930s the Frente Negra was the predominant black organization in São Paulo, and indeed in Brazil. Its detractors, particularly José Correia Leite, had a difficult time creating viable alternatives to the organization and its powerful newspaper. Leite suspended *O Clarim d'Alvorada* in mid-1932, shortly after the Frente's attack on his workshop. He attempted to continue his internationalist pursuits in a series of short-lived newspapers with which he subsequently collaborated (including some of the ones cited above) and by creating an alternative black organization, the Clube Negro de Cultura Social, which he soon thereafter abandoned due to its increasingly recreational character.[125] The Frente Negra, by contrast, enjoyed broad support, probably because its politics articulated more easily with those of the Vargas regime. Its leaders espoused compelling, if extreme and simplified, messages that resonated with dominant nationalist and regionalist ideologies, while continuing to push for racial recognition and advancement.

In 1936 the Frente registered as a political party. Yet it was precisely the Frente's success in obtaining this formal status that made it vulnerable in

1937, when Getúlio Vargas staged the internal coup that inaugurated the most repressive phase of his regime. Under the Estado Novo or New State (a name borrowed from the fascist dictatorship of Antonio de Oliveira Salazar in Portugal), Vargas built up the secret police and the army, increased censorship of the media, and outlawed all political parties. The Frente Negra ceased to exist.[126] Some members attempted to reconfigure as a cultural club, but they failed to draw a wide membership. Straggling members of the Frente Negra held their last meeting in 1938, in time for the fiftieth anniversary of the abolition of slavery. In the seven-year dictatorship that followed, explicitly political black organizations and publications in São Paulo and elsewhere virtually ground to a halt, until the fall of Vargas and the return of democracy in 1945.

Bahian *Negros*

São Paulo did not have an exclusive claim on explicitly "black" politics in the 1930s. Indeed, the events that had marked the political thought and activism of self-defined *negro* men in São Paulo since the late 1920s—in particular, the Mãe Preta celebrations and the Frente Negra—had repercussions elsewhere. Even in the far-off city of Salvador da Bahia, with its strong traditions of activism based on the defense of African culture, a group of men of color with connections to São Paulo's black activist institutions developed a Paulistano-style racial politics as culturally unmarked, Catholic black Brazilians. Yet the brevity and limited visibility of their endeavors illustrates how political strategies developed with success in the specific social context of one city were transformed, in their meaning and resonance, as they crossed into another.

One of the most notable examples of such cross-regional political borrowings momentarily takes us back to 28 September 1929. On that date, a year after José Correia Leite had proposed the creation of a holiday for the Mãe Preta in São Paulo's *Clarim*, a group of Bahians of color led by one Ascendino Bispo dos Anjos helped organize city-wide celebrations in honor of the Mãe Preta, securing the support of Salvador's most prominent politicians, intellectuals, journalists, artists, musicians, religious leaders, and educators. The festivities began with celebratory gunfire at dawn, followed by a special mass at Salvador's Basilica and a civic procession that wound through the streets of the center city. During the procession, public figures made speeches and read poems about the Mãe Preta as a symbol of the black race's contributions to Brazil, echoing the articles politicians and intellectuals in Rio de Janeiro had produced in support of their monument project three years earlier. Schoolchildren sang a hymn to the Mãe Preta that stressed her equal love of her black and white children. Foremost among the participants in the procession were the dark-skinned members of the Centro Operário (Workingman's Center), who had the honor of escorting Bahian artist Presciliano Silva's painting of the Mãe Preta, specially commissioned for the occasion, through the streets of downtown Salvador. The day ended with a "solemn session" at the Centro Operário, though judging from their exceedingly brief mention of this portion of the otherwise lavishly detailed celebrations, it seems that no journalists for Bahia's mainstream newspapers attended the event run by working-class Bahians of color. The speeches by Centro Operário leaders in honor of the Mãe Preta do not appear to have survived.[127]

Who were Ascendino dos Anjos and the men of the Centro Operário, and what can their role in these celebrations tell us about the variety of views on race and culture among Bahians of color? Relatively little is known of Ascendino dos Anjos. Bahian historian Cid Teixeira describes him as a "black leader [liderança negra]," and O Clarim d'Alvorada described him as a clerk at Salvador's Polytechnic Institute and a part-time journalist, declaring him a "figure of great renown among our class [of color] in the Bahian capital."[128] To plan the Mãe Preta events, Anjos joined forces with the Centro Operário, a trade-based organization founded in 1893 by workers of color to "organize and unify" the "trades, crafts, and proletarian classes."[129] It is unclear whether Anjos himself was a member of the Centro, though contemporary reports mention he was known for his efforts to create a school for workers—a project that may well have taken place within the Centro itself.[130] The Centro, for its part, was one of several collectives for preto men in the Bahian capital, like the more famous Sociedade Protectora dos Desvalidos (a mutual aid society) which, though not explicitly dedicated to racial activism, had an exclusively preto membership and was committed to improving the lot and reputation of its members as people of color. The Centro, unlike the Sociedade, does not appear to have made preto skin a prerequisite for membership, but like other trade associations, it nonetheless acquired a largely African-descended membership because of the concentration of people of color among tradesmen, port, and unskilled workers in contemporary Salvador. Kim Butler has shown that the Centro Operário and the Sociedade Protectora shared leaders and members, suggesting some overlap in a vision for race-based collective activism through these organizations.[131]

Though contemporary accounts make clear Anjos's and the Centro's leading roles in organizing Bahia's Mãe Preta celebrations, only São Paulo's O Clarim d'Alvorada made mention of their race, calling them "Bahian negros."[132] The Bahian press's coverage of the events gives too little insight into the motivations of these men of color to know whether they themselves would have adopted the term *negro*, along with the overtones of racial distinctiveness and pride the term was then acquiring in São Paulo. But the outlines of the event they helped to plan provide a glimpse into their possible racial politics. Like celebrations of the Mãe Preta championed by most black writers in São Paulo, the Bahian festivities of 1929 largely stressed the integration of people of color into mainstream Bahian culture through displays of fluency in dominant cultural, civic, and religious norms. That they sought out the patronage and participation of the highest Bahian political and cultural figures, including the Catholic Church, suggests that Anjos and others at the Centro Operário wished to portray the descendants of the Mãe Preta as a legitimate part of a broader Bahian, and Brazilian, identity, even (or especially) in a city where a separate, African-based cultural and religious identity was a real alternative. Indeed, the choice to celebrate the Mãe Preta in Salvador would have had particularly integrationist meanings, given local officials' obsession with "de-Africanizing" the city's public spaces in the last decades of the Republic. In contrast to the black street vendors, Candomblé priestesses, or prostitutes these reformers vilified, the Mãe Preta provided a respectable example of Brazilian blackness, a dark-skinned embodiment of the self-sacrificing dedication to children demanded of the "honorable" women of Bahia's upper classes.

The greatest parallel between the celebrations organized by Salvador's and São Paulo's men of color lay in the specific iconography through which both chose to represent the Mãe Preta. The painting that members of the Centro Operário paraded down the streets of Salvador was an exact replica, by a Bahian artist, of a work by (white) artist Lucílio de Albuquerque (1912), which portrayed a seated Mãe Preta breastfeeding a white child while gazing longingly at her own black baby lying vulnerably at her feet. This painting had once appeared on the front page of Rio's *A Notícia* as part of its monument campaign in 1926. Aside from the iconic drawing *O Clarim* published yearly after 1928 for its Mãe Preta campaign, this appears to have been the only other image of the Mãe Preta then in circulation that included the mother's own black child. In São Paulo, the inclusion of the black child in that picture had set the tone for asserting the distinctiveness of otherwise equal black and white races; perhaps it had the same meaning for the men of color who organized the Bahian festivities and placed the painting at their center.

The Mãe Preta celebrations suggest that a group of socially active men of color in Salvador embraced an identity and politics as Catholic, culturally Brazilian *negros* similar to the identities developed in Paulistano black organizations and newspapers like *Clarim*. Indeed, *Clarim* may have directly influenced the Bahian group's politics. Since the beginning of its "second phase" in the late 1920s, *Clarim* had reached out to readers in other states. In Bahia the paper had secured a group of local contributors, all men of color—Urcino dos Santos, Marciano P. da Paixão, J. Soter da Silva, and Mário de Vasconcelos (the translator of Garvey's *The Negro World*). According to *Clarim*'s editors, by 1930 their paper had reached an "elevated" number of readers in the Bahian capital, thanks to its placement in the newsstands of a "very popular" news agency.[133] Given that mainstream Bahian papers gave no coverage either to Cândido de Campos's monument campaign in 1926 or to *Clarim*'s holiday proposal in 1928, it is quite possible that Ascendino dos Anjos got his idea for a Day of the Mãe Preta directly from *Clarim*'s recurring campaigns. In any case, Anjos and the Centro received coverage of and direct support for their Mãe Preta celebration from *Clarim* on a number of occasions.[134]

Three years after the Mãe Preta celebrations, in another salient example of the far-reaching repercussions of Paulistano black politics, the Frente Negra came to Salvador. Marcos Rodrigues dos Santos, the founder of and inspector general for the state chapter, was a small-town Bahian by birth, but he had spent much of his youth traveling across his state as well as in São Paulo and Minas Gerais. In the city of São Paulo in the late 1920s, Santos had joined the Centro Cívico Palmares, where he met José Correia Leite as well as two men who turned out to be Santos's distant relatives: Arlindo and Isaltino Veiga dos Santos, future leaders of São Paulo's Frente Negra. In the early 1930s Marcos Rodrigues dos Santos moved to the Paulista port city of Santos, where he founded the local Frente Negra chapter (known for its working-class, socialist leanings). In late 1932 he returned to his adopted home of Salvador, bringing with him many of the ideas and strategies he had learned in the *negro* organizations of the South.[135]

The Frente Negra da Bahia opened its doors in November 1932. In public meetings and in interviews with Bahia's press, Marcos dos Santos presented the goal of his organization as the "moral uplift of the race" through the promotion of literacy and employment.[136] Though operating on a much smaller scale and budget than the São Paulo branch, Salvador's Frente Negra provided a similar range of services and events, including classes (elementary education, adult literacy, languages, and typing), fundraising parties, a music band, a women's group, and an employment agency.[137] Also like its Paulista counterpart, the Bahian branch sought to become active in national politics, proposing a black candidate for the Constituent Assembly and staging frequent political rallies in downtown Salvador.[138] *A Frente Negra*, a weekly publication dedicated to the "general interests of the men of color," helped spread the word about the organization and its political programs.[139]

Bahia's Frente Negra was ideologically similar to São Paulo's, though with the significant absence of militarized or fascist rhetoric. As in São Paulo, Frente leaders in Salvador aimed for the full integration of blacks—as racially distinct but culturally unmarked citizens—into the dominant society, and saw themselves as the elite chosen to guide the black masses in the project of uplift. In his interviews with the Bahian press, Marcos Rodrigues dos Santos presented himself as an educated man and a "Catholic" and emphasized the importance of teaching "our savages"—that is, poor and uneducated blacks—to "believe in, love, and venerate a civilized Brazil."[140] Santos, whose Frente Negra operated in an even more traditional and patriarchal society than its Paulista counterparts, placed particular emphasis on the sacredness of a "legitimately constituted family" in elevating the morality of the black race. Echoing the concerns that appear to have animated black organizers of the Mãe Preta celebrations in Bahia, Santos emphasized the role that proper training of "the black female elite" would play in securing the respectability of Bahians of color.[141]

In his speeches and events, Santos, like his distant cousins the Santos brothers in São Paulo, highlighted the role blacks had played and would continue to play in Brazil's "national greatness." On the anniversary of the abolition of slavery in 1933, for instance, the Frente held a "civic session" in which orators remembered the great abolitionist figures of 1888 and placed flowers at the graves of Bahians they considered central to the antiracist struggle. Beginning with renowned mulatto poet and abolitionist Castro Alves, their procession then visited the graves of Ascendino dos Anjos (who passed away in 1931, not long after organizing the Mãe Preta celebrations), Manoel Querino, and Maxwel Porphírio de Assumpção.[142] Querino was a famous mulatto politician and intellectual—a founder of modern Afro-Bahian anthropology, an advocate for the cause of Bahians of color, and a member of leading preto organizations like the Sociedade Protectora dos Desvalidos and the Centro Operário. Maxwel de Assumpção was a lawyer and a member of one of Bahia's most distinguished families of African descent, the Alakijas. On several occasions throughout the 1920s, he wrote open letters to Bahian newspapers affirming his pride in the negro race and protesting racist acts, such as Congress's proposed bans on black immigration in the early 1920s.[143] By honoring the graves of these men, the Frente's members expressed their shared commitment to the political project of defending and uplifting the black race in Bahia.

Yet however consonant with the goals of many black Paulistano activists, the Bahian Frente Negra's focus on racial uplift and unification, and its explicitly antiracist stance, were a rarity among *preto* organizations in the city of Salvador. In the majority African-descended capital of Bahia, as we have seen, a unified notion of "race" or "blackness" was neither the primary vector of discrimination nor the primary identity around which most people of color sought to organize. Even organizations like the Sociedade Protectora dos Desvalidos or the Centro Operário, which in some senses functioned as race-based collectives, were far from gaining the adherence of a majority of *pretos* in the city.[144]

For these reasons, scholars of the Frente Negra in Bahia have argued, the organization failed to attract the cross-class, cross-color constituency of its Paulistano counterpart.[145] The Frente's strong *negro* identity and program of uplift gained some support from working-class Bahians of color (mostly *pretos*), who were suffering from the economic depression and from government efforts at worker repression and co-optation in the early 1930s, and for whom racial issues were one of several historically important aspects of labor activism. Yet the Frente failed to attract upwardly mobile *pretos* and *pardos* in Bahia, most of whom preferred what they saw as more respectable, non-confrontational mechanisms of social ascension. A "mulatto informant" told researcher Thales de Azevedo in the early 1950s that dark-skinned people of higher social ranks had looked on many of the Frente's actions with distaste, as in the case of a parade of poor blacks down one of Bahia's main thoroughfares designed to display the misery in which people of color lived. The informant added that the Frente was "destined to failure from its very birth," since it had been organized "as a sort of revolt."[146] Lacking the moral and economic support of middle-class people of color (so fundamental to the success of São Paulo's black organizations), and increasingly under pressure to fold into the twenty or so labor unions controlled by the local government, the Frente Negra closed its doors in August 1933, less than a year after it was founded. Around the same time, the Centro Operário also shut down, a casualty of government co-optation and of the increasing redundancy of mutual-aid organizations in an era of expanding government-based social security.[147]

The experiences of Bahia's Frente Negra and Centro Operário suggest that a group of Bahians linked directly or indirectly to the black politics of São Paulo adopted those activists' defense of a proud, distinctly "black" Brazilian identity in the face of dominant discourses of racial mixture in the late 1920s and early 1930s, and in a city with strong African traditions. Yet this Bahian contingent remained very small. The Frente Negra, in its 13

May 1933 celebrations, did not have many black leaders' tombs to revere, and some of the figures they honored (like Ascendino dos Anjos and Maxwel de Assumpção) have remained largely obscure. Likewise, despite the commitment of *Clarim*'s Bahian contributors, the fact that they had to publish in a paper based in far-off São Paulo reveals the absence of viable comparable publications in Salvador. The scarcity of these kinds of black organizations in Bahia, together with the greater visibility of culture-based activism and its resonance with shifting ideas of national culture contributed, from the 1930s onward, to cementing Bahia's profile on a national stage as the seat of Brazil's African traditions.

POLITICAL, CULTURAL, AND INTELLECTUAL transformations in Brazil in the 1930s and 1940s allowed people of color in places like Salvador da Bahia and São Paulo newly to imagine themselves as Brazilian nationals. In many ways, the ideas of black belonging emerging from these two cities starkly contrasted. Building on "two race" ideologies from earlier in the century, black journalists and activists in São Paulo sought to make a culturally unmarked blackness and a history of participation in nation building the basis of their identities as Paulistanos and, more broadly, as Brazilians. Leaders of the Frente Negra in particular, eager to show their patriotism, vehemently rejected any ties to Africa, Africans, or blacks elsewhere in the diaspora. This position was not shared universally among São Paulo's activist community, many of whom continued to report on contemporary African and pan-African events. What was shared among black leaders as different as Arlindo Veiga dos Santos and José Correia Leite was a sense of black Paulistanos' position as modern political subjects—a position increasingly crafted through contrasts involving racial, religious, and regional identities, and one which gained meaning in direct opposition to practices, such as Bahian Candomblé, these thinkers considered primitive and politically damaging. Southeastern activists would sharpen this critique of both Afro-Brazilian religion and Bahia throughout the 1940s and into the 1950s.

In Salvador only a small minority of people of color adopted the vision of black belonging championed by São Paulo's black thinkers. Many more Bahians, like Candomblé leaders, their followers, and the anthropologists with whom they collaborated, put forth a view of belonging primarily defined not by race or blackness but by a pure and unmixed African culture. Unlike their Paulistano counterparts, these religious thinkers and activists argued implicitly for the right to be considered Brazilian nationals by embracing what they construed as traditional African practices. Though they did not comment explicitly on the contrast, they clearly rejected Paulistano activists' paths toward inclusion through the denial of all African cultural connections. Undoubtedly, they would have objected to those activists' belittling of Candomblé as apolitical and backward.

Whether presenting themselves as "blacks" or as "Africans," however, black thinkers in the cities of both São Paulo and Salvador in the 1930s and 1940s productively used the acceptance of Brazil's African past by a new generation of nationalist intellectuals. In Salvador, the Candomblé community won the right to practice its religion freely and made inroads in the battle against pervasive cultural discrimination. In São Paulo, activists pushed further than before their demands to be full Brazilians with equal access to jobs, public spaces, and dignity. Above all, both groups struggled to assert their rightful inclusion as nationals (either as *negros* or as members of an African ritual community) while resisting the racially and culturally assimilationist aspects of official *mestiço* identities emanating from Rio de Janeiro.

Both groups found opportunities as well as challenges in the tumultuous period between 1930 and 1945. The Frente Negra, which flourished in the first few years of Vargas's regime, eventually fell victim to the Estado Novo, as did all other formal black social and political associations in São Paulo and across Brazil. Leaders of Bahia's most famous Candomblés forged a newly supportive environment for themselves by the end of the 1930s, but they would face increasing obstacles as World War II cut the ties to Africa that had sustained their claims to legitimacy. With the end of the war and Brazil's return to democracy in 1945, activists in both places—together with new colleagues in Rio de Janeiro—would eagerly take up their struggles in a new political and cultural context.

4. Democracy
São Paulo and Rio de Janeiro, 1945–1950

In 1945 growing opposition in Brazil helped bring down Getúlio Vargas's dictatorship, inaugurating a Second Republic (1946–64) that deepened and expanded Brazil's historically weak democratic institutions.[1] This transformation coincided with the Allied victory in World War II, which brought the end of totalitarian regimes in Europe and fueled enthusiasm for democracy across Latin America. In Brazil, democracy, and how it should be defined, became a central issue of national politics for the rest of the decade.

In the cities of São Paulo and Rio de Janeiro, black thinkers took full advantage of reinstated freedoms of speech and association to resume older organizations and publications, and to form new ones. Even the titles of their newspapers, like *Alvorada* (*Dawn*), *Novo Horizonte* (*New Horizon*), and *Mundo Novo* (*New World*), reflected the prevailing mood of hope and renewal. "In São Paulo, as in the rest of Brazil," one postwar Paulistano black newspaper proclaimed, "the black man is in motion, trying to get back to the work of definitively conquering those fundamental citizenship rights . . . once dreamed of by our great family."[2] Yet even as they returned, after a seven-year hiatus, to their long-standing project of publicly demanding full citizenship for Brazilians of color, black thinkers framed their politics of belonging in distinctly new terms. In place of an older language of fraternity or a more recent turn to nativist nationalism, their publications and public declarations made the language of democracy central to claims for racial inclusion.

The widespread currency of the ideal of democracy in postwar Brazil reflected significant transformations in ideas about both politics and race in the mid-1940s, nationally as well as abroad. The genocide perpetrated by Nazi Germany had contributed to discrediting scientific racism along with totalitarianism in much of the West. In the wake of the Nazis' defeat, a group of prominent organizations, leaders, and scholars in the emerging international community made the eradication of racism an integral component of the project to uphold democracy and human rights worldwide. As international organizations enlisted social scientists to address the problem of racism and to find models of harmonious race relations, Brazil, where antiracism had become state doctrine, received new visibility. It was in this context that Brazilian and foreign intellectuals, including black thinkers, restated an older idea of Brazilian racial harmony in the dominant political language of the times: Brazil's extensive mixture and lack of institutionalized racism made it a "racial democracy." Prominent *negro* activist and sociologist Alberto Guerreiro Ramos voiced the sentiments of many of his fellow black thinkers when he claimed in 1950 that "Brazil should assume a leadership role in teaching the world the politics of *racial democracy*. Because it is the only country on earth that offers a satisfactory solution to the racial problem."[3]

It was precisely this sort of sanguine endorsement of ideas of racial democracy that black thinkers in later years, looking back from the other side of a brutal military dictatorship that invoked racial democracy to silence dissent, would regret as naive or deeply compromised. Yet in the heady years following the end of the Estado Novo, widespread enthusiasm for new ideas about both race and democracy seemed to, and in many ways did, offer black thinkers in São Paulo and Rio de Janeiro a more powerful set of tools with which to demand inclusion than earlier claims based on brotherhood or nativist nationalism. Institutionally, black thinkers in these cities seized the openings created by political democracy—like freedom of assembly and the press, a new constitution, expanded party politics, an emerging international consensus about human rights, and alliances with white politicians—to pursue and defend their participation, as black Brazilians, in the civic life of their nation. They used their new papers and organizations to promote black candidates, to encourage fellow Brazilians of color to vote, and to push for a law criminalizing racial discrimination. Rhetorically, black thinkers in this period also upheld racial equality as the ultimate test of Brazil's fledgling political democracy. As long as discrimination persisted, they argued, Brazil's much vaunted transition to democracy was incomplete.

Finally, in São Paulo and Rio de Janeiro, black intellectuals availed themselves of transformations in social scientific inquiry about race, and of alliances with progressive white intellectuals, to bolster their politics of inclusion. Unlike earlier in the century, when the social and medical sciences heavily underwrote ideas about black inferiority, much social scientific work in the postwar period was self-consciously opposed to scientific racism. Social science, in this context, provided black thinkers with new authority and a new logic through which to frame their claims for citizenship. In particular, an expanding field of sociological studies of Brazilian race relations appealed to Paulistano and Carioca black thinkers for its portrayal of *negros* in the cities of the Southeast as politically active protagonists of Brazil's modernity—a useful counterpoint to an earlier anthropological literature that had inconveniently, in their view, celebrated the primitive African cultures of blacks in the Northeast. Far from being dupes of a cynical elite political project, then, black thinkers at midcentury were vigorous participants, and major stakeholders, in the project of reframing long-standing ideas of Brazilian racial harmony as "racial democracy."

"The black man is in motion"

In many ways, it was civil society, unevenly repressed during the Estado Novo, that finally brought down Vargas's dictatorship and ushered in a more democratic regime. In August 1942, Brazil declared war on the Axis, becoming one of the most prominent Latin American contributors to the Allied effort. Though this gesture raised Vargas's profile internationally, it contributed to eroding his power at home. Intellectuals, opposition politicians, and military officers in Brazil increasingly chafed at the contradiction between battling dictatorship in Europe and living in one themselves. As the Allies marched toward victory in Europe, Vargas's critics began to speak and act against his regime. Protest, initially confined to political oratory and intellectual manifestos, soon overflowed into public spaces.

This public pressure from a growing opposition, which drew legitimacy from international events, forced Vargas to prepare for a transition to democracy and gradually to ease the reins of power. Over the course of 1945, Vargas relaxed political censorship, allowed for voter registration, and prepared the nation for competitive elections that December. The electorate for this contest had expanded threefold since the previous election (1930), thanks to the electoral reform of 1932 that gave women the vote and lowered the voting age from twenty-one to eighteen. Over the course of 1945, three major and several minor political parties emerged. Two of the major parties were largely controlled by Vargas and drew on his still broad bases of support (which included many workers, peasants, civil servants, industrialists, and reformist military officers). A third major party, the União Democrática Nacional (UDN, or National Democratic Union), brought together conservative anti-Vargas politicians. In part because of the continuing loyalty that the many voters who had been excluded from national politics during the Republic still felt for the man who had given them a voice, one of Vargas's parties, the rural-based Partido Social Democrático (PSD, or Social Democratic Party), took 55 percent of the national vote and a majority in both houses of Congress. In January 1946 General Eurico Dutra, former minister of war and Vargas's preferred candidate, became the first president of Brazil's Second Republic.[4]

The political transformations that ended the Estado Novo and inaugurated a democratic Second Republic thus did not fully end Vargas's influence over national politics. But they marked a significant achievement in a nation that had limited experience with competitive elections and popular suffrage. The period after 1945 saw the growth of vigorous parties, a broad active elector-ate, and a respect by parties and candidates for electoral results. As impor-tant, in 1946 the new Congress sat as a Constituent Assembly charged with drafting a constitution and returning Brazil to the rule of law. Promulgated in September of that year, the constitution preserved a powerful executive but included some protections against its abuse, like strong legislative and judiciary branches.

In particular, the restitution of rights of political dissent and free speech marked a significant departure from the repressive Estado Novo. It was this aspect of the democratic opening, more than a uniformly shared ideological opposition to Vargas, that would unite black activists of different generations and political persuasions in São Paulo and Rio de Janeiro in the mid-1940s. In the wake of Vargas's fall, it was not just black thinkers identified with the previously persecuted Left who condemned the Estado Novo's suppression of formal black organizations and publications but also former members of the generally pro-Vargas Frente Negra. This shared rejection of Vargas's tactics (if not necessarily of his nationalist ideology) highlights a significant differ-ence between the men of color who became politically active in race-based organizations after 1945 and the much broader population of Brazilians of color they aspired to represent. Well after Vargas's fall, many poor and work-ing-class Brazilians of color continued to revere him as their benefactor, see-ing his extension of jobs to black workers, his inclusion of poor people of color in political patronage networks, and his crackdown on immigrants as just restitution for a longer history of slavery and marginalization.[5] Whereas most poor and working-class beneficiaries of Vargas's regime would there-fore continue to work through the cross-racial parties and unions still asso-ciated with the deposed leader after 1945, the men who saw themselves as black thinkers and activists, regardless of their political sympathies, would instead invest their energy in rebuilding the kinds of race-based institutions and publications that the Estado Novo had shut down.[6] This difference in approaches to social advancement—one defined by racial identity, the other couched within broader class-based, multiracial clientelistic networks—helps explain why the new black organizations that sprung up during this period, however energetic and ambitious, would not command the loyalties of most Brazilians of color.

The story of the rebirth of black activism in postwar São Paulo and Rio de Janeiro begins during the Estado Novo itself. As with civil society more generally, the Estado Novo had not succeeded in closing down all spaces of black politics, despite the state's suppression of explicitly political black organizations like the Frente Negra. Black activists and thinkers had continued to organize after 1937, though with a much lower profile. Some former members of the Frente Negra, as we saw in chapter 3, reconvened in cultural organizations dedicated to performing the sorts of Afro-Brazilian dances or carnival parades deemed acceptable by the regime. Others pursued causes that were more openly political in nature. Former *O Clarim d'Alvorada* editor José Correia Leite, whose memoirs provide one of the few sources of information on black organizing in São Paulo during Vargas's dictatorship, recalled that his home "became a sort of headquarters for the discussion of black issues" among dedicated writers and activists of color. Elsewhere, the Jabaquara Club, a Marxist-inspired group led by activist Luiz Lobato, brought together former writers for *Clarim* and former members of the Frente Negra. According to Leite, the Jabaquaras advocated the resolution of racial problems within a broader struggle for class equality and social justice.[7] A larger group, the Associação José do Patrocínio, was founded in 1941 to continue aspects of the Frente Negra's work—particularly advocating for and protecting women of color who were domestic workers. The association, named after the famous nineteenth-century journalist and abolitionist of color, monitored and protested advertisements for domestic employment that specified a preference for white or light-skinned workers.[8]

These spaces of muted activism fueled a resurgence of black politics in São Paulo in the final months of the Estado Novo, as Vargas loosened his hold on power. They also provided opportunities for black thinkers to begin to reconcile the ideological differences that had proved so divisive in the previous decade. Toward the end of Vargas's dictatorship, Leite recalled, a group of former writers for *Clarim*, as well as former members of the Clube Negro de Cultura Social (CNCS, or Black Club for Social Culture) and the Frente Negra, began to meet at the downtown workplace of Raul Joviano do Amaral. In the early 1930s Leite and members of his group at *Clarim* had created the

CNCS when they broke off from the Frente Negra due to personal and ideological differences with its leadership. In his youth Raul Amaral had joined the dissident CNCS and befriended Leite. But he subsequently left the CNCS for the Frente Negra, possibly yielding to pressures from his father, a staunch *frentenegrino*.[9] Perhaps it was Amaral's status as a former member of both factions of São Paulo's black movement that positioned him to bring together veterans of the *Clarim* group, like Leite and his colleague Fernando Góis, with former leaders of the Frente, like Francisco Lucrécio. According to Leite, the new group convened to "try to recover the work we had lost since '38," referring to the date when the Estado Novo drew the curtain on black (and most other) independent political organizing in Brazil. After a series of meetings, Amaral, Leite, and the others resolved to create a new black organization, modeled after the principles and goals of the Frente Negra but tailored to the new democratic context. In 1945 the Associação do Negro Brasileiro (ANB, or Association of Black Brazilians) opened its doors, offering programs ranging from social assistance to sports, culture, arts, and a women's wing.[10]

In April 1945, as Vargas prepared to step down, the ANB's leaders laid out their goals in a "Manifesto in Defense of Democracy," published in the *Jornal de São Paulo*. The document reveals how essential the ANB's leaders believed the return of liberal democracy to be for the pursuit of black politics. "The reactionary and Fascist measures adopted by the regime of 1937," it began, "including the prohibition of political parties, censorship of the press, and limitations on freedom of assembly, have directly contributed to undermining the efforts of the Brazilian *negro* to integrate himself into the mainstream of national life." Availing themselves of their new rights under a democratizing regime, the document's signers (Leite, Lucrécio, Amaral, Góis, and others) proclaimed their intention to "unite the *negros* of São Paulo in order to demand freedom of speech and freedom of assembly; combat all manifestations of racism in Brazil; . . . demand that labor laws be extended to include domestic servants and rural workers [most of them people of color]; fight for unconditional amnesty for all political prisoners; demand the elimination of racial discrimination in the military academies and in the diplomatic service; demand special penal legislation directed at these institutions and at individuals who discriminate; demand the freedom to unionize and the right to strike; [and] fight for universal education at all levels."[11] In its concern with labor laws, unionization, universal education, and amnesty for political prisoners (most of whom were communists), the manifesto displays the leftist leanings of the ANB, shared by older members like Leite and, increasingly, by younger activists.[12] But beyond representing the specific concerns of the

ANB, the manifesto, with its demands for racial equality framed in the language of democracy, political institutions, and legal rights, announced the broader changes in black formulations of belonging that would take place at midcentury. Calling for legislation against racist acts was different indeed from earlier antiracist claims based on interracial brotherhood or rights of native birth.

Along with the reinvigoration of black political and social organizations, the end of the repressive Estado Novo led to the rebirth of São Paulo's black press, which had fallen almost completely silent after 1937. As part of the statutes of the ANB, Leite, Amaral, and Góis had declared their intention "to reestablish the paper *O Clarim d'Alvorada*." They fulfilled this goal in September 1945 with the appearance of *Alvorada* (so called to distinguish it from its predecessor).[13] *Alvorada* was soon joined by other papers, like the one founded in May 1946 by Aristides Barbosa. A former Frente Negra member, Barbosa had participated in several of the cultural groups that replaced the Frente after 1938, but he had grown disenchanted with their transformation into recreational clubs. A man who later described himself as an "intellectual" who had "completed secondary school" (revealing the rarity of a secondary education for black men in São Paulo at the time), Barbosa had greater ambitions. In the course of his work as a janitor in São Paulo's state aviation school, he met North American flight instructors who introduced him to the U.S. black magazine *Ebony*. That publication inspired Barbosa to gather together a group of former Frente members, along with veterans of São Paulo's early-twentieth-century black press (like poet Lino Guedes of *Clarim*) and younger writers (like journalist Geraldo Campos de Oliveira and poet Oswaldo Camargo), and to found his own black paper, *O Novo Horizonte*.[14]

Though many black thinkers, particularly from the vantage point of a democratizing Brazil in the mid-1940s, looked back on Vargas's dictatorship as a period that interrupted black militancy, it was under Vargas that *pretos* and *pardos*, and especially the less privileged among them, made many of the gains for which black thinkers had long advocated. In São Paulo state, the advancement of people of color was most prominent in the industrial sector, where the politics favoring "national" workers after 1930 allowed *pretos* and *pardos* to enter the labor force in numbers that approached their representation in the broader population. The fact that most factory jobs were concentrated in the city of São Paulo made the entrance of *pretos* and *pardos* into the industrial proletariat particularly visible there, despite their relatively low numbers in the city's overall population (9%, as opposed to 12% statewide in the 1940 census).[15] By 1940 *pretos* and *pardos* in São Paulo state also approached parity with their white counterparts in public sector jobs—the same modest subset of public employment (janitors, office messengers, street sweepers) that had sustained the city's precarious black middle class in the early years of the twentieth century and which subsequently formed the basis of the patronage networks of the Vargas regime.[16]

Yet people of color in São Paulo still had a long way to go. In 1940 *pretos* and *pardos* in that state continued to lag behind whites in literacy rates and remained sharply underrepresented among high school and college graduates.[17] Despite breaking into the industrial working class, *pretos* and *pardos* had a particularly hard time getting white-collar jobs.[18] Furthermore, even by the transition to democracy in 1945, key areas of Paulistano and Brazilian society—notably the military, civil service, diplomatic service, and many restaurants and public spaces—remained in a state of de facto segregation.

In the city of Rio de Janeiro, *pretos* and *pardos* (who made up 11% and 17% of the population in 1940, respectively) in many respects fared even better under Vargas than their counterparts elsewhere in the country. Gains were most striking in the area of education, thanks to the expansion of public schools in the Federal District under Vargas. Literacy rates for *pretos* and *pardos* in the city of Rio de Janeiro in 1940 far outpaced the national average for people of color, and although they were lower than the rates for whites in Rio, they actually exceeded rates for whites in some areas of the nation.[19] In terms of employment, *pretos* and *pardos* also benefited somewhat from Rio's expansion as an administrative, commercial, and industrial center over the course of the Vargas years. Most people of color who found jobs did so in agriculture, industry, manual trades, and the service economy, and indeed they were overrepresented in these areas. As in São Paulo, public sector jobs remained an important area of upward mobility for some people of color in Rio, with the difference that in Rio, according to midcentury accounts, employers distinguished clearly between *pardos* and *pretos* and consistently privileged the former for many public service posts.[20] Yet people of color remained greatly underrepresented in areas like commerce and the liberal professions, given their overall numbers in the city's population.[21]

On the one hand, the relative mobility of *pardos* in Rio suggests that in that city, the divide between whites and nonwhites was less sharp than in São Paulo, where by midcentury *pardos* generally fared no better than *pretos* in terms of employment. On the other hand, many employers' apparent predilection for lighter-skinned *pardos* over *pretos* suggests the existence of a significant color prejudice in Rio (if not a racial one, as in São Paulo). Indeed, despite the visible upward mobility of some sectors of Rio's population of color, the city was becoming highly segregated by space, color, and class by midcentury. In the first decade of the century, as we saw in chapter 2, the reforms of Mayor Francisco Pereira Passos had begun to beautify Rio's downtown spaces and remove its poor and dark citizens to the shanties and suburbs. Since then, the city's well-to-do citizens had relocated to the elegant beachside neighborhoods (like Flamengo, Botafogo, Copacabana, and Ipanema) south of the center city, while the poor were forced to places distant—horizontally or vertically—from the center and the wealthy South Zone. Some of Rio's poor and working-class people settled the areas north and west of the center city, giving rise to large industrial suburbs, while others continued to build precarious shanties on the slopes of the city's hills, or *morros*. By the postwar period, Rio de Janeiro was a largely segregated city, with a nonwhite, poor majority—swollen by the influx of hundreds of thousands of immigrants from the Northeast—inhabiting either the *morros* or the North Zone's *subúrbios*. This segregation was neither legalized nor watertight; many *morros*, for instance, were located on the edges of Rio's wealthy neighborhoods, and *preto* and *pardo* service workers from an array of neighborhoods entered Rio's center city and South Zone on a daily basis. Nonetheless, as one contemporary researcher noted, social distance along the intersecting lines of race and class mapped clearly onto spatial distance in midcentury Rio de Janeiro.[22] For all of its growing fame as the cradle of a *mestiço* national culture and an emblem of Brazil's interracial harmony, postwar Rio de Janeiro embodied perhaps better than any other Brazilian city the overlapping race and class inequalities that divided Brazilian society.

The growing ranks of educated people of color and the reopening of civil society in Rio de Janeiro gave rise to several explicitly race-based organizations and publications in that city, where few had existed during the First Republic and where, by all accounts, the Frente Negra of the 1930s had few members.[23] In 1949 Joviano Severino de Melo and José Bernardo da Silva founded a chapter of the União dos Homens de Cor (UHC, or Union of Men of Color) in Rio de Janeiro. Though part of a broader organization that emerged from the state of Rio Grande do Sul and spread to at least ten other states after 1943, Rio's chapter of the UHC appears to have been somewhat idiosyncratic in its goals and outlook. The UHC's national statutes highlighted, above all, the objective of "elevating the economic and intellectual level of people of color across the national territory, preparing them to enter the social and administrative life of the country, in all of its activities." Across several Brazilian states, the UHC sought to attract polished, presentable black professionals who would uphold the group's image as a promoter of liberal, middle-class values of racial uplift.[24] This perspective, so reminiscent of the politics of most of São Paulo's black thinkers since the early decades of the century, is not surprising given that the organization was created in Rio Grande do Sul, a state where the separation between a tiny black minority and a white immigrant majority was even sharper than in São Paulo. Yet in Rio de Janeiro, the UHC appears to have been more concerned with reaching out to poor Brazilians of color than with promoting middle-class values among its own membership. Indeed, on several occasions, its leaders expressed discomfort with organizations that appeared to work exclusively for the benefit of an elite of color and that placed race at the forefront of their activism at the expense of class.[25] Instead, leaders of Rio's UHC modeled their group after charitable organizations, working to assist the poor through concrete means like the distribution of food, clothing, and medicine. They also worked as a pressure group, staging protests and writing public letters denouncing instances of racial discrimination.[26]

In large part, the particular character of the Rio chapter of the UHC reflected the influence of José Bernardo da Silva, its cofounder and intellectual "mentor." Silva was a former stevedore who learned to read and write in his late twenties and subsequently became a professional journalist. Despite his education and upward mobility, Silva referred to himself in several articles as an "operário," or laborer, telegraphing his continued identification with his lower-class background and his sympathies for class-based politics.[27] Silva was also the leader of a small spiritualist Christian center, "Jesus no Himalaya," with which the UHC collaborated. The activities of the UHC and the Christian center, chronicled in the small newspaper called *Himalaya: Órgão de justiça social cristã* (Himalaya: Organ of Christian Social Justice), also edited by Silva, suggest that the UHC hoped to bring about "the political, cultural, economic, and moral recovery, within Brazilian society, of the marginalized of our ethnic group" within a broader social-Christian framework.[28] True to this ideal, the UHC's leaders did not publish a separate newspaper dedicated solely to racial issues. Instead, they published a regular column titled "A voz do negro" (its name and illustration sharply reminiscent of the Frente Negra's *A Voz da Raça*) alongside *Himalaya*'s broader coverage of the Christian center's events.[29] It may have been the leadership's admiration for the Frente Negra, one of the few racial organizations to reach out beyond a small middle-class elite, that led José Bernardo da Silva, along with Isaltino Veiga dos Santos and a handful of other black men, to attempt (unsuccessfully) to revive the Frente in Rio de Janeiro in 1954.[30]

Idiosyncratic as Silva's influences might seem, however, the UHC in many ways reflects the specific patterns of black activism that characterized Rio at midcentury and which, as in earlier years, distinguished its black politics from those of São Paulo. After World War II, as in previous decades, most black organizations in São Paulo adopted a strong notion of *negro* racialism, reflecting both the stark division that prevailed in that city between a white majority and a black minority, and the scant spaces that both white racism and black activism left for intermediate color identifications. Light-skinned *pardos*, like veteran newspaperman José Correia Leite, were welcome in Paulistano black organizations as long as they were willing to assume their identities as *negros* and to give up potentially divisive claims to a distinct status based on lighter skin. Yet founders of Rio's chapter of the UHC stressed, on several occasions, that their members included "*pretos, pardos,* and antiracist whites, . . . believers in the dignity of human beings of any color, nationality, political or religious creed, class, level of culture, or social condition."[31] Their express inclusion of both *pretos* and *pardos* underscored precisely those distinctions of color that, contemporary census categories and patterns of discrimination suggest, were meaningful to many whites and nonwhites in Rio de Janeiro at midcentury. The prime role the UHC reserved for "antiracist whites," moreover, also fits with longer-standing patterns of black mobilization in that city, suggesting that in the mid-1940s (as in the 1920s), Rio may have presented greater opportunities for interracial sociability, and therefore for cross-race and cross-class alliances, than São Paulo. Black writers in São Paulo had at times relied on the words of antiracist whites, but they almost never counted these people as members of their *negro* political associations. Yet in Rio, as we have seen, there was a historically strong connection between racial and class-based activism, notably among black port workers like José Bernardo da Silva, who in their unions or political demonstrations often worked alongside whites. And in the area of popular culture and performance, for which Rio came to national prominence in the first half of the twentieth century, the ongoing visibility of dark-skinned musicians and entertainers in a range of often integrated popular settings (such as carnival, samba schools, small clubs and bars, upscale and "dive" theaters, or movie parlors, to name a few), as well as the close (if often extremely unequal) interactions between artists of color and whites in Rio's music industry and professional organizations, provide perhaps the best examples of the sorts of avenues for cross-racial contacts Rio offered at midcentury.[32]

In part because of the possibilities of such interracial alliances in Rio, and because of the historically strong link in that city between racial and class-based activism, very few organizations in the 1920s or in the postwar period framed their work explicitly and exclusively in terms of racial concerns. To be sure, in its express concern with the fate of people of color, going so far as to adopt the racial term *negro* in its publications, Rio's UHC betrays its origins as an import from the immigrant-heavy Brazilian South, where "blackness" emerged as a more sharply defined sociopolitical identity. No doubt, UHC leaders in Rio found this treatment of the racial question appealing, and at times they experimented with placing race in the foreground of their public identities. Yet in its inclusion of white members, its close ties to the Christian center, its antielitist commitment to members "of any level of culture or social condition," and above all, its leaders' insistence that the problems of poverty and racism had to be tackled together, the UHC differed from most black organizations in São Paulo. It reflected instead the sorts of concerns and strategies that had historically driven racial activism in Rio and that continued to shape newer organizations in the postwar period.[33]

The personal and political trajectories of Abdias do Nascimento, who would become a leading figure of Brazilian black thought and politics, further illustrate the distinctive contours of black activism in midcentury São Paulo and Rio de Janeiro.[34] Though Nascimento undertook the work that would make him famous in the Rio de Janeiro of the mid-1940s, his views on race and racial activism, and his own identity as a black intellectual, were shaped by his back-and-forth travels between Rio de Janeiro and São Paulo during his formative years. Nascimento was born in 1914 in Franca, a small town in São Paulo's coffee-growing interior, the grandson of freed slaves. His father was a shoemaker, and his mother worked variously as a cook, a seamstress, and a wet-nurse to the children of Franca's coffee planters. Like São Paulo's José Correia Leite, Nascimento later traced his consciousness of race and racism—above all, his sense of himself as a *negro*—to the experience of growing up in a community heavily populated with Italian immigrant workers, who called him demeaning nicknames like "tição" or charcoal. (Unlike Leite, however, Nascimento also recalled the middle- and upper-class Brazilians of his rural town voicing similar insults.)

As a teenager, Abdias do Nascimento—a young army recruit—moved to São Paulo City, where he joined the Frente Negra. He channeled his anger and youthful energy into what the Frente called "isolated actions," like starting fistfights in barbershops or movie theaters that barred people of color, and was arrested on several occasions. Like other members of São Paulo's Frente Negra, Nascimento soon found himself drawn to Integralism, Brazil's quasi-fascistic nationalist movement, perhaps for its emphasis on martial masculinity (though Nascimento later recalled his admiration for its "anti-imperialist and antibourgeois position"). When he moved to Rio de Janeiro in 1936, he, like several other politically active men of color in that city, joined the local chapter of the national Integralist movement rather than the Frente Negra (which, Nascimento recalled, was nearly nonexistent in Rio, perhaps for the reasons suggested above). Yet the Integralists soon disappointed him for their racist attitudes, and Nascimento began to search for new outlets for his racial politics within the confines of the Estado Novo. He found them in part through ongoing contacts with friends and activists from his São Paulo days. In 1938 Nascimento collaborated with friends in Campinas (the city in São Paulo state whose sharp color line had given rise to the black newspaper *O Getulino* in the 1920s) to stage an academic congress aimed at exposing racial discrimination there. In 1943 Nascimento, by then based in Rio, joined forces with several Paulista black activists to bring to Vargas's attention a local police chief's denial of black people's right to frequent the Rua Direita, a favorite gathering place in downtown São Paulo.[35] This form of protest, with its direct appeal to the executive, seems drawn almost directly from the play-book of São Paulo's Frente Negra.

According to his own accounts, Nascimento's outlook on black activism changed when he took a trip to Argentina in 1943. In Buenos Aires, he witnessed the work of the independent Teatro del Pueblo, which inspired him to think about theater as a tool for political education. Nascimento recalled that the Teatro, in the tradition of anarchist theater, encouraged the audience to participate in and comment on all aspects of the performance (text, direction, acting), thereby serving as a school for *el pueblo*. On his return to Brazil, Nascimento approached black activists and intellectuals in São Paulo with the idea of a theater group designed to raise public consciousness about racial oppression, but he found little support there (despite the fact that earlier black associations in that city, like the Elite and Kosmos clubs, had featured theater groups as part of their activities). He turned instead to friends and acquaintances from Rio de Janeiro—people like Sebastião Rodrigues Alves, a man of color who had also been an Integralist, and an array of other young professionals, artists, and workers of color, both men and women, who enthusiastically backed him.

Years later, Nascimento suggested that Rio's different traditions of black activism made that city fertile ground for his black theater idea. In São Paulo, he noted, black thinkers and activists staged explicit protests against racism and "confronted oppression with a warlike attitude," invoking political principles of "justice and the rights of citizenship." But many of their counterparts in Rio de Janeiro saw cultural elements, particularly in Rio's African-inflected popular culture, like samba or Candomblé, as sites for activism.[36] In the years that followed, Nascimento would skillfully combine his experiences with the explicitly *negro*, independent political activism of São Paulo, and Rio's more fluid integration of Afro-Carioca cultural expression into mainstream spaces and institutions, to create one of the most prominent black Brazilian organizations of the twentieth century.

In October 1944, as an Allied victory in Europe drew nearer and pressure mounted on the Vargas regime to open new spaces for public debate, Abdias do Nascimento and his colleagues founded the Teatro Experimental do Negro (TEN, or Black Experimental Theater) in Rio de Janeiro. Their immediate goal was to cast black actors, both professionals and amateurs, in more dignified roles than the servants, criminals, or prostitutes they had until then embodied in the racially exclusive world of Brazilian theater. The troupe's first show, a performance of Eugene O'Neill's *The Emperor Jones*, débuted at Rio's elite Teatro Municipal on 8 May 1945 (coincidentally, the day the Allies accepted Nazi Germany's unconditional surrender). The TEN then expanded its activities to include popular theater, workshops, and academic events to educate blacks and whites about race and racism in Brazil. TEN members also offered adult literacy courses and taught classes on the history of Africa and Africans in the Americas (which, together, reportedly drew up to six hundred students), and helped coordinate national-level black activism. The TEN and its newspaper *Quilombo* (a term referring to Brazil's runaway slave communities), edited in Rio from 1948 to 1950 and reaching an estimated circulation of two to three thousand copies per issue, would dominate the black intellectual scene in that city well into the 1950s.[37]

As black thinkers and activists in Rio and São Paulo began to revive old institutions and build new ones, they also sought to give black politics a more "national" character by stimulating connections between their two cities. In November 1945, members of Rio's TEN, along with members of organizations from several other cities, traveled to São Paulo for the first Convenção Nacional do Negro Brasileiro, or Black Brazilian National Convention. Convention leaders called on black Brazilians "regardless of sex, age, political or religious belief, to close ranks," and emphasized the importance of "unifying and coordinating our efforts."[38] A month later, the magazine *Senzala* (*Slave Quarters*) began publication out of São Paulo. Though *Senzala* would prove short-lived, its long and varied list of contributors illustrates an emerging spirit of collaboration that was not only about bridging regional distances between vibrant sites of race-based activism (contributors hailed from São Paulo, Rio, and Campinas) but also about healing old political wounds. Along with the names of a newer generation of activists (like Abdias do Nascimento

Abdias do Nascimento, 1955. Coleção Fotos Correio da Manhã, PH/FOT 35917. Acervo do Arquivo Nacional, Rio de Janeiro, Brazil.

of Rio's TEN, Geraldo Campos de Oliveira of São Paulo's *Novo Horizonte*, and Luiz Lobato of São Paulo's Marxist Clube Jabaquara), the list boasted an array of veterans from the black politics of the 1920s and 1930s. These included Jayme de Aguiar, José Correia Leite, and Lino Guedes (all formerly of *Clarim*), as well as former *frentenegrinos* Aristides Barbosa, Francisco Lucrécio, and Isaltino Veiga dos Santos (cofounder, along with his brother Arlindo, of the Frente Negra, and contributor to *A Voz da Raça*). Though far from "national" in a geographical sense, this loose alliance among southeastern black thinkers (itself partly the result of the greater integration of Brazil's core regions after the Vargas regime) helped give black politics higher visibility on a national stage in the years that followed.

"To use those freedoms"

Self-appointed leaders of Rio and São Paulo's new black organizations understood the democratic opening as a challenge and an opportunity to rectify the inequalities affecting people of color in their cities. If, as *Quilombo*'s Alberto Guerreiro Ramos claimed, "Brazilian society grants men of color practically all freedoms," the task then awaiting black thinkers and activists was "training [Brazilians of color], through culture and education, to use those freedoms."[39] One of the principal freedoms black thinkers wished to "train" Brazilians of color to use was the right to vote in an electoral democracy. The newspapers emerging after 1945 expressed much greater interest in electoral politics than did their earlier counterparts, with frequent articles on parties, candidates, and platforms.[40] The papers also began printing paid political advertisements, mostly for black candidates running for local office as part of national party tickets. Several of these candidates were editors of black newspapers, like Geraldo Campos de Oliveira of *Senzala* and José Correia Leite of *Alvorada* (running for office in São Paulo) and Abdias do Nascimento of *Quilombo* and José Bernardo da Silva of *Himalaya* (in Rio). Though none of them were elected, these men's candidacy for local office as members of national mainstream parties signals the gradual emergence of new channels for institutional participation by black Brazilians in this period, especially toward the end of the 1940s.

In some instances, black writers used their newspapers to endorse a particular candidate, such as when *Mundo Novo*'s director, Armando de Castro, backed Geraldo Campos de Oliveira in his bid for the state legislature of São Paulo in 1950.[41] More generally, however, writers limited their advocacy to nonpartisan articles educating readers on the importance of black participation—as both voters and candidates—in the democratic process. "The man of color in Brazil must understand his position at this moment," wrote Abdias do Nascimento in Rio's *Quilombo*. "The enormous contingent of black voters must not let itself be led to the urns like lambs with no consciousness of their electoral power." Nascimento called the vote "a weapon" that "we must use . . . to elect those who truly feel [our] problems and wish to solve them as far as possible," and proclaimed the selection of black candidates to be "a decisive 'test'" of party leaders' commitment to racial equality.[42]

Yet Brazil's postwar democracy, though a remarkable achievement in many ways, had distinct limitations. Though the electorate had expanded significantly under Vargas, the 1946 Constitution still denied the vote to illiterates (approximately 60% of the adult population), military enlisted men, and noncommissioned officers, thus disenfranchising well over half of Brazil's population.[43] Only 22 percent of *pardo* Brazilians and 20 percent of *preto* Brazilians could read in 1950, disproportionately excluding them from voting rights.[44] In Rio, where literacy rates for people of color were considerably higher, the situation was somewhat better. Perhaps this explains why Nascimento described an "enormous contingent of black voters" waiting to unleash their electoral power in that city. But nationwide, only 16 percent of the total population registered to vote in the 1945 elections (a number that would increase, though not enormously, over the next two decades), suggesting that few Brazilians saw voting as a crucial (or even possible) avenue for playing a role in Brazilian politics in this period.[45]

While their leaders sometimes ran for political office or urged people of color to vote, black organizations in both cities in this period generally did not seek to mobilize poor and working people of color, especially when compared to the more assertive efforts of unions and labor-based parties.[46] In ways reminiscent of the earlier social clubs in São Paulo, Rio's TEN, for instance, kept a relatively small, select membership and focused primarily on elite cultural activities like theater or beauty pageants for women of color. The motto on the masthead of *Novo Horizonte* for much of this period captures these aspiring middle-class values of education and culture: "To be a good black man, be cultured—the future of our race demands it."[47] A few organizations, like Rio's União dos Homens de Cor and São Paulo's Associação do Negro Brasileiro and Associação José do Patrocínio, reached out to poor and working-class people with concrete programs of social assistance and advocacy. On several occasions, as mentioned above, leaders of the UHC even expressed disdain for what they saw as elitist middle-class *negro* groups. They were especially critical of the TEN, with its predilection for theater or academic congresses. Nevertheless, even the UHC was not designed to be a mass organization; rather it was conceived as a small group of people dedicated to helping the poor. The educated leaders of the UHC, like their counterparts in the TEN, were selective in recruiting members, and the UHC therefore remained relatively small.[48]

For these reasons, scholars have largely characterized postwar black organizations in Rio and São Paulo as elitist, apolitical, or weak in comparison to the Frente Negra of earlier years or, more pointedly, to the Movimento Negro of later years.[49] And in several ways, leaders of postwar black organizations and newspapers fit this description. Viewing themselves as members of a select intelligentsia of color who believed in an ideology of uplift, or even as Christian social workers, southeastern black thinkers in this period generally acquiesced to their society's limited democracy and only challenged it in ways that would ensure greater education and middle-class values among black Brazilians. Black thinkers and activists did not, for example, challenge the literacy requirement that kept so many Brazilians (of all colors) from voting. Instead, they called for improved black education and in some cases took charge of literacy campaigns. Education, of course, contributed to equality in and of itself, and it had the secondary effect of producing more potentially active citizens of color.[50] Nor did black thinkers in this period attempt to become power brokers in a political machine, leveraging influence for their group by promising to deliver black votes to a particular party. Instead, they tended to see themselves as intermediaries responsible, on the one hand, for presenting a variety of political options to their (very limited) readership and, on the other, for pressuring candidates of all major parties to address social and economic issues affecting black Brazilians.[51]

Yet the story is more complicated than portrayals of elitism and weakness would suggest. Democracy had a range of meanings for midcentury black thinkers. Perhaps most central was the opportunity the democratic opening provided to present themselves (and the broader population of black and brown Brazilians they hoped to represent) as rational and balanced political actors, capable of participating productively in a democratic system. In many ways, this goal took precedence over, and even preempted, any concrete attempt to organize potential legions of black voters. On principle, writers in the postwar black press rarely endorsed specific parties or candidates, arguing that such partisanship could taint the virtue of their activism on behalf of all people of color. Abdias do Nascimento best phrased the potential payoff of this strategy in an article for *Quilombo*: "We have nothing to do with parties, neither the so-called democratic ones, nor those of the Right or Left, which have always engaged in the electoral exploitation of blacks. . . . Even less do we advocate a black politics; what we do express is our will to be Brazilians, with the same responsibilities as other Brazilians."[52] As a private citizen, Nascimento leaned toward the Partido Trabalhista Brasileiro (PTB, or Brazilian Labor Party), a primarily urban party loyal to Vargas, which in November 1946 created a Black Council (Diretório Negro) dedicated to discussing racial issues and selecting candidates linked to Rio's black community.[53] In his public writings, however, Nascimento sought to preserve the appearance of political independence for blacks and the re-emerging black movement as a whole. Several black newspapers at this time, most notably José Correia Leite's *Alvorada*, took a similarly neutral stance toward local and national politics, while extolling the virtues of political and civic participation writ large. For Leite, at least, this choice likely reflected a desire to retreat from the extreme partisan divisions of the previous decade.[54] Only a few papers, like Aristides Barbosa's *Novo Horizonte*, publicly involved themselves in party politics (at one point, *Novo Horizonte* endorsed the governorship of São Paulo's Adhemar de Barros [1947–51]). Political scientist Michael Mitchell argues that though this political affiliation compromised *Novo Horizonte* in the eyes of some readers, it helped ensure the paper's existence for more than fifteen years.[55] By contrast, the editors of *Alvorada*, though widely respected for refusing any political affiliation and attempting to make their paper available for free, were forced to cease publication after three years.[56] Seen as a principle for which black writers were willing to sacrifice even the eventual viability of their publications, then, the choice to remain outside of party politics appears not as passive or apolitical but as a shrewd, if cautious, tactic aimed at showcasing blacks as full and politically responsible citizens.

To midcentury black thinkers, then, democracy was not just about electoral or participatory politics. It was also a discourse and a set of performances through which they attempted to proclaim *pretos'* and *pardos'* political competence and full belonging as Brazilian citizens. Black thinkers in the 1940s and 1950s used the idea of democracy in the ways that an earlier generation of activists had used the idea of fraternity—as an acceptable idiom, a shared symbol, through which to make their claims to full citizenship. And, like the republican ideal of fraternity in an earlier period, the trope of political democracy functioned both to celebrate a national ideal and to make demands on it. Most of the time, black thinkers' rhetoric was just that—passionate writing that reflected their relatively limited political outlets and their particular outlook as an elite of color. But at times, the rhetoric of democracy—combined with pressure applied through the democratic public sphere—proved a powerful resource in the struggle for equality.

A Second Abolition

In the budding black publications of postwar São Paulo and Rio de Janeiro, writers greeted the return of democracy with high spirits and equally high expectations. In the first issue of *Alvorada* (28 September 1945), José Correia Leite ambitiously addressed his potential readers as *"negros* of Brazil," and located Brazil's democratic reawakening in the context of a global transformation: "In front of us, there unfolds the dawn of a new era. People everywhere advocate for the reconstruction of a better world."[57] In another article, *Alvorada*'s editors called the election of 1945 "perhaps the most significant fact of our history as a Republic" and congratulated Brazilians on "our country's return to a democratic regime."[58] Many writers in these newspapers scripted *negros* into what *Senzala*'s Luiz Lobato called "the great starring role of democracy" in Brazil.[59] *Alvorada*, taking a grand historical view, reminded its readers that blacks had been the "advance guard" of freedom in Brazil, from their role in defending the nation against the Dutch in the seventeenth century to their recent participation in the Revolution of 1930 against "dominant oligarchies."[60]

Implicit in this celebration of blacks' position at the forefront of Brazil's steady march toward democracy was the pointed demand that the new democratic regime repay its obligations by making racial equality a reality. Black writers frequently made racial equality the test of Brazil's much vaunted political democracy, and declared it still incomplete. "It is with indescribable grief that we hear our orators proclaim from the heights the word 'Democracy,'" wrote Waldemar Machado of *Novo Horizonte*. "'We are in a full democracy,' they say constantly. What democracy? . . . Until we give better opportunities to the [black] descendants of Henrique Dias . . . it is inadmissible to have it proclaimed in public that we live in a full democracy. Being black in Brazil means living amid severe limitations."[61] Indeed, because the return of democracy at midcentury was generally understood as a dramatic, if still unfinished, washing away of the evils of previous regimes, it provided a perfect juncture to express openly the persistence of racism in Brazil and demand action from the new regime, while still joining patriotically in the chorus of national political rhetoric. Rio's UHC, for instance, declared in its membership pledge that "despite the fact the Imperial Law 3,353 of 13 May 1888 [which abolished slavery] assured equality and rights to all Brazilians, without distinction of color, the black family is placed at the margin of politics and of the high administration of the nation; therefore, it remains in a state of moral and civic slavery."[62] The masthead of *Alvorada* in November 1945 called abolition a "sentimental lie."[63] And Leite warned readers that abolition had been an "incomplete" process, that blacks should "not relax in the belief that they are already fully free."[64] The diagnosis of an "incomplete emancipation" that dogged all people of color, issued by the editors of *O Baluarte* as early as 1903, thus continued to resonate among black writers at midcentury.

Where the Republic and the Estado Novo had failed, however, postwar black writers dared to hope that the Second Republic, helped by the prevailing winds of international democracy, might succeed. Contributors to each of the most important new black papers, like *Alvorada*, *Novo Horizonte*, and *Quilombo*, saw in Brazil's redemocratization a long-awaited "Second Abolition" that would finally fulfill the promises of equality and inclusion.[65] In 1947 Leite explained that just as abolition had been a "door that opened in front of a race that was enslaved and full of hope," so did democracy in his own time carry the promise and the burden of abolishing the slavery of prejudice, "help[ing] the black Brazilian to reach economic, cultural, and social stability in the heart of our national community."[66] Writers like Leite turned the idea that democracy would bring what he called "true emancipation" into a call for black people to take action and make use of the prevailing political opening. Black political participation was a crucial component of a well-functioning political democracy, which "can only be made strong when an organized population conscientiously takes on its duties of cooperation."[67]

If the race-based organizations of the postwar period were unable, for various reasons, to mobilize a broader population of color toward greater political participation, they nonetheless found ways to use the principles and channels of democracy in the service of their struggle. In particular, the language of rights, and the principle of the rule of law, gave black thinkers in this period new traction with which to demand racial equality. In the opening editorial of the first issue of the TEN's *Quilombo* (1948), Abdias do Nascimento argued: "It is a transparent historical truth that the black man won his liberty not through the philanthropy or kindness of whites, but by his own struggle and by the unsustainability of the slave system. . . . The black man rejects humiliating pity and philanthropy, and fights for his right to Rights [*direito ao Direito*]," or, in the broader sense of the term *direito* in Portuguese, the right to the law.[68] For Nascimento, black Brazilians' right to be equally protected by the laws of their country, and to participate equally in the democracy that gave these laws meaning, was the ultimate test of the new political system. To Nascimento, moreover, demanding full citizenship in this language of legal rights marked the distinction between robust, active claims to black belonging based on a history of civic participation and anemic, passive definitions of black citizenship, which depended on the pity and patronage of whites. In principle, this was not a new aspiration. Most black thinkers in the 1920s and 1930s had also sought to frame their claims to citizenship in an active voice, rejecting the "humiliating pity and philanthropy" of whites in favor of narratives that highlighted black economic, military, and cultural contributions to the nation. Yet claims framed through the newly vigorous language of democracy and rights made it easier for black activists at midcentury to demand equality on their own merits than the idioms available to black thinkers of earlier generations. The language of rights, with its claims to universal authority, revealed to many midcentury black thinkers the extent to which earlier strategies, based on appeals to the fraternal sentiments of whites, or to the nativist sentiments of elites in a paternalistic and authoritarian regime, had depended at least in part on a logic of concession.

Nascimento, however, clarified that having a "right to Rights" or a "right to the Law" did not just mean giving blacks "theoretical and codified rights." After all, he noted, the notably racist Republic had already "theoretically" given blacks (as Brazilian citizens) equality under the law; what was still missing was "the active exercise of these rights."[69] For Nascimento, as for other black thinkers of his time, the democratic Second Republic had the obligation to finally close the gap between theory and practice, between what black sociologist Alberto Guerreiro Ramos called "the legal black [*o negro legal*]" and "the real black [*o negro real*]."[70] As soon as they came together at the Black National Convention in São Paulo in November 1945, Paulistano and Carioca activists moved toward making these "theoretical" rights to equality more explicit in Brazil's Constitution, so that they might become realities in the lives of black and brown Brazilians. During the convention, activists wrote a "Manifesto to the Brazilian Nation" detailing a set of demands to be presented to the Constituent Assembly for inclusion in the Second Republic's Constitution. Among these demands, clearly framed in the language of democracy and law, the manifesto's writers included "that race and color prejudice be made a matter of law, as a crime against the fatherland [*crime de lesa-pátria*]," and "that any crime practiced in the above context be made a matter of penal law, applying to private businesses as well as to civic groups and other public and private institutions." By "formulat[ing] and demand[ing] rights that, though granted by [abolition], were not concretely implemented," convention delegates concluded, they would be working "so that the ideal of Abolition can become a reality in all of its terms, today and in the future."[71]

Like the ANB's "Manifesto in Defense of Democracy," issued only a few months earlier, the convention's "Manifesto" shows how significantly activists' view of the law had changed since the 1920s. Then, black thinkers in both Rio and São Paulo had fought to defend the absence of legal discrimination in the nation's codes, a relatively recent gain, from proposed legislation that threatened to reinscribe racism into the law. At a time when the enactment of "theoretical" provisions of equality rested more on interpersonal goodwill than on firm institutional foundations, black thinkers had invoked fraternal sentiments to condemn racial discrimination. By the mid-1940s, however, in a context of national and global transformations that strengthened the real and rhetorical power of institutional democracy, black thinkers changed strategies. No longer content with the "theoretical" and passive absence of racial strictures in earlier constitutions, nor with the power of sentiment and personalistic ties to prevent unjust treatment, black thinkers demanded an explicit legal enforcement of racial equality, along with active state sanctions against private citizens who practiced race prejudice, and affirmative interventions in the area of social rights for Brazilians of color. They newly hoped that the law might prevail where fraternal or nationalist sentiment had not.

"Equal before the law . . . without distinction of race or color"

Like their counterparts in earlier decades, the thinkers and activists responsible for the reinvigoration of black politics after 1945 were talented and ambitious, and enjoyed respect and visibility in their immediate social circles. Yet
they themselves were not members of a political or intellectual elite. As in
an earlier period, gaining access to a broader public sphere, and building
networks of support among more influential Brazilians, was crucial to the
activism of the postwar years.[72] Expanded access to the mainstream press,
for instance, gave participants in the Black National Convention of 1945
the opportunity to make their demands heard on the national stage, and to
build alliances with progressive politicians. In São Paulo, members of black
organizations arranged for the convention's "Manifesto to the Brazilian
Nation" to appear in their city's *Folha da Noite* on 11 November 1945. In
Rio de Janeiro, Abdias do Nascimento, who wrote a weekly column for the
Diário Trabalhista (a prolabor newspaper with close ties to the PTB) on the
"Problems and aspirations of black Brazilians," explained the substance
of the demands of the "Manifesto" in the issue of 15 January 1946.[73] That
Nascimento, a black thinker and activist, could write about racial issues in
his own words in a mainstream newspaper suggests how much had changed
since the 1920s, when black supporters of the Mãe Preta monument in Rio
had appeared in the mainstream press only through short quotations or distorted paraphrases. That the "Manifesto" of 1945 and its demands were read
and taken up by representatives of Brazil's populist and labor parties, moreover, reveals the openings that the democratic process newly afforded black
claims at a time when these parties attempted to appeal to as wide a sector of
the Brazilian population as possible.

In particular, the PTB, with its Black Council and its ties to Vargas, sought
to profile itself as the party most receptive to the concerns of black Brazilians.
Following the appearance of the "Manifesto" in the press, Congressman
Manoel Benício Fontenelle, a PTB deputy from the Federal District (the city
of Rio), took the document and its demand for an explicit antidiscrimination
clause to the Constituent Assembly. He proposed amending article 159 of the
draft Constitution, which read "All Brazilians are equal before the law," by
adding the phrase "without distinction of race or color." Echoing the long-
standing claims of black activists themselves, Fontenelle and his cosigners
contended that the means by which slavery had been abolished in Brazil had
placed African descendants in a position of "social inferiority." And like contemporary black writers, proponents of the amendment boldly maintained

that "racial prejudice in Brazil is a sad reality," citing discrimination in the navy, army, and air force, as well as in commerce, theater, banking, schools, and public service. "This [amendment]," its authors concluded, "is the only path toward definitively extinguishing color prejudice, [by] integrating the noble and virile black race into its legitimate fatherland—Brazil."[74]

Though Fontenelle authored the amendment, it was Senator Hamilton Nogueira, a white representative from the Federal District for the conservative UDN, who became its most outspoken and visible defender.[75] In the tradition of the congressmen who argued against racial restrictions on immigration in the 1920s, Nogueira, in impassioned speeches condemning antiblack discrimination, anti-Semitism, or proposed bans on Japanese immigration, spoke out frequently against racism as a delegate to the Constituent Assembly.[76] Though Nogueira's particular antiracist stance, and his intense public commitment to it, was by no means representative of his party as a whole, it did resonate with important strands of antiracism in Brazilian conservative thought—particularly, the views of Gilberto Freyre, another UDN representative. Like Freyre, Nogueira saw explicit racial discrimination as anathema to the traditional values and fraternal sentiments of a Catholic, *mestiço* Brazil. Yet whatever the origins of Nogueira's broad-based rejection of racism, his chosen language closely mirrored that of contemporary black thinkers in its concern with framing racism as an assault on democracy and an offense against modern international standards of humanitarianism. Also like black thinkers, on several occasions (as when he derailed a complacent, hagiographic discussion of Brazilian abolition on its anniversary in May 1946), Nogueira insisted that antiblack racism was still alive and well in Brazil, in practice if not in the law. In calling for an antidiscrimination clause in the constitution, Nogueira's language amplified that of black activists' 1945 "Manifesto." Where they had called racism a "crime against the fatherland [*crime de lesa-pátria*]," Nogueira condemned racism as "a crime against humanity [*crime de lesa-humanidade*]." For Nogueira, as for black thinkers in the mid-1940s, abolition was not yet a finished process, and the inclusion of an article in the Brazilian constitution spelling out "the equality of all races before the law" would be a test of the "humanist base" of Brazil's democracy, and of its ability to break with an exclusionary past.[77]

The black newspapers of Rio and São Paulo followed Nogueira's activities closely, hailing him as "the Senator of the *negros*."[78] They were disappointed when, in August 1946, a month before the constitution was promulgated, the Assembly voted down Nogueira and Fontenelle's amendment. The majority argued that the amendment was redundant, since the constitution already protected the equal rights of all citizens and therefore did not need to specify racial equality.[79] But a group of dissenting representatives, led by Fontenelle, signed a declaration registering their continued support of the amendment, "being convinced that it was of a profoundly democratic nature," and proclaiming their intent to take the matter up in the future.[80]

Despite the failure of this legislative project, activists continued to work, along with allies in Congress, to make sure instances of racial discrimination were heard and addressed. In February 1949, as Abdias do Nascimento and other TEN actors sought to enter Rio's elegant Hotel Glória to attend an actor's ball, a local policeman (apparently at the instigation of the hotel management) barred the group from entering. Abdias do Nascimento mounted a wideranging publicity campaign to bring this episode to light, tracking his progress through his publication, *Quilombo*. First, Nascimento published an open letter to Brazil's chief of police in several mainstream newspapers, denouncing the offending policeman's racist attitude as "incompatible with democracy."[81] After this, the news spread—Senator Nogueira used Nascimento's case in one of his speeches to the Senate as an example of ongoing discrimination and of the need for antiracist legislation; Representative Barreto Pinto (of the PTB) gave an extensive speech denouncing the event in the Chamber of Deputies; cultural associations appealed in the mainstream press; and in the United States the *Pittsburgh Courier* (a black newspaper whose editor, George Schuyler, had visited Brazil and established a close relationship with Nascimento) published an article on the incident.[82] Perhaps most satisfying for Nascimento in his use of the public sphere to denounce racism was the fact that Edgard da Rocha Miranda, a São Paulo doctor who owned the hotel from which Nascimento was barred, wrote an indignant letter to President Dutra demanding that he take action against such abuses. Dutra's personal secretary responded to Rocha Miranda, assuring him that the policeman in question had been dismissed from his post. *Quilombo* reported on these events under the headline "Dutra against Racism," which cleverly claimed Brazil's president as an ally.[83]

Even more highly publicized than Nascimento's experience of racial discrimination were two cases that, as in the immigration debates of the 1920s, involved people of color from the United States. These incidents, however, publicly threw into question long-standing contrasts between a racially harmonious Brazil and a racist United States. In 1947 U.S. social scientist Irene Diggs, on a visit to Rio de Janeiro, had been refused entrance to the Hotel Serrador because of her skin color. And in 1950 another African American visitor, dancer and anthropologist Katherine Dunham, was barred from entering São Paulo's Hotel Esplanada for the same reason. Thanks to those women's fame and their vocal complaints, these incidents received widespread publicity, causing great embarrassment among Brazilian elites committed to maintaining their country's image of racial harmony. Diggs claimed that while prejudice in the United States was tending to disappear, she believed it was getting stronger in Brazil. And Dunham noted her "disenchantment" with Brazil, which far from being the racial paradise many advertised, was in fact the "Latin American country with the most hateful prejudice."[84] In the mainstream press coverage of these events, a few interviewed black journalists, like São Paulo's Geraldo Campos de Oliveira, noted that such incidents confirmed the existence of racial prejudice in Brazil—an assertion, he strategically argued, made "not by us" black activists but by respected national authorities like Gilberto Freyre and Arthur Ramos, as well as a range of international scholars and observers.[85]

These incidents struck a chord among black thinkers and in Brazilian public life more broadly, largely because of the power that the international context added to arguments against racism in the postwar years. Like Nogueira, black activists frequently sought to amplify their nationalist antiracist arguments by drawing on a new internationalist humanitarian language of rights, particularly in the wake of the United Nations' 1948 Universal Declaration of Human Rights. Drafted to express the world's horrified rejection of totalitarianism and genocide, the declaration emphasized equal rights for all human beings regardless of race. The document resonated with black activists in Rio and São Paulo, who republished segments of it in their newspapers, included it in their organizations' statutes (like those of Rio's UHC), or otherwise made frequent reference to it in the course of their political claims and practices. A journalist for *Quilombo*, for instance, spoke of "our right—a right assured by the Constitution and by the eternal principles of human rights—to seek a place in the heart of the Brazilian collectivity."[86] In addition to national traditions and laws, then, the language of human rights provided a powerful justification—interpreted as universal and timeless—for activists' demands for racial equality and expanded rights.

But it was arguably the comparison with the United States that made the international context of democratization most useful to midcentury black thinkers seeking to expand their constitutional rights. "Fifty-eight years have passed [since abolition]," writer Aristides Negreiros of *Alvorada* proclaimed. "And what Liberty? What Democracy? It is a lying, shameful liberty, where the black Brazilian race must face all sorts of prejudices, in a country built by our own ancestors. . . . What democracy does not allow blacks to enter the diplomatic service?" Brazil was, he added in the most damning comparison

imaginable, "a democracy just like that of the United States."[87] This cautionary reference to the United States helped to specify the kind of democracy
Brazil should be: a "racial" democracy in which racial equality was a fundamental ingredient. A racist democracy, Negreiros implied, was no democracy
at all. Writers in the black press joined him in making this point through
their frequent denunciations of racism in the self-proclaimed "land of liberty
and democracy," or, in one particular case, through an open letter to U.S.
president Harry S. Truman pointing out the position of the United States as
an international pariah in a "postwar world" in which "racial discrimination
was an aberration."[88] Singling out the United States as a place where democracy had failed to redress the problems of racism put black thinkers on the
side of acceptable nationalist discourses that rested on the contrast between a
racist United States and a racially harmonious Brazil. But it also allowed them
to hold Brazil to a higher standard.

The international incidents sparked by the mistreatment of Diggs and
Dunham reopened debate in the Brazilian Congress over legislation against
racial discrimination, eventually resulting in the Afonso Arinos Law of 1951.
The law provided a series of punishments for public and private establishments that refused service to people of color, including fines and up to a year
in prison. Repeat offenders could lose their positions, and establishments
could be shut down.[89] Among the key proponents of the law were Senator
Hamilton Nogueira and Deputy Gilberto Freyre, both of whom had endorsed
black activists' calls for some form of antidiscrimination clause in the 1946
Constitution. Although the bad press that Brazil received internationally as
a result of Diggs's and Dunham's denunciations was decisive in passing the
Arinos Law, Nogueira also used the example of Nascimento's incident in his
arguments.[90] And Afonso Arinos de Melo Franco, who authored the bill,
explained that the incident that motivated him to action involved his chauffeur, who for being dark-skinned was refused service at an establishment in
downtown São Paulo.[91] In other words, discrimination against Brazilians of
color, and not just against higher-profile black foreigners, came to light during this period as an offense demanding legal redress. During the debates,
Freyre argued, in the language he was helping to develop, that failing to use
the political system to punish such racist acts would "betray our duties as
representatives of a nation that has made the ideal, if not always the practice,
of a social and even ethnic democracy one of its reasons for existence and one
of its conditions of development."[92]

Emphasizing the role of Diggs and Dunham in the passage of the Afonso
Arinos Law, scholars have interpreted it as a rearguard, remedial move by

conservative politicians eager to defend Brazil's international reputation as a racial democracy.[93] Yet what has gone relatively unnoticed in the law's history is the extent to which it was also the result of the efforts of Brazilian black activists to make political democracy a vehicle for racial equality in this period. Especially considering the limitations of voting as a mechanism for black activism, Nascimento and other leaders' strategic use of the public sphere (as well as the sympathy of powerful political allies) should be considered an important part of the history of antidiscrimination legislation and a success more broadly of activists' attempts to work within a limited kind of political democracy. Indeed, contemporary black thinkers saw the Afonso Arinos Law as a major step toward Brazil's "second abolition" and claimed it as their own.[94] Since then, enthusiasm for the Afonso Arinos has been eclipsed by the fact that the law went almost completely unenforced in the ensuing years.[95] For black activists in subsequent decades, the law would become a symbol of the failings of Brazil's racial democracy. But in the context of contemporary activists' attempts to harness democracy to the project of racial equality, that law stood among their most important accomplishments, even if it did not transform Brazilian society as they hoped.

Democracia Racial

It was in the midst of the national and international enthusiasm for democracy at the end of World War II that the phrase *democracia racial* made its way into Brazilian public life. According to sociologist Antônio Sérgio Alfredo Guimarães, despite the widespread scholarly and popular attribution of that term to Gilberto Freyre's 1933 *Casa-grande e senzala*, Freyre did not use *democracia racial* in his writings until at least the 1940s.[96] Even then, Freyre was but one of several leading social scientists who collectively helped usher that term and concept into the national public consciousness. Freyre was perhaps the first to use the political metaphor of democracy to describe harmonious relations among the nation's ethnic groups. In a series of lectures he gave abroad in the late 1930s and early 1940s, he called Brazil a *"social and ethnic democracy"* where democracy stood opposed not to aristocracy (the tyrant of his earlier works) but to totalitarianism, and where Brazil's ethnic syncretism stood opposed to the obsession with racial purity at the heart of Nazism and fascism. In 1941 anthropologist Arthur Ramos, a committed antiracist and a prodemocracy activist, spoke publicly of the need for democracy to be not just political but also, among other things, "racial." And in a series of articles for the *Diário de São Paulo* in 1944, French scholar Roger

Bastide described Brazil's "racial democracy" as an example and a balm for the rifts that totalitarianism had opened in Europe.[97]

Over the next few years, Guimarães demonstrates, the idea that Brazil was a racial democracy became a widely held consensus among Brazilians of different backgrounds. The term's power, he argues, lay in its ability to mean different things to different people. To conservatives like Freyre, the term celebrated Brazilians' near-complete achievement of racial equality, just as older discourses of Brazil's racial paradise had done at different times at least since the days of the Empire. In this conservative formulation, Guimarães argues, racial democracy was not a discourse of civil rights, nor did it leave room for race-based activism by people of color. To the contrary, Freyre's use of *democracy* in the late 1930s to signal Brazil's extensive mixture and its freedom from racial strictures stood in for actual political freedoms at a time when Brazil, like the Portugal Freyre idealized, was still a highly undemocratic society. With the return of democracy, Guimarães suggests, black thinkers, together with progressive white political and intellectual figures like Roger Bastide, Arthur Ramos, or Florestan Fernandes, turned away from those older, conservative, self-congratulatory interpretations of racial democracy. They drew instead on the widespread consensus about political democracy and antiracism to frame new, explicitly rights-oriented meanings for the term, using *racial democracy* to make demands toward an unfulfilled ideal of racial equality.[98] In Guimarães's view, in other words, black thinkers left behind *racial democracy*'s traditional, conservative meanings (as defined by thinkers like Freyre) and instead emphasized the term's emancipatory, claims-making potential.

In the black newspapers of São Paulo and Rio de Janeiro in the second half of the 1940s, black thinkers did indeed wield the idea of racial democracy in this explicitly claims-making way. Many writers called for concrete measures, such as antiracist legislation, that would make Brazil's racial democracy a reality. In February 1950, before the ratification of the Afonso Arinos Law, for instance, Abdias do Nascimento called for the discourse of racial democracy to move beyond mere rhetoric into political action. "Democracy of color [*democracia de cor*]," he argued, "must not and cannot be only a luxury in our Constitution, a slogan without content or effect in the daily lives of Brazilians." Nascimento and other black writers also argued that Brazil's commitment to a "democracia de cor" should lead political parties to run more black candidates.[99] For the editors of São Paulo's *Mundo Novo*, support of particular black candidates would help create "the true racial democracy in which we wish to live and which we wish to build."[100]

This rights-oriented use of racial democracy fit in with writers' broader attempts to use political democracy to substantiate racial equality in the years between 1945 and 1950.

But writers in the black press did not always deploy racial democracy as an ideal not yet achieved, a challenge to long-standing ideas of Brazilian racial harmony. At the same time that they used the idea of racial democracy to call for concrete rights, many black writers also invoked what Guimarães suggests were the more conservative meanings of the term: a celebration of Brazil's extensive *mestiçagem* and resolution of racial tensions. Indeed, the line between what we might call "emancipatory" and "conservative" uses of the term was not particularly clear in the writings of black thinkers in the mid-1940s. Black newspapers in this period were peppered with references to Brazil's harmonious racial mixture and to a range of elite scholars and public figures (Gilberto Freyre in particular) whom black writers deemed responsible for popularizing this vision of the nation. Editors of black newspapers frequently let these prominent figures speak for themselves, by running reprints of works from the mainstream press and other published sources, or by commissioning essays and articles. In 1950, for instance, São Paulo's *Novo Horizonte* published a piece by Austregésilo de Athayde, the prominent northeastern-born white journalist and intellectual whose vision of Brazil's potential contributions to social equality and human rights earned him the position of delegate to the U.N. commission that drafted the Universal Declaration of Human Rights. As part of an article commemorating Brazil's abolition of slavery and applauding the nation's racial tolerance thereafter, Athayde wrote, "The absence of ethnic prejudices among us has been universally lauded. Those who know the grave consequences of such prejudices in other countries cannot fail to congratulate themselves on the regime of peace and comprehension that marks the coexistence of men in our land, where skin color is no obstacle to anyone's success."[101]

In Rio, *Quilombo* ran a regular column titled "Democracia racial," in which a range of noted national and international intellectuals reflected on issues of race and racism in Brazil and abroad. Always aware of an international comparative perspective (and of Brazil's potential contributions to humanity), authors typically sounded the theme of Brazil's uniquely friendly interracial relations, historically and in the present. Gilberto Freyre, a fitting inaugural guest writer for this column, contributed an article titled "A atitude brasileira" ("The Brazilian Attitude"), which outlined his classic thesis in the new language of democracy: "It would not be exaggerated to say that an ethnic democracy has been emerging in Brazil, over which the sporadic

Aryanisms . . . that at times have surfaced among us, have yet to prevail." Far from falling prey to the "systematic hatreds" of the United States or Nazi Germany, Freyre argued, his conationals, shaped "since remote times" by a "process of democratization in relations among people and groups," preferred a shared identity as "Brazilians or 'Latins' over each individual's particular [ethnic] origin."[102]

Along with reprinted tracts from Freyre and others, black newspapers published their own celebrations of Brazil's racial democracy. They affirmed the idea that "Brazilianness" included no discrete ethnic or racial identities, that Brazil was singular in its granting of full freedoms to people of color, and that Brazilian culture was fundamentally *mestiço*.[103] Abdias do Nascimento eloquently captured these sorts of uses of racial democracy among his fellow black thinkers in his August 1950 opening speech to the Black Brazilian Congress, a nationwide intellectual convention on black issues sponsored by Rio's TEN: "We note that the widespread mixture [*miscigenação*] practiced as a central feature of our historical formation, from the earliest moments of Brazil's colonization, is becoming—through the inspiration and stipulation of the latest triumphs of biology, anthropology, and sociology—a well-delineated doctrine of racial democracy that will serve as a lesson and model to other nations of complex ethnic formation."[104]

Black writers' embrace of apparently "conservative" interpretations of racial democracy as harmonious *mestiçagem* was more than just a lukewarm or lamentable tactical alliance, as some scholars and activists have subsequently suggested.[105] In the mid-1940s, scholarly celebrations of Brazil's *mestiçagem* were integral to the social sciences' rejection of biological racism, providing an authoritative baseline against which black thinkers could frame their demands for inclusion. More important, black thinkers in Rio and São Paulo welcomed new social scientific studies of race and race relations—inaugurated by Freyre himself and continued by national and international sociologists—as the symbolic bases for a particular model of black citizenship that suited their own identities as modern, educated urbanites.

Modern Scientific Principles, or, the Era of the Sociologists

Black writers in São Paulo and Rio de Janeiro were keen observers of a series of projects of comparative international research that came to Brazil in the postwar period. At least since the early twentieth century, Brazilians of many different backgrounds had used the United States as a foil for discussions of their nation's racial tolerance. Most famously, Gilberto Freyre used this contrast to great effect in his portrayal of Brazil's extensive racial and cultural mixture in his 1933 *Casa-grande e senzala*. In 1942 this comparison received the imprimatur of the U.S. academic establishment when University of Chicago sociologist Donald Pierson's *Negroes in Brazil* (1942) described what its author saw as the relative absence of race prejudice in Bahia in explicit comparison with, and as a critique of, race relations in the U.S. South.[106] After World War II, this emergent scholarly attention to Brazil as a potential model for racial harmony found a new home in the institutions and public sphere that would come to constitute the international community. In particular, the United Nations Educational, Scientific, and Cultural Organization (UNESCO), founded in November 1945, played a salient role in bringing Brazil to the attention of international researchers. UNESCO scholars, guided by the principles laid out in the Universal Declaration of Human Rights, set out in the late 1940s to understand, prevent, and find counterexamples to the racism that had resulted in such atrocities in Europe during World War II. In 1949 Brazilian anthropologist Arthur Ramos, the disciple of turn-of-the-century medical and legal doctor Raymundo Nina Rodrigues who helped revive the study of Afro-Brazilian religions in the 1930s, became director of the UNESCO's Department of Social Sciences. Ramos's appointment would place Brazil squarely at the center of the United Nations' international antiracist projects.

Over the course of World War II, Ramos's work had shifted from a concern with Afro-Brazilian religions to a growing academic and political interest in race relations, racial movements, and the broader structural inequalities affecting people of color in Brazil. As the war drew to an end, Ramos became an outspoken critic of racism, a promoter of the social sciences as instruments of antiracism, and a champion of Brazil as a "racial democracy" and a "racial laboratory" worthy of the world's attention.[107] When he became director of UNESCO's Department of Social Sciences, Ramos brought together a group of leading social scientists to debate the scientific validity of race. Ramos died in 1949, before the group issued its "Statement on Race" (May 1950) calling race a "social myth" with no biological basis. Yet his project to use the social sciences to discredit racism, and specifically, to examine the potential lessons of the Brazilian experience, had a lasting effect. In the early 1950s, Ramos's colleagues at the UNESCO commissioned a group of Brazilian and international scholars to study race relations in several Brazilian cities. As historian Marcos Chor Maio argues, the UNESCO's "radical statement denying the scientific validity of the concept of race was followed by the selection of a country with a population considered the result of miscegenation, and therefore definite proof that miscegenation was universal and a refutation of the concept of a world inhabited by distinct races."[108]

The resulting UNESCO studies presented a mixed verdict on Brazil's celebrated racial democracy. From one perspective, these studies largely discredited the idea of harmonious race relations in Brazil, since most participating researchers agreed that the balance of power and resources was overwhelmingly tipped against Brazil's vast population of color.[109] Yet many researchers, roughly following the conclusions of Pierson's 1942 study, concluded that class, and not race, was the major reason for discrimination in Brazil. Marxist scholars Florestan Fernandes and Luiz de Aguiar Costa Pinto (who studied São Paulo and Rio de Janeiro, respectively), for example, made it clear that racism existed and that it represented a serious obstacle to the advancement of Brazilians of color. Yet in different ways, both scholars subordinated the problem of racism, and the affirmation of black racial identities in response to racism, to broader questions of class discrimination and class struggle.[110] In areas of the Northeast with nonwhite majorities (especially Bahia), UNESCO-sponsored studies tended to downplay the role of race and racism even further than did studies of Brazil's more explicitly racist South and Southeast. Indeed, when the UNESCO set out to use Brazil as a case study of nonracism, organizers had principally imagined conducting research in Bahia, precisely because scholarship since the 1930s had presented that city and state as exceptionally integrated along racial and cultural lines.[111] In this sense, even as the UNESCO studies challenged facile visions of Brazil as a racial paradise, they simultaneously contributed to discounting the role of race and racism as independent factors in creating and sustaining Brazil's social inequalities.[112]

The UNESCO's selection of Brazil as a racial research site at midcentury dramatizes not only a professed faith in Brazil as a "laboratory" of mixture and nonexistent discrimination. It also reflects a broader international moment of faith in the power of the social sciences to address social problems—in this case, what was becoming commonly known as "race relations." In Brazil in particular, these international influences, as well as local forces, contributed to making the 1940s and 1950s what Marcos Chor Maio has called the "era of the sociologists."[113] The context of redemocratization, an increasing pace of industrialization, and Brazil's transformation into a class society guided and shaped academic inquiry. Sociology's "universalist paradigm" became the primary means of understanding, on a level of equality, the variety of forces and actors that brought about these sorts of social transformations in Brazil.[114] Along with intense social change, the strengthening of academic institutions in the postwar period provided the context and opportunity for sociologists to imbue their science with a particular historical mission. Sociologists conceived of their field as "a rational way of knowledge that was equivalent to a superior consciousness. Through it, they would contribute to bringing about a new stage of the civilizing process in Brazil."[115] This sociological turn marked a significant shift away from Brazilian scholars' earlier criminological, folkloric, or anthropological approaches to the study of African-descended Brazilians.[116] Scholars in the new tradition concerned themselves little with the survival of African cultural traits—language, dress, food, or religion—among African descendants in Bahia and other northeastern regions. Instead, researchers like Roger Bastide, Florestan Fernandes, Luiz de Aguiar Costa Pinto, and many others used statistical analyses, interviews, and participant observation to understand the class and color disparities arising from modernization, particularly in the dynamic cities of the Southeast.[117]

This context helps us understand why the line between "conservative" and "rights-oriented" uses of ideas of racial democracy was so often blurred in the writings of midcentury black thinkers. When they invoked Freyrean visions of racial democracy as harmonious *mestiçagem*, black thinkers did so in the context of a broader trajectory of social scientific writing that denied the validity of race and racism and recognized black people as central actors in a modernizing Brazil. In the pages of *Quilombo*, black editors reprinted the writings of UNESCO-associated scholars like Arthur Ramos and Roger Bastide, a prominent scholar of Afro-Brazilian religions and Brazilian race relations teaching at the University of São Paulo, in which these scholars explicitly wielded Brazil's "hybrid vigor" and *mestiçagem* as proof for global audiences that race had no biological basis.[118] In this sense, prescriptively antiracist statements by internationally recognized intellectuals, like Austregésilo de Athayde's claim that "any racist idea carries within it the potential to dissolve [our] nationality . . . [and] is therefore incompatible with Brazil," held out the promise of harnessing the older idea of indissoluble mixture to the newer project of full rights for Brazilians of color.[119]

More specifically, for many black thinkers, social science, beginning with Freyre's works, lent authority to new kinds of claims to citizenship based on black Brazilians' active participation in the nation. Waldemar Machado, in a 1947 article for *Novo Horizonte*, argued that "one must read Arthur Ramos, Nina Rodrigues, Gilberto Freyre, . . . and so many others in order to appreciate the value of the black race in Brazil," a race that should be "undeniably recognized as a primary participant in the formation of our nationality."[120] Writers like Raul Joviano do Amaral, an editor of São Paulo's *Alvorada*, saw these academic studies as a way to teach all members of society about the role blacks had played in Brazilian history. The works of what Amaral generically called "Brazilian culturalists" (possibly in reference to the post-Freyre shift from biological to cultural and structural explanations of difference) had contributed to bringing down "the unjustifiable barriers of stupid prejudices and dogmas inculcated by the mixed-race, aristocratic elites of this land." They had also helped "the black man himself," who, "thanks to his own titanic efforts as an autodidact, begins to perceive the true position he deserves, and his important role in our nationality." Amaral hoped that recent developments in social theory would help shape a new national consensus about people of color's rightful place in Brazilian society. "From the wider divulgation (among all the component classes of our people) of serious sociological, historical, and ethnographic studies and observations of the relevance of the black man's contribution, there must follow a practical recognition of that relevance: granting the black man assistance commensurate with the duties imposed on him under the hard labors of slavery."[121] The social sciences, in other words, would authoritatively showcase blacks' historical contributions, and ensure tangible recompense in the present.

Amaral and many of his midcentury contemporaries expressed the belief that there was a qualitative difference between the opportunities offered by the new sociology and the intellectual resources available to previous black writers. The range of recent "serious" social scientific studies focused on social disparities, Amaral argued, provided a newly "favorable" climate for dealing with the "black question," displacing the "brilliant but useless" ideas of a previous generation of "chroniclers, poets, and fiction writers." Although later critics would see black writing in the 1940s and 1950s as itself too conciliatory, Amaral and other midcentury activists saw themselves as newly forceful and criticized *their* earlier counterparts for appealing excessively to elite sentimentalism. Any concessions gained in this older manner, they reasoned, could only be based on pity or condescension toward people of color rather than on acknowledgment of their hard-earned rights. The new sociological studies, by contrast, set the stage for interpreting black Brazilians' gains not as something "*granted*, in the name of saccharine sentimentalism; but *conquered* by tenacious effort, by [the black man's] persistence in making himself an economic, political, and social force to be reckoned with."[122] This use of a sociological turn in the literature on black Brazilians to highlight black subjecthood and agency is consistent with efforts more broadly, in the black press of the period, to base activism increasingly on what Nascimento called "a right to Rights" instead of on what Leite called "the sentimentalism . . . of dilettantes who sing the praises of black Brazilians as builders of the foundations of our nation's wealth."[123]

In this context, the Mãe Preta—once a cherished symbol for black thinkers seeking precisely to use "sentimentalism" to affirm their role as builders of the nation—fell even further out of favor. Already in the 1930s, most black thinkers in São Paulo had shifted their politics of belonging from appeals to the fraternal sentiments of their conationals to assertions of their own status as nationals through invocations of military or filial duty to the nation. If the latter strategy had already narrowed the space for the black wet-nurse to function as a useful symbol of black inclusion, the efforts of black writers in the second half of the 1940s to replace older appeals based on sentiment with newer arguments based on democratic rights and sociological truths made the Mãe Preta even less relevant as a symbolic resource. In the postwar years, only a very few black writers in Rio de Janeiro and São Paulo still mentioned the Mãe Preta. Leite's *Alvorada*, in particular, continued to celebrate her holiday every 28 September. Yet even those writers had to update the symbol's meanings to make it resonate with the new mood. In an article titled "Black Man, You Are Important!," *Novo Horizonte* director Arnaldo de Camargo invoked the Mãe Preta through older tropes of black males' soldiering and labor, but added a boldness of demand and a language of rights that reflected the racial politics of his own time: "When we remember that our glorious fatherland is splattered with the brave and heroic blood of black people; when we know that the national economy always rested on the strong shoulders of the sons of the Mãe Preta, it makes us want to scream at the top of our lungs, 'Give us what belongs to us. Our rights are equal.'"[124] Others, like *Alvorada*'s Sofia Campos Teixeira (one of a handful of women writing in the midcentury black newspapers and an active participant in black politics since the Black National Convention of 1945), celebrated the Mãe Preta as a humanistic figure but sharply criticized the shortcomings of the Law of the Free Womb, which earlier activists had chosen as the symbolic foundation of black citizenship and freedom.[125]

For many other writers, however, the Mãe Preta's inherent sentimentalism sent the wrong political message altogether. *Novo Horizonte*, for instance, ran an article by Austregésilo de Athayde, the prominent writer and defender of human rights, who argued that the struggle to ensure racial equality should not take place on just any set of terms. Politics was more powerful than sentiment: "I do not want to invoke the principle of gratitude that white Brazilians should have for their 'nannies' and Mães Pretas. They [the Mães Pretas] would only appeal to those with well-trained hearts, whose emotions have not been desensitized by stupid pride. I prefer political reasons, drawn from the fact that three races contributed to the formation of the Brazilian people, and [that] each has merits that we must recognize and respect." Black thinkers from the 1920s might have retorted that the "political" idea that three races participated in the "formation of the Brazilian people" was exactly the point they had been trying to make with the Mãe Preta. Indeed, in their time, they had used appeals to sentiment to counteract racist ideas supported by purportedly objective science. But by the 1940s and 1950s, the political valence of science and especially social science had largely shifted in black writers' favor. For Athayde, and presumably for the *Novo Horizonte* editors who republished his article from a leading news magazine, it was recent scholarly production on black Brazilians that should provide the new source of authority for claims to black inclusion: "Those who have studied this issue maturely and at length stand ready to proclaim the veracity of the black man's cooperation toward the success of Brazilian culture and what little originality it may have."[126] A writer from the city of Santos whose article was also reprinted by the editors of *Novo Horizonte* similarly argued that "tenderness for the Mãe Preta has not yet resolved the black question." It fell on sociology, he claimed, to provide the scientific understanding that would dispel tenacious racism: "Where sentiments fail, the rigor of a sociological principle will indicate the solution."[127] In this way, "rigorous" sociological studies of black Brazilians—built on what one black writer called "modern scientific principles"[128]—replaced sentiment as a new, objective source of authority for black thinkers' claims to being full and active citizens with equal rights, rather than supplicants subject to the whims of condescending patriarchs or paternalistic dictators.

Sometimes, in their enthusiasm for works that included black Brazilians as central contributors to the nation, writers (like Waldemar Machado, above) failed to discriminate between the derogatory, exoticizing perspective of a Nina Rodrigues and the evolving social scientific perspective of scholars like Arthur Ramos. But for most black writers who addressed the subject of the social sciences, this distinction was crucial. The new sociological consensus was attractive precisely because it allowed them to challenge the anthropological and folkloric depictions of black Brazilians that had gained such wide circulation in the 1930s, particularly those that portrayed people of color as exotic, primitive Africans—a characterization many Paulista activists in particular had worked to reject since the early twentieth century. In the September 1946 issue of *Novo Horizonte*, for instance, W. D. Silva noted that "there has been a great and undeniable interest—though merely an interest—in the black Brazilian; bookstores are crammed with studies about our race; but what does this literature deal with? It deals with our folklore, with what is picturesque about us, as if we were ever available exotic themes for the delight of readers of fantastical stories of Zulus, Zumbis, and who knows what else." Not only, Silva objected, were these works "written with an attitude more of curiosity than erudition," but blacks everywhere were then expected to act in this folkloric fashion: "They blame us for being negligent—for not having been good at continuing the practices of our grandfathers, with their 'candomblés,' 'pais de santo,' and the like."[129] Several years later, looking back on early-twentieth-century studies of black Brazilians, José Correia Leite reached a similar verdict: "We know that since Nina Rodrigues, the analysis in these works was linked to the collection of anthropological and historical material about the process of integrating Africans into Brazil." This "Afro-Brazilian" tradition, Leite noted, reached its peak with the Afro-Brazilian Congresses of Recife and Bahia in the 1930s. "But we must note that these works' central point of interest had . . . to do with the bizarre, the picturesque and exotic to be found in the rich color of our folklore." In the end, Leite argued, much of what was "said, studied, and researched about the black Brazilian" in that heyday of anthropological investigation ultimately cast people of color as outsiders in their nation. Those studies were more about "the black than the Brazilian."[130]

These statements reflect a continued, even deepening, conviction among many black thinkers that associations with exotic Africa, even when couched in terms of Brazilian folklore, tarnished their status as "Brazilians." Particularly among Paulistano black writers, any interest in Africa—which a handful of writers like Leite had staunchly maintained throughout the 1930s—sharply declined in the postwar years. This change was most visible in Leite's "O mundo negro" columns, which after appearing in O Clarim d'Alvorada in the early 1930s reemerged with significantly different content in Alvorada in the mid-1940s. Originally inspired by Garvey's writings in The Negro World and a space fervently dedicated to promoting the "unity of old and new world blacks," the column in the mid-1940s became almost exclusively devoted to following racial affairs in the United States. In part, as the editors claimed, this shift had to do with the notable progress that black North Americans had begun to make after the end of the war.[131] But it also reflected transformations in the international academic environment. In the 1930s Leite had worked to portray Africa, and diasporic and pan-African politics in particular, as dynamic and modern. His coverage of Garvey's movement had been central to that attempt. But his efforts swam against the current of prevailing perceptions, among black thinkers and Brazilians more broadly, of Africa's inherent primitivism—perceptions, Leite and others believed, enhanced by prominent anthropological studies of Afro-Brazilian culture and religions. By the 1940s, even Leite appears to have greeted with some relief the emergence of sociological studies that left Africa entirely aside and instead approached the study of race in Brazil within the same comparative framework as the modern, industrialized United States.

If Leite's column hardly mentioned Africa in this period, the few authors who did evinced mostly disdain for the continent. One writer in *Novo Horizonte*, for instance, confessed his "nostalgia" for the "Motherland from which our ancestors came" but went on to demarcate his deep cultural distance from Africa. Referring to a photo of a smiling young African girl dressed in beads and animal skins, the author exclaimed, "At least she is happy, because she is barbaric, savage, and without consciousness of what we call civilization."[132] And an article in *Senzala* included a joke about an African native who, taking to heart a missionary's injunction against polygamy, proceeded to eat all but one of his wives.[133]

If they occasionally belittled and mostly ignored Africa, writers in the post-war black press were noticeably more vocal about their dislike for the Brazilian Africanisms that had risen to national notoriety through the anthropological writings of the 1930s. Black writers emphasized their own status as civilized, modern, cultured Catholics, distinguishing themselves as much as possible from the subjects of Afro-Brazilian anthropology. Even in Rio de Janeiro, where the practice of African-derived religions had been more widespread than in São Paulo in the first half of the century, outright denunciations of Candomblé or Macumba were not uncommon. João Conceição, a special contributor to *Quilombo*, drew a bold line between progress and the "primitivism" of African religions. He argued that in order to "move forward," people of color themselves had to "correct many of our errors and ways," among them "certain primitive habits, the mystifications of African religions."[134] In São Paulo, José Correia Leite called for black activists to challenge "the stigmas of atavistic inheritances that have undermined a forward-looking image of blacks in national life."[135] The advancement of blacks as modern citizens, in these formulations, stood in direct tension with the persistence of African "atavisms" and religious practices.

These anti-African pronouncements had a clear regional component, one that had already begun to emerge in the writings of some black Paulistanos in the 1930s. Black writers in postwar Rio and São Paulo made a clear distinction between themselves, as representatives of a modern, industrial, truly Brazilian South, and the inhabitants of the distant Northeast, with their "earthly and uncivilized pleasures of exotic and sensual dances to the tune of barbaric music."[136] Against the grain of the anthropologists of the 1930s, and much more consistent with a previous generation of thinkers influenced by scientific racism, they took the position that these primitivisms should be eradicated. "It is in Bahia," a reprinted article in *Novo Horizonte* declared, "that we find the greatest [African] religious influence, even making it necessary for the local police to take action, initiating persecutions against those sorts of base spiritism—candomblé and macumba."[137] This image of a barbaric, backward Afro-Bahia thus provided a foil against which many southern black intellectuals constructed their own identities as modern nationals.

What bothered black writers from São Paulo and Rio de Janeiro about anthropological or folkloric approaches to the study of African-descended Brazilians was not just the harmful associations they appeared to establish between blackness and barbarism. In the eyes of many southeastern black thinkers, anthropological studies of Afro-Braziliana (much like the "sentimentalism" many of them disdained) cast people of color as objects, rather than as active subjects, and zeroed in on black cultural difference at the expense of the kinds of race-based political activism they themselves practiced. As early as 1940, in a rare issue of *O Clarim d'Alvorada* edited in the midst of the Estado Novo, writer Luiz Bastos published a critique of the study of Africanisms in Brazil that foreshadowed the mood of the upcoming decades. Titled "Where Is Afrology Heading?," Bastos's article denounced the transformation of black Brazilians into material for "aspiring Afrologists [*candidatos a afrologistas*]" who, seeking to advance their careers, could simply "go to the *terreiro*, watch the *batucadas* [ritual drumming] . . . and then run to the library to write a formidable article 'about the blacks' with several citations in English, German, and Latin." For Bastos, "underneath that superficiality that sees the black man as a thing and not a living being, what we find is an accentuated race prejudice."[138] He concluded his critique by exhorting "Afrologists" to "set themselves a more concrete and perhaps more fruitful task: becoming militants in the cause of uplifting the black man socially and morally and . . . at last, incorporating him into the Brazilian Nation."[139]

In 1950 the editors of *Quilombo*, Abdias do Nascimento and Alberto Guerreiro Ramos, echoed Bastos's critique. As they put it in one of their columns, "ethnological" studies of Brazilians of color had turned their subjects into no more than "primary material for scholars." These works, they added, presented an image of black Brazilians as nearly mummified creatures, frozen in a distant past: "Every time that blacks were studied, it was with the evident purpose or the ill-disguised intention of considering him a distant being, almost dead, or even packed up in straw like a museum piece." By contrast, in the period between 1945 and the early 1950s, the sociological approach seemed to offer a politically engaged alternative to anthropology's static objectification of people of color. Announcing the objectives of their First Black Brazilian Congress of 1950, Nascimento and Guerreiro Ramos explicitly contrasted their planned academic event to the northeastern anthropological congresses of the 1930s run by Gilberto Freyre and Édison Carneiro: "Our event has no links—except very remote ones—with the Afro-Brazilian Congresses of Recife (1934) and Bahia (1937). Those congresses were, in a sense, academic—mostly distant from popular cooperation and participation." The Black Brazilian Congress of 1950, they hoped, would be significantly different from those earlier anthropological endeavors. "A sociological congress par excellence, ours aims to discover mechanisms that will accelerate the process of integration among blacks and whites begun by our historical evolution." They expressed the hope that the politically informed works presented at the event (most of them by people of color themselves) would fundamentally change the ways academics approached the study of Brazilians of color. Sociology, with guidance from black intellectuals like Nascimento and Guerreiro Ramos, would show people of color no longer as "primary material for scholars" but as active agents, "builders of their own conduct, of their own destinies."[140]

Consistent with their critique of the TEN as an elitist cultural organization, Rio's União dos Homens de Cor favored the new sociology on slightly different terms. Like most other writers in the postwar black press, the UHC's leaders drew on social science for the authority it gave to antiracist claims. On the cover page of their 1953 special supplement A Voz da Negritude, for instance, the editors cited sociologist Donald Pierson's assertion that "underneath [the world's] cultural diversity is a common human nature, universal to the human species."[141] Yet for the UHC's leaders, sociology was a remedy not primarily for the excesses of cultural anthropologists but for the excessive focus that many black thinkers placed on elite cultural productions, such as plays and academic events. José Bernardo da Silva's participation in the TEN-sponsored Black Brazilian Congress of 1950 stressed the need for fewer "cultural congresses" and more "objective" action on behalf of black Brazilians—a goal he believed was being ignored in favor of high theory.[142] Those cultural movements, his colleague Joviano Severino de Melo explained in an article, "are very interesting and useful for showing the dominant class the value, the culture, and the creative capacities of blacks," but they did little for the people as a whole.[143] Sociology, the UHC's leaders held, should provide a tool for valorizing and helping less fortunate people of color rather than for buttressing the status of a black intellectual elite. As Silva argued elsewhere, "It is wrong to believe that only the cultured blacks of our land can think correctly. Afro-Brazilians of the popular classes are simple men but have extremely acute observational skills." He called for "a meticulous study of the psychology of black popular classes [to] give sociologists a better comprehension of that ethnic group."[144]

As these statements illustrate, black thinkers in this period expected to be much more than passive recipients of the benefits of broader academic transformations. Like their colleagues from the TEN or the UHC in Rio, men of color in São Paulo also attempted to seize and to shape the emerging sociological field of "race relations" studies. In the early 1950s José Correia Leite, Jayme de Aguiar, Francisco Lucrécio, and several other veterans of the city's black movements participated as informants in the research projects of leading white sociologists like Florestan Fernandes and Roger Bastide.[145] Indeed, when José Correia Leite looked back in the early 1960s on transformations in "black studies" at midcentury, he argued that black activists in Rio and São Paulo, then "in the midst of great activity," had played a crucial role in the shift from a primarily anthropological perspective in black studies to a dominantly sociological one. Leite dated this transformation to Arthur Ramos's 1938 visit to São Paulo when, in Leite's words, Ramos encountered "an intense black movement of ideological content." (Ramos had, in fact, visited and corresponded with leaders of the Frente Negra since the mid-1930s).[146] In Leite's view, it was this "intense black movement" that accounted for Ramos's intellectual shift toward the study of race relations and his closer involvement with black politics. More broadly, Leite's reminiscences portrayed works focusing on southeastern activism's "ideological content," rather than on the Northeast's "religious cults, dances, music, cuisines, and things of folklore," as responsible for the shift away from "poetic sentimentalism" in the study of black Brazilians. Indeed, the academics who figure most prominently (and positively) in the black press in this period—Arthur Ramos, Édison Carneiro, and Roger Bastide—all transitioned in the postwar years from studying African cultural traits to studying issues of race and race relations and became closely associated with or involved in the black politics of the 1940s and 1950s.[147]

As a whole, then, writers in the black newspapers of São Paulo and Rio de Janeiro in the second half of the 1940s showed a dramatic preference for sociological scholarship over the anthropological approach to the study of black Brazilians that had taken hold in the 1930s. This may seem surprising today, given the evolution of anthropology to reject the notion of the primitive and to recognize that all cultural forms are the product of an active process by which people construct meaning in their lives. But at the time, sociology seemed more powerful to black thinkers on several levels. The shift to sociology further discredited an earlier consensus on biological racism and whitening with a celebration of not just mixing but also explicit antiracism. It helped to shift the focus of research on race from African subcultures to modern social structure. It highlighted the dynamic racial politics of southeastern activists. Finally, it supported interpretations of citizenship based on agency and rights rather than pity or patronage. But as the pronouncements of black thinkers like Nascimento, Guerreiro Ramos, and Leite suggest (and as leaders of the UHC astutely observed), the sociological perspective conferred agency on people of color not by granting a new role to the black masses but by creating a formal space for the interventions of black thinkers and activists into national intellectual life. In the sociological works that postwar black thinkers embraced, the "black man" who was to become an agent in modernity looked very much like themselves. For southeastern writers, who often expressed disdain for African religions and their practitioners, the question of whether black Brazilians were cast as active agents or passive subjects did not necessarily reflect an inclination to defend the black practitioners of Candomblé. Rather, it reflected a concern for their own role as intellectuals who would represent and help guide their race. In many ways, then, southeastern black intellectuals' preference for sociology illustrates their position in between white intellectuals and the black masses, as they attempted to define black Brazilian citizenship in their own image in the heady first years of democracy's return.

IN 1982, at a moment when black activists in Brazil firmly dismissed racial democracy as a deceitful myth, an older Abdias do Nascimento expressed his distaste for his and other activists' "excessively conciliatory behavior toward liberal whites" at midcentury. Nascimento particularly singled out his own assertion, in his pronouncement to the Black National Congress of 1950 that racism did not exist in Brazil. "We know this to be contrary to historical truth," he declared three decades later, "and I can only, at this moment, berate myself for those excesses of tolerance toward the racists of this country."[148] Yet in the second half of the 1940s, black thinkers in São Paulo and Rio de Janeiro used the widespread idea of racial democracy, and even of Brazil's indissoluble racial mixture, to push forward their demands for racial equality. Nascimento and others linked the emerging discourse of racial democracy with an international language of rights and political freedoms to craft seemingly universal and scientific claims for black inclusion that, they believed, exceeded the reach of earlier claims based on sentimental, familial metaphors like fraternity or filial duty. Black thinkers in these years also established close ties with leading social scientists, helping to redefine scholarship about race in ways that suited their own political and intellectual goals and reflected their own racial, class, and regional identities. And at times, as in the case of antiracist legislation, black intellectuals in this period were able to leverage the dominant discourse of racial democracy to effect legal and political change.

By 2002, when Nascimento republished *Quilombo*, he looked back on this period once again, and saw it with new eyes. "The appeal to the principle of democracy," he explained, "constituted, at that point, the most powerful weapon for social demands and political struggles. The motto of racial democracy fit into that context, and the leadership of the black movements brandished it like the banner of Ogum [the *orixá* or deity of justice in Candomblé]."[149] Placed in the context of the democratic promise of the immediate postwar years, Nascimento realized, black leaders' engagement with ideologies of racial democracy was not a shameful betrayal of the cause of racial justice but a crucial part of their struggles for that cause. Understanding why black leaders embraced the promises of racial democracy in these years helps us see the black movement's rejection of racial democracy in the 1970s not just as the product of a different political consciousness among a later generation of activists but also as the result of many older activists' intense disillusionment with the shortcomings of the racial democracy that had appeared possible at midcentury.

Indeed, the intensity and visibility of black leaders' attempts to claim the language of democracy for race in this optimistic half-decade in many ways sparked the beginnings of the conservative backlash against which activists like Nascimento would later mobilize. The bold demands of black thinkers, black newspapers, and black organizations in the second half of the 1940s quickly revealed the ideological fissures in the apparent consensus surrounding Brazil's racial democracy. The more insistent black thinkers became in their attempts to brandish the banner of democracy for antiracism, the more energetically conservative proponents of racial democracy used similar ideas to delegitimize black demands. By the early 1950s, as the high hopes surrounding Brazil's new democracy began to wear off, black thinkers across Brazil would find themselves fighting not just to encourage a progressive ideal of racial democracy but, increasingly, to resist complacent or repressive definitions of racial democracy that stressed cultural, racial, and political assimilation.

5. Difference
São Paulo, Rio de Janeiro, and
Salvador da Bahia, 1950–1964

The language of an antiracist, unified Brazilian identity permeated Brazilian public life so thoroughly in the years following the return of democracy in 1945 that black organizations themselves soon came under suspicion as racist entities. In July 1949 a writer in Rio's *Diário Carioca* accused black thinkers of sowing "seeds of hatred." In April 1950 a front-page editorial in Rio's *O Globo* accused black organizations of "*preto* racism." "From the most remote times of our formation," this writer declared, "*pretos* and whites have treated each other cordially. . . . Yet for some time now, we have seen the emergence of elements concerned with giving *negros* a separate situation. . . . *Negro* theater, *negro* newspapers, *negro* clubs." These organizations, the product of "pure and simple imitation" of foreign, North American racial ideas, were having a "pernicious effect" on Brazil, "creat[ing] among us a problem that never before existed."[1]

The problem with *negro* theater, *negro* newspapers, and *negro* clubs, to critics like these, was not just that they undermined the idea that Brazil was truly a society without racism and therefore without need for social transformation. Perhaps more ominously, groups or publications built around distinctly *negro* racial identities threatened the increasingly widespread idea of a unified Brazilian identity blessed by the absence of racial divisions. At midcentury, this idea was dear not just to conservatives like the *Globo* editorialist, who, from the extreme position of denying that Brazil ever had racism, saw *negro* organizations of any kind as out of place and even treasonous. It was also dear to moderate and progressive social scientists committed to democracy and antiracism, and even to leftist thinkers and politicians who aspired to foment cross-racial alliances among the Brazilian *povo*.

Over the course of the 1950s and early 1960s, as more and more Brazilians from across the political spectrum subscribed to the consensus that Brazil was a society uniquely graced by racial equality—an image partially buttressed by the deepening social democracy of the Second Republic—black intellectuals encountered more and more public formulations of racial democracy that placed limits on black politics, especially politics based on cultural or racial difference. An article by Gilberto Freyre in the black Carioca magazine *Quilombo* spelled out, in 1948, what many Brazilian thinkers and politicians in subsequent years would come to see as the rightful price of belonging in a racial democracy. Freyre granted that Brazilians of different ethnic backgrounds "might, and even should, preserve, from their mother culture or 'race,' values that can be useful to the whole." But he warned Brazilians to be "vigilant" against any divisions along racial or ethnic lines, to avoid behaving "as if the descendant of the African [were] a neo-African surrounded by enemies, and the descendant of Europeans . . . a civilized neo-European surrounded by savages." Brazilians, Freyre urged, "should behave as Brazilians," subordinating any racial or ethnic affiliations to "the *mestiço*, plural, and complex culture of Brazil."[2]

Ironically, the same social transformations that had allowed black thinkers to use both democracy and antiracism to sharpen their race-based demands in the second half of the 1940s made it increasingly difficult for them, in subsequent years, to discuss racial inequality, organize around distinct racial identities, or call into question their fellow citizens' much vaunted racial tolerance. Claiming difference, or exposing differential treatment, became a tricky proposition in a purportedly postracial society. These constraints, however, did not make racial democracy simply an oppressive myth, any more than black thinkers' initial enthusiasm for racial democracy had made it a reality. Black intellectuals in São Paulo, Rio de Janeiro, and Salvador da Bahia in the 1950s and early 1960s found different ways to continue making use of widespread antiracist rhetoric in Brazilian public life, while asserting their rights to independent organizing and to countervailing ideas of racial or cultural difference from what Freyre called the *mestiço* "whole."

As in earlier years, black politics took on different casts in different cities. The supposed problem of "*preto* racism," raised by the visibility of "*negro* theater, *negro* newspapers, and *negro* clubs," was of concern to white observers particularly in the cities of São Paulo and Rio de Janeiro, where a number of specifically race-based organizations flourished at midcentury. In both cities, leaders of race-based organizations and publications held on to the hope that a broad antiracist consensus would ultimately help their cause, even as they worked to expose the hypocrisies of dominant notions of racial democracy and to define their own ideal version more closely. Here is Abdias do Nascimento in 1950, clearly at pains to portray his organization as compatible with dominant ideas of mixture and harmony: "In our country, everything has the indelible mark of that happy melding of races, and the black man has no interest in disturbing the natural march of our *mestiçagem* of blood, culture, religion, art, and civilization." Race-based organizations, he indignantly clarified, were "simply complementary measures, and it is neither just nor honest that the balanced movement of black affirmation, inspired in the ideas of cooperation, unity, and of increasingly perfect integration of blacks and whites, be defamed or disrespected."[3] Nascimento's Paulistano colleagues adopted different styles and strategies when defending their right to organize from white conationals' accusations of reverse racism. In São Paulo, where the color line was by all accounts sharper, black thinkers began to defend themselves against charges of "*preto* racism" even earlier and in more confrontational language that openly challenged dominant ideas of a harmonious *mestiço* Brazil. In both cities, by the 1950s and early 1960s, the struggle to assert blacks' racial or ethnic difference would lead black thinkers, in one way or another, back to Africa, then in the grip of vast political and cultural transformations.

In Rio and São Paulo, black thinkers' frustrations with the oppressive aspects of dominant discourses of racial democracy would also intersect with a changing attitude toward the social sciences, which had proven so useful to their antiracist agenda in the immediate postwar years. Beginning even in those years, and increasingly over the course of the 1950s and early 1960s, black thinkers in Rio and São Paulo raised their expectations of social scientists and their disciplines. They demanded participation as makers of knowledge about race and race relations rather than as mere informants or subject material and criticized what they saw as the social sciences' tendency to downplay the role of race and racism in explanations of social inequality. These were pressing concerns for black thinkers at a time when rapid social and economic change masked, in the eyes of many of their conationals, the persistent role of racial discrimination in preventing people of color from benefiting proportionately in Brazil's development.

In Salvador da Bahia, a majority black and brown city where candomblés were the most prominent ethnocultural organization for African-descended Brazilians, the opportunities and limitations black leaders faced in the postwar period were different than in the Center-South, where explicitly *negro* social and political organizations were more common. For Candomblé leaders in Bahia, the return of democracy did not add substantially to the religious freedoms obtained in the 1930s and 1940s under Vargas. Moreover, even as Candomblé leaders and followers openly marked their ethnic difference by adhering to African cultural practices, they did not face the sorts of accusations of separatism that their southeastern counterparts did. In large part, this was because their organizations were defined not in terms of race but of African culture and religion—the sorts of traits mainstream thinkers deemed acceptable objects of celebration since the 1930s. Yet if, in contrast to Paulistano and Carioca black writers, Bahian Candomblé leaders did not explicitly comment on political democracy, racial democracy, antiracist social science, or the political and cultural winds of change sweeping the African continent, they nonetheless took advantage of these very same transformations to define Brazil's African traditions in ways that raised the visibility, legitimacy, and prestige of their religion and their specific *terreiros*.

The Best of Times, the Worst of Times: Brazil, 1950–1964

All of these strategies evolved in the years between 1950 and 1964, as Brazil's political democracy broadened with successive populist and reformist governments. Though the government of General Eurico Dutra (1946–51) ushered in the first democratic reforms, changes were initially gradual and cautious. The electorate, though greatly expanded since the Republic, was still restricted to less than half the population in 1945. And despite democracy's theoretical protection of a wide range of political organizations, Dutra had outlawed the Communist Party and purged suspected leftists from Brazil's labor unions early in his term. But the return of a reformed Getúlio Vargas to the presidency (from 1951 until his suicide in 1954) buttressed the power of the *povo*, particularly urban union workers and the PTB, making them increasingly important actors in Brazilian politics over the coming years.

The pace of social and economic change quickened in the late 1950s. Between 1956 and 1961, President Juscelino Kubitschek embarked Brazil on a massive government-sponsored program of economic modernization that yielded mixed results. Its successful stimulus of industry (particularly in and around the cities of the Center-South), and its bold programs of infrastructure development and urban construction (foremost among them, the inauguration of a modernist new capital in Brasília in 1960), created new jobs in these growth sectors and instilled optimism among many about Brazil's ability to become a modern, developed nation. At the same time, however, modernization increased income disparities among Brazilians. It primarily benefited those employed in boom sectors and widened the economic gap between urban, industrial regions (the Center-South) and rural ones (especially the Northeast). By 1961, following the resignation of Jânio Quadros from his brief stint as president that year, Vargas's former minister of labor, João Goulart, took the reins of government. From 1961 to 1964, Goulart presided over an increasingly mobilized and polarized polity, as labor and the left multiplied and radicalized their demands while conservatives and the military watched apprehensively. Though Goulart would not remain long in power, his populist style and increasingly left-leaning rhetoric responded to many Brazilians' heightened expectations for economic prosperity and political participation. Since 1945, Brazil's electorate had grown from 5.9 million voters (with a 16% registration rate) to 11.7 million in the 1960 election (with a 25% registration rate).[4]

The democratic reforms and economic growth of the 1950s and 1960s afforded new opportunities for some Brazilians of color, particularly in south-central cities like Rio de Janeiro and São Paulo. The census of 1960 did not collect data on race, and there was no census the following decade. But Carlos Hasenbalg's study of national household surveys from 1976 shows marked improvements for Brazilians of color since the census of 1950, improvements he attributes primarily to the reforms of the 1950s and especially early 1960s. Literacy rates for *pretos* and *pardos*, for instance, more than doubled from a national average of 25.7 percent in 1950 to 59.8 percent in 1976. This advanced one of black intellectuals' principal goals during the Second Republic, since literacy was a basic requirement for voting. In the same period, Brazilians of color maintained their relative participation as industrial workers and increased their participation in the areas of commerce, transportation, and communication. In areas in which Brazilians of color had been almost entirely absent in 1950—such as the professions, banking, real estate, education, and health—rates of employment for nonwhite Brazilians grew faster than for their white counterparts.[5]

Yet the populist and centrist economic reforms of this period—focused primarily on alleviating class inequalities—failed to fully address disparities and discrimination due specifically to race. Though economic growth and the rise in educational opportunities for people of color allowed for their greater participation in national life as producers or as voters, they remained disproportionately excluded from the benefits of Brazil's growth. Despite the rise in literacy for Brazilians of color, for example, improvements in access to education between 1950 and 1976 dropped off sharply at the level of high school and college. Literacy rates were much lower for rural areas, where much of Brazil's nonwhite population was concentrated, than for urban ones.[6] Indeed, by analyzing Brazilian development in the 1950s and 1960s, a new generation of sociologists in the 1970s, like Hasenbalg himself, would demonstrate the extent to which industrial capitalist development reinscribed racial differences even as it created some new opportunities for social mobility.[7] According to these thinkers, the unequal status of nonwhite Brazilians was not a holdover from slavery, destined to disappear with the maturation of a class society (as Florestan Fernandes had argued), nor, as many other scholars affiliated with the midcentury UNESCO studies maintained, was the ongoing marginalization of people of color due primarily to class rather than racial inequality. Rather, it was the persistence and generational reproduction of specifically race-based discrimination, in addition to class-based inequality, that kept people of color from participating equally in the growth of the 1950s and 1960s. This was precisely the point that black thinkers themselves insisted on as they lived through these years of intense political, social, and economic transformation.

The symbolic dimensions of black incorporation into national life also shifted over the course of these decades, particularly under the reformist governments of Quadros and Goulart in the early 1960s. During their administrations, the rhetoric of a Brazilian racial democracy reached new heights of institutionalization and international visibility, and took on new contours. As these leaders sought to reposition Brazil on the world stage as a bridge between First and Third World nations, particularly Africa, they would make racial democracy a central component of Brazil's foreign policy. Specifically, they would incorporate into official discourses many of the newer ideas about African cultural purity that emerged from interactions between Bahia's Candomblé leaders and social scientists in the 1940s and 1950s. In the early 1960s, as Brazil's Foreign Ministry sought to present Brazil to its new African diplomatic partners as an Africanized nation, this vision of Bahia's undiluted African culture increasingly disputed the spotlight with older iterations of racial democracy based on cultural mixture. Like other major transformations in this period, this shift opened some doors for black intellectuals seeking to claim inclusion as black or African Brazilians, even as it silently closed off others.

"Racism pure and simple"

Perhaps because of the particularly stark racial discrimination that had historically prevailed in São Paulo, black thinkers in that city found themselves fending off accusations of *racismo às avessas*, or reverse discrimination, almost as soon as they reentered the public sphere in 1945. Appealing to the prevailing national mood, Raul Joviano do Amaral, writing for São Paulo's *Alvorada* in October 1945, attempted to head off accusations of racial separatism by casting black activist organizations as useful components of a pluralistic, democratic society. "As a minority—and a minority situated at the bottom of the social pyramid—[*negros*] cannot constitute a 'danger' and do not wish to exchange one form of prejudice for another. What the community wants is to educate itself, instruct itself, working democratically to form an integral part of Brazilian society, as is justly their due."[8] While making this defensive appeal to democracy, however, Amaral did not hesitate to call out accusations of reverse racism for what they were: repressive uses of racial democracy intended to deny racism and silence black claims for redress. "Each time that blacks begin to escape their somnolence, the most absurd and outlandish invectives are raised against them. And—as in earlier days—the well-worn arguments rear their heads: 'Blacks don't have a problem,' 'We are a people who do not have racial prejudices,' 'We do not have barriers based on color.'"[9] In August 1947 another article in *Alvorada* denounced allegations of reverse racism as "a ridiculous concept" that arose as a direct response to the reemergence of black activism in São Paulo after 1945. "All other groups have a right to deal with their problems. Except for blacks. When the black man lifts his head, he is immediately singled out as aggressive."[10] By 1954 an article by veteran black journalist José Correia Leite lamented the effectiveness of such accusations in cowing some black leaders into inaction: "With the escape valve of not being racist," he wrote, some black leaders "preach inertia [and] cowardice."[11]

Against this backdrop, writers in São Paulo's black press set out to disprove prevailing assertions that Brazil was free of racism and that blacks faced no "specific" problems based on their race. As early as 1945, *Alvorada*'s Amaral attempted to "debunk the false supposition that blacks do not have their own issues within the broader human problems . . . of the Brazilian community."[12] And in March 1947 Leite responded to the barring of African American scholar Irene Diggs from a Rio hotel on account of her race by inverting the traditionally flattering comparison between Brazil and the United States. "There [in the United States], blacks are imposing their progress; and here, we are being swallowed by the sentimental lie that in Brazil there is no prejudice. But in fact [Brazil] continues to be a vast slave quarters, with just a few blacks in the Big House."[13] Leite's use of "slave quarters" and "Big House" (*senzala* and *casa-grande*) directly referenced Gilberto Freyre's famous work, widely credited with popularizing the idea that Brazil was free of racism. By using these terms to draw attention to Brazil's racial separation rather than to its history of mixture and conviviality, Leite took aim at one of the most sacred pillars of mainstream celebrations of racial democracy. Denunciations such as these continued into subsequent decades, revealing waning enthusiasm among São Paulo's black thinkers for the promises of racial democracy.[14]

Paulistano black writers in the postwar period were no less critical, when they felt it necessary, of the new sociological consensus around Brazil's race relations. Although many black thinkers after 1945 celebrated the shift from anthropological to sociological perspectives on race, they objected forcefully to the new sociology when it denied the independent power of race and racism in Brazilian social relations, and when it threatened black people's rights to racial activism. As we saw in chapter 4, many of the sociological studies of the 1940s and 1950s, especially those sponsored by the UNESCO, contributed to upholding class, and not race, as the main category for understanding black and brown Brazilians' comparably lower social status. Even Florestan Fernandes, whose studies of São Paulo made the clearest case for the continued existence of racial prejudice, portrayed prejudice as a remnant of slavery, preserved in Brazil's incomplete transition to capitalism. The solution, sociologists generally concluded, was to speed Brazil's process of modernization and incorporate the sectors that had been left behind.

Although the sociologists working on race at midcentury were avowed antiracists who often had friendly relations with black intellectuals, such conclusions particularly rankled writers in São Paulo's black press. As residents of a majority white city in which members of a black minority were frequently treated with hostility regardless of their wealth, connections, or learning, several of São Paulo's black writers reacted energetically against the demotion of race as an independent factor in explanations of (and potential solutions to) black marginalization. In June 1947 Amaral inveighed against "the profoundly mistaken thesis that color prejudice proper does not exist in Brazil, but that it is dislocated onto a class prejudice that affects all nonelite sectors of the population." Perhaps, Amaral admitted, this could be true of some regions of the nation, such as the Northeast, where people of color were in the majority, making class and racial discrimination more difficult to disentangle. But "from the middle of Brazil to the South, what there is—let's have the courage to admit it—is racism pure and simple, fascist discrimination, race prejudice."[15] He noted that it was common knowledge that a poor but well-dressed white person could break through class prejudice, while no amount of sartorial magic could guarantee a black person equal treatment. In the direct style that prevailed in São Paulo's postwar black press, Amaral tried to preserve the ideal of a "true" racial democracy by calling out the failures of its particular incarnation in his time: "Any conscientious analyst who spends the necessary time will see that our democracy, this Brazilian racial democracy, is a tremendous failure, an advertisement put up *para inglês ver*."[16] "*Para inglês ver*," literally "for the English to see," is a Brazilian expression meaning "for show," or "for public consumption." It dates back to the mid-1830s when Brazilian elites, having signed a treaty with Britain agreeing to end the slave trade, developed a series of public practices "for the English to see" that disguised their continued involvement in the trade. In Amaral's usage, it provides one of the earliest critiques by black thinkers of Brazil's racial democracy as window dressing, a public veneer constructed specifically for the consumption of foreign researchers and the international community.

Perhaps as much as it reveals the specific workings of race in São Paulo, Amaral's line of argument sheds light on the particular class position from which that city's black journalists viewed the line between class and racial prejudice. Because they were not members of the vast working class but shared in the educational and employment opportunities of a modest middle class, they had a privileged view of how race in particular operated to keep blacks out of certain social spaces. At the same time, their focus on racial prejudice might have led them to underestimate the role of extreme economic exclusion in the lives of most Paulistanos of African descent—something sociologists like Florestan Fernandes made central to their analyses.

The second aspect of Paulistano black writers' critique of sociology and of social science more broadly had to do with these disciplines' potential effects on black activism. Black thinkers were aware of the power sociology enjoyed at midcentury and of sociologists' own belief in their ability to impel social change in Brazil. Indeed, this potential to bring about concrete social change led many black writers to celebrate what they saw as the triumph of sociology over anthropology in the literature of race in Brazil. Yet sociologists' notion of what would transform society did not always match up with black activists' political projects. Many scholars of race relations in this period, like Luiz de Aguiar Costa Pinto or Thales de Azevedo, were critical of specifically black social and political organizations, pointing out their limited appeal among most Brazilians of color. Costa Pinto, in his study of Rio de Janeiro, argued that since most blacks were proletarians, they should (as many in fact did) pursue solutions as a class rather than as a race, demanding the benefits of economic modernization through institutions like parties and labor unions.[17]

These arguments were often articulated by well-meaning social scientists who sought to balance their desire to improve conditions for Brazilians of color with their faith in the uniqueness of a Brazilian identity based on racial mixture and integration. Arthur Ramos, whom São Paulo's and Rio's black writers treated as an ally and saw as an exemplar of academic engagement with black movements, disappointed several black intellectuals when asked in an interview with *Senzala* in 1946 what he thought about the recent Black Brazilian National Convention. Ramos responded with an attempt to contain black activism within boundaries consistent with the idea of *mestiçagem*. No one ethnic group, he implied, could have exclusive grievances: "I am in full agreement with the courageous and timely declarations of the Convention, especially insofar as these demands do not entail the danger of forming *ethnic cysts*, with the intransigent positing of an exclusive 'black question,' which would invert the terms of the problem. Very wisely, the Convention demands the rights of blacks alongside those of other ethnic groups, on equal footing."[18] The use of the term *ethnic cysts* dates back to the 1910s and 1920s, when some nationalist ideologues argued for closing Brazil's borders to foreigners from regions, ethnic groups, or religions deemed difficult to assimilate.[19] In 1923, congressional deputy Fidelis Reis had used the phrase "cysts" in the "national organism" to describe potential black migrants from the United States in his anti-immigration bill, which had led black writers like Theophilo Camargo to fear that Brazilians of color would soon also be seen as unwelcome foreigners. Ramos's use of "ethnic cysts" in relation to black Brazilians not only revealed his discomfort with race-based organizing but also (however unwittingly) raised the specter of foreignness that had dogged black writers in São Paulo since the early decades of the century. Wary of this connotation, writers in São Paulo's black press were quick to describe themselves as long-standing Brazilians. In their inaugural issue, several months after Ramos's interview, *Novo Horizonte*'s editors argued that "our demands, as well as our calls for blacks' moral and intellectual uplift, can in no way be seen through the erroneous prism of 'cysts' disturbing the nation's harmony. We simply want to claim what belongs to us. We want to enjoy our rights as Brazilian citizens . . . always and forever."[20]

In order for academic research on race to be helpful to their cause, many Paulistano black writers believed, it had to be accompanied by independent black organizing that would result in intellectual, moral, and material uplift. In 1947 Leite called for sociologists, many of whom were his frequent interlocutors, to "substantiate" their studies of race "in the solution of our problems, searching for ways of bringing about our organization."[21] In a 1960 article looking back on "Brazilian Black Studies," Leite admitted to disappointment with the extent to which the social scientific studies of the previous decades had achieved this goal. "It is difficult to see . . . what exists in them that is positive, in terms of concrete solutions to [black] problems, given the importance that that subject represents in the field of social sciences."[22] The modernization projects that sociologists favored, and which influenced state policy in the 1950s with mixed results for Brazilians of color, did not count as "concrete solutions" in Leite's formulation. For a man long concerned with building distinctly black social organizations, studies that did not directly advance that cause by highlighting the problem of discrimination and the need for race-based organizing ultimately addressed the problem of race at an unsatisfactorily abstract level. Leite's colleague Amaral foresaw this problem as early as 1945, at a time when many black thinkers eagerly embraced the symbolic new terms through which social scientific studies of race configured black citizenship. He worried that the increasingly open celebration of black and African contributions to Brazil in intellectual works would come to stand in for, or even discourage, actual black activism.

> The black community must not feel satisfied by the academic—and merely academic—recognition bestowed on it by our greatest sociologists, musicians, poets, historians, journalists, etc., as they speak of the magnanimous and constructive effort our race exerted in the past, contributing to solidifying the foundations of Brazil's greatness. It is painful to note that this recognition of blacks' role in the formation of our nationality, their much vaunted contributions, has created an artificial *climate*, to the extent that today, blacks are presented under the false guise of living happy, satisfied, and unpreoccupied.[23]

São Paulo's black writers had long made symbolic inclusion "in the formation of [Brazil's] nationality" central to their politics. Yet over the course of the Second Republic, even veteran thinkers like Leite came to distrust mainstream Brazilian intellectuals' celebrations of blacks' contributions, seeing this rhetoric as a poor substitute for sustained attention to specifically racial problems.

Although these polemics highlight the contrast between left-leaning sociologists, who largely saw the solution to black disadvantage in class-based strategies for social transformation, and black intellectuals, who focused on the primarily racial exclusions they experienced as members of a middle class, the dividing lines between race and class were not always so clear in practice. Some Paulistano black thinkers active in race-based organizations and newspapers nonetheless sought to place the issue of racial equality within a broader context of class struggle. Sofia Campos Teixeira, Luiz Lobato (founder of the Marxist Clube Jabaquara), Francisco Lucrécio (a former Frente Negra leader), and Geraldo Campos de Oliveira (an editor of *Senzala* and contributor to several other postwar black newspapers), for instance, were all active in the Socialist Party.[24] Indeed, when Geraldo Oliveira ran for office in São Paulo's state legislature as a socialist in 1950, the black paper *Mundo Novo* published an article by a group of black university students involved in Oliveira's campaign that outlined his and his supporters' stance on race. "Black man," the article proclaimed, "the solution to your racial problem depends on the solution of your problem as a worker in the capitalist system. The class struggle is greater than the color struggle."[25]

Adopting the class analyses of the labor movement and Socialist Party did not, however, mean passively accepting the notion that there were no *negros* in Brazil or that race was insignificant to their suffering. Though Armando de Castro, *Mundo Novo*'s editor and an avid supporter of Oliveira's candidacy, pronounced himself against "the racism of some blacks tormented by injustice and continued humiliations" (by which he presumably meant the tendency of some black thinkers to foreground race in their political struggles), he also considered it "urgent" to combat "the negation of race prejudice by whites."[26] The Marxist Luiz Lobato spent part of the 1950s as a contributor to the Rio newspaper *Vanguarda Socialista*, from which he criticized what he saw as the narrow politics of *negro* newspapers and organizations like Leite's.[27] Yet in the late 1950s, when he took on the editorship of a small black newspaper in Santos (a port city in São Paulo state with a history of strong ties between black organizations like the Frente Negra and the Socialist Party), he also highlighted the importance of race in the broader question of class struggle. "We are not a racist newspaper. . . . Yet no reasonable person can deny certain peculiarities intrinsic to *negros* and that only we *negros* can understand."[28] In the context of accusations that specifically black organizations represented separatism, situating the racial problem in a broader popular or class context thus provided some self-identified *negros* with an alternative. Though the Left had historically placed its own rhetorical limits on the possibilities for independent *negro* struggles, these limits were as open to negotiation as those imposed by nationalist Brazilian discourses of racial harmony.

Whether they favored race-based organizing or thought of themselves as *negro* members of a multiracial working class, most black Paulistano writers' ideas about race and politics during the Second Republic resembled the "two races" approach that dominated celebrations of the Mãe Preta in the Paulista black press of the 1920s, and which had continued to shape black politics in São Paulo in the intervening decades. As in earlier years, black intellectuals in midcentury São Paulo used the term *negro* as a unified racial category, inclusive of both *pretos* and *pardos* and aimed at drawing a clear distinction between whites and nonwhites. They distrusted the notion of *mestiçagem* when it was deployed in ways that undermined a distinct and unified *negro* identity or encouraged whitening. The Paulistano black press's close attention to the individual and collective gains of African Americans in this period, which I explored in chapter 4, is consistent with this binary view of race. Specifically, black Paulistano writers who compared Brazil to the United States openly admired their North American counterparts' tendency to preserve their "black" identities despite their social and economic successes, and lamented the fact that in Brazil, any high-achieving person of color would immediately be called "mulatto" or "white."[29] Moreover, the overwhelming presence of references to the United States in São Paulo's black press for much of the postwar period, at the expense of earlier references to Africa, suggests writers' desire to prove their credentials as Brazilians different only in race, not in culture or ethnicity.

Once again, the particularities of the regional context in which these thinkers operated played a central role in shaping their views of race and racial activism. Not only did they live in a city they perceived as sharply divided between a white majority and a *preto* minority (despite São Paulo's significant ethnic diversity and its growing population of nonwhite immigrants from the nation's Northeast), but they also lived in a city whose political and intellectual leadership vigorously resisted the messages of racial and cultural mixture broadcast from Rio de Janeiro since the 1930s. Even as official formulations of Brazilian culture and national identity increasingly embraced an African heritage after the end of the First Republic, São Paulo's intellectual, cultural, and political elites continued to present their state as primarily European and unmarked by a history of black slave labor. These images of a white, modern, culturally superior São Paulo had flared up during the 1932 Constitutionalist revolt against Getúlio Vargas's central government, which insurgent Paulistas had tarred as a *dictanegra*, or black dictatorship. Similar images resurfaced in 1954, during celebrations for the fourth centennial of the founding of the city of São Paulo. To mark the occasion, the city's major newspapers issued massive commemorative editions honoring São Paulo's history, particularly its *bandeirante* past. Alongside extensive historical articles, full-page advertisements depicted *bandeirantes* (the leaders of the prospecting and Indian slave-raiding expeditions traditionally considered the state's pioneers) in the company of Jesuit priests and native Brazilians, evoking episodes from the city's foundation and its inhabitants' early and intrepid exploration of the hinterlands. As during the Constitutionalist uprising of 1932, these histories and advertisements portrayed São Paulo City as the spearhead of the nation's industrialization and whitened modernity.[30]

Whereas the copious historical articles in these special editions predictably celebrated European immigrants' contributions to the city's grandeur (and even made positive if brief mention of Japanese and Syrio-Lebanese communities), they made almost no mention of slaves, black migrants, or black contributions to the city's history.[31] Particularly galling to black thinkers in the state with the largest black press in the nation must have been the *Estado de São Paulo*'s article, "127 Years of a Paulista Press," which ignored half a century of black newspapers.[32] The only images of black Paulistas in these papers were as soccer players, or as occasional subjects of the works of the state's much celebrated modernist painters, the Italian-descended Cândido Portinari and Emiliano di Cavalcanti.[33] To *negro* observers like Leite, blacks' absence from celebrations of the city's history "while *colônias* of foreigners appeared as those responsible for [its] development and progress" was lamentable proof of local elites' ongoing "Aryanist" and "prowhitening" views.[34] As voices of a discriminated minority in a city that all but erased them from its history and asserted a white(ned) past, Paulistano black writers of the 1940s and 1950s, like their counterparts in earlier decades, found little of use in "national" discussions of racial mixture, and they continued to propose a vision of Brazil as primarily marked by the cleavage between a black and a white race.

It might seem odd that in this atmosphere celebrating São Paulo's white heritage members of the city's black community finally got the tribute they had once so ardently demanded: a statue to the Mãe Preta, and in their very own city. After it died a quiet death in late 1920s Rio, the monument project was revived in the postwar years by members of the Clube 220, a black social club in São Paulo. Under the leadership of Frederico Penteado Júnior, and with the help of representative Elias Shammas, a Brazilian of Lebanese descent, the Clube 220's monument commission was able to usher the project through the São Paulo city legislature in 1953, successfully overriding a veto by the city's mayor, Jânio Quadros. Perhaps Shammas, like the members of the Syrio-Lebanese community who built a monumental statement of their identity as ethnic Brazilians in the early 1920s, saw the importance of the Mãe Preta monument for a black community intent on celebrating its distinct contributions, in a way that Quadros, a white (adoptive) Paulistano, did not. In any case, by 1955, following a public contest, the winning design for the long-desired Mãe Preta monument was unveiled in the Largo do Paissandú, a

Statue of the Mãe Preta (1955), in Largo do Paissandú, downtown São Paulo. Photograph by the author.

small square that was also home to São Paulo's oldest historically black religious brotherhood, Nossa Senhora do Rosário dos Homens Pretos.[35] After repeatedly petitioning the quadricentennial planning commission, Penteado even managed to obtain official recognition for the monument unveiling as part of São Paulo's year-long celebrations.[36]

We might expect Leite, of all people, to have greeted this much-anticipated development with joy. Yet the statue, a central goal for black thinkers in earlier decades, failed to impress Leite and his fellow Paulistano black thinkers in the mid-1950s. Perhaps this was because, as Leite recalled in his memoirs, the monument portrayed the Mãe Preta in an exaggerated realist idiom (blunt, squarish features, oversized hands and feet), which he found insulting to black Brazilians: "If she had been white, they would never have permitted an artist to create a figure as deformed as that. . . . Why design such a grotesque *negra*, when everyone knows that a *negra* like that, with such big feet, would never have been selected to suckle the child of the master?"[37] More important, however, the fact that the monument failed to garner the sympathies (indeed the notice) of writers in the black press illustrates how much had changed in the strategies and priorities of black writers since the 1920s. The statue represented an older political strategy celebrating an idealized and sentimentalized racial fraternity, which, Leite and others now believed, made blacks into supplicants rather than agents of change. To thinkers like Leite, Penteado and the men of the Clube 220 were a lamentable reminder of this older sort of politics and of the rifts that still plagued the city's black movement. The Clube 220 spent its energies on social events like beauty pageants or 13 May celebrations at a time when writers in the black press were calling for political engagement and formulating ever sharper denunciations of the failures of abolition and the shortcomings of official histories. (Leite recalled that Clube 220 members, for their part, derisively called him and his colleagues communists.)[38] Perhaps, in the end, the black press's silence on this otherwise remarkable achievement is telling of contemporary Paulistano thinkers' growing disillusionment with the ways that ideas of racial democracy, at least in São Paulo, ultimately reinforced long-standing ideals of whiteness.

Particular Values

In the years after 1945, the problem of fighting discrimination and highlighting the specific problems of *negros* while avoiding accusations of reverse racism weighed heavily on black thinkers in the city of Rio de Janeiro as well. Perhaps with even more frequency than in São Paulo, in Rio de Janeiro several prominent *negros* involved in the struggle against racial discrimination dealt with this dual burden by couching their racial claims in broader struggles for social equality, in social and cultural organizations or left-wing parties. The Constituent Assembly's 1946 discussions on the possible inclusion of an antidiscrimination clause in the Constitution provide an early opportunity to glimpse this alternative perspective, and to understand why some black thinkers adopted it. When, in 1946, Senator Hamilton Nogueira first presented the Black National Convention's demands that the article declaring all Brazilians "equal before the law" include the specification "without distinction of race or color," he encountered opposition from other legislators who believed the clause was redundant. Congressman Jurandir Pires, for instance, argued that since people of color (whom he called "mestiços," reflecting his adoption of prevailing nationalist ideologies) were Brazilians, there was no need to further specify their rights to equality. Others, like Eduardo Duvivier, claimed that such an amendment would be necessary only "if there were any racial issue among us." But such an affirmative stance on race, he implied, made no sense in a nation with no past history of racial struggles. Still others contended that the law was entirely the wrong place to fight racial discrimination—this was more properly an issue of "morality and good education," a question for private citizens. These discussions reveal how the emerging consensus about Brazil's racial harmony, buttressed by the postwar discourse of racial democracy, could restrain affirmative efforts in favor of people of color.

In this context, Claudino José da Silva, a black representative for the Brazilian Communist Party from the state of Rio de Janeiro, took a third position. He agreed with Nogueira (and, implicitly, with the members of the Black National Convention) that the antidiscrimination clause should be included in the Constitution to defend against frequent acts of prejudice. "When people of color try to enter some institutions of higher learning, they are not granted that right, and have no recourse, for lack of an explicit law in the Constitution." But, he explained to Nogueira, "I find Your Excellency's proposed amendment to be restrictive insofar as other social and class problems are concerned." Silva did not deny race prejudice, but as a Communist, he believed it to be part of a broader pattern of oppression against poor and working-class Brazilians, something the new antidiscrimination clause should also address.[39] In taking this stance, Claudino da Silva prefigured the concerns of the leaders of Rio's União dos Homens de Cor, who only a few years later began their Christian charitable activities in favor of not just black Brazilians but Rio's poor and dispossessed more generally.

The *negro* poet and theater director Solano Trinidade, a fellow Communist Party member and a defender of black cultural traditions, took a similar position in the 1940s and 1950s.[40] Trinidade was born in Recife (the capital of the northeastern state of Pernambuco) in 1908, the son of a cobbler and a street vendor. As a young man, Trinidade became deeply interested in Afro-Brazilian culture, particularly religious traditions like Candomblé, at a time when these themes became central to northeastern literary and academic production. He attended Freyre's 1934 Afro-Brazilian Congress in Recife and subsequently founded his own Center for Afro-Brazilian Culture in that city. Yet Trinidade was also closely involved with the sorts of black politics coming out of Brazil's South in the 1930s—at the age of twenty-six, he became one of the founding members of Recife's Frente Negra chapter (likely a small group similar to the one in Bahia). In the early 1940s, Trinidade and his family moved to Rio de Janeiro, where he obtained a modest but stable post at a census bureau. His interest in black culture and politics led him to collaborate with the Teatro Experimental do Negro on several occasions, as in his direction of a *maracatú* (an Afro-Brazilian dance) at the Teatro Folclórico Brasileiro (an offshoot of the TEN) and his poetry readings sponsored by *Quilombo*, the TEN's publication.[41] Yet poems such as his 1958 "Negros" made it clear that his commitment to racial issues was secondary to a broader fight against economic exploitation: "Blacks who enslave / and sell Blacks in Africa / are not my brothers / Black bosses in America / in the service of capital / are not my brothers / Black oppressors / in whatever part of the world / are not my brothers / Only oppressed Blacks / enslaved / struggling for freedom / are my brothers."[42] This perspective not only marked Trinidade's difference with Paulistano writers who admired successful black "race men" in the United States but often put him at odds with his friend and colleague Abdias do Nascimento, whose black theater not only was an explicitly race-based organization but also was committed to promoting black culture through erudite rather than popular means. For Trinidade, the TEN was guilty of what he saw as the failings of Brazilian theater more generally: "the *povo*, the workers don't go to the theater because they don't understand its language" or its overly intellectual, bourgeois themes.[43] When Trinidade created his own activist Teatro Popular Brasileiro in the late 1950s, it reflected his working-class sensibilities. It was not, like Nascimento's, an "experimental" theater with a strong academic component but a theater that focused on portraying aspects of black Brazilian culture as part of the culture of a broader Brazilian *povo*.[44]

Black leftists' critique of black organizations' middle class and "narrowly" racial outlook seems to have been sharper in Rio de Janeiro, where, especially in the postwar period, people of color were somewhat better integrated into the city's economic and social life, than it was in São Paulo, where black thinkers were a smaller, more embattled group. In Rio in particular, leftist critiques of black organizations—primarily the TEN—turned on not just questions of class versus race but the issue of elitism. For men like Solano Trinidade, the TEN's cerebral Eugene O'Neill plays and erudite academic congresses were misguided in a city where black popular culture (samba, carnival, or Macumba) was so rich and widespread. For the leaders of the União dos Homens de Cor, the TEN's focus on theater was misplaced in a city where the real-life drama of poverty made food, jobs, housing, and basic literacy far more pressing concerns. Yet precisely because of its leaders' high-culture intellectual tendencies and its successful links with powerful mainstream intellectuals and politicians, the TEN became the most visible of Rio's postwar black activist organizations, and it left behind the most prolific written record of its activities.

This fame and visibility, however, had its drawbacks. As the leading explicitly black organization in Rio de Janeiro—a city with a history of few such groups, and a place that symbolized the nation's purported racial mixture and harmony—the TEN bore the brunt of contemporary accusations of reverse racism. Like their counterparts in São Paulo, black intellectuals at the TEN used their journal *Quilombo* (and, unlike black Paulistanos, occasional contributions to the mainstream press) to counter these accusations and to debunk the notion that Brazil's commitment to racial democracy made racism a nonissue. But though the TEN, as one of the few explicitly *negro* groups in Rio, was in many ways the black organization most similar to the race-based groups prevalent in São Paulo in the postwar years, its leaders' political strategies set it apart from its peers in the Paulista capital. In particular, the TEN's leaders sought to avoid the combativeness that characterized their Paulistano counterparts' approach to fighting racism and advocated instead a more strategic, indirect course of action. In his inaugural speech for the Black National Conference of 1949, Abdias do Nascimento contrasted the TEN with other leading black associations, past and present (most of which were based in São Paulo). Though he expressed his respect for the latter's goals, he concluded that most had "failed precisely for lacking what we might call a sociological attitude," or a second-order tactical approach. "They were born of revolt and organized themselves only to fight—directly and immediately—against injustice and racial discrimination." Yet this confrontational style had only "aggravated . . . the problem" by leaving them vulnerable to accusations of reverse racism.[45] In a later issue of *Quilombo*, writer Péricles Leal elaborated on Nascimento's point, explaining why a method of "direct struggle" had always been, and would continue to be, "unfruitful." Leal shared with contemporary Paulistano black writers the frustrations of attempting to point out ongoing racial discrimination in a society many blithely declared to be a full-fledged racial democracy.

> The black problem in Brazil is one of the most complex that ever was. Simply because, from the start, we are faced with a paradox: *there exists and does not exist a problem for our people of color!* It exists because it has been showing its obscene face in several places, manifesting itself in various guises, in small things that together form a whole. . . . And it does not exist because there is no law that discriminates [against blacks], nothing printed in this respect and, to all appearances, any man, as long as he is a born Brazilian, has all rights.

Precisely because racism was so slippery, Leal believed that openly calling it out would only hurt black thinkers' cause: "A direct struggle would be scarcely recommendable, and should even be condemned, since those attacks could be used against the attacker, and since there is nothing written that can prove—prove, it must be noted—the existence of such barriers."[46]

Rather than expending their energies on trying to prove the existence of racial discrimination, TEN leaders Nascimento and Guerreiro Ramos developed a multifaceted, "sociological" approach to activism, designed to integrate people of color more thoroughly into Brazilian society, while making Brazilian society itself more inclusive of black people and cultures. Their view of theater as a "generic methodology for the treatment of racial questions"[47] exemplifies this outlook. By placing blacks in leading theatrical roles, allowing them to occupy the position of a universal "everyman" despite their race, Nascimento and Guerreiro Ramos hoped to create positive experiences for black actors as well as positive role models for black audience members. In dealing with racial questions explicitly in its plays, the TEN hoped to educate white and black audiences about racial integration while producing a "catharsis" of racial tensions. In addition to staging plays, the TEN ran a series of theatrical workshops, literacy classes, group therapy sessions, and black beauty pageants, often coordinated through their Instituto Nacional do Negro (Black National Institute), which was devoted to research and pedagogy on black issues. Much of this work aimed to train people of color "in the behavioral styles of the most elevated classes in this country," thereby improving their chances for upward mobility.[48] TEN leaders also sought to create articulations between the black community that was their base and the white elites with whom they had developed extensive connections. Through their guest contributors to *Quilombo* (as in the column "Democracia racial"), their political contacts (like Senator Nogueira), their theatrical events (which brought "humble domestic and factory workers to the greatest theater in Brazil" alongside "Rio's highest society"),[49] and their momentous intellectual congresses (like the Black Brazilian Congress of 1950, which brought together black and white intellectuals), the TEN sought to insinuate the themes of antiracism and black culture into the mainstream of Brazilian public life—all "without aggressiveness."[50] These activities fulfilled the TEN's commitment to fight "color and race discrimination in Brazil" not by attacking "those who deny our rights" but by "motivating blacks themselves to remember or acquaint themselves with their rights to life and culture."[51]

In part, TEN leaders took this approach in the hopes of distinguishing their group from both confrontational race-based organizations and revolutionary leftists. "Do not confuse us with them. . . . Do not see us through a stereotype," urged Nascimento in an article for the daily *Folha do Rio*, his response to *O Globo*'s accusations of reverse racism. "Get to know us first, and define us later. Our movement is not a protest: it is an affirmation. It is inspired not by class struggle, but by the idea of cooperation. Its motto is not segregation but unification."[52] But this approach also reflected the personal backgrounds and evolving philosophies of race of the TEN's leaders. For sociologist Alberto Guerreiro Ramos, the commitment to improving the situation of people of color through nonconfrontational strategies and cross-cultural, interracial interactions echoed his own intellectual trajectory as a former Integralist and Catholic activist, long suspicious of explicitly race-based organizations.[53] Guerreiro Ramos, a light-skinned Bahian *pardo* who rose to academic prominence from a poor background, believed that region, class, and culture, and not just race or color, were important factors in understanding Brazil's "black problem." Though he overcame his reluctance to engage in explicitly *negro* politics by the late 1940s when he joined the TEN (a move historian Marcos Chor Maio interprets partially as a result of his desire to increase his professional visibility as a sociologist of race), Guerreiro Ramos maintained an integrationist approach to racial politics, explicitly contrasting Brazil's situation to the black/white polarization of the United States.[54] Guerreiro Ramos saw blacks not as a distinct race but as the *povo* or people—a vision common among black thinkers and activists in Rio at midcentury[55] and perhaps, too, one influenced by Guerreiro Ramos's experience in his native Bahia (a city with a majority black and brown population). For Abdias do Nascimento, personal, intellectual, and regional trajectories also appear to have led him to choose a method of "indirect attack" that was engaged with, rather than pitted against, a broader white mainstream. As we saw in chapter 4, Nascimento recalled noticing a significant difference in the 1930s and 1940s between assertive, explicitly political black organizations in São Paulo and the culturally based organizations of Rio de Janeiro, which were not separate but integrated into the popular and high culture of the city. It is possible that Nascimento's idea for a "sociological" approach to activism in the TEN mirrored his personal attempts to mediate between the cultures of black activism in these two cities, leaving behind confrontational methods (like the public fistfights for which he had been arrested as a young member of São Paulo's Frente Negra) and adopting a stance better suited to the particular style and parameters of racial activism in Rio.

If, in contrast to Paulistanos' open attacks, the TEN's indirect cultural approach to combating racism reflects the delicate balance of black organizing in a city that prided itself on its racial integration, it also points to the comparably greater avenues for contact between black thinkers and a white political and intellectual elite in Rio de Janeiro. Indeed, the intensity of racism in São Paulo, in contrast to Rio (and much of the rest of the nation), was something contemporary black intellectuals in both cities openly discussed, often comparing patterns of racial discrimination in São Paulo to the extreme black/white polarization they understood to prevail in the United States.[56] By the same token, however, the relatively greater opportunities for political, economic, and educational integration for people of color in Rio de Janeiro help to explain the TEN's relative rarity as an explicitly black organization in that city. Much more widespread and popular in this period, as in earlier decades, were neighborhood sporting or recreational clubs, like the famous Clube Renascença, or organizations like samba schools, which were made up mostly of people of color, and responded to the need and desire for race-specific sociability, but did not make race and antiracist activism explicit conditions of membership.[57] In the case of samba schools, these organizations were closely incorporated into the city's public celebrations and political patronage networks in a way that the TEN was not.

The particular style and parameters of black politics in Rio de Janeiro also shaped how leaders of the TEN criticized the social science consensus they often admired when it worked against their goals as black intellectuals. In São Paulo, many black thinkers objected to social scientific studies on race when they failed to recognize race as a problem independent of class, or when they discouraged independent black organizing as a solution to Brazil's racial problems. Yet Paulistanos like José Correia Leite, long used to conducting their activism on the farthest margins of public life, took pride in the role they had been able to play as informants in the UNESCO studies. In Rio, however, where a handful of people of color were historically able to establish alliances with, or themselves enter the ranks of, the nation's political and intellectual elite, black thinkers expected to be more than just informants. During the Black National Congress of 1950, for instance, sociologist Alberto Guerreiro Ramos called for the UNESCO to host an international congress on race relations in Brazil, in which members of the TEN and other black thinkers would participate as producers of knowledge alongside activists and scholars from around the world. Guerreiro Ramos saw his and other black intellectuals' inclusion in these proposed academic discussions as a key step toward racial justice in Brazil. His hopes for academic parity were dashed, however, when a white scholar, Luiz de Aguiar Costa Pinto, announced that the UNESCO had decided (partly on his own advice) to sponsor a substantially different project—a study of race relations in Rio de Janeiro (part of the broader studies the UNESCO was then conducting across Brazil). Costa Pinto himself, and not any of Rio's black intellectuals, would conduct the study.[58] For Guerreiro Ramos and other TEN members, the difference between the two projects was enormous. Guerreiro Ramos's proposed world congress on race relations would have given black thinkers from the TEN and other nationwide organizations a position as active and equal participants—experts on race relations and narrators of their own experiences—in a prestigious event backed and funded by the United Nations. Studies *about* race relations, carried out by accredited white scholars like Costa Pinto, threatened to treat black activists as raw material—just like the anthropology to which they had previously objected.[59]

Over the course of his earlier research, Costa Pinto had developed close ties with Nascimento and Guerreiro Ramos, participating, as we have seen, in their 1950 Black National Congress. Yet tensions between these intellectuals mounted after 1953, when Costa Pinto completed and published his study, *O negro no Rio de Janeiro*. His book ultimately portrayed the TEN as an elitist organization composed of a tiny black intelligentsia, distant from the masses, and far too focused on black cultural distinctiveness—something Costa Pinto considered harmful to the cause of racial equality, casting blacks as outsiders to the nation rather than as integral parts of a modern class society.[60] Guerreiro Ramos, in yet another demonstration of TEN leaders' access to the mainstream public sphere, responded with an editorial in Rio's *O Jornal* in early 1954, in which he declared that the book confirmed Costa Pinto's sociological "incompetence" and "lack of integrity." Guerreiro Ramos's falling out with Costa Pinto was not primarily over substance. Both shared a critique of studies that emphasized a separate "black problem," or that focused on black folklore or "spectacle" at the expense of structural problems like poverty, unemployment, illiteracy, malnutrition, and so forth.[61] Their confrontation was, instead, about power in intellectual production, about asserting black intellectuals' right to be agents, rather than mere subject matter, in the study of race relations. In Costa Pinto's book, Guerreiro Ramos and other members of Rio's TEN were demoted from engaged, internationally visible black thinkers to a frivolous "black elite" subject to the criticism of a white "expert" on race relations.

In his attack on Costa Pinto in Rio's *O Jornal*, Guerreiro Ramos accused the white scholar of stealing and plagiarizing the papers and proceedings from the 1950 Black National Congress, which had been loaned to him while he prepared his book.[62] The accusation of "plagiarism" was telling: Guerreiro Ramos saw the papers as original intellectual production belonging to black writers, while Costa Pinto saw them as primary source material about black thinkers. Costa Pinto himself, in fact, was quite explicit about the extent to which he considered black intellectuals subject material rather than colleagues. In an earlier article for *O Jornal*, he complained that it was a singular, and not entirely welcome, trait of the social sciences that a researcher could "see how his material, or a part of it, reacts to the conclusions of a study conducted about it. I doubt that there are biologists who, after having studied, say, a microbe, had the opportunity to watch that microbe take up the pen and publish nonsense about the study in which it participated as laboratory material."[63]

This kind of attitude suggested to many black thinkers that the social sciences had not fully internalized their own critique of racism. For Sebastião Rodrigues Alves, a member of the TEN and longtime friend of Abdias do Nascimento, Costa Pinto's derision of black intellectuals suggested that social scientists' fascination with "race relations" was simply self-serving: "Everything leads us to believe that those adventurers have the goal of belittling blacks, and of remaining in their customary position as 'masters.' This industrialization of Afro-Brazilian studies and of race relations is a very profitable pursuit, not only in an economic sense but also in terms of the advancement of the 'scholars' who become owners of the black problem."[64] From 1953 onward, Guerreiro Ramos mounted increasingly visible attacks on sociological studies of race in Brazil, culminating in his 1957 *Introdução à sociologia brasileira*. In this work, he declared that all studies of race in Brazil conducted by white thinkers—from Nina Rodrigues to the UNESCO studies—had in the long run turned black Brazilians into mere subjects of study (what he called "o negro-tema")—"a thing to be examined, looked at, seen, as a mummified or curious creature."[65]

Aside from demanding the right to be producers of social scientific knowledge about race, black intellectuals from Rio's TEN increasingly targeted the idea that integration—put forth by many social scientists as the solution to the so-called black problem—should necessarily mean cultural assimilation. They began to unravel the long-standing presumption that the equality of black people was demonstrated through the acquisition of superior European culture, or of a mixed national culture in which European civilization was dominant. In October 1954, following Guerreiro Ramos's acrimonious exchanges with Costa Pinto, Abdias do Nascimento published his own article in Rio's *O Jornal*, titled "'Deacculturated' Sociology." In it he asked: "Why should we erect whiteness as the only measure of value, as the true ideal of life and the supreme template of beauty? Why should we passively accept the impositions of an erroneous sociology that preaches acculturation as the natural form of the 'solution' to the black problem in Brazil? That racism, disguised by the mystification of science, is the most shocking and subtle form of violence that blacks will face in their struggle *for the survival of their particular values.*"[66]

Like Guerreiro Ramos's sharpest critiques of sociology, Nascimento's accusation of sociology's "racist" requirements for cultural whitening or assimilation came a few years after the final issue of *Quilombo* in 1950. But in terms of ensuring the survival, in the face of assimilation, of blacks' particular cultural values, *Quilombo* had been at the center of the TEN's counterstrategy. Even as it preached integration and upheld mainstream ideas of racial democracy, especially in terms of cultural mixture, *Quilombo* developed a complementary discourse that challenged the idea that black incorporation into the nation meant cultural whitening. In the very first issue of *Quilombo*, Nascimento wrote in defense of blacks' "culture, a culture with African accents and intuitions . . . that is being abandoned, ridiculed by the leaders of 'whitening,' even as those 'aristocrats' forget that ethnic, cultural, religious, and political pluralism is what gives vitality to our national organism, constituting the very blood of democracy."[67] Nascimento cited Gilberto Freyre in support of that assertion, displaying his expertise in the strategies of indirect confrontation. But the measures the TEN deployed to highlight the "African accents" of Brazilian culture also challenged Freyre's sense of a mixed but ultimately whitened Brazilian culture.

In the pages of *Quilombo*, Nascimento and Guerreiro Ramos turned toward African cultural values to mark the distinctiveness, and greatness, of blacks' specific contributions to a plural national culture. Their problem with dominant academic ideas of Brazil's Africanness was not, as for many Paulistano black writers, the suggestion that blacks were bearers of a different African cultural heritage. To the contrary, *Quilombo*'s editors embraced a distinct African heritage; what they objected to was the way both anthropology and sociology presented and defined it. The Africa they turned to was most certainly not the primitive, "museum"-like, anthropological one they frequently worked to discredit. Rather, it was a modern Africa, inspired in the *négritude* literary movement of francophone African writers like Léopold Sédar Senghor, Aimé Césaire, and Léon Damas, with the support of French existentialists like Jean-Paul Sartre and Albert Camus. The *négritude* movement revalued traditional African cultures in a vanguardist framework, positing this cultural heritage as a shared basis for a diasporic movement of cultural and political decolonization. *Quilombo* editors demarcated the modern, international contours of their chosen Africa by maintaining regular correspondence and exchanges with the editors of the West African magazine *Présence Africaine*, publishing an excerpt from Sartre's "Black Orpheus," and hosting Camus when he visited Rio.[68] From this vantage point, *Quilombo*'s editors looked at Rio's own rich African cultural expressions with new, at times exoticizing, interest. When Camus came to town, for example, Nascimento took him to see what *Quilombo* called "macumba rituals (a centuries-old inheritance from Africa)," to dance samba, to watch black dancer Mercedes Batista and her "Afro-Brazilian ballads," and to listen to the Orquestra Afro-Brasileira's "black rhythms."[69] By presenting these (often highbrow) incarnations of Rio's African culture to the Algerian-born Camus (himself an "African" intellectual, *Quilombo* noted), Nascimento not only claimed a space for Brazil in the transnational world of African representations that made up the content of *négritude* but inserted his circle of black thinkers and artists in the elite intellectual milieu that defined the movement.

In formulating their idea of a Brazilian modernity based on distinct African contributions in the late 1940s, the editors of *Quilombo* simultaneously battled the assimilationist tendencies of contemporary sociology and the rigorously de-Africanized definitions of culture and modernity of their Paulistano counterparts. The African traits that TEN leaders celebrated were not, in their eyes, static markers of difference or obstacles to modernity but tools for integrating people of color more fully into Brazilian society while respecting their particular heritage. In his opening speech to the 1949 Black National Conference, Abdias do Nascimento described the TEN's intended strategy of tapping into Rio's rich Afro-Brazilian culture to reach and mobilize a broader population of color: "*Candomblé* houses and samba schools are black institutions of great vitality and with deep roots. . . . We can only bring together masses of people of color by manipulating these paideian [i.e., collective cultural] survivals . . . linked to African cultural matrixes."[70] Drawing on the francophone concept of *négritude*, black intellectuals associated with the TEN coined the Portuguese word *negritude* to describe their celebration of an African life force at the center of Brazilian culture. In *Quilombo*, Guerreiro Ramos stressed that *negritude* was not "a ferment of hatred," not "a schism," but rather "a subjectivity, a lived experience, an element of passion emerging from the classic categories of Brazilian society, which enriches them with human substance."[71] The deep cultural "passion" of *negritude* was not a barrier to blacks' becoming modern; it was the essential building block of all avant-garde Brazilian expression. This meant that black Brazilians had a special role in moving national culture forward—and, perhaps, that Brazilians who did not claim African descent or did not identify with an African-inflected culture were not true Brazilians at all.

In many ways, the ideas about *negritude* developed by thinkers and artists associated with the TEN built on the traditions of the aesthetic vanguard that had, since the 1920s, proposed that local African cultures could be a resource for new visions of Brazilian identity. In that decade, as Hermano Vianna has shown, modernist intellectuals in Rio de Janeiro "discovered" the value of African influences in part by showing French intellectual Blaise Cendrars (a leading figure in France's own early-twentieth-century interest in Africanisms) around their city, proudly introducing him to Afro-Carioca food and music.[72] The TEN echoed these gestures, as well as the official pronouncements of the Vargas regime, which had promoted black culture as part of Brazilian culture. Yet intellectuals in the TEN did more than celebrate white thinkers' appropriation of black culture. To them, *negritude* meant that they themselves, as black thinkers, were crucial conduits for defining contemporary Brazilian culture. Blacks could be producers of a modernist aesthetic and not just primitive inspiration for a white modernism that called itself *mestiço*. In contrast with mainstream definitions of *mestiçagem*, which often imagined racial and cultural mixture as a progressive whitening of Brazil's population, the idea of *negritude* recast cultural mixture as "blackening" or "Africanizing." These definitions of *negritude* were consistent with the TEN's broader attempts to define black Brazilians not as a race clearly apart (as many black Paulistano writers did), but, through racial and cultural mixture and political integration, as the essence of the Brazilian *povo* or people itself.

If the strategies of many postwar Paulistano black writers for asserting difference in the face of assimilationist discourses resembled the "two race" model of citizenship that emerged in the black press of the 1920s, the positions of their Carioca counterparts reveal marked continuities with the minority "one race" model. This was true of TEN intellectuals, who sought to make a highly abstract and modernist black or African culture the essence of a mixed national identity, and it was true in a different sense of leftist black thinkers in groups like Solano Trinidade's Teatro Popular Brasileiro, which produced an intentionally unrefined Afro-Brazilian folklore in the name of the Brazilian *povo*. In either case, compared to what prevailed in São Paulo, Rio's larger population of color, its somewhat less restrictive racial barriers, its claims to being the center of a *mestiço* Brazilian identity, and its position as the national capital may have reinforced Carioca black thinkers' demands for rights and recognition as part of a mixed-race *povo*, rather than as a distinct minority.

African Embassy

Although many black thinkers in São Paulo and Rio de Janeiro developed critiques of sociology and its practitioners in the postwar period, generally, as we have seen, they celebrated the shift away from an anthropological focus on African religions that, they believed, relegated Brazilians of color to the status of "museum pieces." However, for some Candomblé leaders in Salvador da Bahia, where alliances with a local and foreign intelligentsia since the 1930s had contributed to the legitimization of Afro-Brazilian religions and to the prestige of particular *terreiros*, the story was different. Not only did leading Candomblé figures not object to being the subjects of anthropology and social science as these disciplines evolved in the postwar years, but they quite manifestly were not the passive and primitive "raw material" for scholars that Paulistano and Carioca activists imagined them to be. Like those activists, if through different means, Candomblé leaders—specifically Mãe Aninha's successor at the Ilê Axé Opô Afonjá—laid claim to their rights to ethnic and cultural difference by inserting their voices into contemporary academic discussions about Brazil's African heritage.

Maria Bibiana do Espírito Santo, or Mãe Senhora, assumed leadership of the Opô Afonjá in 1942, shortly after Mãe Aninha's death. Senhora was chosen as a successor to the formidable Aninha for her strength and character, and for her familial and spiritual lineages, which could reputedly be traced back to the female founders of Bahia's first candomblés.[73] Yet Senhora faced a difficult set of circumstances. The onset of World War II had shut down the already waning world of transatlantic contacts that had sustained the prestige of Candomblé houses like the Opô Afonjá in the first decades of the century. The loss of spiritual and material connections to Africa during the war placed a significant constraint on the practice of religious ritual at the Opô Afonjá, on the *terreiro*'s prestige, and potentially on Senhora's authority itself.

It was against this backdrop that Mãe Senhora met Pierre Verger. Before he settled in Salvador in 1946, Verger was a Paris-based photojournalist who had traveled extensively in Europe, Asia, Africa, and Latin America, working for international news agencies and magazines like *Life* and *Paris-Soir*. By the early 1940s, Verger had visited Brazil and become one of the many foreign intellectuals who, at midcentury, were seduced by its reputation of peaceful racial coexistence and vibrant cultural mixture.[74] As Verger became increasingly interested in the study of African-descended Brazilians and their cultures, he made his way to Bahia, securing a contract from the leading Rio-based news magazine *O Cruzeiro* as a support and outlet for his work. Verger developed close relationships with other foreign intellectuals central to the study of Brazil's race relations at midcentury, like Roger Bastide and Swiss anthropologist Alfred Métraux, who headed the UNESCO studies on race relations in Brazil.[75] In the early 1950s, Verger participated in these studies as a photographer for what would become two of the classic works on Bahia: Charles Wagley's *Race and Class in Rural Brazil* (1952) and Thales de Azevedo's *Les élites de couleur dans une ville brésilienne* (1953).[76] Despite contacts with some foreign researchers, Verger always remained somewhat of an outsider to Bahia's academic establishment. He chose instead to learn about Bahia's African influences directly from the *povo de santo*, as Candomblé practitioners are known.[77]

In 1948 Verger's emerging interest in the history of mutual influences between Bahia and the west coast of Africa led him to Senhora's candomblé, by then well established as one of the most famously "African" of all the *terreiros* in Bahia. Senhora continued the practice, begun under her predecessors, of welcoming Brazilian and international intellectuals into her fold as a way of earning respect, visibility, power, and a degree of protection for her candomblé. Yet Verger offered something substantially different from other contemporary academics in Bahia: the possibility of renewed contacts with Africa. With a grant from France's Institut Fondamental de l'Afrique Noire and his French passport in hand, Verger prepared in 1949 to travel to West Africa to conduct research on the history of mutual exchanges between Bahia and the coastal area along the Bight of Benin. Senhora seized the opportunity. She consecrated Verger's head to Xangô (the reigning *orixá* or deity of her candomblé), adopting him as her initiate or spiritual "son," and sent him off as what she called her very own "ambassador" to renew contacts with a land that had, in the recent past, become truly distant.[78] Senhora's choice of word is suggestive of the continuing power of *nações* or African ethnic groups to structure identities and allegiances in the world of Candomblé. Brazil would not establish its first embassies in sub-Saharan Africa for another decade. But she, a religious leader in Bahia who claimed a Yoruba ethnic and spiritual lineage, appointed her own ambassador to that region on behalf of not her nation-state but her *nação*. Senhora's language echoed that of the "African Embassy," the carnival revelers who in early-twentieth-century Bahia had similarly played on the language of diplomatic representation to mark their allegiance to an African "nation" and to appoint themselves legitimate representatives of African peoples before a Bahian public.

Senhora and other Candomblé leaders whose prestige and religious practice depended on direct contact with Africa found in Verger a worthy successor to the travelers and merchants who had kept transatlantic contacts alive into the late nineteenth and early twentieth centuries. As he set out, for his own intellectual purposes, to reconstruct the history of these intermediaries—both of the travelers from Bahia and of the *agudás* or Brazilian returnees who settled along Africa's west coast—Verger collected valuable information and ritual objects for leaders of Bahia's candomblés. "I got presents for the Babalorishas [Candomblé priests] of Bahia," Verger wrote in a letter to his friend and colleague Melville Herskovits in 1950, "that I hope they will appreciate—as: 'genuine pebbles of the river Oshun and two bracelets' given to his people of Brazil by the *Ataoya* [king] of Oshogbo [in Eastern Nigeria] and taken from the altar of his own palace; 'Thunder stones' for my friends of Shango; 'Irons' for other ones of Ogun and some more 'divines' [*sic*] presents."[79] Verger took evident care to gather "divine" gifts representing the characteristics of the particular *orixá* each Bahian religious leader worshipped—river pebbles for worshippers of Oxum the river goddess, thunder stones for followers of Xangô, iron for followers of Ogun. But these divine gifts were also laced with temporal power. Some, like the gifts sent "to his people of Brazil by the *Ataoya* of Oshogbo," actually performed the sort of diplomatic duty Senhora envisioned, linking the heads of Bahian candomblés to political leaders in Africa (and allowing these African leaders, in turn, to claim subjects in Brazil).[80] Verger also shared with Candomblé leaders what he called, in his excellent but idiosyncratic English, the "enormous quantity of informations" about ritual practices that he "caught" in Dahomey and Nigeria.[81]

Senhora's own prestige, in particular, increased immensely over the course of Verger's travels to Africa. On his next trip to Africa in 1952, Verger visited Hadji Adeyemi II, *alafin* (king) of the city of Oyo, the former seat of a Yoruba empire that became particularly powerful in the seventeenth and eighteenth centuries. It is not clear whether Mãe Senhora sent Verger on this visit, once again entrusting him as her "ambassador" with a particular gift or message, or whether the visit took place at Verger's own initiative. The only written description of the event is a letter addressed to Senhora by the *alafin* of Oyo himself, a copy of which is preserved among Verger's personal papers. In the letter, the *alafin* of Oyo expresses his great pleasure at receiving from Verger a photograph of Senhora (presumably one of Verger's own striking black and white images, which accounted for most of the likenesses taken of her in the 1950s). Also according to the *alafin*'s letter, Verger visited Oyo during the festival of the *orixá* Xangô, the reigning deity both of Oyo and of Senhora's *terreiro*. During this festival, Verger "has seen and gather [*sic*] informations about sacificing [*sic*] to 'Sango' in the proper way for the information of you the 'Iyanaso' and members of the 'Sango' worshippers in Brazil." The timing of Verger's visit suggests his intention to establish this *orixá*'s worship as a point of convergence between Senhora's *terreiro* and Oyo locals, while conducting valuable research, on Senhora's (and his own) behalf, about the ways Xangô was worshipped in Africa.[82]

The king of Oyo evidently believed that Verger's collection of information on Xangô worship was intended for didactic purposes—to teach Senhora and her followers the "proper" way it was done. If there was a touch of condescension in his tone, however, his idea that Senhora would be interested in learning about what was considered "proper" in Africa was not far off the mark. Far from belittling the ritual practices of Senhora and other "members of the 'Sango' worshippers in Brazil," Verger's visit to the "source" of Xangô worship, and the letter and tokens he brought back with him, had quite the opposite effect. The *alafin*, according to his letter, gave Verger "one each 'edun ara [thunder stones]' and 'Sere [an elongated musical instrument, made from a gourd with small seeds inside]' from the 'Sango' Hall in Mogba's house, Oyo, which simbolise [*sic*] his [Verger's] true visit to Oyo, to be shown to you and members of 'Sango' worshippers in Brazil, and these 'edun ara' and 'Sere' can be kept in the hall of your society cult in Brazil." These ritual objects were likely among the first to be brought from Africa to Bahia since transatlantic contacts began to dwindle in the 1920s and 1930s, and they were probably the only ones sent exclusively to a Candomblé priestess by Yoruba royalty. But in this case, as with other gifts Verger relayed, it was not necessarily the material objects that brought greatest status to the receiver. In his letter, the king of Oyo addressed Senhora as "the 'Iyanaso' . . . of the 'Sango' worshippers in Brazil." This title conferred on Senhora the coveted status of priestess of Xangô in the royal court of Oyo, symbolic seat of Yoruba power.

Since Senhora received this famous letter, specialists have argued about the significance of the title *Iyanaso*. Some hold that its power derives from being a highly honorific title reserved for the select women who keep charge of the cult of Xangô—the king's personal deity and, in the period of Oyo's regional dominance, one of the most powerful in the Yoruba pantheon. In this sense, to be designated an *Iyanaso* was a spiritual and political honor for Senhora, marking her as a prominent religious leader in the greater Yoruba world.[83] Others, like Verger, contended that the title had particular meaning in Brazil, aside from the meanings originating in Africa. "Iyá Nassô" was the name given to the legendary women who founded Bahia's first candomblés, from which all contemporary candomblés derived. In the world of Afro-Bahian ritual, Senhora's new title authoritatively confirmed her familial and spiritual descent from those women of mythical stature. But beyond this, Verger argued, Senhora's distinction as *Iyanaso* superseded that previous history, symbolically establishing her as the spiritual founder of all Ketu-derived candomblés in Bahia.[84] In writing a history of the Ilê Axé Opô Afonjá, Senhora's son, Deoscóredes M. dos Santos, provided yet another interpretation of the title's significance, one that highlighted the transatlantic connections so central to that *terreiro*'s prestige and identity: "This event marks the resumption of older religious relations between Africa and Bahia, which would be broadened in the future, as Mãe Senhora went on to maintain a constant exchange of presents and messages with kings and other religious personalities in Africa."[85]

Yet it may not be necessary to choose one interpretation, since all three meanings—from the intertwined worlds of Bahian Candomblé and a broader Yoruba world—combined to consolidate Senhora's position as one of the most powerful religious figures of her time. Senhora recognized the import of her new title. She made the *alafin*'s letter public with a large celebration on 9 August 1953, inviting all of her followers, members of other houses, intellectuals, journalists, and other friends of the Opô Afonjá. By 1958, when Senhora celebrated a party for the fiftieth anniversary of her initiation, a range of Brazilian personalities from the intellectual and political world— including representatives sent by President Kubitschek—were in attendance.[86] Later that year, Senhora appeared in Rio's newspapers on the occasion of her trip to that city, where she stayed with her friend and spiritual son, Bahian novelist Jorge Amado, and met with other leading cultural figures, like bossa nova composer Vinícius de Morais.[87] Finally, aside from boosting Senhora's visibility and prestige, the relationship with Verger, like Mãe Aninha's relationships with returnee merchants in earlier years, sustained Senhora and her candomblé economically. Senhora sold African imports—mostly ritual objects—from her stall at the Mercado Modelo, located by the port in downtown Salvador.[88] In the 1950s and 1960s, Verger made contacts for Senhora with commercial firms in Africa and sent or delivered care packages filled with ritual objects for her own use, and possibly for sale.[89]

Acting as Senhora's personal ambassador benefited Verger as well. His status as an ethnographer in Brazil and Africa greatly increased through his privileged access to Senhora and other Candomblé leaders. In a letter to Herskovits written on his way back from Africa in January 1950, Verger hinted at the power he expected his transatlantic "messages" to carry: "In Africa I could too be admited [sic] among the members of the so called secret society of the 'Eguns' and I return with a message for the same society still existing in Bahia. I hope that all this [in addition to the aforementioned gifts] will help me on my return there."[90] In another letter to Herskovits, written on his return to Bahia, Verger described his distribution of news and gifts to "our friends of 'Candomblé,'" and confessed, "I am rather well received and admitted among them due to the 'prestige' of the pilgrimage to their fathers' land."[91]

The importance that Senhora and other contemporary Candomblé leaders placed on direct and contemporaneous exchanges with Africa shaped Verger's research in tangible ways. His interactions with people on both sides of the Atlantic became the basis for a unique research practice, which ethnomusicologist Angela Lühning has called "transatlantic dialogue as research method."[92] Aside from transporting letters and objects back and forth, Verger began to use several forms of mechanical reproduction, like photography and sound recordings, to allow Africans and their descendants in different parts of the diaspora to represent themselves to each other as well as to broader audiences. In December 1958, for instance, Verger made two successive appearances on a popular Bahian radio program, *Vamos cantar a Bahia*. In one of these, he had the host play a recording of Nigerian ritual drumming, followed by recordings of corresponding rhythms from Senhora's candomblé, to highlight the similarities between them. In his other appearance, Verger played recordings of his interviews with two African-descended Brazilian women, Maria Ojelabi and Romana da Conceição, who as young girls in the early 1900s "returned" with their African-born elders to Lagos, Nigeria, where they would spend the rest of their lives. Through this interview (the tapes and transcript of which have been lost), a sector of the Bahian public heard the voices of women from across the Atlantic with whom they shared a birthplace, language, culture, and religion (the women, like most Brazilian returnees, were Catholic).[93] In the course of researching the history of African-Bahian connections and facilitating these connections for a group of Candomblé leaders in Bahia, then, Verger helped portray Bahia's African culture as not just pure and undiluted but vibrantly linked to a contemporaneous Africa.

To "link what has been severed"

Verger's approach to the study of African-descended people in Bahia was distinct from the dominant anthropological and sociological perspectives of the time. Since the 1930s, as we have seen, anthropologists working on Bahia's African traits had celebrated their "purity." But by and large, scholars like Melville Herskovits or Arthur Ramos had viewed these remarkably unadulterated traits as "survivals" from the days of the slave trade, when both sides of the Atlantic were closely connected. Africa and Brazil, in the eyes of many of these scholars, were not coeval—rather, the purity of Bahia's African traits was preserved largely through memories of, or traditions handed down from, a distant past.[94] Verger's research methods and academic productions, however, portrayed Candomblé leaders and their African interlocutors as agents active not in the preservation of crystallized traditions, but in the reinvention of ritual practices through ongoing transatlantic contact. His work also provided an alternative to the sociological perspective (embraced by many southeastern black intellectuals in the postwar period) that emphasized modernization, industrialization, and the development of a class society as the processes that would complete the transformation of Brazil's "Africans" into modern citizens.

Though Senhora and (to a lesser extent) Verger became increasingly well known throughout the 1950s, their attempts to revive and celebrate Bahia's direct African connections remained marginal to national public life in this period. Verger, who did not obtain his doctorate from the Sorbonne until 1958, continued to be largely an outsider to Brazil's academic establishment. Nor did Verger's principal employer, the Rio-based *O Cruzeiro*, provide a fruitful outlet for his particular perspective on Bahia's African connections. His dozens of proposed articles on African-Brazilian relations or contemporary African affairs failed to capture the imagination of the magazine's editors, who, as Angela Lühning suggests, probably saw such topics as incompatible with the "modern" Brazil they attempted to portray.[95] This situation began to change, however, in the late 1950s, with shifts in Bahia's academic establishment and, more broadly, with a transformation in Brazil's foreign policy toward Africa.

In 1959 a Portuguese intellectual residing in Bahia, George Agostinho da Silva, founded the Centro de Estudos Afro-Orientais (CEAO, or Center for Afro-Oriental Studies) at the University of Bahia. The reference to the "Afro-Oriental" or "Afro-Asian" world, common to several of the African studies centers that emerged in Brazil in those years, reflected a sense of global politics that issued from the 1955 Bandung Conference in Indonesia, in which colonized nations affirmed their rights to sovereignty and their nonaligned status. Like other similarly named centers in Brazil to this day, however, Bahia's CEAO focused almost exclusively on African or Afro-Brazilian topics.[96] From its inception, the CEAO worked to establish ties with other African studies centers around the world and, as they gradually emerged, in Brazil as well.[97] Silva conceived of the center as a kind of political think-tank aimed at spreading public knowledge about, and proposing policy initiatives toward, contemporary Africa at a time when the continent was moving toward decolonization. He hoped that the center could accomplish what, in 1959, Brazilian diplomatic officials were still reluctant to do: capitalize on Brazil's African cultural ties to assure it a place of primacy among Africa's emerging nations.[98]

In many ways, the CEAO's perspectives on Brazil's African culture built on earlier traditions of Afro-Bahian anthropology. In particular, Silva held beliefs about the power of Brazil's racial mixture to foster tolerance that echoed Gilberto Freyre's own, increasingly conservative, views. Both men's conviction that Brazil, and specifically Bahia, had something to offer the fledgling nations of Africa grew out of their shared belief in Brazil's relatively benevolent experience with slavery, race relations, and cultural mixture.[99] In the early 1950s Freyre's theory of "lusotropicalism"—the supposedly unique capacity of the Portuguese to thrive in foreign, tropical settings because of their innate openness to sexual and cultural mixture—took a turn to the right, as Freyre toured Africa at the behest of Portuguese dictator Antonio de Oliveira Salazar, praising the wonders of Portuguese colonialism.[100] Similarly, in the late 1950s, Silva looked forward to the rise of a Luso-Brazilian "Empire" in the tropics, in which Brazil (itself a bridge between Europe and Africa) would gradually usurp Portugal's role as the bearer of lusophone civilization to Africa.[101]

Yet the CEAO also opened up space for a new, rather unorthodox set of ideas about African-Brazilian connections to gain official stature in Brazil. For all of its resonance with Freyre's conservative and colonialist views, Silva's vision of Brazil's role in the Atlantic world had quite different political roots and implications. If Freyre's lusotropicalism implied a commitment to colonial authority and a celebration of an ultimately unequal racial status quo, Silva's ideas about a Brazilian-led lusophone "Empire" had a distinct mystical and revolutionary bent. For him, the desired "Empire of the Holy Spirit" would constitute "what others call a society without classes," a brotherhood predicated on the shared struggle for social, economic, and racial equality.[102]

Silva's unique perspective on African-Brazilian relations led him to put together a team of scholars who recognized and valued direct connections between Bahia and Africa not just in the past, as a previous generation of scholars had, but in the present as well. Not surprisingly, given this goal, one of the first people Silva approached after founding the center was Pierre Verger, at the time the only Bahian-based scholar with extensive firsthand knowledge of, and contacts in, Africa. Over the next few years, Verger became a guide for a new generation of scholars who wished to travel to Africa for their research, and who, like him, interpreted Bahia's African culture as the outcome of ongoing, rather than ancient and truncated, transatlantic ties.[103] CEAO anthropologist Vivaldo da Costa Lima summarized this view in an interview with the Bahian press in 1960. When asked whether the CEAO's new Yoruba course—intended for Candomblé devotees but taught by visiting Nigerian professor Ebenezer Lasebikan—would corrupt the Yoruba traditionally spoken in Bahia's candomblés, Costa Lima responded, "It is precisely against this cultural nostalgia that we struggle." Far from fearing ruining the "purity" of the Bahian experiment—or slowing the process of national integration—by exposing Afro-Bahian culture directly to African culture, Costa Lima and others like him at the CEAO expressed the belief that Bahia's African culture would only be strengthened by the renewed contact. The Yoruba course, Costa Lima explained, brought dozens of Bahians of African descent to study the language of their ancestors "in order to remake the broken cultural bond," to "link what has been severed."[104] This was precisely the vision of Bahia's African connections that had guided leading practitioners of Candomblé, like Mãe Aninha and Mãe Senhora, since the early decades of the century.

These formulations of Bahia's African culture escaped the debates about the permissible levels of black cultural or racial difference that constrained black thinkers in São Paulo and especially Rio de Janeiro in the same period. Senhora's religious practices, though constructed through direct ties to Africa and in alliance with African political leaders, did not raise suspicions of creating an "ethnic cyst." As one of the African cultural traits celebrated as essential to a *mestiço* Brazilian nationality since the 1930s, Candomblé had the advantage of being accepted as "national," whereas race-based *negro* organizations were denounced as unwelcome foreign imports. Moreover, candomblés like Senhora's, though made up primarily

Ebenezer Lasebikan of Nigeria, teaching his Yoruba course at the Centro de Estudos Afro-Orientais of the University of Bahia, early 1960s. Pierre Verger, © Fundação Pierre Verger.

of African-descended followers, defined their membership not by race but by cultural and religious practices that people of any racial background could follow. Nor did they focus their activities on explicit denunciations of racism in Brazil. They thus did not pose the same kind of political threat that southeastern race-based organizations did in this period. This is not to say, however, that candomblés presented no challenges to dominant notions of black citizenship and culture at midcentury. The idea of Bahia as the nexus between Brazil and Africa, tirelessly cultivated by priestesses like Aninha and Senhora, made its way, through the mediation of scholars like Verger and Costa Lima, into Bahian public life at a time when most Bahian elites still imagined their city's culture as predominantly European.[105] In the early 1960s this vision of Bahia's African purity—which stood in tension with older ideas of cultural *mestiçagem*—would earn the attention of the

Mãe Senhora at her *terreiro*, with visiting Yoruba professor Ebenezer Lasebikan of Nigeria, early 1960s. Pierre Verger, © Fundação Pierre Verger.

Brazilian government, as it reconfigured its foreign policy toward a decolonizing Africa.

"Africa's Awakening"

In the 1950s and 1960s Africa itself was the source of one of the most significant shifts in the ways Brazilians discussed their racial democracy and cultural diversity. The decolonization movement that spread across the continent after World War II, and which intensified over the course of the 1950s, yielded more than thirty newly independent African nations by 1964. Most of these were former British and French colonies in sub-Saharan Africa (Portugal would hold on to its African territories until the mid-1970s). In the late 1950s and early 1960s, the saga of Africa's decolonization produced a dramatic transformation in the ways São Paulo's black journalists viewed the continent. For the greater part of the century, most Paulistano black writers had shunned Africa. News from the continent, filtered through colonialist journalism, seemed to confirm the inferiority of black people subjected to colonial white governments. For much of the century black writers in São Paulo (with a few notable exceptions, like Leite in *O Clarim* and some contributors to *O Progresso*) had also worked vigorously to assert their *brasilidade* and to distance themselves from any foreign, African association.

Over the course of the 1950s, however, the news from Africa began to change, and Leite, who had always been more interested in topics like Garveyism and Ethiopia than most of his contemporaries, led the way in a new effort to tie African politics to the black struggle in Brazil. In 1958 Leite's Associação Cultural do Negro (ACN, or Black People's Cultural Association), the successor to the Associação do Negro Brasileiro of the previous decade, staged a public protest against racial discrimination in South Africa and suggested creating a committee to express black Brazilians' solidarity with decolonizing African peoples. The committee did not materialize, but Leite's gesture led the ACN to establish correspondence with African independence groups, like Angola's Movimento Popular da Libertação de Angola (Popular Movement for the Liberation of Angola).[106] By 1960, when he founded the newspaper *Niger*, Leite revived his "Mundo negro" column (the vector for his Garveyist and pan-Africanist musings in the early 1930s) as a site for exploring his renewed interest in African politics. "Though Africa is an old continent," Leite wrote in an installment of "Mundo negro" subtitled "The African Renaissance," "it seems that we are now witnessing the discovery of a new world." Africa, he pronounced, was suddenly and momentously "assuming its consciousness and its responsibilities to black values." Between 1945 and the early 1950s, in the midst of new enthusiasm for the ideals of political democracy, a colonized and passive Africa had held no interest for black thinkers. But as Africa began to take a leading role in the narratives of democracy, human rights, and antiracism that black thinkers held dear, it provided Leite and others with a new source of inspiration for their racial politics and identities. African events "make us, in Brazil, feel compelled by those who once seemed so distant."[107]

As early as 1950, an array of Paulista black newspapers began to cover African topics like elections in Ethiopia (held up as a model of "true democracy" for the rest of the world), racial discrimination in South Africa, and, above all, what the Campinas newspaper *Hífen* called "Africa's Awakening": the national processes of independence.[108] In stark contrast to the silence (and occasional reference to primitiveness) surrounding Africa in São Paulo's black press in much of the first postwar decade (when the United States became a preferred source of inspiration), newspapers like *Mundo Novo* (1950), *Notícias de Ébano* (1957), *Hífen* (1960–62), *Ébano* (1961), and especially Leite's *Niger* (1960) exhibited detailed knowledge about leaders and events in places like the French and Belgian Congos, Madagascar, Kenya, Angola, and Ghana. These articles, along with pointed demands that Africa receive better coverage in the Brazilian and international press, evince a new sense of ownership toward Africa and its politics among São Paulo's black journalists.[109]

In a *Niger* article titled "The Congo and Us," from the August 1960 issue that featured Congolese independence fighter Patrice Lumumba on its cover, Leite drew the outlines of this African inspiration more closely.

> If we blacks were to analyze the events that are taking place in the
> African world and to draw practical conclusions for our own milieu, we
> would inevitably arrive at very serious thoughts. . . . It would be sad if
> Brazilian blacks made no attempt to free themselves as well—not from
> colonial masters but from the specter of disillusionment that dogs black
> thought. It would be sad not to adapt our own case to the struggle of
> the Congolese and to attempt, with sacrifice and even with heroism, to
> affirm ourselves as blacks, and above all, as humans.

Leite's description of Africa's struggle was consistent with black Paulistanos' ideas of belonging to their nation, and to the world, as "universal" political subjects. He was careful, however, to qualify exactly how his enthusiasm for "heroic" African armed struggles might translate into black political action at home. "Lumumba can be almost a symbol, even though our solutions and means of struggle are not the same. If Lumumba expelled the Belgians from black territory, we do not mean to expel anyone; on the contrary, we will let the hope of better days grow among us."[110] The comparison with Africa made black Brazilian activists, who demanded "hopeful" inclusion in a multiracial Brazil rather than the creation of an exclusively "black territory," seem tame by comparison. At the same time, Africa's battle against what Leite called "the obscurantism of centuries of exploitation" provided a new source of legitimacy for a Paulistano black movement seeking to rectify racial injustice without being tarred as racist or separatist.[111]

This new sense of closeness between Brazil and Africa spilled over into Leite's terminology for black Brazilians themselves. Witnessing the "African Renaissance," Leite enthused, "We cannot remain closed off and limited by our distance in the face of these events, which excite our sentiments as

Afro-Brazilians."[112] Originating in the anthropology of the 1930s as an adjective describing African cultural heritage in Brazil, the term *Afro-Brazilian* (*afro-brasileiro*) appeared only occasionally in the midcentury Paulistano black press, and then not usually as a noun referring to people but as an adjective qualifying certain black cultural events and organizations.[113] The term was more common in Rio, where it was consistent with intellectuals' more cultural uses of Africa in the 1940s and 1950s. Leite's use of the term to refer to black Brazilians rather than to African cultural manifestations therefore stands out, especially in São Paulo, where black thinkers largely referred to themselves as *negros*, in keeping with their own sense of racial distinctiveness and their rejection of a foreign cultural identity. This usage seems to signal a new acknowledgment of Africa as a component of black Brazilians' racial and political heritage—one visible as well in the choice of the name of Leite's newspaper, *Niger*, which, he explained, was both an African nation and the Latin word for *negro*.[114]

All of this draws attention to the ways that shifting African politics in the 1950s and early 1960s simultaneously excited interest among black thinkers in Rio de Janeiro, Salvador, and São Paulo, though in distinct ways. Black Carioca thinkers, especially in the TEN, focused on the intellectual currents emerging from decolonization, especially the psychological and literary elements of *négritude*, which presented a modern, elite version of African culture and supported blacks' (and particularly black intellectuals') claims to being unique participants in the development of Brazilian identity. Black religious leaders in Bahia tapped into Yoruba ethnic nationalism, itself part of a longstanding decolonization effort, as they renewed their ties to Africa. In São Paulo, however, the Africa black thinkers adopted in these years continued to avoid any hint of cultural difference. As with *Clarim* or *Progresso*'s interest in Garveyism and pan-Africanism in the early decades of the century, the Africa Leite and others admired in the 1950s and early 1960s was a politicized one, now undergoing a widespread process of decolonization that could support black Brazilians' claims for inclusion based on human rights, democratic participation, and self-determination.

Protagonists of Negritude

Among Brazilian politicians, especially those allied with leftist or reformist sectors, anticolonial struggles in Africa produced a shift in foreign policy and, eventually, in representations of racial democracy itself between 1960 and 1964. Brazil had not maintained official diplomatic contacts with sub-Saharan

Africa since the end of the slave trade. For the first half of the twentieth century, Brazil's stance toward colonial Africa reflected the nation's pro-Western orientation more generally, and throughout the 1950s, Brazil officially supported Portugal and other European powers in their colonial endeavors. But a small, dissenting group of Brazilian diplomats in the late 1950s began to argue that the emergent independence movements of the Afro-Asian world provided an opportunity for Brazil to break out of its subordinate position in the Cold War order. If Brazil could position itself as a mediator between the colonial and colonized, First and Third World, nations, it might secure for itself a more prominent profile in international affairs. Africa in particular, they believed, could provide Brazil with important commercial and diplomatic opportunities.[115]

The election of Jânio Quadros to the presidency in late 1960 put these dissenters in control of Brazilian foreign policy toward Africa. Officials at Itamaraty, the Brazilian Ministry of Foreign Affairs, raced to design and implement what Quadros declared to be an "independent" foreign policy toward Africa—one that broke with traditional support for Portugal and asserted Brazil's new anticolonial, antiracist position of solidarity with Third World countries. Beyond solidarity, however, one of the major goals of Brazil's new Africa policy was to position Brazil as a compelling commercial partner for the emerging African nations.[116] Itamaraty's yearly reports for this period document a flurry of diplomatic activity to this end: creating an Africa Division in Itamaraty to guide the new policy; opening new consulates, embassies, and commercial missions; organizing exhibitions of Brazilian manufactures; and signing agreements on economic and cultural exchanges.[117]

The outlines and goals of Quadros's new foreign policy reflected transformations in Brazilian politics by the early 1960s. Ideologically, Quadros's (and his successor João Goulart's) pursuit of an independent foreign policy reflected a reformist, nationalist rejection of traditional alliances with Europe and the United States and an attempt to find alternative partners within the narrow parameters of Cold War politics. Their anticolonial, pro–Third World stance in particular echoed the leftward shift of Brazilian politics at the start of the new decade. Pragmatically, Quadros and Goulart's search for new markets responded both to the significant growth in Brazilian industry in the second half of the 1950s under President Kubitschek and to the enormous foreign debt, inflation, and economic crisis that resulted from his ambitious modernization policies. Overtures toward the emerging nations of Africa, the Quadros and Goulart administrations hoped, might result in the sort of South Atlantic influence that could earn Brazil greater economic stability without excessive reliance on the International Monetary Fund and other financial institutions dominated by Europe and the United States.

Brazil's new African foreign policy, though notable, had limited concrete effects on Brazil's economy and international status in the early 1960s. But Africa's symbolic influence on official Brazilian discourses, both at home and abroad, was disproportionately great. Diplomats, politicians, and intellectuals used Brazil's history of contacts with Africa to recast the nation's identity in ways that would simultaneously fuel and naturalize the new diplomatic connections. In 1961, for example, Quadros published an article in the U.S. journal *Foreign Affairs* intended to increase the profile of Brazil's foreign policy and to stake out Brazilian claims to a special role in Africa's destiny, based on long-standing ties in the past. "We are linked to that continent by our ethnic and cultural roots," Quadros explained, "and share in its desire to forge for itself an independent position in the world of today." Quadros urged Brazil to "become the link, the bridge, between Africa and the West, since we are so intimately bound to both peoples."[118] Under Quadros, ideas of Brazil's "ethnic and cultural roots" in Africa—extensively disseminated in intellectual circles since the appearance of Gilberto Freyre's works in the 1930s—would penetrate the traditionally white, pro-Portuguese realm of foreign policy, acquiring a new level of official status. In the process, the notion of African ethnicity in Brazil would itself undergo significant modifications.

Between Quadros's election and the 1964 coup that removed his successor, leading experts on Africa (the architects of Itamaraty's new foreign policy) relied on what diplomatic historian José Flávio Sombra Saraiva has called the "culturalist discourse" of Brazil's "natural African vocation" to forge diplomatic ties with the continent.[119] Eduardo Portella, the intellectual at the head of Itamaraty's newly founded academic institute for the study of Africa, explained the deep ties of race and culture that made Brazil the only country capable of leading an "authentic cooperation" with the continent: "We are the only country possessing the conditions to execute such a program without 'deculturizing' Africa. Banishing, exterminating its specific ingredients. Our collaboration will not be that of strangers, but of people who carry a culture that is not oppressive. . . . We will bring them a culture that they themselves helped to build, one that is also theirs, one that can be confused with theirs."[120]

Officials like Portella drew on a range of more- or less-clearly expressed similarities with Africa—including a shared past, a shared geopolitical and economic situation, and especially shared racial and cultural traits—to make claims for Brazil's inherent suitability to guide Africa into world trade and politics. Portella succinctly captured the prevailing mood among officials and diplomats in the Quadros administration when he declared, in one of his speeches, that Brazil was "the largest African nation outside of Africa."[121]

To be sure, most of the Brazilians who designed and carried out foreign policy in Africa were white. But the prevailing discourse of racial democracy held that Brazil was unique precisely because it produced racially white subjects who could, because of historical patterns of easy racial and cultural mixture, nevertheless claim antiracist credentials as well as fluency in black culture. "The white Brazilian, or better yet, the Brazilian," Portella asserted, "is a protagonist of *negritude*. . . . The African countries understand this reality. This is why they prefer us."[122] This was, in effect, a reiteration of Alberto Guerreiro Ramos's definition of *negritude* in *Quilombo* a decade earlier, though predictably stripped of the *negro* sociologist's sharp critique of white intellectuals and policymakers' sense of ownership of Brazil's African culture. Proponents of the new foreign policy, notably President Quadros himself, argued that Brazil should use its history of harmonious ethnic mixture as a foreign policy tool: "Insofar as we can give the nations of the Black continent an example of complete absence of racial prejudice, together with successful proof of progress without undermining the principles of freedom, we shall be decisively contributing to the effective integration of an entire continent in a system to which we are attached by our philosophy and historic tradition."[123] In this vein, Quadros chose as his minister of foreign relations the white senator Afonso Arinos de Melo Franco, famous for writing the 1951 law that made racial discrimination a punishable offense.[124]

By the early 1960s, then, one of Itamaraty's projects was to produce demonstrations of Brazil's racial democracy and cultural affinity with Africa that would, as one famous historian of Brazilian-African relations put it, "seduce the African masses."[125] Yet attempts to deliver on this seduction revealed certain limitations in Brazil's diplomatic institutions. President Quadros wished, for instance, to send a black ambassador to Brazil's new embassy in Accra, Ghana, but was faced with the reality of the total absence of blacks in the informally segregated Foreign Service. To "fix" that public relations problem, Quadros selected Raymundo Souza Dantas, a writer of color, to fill the post.[126] (To this, Ghanaian President Kwame Nkrumah retorted that the true measure of Brazil's racial democracy would come when Brazil appointed a black ambassador to a white nation.)[127]

A similar situation arose as Itamaraty sought to obtain knowledge about Africa after a century of silence about the continent in foreign policy circles. Brazilian experts in African history or in African-Brazilian relations were rare in the early 1960s. To address this lacuna, President Quadros created in

1961 the Instituto Brasileiro de Estudos Afro-Asiáticos (IBEAA, or Brazilian Institute for Afro-Asian Studies). Like Bahia's CEAO, the IBEAA's reference to the Afro-Asian world shows contemporary officials' and academics' desire to signal their solidarity with leftist, anticolonial, Third World causes. Once again revealing the saliency of the "Afro" in Brazil's "Afro-Asian" initiatives in this period, the IBEAA functioned largely as a pro-Africa lobby, and its intellectuals wrote Brazil's first books on African politics and African-Brazilian relations.

Brazilian diplomats knew little about the African cultures of Brazil they now claimed as their own, beyond Gilberto Freyre's general formulations, which became standard reading in diplomatic circles by the early 1960s.[128] They turned, therefore, to the pioneering intellectuals at Bahia's CEAO, whose academic work on and contacts with Africa outpaced Itamaraty's. This collaboration began in earnest in 1961, when Itamaraty created a series of scholarships to fund West African students for four years of university studies in Brazil and partnered with the CEAO to develop and implement the program. Itamaraty officials hoped that the CEAO would provide, first, the professional expertise and personal contacts they needed to attract and welcome the African students and, second, the institutional setting for a three-month program in Portuguese language and culture that scholarship recipients would be required to attend on their arrival in Brazil, before heading off to their respective universities.[129] This proposed role recognized founder Agostinho da Silva's goals for the CEAO, which included increasing opportunities for interaction between Africans and Brazilians, and providing Africans an alternative to European academic institutions.[130] Beyond these practical attractions, however, the partnership with Bahia's CEAO also held powerful symbolic appeal for Itamaraty officials. In December 1961, just before the students' arrival, Minister Lauro Escorel de Moraes, head of Itamaraty's Cultural Department, spoke to the CEAO and other members of the university community. "Brazil's cultural policy in Africa will rely fundamentally on the University of Bahia and on this state's cultural ambience," which, combined with "traditions in the field of Afro-Brazilian studies since Nina Rodrigues," resulted in their "primacy in the cultural and human contacts with the young African nations."[131]

The CEAO, in other words, had the knowledge and the cultural setting (Bahia) needed to show African visitors an African Brazil. Itamaraty's mission seemed accomplished a year later, when the visiting African students reported to the Bahian press their strange sensation, on arriving in Bahia, of never having left Africa at all. Akinkunmi Oladepo Akinpelu, a Nigerian medical student, remarked that "Brazil has many things in common with Africa. . . . The people are easy to understand. Their way of dressing, most specially the women, resembles the native dressing along the West Coast of Africa." One of the newspapers in which these interviews appeared was a "Special" English-language edition of the *Jornal da Bahia*, written in conjunction with CEAO scholars and staff and intended for distribution in Africa, where it might convey news of Bahia's Africanness.[132] In exposing the students to Bahia's Africanness, and ensuring press coverage (in Bahia and in Africa) of their impression that Bahia was familiarly African, the CEAO helped Itamaraty with its broader goal of "seducing" African audiences. This also suited the CEAO and some journalists in the Bahian press, who in the early 1960s worked together to advocate for the CEAO's and Bahia's "primacy" in Brazil's nascent African relations.[133] One editorial, for instance, praised the CEAO for recognizing Brazil's obligation to the new African nations "even before Itamaraty itself." "And it is not by accident," the writer concluded, "that this comprehension should have arisen in the cultural medium of Bahia, a state that has constituted itself as one of the foci irradiating African influence across our ethnic and cultural formation."[134] As in the 1930s, when northeastern intellectuals faced with Bahia's slipping position in the nation touted the purity of Bahia's African traditions as emblems of regionalist pride, CEAO intellectuals and their allies in the Bahian press in the early 1960s hoped that Africa's ascendancy in Brazil's foreign policy would bring positive attention to a state whose marginality in national affairs was exacerbated by the uneven economic modernization of the Kubitschek years.

For a brief period between 1961 and 1964, collaborations between Itamaraty and the CEAO helped to make Senhora and Verger's vision of Bahia's "pure" African traits, preserved through ongoing and direct transatlantic contacts, central to official formulations of Brazil's racial democracy. Though discourses emphasizing mixture and assimilation were still widespread in Brazilian public life, the Bahian vision of African purity took the spotlight in Itamaraty's African initiatives. During these years, Itamaraty made Bahia a featured stop on the itineraries of African students, ambassadors, and other distinguished figures who visited Brazil, hoping to expose them to what they considered the nation's most authentic African traditions.[135] Though Mãe Senhora herself remained distant from the academic and political negotiations behind these visits, through her candomblé she, like Aninha before her, maintained ties to important intellectual and political figures in Bahian and Brazilian public life. Some of these people, like Antonio Olinto, were directly connected with Brazil's foreign policy. In the early 1960s, Olinto, a writer and scholar of the history of Bahia's transatlantic connections, and a prominent patron and member of Senhora's candomblé, became Brazil's cultural attaché in Lagos, Nigeria. Through connections like these, Senhora's candomblé became an obligatory stop for African guests of the state in the early 1960s. Itamaraty's first crop of African scholarship recipients visited her, as did ambassadors Louis Inácio Pinto (of Benin) and Henri Senghor (of Senegal). In 1963 Antonio Olinto and Pierre Verger helped to arrange a state-sponsored visit to Brazil for Romana da Conceição, an elderly Brazilian who was among the last descendants of slaves to make the "return" voyage to Africa with her family and was one of two women who had shared their stories with Bahians through Verger's 1958 radio broadcast. On this trip, itself a high-profile public relations event intended to showcase Brazil's unique connections to Africa, Romana too made the obligatory pilgrimage to Senhora's candomblé.[136] In this way, Senhora, who over a decade earlier had sent Verger as her own "ambassador" to Africa, came to play an important role in Brazil's diplomatic functions, hosting African ambassadors and cultural emissaries at her candomblé, and representing for them, in turn, Brazil's internal Africa.

THE RISE OF constraining interpretations of Brazil's racial democracy in the years between 1950 and 1964 in many ways supports later scholars' and activists' critique of racial democracy as a repressive myth. Yet black intellectuals in São Paulo, Rio de Janeiro, and Salvador da Bahia were not entirely without resources to develop explicit critiques of, or alternatives to, views of racial democracy that restricted their subjecthood and their rights to cultural or racial difference. Faced with the enduring problem of asserting their Brazilianness while protecting their particular identities as blacks and Africans, black intellectuals in São Paulo and Rio de Janeiro updated strategies that had served earlier generations: "two race" theories of citizenship that emphasized racial (but not cultural) distinctiveness and "one race" theories of citizenship that emphasized racial fusion but preserved specificity through an appeal to African culture. Although not articulated as a critique of racial democracy, in Salvador, Mãe Senhora (in association with Pierre Verger and CEAO intellectuals) presented yet another configuration of these ideas, also based on the longer-term historical patterns of black identity and activism in that city. Senhora's self-definition stressed a kind of ethnic "purity" and distinctiveness that relied not on a strictly racial community but rather on cultivating ongoing cultural and spiritual connections with Africa. Though a discourse of *mestiçagem* based in the experience and popular culture of Rio de Janeiro dominated expressions of Brazil's racial democracy in the postwar period, this vision of Bahia's direct, undiluted African connections enjoyed national and international visibility during a brief period in the early 1960s, when Brazilian officials sought to portray their nation as "the largest African nation outside of Africa."

Senhora's rise as a national and international symbol of Brazil's African connections reached its apex just after the military coup of 1964 put an end to Quadros and Goulart's independent foreign policy and, more broadly, to Brazil's democratic Second Republic. On 13 May 1965 (the anniversary of the abolition of slavery and, coincidentally that year, Mother's Day), Mãe Senhora was the guest of honor at a festival in Rio de Janeiro's Maracanã Stadium celebrating Brazil's African traditions. The festival, cosponsored by the UNESCO, the national government, and Rio's municipal government, featured Afro-Brazilian religious and popular music and dances, and brought together high-ranking guests from the rest of Latin America. At this festival, Mãe Senhora became the first recipient of a new honorific national title. In a special ceremony, with thousands of people looking on, a UNESCO representative dubbed Mãe Senhora the "Mãe Preta" of Brazil—the living embodiment of Brazil's historical and emotional ties to the African continent.[137] This familial metaphor was appropriate for a woman who, as a religious authority, had adopted leading white public figures, from Jorge Amado to Pierre Verger, as her "filhos de santo" or spiritual sons. For Senhora, it no doubt resonated with her own and her predecessors' efforts to establish their respectability as black women through one of the few positive images available to them: the spiritually, culturally, and physically nourishing Black Mother, who admitted both black and white Brazilians into her proverbial arms. On receiving her new title, Senhora stepped comfortably into the nostalgic, harmonizing, and nationalistic role of the Mãe Preta, but not without giving it an explicitly African and religious twist: "In the name of all of the *orixás*, I bless my black and white *filhos* [sons/children] from all over Brazil . . . which is the best land in the world."[138]

It is perhaps not surprising that the Bahian vision of Brazil's African connections was so alluring to the national government in the early 1960s. This vision cast Africa in cultural terms (rather than in the political or racial terms of Paulistano black thinkers) and, specifically, in terms that portrayed African culture as part of a traditional Brazilian culture (and not as part of an international vanguard, as intellectuals in Rio's TEN depicted it). The ascendancy of Bahian Candomblé as an icon of an African Brazil in some ways afforded African culture the specificity and difference within Brazilian culture that many Candomblé leaders had long advocated. Yet at the same time, the national government's celebration of Bahia as the embodiment of Brazil's pure African traits in the service of foreign policy sequestered an African Brazil in a place distant from the cultural, political, and economic capitals of Rio, Brasília, and São Paulo, which remained icons of modernity.

The repressive potentials of this vision, largely latent in a period of left-populist rule, would become manifest once the post-1964 military dictatorship redeployed Brazil's African heritage to enforce an authoritarian vision of Brazil's racial democracy, and to shut down debates about racial discrimination. By the mid-1970s, a new generation of black thinkers in Rio de Janeiro, São Paulo, and Salvador da Bahia would make the dictatorship governments' celebrations of an apolitical Africa and of racial democracy the main targets of their activism. In different ways, they would take Africa's struggles for independence and self-determination as ever more explicit models for their own cause, demanding their equal rights as citizens of what they too portrayed as the largest African nation outside of Africa—one of the few still awaiting decolonization.

6. Decolonization
Rio de Janeiro, Salvador da Bahia,
and São Paulo, 1964–1985

Until 1964 most black thinkers remained committed to turning the dominant idea of racial democracy to their advantage, refining and contesting its meanings in a democratic public sphere. This situation changed drastically after the military coup in late March of that year. The coup put an end to the democratic Second Republic and inaugurated a succession of authoritarian governments that repressed black thinkers and organizations, along with unions, student groups, and leftists, as subversive threats to national security. By the end of the 1960s, most race-based organizations in Rio de Janeiro and São Paulo disbanded, and the black press fell silent.

The military officers who took power after 1964 adopted racial democracy as an official state ideology. But their vision of racial democracy, adapted to the needs of a right-wing nationalist regime, was a far cry from the one that had inspired black thinkers and activists at midcentury. Representatives of the authoritarian state used the idea that Brazil was a racial democracy to shut down public discussions about racial discrimination and to justify state suppression of race-based organizing. Architects of the regime's cultural policies leaned on select aspects of Brazil's African heritage—particularly those deemed quaintly folkloric and politically unthreatening—to illustrate Brazil's racial harmony, even as the state produced this apparent absence of racial grievances through censorship and police intimidation. Finally, backed by the threat of military force, the state's idealization of *mestiçagem* stifled the claims to racial and cultural difference black thinkers had insisted on in previous decades.

To black thinkers who had sought to make racial democracy a vehicle for social change in the emerging political democracy of the Second Republic, the dictatorship governments' cynical and disempowering deployment of racial democracy drained the idea of its earlier attractions. By the mid-1970s, as the dictatorship entered a phase of decompression that allowed for the gradual reemergence of political and social movements, veteran black thinkers, together with a new generation of college-educated people of color, announced a transformed black politics. Racial democracy was not a path toward inclusion, they contended, but a "myth"—an insidious mirage disguising a bleak and violent landscape of racism. Even worse than the notorious institutionalized racism of South Africa or of Portugal's remaining African colonies, Brazilian-style racism, masquerading as racial harmony, had kept people of color passively subjected to a centuries-long succession of racist governments, of which the present dictatorship was but the latest unfortunate example. Like their still colonized African brethren, these writers therefore argued, what black Brazilians needed was not "inclusion" in a mixed or whitened nation but decolonization: liberation from the political, economic, and ideological domination of an illegitimate white minority. Only then, and with the return of democracy, could Brazilians build a new social order true to Brazil's status as the largest black nation outside of Africa.

In Rio de Janeiro, Salvador da Bahia, and São Paulo, new black political and cultural organizations drew inspiration from African decolonization movements, as well as from the international Left and the U.S. civil rights movement, to criticize the dictatorship and dominant racial ideologies. In all three places, black thinkers sought to denounce racism, expose racial democracy as a "myth," and mobilize Brazilians of color around specifically *negro* (rather than mixed) identities, in order to reveal Brazil as a majority black nation. As at other moments in the twentieth century, black thinkers and community leaders in each of these places pursued their work from within distinct regional traditions of activism. But the 1970s and early 1980s provided increased opportunities for exchange and convergence among black thinkers in different parts of the country. Seeking to build a wide front of opposition to the regime, black intellectuals in Rio, Salvador, and São Paulo looked toward one another and began to establish personal and institutional connections with their counterparts in these (and other) cities. One of the outcomes of this exchange was a new openness to styles and strategies of racial politics long associated (positively or negatively) with a particular city or region. Specifically, in all three places, black thought and politics in the 1970s and early 1980s witnessed a new synthesis between the explicitly political, race-based, culturally unmarked activism that São Paulo's black thinkers had adopted as their trademark for most of the century, and the emphasis on different kinds of African-inflected culture that had figured so prominently in the activism of black Cariocas and Bahians since the early 1900s.

This cross-pollination of political and cultural concerns—abetted by activists' shared point of reference in African decolonization movements that stressed both aspects of self-determination—gave black Brazilian politics a more national cast than ever before. It also gave black thinkers in each city a new and forceful language through which to communicate their criticism of the regime and of reigning racial ideologies. In Rio de Janeiro, activists' adoption of a militant rhetoric of blackness was a particularly provocative rejoinder to the national traditions of racial and cultural *mestiçagem* purportedly embodied in that city and its popular culture—a vision dear not just to conservatives, but also, as in earlier years, to many on the left. In Salvador, emerging carnival associations newly (and controversially) associated the African traditions of Candomblé with an explicit politics of *negro* identity and with open denunciations of racism. And in São Paulo, black thinkers found new value in the African cultural and religious traditions they had once denigrated, as they sought to extend the appeal of their racial politics in and beyond their city.

The emerging black movement of the 1970s in many ways marks a break with previous patterns of black mobilization in Brazil. In terms of scale and organization, the struggle against racial discrimination expanded and gathered unprecedented momentum in these years. Through collaborations between veteran activists and the first generation of college-educated black students, through the multiplication of black cultural and political groups across Brazil, and through increased efforts at cooperation and centralization, black thinkers achieved their highest national profile since the days of the Frente Negra. The self-perception of members of black organizations in these years shifted as well. Hoping to reach out to constituencies broader than those many of the black thinkers of previous decades had been able to attain, and embracing an oppositional relationship to the state and dominant society, these men and women described themselves not as black intellectuals (though intellectuals they often were) but as *militantes negros*—black activists. Finally, by breaking with longstanding attempts by black thinkers to find the antiracist potential in national ideologies of racial inclusiveness, members of the emerging Movimento Negro expressed the conviction that they were coming to true political consciousness. What the dictatorship had done by presenting the oppressive aspects of racial democracy in such pure form, they believed, was to open their eyes to a reality that had eluded earlier generations of black thinkers, enabling them, at last, to take a radical stand against racial oppression.

This moment in Brazilian black politics, perhaps the most widely discussed, remembered, and studied for twentieth-century Brazil, presents a challenge of historical interpretation. Tracing the remarkable range of organizations that emerged in Brazil in the mid-1970s, and the incisive critiques they offered, it is tempting to adopt these activists' assessment of racial democracy as mere myth and to accept their implicit (and in a few cases, explicit) characterization of earlier modes of black politics as weak and compromised. Yet to do so would be to adopt the perspective of a singular generation of black thinkers, at a particular historical moment, as the standard for black thought and activism across vastly different terrains of time, place, and circumstance. Compelling as their claims to clear-sighted historical critique may be, the black politics of the dictatorship era do not stand above or apart from earlier attempts to claim racial fraternity and racial democracy as inclusive, antiracist ideals. Only by connecting these moments in the longer history of black thought and politics can we can understand why, when an authoritarian regime flagrantly betrayed these long-standing ideals, black thinkers turned so sharply against them.

"Brazil has no minorities"

The military took power in 1964 in response to a leftward turn in João Goulart's democratic government. In the face of intensified pressure from popular sectors to expand Brazil's democracy, Goulart had proposed measures ranging from land expropriation and the nationalization of oil refineries to the expansion of the vote to illiterate citizens. Brazilians had always been deeply divided in their support for Goulart, who was not elected president but had succeeded to the post after the resignation of the democratically elected Jânio Quadros. Over the course of his short term, Goulart's increasing radicalism, his apparent concessions to the bold demands of unions and other leftist groups, and a persistent economic crisis during which inflation exceeded 100 percent alienated conservatives, the military, and many middle-class Brazilians. What to some seemed like a democratic opening backed by a commitment to social equality to others seemed like a less-than-democratic breakdown of the social order. Between 31 March and 1 April 1964, in a quick and largely bloodless coup, the military took over government offices.[1]

General Humberto de Alencar Castello Branco, who assumed the presidency in April 1964, was a relative moderate, concerned with the appearance of legality and legitimacy. Though he replaced Brazil's political parties with an official two-party system and purged government institutions of leftists, in the first two to three years of military rule, the opposition had some room to maneuver. Workers, students, intellectuals, and artists frequently expressed their discontent with the regime through strikes, public protests, and the media. Indeed, though the paucity of new black organizations and publications in this early period of military rule suggests that it was not the most propitious time for race-based organizing, these activities were not specifically forbidden. In São Paulo, for instance, José Correia Leite remained at the helm of his ACN until 1965, when ill health forced him to retire. But the ACN continued its activities (albeit less vigorously than before the coup) under new leadership until 1969.[2] In Rio, Abdias do Nascimento's TEN continued to function until 1968.[3]

The situation began to change after 1967, when hard-line sectors of the military took over, installing General Artur da Costa e Silva as president. To Costa e Silva and his supporters, the first regime had not gone far enough in imposing order and restraining the people. For them, Brazil's ills ran deep; democracy was corrupt and untenable, and only a long period of authoritarian rule could heal a sick society and restore it to a proper patriarchal, Christian order. In December 1968 the regime issued Institutional Act 5, which greatly expanded the state's powers, shut down Congress, instituted intense media censorship, and renewed purges in government offices and universities. By 1969, as government repression grew, so did armed resistance to the regime, in the form of urban and rural guerrillas. Under General Emílio Garrastazu Médici (1969–74), the dictatorship entered its most repressive phase, stamping out "subversion" through kidnappings, detentions, torture, and assassinations, and sending thousands of Brazilians—including many middle- and upper-class students, artists, and intellectuals—into voluntary or forced exile.

It was in this period that the regime began to back the ideology of a harmonious, *mestiço* Brazil with the state's repressive apparatus. In 1969 the National Security Council declared it an act of "leftist subversion," aimed at "provok[ing] new sources of dissatisfaction against the regime and . . . the duly constituted authorities," to write or speak about the issue of racial discrimination.[4] Through countless pronouncements, publications, and cultural policies, regime ideologues proclaimed racial and cultural *mestiçagem* to be a pillar of national order, strength, and security.[5] In keeping with this official stance on race, the National Census Commission opted to exclude color categories from the census of 1970, for the first time in decades.[6] Between the late 1960s and the mid-1970s, moreover, government censors were instructed to keep any reference to U.S. racial movements out of movies entering Brazil, and to control the media and public events more broadly for any views that might contradict the official image of Brazil's racial democracy.[7] The armed forces and political police participated actively in these tasks. In 1971, for instance, on reading press reports of the recent opening in Rio of a show by a black U.S. dance troupe, the Army sent a letter to Rio's secret police warning them that the dancers might attempt to preach Black Power ideologies to their audiences. "Measures must be taken to avoid that sort of propaganda, and to prevent the introduction within our population of foreign problems that do not exist in Brazil and that under no circumstance should be raised or instigated."[8] Several leading academics lost their jobs in the wake of these censorship laws; in 1969, to cite a famous example, state-led purges at the University of São Paulo resulted in the forced retirement of sociologists Florestan Fernandes, Octavio Ianni, and Fernando Henrique Cardoso—three prominent researchers into, among other things, racial inequality.[9] In this suffocating climate, most leading activists lowered their profiles or went into exile. Abdias do Nascimento, whose TEN had weathered the first four years of the dictatorship, fled to the United States, taking up a position as professor at SUNY-Buffalo.[10]

By the early 1970s the breadth and depth of repression had eroded most middle-class support for the dictatorship, setting the stage for a return to democracy. When General Ernesto Geisel assumed power in 1974, he responded to the public mood by promising a gradual easing of government repression. This period of political decompression (*distensão*), which lasted through the end of Geisel's rule in 1979, allowed for the reemergence of a civil society marked by the return of older social and political movements (such as labor) and the rise of new ones. Under Geisel's successor, General João Baptista de Oliveira Figueiredo (1979–85), Brazil entered a period known as the *abertura* (opening), a broad-based popular push for a return to democracy. Figueiredo continued to roll back censorship, began to respect basic political and civil liberties, and slowly prepared Brazil for the election of a civilian president. Yet even as the easing of government repression under Geisel and Figueiredo legally allowed for the emergence of black racial and cultural organizations across Brazil, these regimes maintained earlier military governments' view of racial democracy as a discourse of order, assimilation, and submission. Though no longer overtly persecuted in the period of political decompression, black organizations, as we will see, were nonetheless heavily discouraged as traitorously un-Brazilian, and closely policed as an ongoing threat to national security.

Just as the ideology of racial democracy served as a tool for social control at home, related ideas about Brazil's racelessness and deep African cultural traditions served the regimes' foreign policy goals abroad. By the late 1960s, successive military administrations returned, after an initial moment of cooled relations with Africa under Castello Branco, to a version of the African foreign policy developed by President Quadros in the early 1960s.[11] This was, to use those officials' own term, a "pragmatic" approach to Brazilian-African relations, one that subordinated ongoing geopolitical concerns about the region's many left-leaning governments to Brazil's pressing search for new markets and trading partners. During what historian José Flavio Sombra Saraiva has termed the "Golden Years" of Brazil's Africa policy (1967–79), trade with West Africa (especially Nigeria) and eventually with the former colonies of Portugal (especially Angola) became the express goal of Brazil's Africa policy. Brazilian diplomacy once more quickened its pace, promoting trade accords with Africa, opening new consulates and embassies on the continent, and arranging reciprocal visits of statesmen and businessmen.[12] The media, for its part, began in the mid-1970s to present Africa as a land of opportunity for Brazilian businessmen. As one reporter put it, Brazilians in this period were "fazendo a África" or "making it in Africa," in reference to the phrase *fazendo a América* used to describe the wild economic successes of European immigrants to Latin America in the nineteenth and early twentieth centuries.[13] For Adalberto Camargo, a black congressman from São Paulo and the president of a newly established Afro-Brazilian Chamber of Commerce (1968), this period was a veritable "return to Africa."[14]

The push to penetrate emerging African markets gained pace after 1975 when, in the wake of an internal revolution that put an end to the dictatorship of Antonio de Oliveira Salazar, Portugal granted independence to its African colonies. Brazilian policymakers rushed to fill the power vacuum, promoting their nation, larger and more economically powerful than Portugal, as the premier diplomatic, cultural, and commercial partner for the former Portuguese colonies. They simultaneously sought to dispel Brazil's image (cemented under Castello Branco) as a supporter of Portuguese colonialism and of South Africa's racist policies. In this spirit, between 1975 and 1980, Brazil worked to recognize the Marxist government of independent Angola, stepped up its public condemnations of apartheid, sponsored the visits of growing numbers of ambassadors and other dignitaries from Africa, and eventually withdrew from discussions of a South Atlantic pact with South Africa and Argentina.[15] These overtures paid off: from 1975 into the early 1980s, Brazil became "the prime beneficiary in all bilateral trade relations with African nations."[16] The "pragmatic" nature of these gestures becomes evident, however, when we consider that throughout this period, Brazil refused to break its diplomatic and (lucrative) commercial ties with South Africa despite its vocal condemnation of apartheid, and that it opened its doors to white colonizers (self-styled "refugees") fleeing independence revolutions in Portuguese Africa and the Belgian Congo.[17]

Against this backdrop of renewed commercial and diplomatic interest in Africa, what Saraiva calls the "culturalist discourse" of a shared heritage between Brazil and Africa reemerged with vigor in official circles and in Brazilian public life.[18] State-owned and private enterprises in this period flooded Africa, and especially the emerging markets of large Portuguese-speaking nations like Angola and Mozambique, with the products of officially sanctioned Brazilian popular culture—from mass education programs to *telenovelas*, from MPB (*música popular brasileira*, or Brazilian popular music) to the novels of Jorge Amado.[19] These cultural productions portrayed Brazil as an African-influenced, "tropical" lusophone nation akin to the former Portuguese colonies (if more modern, experienced, and developed), and therefore ideally suited to become their main diplomatic and commercial partner. Though primarily directed at new audiences in central and southern Africa, these portrayals of an Africanized Brazil, much like those the state exported in the early 1960s, relied heavily on older icons of Afro-Brazilianness drawn from a West African (especially Yoruba) heritage.

Perhaps nowhere is the substance and style of this culturalist discourse toward Africa more evident than in documents surrounding Brazil's participation in the Second World Black and African Festival of Arts and Culture (FESTAC II) in Lagos, Nigeria, in 1977. Itamaraty, the Brazilian Foreign Ministry, coordinated Brazil's presence at the event, and selected Clarival do Prado Valladares, a prominent Bahian art critic specializing in Afro-Brazilian art, to author the official publication describing the Brazilian delegation. *The Impact of African Culture on Brazil* (released in advance of the festival) guided the reader through the many planned performances and exhibits intended to highlight a range of African contributions to Brazilian culture. A section on modern art, the centerpiece of the delegation's offerings, was perhaps the closest to the vision of cultural similarity between Brazil and Africa developed in the early 1960s. As Valladares described the logic behind the selection of each artist to represent Brazil in Nigeria (besides the festival's own requirement he or she be of African descent), or as he explained why each body of work qualified as "African culture," Valladares invoked their connections with what had emerged in that previous period as the classic sites for measuring and displaying Brazil's African heritage: codified elements of Yoruba culture, notably Candomblé.[20] Working with scholars like Valladares, officials at Itamaraty put together an exhibit of Brazil's Africanness that would have exceeded the expectations of their counterparts in the early 1960s.

But for all its continuity with previous displays of Brazil's Africanness, Itamaraty's 1976 publication demonstrates how ideas about Brazil's African culture took on significantly different meanings under military rule. Diplomats and scholars of the early 1960s had circulated a view of African culture in Brazil that emphasized the importance of ongoing contacts in maintaining that culture's strength and "purity," and that reflected the claims to cultural and racial distinctiveness of some black Brazilians. Valladares's account, by contrast, portrayed African culture as a thing of the past, no longer physically linked to Africa or even necessarily to people of African descent in Brazil. He wrote, abstractly, of "African prototypes," the "heritage of the ur-culture of African origin," and the "inspirational force stemming from African, ancestral aesthetic realities."[21] The African "impact," for Valladares, was a sort of historical collision among cultures that bequeathed Brazil a disembodied, ethereal African cultural sensibility.

This perspective on Brazil's African heritage as a thing of the past was consistent with a more general "backward look" in ideas about national culture among state intellectuals at the time. The dictatorship governments sought to portray Brazilian history after 1964 not as a rupture with the past, but as the restoration of traditional, hierarchical, sociopolitical structures. Specifically, anthropologist Renato Ortiz argues, the military governments turned to "traditional intellectuals" (conservative scholars in places like academies of letters or historical and geographical institutes, such as Gilberto Freyre) to catalog and preserve "expressions and manifestations configured in the Brazilian past." Examining the writings of the Conselho Federal de Cultura (CFC, a body created in 1965 to coordinate the state's cultural policy, and composed largely of these kinds of conservative intellectuals), Ortiz concludes that national culture, for much of the dictatorship, was imagined as an unchanging patrimony, "a group of spiritual and material values accumulated throughout time."[22] Not surprisingly, the author of Itamaraty's exhibition booklet, Valladares, was himself a member of the CFC, actively engaged in the official project to preserve and "defend" Brazilian culture against modernization and foreign influences—a task he considered crucial to protecting Brazil's "national security."[23] In the context of this right-wing cultural nationalism, Africa was not the revolutionary continent that had whetted the political aspirations of black Paulistano activists in the previous decade, or the inspiration for the artistic vanguards that fueled black Cariocas' claims to difference in a culturally mixed Brazil, or even the source of the religious connections through which Bahia's Candomblé leaders composed a distinct identity as African Brazilians. Rather, as portrayed by the state, Brazil's Africanness was a folkloric, ancient, and depoliticized presence, heavily mediated by cultural and racial mixture, and contained by processes of nationalization—an Africa barely suitable for racial or ethnic mobilization.

Itamaraty's official publication for the FESTAC also illustrates the ways intellectuals affiliated with the military regime used ideologies of *mestiçagem* to promote a homogeneous, organic nation and to blot out claims to black cultural or racial distinctiveness. In response to the FESTAC's requirement that all artists included in the Brazilian delegation be of African descent, Valladares and his patrons at Itamaraty let it be known that in Brazil, African cultural traits did not belong exclusively to African-descended Brazilians, but were the shared patrimony of a *mestiço* nation (whose leaders and official representatives only happened to be white). The head of the Brazilian delegation, Ambassador Francisco de Assis Grieco, boasted in Valladares's publication that "Brazil has no minorities. We are a *mestizo* [sic] people and a people of African culture."[24] Elsewhere in his text, Valladares explained the roots of this phenomenon. Over time, "the predominance of the Negro declined in the face of the natural ascendcy [sic] of his *mestizo* [sic] descendants." Yet "even as miscegenation waters down the ethnical [sic] characteristics themselves, the marks of African ascent gain greater weight in the entire basic structure."[25] Intellectuals from Rio's TEN at midcentury might have agreed with such celebrations of Brazil's racial mixture and African culture, and even with the idea that Brazil's African-descended population was not a minority but the *povo* itself. They, however, had made those claims while asserting their rights to distinctiveness as black intellectuals uniquely positioned to interpret Brazil's mixed culture. Public officials and intellectuals during the dictatorship invoked ideas of *mestiçagem* to a much different end: to declare illegitimate any claims to racial or cultural difference, and by extension, any politics based on specifically racial or ethnic grievances.

These sorts of repressive, instrumental uses of Brazil's African culture and purported racial harmony led black thinkers and activists, once they were able to regain their voices in the decompression of the mid-1970s, to break with black thinkers' earlier endorsements of national ideologies of racial inclusiveness. Both for veteran activists who had experienced the progressive potential of racial democracy at midcentury only to see it hopelessly shattered under military rule, and for a new generation of black student radicals who came of age during the dictatorship's most repressive years, racial democracy appeared as not an unfulfilled ideal worth fighting for but an outright lie. To Abdias do Nascimento, who spent many of the dictatorship years in exile abroad, attempts by government officials and diplomats under successive military regimes to present Brazil as a racial democracy were particularly insulting and injurious, closing off potential networks of international support for black Brazilians in their struggle against a racist regime and society.

Nascimento had begun his public attacks on the dictatorship's racial politics as early as 1966. That year, as director of the TEN, still living in Brazil, he sent an open letter to the first World Festival of Black Arts, held in Dakar, Senegal, denouncing Itamaraty's failure to send any black representatives to the event even as the Foreign Ministry's official publication praised *Africa's Contribution to Brazilian Civilization*.[26] By 1977, when the Brazilian government attempted once more to sell itself as a racial democracy to the international audiences gathered at the second FESTAC in Lagos, Nascimento, who had been living in Nigeria as a visiting professor since September of the previous year, seized the opportunity to correct that impression. Appointing himself an unofficial member of the Brazilian delegation, Nascimento delivered a paper titled "'Racial Democracy' in Brazil: Myth or Reality?," in which he laid out the searing public attack on the "myth" of racial democracy that I briefly discussed in the introduction.

"Brazil, as a nation," Nascimento's paper began, "proclaims itself to be the only racial democracy in the world, and much of the world respects it as such. Yet a close examination of its historical development reveals the true nature of its social, cultural, and political structures: they are essentially racist, and vitally threatening to blacks." Racial democracy, Nascimento contended, was nothing but a spurious myth, an elite ideology of domination "diametrically opposed" to Brazil's realities of inequality, and deployed in order to hide them. Throughout his paper, Nascimento set out to demolish the main arguments that sustained this "myth," exposing them as part of a systematic attempt on the part of Brazilian elites to erase black people and their culture from the nation. He denounced interracial marriage—long a measure of Brazil's supposed racial tolerance—as the sexual exploitation of African women, and called the much idealized process of *mestiçagem* a "strategy of genocide." Nascimento expressed his disgust with cultural politics, like Valladares's, that celebrated the "ascendancy" of African culture in Brazil. In his view, such celebrations—part of a broader scheme to "immobilize" and "marginalize" African culture as "mere folklore"—simply signaled the co-optation of that culture by white elites. Moreover, Nascimento pointed out, these celebrations of Brazil's Africanness hid the fact that any "persistence" of African culture in Brazil took place *despite* the active and vicious persecution it suffered for centuries. To Nascimento, the combination of hegemonic discourses of *mestiçagem* and racelessness, together with strategic celebrations of the nation's Africanness, had the disastrous effect of "denying [blacks] the means of racial identification"—the crucial self-recognition necessary to begin to resist racial domination.[27]

Nascimento's intervention at the 1977 FESTAC was perhaps the most vocal and well-publicized attack, by a black activist in his time, on Brazil's image as a racial democracy. Expanded soon thereafter and published in Portuguese as *O genocídio do negro brasileiro* [*The Genocide of Black Brazilians*], Nascimento's piece became a manifesto of the black thought and politics of the 1970s and 1980s, an icon of the sea change that had taken place in black thinkers' relationship to dominant ideologies of race. Though Nascimento, as an exile, partly developed this critique in dialogue with scholars and activists in the United States and Africa, it also reflected his close and ongoing ties with black activists back home, then in the midst of great political ferment.[28] In Brazil, a new generation of college-educated black thinkers who came of age at the height of the dictatorship's repression also contrasted their reality, and that of other, less fortunate black Brazilians, to the rosy discourses produced by regime-affiliated intellectuals like Valladares. Just as the regime drew on Africa (the place and its people, culture, and politics) to compose and disseminate its vision of a racially harmonious Brazil, so too did these young thinkers, often in dialogue with veterans like Nascimento, rely on Africa to expose this vision as a myth veiling a much bleaker reality.

Breaking the Monopoly on Africa

Even as official intellectual life and diplomatic practice shifted to the right after 1964, the African studies and international relations establishment of the early 1960s persisted in pockets, paving the way for the black activism of the 1970s. In Rio de Janeiro, during the political decompression of the mid-1970s, black activism reemerged in the spaces afforded by the fledgling Centro de Estudos Afro-Asiáticos (CEAA, or Center for Afro-Asian Studies) of the private Cândido Mendes University. In the early 1960s, Cândido Mendes de Almeida, the grandson of the university's founder, had himself been a founding member and the second director of the IBEAA, the academic organization set up to advise President Quadros on Brazil's independent foreign policy toward Africa. Mendes was part of the cohort of politically engaged white intellectuals, like Agostinho da Silva in Salvador, who in the early 1960s sought to reshape Brazil's foreign policy and academic institutions to reach out to decolonizing African nations and to better reflect Brazil's African heritage. In 1967 Castello Branco's government shut down the IBEAA. But in 1973 Mendes—protected by powerful family connections and close ties to the Catholic Church—took the spirit of the IBEAA, as well as its collection of books, to a suite of offices in the well-to-do neighborhood of Ipanema, where he founded the small but dynamic CEAA. The CEAA reflected the interests of Mendes and of his close collaborator, José Maria Nunes Pereira, a white Brazilian who had pursued his university studies in Portugal and who, as a member of an organization for students from Portuguese colonies in Lisbon (the Casa dos Estudantes do Império), had established friendships with many Portuguese-speaking Africans and become interested in their decolonization struggles. Like the architects of Brazil's independent foreign policy in the early 1960s, Mendes and Pereira envisioned their responsibility toward Africa in terms of the spirit of the 1955 Bandung conference on decolonization: Third World solidarity, national self-determination, liberation, and antiracism. They were primarily interested in emerging nationalist movements in Portuguese-speaking Africa (Angola, Guinea-Bissau, Mozambique, and Cape Verde) and were involved in antiapartheid activism.[29]

It was these issues of African decolonization and Third World solidarity, rather than questions of race and discrimination in Brazil, that had originally guided Mendes and Pereira's work at the CEAA. But in 1974 a small group of black students from Rio's Universidade Federal Fluminense, under the leadership of historians Maria Maia Berriel (a professor) and Beatriz do Nascimento (a graduate student), visited the center's library to conduct research on the history of race relations in Brazil. In addition to works on Afro-Brazilian politics and culture, they discovered a wealth of information on Africa and Brazilian-African relations. They began to hold informal weekly meetings at the CEAA to discuss these topics and the relationships among them. At first, José Maria Nunes Pereira recalled, the Saturday meetings that began in April 1974 were small—just over ten people. But a few weeks later, almost one hundred students of color from several of Rio's universities crowded into the CEAA's small Ipanema offices. Guided by their own emerging interests, the students investigated the history of black movements in Brazil and read the works of Brazilian black intellectuals like Alberto Guerreiro Ramos, Abdias do Nascimento, or Solano Trinidade.[30] These were formative experiences for these young university students. Amauri Mendes Pereira, an early active participant in the CEAA group, recalled that until those meetings, he and many of his colleagues knew little or nothing about the history of organized racial struggles in Brazil. He himself had never before heard of explicitly black groups like the Frente Negra or activists like Abdias do Nascimento. Carlos Alberto Medeiros, another young activist who participated in these events, remembered, "It was as if we were starting from zero, even though we weren't."[31]

These students' sense that they were "starting from zero" as they set out to learn the history of racial struggles in Brazil is telling of the political moment in which they lived. As young university students in the mid-1970s, many of them came of age during the most repressive phases of the dictatorship, when the state had shut down race-based organizations and banned public discussions of racial discrimination. Yet even in the absence of information about the history of racial politics in Brazil, their own experiences as college students and young professionals would have made them highly aware of the racial barriers that kept them, despite their qualifications, from fully enjoying the benefits of Brazil's "economic miracle." After 1968 Brazil entered a period of intense economic growth, in which the national economy expanded at a rate of just over 10 percent a year. As with the development boom of the late 1950s, the benefits of this economic expansion accrued highly unevenly across Brazil, with industry receiving the lion's share of growth and wealth. In industrialized regions of the country, like São Paulo and Rio de Janeiro, or newly industrializing ones, like Bahia, the "miracle" helped improve the lives of some Brazilians who were not already wealthy, through reductions in infant mortality, increased literacy rates, access to new jobs, and an expanded university system.[32] To an extent, it also benefited people of color who lived in these regions and aspired to, or had achieved, middle-class status, providing them with increased access to professional and white-collar jobs, and to secondary and college educations. But even as the economic growth of the late 1960s and 1970s broadened a modest black middle class, it widened the gulf, in terms of employment rates and salary, between blacks and whites in similar occupations. This gulf was particularly evident in the sorts of jobs to which college-educated young black men and women aspired, such as office work and the professions.[33] It is no wonder, then, that to this increasingly qualified yet still discriminated group of black students and recent graduates living under an authoritarian regime, the rhetoric of Brazil's "racial democracy" began to ring hollow.

The weekly meetings at the CEAA sharpened these students' awareness of racial inequality in more ways than one. Because of the CEAA's internationalist focus, the students who met there each week developed an understanding of racial politics in Brazil as part of a broader struggle for freedom, dignity, antiracism, and self-determination among Africans and African-descended people worldwide. Alongside the history of the Frente Negra or the Teatro Experimental do Negro, they discussed African liberation movements, pan-Africanism, cultural colonialism, négritude, and black socialism. The works of African and diasporic intellectuals like Kwame Nkrumah, Albert Memmi, Aimé Césaire, Amílcar Cabral, George Padmore, Léopold Senghor, Sékou Touré, Agostinho Neto, Julius Nyerere, and, above all, Frantz Fanon, made up the core of their curriculum. Fanon's *Wretched of the Earth* had been banned by the dictatorship's censors, but it was nonetheless widely read (just as African guerrillas and liberation movements were safely discussed) within the CEAA. Mendes's renown in government circles afforded him some leeway, which he used to carve out protected spaces for these conversations in the repressive atmosphere of Brazil's military dictatorship.[34] But he did not operate the center entirely free of restraints. According to one historian of the CEAA, in the highly segregated space of Rio de Janeiro's mostly white, wealthy Zona Sul, the presence of "a group of nearly one hundred black students exiting the Cândido Mendes School in Ipanema all at once, at 9 o'clock [after the Saturday night meetings], ended up attracting notice." Mendes continued to allow the meetings, but when "pressures mounted, he recommended that some whites be incorporated into the group as well."[35] In addition to providing black students a safe site for new conversations about the forbidden topic of race in Brazil, crucially articulated alongside conversations about African decolonization, the experience of gathering weekly in the mostly white neighborhood of Ipanema—and of being reprimanded for their excessively "black" (and potentially subversive) profile—must also have taught the students valuable lessons about the limits of social and geographical mobility for people of color in their own city and country.

However nurturing and protective a space for emerging racial activism, the CEAA was nonetheless an organization run by white academics whose expertise was in African, not Afro-Brazilian, issues. Eager to create their own, explicitly activist organizations, aspiring leaders of the emerging black student movement "began little by little to establish our own contacts [with Africa] and to break, at least in Rio, the monopoly held by the Centro de Estudos Afro-Asiáticos."[36] Young activists' desire to break their white mentors' monopoly on Africa, to claim ownership of Africa for themselves, confirms the importance of that continent for these students' emerging racial politics—as well as the extent to which these politics had been shaped by the CEAA's priorities. The weekly meetings at the CEAA gave rise to two of the leading black organizations in mid-1970s Rio de Janeiro: the Sociedade de Intercâmbio Brasil-África (SINBA, or Society for Brazilian-African Exchange) and the Instituto de Pesquisas das Culturas Negras (IPCN, or Institute for Research in Black Cultures). At its height, SINBA had an estimated 150 members, while the IPCN (according to one scholar, the most popular of Rio's black activist organizations in the mid-1970s) had more than two hundred.[37] Though they pursued the same goals, and at several times joined forces, SINBA and the IPCN worked through quite distinct, and often opposing, political strategies.

Brazilian-African Exchange

SINBA provides the clearest example of how engagement with African politics helped the new generation of black thinkers to articulate their own politics of opposition and racial distinctiveness in the period of political decompression. Amauri Mendes Pereira and Yedo Ferreira, black graduates of the Universidade Federal do Rio de Janeiro (UFRJ) and participants in the early meetings at the CEAA, founded SINBA in late 1974. Pereira, in his early twenties, had just finished a degree in physical education. Though he claimed to know very little about the history of formal racial activism in Brazil when he first arrived at the CEAA, his family history had nonetheless made him strongly aware of how race and racism shaped the lives of generations of Brazilians of color. Pereira's maternal grandmother was a freed slave, and his grandfather often sang the praises of Getúlio Vargas for having "blackened" (*empretecido*) the labor force through his "two-thirds" law in 1930.[38] Pereira's colleague, Yedo Ferreira, had, by his own account, given the topics of racial discrimination and racial activism relatively little thought for most of his life. A postal worker turned mathematics student (he was in his forties, much older than the others), Ferreira instead had directed his political energies primarily toward the question of class struggle. Until the onset of the dictatorship, he had been a staunch member of the Communist Party. Though he later criticized the Communists' excessive emphasis on class inequality to the detriment of racial questions, he also remembered that the Communist Party denounced the assassination of Congolese freedom fighter Patrice Lumumba in the early 1960s as a vicious colonialist act. This episode, he later recalled, began to "sensitize" him to the issue of racism and its intimate relationship with questions of class and colonial domination.[39] As students at the UFRJ, Ferreira and Pereira participated avidly in discussions of racial issues, both on campus and through the CEAA. They created SINBA as a way to explore, attract attention to, and create spaces for public debate about racial problems in Brazil and worldwide.[40]

Like their predecessors in early-twentieth-century São Paulo, these activist intellectuals sought to use the printed word as the primary medium for racial activism at a time when their access to organized politics and civil society was particularly limited. Pereira and Ferreira produced five issues of the newsletter *SINBA* between 1977 and 1980, hoping to get their message out to broader audiences. Yet their newspaper struggled with exactly the kinds of problems that had historically afflicted the black press in Brazil. *SINBA* was a small operation, with Ferreira and Pereira authoring the vast majority of the paper's unsigned articles.[41] Funds were limited, for the paper was sold for a symbolic fee, and sometimes given away. If editors of publications for "the class of color," "pretos," or "negros" in Brazil had always faced the challenge of reaching a broad readership—whether because of their intended audience's poverty, illiteracy, or lack of identification with race-based concerns—*SINBA*'s editors faced the additional hurdle of censorship under the dictatorship, which made distributing their clandestine publication both difficult and dangerous. Pereira remembered that members of various military police intelligence organizations routinely visited the city's printing presses (*SINBA* was published at a press formerly owned by the Communist Party) to collect, inspect, and possibly confiscate anything deemed subversive. To avoid the police's notice (unsuccessfully, as it turned out), Pereira and other SINBA members would "grab a stack of newspapers, hop in a taxi, get out somewhere else, and then take another taxi" in order to distribute their paper at various points throughout the city.[42]

Despite these challenges, *SINBA* quickly became one of the most influential black activist publications of its time (even reaching the attention of Abdias do Nascimento in exile), and it remained an important point of reference for the Carioca black movement through the end of the century.[43] Its articles also offer a clear view of the kinds of racial politics that the new generation of activists began to develop in the mid-1970s. Building on the discussions at the CEAA, *SINBA* helped consolidate a new black politics around two issues: "movements that are fighting against racism and colonialism, with special attention to news about the situation of African peoples," and "the struggle against racism and the centuries-long submission of blacks in Brazil."[44] For *SINBA*'s writers, these two issues were inseparable. African struggles against colonialism and racism were part of the broader global context in which their own battles against discrimination took place. From their first issue, writers argued that information on Africa's "current reality" was crucial for Brazilians' understanding of their common destiny with "the people of the Third World."[45] And they maintained that "exchanges" of knowledge and experiences (SINBA, after all, was the Society for Brazilian-African Exchange) would help brothers-in-arms on both sides of the Atlantic in their fight against racial inequality.

As *SINBA* writers developed their critique of the dictatorship and of dominant racial ideologies, they mounted an offensive against what they called "culturalism." In a definition that almost exactly described Valladares's tract on Brazil's representation at the 1977 FESTAC, Pereira and Ferreira explained that culturalism was "the idolatry of culture, the act of rendering it homage as a collection of values, in isolation, without considering the lived reality of the people who produce it." They did not deny the power of culture for transformation. As readers of Fanon from their days at the CEAA, Pereira and Ferreira believed that culture could and should be a powerful source of resistance to domination. But precisely because of this, they lamented the appropriation of popular culture—by which they meant the culture of an African-descended *povo*—by dominant elites. "Those who are in power (and Brazil is an excellent example) make use of countless stratagems in order to strip popular cultural manifestations of their character, because a people's culture is its most powerful source of mobilization, and of formation of a social conscience."[46] Key manifestations of what should rightfully be considered black culture, such as samba, the editors noted elsewhere, had been taken over by the middle classes as objects of consumption, by the state as mechanisms for social control, and even by the nationalist Left as purportedly authentic manifestations of national culture.[47] Much like Abdias do Nascimento in his polemic paper for the FESTAC, then, *SINBA* writers lamented that African cultural traits had been sequestered as folklore, co-opted by a white dominant class, stripped of their political content, and deployed in the service of a racist system. African or black culture was no longer a viable touchstone for racial politics.

SINBA writers were therefore dismayed that so many of the black organizations that blossomed in mid-1970s Rio were built almost entirely around what Pereira and Ferreira called "manifestations of black culture."[48] They might have been thinking of some of the better-known groups in Rio's contemporary black movement, like the progressive samba school Quilombo, which attempted to resist commercialization and links with Rio's tourism office, or the African-inspired dance group Olorum Baba Mim, or even the Instituto de Pesquisas das Culturas Negras, the offshoot and sometimes rival of SINBA, which boasted a full calendar of conferences, film screenings, research activities, shows, and social gatherings on various aspects of *cultura negra*. The impulse to engage in a cultural "'return-to-the-roots,'" *SINBA* writers recognized, was common to "practically all emergent movements among colonized peoples, a form of confrontation . . . of the colonizer."[49] But Pereira and Ferreira warned that these groups' well-meaning promotion of African culture ultimately risked reproducing established images of a quaint, folkloric Africa that severely undermined black politics in Brazil. "To speak of Africa as the land of our slaves, mother of our folklore, and other commonplaces, is to try to maintain an image that has been completely superseded in time."[50] Black thinkers, they believed, should no longer converse with elites in the language of *mestiçagem*, or try to find the potentially empowering spaces within dominant definitions of Afro-Brazilian culture; these were instruments of "cultural alienation."[51] Rather, at a time when official intellectuals claimed a quaint and ancestral Africa for stifling national ideologies of race, *SINBA* writers sought to reconnect with "[Africa's] recent history, its peoples, its accomplishments, in short its current events."[52] Redefining Africa as an erupting front of revolution and decolonization, rather than as an ancient source of staid culture and folklore, they believed, was the key to a reinvigorated, oppositional black politics in Brazil.

This was a different kind of contemporary link to Africa than the one envisioned by a previous generation of scholars and activists in Rio and Bahia. *SINBA* held that the Africa worth knowing was not one of diasporic literary and artistic vanguards or of venerable Yoruba ritual practices; rather, it was an anticolonial, antiracist, and politically charged Africa, one that remained hidden from Brazilian audiences by the dictatorship state and its heavily censored media. Echoing coverage of Africa in the Paulistano black press of the early 1960s, *SINBA* writers declared that it was "the struggles of the people of South Africa, of Zimbabwe and of Namibia against imperialist and racist domination; the efforts of African peoples to free themselves of neocolonialism; and the national reconstruction efforts of the people who fought for liberty in Angola, Guinea-Bissau, and Mozambique" that "we must be very interested in hearing, reading, and speaking about."[53] Like José Correia Leite in early 1960s São Paulo, *SINBA*'s editors explicitly imagined their links with Africa in terms of "solidarity with the peoples of black Africa who fight against white minority governments."[54]

Of all of these examples of African struggle, *SINBA* writers made the most expansive use of the antiapartheid movement in South Africa. On the front page of their first issue, for instance, they ran an interview with a student leader in the townships of Soweto (outside of Johannesburg), who recounted the strength of the student antiracist movement there, and its confrontations with a repressive regime. Above the article, an image of Africa and Brazil with their coastlines neatly fitted together, and arrows pointing East and West to suggest closeness and dialogue, illustrated this vision of exchange and shared experience.[55] At first, such expressions of solidarity with the revolutionary struggle against South Africa's racist government fell short of actually criticizing the Brazilian government. But increasingly, discussions about South Africa became a tool for exposing and discrediting the idea that Brazil was a racial democracy. On several occasions, *SINBA* criticized the hypocrisy of the Brazilian regime, which proclaimed itself a defender of antiracism and publicly condemned apartheid in international forums, yet maintained commercial and diplomatic ties with the racist dictatorship in South Africa.[56] On others, they argued more forcefully that the alliance with South Africa in international affairs was in fact consistent with Brazilian racial politics; what they mocked as hypocritical were claims, such as the one made by Brazil's ambassador to the United Nations, that "the apartheid regime is the complete antithesis of Brazilian history and culture. Nothing could be more incompatible with the Brazilian people than racism and its institutionalization."[57] In article after article about police brutality, racial discrimination, poverty, forced sterilization, and other forms of social violence disproportionately borne by black Brazilians, *SINBA* writers disproved such claims, exposing the absurd dissonance between discourses of harmony and realities of discrimination in Brazil.[58] Through this work, *SINBA* declared: "We are taking large strides toward unmasking the racial aspect of the domination and exploitation imposed on us. Then we will see that there is not really that great a difference between Brazil and South Africa."[59]

Indeed, beyond exposing the "myth" of racial democracy to withering ridicule, the strategy of comparing Brazil to South Africa symbolically reconfigured Brazil from a racially democratic nation of *mestiços* to a majority black nation ruled by an illegitimate white minority. On one occasion, for instance, *SINBA* wrote approvingly of a talk given at a seminar on racism in South Africa: "Brazil and Apartheid—An Example of Two States Turned against Their Own People."[60] What Brazilian blacks therefore needed, *SINBA* writers argued, was not inclusion but decolonization. Likely influenced by Ferreira's experience with communism as well as by contacts with the student Left in Brazil, the writers in *SINBA* saw African revolutionary struggles as a model for Brazilian blacks, who, they believed, ought to move away from "elitist" and ineffective cultural activities toward a mass political movement to overthrow the white dictatorship. Moving in the leftist political circles of the time, which called for nothing less than socialist revolution, SINBA members

SINBA

ORGÃO DE DIVULGAÇÃO DA SOCIEDADE DE INTERCÂMBIO BRASIL-ÁFRICA

| ANO I | RIO DE JANEIRO, JULHO DE 1977 | N.º 1 |

Depoimento de um líder estudantil de Soweto

AJUEA DÉ CUSTO Cr$ 2,00

(NASHININI)

— A POPULAÇÃO negra sul-africana é constantemente submetida a uma repressão tão grande, que bastam poucas iniciativas para que se alcance certa prática política, passando à luta organizada. Ideologia política seguida pelos negros é na verdade traçada pelas atrocidades a que os brancos nos submeteram. Eomos capazes de identificar com facilidade todos os elementos da opressão que sofremos, e de escolher os meios de combatê-la. Não temos a necessidade de que nos ditem nossa conduta. Sabemos muito bem o que quer dizer "educação bantu": um conceito e uma prática introduzidos pelo regime com a finalidade de ensinar as crianças negras a servirem ao homem branco, assim que elas se tornem membros ativos da força de trabalho. Além disso, nossas escolas foram dididas segundo critérios puramente étnicos, coisa que os estudantes jamais aceitaram. Recentemente, os departamento de administração e educação bantu decidiram que os estudantes negros deveriam aprender a "viver" em duas línguas, inglês e afrikaans, idioma inventado pelo brancos e meio privilegiado de submissão do estudante negro, medida que nos levou a desencadear greves, especialmente nas escolas secundárias, onde essas normas foram aplicadas primeiro. As greves foram de maio a junho. Depois resolvemos partir para uma ação mais concreta e eficiente para denunciar mais essa medida repressiva. Depois de contactarmos várias

escolas secundárias, decidimos organizar uma manifestação pacífica, a 16 de junho, no curso de um dia inteiramente dedicado à revolta contra os africanas: "Não somos Boers", foi o nosso slogan. Havíamos combinado nos encontrar, no fim, em uma escola para um comício, a que se se-

guiria a publicação de um manifesto às autoridades, rejeitando o novo idioma e manifestando nossa intenção de só voltar às aulas quando essa lei fosse revogada. Depois de percorrermos as ruas de Soweto durante a tarde, fomos para o encontro marcado. A polícia havia chegado primeiro

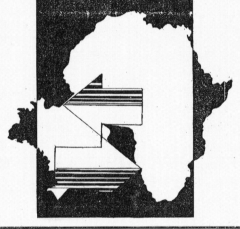

e tentamos parlamentar — mas como única resposta, obtivemos bombas de gás lacrimogênio. Quando começamos a fugir, a polícia abriu fogo, indistintamente. Muitos de nós morreram. O balanço oficial foi de 177 mortos nos três primeiros dias de rebelião, mas sabemos que só em Soweto e

nos arredores morreram 353. Mais de mil foram presos, enquanto muitos eram dados como "desaparecidos".

As "forças da ordem" não esperavam essa revolta: ficaram visivelmente surpreendidos com essa primeira grande manifestação estudantil, fenômeno desconhecido na África do Sul. Compreendemos imediatamente que a polícia e o regime nos haviam declarado guerra, e que não recuaríam diante de nada. Também nós ficamos muito chocados com o morticínio do primeiro dia — mas esse choque transformou-se rapidamente em raiva, um ódio profundo que rapidamente se comunicou a toda a população africana de Soweto. A partir desse momento, tudo o que simbolizava o branco e sua repressão foi destruído: sedes de órgãos municipais, bibliotecas, etc. O regime racista declarou, depois, que entre os estudantes, haviam agitadores comunistas cuja intenção era derrubar o governo. Então nós, estudantes, gritamos em resposta que as leis contra os comunistas são na verdade leis discriminatórias que permitem ao regime dedicar uma soma mínima à educação das crianças negras, enquanto quantias colossais são reservadas nos serviços de segurança ou da defesa.

Diante dessa atitude do governo, depois dos três primeiros dias de protesto, resolvemos continuar nossas manifestações, não só contra a imposição dos afrikaans, mas também a fim de conseguir a libertação dos companheiros presos.

SOWETO — 16 DE JUNHO DE 1976 — MAIS DE 600 MORTOS

Segundo a UNESCO:

— "São poucos na história os exemplos de uma polícia que dispara sobre escolares sem armas e os mata em tal quantidade que o número exato de mortos não pode nunca ser es tabelecido."

— Este ano continua a repressão cada vez mais brutal. E a luta vai continuar até que o racismo seja completamente vencido pelos negros na África do Sul.

SINBA's vision of "African-Brazilian" exchange, on the front cover of *SINBA*, July 1977. Fundo Polícias Políticas, Arquivo do Estado do Rio de Janeiro–APERJ.

argued that bourgeois or individual attempts at improvement were doomed to failure.[61] But SINBA members cautioned that their mass-based revolutionary black politics "could not take place within conventional political molds," not even those of the Left. As in earlier periods (and perhaps even more forcefully in a context of extreme political polarization), in the 1970s, many on the left saw race as an issue that threatened to divide a class-based movement. (Abdias do Nascimento, who in 1968 was picked up by the political police on suspicions of communism, later recalled the irony of that situation: "I was execrated by the communists as a fascist [as a former Integralist] and reverse-racist!").[62] Explicitly black organizations in this period, like SINBA, were thus a response not just to right-wing repression but also to what many contemporary black thinkers perceived as the lack of space in leftist opposition movements for the discussion of racial issues.[63] SINBA leaders therefore advised eschewing participation in a "general [political] struggle" and instead advocated a distinct movement of the "great majority of blacks."[64] In other words, African anticolonial revolutions and antiapartheid movements, with their inseparable combination of leftist and antiracist concerns, provided the ideal model for black politics in Brazil.

In their insistence on the stark division between Brazil's blacks and whites, *SINBA* writers' view of race strongly resembles the "two race" perspective held by many Paulista black writers throughout the century. Yet while those writers had seen themselves as a clearly defined black minority amid their city and state's white majority, SINBA members issued a new version of the "two race" theory that imagined blacks in the majority. In an early editorial about the problem of elitism in black activism, *SINBA* writers established a motto they would return to in subsequent issues: "The black problem in Brazil is the problem of the great black majority of Brazilians."[65] *SINBA's* vision therefore resembled, too, that of the Carioca activists of the 1950s who argued that the true Brazilian *povo* was African-descended. But crucially, they rejected the corollary idea that this *povo* was made up of *mestiços*— Brazil's majority was *negro*.

In the late 1970s getting Brazil's majority officially recognized as black— and thereby statistically debunking the idea of a whitened or mixed nation—became one of SINBA's most urgent tasks. With the census of 1980 approaching, SINBA organized a campaign that included academics and other black activist organizations, like the IPCN, to lobby the Instituto Brasileiro de Geografia e Estatística (IBGE, or Brazilian Geographical and Statistical Institute) to include color in the upcoming census. Racial data had not been published for the 1960 census, and had not even been gathered for 1970.[66] The very inclusion of color, SINBA argued, was "of fundamental importance to all those who have a real interest in collecting true data regarding the situation of different racial groups in Brazil. For us *negros* (blacks and mulattos), it is particularly in our interest because we affirm that we are the majority of the population in Brazil, but we have long been victims of intense campaigns that mystified our true social situation in this country."[67] Census data would reveal the reality behind the state's "racial mystification": Brazil was a majority black nation, yet this majority suffered inequality and marginalization.[68]

Yet while it was relatively simple to attribute the invisibility of Brazil's black majority to the government's resistance to collecting racial data, it was more complicated to explain why, when social scientists did count race, popular identities did not match black activists' expectations. A 1976 household survey that let respondents identify their own color, for instance, famously produced 135 distinct categories—some of which were rare and creative, like "purple," or "dark chocolate." Though 95 percent of respondents favored six of the most traditional color categories, including *branco, pardo, preto,* or *moreno* (a term signifying brown skin), the survey nonetheless confirmed nonwhite Brazilians' preference for intermediate racial categories over terms like *preto* or *negro.*[69] To the writers in *SINBA*, this demonstrated that racial mystification in Brazil had deeply affected Brazilians' sense of themselves, and was not due solely to government efforts to cover up color in its data collection. As in the early days of São Paulo's black press, *SINBA* writers denounced intermediate color and racial categories for the escape they provided from being *preto* or *negro.* Attempting to "hide or deny one's origins," *SINBA* writers argued, was another deep form of "alienation," which only "permits the continuation, the impunity, and the growth of discrimination." SINBA members proposed to fight this problem by inverting, and thereby simplifying, Brazil's system of racial classification. "We must define what is white and what is *negro* objectively, by using the very principle that whites (or so-called whites) have always used to discriminate against those with any amount of blackness in their blood: 'He who fails to pass as white is black.'"[70] What they proposed, in other words, was a definition of blackness reminiscent of the bipolar racial system of the United States, where anyone with "any amount of blackness in [his] blood" (or, as they explained elsewhere, with "the marks of that race" in "the color of his skin, his facial features, or his hair") counted as black.[71] The exclusionary category "nonwhite," actively reclaimed as "negro," could thus be used to their political advantage.

To correct what they saw as the lamentable fragmentation of Brazil's true black majority, SINBA held meetings, research groups, and seminars to persuade the IBGE to end the practice of self-reporting. In its place, black activist groups agreed that they themselves, along with allied academics and the IBGE, should prepare four or five fixed and "objective" color categories, which census workers would be trained to recognize and record. Though the IBGE initially rejected this proposal, ongoing lobbying efforts from black groups and academics eventually prevailed, and the 1980 census included the options of black (*preto*), white (*branco*), brown (*pardo*), and yellow (*amarelo*).[72] After thirty years without public census statistics on race, the inclusion of the color question in 1980 was a victory for many activists. But the use of *preto* and *pardo* color categories, instead of the more unifying, descent-based *negro* favored by activists, still had the effect of splitting Brazil's African-descended population into two different categories. Moreover, the census did not reveal the African-descended majority of which black activists were so certain: 54.2 percent of Brazilians declared themselves white, whereas the total of those identifying as *pardos* and *pretos* accounted for 44.7 percent of the population.[73] For subsequent censuses, black activists would concentrate on "blackening" Brazil's population by educating Brazilians of color to identify with their African ancestry and lobbying the IBGE to replace the color categories of *preto* and *pardo* with the single racial category *negro*.

Despite its articulate critiques of racism, its visibility and influence in activist circles, and its inspiration in broad-based African revolutionary movements, SINBA never managed to create a mass black movement. For most of the poor and working-class Cariocas of color who made up its target audience, ideas of *mestiçagem* were probably still much more familiar than the notion that Brazil was an apartheid state. The commercialized versions of popular culture, like samba and carnival, that SINBA denounced, moreover, were intimately woven into the lives of the people it hoped to attract. Paulo Roberto dos Santos, an activist from the IPCN (SINBA's more culturally oriented rival) later remembered that SINBA idealized a revolutionary solution to racism to the point of impracticality. "They wanted to go straight to the masses, even talking about an armed struggle in the very midst of a military dictatorship, when the myth of racial democracy was in full force." For Santos, the shortcomings of this strategy were obvious: "They lacked the ability to just raise their hand and have people follow."[74] But the intellectual innovations of this group, as it emerged from meetings in the CEAA to help reconstitute Rio's black press and black movement, contributed to a dramatic revision of black politics in Brazil. Its new politics of race responded to the dictatorship's cynical enforcement of racial democracy with a call for decolonization modeled on African revolutionary struggles. *SINBA* writers expressed their belief that there existed an authentic, black Brazilian nation beneath the "mystification" of racial democracy, of European-oriented ethnocentrism, and of culturalism, colonialism, and dictatorship. Their ideal version of a true and inclusive Brazilian nation—one that would perhaps emerge with the return of democracy—accepted its blackness, its links to global struggles, and, most important, its inequalities and its responsibility to right them. This was the transformed vision of black Brazilian activism that Abdias do Nascimento captured and relayed to international audiences from his podium in Lagos in 1977.

Black Racists

This was also the vision of black racial activism that caught the attention of Rio's secret police in the second half of the 1970s, and what they saw made them uneasy. The secret or political police had existed under several guises in Brazil since the early twentieth century, gathering strength under authoritarian regimes such as Getúlio Vargas's Estado Novo (1937–45) and again after 1964. As the dictatorship became increasingly repressive in the late 1960s, Rio de Janeiro's secret police forces (then known as the Departamento Autônomo de Ordem Política e Social [DOPS, or Autonomous Department of Political and Social Order]), worked closely with federal intelligence agencies to assist in the repression of the organized leftist and urban guerrillas. After 1975, with leftist movements disarmed and the decompression under way, the force was reorganized as the Departamento Geral de Investigações Especiais (DGIE, or General Department of Special Investigations), and given the task of collecting intelligence on the new, and largely peaceful, social and political movements that were tentatively permitted.[75]

The secret police had relatively little experience with black activist organizations when they encountered them in the mid-1970s. The Frente Negra of the 1930s or the Teatro Experimental do Negro of the 1940s to 1960s had previously attracted their attention, but only on an ad hoc basis, usually under suspicions of communism; there had been no category for black activism as such on the police's lists.[76] Similarly, in the 1960s and early 1970s, the police did not make it a priority to target black organizations. Though the military state had prohibited racial activism and discussions of race at the height of the repression, other categories of political subversion ("Terrorism," "Communism," "Cuba," to judge from the police's filing system) placed more immediate demands on their energies. And, in any case, very few black organizations survived the coup.

Yet as new activist organizations with bold *negro* identities sprang up in the mid-1970s, police and military intelligence officers, steeped in nationalist ideologies of racial democracy, became suspicious. In late 1977 and early 1978 secret police officers (echoing conservative critics of black organizations in the 1950s) identified the student groups emerging from the CEAA as "black racist groups" or promoters of "black racism."[77] Army and navy intelligence officers (whose work included combing the city's alternative presses in search of subversive publications) sent the DGIE copies of *SINBA*, which they deemed "in all of its topics, to foment racial disaggregation," something that expressly contradicted the ideology of *mestiçagem* put forth by regime intellectuals. The report further remarked that the "newspaper . . . was sold, freely given, or even forced on those who were entirely indifferent to the matter," as if to reinforce how unnatural a politics of racial "disaggregation" was to most Brazilians.[78]

Police agents especially worried that the interest in African exchange expressed by SINBA and other groups served as cover for broader alliances between Brazilian leftists and Marxist revolutionaries in Africa. One report from October 1976 asserted that "Brazilian students are being trained in subversive activities and guerrilla operations in permanent training camps in Angola, by Cuban instructors who form part of the Cuban forces stationed there."[79] A year earlier, the secret police had seized letters and pro-MPLA (Angola's liberation front) manifestos sent from Lisbon's Center for Anticolonial Information and Documentation to José Maria Nunes Pereira of the CEAA. They cited this correspondence as evidence of "widespread international communist infiltration" in Brazil.[80] In 1980, tracking contacts between the Brazilian Communist Party and the revolutionary government of Mozambique, the police warned that "Brazilian commerce with countries under communist regimes may be necessary, but [the foreign policy of] pragmatism aside, it must be conducted with extra care, so that subversive organizations will not be financed through the commissions they earn from this trade."[81]

It is difficult to know exactly how many of these accusations were true, and if they were, how much of a threat to national security these activities could have posed. Certainly, the CEAA and José Maria Nunes Pereira were sympathetic to Marxist decolonization movements in Portuguese Africa, but the assertion that their correspondence with anticolonial groups in Lisbon made them lynchpins of a "widespread international communist infiltration" in Brazil suggests that the police were often misinformed, paranoid, or both. What these documents on the potential exchanges between African revolutionaries and local leftists or racial activists do suggest, however, was that many in the secret police perceived Africa just as *SINBA* writers wished to portray it: as a hotbed of leftist and racial revolution. Though the DGIE expressed general concern about "black racist" entities in the mid-1970s, their surveillance of these groups became particularly intense when members associated themselves, even rhetorically, with African liberation or antiracist struggles. Throughout the 1970s and early 1980s, the secret police infiltrated scores of black organizations' academic and cultural events about Africa—film screenings, group meetings, and academic conferences—transcribing or paraphrasing speeches, gathering the names of attendees, and collecting any printed information available.[82] For in the context of the dictatorship, black organizations' invoked connections with revolutionary Africa made the specter of "black racism"—long a concern for Brazilian nationalists—even more threatening.

Black Culture, Brazilian Culture

When SINBA was founded in September 1974, it initially included everyone present at the original CEAA meetings.[83] Yet this unity did not last long, with other groups—notably the IPCN—splintering off from SINBA that same year. Sebastião Soares, a student from the Universidade Federal Fluminense, explained that the leaders of SINBA "thought there had to be an entity that was specifically dedicated to the question of black political action." The founders of the IPCN, for their part, "thought they should turn toward research, that is, academic-scientific knowledge, as their form of militancy."[84] Several of the IPCN's founders and early members were middle-class professionals who saw SINBA's insistence on revolutionary mass organizing as unreasonable, preferring instead to stage cultural and academic events in the universities and affluent Zona Sul neighborhoods where they studied, worked, and lived. Two of the IPCN's founding members, Paulo Roberto dos Santos (who held a degree in literature from the Universidade Federal do Rio de Janeiro) and Carlos Alberto Medeiros (who held a degree in communications from the same university and worked at the Rio daily *Jornal do Brasil*), had attended the original CEAA meetings. Others came from the world of theater, film, and television, like actress Léa Garcia, formerly of Rio's Teatro Experimental do Negro, and Milton Gonçalves, an actor affiliated with the Globo TV network.[85]

Like those of SINBA, the IPCN's members denounced the ways official appropriation and commercial exploitation deformed black culture and restricted spaces for black citizenship and political opposition. In the first issue of their *Boletim*, or bulletin (dated June 1975), the members of the IPCN introduced themselves as a group of people concerned with the "decharacter-ization" of Brazilian culture. "We are particularly concerned," they explained, "with the lack of historical and scientific information on the facts that con-stitute the archive of Black Culture in Brazilian Culture more generally."[86] Through research and dissemination of information on Brazil's black cul-ture, IPCN collaborators explained in another article in that same issue, they aimed to achieve the "immense task" of "lift[ing] the veil of obscurantisms and prejudices that covers our cultural past, belittles our present horizons, and restricts our paths for future progress."[87] The lack of objective knowledge about black or African culture, or the partial and deformed incorporation of African traits into celebrations of Brazilian culture, in other words, weakened the possibilities for black political action in the present and future.

To this urgent problem of national symbolism, the IPCN proposed a sym-bolic solution: redefining the image of Africa on which official formulations of Brazilian culture and black citizenship rested. But where SINBA privi-leged Africa's contemporary politics as a means for diagnosing and address-ing the problem of black citizenship in Brazil, scorning Afro-Brazilian culture as irremediably tainted and co-opted, the IPCN sought to recover the cultural realm as a sphere for political action. A review of the dance group Olorum Baba Mim, published in the IPCN's *Boletim*, summarizes the group's position on African culture. The IPCN considered the group's show a positive affirmation of black culture from a "nonfolkloric" perspective, one that revealed a multifaceted African culture in Brazil. They quoted Carlos Negreiros, one of the dance group's organizers: "Many people, perhaps even the majority of them, believe that before slavery, Africa had a uniform and rudimentary culture. But on the contrary; manifestations of black culture in Brazil come from distant regions that were absolutely diverse in relation to each other." When most Brazilians talked about Africa, he noted, "it's as if they grabbed blacks in Africa, mixed them in a blender, and tossed them into Brazil under one label: slaves."[88] For activists like historian Beatriz do Nascimento (an early participant in the CEAA meetings and a founder of the IPCN), uncovering the richness of this proud past was central to the process by which blacks would "achieve their cultural autonomy and conse-quently their liberation as individuals."[89] The middle-class professionals in the IPCN also challenged official efforts at celebrating black culture. Secret police investigators noted that when the Museu de Arte Moderna (MAM, or Museum of Modern Art) and the FUNARTE (the government's art fund) planned a series of events "in praise of Black Culture" and in keeping with "the relevance and historical value of the liberation from slavery," the IPCN would not participate because "the events (according to its leaders) present blacks as a folkloric object for consumer society, instead of exhibiting them in terms of cultural evolution."[90]

Rather than reject the idea of an African past or celebrations of black culture as "culturalism," the IPCN activists sought, through scholarship, advocacy, and institution-building, to create positive images of Africa and black culture, which, they hoped, would remain central to definitions of Brazilian culture. "We black Brazilians," they wrote, "have a right to come together to preserve and keep active our culture, which is, in the end, Brazilian Culture. Brazilian Culture, that is, in all that it contains of Black Culture. . . . Who can deny the enormous weight of the cultures of Black Africa [in Brazilian Culture]? Can we look at one without seeing the other?"[91] In one issue of the IPCN's *Boletim*, the editors distinguished the cultural associations of blacks from those formed by descendants of immigrants. They explained that while they supported the ethnic associations of Germans, Italians, and Japanese in their attempts to obtain help from the state in preserving their distinct cultures, black Brazilians were in an entirely different category. "For us, it is a historically and legally established fact, on which there cannot be any controversy, that black Brazilians (of all shades) do not form an immigrant colony or distinct ethnic group in our Nation. We are an integral part of the foundational ethnicities of the Brazilian people."[92] Perhaps sensitive about accusations that black groups were separatist or racist entities, the editors emphasized that their organizations, unlike the "pluralist" ones required by Germans or Japanese, were the holistic outgrowth of an Africanized Brazilian people. People of color, they argued in the tradition of a previous generation of black thinkers in Rio de Janeiro, *were* the Brazilian people; their cultural activism was *Brazilian* cultural activism.

Yet, like those of SINBA, the IPCN's writers went further than their predecessors in their assertion that Brazil was not a *mestiço* but a black nation: "Brazil is the second country in the world in terms of its black population, losing [first place] only to an African country, Nigeria. . . . Over half of Brazil's population is estimated to be of African descent."[93] In an article about Zumbi, the warrior-leader of the seventeenth-century maroon kingdom of Palmares who was killed as a result of betrayal by one of his own (black) officers, Beatriz do Nascimento reminded her readers of the importance of racial solidarity: "It is in the political interest of our oppressors to divide us, for they have always been the minority in Brazil when compared to us." To

Nascimento, Palmares was a metaphor for an authentic, decolonized black Brazil. Members of Palmares, she explained, called it N'gola Djanga, or Little Angola, "yet we, today, could call it Little Brazil, since it was a state that for much of its history was made up of black and indigenous Brazilians. It was a state free of Portuguese or any other kind of domination." As a warrior and a statesman, Zumbi, whom Nascimento called the "first Brazilian hero," had "tried always to maintain the autonomy of the Black state against a society that, in the Brazil of those days, was dominated by Portugal."[94] Zumbi's defense of Palmares at a time when the territory that came to be Brazil was still in the hands of the colonizer made him, in the eyes of Nascimento and many other contemporary black activists, a model for black resistance during the dictatorship, an early hero of the sort of cultural and racial decolonization the new generation of black activists advocated.

Given this view of Brazil as a majority black state colonized by European racial and cultural norms, IPCN writers denounced Brazilians of color who denied their African ancestry. They endorsed, for instance, the impressions of members of a dance troupe from Uganda, the Abafumy Dance Company, of the racial attitudes of many black and brown Brazilians: they were "passive" and "lacked consciousness about their own negritude," straightening their hair, wearing wigs, using lipstick and rice powder to whiten their appearance, all "in order to valorize themselves in front of whites."[95] For the IPCN, as for SINBA, the desire to flee blackness by changing one's appearance, as in the widespread practice of adopting intermediate color categories (like *pardo* or *moreno*), was evidence of the mystifying power of dominant racial ideologies among Brazilians of color. To combat these ideologies, activists from the IPCN joined SINBA in the campaign to include color categories on the 1980 Brazilian census. Beatriz do Nascimento and others in the IPCN also joined forces with black activists from São Paulo and other cities in proposing to make the date of Zumbi's death a "Black Consciousness Day." They hoped that 20 November would supplant 13 May, the day of the abolition of slavery, as the national holiday celebrating black liberation. The new holiday would emphasize active black resistance to colonialism and enslavement, rather than celebrating a day on which elite white Brazilians gifted slaves their freedom.[96] One police report on the IPCN accurately, if unsympathetically, summarized these thinkers' strategy: "They thus try to demystify historical dates that are meaningful for comprehending black culture (13 May, for example), [moving] away from the ways [these dates] were presented and coming up with a modern view of the liberation of slaves as an obligation, and not as an act of charity by the SYSTEM."[97]

At the same time, the IPCN supported cultural and aesthetic expressions that embraced a distinct, proud, and (for Brazil) nontraditional "black" identity and style. This included expressions that came from the United States rather than (as SINBA members preferred) Africa. In the second half of the 1970s the IPCN was the main black activist organization to seek articulation with the soul dances that had become popular among Rio's black youth earlier in the decade. By the mid-1970s, musical groups with names like Black Power and Soul Grand Prix drew several thousand young men and women of color almost nightly to venues across Rio's working-class *subúrbios* (north and west of the center city) to dance to the rhythms of James Brown or Isaac Hayes. When, between 1976 and 1977, these dances came to the attention of a broader mainstream audience, including Rio's secret police, they drew criticism from across the political spectrum.[98] Left-wing critics, concerned with the preservation of authentic national traditions and with the dangers that a race-based movement might pose to the broader class consciousness they championed, contended that soul dancers were nothing more than "alienated" victims of U.S. economic and cultural imperialism. These young dancers had sold out their authentic national cultural traditions (particularly samba) in the pursuit of a foreign fad; the soul phenomenon could therefore never represent a "true" political consciousness.[99] Critics on the right, including Gilberto Freyre and Rio's own military police, initially responded quite differently. They shuddered at the "spirit of opposition," the "bombastic" expressions of racial and socioeconomic warfare, embodied in "Black Rio" (as the phenomenon came to be known). Like conservative critics of black organizations in the 1950s, these right-wing commentators argued that the soul phenomenon represented the insidious importation of U.S.-style racism into a nation where "racism did not exist."[100] One military police officer, having read a multipage exposé on Black Rio in the *Jornal do Brasil*, declared the soul phenomenon, with its U.S.-style blackness, to be a dangerous attack on Brazil's mixed and harmonious identity. "It is fundamental," he wrote, "to remember that in our country there was always harmony among Brazilians, independently of race or religion. The miscegenation of our people—white, *negro*, Indian—is, according to Gylberto [sic] Freyre in *Casa-grande e senzala*, a privilege."[101]

It was precisely because the idea of a mixed national race and culture had become central to both left-wing and right-wing nationalisms by the 1970s that IPCN activist Carlos Alberto Medeiros saw soul as "a fertile area for cultural work." He, like many fellow black activists in Rio, perceived the identities of most Brazilians of color as corrupted by the discourses of racial fusion enforced, on the one hand, by a military state that made *mestiçagem* a pillar of national security and, on the other, by a leftist opposition that idealized a mixed-race "povo" and made little to no room for race-based politics. Samba, for many black defenders of soul, was the perfect example of the ways (as *SINBA* had put it) Afro-Brazilian culture had been co-opted by white elites from across the political spectrum and drained of its political potentials. Soul, Medeiros hoped, with its adoption of a bold and distinct black aesthetic drawn from the confrontational U.S. racial context, "will contribute to the emergence of a *negro* Brazilian identity that was attempted ... through samba, but without success." To leftist critics of soul's cultural "alienation," Medeiros responded, "Of course, dancing soul and using certain kinds of clothes, hair-dos, and greetings does not, in itself, solve anyone's problem. But it could provide the necessary amount of emulation for them to come together and, together, begin to solve their problems."[102]

IPCN activists distributed flyers at soul dances, trying to politicize the dancers and gain some recruits for their own organization. Their success on both counts, one member remembered, was ultimately limited.[103] Yet if, as Medeiros admitted, aesthetic performances of a bold black identity did not in themselves solve Brazil's racial problems, they did help to reveal the short-comings of racial democracy in Rio—specifically, the sharp spatial segrega-tion that belied that city's image as the embodiment of Brazil's racial mixture and harmony. In July 1976 the IPCN sponsored a screening of *Wattstax*, the documentary of a music festival that the Stax record label held in the Watts neighborhood of Los Angeles in 1972 to commemorate the riots there seven years earlier. *Wattstax*, with its long musical numbers and vivid portrayal of black American clothing and hair styles, had become a classic among Rio's soul dancers, with party organizers frequently screening the film before dances or projecting stills from the movie as visual accompaniment to their dance music. The IPCN held its screening of *Wattstax*, however, not at one of many social or athletic clubs in the Zona Norte or the working-class suburbs of Greater Rio but at the prestigious Museu de Arte Moderna, an elite—though increasingly countercultural—institution in downtown Rio.[104] The IPCN's Paulo Roberto dos Santos recalled the symbolic importance of staging a majority-black event—with hundreds of working-class, black soul dancers dressed in extravagant styles—in what was perceived as a white urban space: "People from the Zona Norte came to the Zona Sul. At that time, even we didn't fully believe that our people could enter the MAM. The MAM was almost a temple, belonging to a kind of intellectual bourgeoisie. But these kids came from the most distant *subúrbios*. [That exhibition of] the movie *Wattstax* was a scandal back then!"[105] This invasion of Rio's white, well-to-do Zona Sul by black dancers was a defiant reprise of the initial thrill of the meetings at the CEAA, when black students had flocked to Ipanema and caused their own scandal among the center's neighbors. As an exposé of Brazilian racism and of the hypocrisy of ideas of racelessness, this event was the IPCN's counterpoint to *SINBA*'s profuse written denunciations of the "myth" of racial democracy.

Rio's secret police tracked the IPCN's activities, especially after army intelligence officers sent them a copy of the group's publication, the *Boletim do IPCN*. Army officers accused the IPCN, like SINBA, of "preaching racial struggle" and urged the secret police to investigate the group further.[106] In the seized copy of the *Boletim*, someone underlined Beatriz do Nascimento's admonition to "be alert to any attempts to make use of our weaknesses, by those who are interested in dividing and oppressing us even more."[107] Coupled with what another report called the IPCN's "phase of expansion . . . evidenced by their . . . links of collaboration" with a host of black entities in Rio and elsewhere, Nascimento's call for black unity made the DGIE take notice.[108] The secret police were also sensitive to what they saw as IPCN members' attempts to "break with what has heretofore been observed in terms of the history of blacks in Brazil."[109] In the same marked-up issue of the *Boletim* sent to Rio's secret police by army intelligence, for instance, someone underlined a poem by black writer Éle Semog that pointedly revised established versions of Brazilian history: "The black man was in truth / The strongest arm / in this land; / History stands as proof. / The Indian gathered, / The white man exploited, / And the black man built."[110]

The secret police also (wrongly) worried that the connections between the IPCN and the increasingly popular soul phenomenon might indicate the beginnings of an organized mass racial movement. Police agents reported that "the masses who attend these sorts of dances, which little by little are becoming a rage, gradually are being manipulated for the goals (though merely social) of the movements for black supremacy and valorization. . . . [Soul's] initial idea (appreciating a musical genre) is being displaced by the ideal of black self-affirmation." Their concern was tempered, however, by soul's nature as an imported, commercial phenomenon. The IPCN, the agents added in the same report, supported the "enablers" of this new fad, "because a significant part of the profit thereby obtained is earmarked for their operating expenses."[111] The police were concerned about culture-based "movements for black supremacy and valorization," but they ultimately dismissed the IPCN's activities as "merely social," commercial, and culturally illegitimate (for their association with an "American" fad). Whereas connections with Africa's revolutionary politics sharpened the threat of a group like SINBA in the eyes of the secret police, soul's (and by extension the IPCN's) association with the commercialized popular culture of the United States ultimately cast it as unthreatening and apolitical.

These differences in the secret police's response to each of the groups' political styles and strategies would have pleased members of SINBA. As Amauri Pereira later told interviewers, he and other SINBA members in the 1970s saw the Ipanema-based IPCN cohort as a timid "black petite bourgeoisie" that had the United States, with its integrationist struggles and its "black elites," as its main political referent. Members of SINBA, on the other hand, saw themselves as "black revolutionaries" with "African liberation struggles, armed struggles" as their main referent—a much greater threat to the status quo than the IPCN, with its conferences, film viewings, and soul-music events.[112] But although oral histories of the black movement tend to emphasize rivalries and differences between SINBA and the IPCN, the line between these organizations was rather blurred. Yedo Ferreira, one of SINBA's founders and permanent members, helped draft the statutes for the IPCN.[113] And after a rough patch between 1977 and 1979, during which SINBA was unable to afford space for its headquarters, the IPCN invited the group to share its new offices in the neighborhood of Lapa, purchased with assistance from the Inter-American Foundation.[114] Moreover, SINBA and the IPCN worked together on several initiatives, like the proposed census reform of 1980, and each group's newsletter advertised the other's events and publications. Though SINBA was more vocal, in its own publication, about establishing solidarity and comparisons between Brazil and revolutionary Africa, it was the IPCN (together with the CEAA) that put together most of the conferences on apartheid and African decolonization in this period.[115] By the early 1980s, SINBA folded into the IPCN, with a few former SINBA members assuming positions of leadership in the new organization.[116]

One difference between the groups that is not often mentioned but appears to be significant is the place of women within them. Despite the participation of women in black social and political organizations since the beginning of the century, the leaders of these groups, and the authors of their publications, had been almost exclusively men. The organizations and publications that emerged in the mid-1970s were not much different. Across Brazil in the mid-1970s, black women active in feminist movements, leftist movements, and black organizations began to articulate critiques of their dual discrimination, by race and by gender, in these groups and in society.[117] In 1975, for instance, as Brazilian feminists met at the Congress of Brazilian Women to discuss the shape and direction of a movement that was gathering strength in Brazil and worldwide (the United Nations declared 1975 the "Year of the Woman" and the first year in a "Decade of the Woman"), a group of black women activists issued a "Manifesto of Black Women" that underscored their dual burden. Slavery had made them at once racialized "objects of production" (like their male counterparts) and gendered objects of "sexual reproduction," of "pleasure for the colonizers."[118]

Just as they labored to make the particularities of race visible in broader feminist and leftist movements in this period, black women activists struggled against what they saw as the machismo of many of their counterparts in emerging black organizations. An unsigned article in a 1979 issue of *SINBA* by a black woman (probably staff writer Suzete P. dos Santos) pointed out that because society at large portrayed black women primarily as objects of sexual desire and as the vectors of miscegenation, men in the black movement saw them as being "culturally assimilated," and therefore questioned their commitment to black politics. This led to the "omission" of black women from the movement.[119] Lélia Gonzalez, who became famous for her activism on behalf of women in the emergent black movement, recalled that at the CEAA meetings in the mid-1970s, "there came a point when women began to meet separately" before joining the broader group. Many black men, especially the older ones, were not used to black women being opinionated and political and dismissed their outspokenness and political engagement as evidence of bitterness or sexual repression. "Needless to say," Gonzalez argued, "[male activists'] wives or partners never participated in these meetings, since they were at home taking care of the children."[120]

Although participants in these organizations do not mention it directly in their oral and written histories, it appears that the IPCN attracted more women than SINBA. In part, this difference probably reflects the fact that the IPCN was, by the late 1970s, far more popular, boasting more than two hundred registered members, while SINBA, in the words of Amauri Pereira, was being slowly "dissolved" (its list of active staff and contributors in this period numbered at most a dozen people, only two of them women).[121] But it is also likely that SINBA, with its revolutionary rhetoric of armed struggle developed primarily by two men, was less attractive to women already sensitized to the issue of black machismo than the IPCN, where women like actress Léa Garcia (formerly of the TEN) and researcher Beatriz do Nascimento had visible roles. Interestingly, in this period, several black women published articles on the articulation between feminist and black movements in *SINBA* (a more substantial publication than the IPCN's *Boletim*), but it was through the IPCN that black women activists organized most of their events.[122] The IPCN, for instance, advertised in *SINBA* that it held weekly meetings of black women (led by Léa Garcia, Suzete P. dos Santos, and Pedrina de Deus), which were open to the public. Possibly, this was a venue in which to address one of these women's leading concerns: how to make feminism and racial activism—the province of an educated middle class—relevant to poor women of color. And between September and November 1979 the IPCN, mobilized by the unsigned *SINBA* article on the "omission" of black women in the movement, sponsored a series of conferences and debates on issues facing black women in black organizations and in Brazilian society more broadly.[123] Over the course of the 1980s, black women activists like Lélia Gonzalez, dissatisfied with the inability of both black and mainstream feminist organizations to fully address their needs, would join groups dedicated specifically to combating the multiple and intersecting forms of discrimination facing black women of a range of social classes.[124]

While such differences in membership between SINBA and the IPCN, and the debates that emerged between the groups, are crucial to understanding the ways Rio's new black organizations constructed their politics during the period of political decompression, the differences between them were far less important than the perspectives they shared. Both organizations constructed their ideas of race in the context of a dictatorship that made cynical use of ideas about racial democracy, and that persecuted black organizations as threats to national security and official notions of *mestiçagem*. Both also provided a corrective to oppositional movements, such as leftist or feminist politics, that downplayed the significance of race in struggles against injustice and inequality. In the polarized atmosphere of the dictatorship, Rio's young black activists came to see racial democracy and mixture not as flexible symbols with possibilities as well as limitations for black politics but as harmful lies designed to hypnotize a majority black nation into passive acceptance of racial and economic oppression. Though they honed their political ideas by arguing over the precise ways to expose racial democracy as a myth and to build a true black consciousness in Brazil, they agreed on these goals. And though they debated whether soul styles from the United States or revolution from Africa was the more effective model for developing oppositional black Brazilian identities and politics, both groups were fundamentally marked by their shared experience at the CEAA, where they discovered Africa as a model for a racially and culturally *negro* Brazil. By developing their ideas about a majority *negro* nation plagued by apartheid-style racism in the city that had traditionally been cast as the embodiment of Brazil's easygoing mixture, both groups succeeded in announcing—even to hostile audiences—a transformed black politics, intransigent in its rejection of dominant racial ideologies and in its insistence that a race-based movement was the only political solution.

A Cultural and Political Synthesis

The goals and strategies of black thinkers in Rio de Janeiro from the mid-1970s through the early 1980s in many ways paralleled those of their counterparts in São Paulo and Salvador da Bahia in the same period. Yet looking back on the activism of those years, Lélia Gonzalez, whose own trajectory as an activist began at the weekly meetings at the CEAA in Rio, saw significant regional differences: "Black Paulistas have an incredible political consciousness. They have read Marx, Gramsci, and all of those guys. They discuss those ideas, they make things happen. But if you happen to ask them, Do you know what Yoruba is? . . . Ah! They don't know." Black Paulistas, she concluded, reminded her of black Americans, "with a strong political consciousness, a Western political discourse, . . . but no cultural base. The cultural base has been repressed." In Bahia, in contrast, "there is much more of a cultural consciousness (it is something they exude from their pores) than a political consciousness." She saw her own city, Rio, as "a sort of intermediary between Bahia and São Paulo," a place where "political consciousness exists, [but] there is also great engagement with [black] culture, . . . [like] samba, macumba."[125]

Gonzalez's segregation of "cultural" and "political" concerns might strike us as too neat, given that black intellectuals and community leaders in all three places had long deployed "culture" to political ends. Whether they invoked "pure" African traits, as did some Candomblé leaders in Bahia; a mixed Afro-European or *mestiço* culture, as did members of Rio's TEN; or an unmarked, irreproachably Brazilian culture, as did many writers in São Paulo's black press, culture was central to the terms on which black thinkers demanded inclusion as citizens over the course of the century. Nonetheless, Gonzalez's formulation captures key differences in the ways black thinkers in each of these cities presented their political projects, and in the ways a broader society often received them. São Paulo's style of black activism seemed, to black thinkers and their audiences, explicitly political in its insistence on discrete *negro* identities, race-based social and political organizations, and links to pan-African and other diasporic political movements. Bahian Candomblé leaders, for their part, framed their activities within the realm of religion and culture, which afforded them a certain amount of protection from accusations of racial separatism, and contributed to the eventual acceptance of Candomblé as an icon of an African-inflected Brazilian culture. And in Rio, at least since the days of the TEN, black thinkers based their activities both on what would have then been read as race-based politics and on an array of Afro-Brazilian cultural performances and practices. Even in Gonzalez's day, members of Rio's SINBA and the IPCN defined an authentically *negro* Brazil as one attuned to both its African racial and cultural heritage, to both the political and the cultural affinities with an Africa then in the grip of anticolonial revolutions.

Yet what Gonzalez called a "synthesis between cultural resistance and political claims,"[126] achieved in part through a shared focus on Africa as a site of political and cultural struggle, not only characterized black movements in Rio in this period but extended to those in Salvador and São Paulo as well. Like their Carioca counterparts, black activists in the latter two cities gradually reconvened during the period of political decompression from the mid-1970s onward, with similar goals: to expose racism and reveal racial democracy to be a myth, to assert the specificity of the racial question in the midst of multiplying social movements and claims, and to portray Brazil as a majority black nation too long dominated by a white minority. As in Rio, activists in São Paulo and Salvador relied on connections or comparisons with Africa to achieve these goals. But though the story of black organizations in this period is one of increasing nationalization and convergence, activists in each of these three cities began their work from within distinct regional idioms of black thought and politics.

In Salvador, the struggle against discrimination had historically taken place primarily through organizations based on ethnic or cultural rather than explicitly racial identifications. In addition to Candomblé, carnival celebrations historically provided a space for Bahians of color to express their African cultural identities. As we have seen, late-nineteenth- and early-twentieth-century carnival groups like the Pândegos da África and the Embaixada Africana brought African rhythms and symbols, often linked to Candomblé, to Bahia's streets. In the second half of the twentieth century, this tradition was reborn in the form of *afoxés*, groups recruited from Candomblé houses, which paraded in ritual dress and often staged aspects of Candomblé ritual (primarily chants and drumming) in public. *Afoxés*, the most famous of which is the Filhos de Gandhi (founded in 1949 by unionized *preto* and *pardo* stevedores who, in solidarity with India's independence struggle, refused to unload English ships docked at Salvador's ports), typically designed carnival floats with African or Asian themes. Before the mid-1970s, Bahians of color generally participated in carnival either through the *afoxés* or through *blocos índios*, neighborhood-based groups whose members dressed up as stylized North American or Brazilian Indians, expressing nonwhite solidarity and celebrating (often in highly stereotyped ways) indigenous cultures. While these groups were often associated with African culture, expressive of anticolonial themes, or populated by dark-skinned Bahians, none of them explicitly framed their activities in terms of blackness or antiracism (and many, in fact, avoided these issues).[127] In the 1970s, however, a new crop of expressly *negro* activist organizations emerged in Salvador da Bahia. These were the *blocos afro*, or "Afro" carnival groups, which blended performances of African cultural themes with an explicit politics of antiracism, black unity, and pride.

Like the emergence of activist student groups in Rio, the rise of the *blocos afro* in Bahia reflected, in part, major shifts in Bahian society during the dictatorship's "economic miracle." Building on government initiatives to industrialize the Northeast since the 1950s, the dictatorship's development projects brought a wave of new private and public investment to the region. Most of these projects were concentrated in and around the city of Salvador, which had until then benefited relatively little from the nation's spurts of economic growth. In the early 1970s, Salvador boomed, with high-rise apartment buildings and shopping malls transforming the city's appearance. New industrial infrastructure, like hydroelectric or petrochemical plants, cropped up in areas just outside the city.[128] By 1980, this growth spurt, and accumulated changes since the 1950s, gave *preto* and *pardo* Bahians greater participation in the state's economy, making them the majority of workers in all areas of economic activity, including white-collar work. But as elsewhere in the nation, in Bahia this growth was uneven, with most of the state's population still concentrated in the same low-wage areas (agriculture, industry, service) they had largely occupied three decades earlier. And within these broad economic sectors, perceived skin color continued to circumscribe employment opportunities, especially in the upper ranks of the professions, commerce, and government employment, where lightness of skin—or what employers euphemistically referred to as "good appearance" (*boa aparência*)—was an unspoken requirement. Whites and so-called *brancos da Bahia*, people who would be considered black by the standards proposed by SINBA and the IPCN but who in local terms enjoyed the privileges of their lighter skin, were disproportionately represented in upper-level service jobs or professional positions. The relatively few *pretos* and darker *pardos* who made it into these positions made less money than their whiter counterparts.[129] At the same time, the economic boom integrated Bahians more fully into national and international consumer and media trends. In this context, many young people of color, from the middle classes as well as from Salvador's expanding working-class black neighborhoods, became increasingly receptive to messages of racial solidarity reaching them from abroad or from São Paulo and Rio de Janeiro. They became interested in African revolutionary struggles and in the U.S. civil rights movement, with its appealing aesthetic influences. By the middle of the 1970s, Bahia played host to its own soul and funk dance craze, known as *Black Bahia*.[130]

The popularity of soul and funk among Bahia's youth of color gave rise to a range of local musical styles identified with racial consciousness, including the new "Afro" carnival groups engaged with *negro* politics.[131] In 1974 Antonio Carlos dos Santos (known as Vovô), then an employee at Bahia's new Camaçari petrochemical plant, decided to create a carnival association that would focus on African themes and would be composed only of *negros*—dark-skinned people of color who assumed a black racial identity. His friend and partner Macalé remembered the influences that drove them: "Our ideas emerged during the height of soul, of Black Rio, of Black Power. . . . It was also when . . . we here began to get news of what was going on in Africa."[132] The idea to create a specifically *negro* carnival group appears to have emerged in response not only to trends and events that highlighted the dignity, pride, and self-affirmation of African and African-descended people worldwide but also to these men's situation as residents of a city with a large black and brown majority, and specifically, of a neighborhood, Liberdade, where almost everyone had strong physical evidence of African ancestry. True to the atmosphere of the time, Vovô initially wished to name the *bloco* something along the lines of "black power" or "strong blacks," but he was "advised" by the Federal Police that this would not be a good idea. In the end, he decided on the more acceptable Yoruba name Ilê Aiyê, which means "large house, black world."[133] The *bloco* made its début in the carnival of 1975, but it drew only one hundred members. In the midst of a military dictatorship and in Bahia, a city in which explicitly race-based organizations were historically uncommon, many residents of Liberdade feared an association with what they saw as the Ilê's radical position. Indeed, the Bahian press roundly denounced the Ilê for its "racism," in much the same terms that conservative commentators in Rio de Janeiro then denounced Black Rio: it was sadly imitative of U.S. racial politics and imported tensions that did not exist in Brazil.[134] But the *bloco* steadily gained in popularity, and by the late

1970s Vovô and other Ilê leaders had to limit the organization's membership to three thousand *negros*.[135]

As in the selection of a Yoruba name over an English one, in its carnival celebrations, Ilê Aiyê focused on many of the sorts of traditional, established African cultural traits that by the early 1970s had become acceptable tropes in Bahian public life. They drew on a Yoruba vocabulary, designed clothing evocative of traditional African dress, and encouraged a style of dance and drumming that echoed the movements and rhythms of the candomblés. These were exactly the kinds of cultural expressions that activists in SINBA saw as hopelessly tarnished by long years of official mystification. But Ilê Aiyê used them to convey a political message inspired, like the activism of black Cariocas, by Africa's contemporary movements against racism and for self-determination, and by black power styles in U.S. popular culture. Each year, for instance, Ilê Aiyê paid homage to a different independent African nation, its cultural traditions, and its recent politics.[136] The political message Ilê Aiyê's leaders wished to convey was not, as it was for SINBA, the idealization of armed struggles and leftist politics, or a rejection of culture-based black movements. Rather, Ilê Aiyê sought to make explicit the politics of culture, proudly adopting African styles in clothing, hairdos, and music, and reclaiming them not for Brazilians as a whole (as dominant racial ideologies required), or simply for Brazilians who identified with African culture, but specifically for Brazilians who identified openly—and in the midst of a repressive regime—as racially *negro*.

Though the Ilê's requirement that its members adopt a sharply defined racial identity broke with the candomblés' traditions of allowing white devotees to share in Bahia's pure African heritage, the group nonetheless drew much of its inspiration from Candomblé's cultural politics. Vovô, after all, was the son of Mãe Hilda, a well-loved Candomblé priestess from a *terreiro* in the Liberdade neighborhood, and many of the Ilê Aiyê's members were her followers.[137] In particular, the Ilê borrowed from Bahia's candomblés the long-standing tradition of honoring black women as spiritual and familial leaders, a position that, with the coronation of Mãe Senhora as Mãe Preta of Brazil in 1965, became increasingly identified with the figure of the Mãe Preta among the nation's Candomblé communities.[138] (In 1968, this identification deepened as the Federation of Afro-Brazilian Cults and the Federation of Umbanda remembered Senhora, who passed away in 1967, by building a statue of her in the classic form of the Mãe Preta in the Campo Grande square of Rio de Janeiro.)[139] In 1979 the Ilê drew on this association of black motherhood (biological and surrogate), black spiritual leadership, and the valorization of black women when it wrote a song titled "Mãe Preta" to commemorate Mãe Hilda's thirtieth anniversary of leading the Ilê Axé Jitolu candomblé. From then on, the Mãe Preta became a recurring figure in the *bloco*'s explorations of Brazilian history and culture.

As in earlier moments of Bahian history, in the hands of the Ilê Aiyê, the socially acceptable figure of the Mãe Preta served to defend the honor of black Bahian women. In the 1970s many black women in Salvador were poor or working class, struggled to provide for their families in the very common absence of male heads of household, and faced racial and sexual stereotypes not so different from those their counterparts encountered in the early decades of the century.[140] In a song written for one of the Ilê's celebrations of the Mãe Preta in 1983, the male authors framed that figure as a champion of contemporary black women in the face of multiple hardships: they called for "an end to prejudice," declared their intention to help black women "struggle for their rights" (especially "secretaries and domestic workers," who "faced a bad situation if they admitted to being mothers"), and called for the "Mãe Branca" or White Mother to pay back the services she received from the Mãe Preta in the past by extending respect and help to black women in the present.[141]

Members of SINBA and the IPCN believed that more radical breaks with dominant racial ideologies were necessary to create an oppositional black consciousness and politics. But by injecting newly explicit racial meanings into popular cultural expressions, the Ilê mobilized a much broader working-class base of support than either SINBA or the IPCN. This support base in turn strengthened the *bloco*'s commitment to social projects in favor of educational and economic improvement in its home neighborhood of Liberdade. As Vovô explained to an interviewer, despite being derided by many in the emerging black movement as "false Africans" or mere "drum players," the Ilê engaged in black politics by reaching out to thousands of people, helping them to publicly reaffirm their cultural and racial blackness (a feat SINBA and the IPCN could only dream of). "Just the fact of creating a *bloco* like this is a political act. We do the political together with the cultural."[142] The Ilê thus helped transform the face of black activism in Bahia, sparking a "re-Africanization" of carnival in which African cultural themes were widely brought to bear on questions of racial pride and inequality. In the late 1970s and early 1980s, other *blocos afro* emerged, many of them (like Malê Debalê and Olodum) equally committed to dealing with issues of race and to promoting the social improvement of the neighborhoods from which they sprang. Today, these groups are among the most important black activist organizations in Salvador. Their cultural expertise and neighborhood programs have helped make African racial and cultural pride a central and visible force in Bahian society—even if, as in earlier years, their images of Bahian Africanness also play into the hands of government and commercial interests.[143]

In São Paulo, the process by which a new generation of activists used Africa to combine racial and cultural concerns was in some ways the inverse of the Bahian story. Paulistano activists in the early 1970s inherited the explicitly political and racial concerns of the city's earlier black movement. But as they looked toward Africa and attempted to reach out to popular organizations, they also began to fuse their racial ideas with views of black cultural distinctiveness that would have been anathema to their predecessors. In 1972, just as university students in Rio de Janeiro began to gather at the CEAA, black sociology professor Eduardo de Oliveira e Oliveira founded the Centro de Cultura e Arte Negra (CECAN, or Center for Black Culture and Art) in the São Paulo neighborhood of Bexiga, formerly home to *O Clarim d'Alvorada* and other early black publications and organizations. Throughout the 1970s, the center led a resurgence in Paulistano black thought, politics, and writing. The CECAN focused on promoting and showcasing black art and culture in exhibitions, conferences, and a range of publications, which included the poetry journal *Cadernos Negros* and, by 1978, the black newspaper *Jornegro*.[144]

The CECAN attracted a new generation of black thinkers and activists drawn from the student population of São Paulo's universities. There, as in Rio, students combined an interest in international currents of black activism from the United States and Africa with their own concerns and frustrations as an educated black middle class increasingly aware of the ways race thwarted their advancement in Brazilian society. The black poet and literature scholar Luiz Silva (known as Cuti), who joined the CECAN in the mid-1970s, recalls that, along with the "Communist Manifesto" and Mao Tse-Tung's *Little Red Book*, the students who became involved in the city's black organizations in this period read Eldridge Cleaver's *Soul on Ice*, Frantz Fanon's *The Wretched of the Earth*, and as much literary and political production from revolutionary Portuguese Africa as possible, including "the poems of [Angolan independence fighter] Agostinho Neto, information from Mozambique, Mozambican revolutionary poetry."[145] The CECAN's newspaper, *Jornegro*, reflected this interest in revolutionary, antiracist African movements, with articles denouncing apartheid, Western foreign policy toward Africa, and, as in the Paulistano publications of the early 1960s, biased or insufficient coverage of Africa in the mainstream press.[146] Like the writers for *SINBA*, the *Jornegro* journalists pointed to the ways Brazilian foreign relations with Africa, framed in the language of racial democracy, unintentionally exposed racism in Brazil. One article, for instance, lampooned the Brazilian government's attempt to export to Angola a famous children's show, *O sítio do picapau amarelo* (*The Yellow Woodpecker Ranch*, based on the writings of early-twentieth-century author Monteiro Lobato), as an example of Brazil's proud Afro-European heritage, only to have the Angolan government reject it for its racist depictions of blacks. "This is why Africans, through cultural relations, have much to teach the manipulators of Brazilian cultural exportations," *Jornegro* writers admonished. "Camouflaged racism did not work in Africa. But that is not enough: it also must not work here, inside our own country."[147] Also as in *SINBA*, *Jornegro*'s reports on Africa appeared alongside pieces on the condition of blacks in Brazil—poverty, discrimination, and police brutality—in order to draw parallels between blacks' shared experience of racism and colonialism in both places.[148]

But most important, like both SINBA and the IPCN, writers associated with the CECAN saw in discussions of Africa the potential for stimulating new identities that combined both "political" and "cultural" aspects of blackness. *Jornegro* authors, for instance, wrote enthusiastically about cultural trends inspired by Africa and the diaspora, like the soul movement or the aesthetics of négritude.[149] And like their counterparts at the IPCN, the editors of the CECAN's *Cadernos Negros* (making yet another reference to Fanon) proclaimed Africa to be a new muse for the decolonization of Brazilian blackness: "We are at the threshold of a . . . new life for Africa, with greater justice and freedom. Inspired by her, we too are reborn, tearing off our white masks, putting an end to imitations." *Cadernos Negros* was to be "the living image of Africa on our continent," and through its poetry, its editors pledged to "sow the seeds of consciousness that will create a true racial democracy."[150]

The fascination with contemporary Africa as an inspiration for an oppositional black politics in Brazil ran deep in São Paulo's black organizations in the mid-1970s, shaping many of the activist groups that emerged in and around the city during the decompression.[151] African revolutions, with their combination of race, class, and anticolonial politics, were particularly appealing to a group of black writers associated with the magazine *Versus*, the publication of the São Paulo cell of the Socialist Convergence, a Trotskyist organization.[152] Between 1977 and 1979 Hamilton Cardoso, Jamu Minka, Neusa Pereira, and other members of the Convergence's "black socialist nucleus" published a regular section in *Versus* titled "Afro-Latino-América." The section, which, its editors explained, took as its inspiration São Paulo's decades-old black press, provided some of the most extensive and sophisticated coverage in the contemporary black press of African anticolonial and antiapartheid struggles, as well as of issues affecting blacks in Brazil and the Americas, and the connections between them. In an article titled "Africa," writer Vanderlei José Maria explained that black Brazilian activists "should pay close attention to the paths of the African Revolution, for the example of self-determination and de-alienation with which Africans provide us is a categorical affirmation that we *negros* can and will build a new social order, one that is not under the neocolonial domination of the United States or Europe. We *negros*, at this moment, are historical agents."[153] Above all, by focusing on international currents of antiracism and anticolonialism, Afro-Latino-América authors worked to situate race, and the "specific struggles of *negros*," at the forefront of leftist thought and politics. The problem of racial discrimination, they argued, was a product of capitalist exploitation. It thus fell to blacks to lead the bringing about of a fairer society, "for they are the most oppressed, most revolutionary sector of Brazilian society, due to their economic situation, their centuries-long exploitation, and racial discrimination."[154] These writers' attempts to highlight the problem of race in a Marxist framework, however, would gradually lose ground, after 1978, to independent race-based organizing.

Whereas young black activists in Rio de Janeiro in the mid-1970s relied on the mentorship of progressive white African studies experts, and expressed a sense that they were "starting from zero" in creating an internationally inflected black politics, young Paulistano black activists interacted with several generations of veterans of their city's black politics. This situation partly reflects the deeper history of specifically black organizations in São Paulo, and also, perhaps, the greater historical isolation of race-based struggles in that city, in contrast to Rio's apparently broader opportunities for cross-racial collaboration.[155] In 1970s São Paulo, several leaders of black organizations had extensive experience in the activism of previous decades. CECAN founder Eduardo Oliveira e Oliveira (born in 1928), for instance, had been a member of Leite's Associação Cultural do Negro in the late 1950s. In 1965, when Leite retired due to old age and failing health, Oliveira took charge of the ACN until 1969, when it closed down.[156] Writer Oswaldo Camargo, another CECAN member (born in 1936), had also been active in the black newspapers and organizations of the Second Republic, notably São Paulo's *O Novo Horizonte* and Leite's ACN.[157]

Rediscovering, honoring, and reconnecting with this historic legacy of black activism became a central concern for young members of São Paulo's black organizations in the mid-1970s. Many of them made frequent visits to the homes of veteran black thinkers and writers like José Correia Leite or

Henrique Cunha.[158] During the CECAN's Black Fortnight of May 1977 (an event commemorating eighty-nine years of abolition, and including displays of art and film, as well as public lectures), they cosponsored, along with the state government, a display at the Pinacoteca do Estado (the state art museum) on the Paulista black press of the 1920s and 1930s. The exhibition represented a victory for black thinkers of all ages in a city and state that had officially ignored the black press as part of its cultural patrimony for most of the century. In the booklet that accompanied the exhibition, Oliveira wrote that the event was meant to "pay homage to patriotic Brazilians like Jayme de Aguiar, José Correia Leite, Arlindo Veiga dos Santos, Henrique Cunha, Raul Joviano do Amaral, and Vicente Ferreira," and to "reveal *negros* as people and as creators. In a word: as subjects."[159] In newspapers like *Versus*, young activists published interviews with older activists and laid the groundwork for histories of São Paulo's black organizations.[160] Indeed, it was as a young university student affiliated with the CECAN in the 1970s that writer Cuti began the extended interviews with José Correia Leite, which, since their publication in book form in 1992, have served as one of the main sources for the history of Paulista black activism.[161] It was also from the mid-1970s onward, in the midst of a revived interest in the black activism of earlier decades, that Brazilian and foreign scholars began to collect and microfilm São Paulo's black press, making it available in Brazilian and U.S. libraries.[162]

Perhaps this intergenerational exchange was so successful in São Paulo because earlier Paulistano idioms and traditions of black activism provided the seeds for exactly the kinds of oppositional politics and identities black students and young activists sought to develop in the mid-1970s. Since the early years of the century, writers in São Paulo's black press had emphasized a vision of black racial distinctiveness and difference; had at different times (most recently in the early 1960s) explored the value of contemporary African and diasporic politics; and had, since the mid-1940s, developed an increasingly direct critique of how the discourse of racial democracy could work to hide racism and discredit race-based organizations and politics. São Paulo had also historically been one of the Brazilian cities in which racial discrimination was at its most blatant, where *preto* and *negro* identities were stronger than *pardo* identities, and where activists long spoke of a population starkly divided among blacks and whites. It was, in short, one of the Brazilian cities that best fit that staple of 1970s black activism: the unflattering comparison to South Africa. Indeed, in 1978, the antiblack discrimination historically practiced by the police and by private establishments in São Paulo resulted in two widely publicized incidents: the torture and death of a young black worker (held in police custody with no formal charges) and the expulsion of four black men from an elite boating club. Though events like these were far from uncommon, their unprecedented coverage and the fact that they nearly coincided with celebrations for the ninetieth anniversary of abolition on 13 May 1978 made them especially emblematic of the failures of Brazil's supposed racial democracy.[163]

It was, in a sense, precisely this traditionally Paulistano politics of race that began to inflect the activism of university students in Rio and the carnival *blocos* in Salvador during this period. When young black thinkers and activists in 1970s Rio de Janeiro sought to expose racial discrimination in their city, strategically recasting it as a place starkly divided between blacks and whites, they were effectively adopting a Paulistano "two race" vision in order to undermine the nationalist discourses of racial mixture and harmony enforced by the dictatorship, associated with their city, and strategically celebrated by earlier generations of Carioca black thinkers. Likewise, when Salvador's *blocos afro* began to adopt the rhetoric or requirement of racial blackness, they too were adapting to their local context a long-standing Paulistano discourse that allowed them to make racial distinctions clearer and more salient than they had ever been for most black leaders in the northeastern city.

For these reasons, it is perhaps not surprising that the main development in black politics in this period—the creation of a group aspiring to be a national umbrella organization for black politics—emerged from São Paulo. In June 1978, following the much publicized incidents of virulent racial discrimination in that city, activists from São Paulo's black organizations, including CECAN members and writers for Afro-Latino-América, met to formulate a public response. This meeting gave rise to the Movimento Negro Unificado contra a Discriminação Racial (MNUCDR, or Unified Black Movement against Racial Discrimination, later shortened to MNU), which made its début on 7 July with a public demonstration in downtown São Paulo. The founders of the MNU imagined a national-level, independent organization that would link and unify the concerns of black groups across Brazil. They hoped it would also act as a pressure group in civil society to raise awareness of, and combat, racial discrimination in all its forms. Members of the MNU in São Paulo made contact with activists from Rio (including members of the IPCN and SINBA, as well as Abdias do Nascimento, who had returned from exile in the United States). From Rio, Lélia Gonzalez, Abdias do Nascimento, and others traveled to Salvador, where they helped form a local chapter of the MNU, the Grupo Nêgo, from among the city's many black cultural organizations.

Through these sorts of personal contacts and travels, and through the MNU's efforts to rotate its meetings among various Brazilian cities, the organization reached black groups across Brazil by the early 1980s.[164]

Reflecting the power of the leftist revolutionary ideals that had made Africa so appealing to student activists of this generation, MNU founders initially framed their struggle against racism as part of the wider goal of eradicating capitalism in Brazil. An early version of the MNU's statutes, drawn up by Yedo Ferreira and Amauri Pereira of Rio's SINBA, was inspired in the statutes of the Marxist Frente de Libertação de Moçambique (FRELIMO, Liberation Front of Mozambique).[165] The MNU organized itself after the example of communist cells, assigning small groups called *centros de luta* (struggle centers) to spread out among black communities, leading discussions on racial issues and engaging in "consciousness-raising." The MNU's heavily Marxist bent in these early years alienated many potential supporters and in many ways confirms Lélia Gonzalez's subsequent diagnosis of contemporary Paulistano black activism as so committed to radical politics as to be unaware of other forms of resistance. But the organization's desire to unify black organizations in Brazil acted as something of a counterweight to the tendency, among Paulistano black activists, to define politics narrowly. MNU members attempted to cast a broad net, reaching out to black organizations that were not explicitly political and making an effort to give culture a place in the organization's platform. Its statutes promised to "struggle to defend the *povo negro* on political, economic, social, and cultural fronts."[166] Gonzalez recalls that the MNU set out to establish "struggle centers . . . wherever there are Blacks, such as in work areas, villages, prisons, Candomblé and Umbanda temples, samba schools, *afoxés*, churches, favelas, swamp dwellings, and shanties."[167] It also toned down its radical rhetoric to increase its appeal. At the MNU's first congress, held in Rio in December 1979, MNU members decided to change the name of the "struggle centers" to the more inviting "action groups," realizing that many potential allies of the movement (especially those from poorer backgrounds, more exposed to police repression) might have feared any association with such radical-sounding units.[168]

By attempting to reach out to groups that celebrated African contributions to Brazilian culture, the São Paulo–based MNU departed from the tradition of denying that there was any cultural difference associated with black identities, a mainstay of Paulistano black politics in the previous three quarters of a century. Several factors contributed to this shift. Not least, to be sure, was the MNU's desire to become a viable national organization, which required Paulistanos to travel to Salvador and other regions where they were exposed to different traditions of activism.[169] Building a national movement, to paraphrase Lélia Gonzalez, meant learning what "Yoruba" was. In addition, intensified migration to São Paulo from Brazil's Northeast since midcentury meant that it was no longer a place, as Leite had recalled for the 1920s and 1930s, where Candomblé was invisible and marginal to public life. Indeed, shortly after its inauguration in the mid-1950s, the statue of the Mãe Preta in São Paulo's Largo do Paissandú became a central devotional site for many of the city's Candomblé groups, who staged religious ceremonies there and left votives and flowers around its pedestal.[170] Like their counterparts in Salvador, they had made the Mãe Preta part of an African religious pantheon. MNU activists, then, did not have to travel farther than downtown São Paulo to encounter vibrant expressions of black cultural difference.

Indeed, by the late 1970s, at the Largo do Paissandú young black activists could see Candomblé groups practicing in the shadow of two monuments to that city's long history of black mobilization. One was the Church of Nossa Senhora do Rosário dos Homens Pretos, the city's oldest Catholic black brotherhood, a testament to the sorts of associations that had emerged in earlier centuries among slaves and free people of color and which continued to flourish at the end of the twentieth century. The other was the statue of the Mãe Preta, just beside the church, which stood as a reminder of the campaigns waged in the 1920s (and 1950s) by Paulista black organizations for official recognition of their contributions to Brazilian history and culture. To many activists in the 1970s, including veterans like Leite and the young organizers in the MNU, such politics, and the figure of the Mãe Preta herself, seemed stale and conservative. Yet the members of the Clube 220, the black social club responsible for successfully reviving the monument proposal in the 1950s, continued to celebrate the Mãe Preta, as did other black middle-class clubs like São Paulo's Associação dos Homens de Cor. In the early 1960s, the Clube 220 reached out to the Candomblé groups that frequented the statue, making it the site of jointly sponsored celebrations for the *Dia da Mãe Preta* (28 September) and the abolition of slavery (13 May).[171] In 1968 Frederico Penteado, president of the Clube 220 (and the man behind the project to build the statue in the mid-1950s), successfully campaigned for a state law declaring 28 September a "Day of Gratitude to the Mãe Preta," a holiday commemorating "she who, in captivity, . . . raised the children of others, contributing toward the formation of Brazilians since the time of slavery."[172]

In the late 1970s, the new generation of activists associated with the MNU brought yet another layer of political meaning to the statue. Identifying it as a promising site for black activism, and a fruitful place to reach out to different kinds of black organizations in their city, the MNU in 1979 staged an antiracist protest at the Mãe Preta statue during the Clube 220's 13 May celebrations. The MNU's intention was to sensitize these other groups to the problem of racism and to challenge their ongoing use of 13 May, and of the Mãe Preta, as symbols of black liberation. Two *Versus* writers summarized young black thinkers' views of these earlier sorts of politics: "Penteado's intention is positive, in terms of its concern with registering the participation of black women in society, but it has become increasingly limited to an affective and folkloric vision. A vision that is shackled to the cult of 'achievements' obtained since the time of slavery, and which is distant from the aspirations of the 'new black [*novo negro*].'"[173] For young members of the MNU, steeped in the criticism of racial democracy as a myth, black politics that continued to rely on ideas of racial fraternity or cordiality (like the Mãe Preta), or which appealed to the benevolence of white elites (the celebration of 13 May), were not just hopelessly outdated but dangerously blinded by dominant ideologies. Yet for Clube 220 members who saw the symbols of the Mãe Preta and of 13 May as evidence of black Brazilians' great progress throughout the century, the young MNU members appeared as radical malcontents. One MNU member recalled that he had never been physically harassed at a black movement rally until he attended this demonstration at the Mãe Preta statue—when he was attacked not by authorities but by members of rival black organizations. This incident, revealing the ongoing tensions and conflicting politics among São Paulo's (and indeed Brazil's) very different black associations, illustrates the challenges the MNU would face as it set out to construct an inclusive movement in subsequent years.[174]

WITH THE ADVENT of a military dictatorship in 1964, the idea of racial democracy was no longer open to negotiation and claims-making, as it had been to varying extents in the past. Instead, it had become uniformly prescriptive—an authoritarian declaration of the way things were, largely stripped of the aspirational dimensions that had so engaged activists of previous generations. As they fought against an undemocratic regime and a particularly stultifying incarnation of the discourse of Brazil's racial harmony, black activists in Rio, Salvador, and São Paulo from the mid-1970s to the early 1980s shifted away from the engagement with national racial ideologies that had marked the politics of black intellectuals in all three cities for most of the century.

They developed an explicit critique of racial democracy as a harmful "myth," a sinister ideology that occluded bleak realities of racial discrimination and marginalization. They denounced cultural mixture as a process by which the white middle classes and the state commercialized and contaminated true popular cultures. And they rejected ideas of biological *mestiçagem*, arguing that only a widely accepted black consciousness would reveal the reality of a Brazilian black majority ruled by a white minority.

Just as Africa played a key role in the development of official ideologies of racial democracy in this period, Africa's culture and its revolutionary politics became central to these new black thinkers' criticisms of the military regime's racial order, and of Brazilian society more broadly. For these young men and women, struggles against racism and colonialism in Africa in the mid-1970s provided more than an inspiration for local black activism—they provided a metaphor for Brazil. At a time when military law enshrined a restrictive discourse of racial democracy, black thinkers' denunciations of institutionalized racism, colonialism, and state repression in Africa became commentaries on the illegitimacy of the (white) regime in Brasília. Like Portugal's African colonies or South Africa, they argued, Brazil suffered under a repressive, racist, and colonialist police state that had historically oppressed a majority African-descended *povo*. By the same token, African narratives of liberation helped black thinkers in this period to work through their thorny relationship with leftist movements at home and to more clearly articulate their goal: a "decolonized" Brazil graced by political, racial, and cultural self-determination.

In these years, many black thinkers expressed the conviction that they were finally breaking free of the decades- or even centuries-long mystification that ideologies of *mestiçagem* and "culturalism" had inflicted on previous generations of black thinkers, and indeed, on most of Brazil's African-descended population. It was in the early 1980s, with Brazil under an increasingly discredited military dictatorship, and from the trenches of a growing and vocal Movimento Negro, that Abdias do Nascimento disowned his and other activists' earlier endorsements of racial democracy as a cowardly concession to Brazilian racists. In subsequent years, activists' and scholars' focus on the sharp critiques developed by black thinkers of the 1970s and 1980s contributed to portraying this period as a stark and heroic break with earlier black politics described as episodic, weak, bourgeois, or accommodationist.

Yet despite its apparent and in many ways real singularity, this is but one episode in a longer history of black political thought marked by the struggle to harness national ideologies of racial inclusiveness to antiracist social transformations. Although black thinkers in this period thought of themselves as debunking a myth and putting it to rest once and for all, what they succeeded in discrediting, in the eyes of many, was a particular interpretation of racial democracy that asserted the final achievement of racial equality. The aspirational qualities long attached to the idea of Brazil's racial inclusiveness persisted, reemerging with the return of democracy.

Epilogue
Brazil, 1985 to the New Century

Against the backdrop of military dictatorship, a new generation of black thinkers and activists across Brazil revised their relationship with dominant racial ideologies, rejecting the shared symbols that, in different iterations, had served as the centerpiece of black politics since the First Republic. After 1985 the return to democracy gave black activists the openings they needed to make their denunciation of the "myth" of racial democracy increasingly visible in Brazilian public life. The period of democratic transition in the mid-1980s, like the transition to democracy in the mid-1940s, was a propitious time to question an ideology that had become so closely associated with a discredited dictatorship. It was also, as at midcentury, a time of growth for black cultural and political organizations.[1] In this new environment black groups were able to push for, and frequently win, legal prohibitions against racial discrimination as part of the rebuilding of democratic institutions. The constitution of 1988 reflected these transformations, updating the Afonso Arinos Law of 1951 to make racial discrimination a crime subject to imprisonment without bail, and giving rise to hundreds of antiracist laws at state and municipal levels.[2]

Over the course of the 1980s, new and rebuilt political parties (particularly those on the left) recognized the power of the growing Movimento Negro Unificado. Party leaders included antiracist pronouncements in their platforms, constituted committees to address issues of racial inequality, and ran black candidates on their tickets. In 1982 Abdias do Nascimento went to Brasília as a congressman for the Democratic Labor Party, whose leader, Leonel Brizola, simultaneously won the governorship of Rio de Janeiro based on the slogan of *socialismo moreno*, or "brown socialism."[3] By 1988, the centennial of the abolition of slavery, black activist organizations in Brazil—their numbers greatly expanded since the early years of the decompression—succeeded, through media campaigns, widespread public demonstrations, and scholarship, in putting racial democracy up for serious public debate. As part of this debate, several leading public figures acknowledged the problem of racial discrimination in Brazil and admitted that the discourse of racial democracy often bore little relation to everyday practices of racial exclusion.[4]

Throughout the 1990s, activists in the Movimento Negro intensified their calls for corrective and affirmative measures on race and racism, and continued their campaigns to promote a unified *negro* identity among Brazilians of color. For the 1991 census, for instance, several black organizations (including Rio's IPCN) once again lobbied IBGE officials to use the racial category *negro* in place of both *preto* and *pardo*.[5] They also staged a widespread campaign to shift the racial consciousness of the Brazilian population, encouraging citizens not to lighten themselves in their choice of color category. The first strategy failed. Though black activists succeeded in sparking widespread debate among academics, politicians, and census officials about the viability of the *negro* category, both the 1991 and the 2000 censuses preserved the terms *preto* and *pardo* instead.[6] The second strategy of encouraging Brazilians not to identify with lighter skin categories also had little effect, at least in the short term. The 1991 census continued the trend, begun in 1940, of the "browning" of the Brazilian population—the percentage of *pardos* steadily grew at the expense of the categories of *preto* and *branco*.[7] In other words, despite the efforts of activists, a slightly smaller percentage of Brazilians identified as *preto* in the 1991 census than eleven years earlier.[8] But the debates sparked by the Movimento Negro seem to have contributed to reversing this trend by the 2000 census, which showed a slight increase in the proportions of *brancos* and *pretos* at the expense of the intermediate category *pardo*. It is possible that this preference for polar rather than mixed categories among African-descended Brazilians reflects the outcome of the Movimento Negro's public efforts, through census campaigns and on several other fronts, to promote pride in a unified *negro* identity.[9] And activists' longed-for nonwhite majority may well become a reality in the 2010 census, in which, officials predict, *pardos* and *pretos* will combine to outnumber whites for the first time since the census of 1890.[10]

Perhaps the most visible and successful of the Movimento Negro's efforts was its members' demand, throughout the 1990s and into the new century, for public policies explicitly in favor of nonwhite Brazilians. The move toward affirmative action–style programs began in the mid-1990s, under the presidency of Fernando Henrique Cardoso. Breaking radically with the practices of previous Brazilian governments, Cardoso's administration openly denounced racism in Brazil and helped stimulate a range of compensatory policies in several federal agencies, state and municipal governments, businesses, nonprofits, universities, and other public and private organizations. Though much of the debate about affirmative action in Brazil has focused on the visible and highly controversial adoption of racial quotas by a group of institutions and universities (which have mandated that a percentage, usually 20% to 40%, of their slots go to black candidates in order to mirror this group's representation in the broader population), racial quotas are not the only form of affirmative action initiatives. Some quotas often take race as well as class into account, and many programs are not quota-based at all but range more broadly from special fellowships and preparatory classes for people of color, to the inclusion of racial issues in school curricula, to support for black-owned businesses or black community organizations.[11] Affirmative action programs have continued to expand, and to gain official backing, under the presidency of Luis Inácio (Lula) da Silva (2003–10), whose Worker's Party has strong ties to the black movement.[12] As they become more widespread and more visibly discussed at the highest levels of government, affirmative action policies (particularly quotas) have sparked pitched debates in Brazilian society. They have drawn criticism from conservative sectors and from progressive sectors. The former still see black racial mobilization as threatening, while the latter, including many antiracist scholars, believe that Brazil's unique history of racial mixture and antiracialism provides a better path toward inclusion than the adoption of a system of racial remediation (and of fixed racial identities) borrowed from the experiences of historically segregated societies like the United States or South Africa.[13] Yet however contentious, affirmative action policies and the debates surrounding them have made race, racism, and the *negro* identity proposed by some black thinkers since the early twentieth century central issues in Brazilian public life.

Though black activists are now an established element of Brazil's mainstream public sphere, and though their numbers, in the Movimento Negro and in many other organizations, have expanded significantly since the early 1900s, when a handful of black men in São Paulo gathered to publish their *negro* newspapers, black activists remain a tiny minority compared to the vast African-descended constituency they hope to reach. There are many explanations for the inability of black intellectuals, now and in the past, to create a mass black movement, many of which have been explored in this book. As we have seen, middle-class activists for whom race, not class, was the organizing principle of oppression often articulated visions of racial difference that had little appeal for (or were openly condescending to) working-class populations for whom color and class were intricately intertwined. The historical stigmas of blackness, the more immediate pressures of poverty, and deep ideological and political differences among politically engaged people of African descent over the usefulness of claiming racial versus cultural differences or celebrating mixture have also contributed to fragmenting black activists' imagined constituency throughout the century. The remarkable political legacy of the 1970s, which pushed the Movimento Negro to reject popular notions of race and to embrace at best uneasily the symbols of national identity, popular religion, or mass culture shared by many Brazilians of color, made possible black activists' dramatic interventions in national public life but also limited their effectiveness in mobilizing a broad membership.

This tension is worth noting. For however powerful the black politics of decolonization of the 1970s, and however compelling the narratives of political enlightenment told by veterans of the modern Movimento Negro, we should be wary of confusing the black politics that emerged from the last decade of dictatorship with a final or definitive stage in the development of a black racial consciousness in Brazil. Like the famous protest staged by Abdias do Nascimento in Nigeria in 1977, the politics developed by the IPCN, SINBA, Ilê Aiyê, the MNU, and others, which denounced racial democracy as a myth that hampered the development of a true racial consciousness among Brazilians of color, were a response to the particular historical conjuncture of a waning dictatorship and a promising democratic opening. Pushed to the brink by a regime that made discourses of racial democracy its own, and influenced by a revolutionary ideology that called for the fundamental remaking of society, these activists found much to criticize in the shared symbols of black belonging (from African culture to ideas of racial fraternity and democracy) that earlier activists had used to denounce racist practices or to press for fuller inclusion. Yet these earlier activists were as creative in their responses to the contexts in which they lived as the Movimento Negro was in its historical moment. When, in the 1980s, Abdias do Nascimento and his colleagues looked back on the proracial democracy activism of the 1950s with disdain, they did not do justice to the subtlety and courage of that earlier movement as it sought to work within the constraints of its time—something Nascimento himself recently acknowledged as he reflected on that moment in the history of black activism.[14]

Perhaps a more significant benefit to placing the Movimento Negro in a deeper history of Brazilian racial politics is the lesson that racial democracy itself was only one iteration of the many ideas of racial harmony in twentieth-century Brazil. These ideas, while frequently repressive and "mythical" in exactly the ways the post-1970s black movement criticized, were also much more complicated than the imputation of false consciousness might suggest. Social myths, like religious myths, are not simply falsehoods. They are stories that societies tell and retell about themselves, stories that therefore become crucial common ground for debate and negotiation even as the powerful deploy them to parry demands for social change. Despite black (and many white) intellectuals' tendency since the 1970s to proclaim that ideas of racial democracy and *mestiçagem* were antithetical to the emergence of antiracist politics, in fact, those engaged in black politics over the course of the century, like many Brazilians more broadly, were perfectly capable of deploying one or another version of "reality" or "myth" depending on circumstance—even, at times, simultaneously. In this sense, black activism, though almost always practiced by a small, relatively privileged minority of people of African descent in Brazil, reflects a broader pattern identified by scholars working among less privileged Brazilians of color. As Robin Sheriff has shown in her work on ideas about race among residents of a Rio favela in the late 1980s and early 1990s, belief in the *ideal* of racial democracy and the adoption of mixed color identities does not preclude recognition of racial injustice, including a vision of a society divided between whites and non-whites, and sometimes, the assertion that racial democracy is a myth. Indeed, many of her interlocutors, like many black intellectuals earlier in the century, often invoked the ideal of Brazil's racial harmony to denounce acts of racism as contrary to Brazilian ways of being.[15]

Despite the Movimento Negro's successes in debunking the idea that Brazil is already a racial democracy, the aspirational components of Brazil's long-standing ideas of inclusiveness are thus still very much alive and may still have a role to play. Even as the return to democracy allowed space for highlighting the hollowness of smugly celebratory interpretations of racial democracy, increasing cooperation between activists and the state removed the stark line that had helped to make "myth" seem the diametrical opposite of "reality" under the dictatorship. As cooperation with the state gathered force, activists once again engaged, if less openly and directly than in earlier generations, with the desire among many Brazilian politicians to present their nation as one that held racial inclusiveness as a cherished principle and goal. At the World Conference on Racism in Durban, South Africa, in 2001, the roughly 150 Brazilian black activists in attendance were able to push for concessions from Brazilian officials, like promises of larger-scale federal affirmative action plans, in large part because those officials were committed to upholding (or shoring up) Brazil's international reputation as a racially progressive nation. At home, media coverage of Brazilian representation at the conference produced an unprecedented explosion of articles on race, racism, and affirmative action.[16] In contrast with Abdias do Nascimento's intervention at the 1977 FESTAC in Nigeria, the activists attending the conference in South Africa in 2001 were interacting with a state that had opened discussions about racism in Brazil, and had given black activists a space and a voice within these discussions. In the context of this political opening, Brazil's racial inclusiveness could once again operate as a shared national ideal, an iteration of the way Brazil should be, in favor of which activists could newly pressure for change. Thus, in the early twenty-first century, even as activists make their most significant inroads against Brazil's racial hierarchy, long-standing ideologies of Brazil's racial inclusiveness—significantly transformed through decades of struggle to mean the public acknowledgment of racism and the implementation of corrective measures—might once more become a weapon in the arsenal of black thinkers.

NOTES

Abbreviations

APERJ	Arquivo Público do Estado do Rio de Janeiro / Public Archive of the State of Rio de Janeiro
FGM	Fundação Gregório Mattos / Gregório Mattos Foundation
FNB	Frente Negra Brasileira / Brazilian Black Front
FPV	Fundação Pierre Verger / Pierre Verger Foundation
GTAR	Grupo de Trabalho André Rebouças / André Rebouças Working Group
JB, SEA	*Jornal da Bahia*, "Special Edition for Africa"
NU, MJH	Northwestern University Archives, Melville J. Herskovits Papers
PAIGC	Partido Africano da Independência da Guiné e Cabo Verde / African Party for the Independence of Guinea and Cape Verde
PCB	Partido Comunista Brasileiro / Brazilian Communist Party
SC, MJH	Schomburg Center, Melville J. Herskovits Papers
UBa	Universidade da Bahia / University of Bahia
UFF	Universidade Federal Fluminense / University of Rio de Janeiro State

Introduction

1. See, e.g., Mattos, *Das cores do silêncio*; Sheriff, *Dreaming Equality*; Caulfield, "Interracial Courtship"; Abreu, "Mulatas, Crioulos, and Morenas"; and Fischer, *Poverty of Rights*.

2. See tables in IBGE, *Brasil*, 222; and Manuela Carneiro da Cunha, *História dos índios*, 14.

3. Vainfas, "História indígena," 45; João José Reis, "Presença negra," 82. In some areas, like São Paulo, Indian slavery persisted into the eighteenth century; see John Monteiro, *Negros da terra*.

4. Vainfas, "História indígena," 51; Boxer, *Race Relations*, 98–99.

5. *Alvará* of 7 June 1755, cited in Russell-Wood, *Black Man in Slavery*, 43.

6. Exceptions, however, frequently occurred in practice. Russell-Wood, *Black Man in Slavery*, 67–72.

7. Ibid., 30.

8. Bergad, *Comparative Histories of Slavery*, 1–12, 60–61, 285. These three states together (Minas Gerais, Rio de Janeiro, and São Paulo, in that order) would have just over half the nation's slaves by 1874. João José Reis, "Presença negra," 91.

9. Unlike Spanish America, the former Portuguese colony managed to hold together in the years following independence. But it was by no means free of conflict. For an overview of recent literature questioning the long-presumed "smoothness" of this transition, see Weinstein, "Erecting and Erasing Boundaries," nn. 14–19.

10. The literature on abolition is vast. For a classic overview, see Conrad, *Destruction of Brazilian Slavery*. More recent interpretations stress the role of the enslaved themselves; see, e.g., Chalhoub, "Politics of Disease Control"; Machado, *O plano e o pânico*; and Graden, "An Act 'Even of Public Security.'"

11. Famous examples include von Martius, "How the History of Brazil Should Be Written"; and Alencar, *O guarani*. On this trend, see John Monteiro, "Heathen Castes," 710–13.

12. Manuela Carneiro da Cunha, "Política indigenista," 141–47.

13. Vainfas, "História indígena," 53; Nobles, *Shades of Citizenship*, 104.

14. John Monteiro, "Heathen Castes," 713–16; Sommer, *Foundational Fictions*, 21, 155–56. See also Kraay, "Between Brazil and Bahia."

15. Andrews, *Blacks and Whites*, 129–30; Celia Azevedo, *Onda negra, medo branco*, 64–70; Skidmore, *Black into White*, 38–44; Haberly, *Three Sad Races*. On free people of color during the Empire, see Richard Graham, "Free African Brazilians."

16. Nabuco, *O abolicionismo*, 22–23, cited in Skidmore, *Black into White*, 23.

17. Celia Azevedo, *Onda negra, medo branco*, 77–82; Skidmore, *Black into White*, 21–24.

18. Andrews, *Blacks and Whites*, 36–37. Cf. Elciene Azevedo, *Orfeu de carapinha*; Chalhoub, *Visões da liberdade*; and Grinberg, *Liberata*.

19. Skidmore, *Black into White*, 24. Cf. Grinberg, *O fiador*; and Mattos, *Das cores do silêncio*.

20. The literature on these transformations is extensive (see discussions in chaps. 1 and 2 of this book). For an introduction, see Skidmore, *Black into White*. For an introduction to parallel trends in Latin America more broadly, see Martínez-Echazábal, "Mestizaje."

21. Freyre, *Casa-grande e senzala*.

22. For this critique in Brazil and in Latin America more broadly, see Warren, *Racial Revolutions*, 234–42; Wade, *Race and Ethnicity*, chaps. 2 and 3; Weinstein, "Erecting and Erasing Boundaries"; and Andrews, "Afro-Latin America." The long tradition of studying "race" and "race relations" in Brazil primarily through a black-white continuum (a tradition to which my own work is heir) is evident in leading studies from the 1940s through the 1990s, such as Pierson, *Negroes in Brazil*; Bastide and Fernandes, *Brancos e negros*; Fernandes, *A integração do negro*; Degler, *Neither Black nor White*; Skidmore, *Black into White*; Andrews, *Blacks and Whites*; and Hanchard, *Orpheus and Power*.

23. Excepting the 1970 census, which did not include a color question at all, the categories *índio* and *indígena* appeared only in 1960 and 1991, respectively. Nobles, *Shades of Citizenship*, 104–5. Even *amarelos* (literally "yellows," or people of Asian descent), excluded from the myth of Brazil's three foundational races and making up (together with indigenous people) less than 1% of Brazil's current population, consistently appeared as a census category from the 1940s through 2000. Telles, *Race in Another America*, 45; IBGE, *Brasil*, 222.

24. Guimarães, *Classes, raças e democracia*.

25. Abdias do Nascimento, in "Inaugurando o Congresso do Negro," *Quilombo*, June–July 1950, 1; emphasis mine.

26. For an introduction to these studies and their effects on contemporary views of race relations, see Maio, "UNESCO and the Study of Race"; and Motta, "Paradigms in the Study of Race Relations." I discuss specific studies further in chap. 4.

27. While *pretos* made up 15% of the population in 1890, they were only 6% in 2000. Those classified as *pardo* remained relatively stable at 41% and 40% between those years; and those classified as *branco* rose from 44% in 1890 to become a national majority of 54% in 2000. Figures from João José Reis, "Presença negra," 94. On the many reasons for this trend, see Telles, *Race in Another America*, 38–40, 44.

28. Telles, *Race in Another America*, 91–94; Nobles, *Shades of Citizenship*, chap. 3.

29. Telles, *Race in Another America*, 223–24, 215.

30. Foremost among these studies are Cardoso and Ianni, *Cor e mobilidade social*; Fernandes, *A integração do negro*; Ianni, *Raças e classes sociais*; Thales de Azevedo, *Democracia racial*; Nelson do Valle Silva, "White-Nonwhite Income Differentials"; Hasenbalg, *Discriminação e desigualdades raciais*; Fontaine, *Race, Class, and Power*; Andrews, *Blacks and Whites*; Lovell, *Desigualdade racial*; Reichmann, *Race in Contemporary Brazil*; and Telles, *Race in Another America*.

31. Valladares, *Impact of African Culture*.

32. Cited from the revised and expanded version of the position paper, published as Abdias do Nascimento, "O genocídio," 86, 124, 128.

33. Cited in Abdias do Nascimento, "Sitiado em Lagos," 291; emphasis mine.

34. See, e.g., Degler, *Neither Black nor White*; Toplin, "Reinterpreting Comparative Race Relations"; Toplin, *Freedom and Prejudice*; Andrews, *Blacks and Whites*; Daniel, *Race and Multiraciality*; Skidmore, "Bi-racial U.S.A. vs. Multi-racial Brazil"; Skidmore, *Black into White*; Hanchard, *Orpheus and Power*; Twine, *Racism in a Racial Democracy*; Winant, *Racial Conditions*; Winant, "Racial Democracy"; Marx, *Making Race and Nation*; Mitchell, "Blacks and the *Abertura*"; and Turner, "Brown into Black." For revisionist critiques elsewhere in Latin America, see, e.g., Helg, *Our Rightful Share*; Richard Graham, *Idea of Race*; Wright, *Café con Leche*; and Gould, *To Die in This Way*.

35. See Bourdieu and Wacquant, "On the Cunning of Imperialist Reason"; Bairros, "'Orfeu e poder'"; Fry, "O que a cinderela negra tem a dizer"; Fry, "Por que o Brasil é diferente?"; Matta, "Notas sobre o racismo"; Risério, *A utopia brasileira*; and Denise Ferreira da Silva, "Facts of Blackness."

36. For examples of this critique, see Hanchard, "Resposta"; and French, "Missteps." For a range of Brazilian responses to the Bourdieu/Hanchard polemic, see the special issue of *Estudos Afro-Asiáticos* 24 (2002). For an overview of these debates in the scholarship on Brazil and Latin America, see Wade, "Images of Latin American Mestizaje." In the last few years, these debates over the effects of fusionist vs. segregationist racial systems have been articulated, in Brazil, with debates over the desirability of affirmative action policies and the forms they should take. For a nuanced introduction to these linkages, see Pinho, *Mama Africa*, 10–22.

37. Andrews, "Afro-Latin America," 196.

38. E.g., Telles, *Race in Another America*; Andrews, *Afro-Latin America*; and Chasteen, *National Rhythms*.

39. In addition to the works cited in n. 1, see Costa, *Brazilian Empire*, chap. 9; Fry, "Politics, Nationality"; Tiago de Melo Gomes, *Um espelho no palco*; Seigel, *Uneven Encounters*; and Pinho, *Mama Africa*.

40. De la Fuente, *Nation for All*; de la Fuente, "Myths of Racial Democracy"; Ferrer, *Insurgent Cuba*; Scott, *Degrees of Freedom*.

41. See, e.g., the essays in the issue of *Patterns of Prejudice* devoted to exploring the question of "belonging," especially Kannabiran, Vieten, and Yuval-Davis, "Introduction"; and Yuval-Davis, "Belonging and the Politics of Belonging." See also Kannabiran, Vieten, and Yuval-Davis, *Situated Politics of Belonging*; and John Crowley, "Politics of Belonging."

42. Abdias do Nascimento, "Prefácio à 2a edição," in Abdias do Nascimento, *O negro revoltado* (1982).

43. Burdick, "Lost Constituency"; Andrews, *Blacks and Whites*; Hanchard, *Orpheus and Power*; Telles, "Ethnic Boundaries."

44. For an insightful critique of how "political agents" who advocate for their group's belonging simultaneously "use these ideologies and projects in order to promote their own power positions within and outside the community," see Yuval-Davis, "Belonging and the Politics of Belonging," 205.

45. Cf. Scott, "Public Rights."

46. See, e.g., Skidmore, *Black into White*; Renato Ortiz, *Cultura brasileira*; and Mota, *Ideologia*.

47. Guimarães, *Classes, raças e democracia*, chap. 5; Weinstein, "Racializing Regional Difference."

48. See "A Final Note on Language and Race," in Ferrer, *Insurgent Cuba*, 10–12.

Chapter 1

1. In Brazil, *Paulista* is used to refer to inhabitants of the state of São Paulo (whether or not they live in its capital); *Paulistano* refers only to inhabitants of the city. In chapter 1, which deals with writers in both the city and the state of São Paulo, I therefore use primarily the first term. In subsequent chapters, which focus almost exclusively on writers in the city of São Paulo, I use *Paulistano* more frequently.

2. B. Florencio and F. J. de Oliveira, "Nosso programma," *Baluarte*, 15 November 1903, 1.

3. In 1888, when the monarchy abolished slavery in Brazil, most people of color were already free (by birth) or had been freed through earlier legislation or individual efforts. Though most writers in the early-twentieth-century black press had been born free, some (like Lino Guedes) were the children of slaves (Malinoff, "Modern Afro-Brazilian Poetry," 49); for them, the humiliating memory of the enslavement of one or both of their parents would have given the term "emancipation" especially powerful meaning and might have guided their own activist leanings. Cf. Zeuske, "Two Stories," 192.

4. Andrews, *Blacks and Whites*, 42–53; Love, "Political Participation." Popular participation through political meetings and elections was robust during the Republic, but electoral outcomes were highly managed through networks of clientage. Richard Graham, *Patronage and Politics*.

5. Andrews, *Blacks and Whites*, 42–53; Hahner, *Poverty and Politics*, chap. 6; Mattos, *Das cores do silêncio*; Machado, *O plano e o pânico*. For an overview of recent trends in the study of postemancipation society in Brazil, see Scott, "Brazil."

6. Skidmore, *Brazil*, 72.

7. Maciel, *Discriminações raciais*, 91–92, 98–100; José G. Pereira, "São Benedito," 293–97; Domingues, "Um 'templo de luz.'"

8. On vagrancy, see, among others, Andrews, *Blacks and Whites*; Celia Azevedo, *Onda negra, medo branco*; Chalhoub, *Trabalho, lar e botequim*; Fausto, *Crime e cotidiano*; and Olívia M. Gomes da Cunha, *Intenção e gesto*.

9. Andrews, *Blacks and Whites*, 133–34.

10. On scientific racism and immigration, see Skidmore, *Black into White*; Stepan, *Hour of Eugenics*; Borges, "'Puffy, Ugly, Slothful and Inert'"; and Schwarcz, *O espetáculo das raças*.

11. G. V. de Lapouge, *Les sélections sociales*, cited in F. J. Oliveira Vianna, *Evolução*, 185.

12. On whitening and immigration, see Skidmore, "Racial Ideas and Social Policy"; Skidmore, *Black into White*; Seyferth, "Construindo a nação"; and Andrews, *Blacks and Whites*.

13. F. J. Oliveira Vianna, *Evolução*, 185.

14. Skidmore, *Black into White*; Andrews, "Brazilian Racial Democracy."

15. João José Reis, "Presença negra," 94.

16. Andrews, *Blacks and Whites*, 54–58, 88–89; Love, *São Paulo*, 10–12.

17. Andrews, *Blacks and Whites*, 21; Love, *São Paulo*, 26.

18. Butler, *Freedoms Given*, 69, 71.

19. For the years between 1872 and 1940, the percentage of whites in the state of São Paulo jumped from 51.8 to 84.9, that of *pardos* dropped from 28.2 to only 4.7, and that of *pretos* decreased from 20.1 to 7.3. Andrews, *Blacks and Whites*, 247–54. Figures for Rio are from Costa Pinto, *O negro*, 73. Racially segmented data in Brazil are notoriously complex, since race or color categories are not "real" in an objective sense and since many factors influence how a person is categorized (or self-categorizes). Yet however imperfect, this data consistently shows significant differences in the relative proportions of *pretos*, *pardos*, and *brancos* in the cities of São Paulo, Rio de Janeiro, and Salvador da Bahia over the course of the twentieth century. The differences are worth noting, not just because they suggest the varying proportions of people of African descent in each place, but also because they point to differences in the ways census counters (and subjects themselves) assigned color categories in different regions. In the case of the *pardo/preto* distinction analyzed here, the relatively small number of people categorized as "pardos" in São Paulo (compared to Rio de Janeiro), and the fact that these few *pardos* were (by 1940) outnumbered almost 2 to 1 by *pretos*, suggests the greater statistical and symbolic salience of the category *preto* in that city as a term to designate nonwhites. As several scholars have shown, this more dichotomous pattern of race relations in São Paulo (and indeed, in other cities of the Brazilian South, where European immigration was heaviest), in which the term *preto* came to designate anyone of visible African ancestry regardless of lighter or darker skin (or of social status), corresponds to widespread perceptions that nonwhites (both

pretos and *pardos*) suffered discrimination to a nearly indistinguishable degree in these regions. For a discussion of these studies, and the *pardo/preto* distinction in São Paulo specifically, see Andrews, *Blacks and Whites*, 250–51.

20. Weinstein, "Racializing Regional Difference," 243. See also Sevcenko, *Orfeu extático*, esp. 137–41.

21. Butler, *Freedoms Given*, 67; Fernandes, *The Negro*, 61.

22. On industrialization in São Paulo, see Weinstein, *For Social Peace in Brazil*; and Dean, *Industrialization of São Paulo*. On foreigners as both owners of industry and favored employees, see Butler, *Freedoms Given*, 70; and Andrews, *Blacks and Whites*, chaps. 3 and 4.

23. Hasenbalg, *Discriminação e desigualdades raciais*, 254–55. See also Fernandes, *The Negro*, chap. 1; and Andrews, *Blacks and Whites*, 88–89.

24. Flávio Gomes, *Negros e política*, 28.

25. Fernandes, *The Negro*, 76. The term *Negroes* appears in the English translation (used here) of Fernandes's work, but the informant's original term is *negros*. See Fernandes, *A integração do negro*, 107.

26. Fernandes, *A integração do negro*, 117–18.

27. Andrews, *Blacks and Whites*, 124–28; Fernandes, *A integração do negro*, 117–18.

28. Fernandes, *The Negro*, 77.

29. Male writers in the black press are the most frequent subjects of these photographs, though readers and association members of both sexes sometimes appeared as well; see, e.g., the many photos in *O Clarim d'Alvorada* (hereafter *Clarim*), 24 January 1926, and the portrait of Arlindo Ribeiro, a graduate of a training course at the Força Pública (São Paulo's armed guard), posing in sharp military attire, in *Clarim*, 20 February 1927, 4.

30. Bastide, "A imprensa negra," 55–60; Andrews, *Blacks and Whites*, chap. 5.

31. Andrews, *Blacks and Whites*, 139–43; Butler, *Freedoms Given*, 78–83.

32. J. C. Leite, in Silva and Leite, *E disse*, 45.

33. There are no statistics on the early papers' print runs, but copies of each issue almost certainly numbered well under one thousand—the lower end of the estimate for *Clarim*, probably the most popular paper of the 1920s. See Ferrara, *A imprensa negra*, 246.

34. See F. B. de Souza, "O passado," *Bandeirante*, April 1919, 1; the editors' "Vencendo a encosta," *Bandeirante*, August 1918, 1; A. Rodrigues, [untitled], *Kosmos*, 21 February 1923, 1; and the editors' "Aos leitores," *Alfinete*, 9 March 1919, 1. On the press's fragility, see Mitchell, "Racial Consciousness," 154–55; Bastide, "A imprensa negra," 50; and Andrews, *Blacks and Whites*, 128.

35. Two of the most widely used collections of black newspapers are the microfilm sets made by the Biblioteca Nacional (Rio de Janeiro) and by political scientist Michael Mitchell (see bibliography), both filmed in the 1970s and 1980s from the collections of black press veterans. São Paulo's Biblioteca Municipal and the Arquivo Leuenroth at UNICAMP (Campinas, São Paulo) also house important collections.

36. In addition to the above-cited works on the black press of São Paulo, see also Pinto, "Movimento negro"; Domingues, *A nova abolição*, chap. 1. See Domingues's

introduction for a useful overview of recent works (especially Brazilian M.A. theses and Ph.D. dissertations) on the black press.

37. Bastide, "A imprensa negra," 51.

38. Benedito Florencio of *Baluarte* (later of *Getulino*) was well known among Campinas's and São Paulo's community of color as an orator (see Silva and Leite, *E disse*, 38), as was Abilio Rodrigues of *Kosmos* (see F. B. de Souza, "Um appello aos associados do Gremio," *Kosmos*, January 1923, 1). This trend continued in the 1920s and 1930s (see chaps. 2 and 3). See also J. C. Leite, "História dos nossos periódicos," *Alvorada*, May 1947, 5–6; and Butler, *Freedoms Given*, 92.

39. F. B. de Souza, "O passado," *Bandeirante*, April 1919, 1. See also in the same issue, "Collaboração," 4, on editors' use of their paper to revive the words of a colleague (Joaquim Cambará) "forever quieted by death." Souza appears with the formal title of "orador" in "Centro Smart," *Liberdade*, 4 April 1920, 2–3.

40. F. B. de Souza, "Illusão," *Alfinete*, 9 March 1919, 1. See also A. Rodrigues, "Alfinetadas," *Alfinete*, 30 October 1921, 1; and F. B. de Souza, "Observando," *Kosmos*, 16 March 1924, 1.

41. J. C. Leite, in Silva and Leite, *E disse*, 48, 33.

42. Souza does not specify the woman's identity, though given the name of the venue they rented—Itália Fausta (Magnificent Italy)—it would not be surprising if she were a white Italian immigrant or of Italian descent. F. B. de Souza, "Uma explicação," *Liberdade*, 28 September 1919, 2. On Souza, see also, in the same issue, Matuto, "Vagando," 1.

43. Details about editors' jobs are from "Gentes e fatos de outras épocas," *Voz da Raça*, 1 April 1933, 4, except those regarding Aguiar, which are from Silva and Leite, *E disse*, 41.

44. Fernandes, *The Negro*, 78.

45. See also the story of "F" (most likely Francisco Lucrécio), who had to request money from a relative's former employer to buy dentistry books. Ibid., 150–51.

46. "O Baluarte," *Baluarte*, 15 January 1904, 1; mission statement, *Menelik*, 17 October 1915, 1. See also the editors' aspirations to address a state, national, and global audience, in "Aos leitores," *Alfinete*, 28 August 1921, 1.

47. Editors, "O Menelik," *Menelik*, 17 October 1915, 1. See also the editors' exposition of a mission of "concord" for their newspaper in "Em marcha," *Bandeirante*, April 1919, 1; and Bastide, "A imprensa negra," 51.

48. H. de F. Leite, "Preconceitos de raça," *Alfinete*, 3 September 1918, 1–2.

49. J. M. Latino Coelho, "A palavra," *Kosmos*, 21 February 1923, 1.

50. Editors, "Um reptro de honra," *Xauter*, 16 May 1916, 1; see also T. Camargo's exchanges with Z. K. in *Kosmos*, December–January 1922–23.

51. Other prominent editors and writers who were also poets include Lino Guedes and Gervásio de Moraes of *Getulino* and Jayme de Aguiar of *Clarim*. Leite remembered the importance of intricately metered poetry to "anyone with claims to being an intellectual," in Silva and Leite, *E disse*, 33.

52. On the close ties between status as "men of letters" and citizenship rights in Brazil and Latin America more broadly in the late nineteenth and early twentieth centuries, see Kirkendall, *Class Mates*; and Rama, *Lettered City*, chap. 5.

53. Ferrara, *A imprensa negra*, 58.

54. Even earlier, a news-clipping agency requested copies of *Baluarte* to help "advertise" the newspaper and offered to send *Baluarte*'s editors relevant articles from the mainstream press. Editors, "Echo da impresa [*sic*]," *Baluarte*, 15 January 1904, 2.

55. Skidmore, *Black into White*, 221–22.

56. The exceptions were a very few societies made up of women (these did not leave behind any known newspapers; their stories remain to be told). Butler, *Freedoms Given*, 83. Photos of Lavinia Horta and of Benta de Oliveira, presidents of Grupo das Margaridas and Brinco de Princezas, respectively, appear in *Clarim*, 24 January 1926, 3.

57. S. O., "O Baluarte," *Baluarte*, 15 January 1904, 2.

58. Women appeared occasionally, but very infrequently, as contributors to the black press in the first decades of the century. On the limited role of women, particularly as writers, in the black press, see Pinto, "O movimento negro em São Paulo," 53. As Giovana Xavier's new research suggests, however, women's scarce presence as writers may belie their influence over many aspects of the content and organization of these newspapers. See Xavier, "'Leitoras.'"

59. Editors, "Nosso programma," *Baluarte*, 15 November 1903, 1.

60. A. Oliveira, "Aos nossos leitores," *Alfinete*, 22 September 1918, 1. On the centrality of education and literacy to the project of racial uplift, see also in *Alfinete*, B. Fonseca, "Patrícios!," 22 September 1918, 2; and A. Oliveira, "Aos leitores," 9 March 1919, 1.

61. E.g., B. D. de Campos, "O asseio," *Baluarte*, 15 January 1904, 3–4.

62. Pery-Kito, "A propósito de um texto," *Kosmos*, 20 April 1924, 1; see also the lyrics of Kosmos's anthem, which proclaimed Kosmos an "ideal kingdom," both cited in Andrews, *Blacks and Whites*, 141–42.

63. Weinstein, "Racializing Regional Difference," 244.

64. Writers frequently praised São Paulo in terms that echoed the state's dominant discourse: it was the "cosmopolitan city par excellence"; it was "in the vanguard of almost all national initiatives"; it was a "glorious" state with "formidable progress." See, e.g., "A theoria do preconceito," *Getulino*, 5 October 1924, 1; "Nosso dever," *Progresso*, 26 September 1929, 1; "Os negros da América do Norte," *Clarim*, 5 February 1928, 1; and "Apresentação," *Clarim*, 6 January 1924, 1.

65. On ideas of female honor in mainstream Brazilian society during the Republic, see Caulfield, *In Defense of Honor*.

66. J. d'Alencastro, "Grave erro!," *Bandeirante*, September 1918, 2–3.

67. See "Carta aberta," *Alfinete*, 12 October 1918, 2; "Centro Recreativo Smart," *Alfinete*, 9 March 1919, 3; and "O pessoal do Colombo," *Liberdade*, 14 July 1919, 2. On the broader range of attacks in the gossip columns, see Butler, *Freedoms Given*, 92–93.

68. Cf. Fernandes, *The Negro*, 116–21; and Andrews, *Blacks and Whites*, 69, 84. The black newspapers' gossip columns also closely patrolled the economic behavior of men: for instance, *Alfinete*, 28 August 1921, 3–4.

69. Conde, "14 de julho," *Liberdade*, 3 August 1919, 1. See also M. Assumpção, "Negros retintos no parlamento francês," *Getulino*, 8 June 1924, 1.

70. See, e.g., F. Júnior, "Um depoimento agradável," *Alfinete*, 4 January 1919, 2; and unsigned, "13 de maio," *Kosmos*, 18 May 1923, 1, describing abolition as the "commemoração da fraternidade dos brasileiros."

71. B. Florencio, "O advento da República," *Baluarte*, 15 November 1903, 1. Florencio's praise of the Republic echoed the political sympathies of the teachers and other professionals who made up his literary society in Campinas, among whom were politicians and journalists from the Republican Party. José G. Pereira, "São Benedito," 293–97. On the influence of French Republicanism in the Brazilian Republic, see Carvalho, *A formação das almas*.

72. J. d'Alencastro, "Grave erro!," *Bandeirante*, September 1918, 2–3.

73. A. Oliveira, "Aos nossos leitores," *Alfinete*, 22 September 1918, 1. See also A. Rodrigues, "Preto e branco," *Kosmos*, 18 April 1923, 1. In an unusually early use of that term, Rodrigues dismissed the "true Brazilian *democracy*" (referring in part to equal relations among the races) as "pure illusion."

74. A. Oliveira, "A verdade," *Alfinete*, 12 October 1918, 1; emphasis mine.

75. On these immigration plans and on the government's attempts to block them, see Hellwig, *African-American Reflections*; Meade and Pirio, "In Search of the Afro-American 'Eldorado'"; Skidmore, *Black into White*, 193; Lesser, "Are African-Americans African or American?"; Tiago de Melo Gomes, "Problemas no paraíso"; and Seigel, *Uneven Encounters*, 192–98.

76. Love, *São Paulo*, 11.

77. Skidmore, *Black into White*, 192–98; Seigel, *Uneven Encounters*, 196.

78. Proceedings of 29 July 1921, in *Anais da Câmara dos Deputados* (1923): 623–37.

79. J. d'Alencastro, "Grave erro!," *Bandeirante*, September 1918, 2–3; J. d'Alencastro, "Em ferro frio," *Bandeirante*, April 1919, 4. For interpretations of d'Alencastro's quote that stress racial whitening, see Andrews, *Blacks and Whites*, 136; and Seigel, *Uneven Encounters*, 191.

80. See, e.g., J. d'Alencastro, "Em ferro frio," and the bold denunciations of police racism in G. R. de Silva, "Os agentes de polícia em acção," both in *Bandeirante*, April 1919, 2.

81. Both veterans of the black press (like J. C. Leite in "História dos nossos periódicos," *Alvorada*, May 1947, 5–6) and historians of the black press cite *Getulino* as transformative, the first explicitly activist black newspaper; Ferrara, *A imprensa negra*, 45.

82. It is possible from this phrasing that they also had their own printing press, though this is unlikely given the cost of such machinery. Editors, "O nosso aparecimento," *Getulino*, 5 August 1923, 1.

83. Details on the editors' former employment are from Maciel, *Discriminações raciais*, 91. On Campinas's contemporary press and *O Diário do Povo*, see Mariano, "História da imprensa." On the influence of the labor press on black newspapers more broadly, see Flávio Gomes, *Negros e política*, 33.

84. Florencio, "Cartas d'um negro," *Getulino*, 23 September 1923, 1.

85. Though earlier papers had occasionally mentioned the affairs of people of color abroad (particularly in the United States), the editors of *Getulino* pursued these themes more vigorously, in part due to increased coverage in mainstream Brazilian newspapers of people of color abroad. (Cf. Silva and Leite, *E disse*, 40.) Internal evidence from *Getulino* suggests that editors sought out information about Africa and the diaspora from international publications like *L'Illustration* (France) and *National Geographic* magazine (United States), as well as from correspondents' occasional travels abroad: *Getulino*, 20 January 1924, 1; 8 June 1924, 1. Coverage of Africa and

the diaspora was prominent in the paper: on Ethiopia: 20 January 1924, 1; 6 July 1924, 2; on blacks in France: 8 June 1924, 1; on Garveyism and pan-Africanism: 27 January 1924, 2; 3 February 1924, 2; 17 August 1924, 1; 26 October 1924, 2; 23 November 1924, 4; 30 November 1924, 1; on the Ku Klux Klan: 23 November 1924, 1; on the impact of black participation in World War I on race relations worldwide: 4 November 1923, 1; 10 February 1924, 1.

86. G. de Moraes, "A mocidade," *Getulino*, 5 August 1923, 1.

87. Unsigned, no title, *Getulino*, 12 August 1923, 1.

88. Editors, "Respondendo III," 19 August 1923, 2. For more on the rivalry between *O Getulino* and *A Protectora*, see Maciel, *Discriminações raciais*, 95–96.

89. "A immigração dos negros," *O Paiz*, 11 May 1923, cited in Lesser, "Are African-Americans African or American?," 125. For more on the controversy surrounding Abbott's proposal and his visit, see, in addition to the sources cited in n. 75, Andrews, *Blacks and Whites*, 137.

90. B. Florencio, "Cartas d'um negro," *Getulino*, 23 September 1923, 1 (in which he also indicated that his rivals in *A Protectora* supported Abbott); see also his untitled article, 19 August 1923, 1; "Cartas d'um negro II," 30 September 1923, 1; and "Cartas d'um negro," 21 October 1923, 3.

91. See, e.g., "Cartas d'um negro," *Getulino*, 21 October 1923, 3.

92. Proceedings of 22 October 1923, *Anais da Câmara dos Deputados* (1928): 140–49. Fidelis Reis further detailed his plans for the nation in Reis, *Paiz a organizar*. For more on these debates, see Skidmore, *Black into White*, 194–96.

93. Proceedings of 27 December 1923, *Anais da Câmara dos Deputados* (1929): 378–90. Only three years later, a survey of prominent Brazilians nationwide confirmed Reis's position, with a vast majority expressing a negative view of past and potential African "immigration." Levine, "Some Views."

94. "Os negros americanos," *O Jornal*, 24 November 1923, 1.

95. Proceedings of 27 December 1923, *Anais da Câmara dos Deputados* (1929): 381–82.

96. Moraes published frequently in leading mainstream newspapers on issues related to law, race, and slavery. His books include a comparative study of race relations in Brazil and the United States: Moraes, *Brancos e negros*.

97. Moraes, "Brancos, negros e mulatos," *Getulino*, 30 December 1923, 1; and "Os negros nos Estados Unidos e no Brasil," *Getulino*, 13 January 1924, 1.

98. Ibid.

99. Details about Camargo's employment are from *Voz da Raça*, 1 April 1933, 4, according to which Camargo had, in 1915, edited the black newspaper *O Binóculo* out of the São Paulo neighborhood of Barra Funda (I have not been able to find any issues).

100. See the following exchange of angry letters, all in *Kosmos*: Z. K. (José Martinho de Moura Baptista), "Carta aberta, Exmo. Snr. Sargento Theophilo Fortunato de Camargo," December 1922, 1–2; Theophilo Camargo, "Carta aberta," January 1923, 3; and Z. K., "Carta aberta," 21 February 1924, 2–3. News of the expulsion (Camargo is not mentioned by name, but preceding issues strongly suggest he is the object of the editors' dislike) appears in "Gremio dramático e recreativo Kosmos," 18 April 1923, 3.

101. Aside from Camargo's own articles cited below, see, e.g., the recurring column on national politics, "Política e políticos."

102. Proceedings of 22 October 1923, *Anais da Câmara dos Deputados* (1928): 147.

103. T. Camargo, "Echos do projecto F. Reis," *Elite*, 20 January 1924, 1, reprinted in *Getulino*, 27 January 1924, 2.

104. T. Camargo, "A propósito do projecto F. Reis" (presumably from issue 1 of *Elite*, of December 1923 or January 1924, not available), reprinted in *Getulino*, 20 January 1924, 1.

105. A. de Camargo, "A reação," *Getulino*, 9 November 1924, 1.

106. G. de Moraes, "O negro no século XX," *Getulino*, 20 December 1924, 1.

107. B. Florencio, "Os pretos em São Paulo," *Getulino*, 21 September 1924, 1; see also articles with the same title on 28 September 1924, 1, and 5 October 1924, 1; as well as B. Florencio, "Carta aberta," 2 November 1924, 1.

108. B. Florencio, "Carta aberta," *Getulino*, 2 November 1924, 1.

109. B. Florencio, "Os pretos em São Paulo," *Getulino*, 28 September 1924, 1.

110. Ibid.; T. Camargo, "Echos do projecto F. Reis," *Elite*, 20 January 1924, 1; G. de Moraes, "O negro no século XX," *Getulino*, 20 December 1924, 1.

111. The article, from *A Gazeta* of 24 September 1924, is partially reprinted in E. Oliveira, "A theoria do preconceito," *Getulino*, 5 October 1924, 1.

112. E. Oliveira, "A theoria do preconceito," *Getulino*, 5 October 1924, 1; B. Florencio, "Os pretos em São Paulo," *Getulino*, 21 September 1924, 1.

113. G. de Moraes, "Carta de um negro," *Clarim*, 13 May 1927, 7–8. The term *foreigner* and the phrase "foreigners in the land of their birth" entered some of the scholarship on race in Brazil as well, perhaps through black informants. Florestan Fernandes described the position of blacks in early-twentieth-century São Paulo as "strangers in a foreign city." Fernandes, *The Negro*, 32.

114. Editors, "A miséria," *Baluarte*, 15 January 1904, 1; A. Oliveira, "Aos nossos leitores," *Alfinete*, 3 September 1918, 1; Editors, "Os desejáveis," *Getulino*, 7 October 1923, 1. The *Getulino* editors' idea that blacks should take responsibility for their own low position in society was yet another source of their ongoing polemic with rival *A Protectora*; see "Respondendo IV," *Getulino*, 26 August 1923, 2.

115. See, e.g., "Prefere-se branca," *Getulino*, 11 November 1923, 1. For examples of these racist advertisements, see Freyre, *Ordem e progresso*, 224–26.

116. E. Oliveira, "A theoria do preconceito," *Getulino*, 5 October 1924, 1. See also the mock-dictionary entry for "nacional" (defined as "a synonym for *preto* or mulato in the jargon of certain journalists") in *Getulino*, 5 August 1923, 3.

117. B. Florencio, "Os pretos em São Paulo," *Getulino*, 28 September 1924, 1, and 5 October 1924, 1.

118. These details are from Silva and Leite, *E disse*, 23–53. On children of color working as *agregados* in the homes of Italians in this period, see Fernandes, *The Negro*, 37.

119. Silva and Leite, *E disse*, 25, 52.

120. Leite re-creates a fictional version of such an encounter between an Italian and a Brazilian of African descent (set against the backdrop of a cosmopolitan "Babel"-like *cortiço* or tenement) in his stylized account of his experiences as a young black activist, *O alvorecer de uma ideologia*. Ibid., 52, 281.

121. Ibid., 52. See also Fernandes, *A integração do negro*, 211.

122. Indeed, in early-twentieth-century Bahia, mainstream newspapers ran articles mocking Menelik's pretensions to greatness and civilization, presenting him as an object of exotic ridicule. Albuquerque, "Esperanças de boaventuras," 223–24.

123. Silva and Leite, *E disse*, 27.

124. Ibid., 33.

125. M. Cintra (pseud. for Jayme de Aguiar), "Um dever," 2 March 1924, 2–3; H. da Cunha, "Evolução," 24 July 1926, 1; J. C. Leite, "E, após a liberdade," 30 August 1925, 1, all in *Clarim*.

126. Butler, *Freedoms Given*, 73–74; Silva and Leite, *E disse*, 23–25.

127. See n. 42.

128. B. H. Ferreira, "Que atrevimento!," *Getulino*, 4 November 1923, 2.

129. B. Florencio, "Os pretos em São Paulo," *Getulino*, 5 October 1924, 1.

130. Ferreira further tarred the *Pasquino* writer as "a buffoon and an outsider, who comes to criticize those [black people] to whom their country's constitution has granted liberty and equality!" B. H. Ferreira, "Que atrevimento!," *Getulino*, 4 November 1923, 2.

131. B. Florencio, "Os pretos em São Paulo," *Getulino*, 5 October 1924, 1. Like Ferreira, Florencio suggested that foreigners' racism was "criminal" as well as "barbaric"—this latter term a classic designation of foreignness.

132. B. H. Ferreira, "Que atrevimento!," *Getulino*, 4 November 1923, 2.

133. Andrews, *Blacks and Whites*, 85–89. On Rio de Janeiro, see McPhee, "'New 13th of May.'"

134. "Concurso de beleza," *Getulino*, 21 October 1923, 1.

135. U. C., "Fusão das raças," 7 October 1923, 1, and 2 March 1924, 1; E. Oliveira, "A theoria do preconceito," 5 October 1924, 1, all in *Getulino*.

136. Unsigned [Leite], "Naziunale," *Clarim*, 6 January 1924, 4.

137. Bananére, *La divina increnca*.

138. See Matuto's columns "Chegando," 23 November 1919, 3; and "Narração de um caipira," 12 September 1920, 2, and 31 October 1920, 2, all in *Liberdade*.

139. J. d'Alencastro, "Grave erro!," *Bandeirante*, September 1918, 2–3.

140. D. Nascimento, "O Menelik," *Menelik*, 17 October 1915, 1.

141. Lesser, "Are African-Americans African or American?"

142. T. Camargo, "A propósito do projecto F. Reis," reprinted in *Getulino*, 20 January 1924, 1.

143. C. Guerra, "Cartas negras," *Getulino*, 20 December 1924, 13.

144. A. Vasconcellos, "Correio de Lisboa," 27 January 1924, 2, and 3 February 1924, 2; unsigned, no title, 21 September 1924, 2; C. Guerra, "Cartas negras," 20 December 1924, 13, all in *Getulino*.

145. See, e.g., "A Abyssinia," 20 January 1924, 1; "A Rainha de Sabá era negra," 6 July 1924, 2; "Um grande homem de raça negra: O chefe dos Bamanguatos," 28 October 1923, 3; "Um congresso monstro de negros," 26 October 1924, 2, all in *Getulino*.

146. Maciel, *Discriminações raciais*, 192.

147. A. Marques, "A nossa missão," *Getulino*, 20 December 1924, 13.

148. Mary Santos, "Luz e liberdade," *Getulino*, 26 August 1923, 1.

149. *Getulino*, 13 May 1926, 1.

150. E. Oliveira, "A theoria do preconceito," *Getulino*, 5 October 1924, 1.

151. Unsigned, "Os negros," *Clarim*, 26 July 1925, 4.

Chapter 2

1. For discussions of the Mãe Preta campaign on different grounds, see Seigel, *Uneven Encounters*, chap. 6; Tiago de Melo Gomes, *Um espelho no palco*, chap. 4; and Barros, *Corações de chocolat*, 268–82. On the deceptively similar figure of the Black Mammy in the United States, and attempts to monumentalize her, see Manring, *Slave in a Box*; and McElya, *Clinging to Mammy*, chap. 4.

2. On the history of these reforms and popular responses to them, see, e.g., Benchimol, *Pereira Passos*; Needell, *Tropical Belle-Époque*; Needell, "*Revolta contra vacina*"; Meade, "*Civilizing*" *Rio*; and Carvalho, *Os bestializados*.

3. Cândido de Campos, "O Brasil deve glorificar a raça negra, erguendo um monumento à Mãe Preta: A significação desta figura luminosa," *A Notícia*, 5 April 1926, 1.

4. Many of the articles Campos reprinted in *A Notícia* originally appeared in a wide range of other publications, mostly from Rio but often from other Brazilian cities. I indicate the provenance of the original only when relevant to my argument. Unless otherwise noted, all articles from the Mãe Preta campaign cited in this section are from *A Notícia*. Further, for the many articles that formally begin with the headline "Monumento à Mãe Preta," I cite only their first subtitles, when available, in the interests of space and clarity.

5. Cf. Mitchell, "Miguel Reale."

6. C. Esher, "Monumento à Mãe Preta," *Diário Nacional*, 1 November 1928, 3.

7. Sandra Lauderdale Graham, *House and Street*, 117–31.

8. Campos, "O Brasil deve glorificar a raça negra," 5 April 1926, 1. See also Cândido de Campos, "Como repercutiu a idéa de 'A Notícia' no seu editorial de hontem," 6 April 1926, 4; unsigned, "O monumento à Mãe Preta," 7 April 1926, 3; and unsigned, "Glorificando a raça negra," 9 April 1926, 4.

9. Campos, "O Brasil deve glorificar a raça negra," 5 April 1926, 1.

10. W. Luís, "Carta do Dr. W. Luís, presidente eleito da República, a Vicente Ferreira," 23 April 1926, 1.

11. Ibid.

12. Campos, "O Brasil deve glorificar a raça negra," 5 April 1926, 1.

13. For firsthand accounts of elite men's experiences with *amas de leite* in the late nineteenth and early twentieth centuries, see Sandra Lauderdale Graham, *House and Street*, 35.

14. From *Diário da Noite*, 27 September 1928, in *Clarim*, 6 January 1929, 2. See also in the same issue of *Clarim* (p. 2), a reprint of an article from *Correio Paulistano* (date unclear; 27 September 1928?) on "the sweet *Mãe Negra*, all goodness, who with her white milk fed the 'little master' and made him sleep with her songs and stories."

15. Caulfield, *In Defense of Honor*, 79–81; Besse, *Restructuring Patriarchy*, chap. 1; Sevcenko, *Orfeu extático*.

16. Caulfield, "Getting into Trouble," 155–56.

17. A. de S., "Uma idéa feliz," reprinted 15 May 1926, 3. See also M. Rodrigues, "Mãe Preta," 9 and 10 April 1926, 3, calling her a symbol of "the good times, when Brazilian society had not yet fallen into this degradation." Another writer complained of the "tormented evolution through which, unhappily, our family life has been moving, [which has] led to the disappearance of that figure"; unsigned, "Monumento à Mãe Preta," 15 April 1926, 4.

18. On nativist sentiments in São Paulo and Rio, see Andrews, *Blacks and Whites*, 151–52; Fausto, "Imigração e participação"; McPhee, "'New 13th of May,'" 165–67, 174–76; and Sevcenko, *Orfeu extático*, 138–40, 238–50. Cf. Caulfield, "Getting into Trouble," 166–68.

19. B. Costallat, "Monumento à Mãe Preta," reprinted 24 April 1926, 3. See also A. de S., "Uma idéa feliz," 15 May 1926, 3.

20. C. Carneiro, "Uma carta de applauso e um donativo enviados à 'A Notícia,'" 8 April 1926, 4. See also Coelho Neto, "A Mãe Preta," 23 April 1926, 3.

21. See A. Torres, "Gratidão à raça negra," 4 May 1926, 3; and Cândido de Campos, "O Brasil deve glorificar a raça negra, erguendo um monumento à Mãe Preta: O applauso de cinco illustres escriptores," 13 April 1926, 1.

22. Abreu, "Mulatas, Crioulos, and Morenas"; Seigel, "Point of Comparison," 228–30.

23. Campos, "O Brasil deve glorificar a raça negra," 5 April 1926, 1.

24. Ibid.

25. Rodó, *Ariel*; Martí, *Cuba, Nuestra América*.

26. Vasconcelos, *Cosmic Race*.

27. Fernando Ortiz, *Contrapunteo cubano*.

28. For an overview of these works, see Martínez-Echazábal, "Mestizaje."

29. For the "Manifesto antropófago" (1928), see Andrade, *Obras completas*. On the modernist movement, see Dunn, *Brutality Garden*, chap. 1; and Skidmore, *Black into White*, 176–79.

30. Skidmore, *Black into White*, 185–90.

31. Campos, "O Brasil deve glorificar a raça negra," 5 April 1926, 1. Nearly every promonument article reprinted by Campos mentioned blacks' "affection"; the following refer specifically to Comte's "affective race": J. Santos, "Uma idéa em marcha," 22 April, 1926, 3; J. de O. Brasil, "A 'União da Alliança' abre uma subscripção entre os seus socios," 1 May 1926, 4; P. Calmon, "Mãe Preta," 27 May 1926, 4; E. de Moraes, quoted in Campos, "O Brasil deve glorificar a raça negra, erguendo um monumento à Mãe Preta: O applauso ardente do Dr. Evaristo de Moraes à suggestão de 'A Notícia,'" 7 April 1926, 1. See also S. de Navarro, "13 de maio," *Clarim*, 13 May 1927, 1.

32. On the later Comte's influence on Republican thought, see Carvalho, *A formação das almas*, 21–31. On Comte's ideological shift, see Pickering, "Angels and Demons."

33. Brasil, "A 'União da Alliança,'" 1 May 1926, 4.

34. Unsigned, "Monumento à Mãe Preta," 15 April 1926, 4; A. de S., "Uma idéa feliz," 15 May 1926, 3.

35. A. de S., "Uma idéa feliz," 15 May 1926, 3.

36. A. Torres, "Gratidão à raça negra," 4 May 1926, 3.

37. Unsigned, "Mãe Preta," reprinted 17 April 1926, 3. See also Coelho Neto, "A Mãe Preta," 23 April 1926, 3.

38. Cf. Seigel, "Point of Comparison," 219–21.

39. Campos, "O Brasil deve glorificar a raça negra," 5 April 1926, 1.

40. S. de Laboreiro, "Mãe Preta," 3 June 1926, 3.

41. Moraes, in Campos, "O applauso ardente," 7 April 1926, 1. See also E. de Moraes, "A propósito da raça negra," 27 May 1926, 4.

42. On nationalism and anti-U.S. sentiment in the 1920s, see Skidmore, *Black into White*, chap. 5.

43. Moraes, in Campos, "O applauso ardente," 7 April 1926, 1.

44. Cândido de Campos, "Como repercutiu a idéa de 'A Notícia,'" 6 April 1926, 4.

45. See Silva and Leite, *E disse*, 70–71. Visits to newspaper offices appear to have been a common strategy, at least in Rio, by popular sectors (like members of black carnival clubs) seeking coverage of their activities or free advertising. Coutinho, *Os cronistas de Momo*, 63–64.

46. Silva and Leite, *E disse*, 61. Information on Ferreira in this and the next paragraph is drawn from Silva's interview with Leite, 61–66.

47. Campos, "Como repercutiu a idéa de 'A Notícia,'" 6 April 1926, 4.

48. On this lecture and Ferreira's participation, see also "Dr. Baptista Pereira," *Clarim*, 1 July 1928, 1.

49. A speech Ferreira delivered in São Paulo's Centro Cívico Palmares in 1927 in honor of Cândido de Campos, titled "Mulher Negra," includes these elements and provides some insight into his thought. It is partially reprinted in *Clarim*, 28 September 1929, 3, and 27 October 1929, 3. See also his "O Dia da Mãe Negra," *Clarim*, 13 May 1928, 10.

50. Mentions of São Paulo's FHC appear in *Clarim*, 22 June 1924, 1; *Menelik*, 17 October 1915, 3; and *Clarim* of 27 October 1929, 4 (mentioning a "Confederação dos Homens de Cor"). On Rio's, see *Getulino*, 21 September 1924, 1. *Chicago Defender* owner-publisher Robert Abbott was inducted into Rio's FHC on his visit to Brazil in the early 1920s, according to an article in that paper of 14 April 1923, 2. Seigel, *Uneven Encounters*, 227.

51. J. B. de Camargo, quoted in Campos, "Um officio da Federação dos Homens de Cor a 'A Notícia,'" 14 April 1926, 2.

52. *A Federação* does not appear to have survived in archives or collections of Brazil's black press, nor does it appear in most secondary works on Brazil's black press, with the important exception of Seigel, *Uneven Encounters*, 182, 220.

53. As historian Marc Hertzman insightfully points out, Rio is a "missing middle" in most histories of early-twentieth-century black politics, activism, or "race relations" in Brazil, lost between attention to São Paulo's race-based organizations and Bahia's Afro-Brazilian religious entities. Hertzman, "Celebration and Punishment," introduction. Defining racial activism in ways that exclude Rio's patterns of racial identification and politics in the early twentieth century could reinforce ideas about the political passivity of poor and working-class Cariocas more generally (see, e.g., Carvalho, *Os bestializados*). For a critique of images of "passive,

moderate" Carioca workers, particularly blacks, see Velasco e Cruz, "Puzzling Out Slave Origins," 206–8.

54. Fernandes, *The Negro*, 189–205, 209.

55. Cited in Costa Pinto, *O negro*, 73.

56. Coutinho, *Os cronistas de Momo*, 89–141.

57. Skidmore, *Black into White*, xvii; Costa, *Brazilian Empire*, 241.

58. As I noted in chapter 1, Bernardo Vianna, a worker who moved from Rio to São Paulo in the 1920s, claimed to be "shocked" by his inability to find a job as a factory worker in that city, a situation he attributed to São Paulo's extreme racism. "Os pretos em São Paulo," *Getulino*, 21 September 1924, 1. See also the story by a young migrant who claimed that "São Paulo is the worst place for Negroes. In Rio there is more tolerance than there is here." Fernandes, *The Negro*, 398.

59. See, e.g., Meade, *"Civilizing" Rio*; Carvalho, *Os bestializados*; Needell, *"Revolta contra vacina"*; Chalhoub, *Cidade febril*; Álvaro Nascimento, "Um reduto negro"; McPhee, "'New 13th of May'"; and Velasco e Cruz, "Puzzling Out Slave Origins."

60. McPhee, "'New 13th of May,'" 158.

61. Chalhoub, *Trabalho, lar e botequim*.

62. On the role of African-descended people in the development of Rio's samba and carnival, see Roberto Moura, *Tia Ciata*; Hermano Vianna, *Mystery of Samba*; Raphael, "Samba and Social Control"; McCann, *Hello, Hello Brazil*; and Sandroni, *Feitiço decente*. On musical and theatrical precursors to the themes expressed in this period, see Abreu, "Mulatas, Crioulos, and Morenas"; and Erminia Silva, *Circo-teatro*. On the often tense but nonetheless extensive collaborations between whites and musicians of color in Rio's nascent music industry, see Hertzman, "Surveillance and Difference," esp. part 3.

63. On samba, see H. da Cunha, "Os homens pretos e a evolução social," *Clarim*, 20 February 1927, 2; J. C. Leite, "Evocações," *Clarim*, 13 May 1924, 2; and J. Dantas, "Salomés negras," *Progresso*, 13 January 1929, 6. I am grateful to Marc Hertzman for this wonderfully insightful contrast (personal communication, 7 August 2009) and for the broader suggestion to include performers of color more thoroughly in the category of Carioca "black intellectuals" (something I have barely begun to do here, due to constraints of time and space).

64. Hertzman, "Making Music and Masculinity."

65. J. C. Leite remembers Jayme Camargo, the president of Rio's FHC, as a Paulista who founded the FHC as one of the many race-based organizations in his native city. Silva and Leite, *E disse*, 43–44.

66. Articles about the brotherhood and its Mãe Preta–related activities appeared in *A Notícia* on (among other dates) 10 April, 17 April, 21 April, 30 April, 1 May, 3 May, 14 May, and 19 August 1926.

67. For a historical overview, see Kiddy, *Blacks of the Rosary*. On Rio in particular, see Soares, *Devotos da cor*.

68. Cândido de Campos, "Louvando a idéa do monumento à 'Mãe Preta,'" 17 April 1926, 1.

69. Gomes and Seigel, "Sabina's Oranges," 22; Barros, *Corações de chocolat*, 268–82.

70. Though lay brotherhoods were important institutions in São Paulo's black community—even for some members of the class of color—they did not enjoy this sort of prominence among city elites. See Amaral, *Os pretos do Rosário*.

71. O. de Castro, quoted in Cândido de Campos, "A solennidade religiosa de hoje na Igreja do Rosário," 3 May 1926, 1.

72. Cândido de Campos, "O Brasil deve glorificar a raça negra, erguendo um monumento à Mãe Preta: Palavras do cónego Olympio de Castro, vigário da egreja do Rosário e S. Benedicto dos Homens de Cor," 10 April 1926, 1.

73. Information on Santos is from *Clarim*, 6 January 1929, 4; and Flávio Gomes, *Negros e política*, 54.

74. J. C. Leite, quoted in Butler, *Freedoms Given*, 103.

75. Ibid., 104.

76. S. de Navarro, "13 de maio," *Clarim*, 13 May 1927, 1. Cf. Wexler, *Tender Violence*, 63–65.

77. Ivan, "Monumento symbolico à Mãe Preta," *Getulino*, 13 May 1926, 3.

78. Moysés Cintra (Jayme de Aguiar), "A Mãe Preta," *Clarim*, 25 April 1926, 1.

79. See, e.g., S. de Navarro, "Mãe Preta," *Clarim*, 13 May 1927, 1; and Ivan, "Monumento symbolico à Mãe Preta," *Getulino*, 13 May 1926, 3. This tendency continued for the rest of the decade; see Helios [Menotti del Picchia], "Monumento à Mãe Preta," *Clarim*, 28 September 1929, 4; and D. R. de Castro, "Mãe Negra," *Progresso*, 19 August 1928, 2.

80. Cândido de Campos, "Está constituida a commissão central para a effectivação da idéa," *A Notícia*, 11 May 1926, 1.

81. *Annaes do Conselho Municipal do Rio de Janeiro*, 1 June–31 July 1926 (1926): 484; *Annaes da Câmara dos Deputados* 1926, vol. 12 (1929): 15–21, 40–41. See also the speech by Congressman Gilberto Amado, reprinted in Cândido de Campos, "Luminoso parecer do deputado Gilberto Amado na Commissão de Finanças," *A Notícia*, 8 November 1926, 1.

82. A monument to the Mãe Preta was eventually built in downtown São Paulo in the 1950s, though in a very different style than the one proposed for Rio in the 1920s. I discuss the monument in chapter 5.

83. Black newspapers in São Paulo expressed disappointment at the unraveling of the monument plans; see, e.g., Lino Guedes (no title), *Clarim*, 15 January 1927, 3; and their reprinting of Vagalume, "E o monumento?," 28 September 1929, 1.

84. Editors, "Vida nova," *Clarim*, 5 February 1928, 1.

85. J. C. Leite, "O negro para o negro," *Clarim*, 1 July 1928, 1.

86. Particularly clear examples of this conscious shift include "Palavras aos paes negros," *Clarim*, 13 May 1927, 3; and F. B. de Souza, "Na Penha," *Clarim*, 28 September 1929, 1.

87. Unfortunately, the text of Ferreira's speech has been lost, but an adaptation of his speech and an account of the history of the Mãe Preta campaign in Rio can be found in *Clarim*, 6 January 1929, 1–2, as well as in Silva and Leite, *E disse*, 40–41.

88. Ibid., 40.

89. Leite, "O Dia da Mãe Preta: Apello à culta imprensa brasileira," *Clarim*, 28 September 1928, 1.

90. Silva and Leite, *E disse*, 40. *Clarim* received congratulatory notes and articles from papers including (from São Paulo): *Correio Paulistano, Diário da Noite, São Paulo Jornal, Jornal do Commercio, Nota do Dia, Folha da Manhã, Folha da Noite, Diário Nacional,* and *O Estado de S. Paulo;* (from Campinas): *O Correio Popular;* (from Santos): *A Tribuna, A Folha;* (from Rio): *O Jornal, O Globo,* and *A Notícia,* "and many others from the interior and from other states, which we cannot mention for lack of space." *Clarim,* 6 January 1929, 1.

91. Unsigned, "O Dia da Mãe Preta," *Progresso,* 12 October 1928, 2. See also J. C. Leite, "O Dia da Mãe Preta," *Clarim,* 28 September 1928, 1.

92. Silva and Leite, *E disse,* 41.

93. J. C. Leite, "O Dia da Mãe Preta," *Clarim,* 28 September 1928, 1.

94. Unsigned, "Idea erronea da raça opposta," *Clarim,* 18 August 1929, 4.

95. Silva and Leite, *E disse,* 73–76; Butler, *Freedoms Given,* 104–6.

96. Leite, "À mocidade negra," *Clarim,* 13 May 1929, 4.

97. See A. V. dos Santos, "Congresso da Mocidade Negra Brasileira: Mensagem aos negros brasileiros," *Clarim,* 9 June 1929, 1; and Leite's series of articles titled "À mocidade negra" in *Clarim* on the following dates in 1929: 3 March, 7 April, 13 May, 9 June, 14 July, 18 August.

98. Leite, "À mocidade negra," *Clarim,* 7 April 1929, 1.

99. For examples, see Carlos Moura, *A travessia,* 350, 363, 382, 383, and 387.

100. On the "genre" of wet-nurse photographs, see Filha, *A fotografia e o negro,* 71. For examples, see Carlos Moura, *A travessia,* 627, 636; and Ermakoff, *O negro na fotografia,* 98–103.

101. On debates surrounding this painting's provenance and the identity of its subjects, see Schwarcz, *Emperor's Beard,* 26. Historian Roderick Barman suggests that whether or not the painting is actually of Pedro II, it would have been understood as such in the 1920s (Barman, personal communication, 11 January 2008). Members of São Paulo's black press at the time of the holiday campaign certainly saw it this way; see the reprint of this portrait, and its description as "Pedro II in the arms of his *babá* [nanny]," in G. de Moraes, "Mãe Preta," *Auriverde,* 13 May 1928, 2; and "O Dia da Mãe Negra," *Tribuna Negra,* September 1935, 2.

102. For an example of the emperor's popularity in this period, see Alves de Lima, *Recordações.* I am grateful to Roderick Barman for this reference.

103. Vagalume, "E o monumento?," *Clarim,* 28 September 1929, 1.

104. D. R. de Castro, "Mãe Negra," *Progresso,* 19 August 1928, 1–2.

105. Y. de Camargo, in "O Dia da Mãe Preta em Botucatu," *Clarim,* 27 October 1929, 3.

106. D. de Campos and Y. de Camargo, in ibid.

107. Unsigned [Leite?], "A Bahia assistiu no dia 28 de setembro, uma manifestação inédita no Brasil," *Clarim,* 24 November 1929, 4; see also M. Cintra [J. de Aguiar] "A Mãe Preta," *Clarim,* 25 April 1926, 1.

108. Unsigned, "Os reparos do *Fanfulla* reflectem nova investida do fascio [*Fanfulla*'s criticisms reflect renewed fascist attack]," *Diário Nacional,* 10 October 1929, 1.

109. L. de Sousa, "A imprensa independente de São Paulo, sempre vigilante e patri-ótica, mais uma vez, demonstrou que, 'O Brasil ainda é dos Brasileiros,'" *Clarim*, 27 October 1929, 1, 4. See also Leite, "À mocidade negra," *Clarim*, 13 May 1929, 4.

110. Santos, "Congresso da Mocidade Negra Brasileira," *Clarim*, 9 June 1929, 1.

111. "Concurso de beleza," *Getulino*, 21 October 1923, 1. (See chap. 1.)

112. The black press perceived, and commented on, this shift of opinion among the Paulista elite. Andrews, *Blacks and Whites*, 87–88.

113. Fausto, "Imigração e participação," 22–23. Fausto describes several earlier episodes in which the *Diário Nacional* denounced Italian immigrants' fascism.

114. Unsigned, "Os reparos do 'Fanfulla,'" *Diário Nacional*, 10 October 1929, 1.

115. "Cultuando a Mãe Preta," *Correio Paulistano*, 28 or 29 September 1929 [date unclear], cited in "A nossa victória do 28 de setembro," *Clarim*, 6 January 1929, 1–2. See also the reprint of an article from the *Diário Nacional* [n.d.]: "Centenário do café: O Hércules de ébano. A raça soffredora e forte na glorificação mais alta: a do trabalho," *Clarim*, 15 October 1927, 1. On nativism as a shared ideology among Brazilians of color and a subset of white elites in early-twentieth-century Rio de Janeiro, see McPhee, "'New 13th of May.'"

116. Unsigned [Leite?], "Do passado consciência . . . ," *Clarim*, 21 October 1928, 1.

117. Raul, "Há negros no Brasil, sim," *Clarim*, 6 January 1929, 2. See also Leite, "A nossa raça é uma raça mestiça superior," *Clarim*, November 1928, 2.

118. See Ferrara, *A imprensa negra*, 57.

119. Ivan, "Monumento symbolico à Mãe Preta," *Getulino*, 13 May 1926, 3.

120. Helios, "Mãe Preta," *Clarim*, 28 September 1929, 4.

121. Ferrara, *A imprensa negra*, 57.

122. Ivan, "Monumento symbolico à Mãe Preta," *Getulino*, 13 May 1926, 3.

123. Booker, "O continente negro," *Clarim*, 15 January 1927, 4. See also unsigned, "A África berço da humanidade," *Progresso*, 31 August 1929, 2; and unsigned, "Na África," *Progresso*, 13 January 1929, 3.

124. A. H. Mattar, "O unico povo livre do occidente africano," *Clarim*, 1 July 1928, 2.

125. See, e.g., *Progresso*, 31 August 1929, 3, on pan-Africanism; on enthusiasm for black culture in Europe, see *Progresso*, 13 January 1929, 6; 24 February 1929, 1; and 24 March 1929, 1.

126. On Ethiopia (Abyssinia), see *Clarim*, 15 January 1927, 4, and 24 November 1929, 1; and *Progresso*, 13 January 1929, 5; 28 April 1929, 2; and 23 June 1929, 2. Ras Tafari, as Haile Selassie, would become even more famous in the Brazilian black press (as elsewhere in the world) after 1930, when he was named emperor of Ethiopia, and during the second Italo-Ethiopian war (1935–36).

127. Leite, "Cinco annos de clarinadas," *Clarim*, 6 January 1929, 1. See also H. Cunha, "Evolução," *Clarim*, 24 July 1926, 1.

128. Unsigned, "Gesto nobre," *Progresso*, 7 September 1928, 3. On the symbolism of the Syrian-Lebanese monument, see Lesser, *Negotiating National Identity*, 55.

129. Unsigned, "Gesto nobre," *Progresso*, 7 September 1928, 3.

130. On the statue of Gama, see *Progresso*, 31 August 1929, 2; 31 October 1929, 1–2, 4–5; and 24 November 1929, 1; on the creation of *Progresso* as an instrument for

drumming up support for the Luiz Gama bust, see Silva and Leite, *E disse*, 88. On their support for the Mãe Preta monument, see *Progresso*, 19 August 1928, 1–2; 12 October 1928, 1–2; and 26 September 1929, 2.

131. Kim Butler argues, for instance, that awareness of the Syrio-Lebanese monument sparked *Progresso*'s fund-raising initiative for the Gama bust. Butler, *Freedoms Given*, 110. A bust of Luiz Gama was installed in São Paulo's Largo do Arouche in the early 1930s. Michael Mitchell, personal communication, 25 June 2010.

132. The details of the monument are from Lesser, *Negotiating National Identity*, 55–59.

133. Silva and Leite, *E disse*, 40.

134. Helios, "Monumento symbolico à Mãe Preta," *Clarim*, 28 September 1929, 4.

135. See chap. 5.

Chapter 3

1. On the Vargas regime, see, among others, Fausto, *Revolução de 1930*; and Levine, *Vargas Regime*. On paternalism in particular, see Levine, *Father of the Poor?*; and Wolfe, "'Father of the Poor.'"

2. Quoted in Wolfe, "'Father of the Poor,'" 84.

3. On ideologies of *brasilidade*, see Williams, *Culture Wars in Brazil*; Lenharo, *Sacralização*; Angela de Castro Gomes, *A invenção do trabalhismo*, chap. 6; and Dávila, *Diploma of Whiteness*. On antiracism in government propaganda, see Raphael, "Samba and Social Control," 106–8.

4. Freyre directly credits Boas's view in Freyre, *Casa-grande e senzala*, 7. On Freyre's intellectual trajectories, see Needell, "Identity, Race, Gender"; Skidmore, "Raízes"; and Benzaquen de Araújo, *Guerra e paz*.

5. On Boas's influence in anthropology, see Stocking, *Shaping of American Anthropology*.

6. Freyre, *Casa-grande e senzala*, 301.

7. Romo, "Rethinking Race and Culture," 32n2. Elsewhere in his text, Freyre lauded the "superiority of the black to the Indian" (Freyre, *Casa-grande e senzala*, 302).

8. Costa, *Brazilian Empire*, 244–46; Needell, "Identity, Race, Gender."

9. Freyre, *Casa-grande e senzala*. On black and white children, see 344–45; on *amas de leite*, see 339–44; quote is from 9; on fraternity or fraternization (*confraternização*), see also, e.g., 341 and 344.

10. The term is from Matory, *Black Atlantic Religion*, chap. 4.

11. Landes, *City of Women*, 7.

12. Details from Freyre's night on the town, including his journal entries and an excerpt from his article, appear in Hermano Vianna, *Mystery of Samba*, 1–9.

13. On the reception of Freyre's work, see Benzaquen de Araújo, *Guerra e paz*.

14. Borges, "Recognition of Afro-Brazilian Symbols"; Raphael, "Samba and Social Control"; Hermano Vianna, *Mystery of Samba*; McCann, *Hello, Hello Brazil*.

15. McCann, *Hello, Hello Brazil*, chap. 2; Raphael, "Samba and Social Control," chap. 3. McCann not only highlights these restrictions but shows how sambistas worked within and against them.

16. Dávila, *Diploma of Whiteness*; Lenharo, *Sacralização*; Lesser, "Immigration and Shifting Concepts."

17. On the revolt, see Weinstein, "Racializing Regional Difference."

18. McCann, *Hello, Hello Brazil*, chaps. 2 and 3.

19. Roberto Moura, *Tia Ciata*.

20. Harding, *Refuge in Thunder*, 13.

21. On the meanings of *ethnicity* or *nação* in the Brazilian context, see Nishida, *Slavery and Identity*; Verger, *Fluxo e refluxo*; Lima, "O conceito de 'nação'"; and Maria Ines C. de Oliveira, "Quem eram os 'negros da Guiné'?"

22. On this and previous slave revolts in Bahia, see João José Reis, *Slave Rebellion*.

23. João José Reis, "Candomblé," 118.

24. Albuquerque, "Esperanças de boaventuras"; Fry, Carrara, and Martins-Costa, "Negros e brancos"; Butler, *Freedoms Given*, 171–89.

25. Butler, *Freedoms Given*, 53–55, 170–71; Harding, *Refuge in Thunder*, esp. 13–14, 55.

26. I capitalize Candomblé when referring to the religion and lowercase it when referring to communities and spaces of worship. Cf. Harding, *Refuge in Thunder*, xix; João José Reis, "Candomblé," 132n2. On the broader social roles of *terreiros*, see Butler, *Freedoms Given*, 47, 194–200; Harding, *Refuge in Thunder*, 78–79, 108–16; and Paul Johnson, *Secrets, Gossip, and Gods*, 35–51.

27. Landes, *City of Women*, 16, 50. Cf. Mattos, *Das cores do silêncio*.

28. Butler, *Freedoms Given*, 50–59. Census figures in this paragraph are from 134.

29. Bairros, "Pecados no 'paraíso racial.'"

30. "A hierarquia das raças—cor, trabalho, e riqueza após a abolição em Salvador," and "A Frente Negra Brasileira na Bahia," in Bacelar, *A hierarquia das raças*, 41–87, 143–57; Thales de Azevedo, *Les élites de couleur*.

31. Freyre, *Ordem e progresso*, cxxxvii.

32. *A Tarde*, 18 August 1917, cited in Albuquerque, "Santos, deuses e heróis," 104. See also newspaper reports decrying the Africanness of Bahian carnival at the turn of the century in Raymundo Nina Rodrigues, *Os africanos*, 237–38. Cf. Filho, "Desafricanizar as ruas," 241; Albuquerque, "Esperanças de boaventuras"; and Fry, Carrara, and Martins-Costa, "Negros e brancos."

33. See the summaries of newspaper reports in Raymundo Nina Rodrigues, *Os africanos*, 353–72; and Ramos, *O negro brasileiro*, 106–9. On the repression of nineteenth-century Candomblé, see Harding, *Refuge in Thunder*; and João José Reis, "Candomblé."

34. Raymundo Nina Rodrigues, *Os africanos*; Raymundo Nina Rodrigues, *O animismo*.

35. Lühning, "'Acabe com este santo.'"

36. Ramos, *Negro in Brazil*, 26–27, 99–103, 124. Cf. Dantas, *Vovó nagô*, 150–61; and Matory, *Black Atlantic Religion*, chap. 4. On Ramos's work in the 1930s, see Campos, *Arthur Ramos*.

37. Risério, "Bahia com 'H.'"

38. Gilberto Freyre, *Manifesto regionalista* (1926), quoted in Dantas, *Vovó nagô*, 159.

39. Ibid., 196–97. Borges dates this process even earlier. Borges, *Family in Bahia*, 31.

40. "As festas da Mãe Preta," *Diário de Notícias*, 30 September 1929, 1.

41. See, e.g., "Brasilidade," *Diário da Bahia*, 26 November 1932, 4.

42. Butler, "Africa"; João José Reis, "Candomblé"; Harding, *Refuge in Thunder*, 72–73.

43. Olinto, *Brasileiros na África*; Guran, *Agudás*; Manuela Carneiro da Cunha, *Negros, estrangeiros*; Verger, *Fluxo e refluxo*; Freyre, "Acontece"; Laotan, *Torch-Bearers*; Matory, *Black Atlantic Religion*, 38–72; Mann, *Slavery and the Birth of an African City*.

44. Matory, *Black Atlantic Religion*, 118–20, 306–7n31; Pierson, *Negroes in Brazil*, 243; Olinto, *Brasileiros na África*, 168, 265–67.

45. Matory, *Black Atlantic Religion*, 38–72.

46. Butler, *Freedoms Given*, 200–201; Matory, *Black Atlantic Religion*, 118–27; Dantas, *Vovó nagô*, 202–3. See also Martiniano do Bomfim, "Os ministros de Xangô," in Congresso Afro-Brasileiro, *O negro*, 233–36.

47. Quoted in Matory, *Black Atlantic Religion*, 115.

48. Cf. Paul Johnson, *Secrets, Gossip, and Gods*.

49. Butler, "Africa," 144; Olinto, *Brasileiros na África*, 265–67.

50. Butler, "Africa"; Paul Johnson, *Secrets, Gossip, and Gods*, 75–76. For different perspectives on this point, see Capone, *La quête*; Dantas, *Vovó nagô*; Matory, *Black Atlantic Religion*, chap. 1; and Serra, *Águas do rei*.

51. Dantas, *Vovó nagô*, 203.

52. Matory, *Black Atlantic Religion*, 46, 62; Braga, *Na gamela do feitiço*, esp. chap. 2.

53. Herskovits, *Myth*; Herskovits, "Social Organization."

54. Pierson, *Negroes in Brazil*, 238. Landes similarly praised "the unique quality of [Bahia's] Negro folk life"; Landes, *City of Women*, 7.

55. Congresso Afro-Brasileiro, *Estudos*; Congresso Afro-Brasileiro, *O negro*. On the congresses, see Levine, "First Afro-Brazilian Congress"; Romo, "Rethinking Race and Culture"; Butler, *Freedoms Given*, 206–9; and Dantas, *Vovó nagô*, 192–201.

56. Carneiro, quoted in Dantas, *Vovó nagô*, 195. For transcriptions of some of that radio and newspaper coverage, see Lühning, "'Acabe com este santo,'" 216–17.

57. Butler, *Freedoms Given*, 203–4. On the changing gender composition of Candomblé leadership, see João José Reis, "Candomblé."

58. Filho, "Desafricanizar as ruas," 254–55. Cf. Joaquim, *O papel da liderança religiosa feminina*.

59. Matory, *Black Atlantic Religion*, 60; Velho, *Guerra de orixá*, 14.

60. Weinstein, "Racializing Regional Difference."

61. Unsigned, "Samba, o hymno nacional da malandragem," *Progresso*, 31 July 1931, 4.

62. See, e.g., the following in *Progresso*: "A musa negra e os seus triumphos na Europa," 13 January 1929, 2; "Salomés negras," 13 January 1929, 6; "Na civilizada Europa, os rhythmos da música negra provocam enthusiasmo e reclamam applausos," 24 March 1929, 1; and "Villalobos," 26 September 1929, 3.

63. Getúlio Vargas, interview with the press on 10 October 1938, quoted in Lenharo, *Sacralização*, 113. On Vargas's immigration policies and actions against internal immigrant groups, see Levine, *Vargas Regime*, 167; and Dávila, *Diploma of Whiteness*, 65.

64. See, e.g., *Clarim*, 7 December 1930; and *Progresso*, 30 November 1930.

65. Butler, *Freedoms Given*, 113.

66. "Estatutos da FNB," *A Voz da Raça*, 15 April 1933, 3.

67. Andrews, *Blacks and Whites*, 148–49; Butler, *Freedoms Given*, 115–17; Mitchell, "Racial Consciousness," 131.

68. *A Voz da Raça*, 29 April 1933, 1.

69. Following a meeting of suffragist women with Vargas, the new electoral code of 1932 enfranchised women (subject to the same literacy restrictions as men). Hahner, "Feminism, Women's Rights," 101.

70. Butler, *Freedoms Given*, 118–19; Andrews, *Blacks and Whites*, 151. See also Francisco Lucrécio's testimony in Barbosa, *Frente Negra Brasileira*, 54–55.

71. See "Judas da Raça," "O que necessitamos," and "A leaderança" in *Clarim*, 8 November 1931.

72. See Leite's accounts in Barbosa, *Frente Negra Brasileira*, 66–68; and Silva and Leite, *E disse*, 94–104.

73. See "Correspondencia," "Agora vae," "Um caso anormal," and "Um caso sério," *Chibata*, February 1932.

74. "O nosso pasquim e o Dr. Veiga dos Santos," *Chibata*, March 1932.

75. See *Clarim*, 27 March 1932; Leite in Barbosa, *Frente Negra Brasileira*, 68–69; and Silva and Leite, *E disse*, 99–100.

76. "O empastellamento d'*A Chibata*," *Diário Nacional*, 22 March 1932; see also *Folha da Manhã* of the same day.

77. See A. V. dos Santos, *As raízes históricas do patrianovismo*.

78. See, e.g., "Eduquemos nosso povo," *Clarim*, 13 May 1932, 2; and "Patriavelha" (a playful comment on the conservatism of "patrianovismo"), *Chibata*, February 1932, 1.

79. He also called freedom of the press "liberal stupidity" and "freedom of libel," in A. V. dos Santos, "Critiqueiros," *A Voz da Raça*, 22 April 1933, 1.

80. Domingues, "'Pérolas negras,'" 207.

81. Silva and Leite, *E disse*, 103–4; Barbosa, *Frente Negra Brasileira*, 70. On the Frente's support for Vargas in this revolt, see Olavo Xavier, "Milicianos de fé," *A Voz da Raça*, 29 April 1933, 4. On the Black Legion (and its split with the Frente), see Domingues, "'Pérolas negras.'"

82. Ferrara, *A imprensa negra*, 68.

83. See, by A. V. dos Santos, "Em marcha," 3 June 1933, 1; "A árvore da FNB," 25 March 1933, 2; "Alerta!," 1 April 1933, 1; by Menelik, "Do meu canto," 22 April 1933, 4; and by J. B. Feliciano, "A união faz a força," 22 April 1933, 2; all in *A Voz da Raça*.

84. A. V. dos Santos, "Aos frentenegrinos, aos negros em geral e aos demais patrícios, especialmente trabalhadores e produtores," *A Voz da Raça*, 29 April 1933, 1.

85. I. V. dos Santos, "Liberdade utópica," *A Voz da Raça*, 13 May 1933, 1. Euclydes de Oliveira (who helped popularize the phrase in the mid-1920s) also expressed hope that the Revolution of 1930 would reverse his situation as "a foreigner in my own homeland." "A arrancada para o infinito," *Progresso*, 30 November 1930, 1.

86. In *A Voz da Raça*: Santos, "Aos frentenegrinos," 29 April 1933, 1; "Apelo à economia," 28 October 1933, 1. On Jews as communists, see also A. V. dos Santos,

"Resposta a um boletim," 9 December 1933, 1. Ironically, São Paulo's secret police, who often confused black activism with communism, arrested Arlindo's brother Isaltino on charges of communism in 1936. Police files record Isaltino's fervent rejection of this accusation and his assurances of national loyalty. Carneiro and Kossoy, *A imprensa confiscada*, 54–55.

87. On the Frente's support for Vargas, see "O memorável pleito de 3 de maio," *A Voz da Raça*, 6 May 1933, 1.

88. A. V. dos Santos, "A situação aparente dos negros," *A Voz da Raça*, April 1936, 1. Arlindo Santos laid out his monarchist ideas in his *Idéias que marcham no silêncio*.

89. Cf. Oliveira, "Quem é a 'gente negra'?," 64, 90.

90. Santos, "A situação," *A Voz da Raça*, April 1936, 1.

91. The militarized call for members to participate as "soldiers" of "disciplined battalions," with Frente leaders as commanders, appears at its clearest in A. V. dos Santos, "Aos frentenegrinos!," *A Voz da Raça*, 18 March 1933, 1. See also P. P. Barbosa, "Com que interesse?," *A Voz da Raça*, 8 April 1933, 1.

92. A. V. dos Santos, "Que o negro brasileiro não se iluda! . . . ," *A Voz da Raça*, 15 December 1934, 1; on militias, see *A Voz da Raça*, 29 April 1933, 3–4.

93. The lyrics of the Frente's hymn appear in *A Voz da Raça*, 29 April 1933, 3. Cf. Fernandes, *The Negro*, 211–12; and Butler, *Freedoms Given*, 121–23.

94. Interview in Barbosa, *Frente Negra Brasileira*, 37–38.

95. Ibid., 18, 42, 50–51.

96. "Secção feminina," *A Voz da Raça*, November 1937, 3.

97. A. V. dos Santos, "A afirmação da raça," *A Voz da Raça*, 10 June 1933, 1; Santos, "Resposta," *A Voz da Raça*, 9 December 1933, 1. Support for Italy and Germany's fascist regimes continued in later years; see (in *A Voz da Raça*) A. V. dos Santos, "Fogo neles!," 6 January 1934, 1; C. Gonçalves's call for a "fuherer [*sic*] for the black race," November 1936, 1, 4; and P. P. Barbosa, "Apreciando," October 1936, 1–2.

98. Santos, "A situação," *A Voz da Raça*, April 1936, 1.

99. Butler, *Freedoms Given*, 118, 123; Barbosa, *Frente Negra Brasileira*, 17–18.

100. Mitchell, "Racial Consciousness," 135–37.

101. Levine, *Vargas Regime*, 73–79.

102. Much work still remains to be done on the role of blacks in leftist organizations. According to Édison Carneiro in 1933, "It is well known that blacks have constituted an enormous contingent of the ranks of the Brazilian Communist Party." Congresso Afro-Brasileiro, *Estudos*, 240. Cf. Risério, *Uma história*, 498–504. People of color appeared far more frequently in the records of São Paulo's political police for their links to the Left and labor unions than for involvement in specifically race-based activities; see Carneiro and Kossoy, *A imprensa confiscada*, 54–55.

103. Interview with M. O. Ribeiro, in Barbosa, *Frente Negra Brasileira*, 90.

104. In *A Voz da Raça*: J. B. Mariano, "Chegou o momento," 22 April 1933, 1; Santos, "Em marcha," 3 June 1933, 1; J. B. Feliciano, "Em defesa de Palmares," 20 May 1933, 1; H. Costa, "Bandeira da FNB," August 1936, 1; A. V. dos Santos, "Datas históricas," April 1937, 1.

105. A. V. dos Santos, "Marchando," *A Voz da Raça*, 28 April 1934, 4.

106. In *A Voz da Raça*: A. V. dos Santos, "A afirmação da raça," 10 June 1933, 1; also A. V. dos Santos, "Irmãos negros," 15 April 1933, 1, on our "African and Indigenous [*Bugre*] ancestors"; and Henrique Dias, "Discurso que eu não disse," 14 April 1933, 1.

107. A. V. dos Santos, "O mulato," *A Voz da Raça*, 29 April 1933, 3.

108. On the black race as a "family" united "across time and space," see, in *A Voz da Raça*, A. V. dos Santos, "A árvore da FNB," 25 March 1933, 2. On pride in black "blood," see the recruitment ads on 8 April 1933, 3.

109. Santos, "Aos frentenegrinos," *A Voz da Raça*, 29 April 1933, 1.

110. A series of early articles in *A Voz da Raça* reveals the process by which "fraternity" and "equality" quickly shifted from guiding principles to empty fictions of the Republic: A. V. dos Santos, "Alerta!," 1 April 1933, 1; J. B. Feliciano, "A união faz a força," 22 April 1933, 2; H. de Campos, "O destino da raça negra no Brasil," 9 December 1933, 1. For a denunciation of "Brazilian sentimentalism," see J. B. Feliciano, "O negro na formação do Brasil," 24 June 1933, 1.

111. Santos, "Marchando," *A Voz da Raça*, 28 April 1934, 4.

112. Silva and Leite, *E disse*, 97–99. See *Clarim*, issues of 28 September 1930, 1931, 1940.

113. J. Guaraná de Santana, "Manifesto," *Correio de São Paulo*, 21 July 1932, reproduced in Flávio Gomes, *Negros e política*, 71–72. On citizenship as soldiering in the Black Legion, see Flávio Gomes, *Negros e política*, 68–74.

114. A. V. dos Santos, "A FNB e um artigo do Snr. Austregesilo de Athayde," *A Voz da Raça*, 25 March 1933, 1.

115. Interview with Francisco Lucrécio, in Barbosa, *Frente Negra Brasileira*, 46.

116. "Menelik," "Do meu canto," *A Voz da Raça*, 22 April 1933, 1. A retrospective article on the newspaper *O Menelik* (*A Voz da Raça* of 31 March 1934, 4) conspicuously omits discussion of its African namesake. A letter from Mário Ferreira of the *Tribuna d'África* in Lourenço Marques expressing a desire to receive issues of *A Voz da Raça* appears on 18 March 1933, 4, but *A Voz da Raça*'s editors do not reciprocate by reprinting anything about Portuguese Africa.

117. See *Clarim*, 25 January 1930, 4; 13 April 1930, 3–4; 23 August 1930, 4; and 28 September 1930, 4. *O Progresso* also continued its coverage of Africa and the diaspora: "Continente Negro," 31 January 1930, 5; "O nascimento da questão racial da África do Sul," 31 July 1930, 1; "Throno preto," 31 July 1930, 2; "Curiosa confederação economica dos negros africanos," February 1931, 3; "Alheios a pecuinhas, com o seu trabalho, Africanos assombram a Europa," 31 July 1931, 2.

118. *Clarim*, 7 December 1930, 4.

119. See esp. *Clarim*, 26 July 1931, 4; 28 September 1931, 4; 20 December 1931, 4. Leite describes his interest in Garveyism, despite its limited appeal in contemporary São Paulo, in Silva and Leite, *E disse*, 77–82.

120. On Ethiopia, see "O caso da Abyssinia e o mundo negro," *Clarim*, March 1935, 1; and J. C. Leite, "Mundo negro," *Tribuna Negra*, September 1935, 3. Other diasporic references appear in *Tribuna Negra*, September 1935, 2; and *Cultura*, March 1934, 3–5.

121. A. V. dos Santos, "Alerta!," *A Voz da Raça*, 1 April 1933, 1; Santos, "A afirmação," *A Voz da Raça*, 10 June 1933, 1. See also the exoticizing poem "Macumba,"

casting its practitioners as "barbarous" and "infantile," in *A Voz da Raça*, November 1937, 3.

122. Castelo Alves, "Flores do campo," *A Voz da Raça*, 20 May 1933, 1.

123. Silva and Leite, *E disse*, 141.

124. Prandi, *Os candomblés de São Paulo*, 21.

125. Silva and Leite, *E disse*, 113–17.

126. Scholars emphasize different reasons for the Frente's eventual demise, ranging from the national political climate to authoritarian tendencies within the organization itself. See, e.g., Butler, *Freedoms Given*, 126–27; Fernandes, *The Negro*, 220–21; and Andrews, *Blacks and Whites*, 155.

127. Coverage of the Mãe Preta celebrations appears in *Diário de Notícias*, 27, 28, and 30 September 1929; *Diário da Bahia*, 27 and 29 September 1929; and *A Tarde*, 27 and 29 September 1929.

128. Cid Teixeira, cited in Bacelar, *A hierarquia das raças*, 148. "A Bahia assistiu no dia 28 de setembro, uma manifestação inédita no Brasil," *Clarim*, 24 November 1929, 4.

129. Letter from members of the Centro Operário to the Sociedade Protectora dos Desvalidos, 1 July 1893, cited in Butler, *Freedoms Given*, 140.

130. "A Bahia assistiu," *Clarim*, 24 November 1929, 4.

131. Butler, *Freedoms Given*, 138–39. See also "O Centro Operário e o seu 32 anniversário," *A Noite*, 8 May 1926, 1.

132. "A Bahia assistiu," *Clarim*, 24 November 1929, 4.

133. "*O Clarim d'Alvorada* na Bahia," *Clarim*, 23 August 1930, 1.

134. "Grandes homenagens serão prestadas hoje à Mãe Preta na Bahia," *Clarim*, 28 September 1929, 4; "Um apello aos negros bahianos" and "A Bahia assistiu," *Clarim*, 24 November 1929, 1, 4; obituary of Ascendino dos Anjos, *Clarim*, 21 June 1931, 2.

135. Bacelar, *A hierarquia das raças*, 145–46; Butler, *Freedoms Given*, 129–30.

136. "Os intuitos da 'Frente Negra da Bahia,'" *Diário da Bahia*, 26 April 1933, 3.

137. See coverage of the Frente Negra da Bahia's activities in *Diário da Bahia*, 10 May 1933; 3, 17, and 21 June 1933. Cf. Bacelar, *A hierarquia das raças*, 147.

138. See, e.g., *Diário da Bahia*, 2, 14, 21, and 31 March 1933. Cf. ibid., 149.

139. I have not found any issues of this newspaper; a brief description appears in *Diário da Bahia*, 16 and 17 February 1933, 2.

140. "Os intuitos," *Diário da Bahia*, 26 April 1933, 3; and "A 'Frente Negra,' pretos novos na própria terra," *Diário da Bahia*, 28 December 1932, 3.

141. "Os intuitos," *Diário da Bahia*, 26 April 1933, 3.

142. "O dia 13 de maio na Frente Negra," *Diário da Bahia*, 13 May 1933, 3; and "Realisado o programma a 'Frente Negra' traçou para o 13 de maio," *Diário da Bahia*, 14 May 1933, 2.

143. See cites in Bacelar, *A hierarquia das raças*, 148. See also M. P. de Assumpção [Alakija], "Negros retintos no parlamento francês," *Getulino*, 8 June 1924, 1.

144. Butler, *Freedoms Given*, 142.

145. Ibid., 131; Bacelar, *A hierarquia das raças*, 150–55.

146. Thales de Azevedo, *Les élites de couleur*, 98.

147. Conceição, "Cultura como alienação," 2.

Chapter 4

1. In calling the period between 1946 and 1964 the "Second Republic," I follow the nomenclature employed by most U.S.-based scholars of Brazil. Note that in Brazil this period is most commonly known as the "Fourth Republic" (with the Second being Vargas's years as provisional and constitutionally elected president [1930–37] and the Third being the Estado Novo [1937–45]), though practices also vary.

2. R. J. Amaral, "Combatamos o bom combate," *Alvorada*, January 1946, 1.

3. A. Guerreiro Ramos, "Apresentação da negritude," *Quilombo*, June–July 1950, 11; emphasis mine.

4. On this transition, see Fausto, *Concise History*, 229–33; Skidmore, *Politics in Brazil*, chap. 2.

5. For a brief overview of the scholarship on this subject, see Andrews, *Blacks and Whites*, 147n59. Cf. Fischer, *Poverty of Rights*, part 2, chap. 3. See also the oral histories in Mattos and Rios, *Memórias do cativeiro*, 248–49. Prominent black thinkers associated with the Frente Negra of the 1930s shared this positive view of Vargas; see, e.g., interviews with F. Lucrécio and M. O. Ribeiro, in Barbosa, *Frente Negra Brasileira*, 55, 87. Yet they expressed almost unanimous disappointment at Vargas's decision to shut down independent black political organizations (see interviews with A. Barbosa, F. Lucrécio, J. C. Leite, and others).

6. Andrews, *Blacks and Whites*, 186–88.

7. Silva and Leite, *E disse*, 138.

8. Mitchell, "Racial Consciousness," 141.

9. Silva and Leite, *E disse*, 111.

10. Ibid., 142–44; Butler, *Freedoms Given*, 126; Mitchell, "Racial Consciousness," 142. See also *Alvorada*, September 1945, 2.

11. "Manifesto da democracia," *Jornal de São Paulo*, 13 April 1945, cited in Mitchell, "Racial Consciousness," 143.

12. Bastide, "A imprensa negra," 54.

13. Mitchell, "Racial Consciousness," 143. Leite, like editors of other black newspapers, largely gave up publishing *O Clarim* during the Estado Novo (though at least one issue, from 28 September 1940, came out of this period).

14. Interview with Aristides Barbosa, in Barbosa, *Frente Negra Brasileira*, 27–29.

15. IBGE, *Recenseamento geral de 1940. Censo demográfico: Estado de São Paulo* (Rio de Janeiro, 1950), table 30, p. 24, cited in Andrews, *Blacks and Whites*, 101.

16. Ibid., 126–27.

17. In 1940, out of a total *preto* and *pardo* population of 862,255 statewide, only 344 *pretos* and *pardos* had graduated from college, and 1,717 had graduated from high school. By 1950, the high-school graduation figures had doubled, but the number of college graduates dropped (to 265). IBGE, *Recenseamento, 1940: São Paulo*, table 25, p. 18; IBGE, *Recenseamento geral de 1950. Censo demográfico: Estado de São Paulo* (Rio de Janeiro, 1954), table 21, p. 24, both cited in ibid., 159.

18. Figures on employment rates by type of employment are from IBGE, *Recenseamento, 1940: São Paulo*, table 30, pp. 24–25, cited in ibid., 126–27.

19. Literacy rates were for Brazilians over age five: *pretos*, 59% for men and 44% for women; *pardos*, 76% for men and 64% for women. Figures from "Alfabetização em relação à cor, nos estados," Gustavo Capanema Collection, CPDOC, cited in Dávila, *Diploma of Whiteness*, 73. The national average in 1940 for *pretos* was 15.8%, for *pardos*, 21.5%, and for whites, 39.5%. IBGE, *Recenseamento geral de 1940. Censo demográfico: Estados Unidos do Brasil* (Rio de Janeiro, 1950), table 17, pp. 28–29, cited in Andrews, *Blacks and Whites*, 255.

20. In some areas of public service, *pardos* outnumbered both *pretos* and whites, though they likely occupied lower-rank positions than their white counterparts. Costa Pinto, *O negro*, 94.

21. Census figures from 1940 on the employment of people over age ten in the city of Rio showed, for instance, only 343 *preto* men and 996 *pardo* men working in liberal professions, compared to 12,837 white men. Ibid., 91.

22. Ibid., 125–49. Cf. Fischer, *Poverty of Rights*.

23. See "A Frente Negra solidária com o Ministro de Trabalho," *A Noite* (Rio de Janeiro), 25 January 1937; and Semog and Nascimento, *Abdias Nascimento*, 88.

24. Joselina da Silva, "A União dos Homens de Cor," 223–24.

25. See J. S. de Melo's and J. B. da Silva's interventions in the first Congresso do Negro Brasileiro (Rio de Janeiro, 1950), in Abdias do Nascimento, *O negro revoltado* (1968), 228, 240–41. Cf. Costa Pinto, *O negro*, 260–63.

26. On the UHC's activities (and those of a spin-off group often confused with the UHC, the União Cultural dos Homens de Cor), see Costa Pinto, *O negro*, 260–64.

27. Indeed, a document from Rio's political police (dated 28 June 1978) identified Silva as having been a member of the Communist Party in 1945 and 1956. APERJ, Fundo Polícias Políticas, Setor Informação 146, p. 1431.

28. J. B. da Silva, "Patrocínio, o visionário," *A Voz da Negritude*, 2 (special supplement), in *Himalaya*, 8 October 1953.

29. According to Costa Pinto's interview with J. S. de Melo in 1952, the group was getting ready to launch the occasional supplement *A Voz da Negritude* as an independent newspaper; this does not appear to have happened. Costa Pinto, *O negro*, 259.

30. "Reorganização da Frente Negra Brasileira," *A Luta*, 29 April 1954.

31. J. B. da Silva, "Patrocínio, o visionário," *A Voz da Negritude*, 2, in *Himalaya*, 8 October 1953. See also Joselina da Silva, "A União dos Homens de Cor," 224.

32. Many thanks to Marc Hertzman for his help in elaborating this point. On the music industry in this period, and tensions and alliances between black artists and white artists and managers, see McCann, *Hello, Hello Brazil*, chap. 4; and Hertzman, "Surveillance and Difference," chaps. 5 and 8.

33. Much like UHC members, the editors of and contributors to a contemporary Carioca black publication, *Redenção*, considered themselves to be "foremost among those who believe that the black problem in Brazil is more of an economic nature, and about education, than it is about race or color" (Unsigned [editors], "Qualquer brasileiro pode ser oficial de nossa marinha de guerra," *Redenção*, 30 December 1950, 1; see also Aloysio da Silva, "Racismo," same issue and page, and Miguel Guilherme Cavalieri, "A questão dos negros nos colégios," *Redenção*, 9 December 1950, 5). Article after article in the two known issues of this paper, dated 9 and 30 December 1950, stress

the importance of education, economic integration, or political participation in the advancement of people of color. Also like members of the UHC, the editors of *Redenção* emphasized on several occasions that though their journal was dedicated to *"negros"* and to the "moral, economic, and cultural uplift of their ethnic group," its contributors were "a group of men of goodwill: *negros, brancos,* and *pardos*" (José Bernardo, "Não somos de promessas," and João Conceição, "Convocação," in *Redenção,* 9 December 1950, 1; see also José Bernardo, "Sou o que sou," *Redenção,* 30 December 1950, 1). Though in these and other articles writers conceded that specifically race-based prejudice continued to exist in some sectors of Brazilian society, they overwhelmingly cast the problem of black and brown Brazilians as the problem of political and economic exclusion, shared across a Brazilian "povo" made up of many races.

34. My discussion of Nascimento's life in the next few paragraphs is drawn from Semog and Nascimento, *Abdias Nascimento.*

35. Cf. Silva and Leite, *E disse,* 140–41; Alves, "We Are All Equal," 181. Nascimento gives the date (incorrectly, it appears) as 1937. Semog and Nascimento, *Abdias Nascimento,* 78.

36. Semog and Nascimento, *Abdias Nascimento,* 87–88.

37. Figures are from Ferrara, *A imprensa negra,* 268.

38. "Manifesto da Convenção Nacional do Negro Brasileiro," in Abdias do Nascimento, *O negro revoltado* (1982), 111–12.

39. A. Guerreiro Ramos, "Apresentação da negritude," *Quilombo,* June–July 1950, 11.

40. Cf. Ferrara, *A imprensa negra,* 142; Bastide, "A imprensa negra," 54.

41. Unsigned, "Aos negros de São Paulo, ao povo em geral," *Mundo Novo,* 23 September 1950, 7; and Armando de Castro [director of *Mundo Novo*], "Um representante do negro no legislativo bandeirante," ibid., 2.

42. Unsigned [Nascimento?], "Os negros e as eleições," *Quilombo,* January 1950, 3; Nascimento, "Candidatos negros e mulatos," *Quilombo,* February 1950, 1. On the TEN's political activism, see Darién Davis, *Avoiding the Dark,* 201–3.

43. Burns, *History of Brazil,* 387; Skidmore, *Politics in Brazil,* 64.

44. Figures from IBGE, *Recenseamento geral de 1950. Censo demográfico: Estados Unidos do Brasil* (Rio de Janeiro, 1956), table 17, pp. 20–21, cited in Andrews, *Blacks and Whites,* 255.

45. Burns, *History of Brazil,* 396. By 1962, 25% of the population was registered to vote.

46. Andrews, *Blacks and Whites,* 188.

47. In *Novo Horizonte,* issues between May 1946 and September 1947.

48. Costa Pinto, *O negro,* 263.

49. See, e.g., Andrews, *Blacks and Whites,* 181–88; Hanchard, *Orpheus and Power,* 104–9.

50. On literacy campaigns, see "Teatro Experimental do Negro," *Quilombo,* December 1948, 7; and *Alvorada,* September 1945, 4.

51. Nascimento, for instance, addressed a letter to the heads of all major political parties in 1950, requesting information on any black candidates in order to advertise their positions for free in *Quilombo.* "O TEN dirige-se aos partidos políticos," *Quilombo,* March–April 1950, 5.

52. Nascimento, "Nós," *Quilombo*, December 1948, 1, 6. See also the opinions of Ironides Rodrigues, a law student who later collaborated with *Quilombo* and stressed a nonpartisan approach to "black valorization," in Guimarães and Macedo, "*Diário Trabalhista*," 147.

53. Nascimento attempted an alliance with the Communist Party early on in his efforts to organize the TEN but soon turned away, angered by the party's failure to address race as a problem independent of class. Semog and Nascimento, *Abdias Nascimento*, 147–49. On Nascimento's eventual preference for the PTB, see Guimarães and Macedo, "*Diário Trabalhista*," 163.

54. See, e.g., unsigned [Leite?], "Nem tudo que reluz é ouro," *Alvorada*, April 1946, 4; and J. S. de Melo, "A voz da negritude: Um toque de reunir," *Himalaya*, 12 August 1950, 2. Cf. Andrews, *Blacks and Whites*, 186.

55. Mitchell, "Racial Consciousness," 157.

56. Silva and Leite, *E disse*, 149.

57. Unsigned [Leite?], "Declaração aos negros do Brasil," and "Nossa obra é de solidariedade humana," *Alvorada*, September 1945, 1. See also J. de Oliveira, "Hino à nova Alvorada," *Novo Horizonte*, June 1946, 2.

58. Unsigned [Leite or Amaral], "As eleições de 2 de dezembro," *Alvorada*, December 1945, 4. Such celebrations of Brazil's democratic process (and of President Dutra as the victor) were common in 1945–46; see, e.g., "Parabéns ao Brasil," *Alvorada*, December 1945, 1; and *Senzala*, January 1946, 5.

59. L. Lobato, "Advertência," *Senzala*, January 1946, 14.

60. Unsigned [Leite or Amaral], "As eleições de 2 de dezembro," *Alvorada*, December 1945, 4. On blacks' inherent sense of democratic and civic duty, see also unsigned [Amaral?], "Novos tempos," *Alvorada*, February 1947, 1; Amaral, "O negro não tem problemas?," *Alvorada*, September 1945, 1; and "Civismo e compreensão," *Alvorada*, December 1945, 1.

61. W. Machado, "Desapareceu o vermelho da folhinha," *Novo Horizonte*, June 1947, 1. For more criticisms of Brazilian democracy, see O. P. dos Santos, "A campanha deve ser iniciada," *Novo Horizonte*, June 1950, 2; and A. de O. Camargo, "Diretrizes," *Senzala*, January 1946, 11.

62. Cited in Costa Pinto, *O negro*, 270n35.

63. *Alvorada*, November 1945, 1.

64. Leite, "Nosso ideal de liberdade," *Alvorada*, May 1947, 1. See also Leite, "A nova abolição," *Alvorada*, May 1946, 1; J. P. Teixeira, "Problemas específicos dos negros brasileiros," *Novo Horizonte*, September 1954, 5; L. Guedes, "O eterno desamparado," *Novo Horizonte*, July 1947, 1; unsigned, "Os negros que se previnam," *Alvorada*, March 1946, 1; A. do Nascimento, "Problemas e aspirações do negro," *Diário Trabalhista*, 23 January 1946, 5, cited in Guimarães and Macedo, "*Diário Trabalhista*," 148–49; and J. Conceição, "Convocação," *Redenção*, 9 December 1950, 1.

65. See, e.g., A. Negreiros, "Que liberdade, que democracia?," *Alvorada*, September 1946, 4; Costa Rego, "Venha uma segunda abolição!," *Novo Horizonte*, March 1948, 4; unsigned, "Despertar na conciência nacional," *Quilombo*, June–July 1950, 3; and unsigned, "Vitória grandiosa de 'Redenção' no seu primeiro número," *Redenção*, 30 December 1950, 4. The idea and phrase "second abolition" had made appearances in

the black press of earlier years (see, e.g., Kössling, "O discurso policial"). But it moved to center stage in this period.

66. Unsigned [Leite?], "13 de maio," *Alvorada*, May 1947, 1. See also "A nova abolição," *Alvorada*, May 1946, 1; "Tribuna, imprensa e abolição," *Alvorada*, May 1946, 4; and J. C. Leite, "As duas etapas da liberdade," *Novo Horizonte*, November–December 1954, 1.

67. Unsigned [Leite?], "Os negros e a democracia," *Alvorada*, January 1946, 1.

68. Interestingly, this predates Hannah Arendt's famous formulation of the "right to have rights" in Arendt, "The Rights of Man"; and Arendt, *The Origins of Totalitarianism*.

69. Nascimento, "Nós," *Quilombo*, December 1948, 1.

70. Cited in Maio, "A questão racial," 183.

71. "Manifesto da Convenção Nacional do Negro Brasileiro," in Abdias do Nascimento, *O negro revoltado* (1982), 111–12.

72. Cf. Guimarães and Macedo, "*Diário Trabalhista*," 150.

73. Nascimento, "Os negros brasileiros lutam por suas reivindicações," *Diário Trabalhista*, 15 January 1946, 5, cited in ibid. 149–50. According to the authors, Sebastião Rodrigues Alves, Aguinaldo Camargo, and Ironides Rodrigues, close colleagues of Nascimento, probably contributed to this column. In Rio, Nascimento and others also distributed the manifesto directly to the offices of leading political parties. Abdias do Nascimento, *O negro revoltado* (1982), 84–85.

74. The proposed amendment and its justification appear in proceedings of 17 June 1946, *Anais da Assembléia Constituinte* (1948): 278–79. Though the PTB became the party most closely linked to black demands in this period, even its members, and Fontenelle in particular, were initially cautious about publicly taking on the topic of racial discrimination. Guimarães and Macedo, "*Diário Trabalhista*," 162–63.

75. Nogueira had initially proposed a narrower amendment (proposal 1087), which specified that "any citizen, without regard to color," would be allowed "entrance into the Diplomatic, Military . . . , and Civil" professions. Gilberto Freyre was a cosigner of this proposed amendment. By 22 August 1946, however, Nogueira appeared together with Fontenelle as the sponsor of Fontenelle's original, broader amendment (proposal 1089), which was more closely in line with black activists' original demands. Proceedings of 24 August 1946, *Anais da Assembléia Constituinte* (1950): 410.

76. On Japanese immigration, 27 August 1946, *Anais da Assembléia Constituinte* (1950): 71–76; on anti-Semitism, 9 July 1946, *Anais da Assembléia Constituinte* (1949): 40–44. For more on Nogueira's background, see Guimarães and Macedo, "*Diário Trabalhista*," 176.

77. 13 May 1946, *Anais da Assembléia Constituinte* (1948): 408–14. See also Nogueira's speeches of 15 March and 24 August 1946.

78. See, in *Alvorada*: "Questão racial no Brasil," March 1946, 4; "Tribuna, imprensa e abolição," May 1946, 4; "Preconceito," June 1946, 4; "Sem distinção de raça ou de côr," September 1946, 8; and Arlindo Alves, "Preconceito de côr é crime de lesa-patria?," March 1947, 4. See also O. Paraná, "Preconceitos," *Novo Horizonte*, June 1947, 4; "Prossegue a cruzada para a segunda abolição," *Quilombo*, June–July 1950, 9; and S. Campos, "Muito pouco para nós," *Novo Horizonte*, September 1946, 2.

79. 24 August 1946, *Anais da Assembléia Constituinte* (1950): 410–13.

80. *Diário da Assembléia*, 28 August 1946, 4,404, cited in Abdias do Nascimento, *O negro revoltado* (1982), 85–86.

81. For the full text of the letter and details of its publication, see ibid., 109–11.

82. For the text of Barreto Pinto's speech, see *Quilombo*, May 1949, 6. For U.S. coverage: Special to the *Pittsburgh Courier*, "[Police?] Chase Negro Actors from Big Rio Hotel: Jim Crow in Brazil Protested," *Pittsburgh Courier*, 12 March 1949, 1–2. For exchanges between the *Courier* and *Quilombo*, see *Quilombo*, December 1948, 1; June 1949, 6–7; and May 1950, 5.

83. "Dutra contra o racismo," *Quilombo*, February 1950, 4.

84. For a fuller account of these events, see Abdias do Nascimento, *O negro revoltado* (1982), 71–72; Andrews, *Blacks and Whites*, 184–86. The black press also commented on them extensively: "Corajosa afirmação," *Alvorada*, February 1947, 1; Leite, "Preconceito casa grande e senzala," *Alvorada*, March 1947, 1; A. Alves, "Preconceito de côr é crime de lesa-patria?," *Alvorada*, March 1947, 4; "O pagóde racial no Brasil," *Alvorada*, April 1947, 4; R. de Queiroz, "Linha de Côr," *Quilombo*, December 1948, 2 (reprinted from *O Cruzeiro*, 24 May 1947); "Prossegue a cruzada para a segunda abolição," *Quilombo*, June–July 1950, 8–9.

85. Oliveira, quoted in unsigned, "O preconceito existe!," *Correio Paulistano*, 16 July 1950, 7–8. See also "Apresentado projeto cominando penas para discriminação racial," *Correio Paulistano*, 18 July 1950, 3.

86. Unsigned, "Despertar na conciência nacional," *Quilombo*, June–July 1950, 3. An article by W. Machado takes the absence of these universal rights to be a measure of racial discrimination: "Black people do not enjoy the Rights of Man"; "Desapareceu o vermelho da folhinha," *Novo Horizonte*, June 1947, 1. See also "A Declaração dos Direitos do Homem," *Quilombo*, June 1949, 9; "União dos homens de côr do Rio de Janeiro," *Novo Horizonte*, October 1954, 1; "Democracia racial," *Quilombo*, June 1949, 7; and A. E. dos Santos, "História são fatos discursivos de uma nacionalidade," *Redenção*, 9 December 1950, 2; Bernardo, "Não somos de promessas," *Redenção*, 9 December 1950, 1; Costa Pinto, *O negro*, 262.

87. A. Negreiros, "Que liberdade, que democracia?," *Alvorada*, September 1946, 4.

88. R. J. Amaral, "Vacillantes primeiros passos," *Alvorada*, June 1946, 1. The hundreds of signers of the letter to Truman included Abdias do Nascimento of the TEN; Abigail Moura of the Afro-Brazilian Orchestra; Solano Trinidade, poet and president of the Center for Afro-Brazilian Culture; and Aguinaldo Camargo, president of the Black National Convention. The letter asked for Truman's intervention in the case of three black U.S. citizens who had been condemned to die in the electric chair in Georgia. The authors of the letter, speaking on behalf of the "democratic conscience of the black Brazilian," called this a "legalized lynching," a "crime against democracy, which guarantees the respect of life and liberty to all men, regardless of color or racial origin"; "Protestam diretores de diversas entidas [*sic*] brasileiras," *Novo Horizonte*, May 1948, 1–2. On the comparison with the United States, see also "Civilização ou barbárie?," *Alvorada*, August 1946, 4; and José Soares, "Contraste," *Novo Horizonte*, July 1946, 3.

89. For the full text of the law and its justification, see *Diário do Congresso Nacional*, July 1950, 5513.

90. "O Senado condena a discriminação de cor," *Quilombo*, May 1949, 2.

91. *Diário do Congresso Nacional*, June 1950, no. 115. Cf. Hanchard, *Orpheus and Power*, 181n15.

92. Quoted in unsigned [Nascimento or Guerreiro Ramos?], "Prossegue a cruzada para a segunda abolição," *Quilombo*, June–July 1950, 8.

93. The most compelling evidence for this interpretation appears in Andrews, *Blacks and Whites*, 184–85. See also Hanchard, *Orpheus and Power*, 108.

94. See, e.g., unsigned [Nascimento or Guerreiro Ramos?], "Prossegue a cruzada para a segunda abolição," *Quilombo*, June–July 1950, 8; and "O projeto-lei Afonso Arinos," *Himalaya*, 12 August 1950, 5.

95. Andrews, *Blacks and Whites*, 185.

96. Guimarães, *Classes, raças e democracia*, 137. See also "The Myth of Racial Democracy," in Costa, *Brazilian Empire*, 234n1. The vast majority of secondary sources that attribute the term to *Casa-grande* do so in a general way, as received knowledge. Those which specifically cite the term's appearance, with page numbers, reference editions of Freyre's major works from the 1940s (usually the 1946 English translation, *The Masters and the Slaves*, for which Freyre wrote a new preface that does include the term *racial democracy* [xii]). See, e.g., Andrews, "Brazilian Racial Democracy," 6n13.

97. Bastide's influential articles, titled "Itinerário da democracia," appeared in the *Diário de São Paulo* on 17, 24, and 31 March 1944. Guimarães, *Classes, raças e democracia*, 145–46. On Ramos, see Campos, *Arthur Ramos*, 204–5, 255n19; and Guimarães, "Africanism and Racial Democracy," 70–71.

98. Guimarães, *Classes, raças e democracia*, 145–46.

99. Nascimento, "Candidatos negros e mulatos," *Quilombo*, February 1950, 1.

100. "Aos negros de São Paulo, ao povo em geral," *Mundo Novo*, 23 September 1950, 7.

101. A. de Athayde, "Comemoração do abolicionismo," *Novo Horizonte*, June 1950, 2.

102. Freyre, "A atitude brasileira," *Quilombo*, December 1948, 8.

103. See, e.g., G. de O. Barbosa, "Preconceito," *Notícias de Ébano*, October 1957, 3; A. Guerreiro Ramos, "Apresentação da negritude," *Quilombo*, June–July 1950, 11; and J. C. Leite, "Em pé na cozinha," *Alvorada*, March 1948, 4.

104. Nascimento, quoted in "Inaugurando o Congresso do Negro," *Quilombo*, June–July 1950, 1.

105. E.g., "Prefácio à 2a edição," in Abdias do Nascimento, *O negro revoltado* (1982), 9–10; Guimarães, *Classes, raças e democracia*, 95.

106. Pierson, *Negroes in Brazil*. On the effects of Pierson's U.S. experiences on his Brazilian research, see Bacelar, *A hierarquia das raças*, chap. 3.

107. Maio, "UNESCO and the Study of Race," 121–24; Campos, *Arthur Ramos*, 202–6. For an example of Ramos's later approach to the study of black Brazilians, see Arthur Ramos, *Aculturação negra*. For examples of his antiracist and pro–social science tracts, see Ramos, *Guerra*; and Ramos, *As ciências sociais*.

108. Maio, "UNESCO and the Study of Race," 122–24.

109. For this interpretation, see Telles, *Race in Another America*, 42–44; Maio, "UNESCO and the Study of Race"; Wade, *Blackness and Race Mixture*, chap. 2; and Andrews, "Brazilian Racial Democracy."

110. For Fernandes, who saw racism as an anachronism left over from slavery, racial discrimination would tend to disappear as Brazil became a more developed capitalist society and as blacks became more fully integrated into the broader working class. While Costa Pinto was much more skeptical about the market's ability to improve race relations (he feared capitalism would worsen racism in subsequent decades), he nonetheless saw racism not as an independent phenomenon but as a distorted manifestation of class competition. Fernandes, *A integração do negro*; Costa Pinto, *O negro*. See also Wagley, *Race and Class*; and Thales de Azevedo, *Les élites de couleur*.

111. Maio, "UNESCO and the Study of Race," 124.

112. For this perspective, see Motta, "Paradigms in the Study of Race Relations"; and Bacelar, *A hierarquia das raças*, chap. 3.

113. Marcos Chor Maio, "Costa Pinto e a crítica ao 'negro como espetáculo,'" in Costa Pinto, *O negro*, 40.

114. Villas Bôas, "Passado arcaico," 58.

115. Maio, "Costa Pinto e a crítica ao 'negro como espetáculo,'" in Costa Pinto, *O negro*, 40.

116. Wade, *Blackness and Race Mixture*, 38.

117. See, e.g., Bastide and Fernandes, *Relações raciais*; Fernandes, *A integração do negro*; Costa Pinto, *O negro*; Wagley, *Race and Class*; and Thales de Azevedo, *Les élites de couleur*.

118. A. Ramos, "A mestiçagem no Brasil," from "Democracia racial," *Quilombo*, May 1949, 8, and R. Bastide, "O movimento negro francês," from "Democracia racial," *Quilombo*, May 1950, 3.

119. A. de Athayde, "Homens como nós," *Novo Horizonte*, July 1947, 4 (from *O Cruzeiro*, 8 March 1947).

120. W. Machado, "Desapareceu o vermelho da folhinha," *Novo Horizonte*, June 1947, 1.

121. R. J. do Amaral, "Apêlo ao bom senso," *Alvorada*, April 1946, 1.

122. Ibid.; emphasis mine.

123. J. C. Leite, "As duas etapas da liberdade," *Novo Horizonte*, November–December 1954, 1. See also an article by Ruth Guimarães arguing against the ongoing folklorization of blacks and against depictions of blacks as seekers of favors; through education, Brazilians of color could "conquer the right" to enter into all areas of Brazilian society: "Nós, os negros," *Novo Horizonte*, March 1948, 4.

124. A. de Camargo, "Negro, você é importante!," *Novo Horizonte*, July 1947, 1.

125. S. C. Teixeira, "28 de setembro," *Alvorada*, October 1947, 3.

126. A. de Athayde, "Homens como nós," *Novo Horizonte*, July 1947, 4 (from *O Cruzeiro*, 8 March 1947).

127. C. Rego, "Venha uma segunda abolição," *Novo Horizonte*, March 1948, 4 (from *A Tribuna de Santos*, 19 March 1948).

128. G. Campos, "Que virá depois," *Novo Horizonte*, June 1946, 1.

129. W. D. Silva, "E assim viemos," *Novo Horizonte*, September 1946, 2.

130. Unsigned [Leite?], "Estudos brasileiros sobre o negro," *Niger*, September 1960, 5.

131. "Mundo negro," *Alvorada*, April 1947, 3. In general, the column tracked the accomplishments of U.S. blacks in the arts, in the military, in sports, and in

labor politics, as well as their experiences of racism. Twice there appeared articles on Africa—Liberia, specifically. But these highlighted Liberia's history as part of a broader history of African Americans (in the narrow sense). See "Centenário da Libéria," *Alvorada*, August 1947, 3; and "Écos do centenário da Libéria," *Alvorada*, October 1947, 3.

132. "Um sorriso d'África," *Novo Horizonte*, December 1946, 3.

133. "Na África," *Senzala*, February 1946, 13.

134. J. Conceição, "Para frente, todos!," *Quilombo*, May 1949, 5.

135. Unsigned [Leite?], "Nossa obra é de solidariedade humana," *Alvorada*, October 1945, 1.

136. A. Z., "A situação social do negro," *Novo Horizonte*, June–July 1949, 4 (from *Jornal de Debates*).

137. Ibid.

138. L. Bastos, "Para onde vae a afrologia?," *Clarim*, 28 September 1940, 4.

139. Ibid. See also A. Z., "A situação," *Novo Horizonte*, June–July 1949, 4.

140. Unsigned [Nascimento and/or Guerreiro Ramos], "O 1º Congresso do Negro Brasileiro," *Quilombo*, January 1950, 1.

141. "Universalidade da natureza humana," *A Voz da Negritude*, 1, in *Himalaya*, 8 October 1953.

142. See J. B. da Silva, "A inutilidade dos congressos," in Abdias do Nascimento, *O negro revoltado* (1982), 239–45. Silva's original speech was not preserved, but his interventions in the ensuing debate were. See also J. B. da Silva, "Guerreiro Ramos," in *Himalaya*, 30 September 1953, 4; and Costa Pinto, *O negro*, 261.

143. J. S. de Melo, "A voz do negro: Um toque de reunir," *Himalaya*, 12 August 1950, 2.

144. J. B. da Silva, "Salgado Filho e os negros," *Himalaya*, 12 August 1950, 2.

145. Silva and Leite, *E disse*, 153. According to Leite, it was Jorge Prado Teixeira, a young black man from São Paulo's interior active in São Paulo's black press, who facilitated contacts between black activists and UNESCO researchers—most famously, as informants for Fernandes's *A integração do negro*.

146. Guimarães, "Africanism and Racial Democracy," 71.

147. Unsigned [Leite?], "Estudos brasileiros sobre o negro," *Niger*, September 1960, 5. See, among many references, an article in *Alvorada* calling Ramos a "great friend of black Brazilians" ("Servindo à humanidade," September 1945, 4); one in *Quilombo* on Ramos's death titled "A morte de um grande amigo" (January 1950, 3); and one in *Novo Horizonte* hailing Bastide as a "sincere friend of the blacks of São Paulo" (October 1945, 1).

148. "Prefácio à 2a edição," in Abdias do Nascimento, *O negro revoltado* (1982), 9–10.

149. Nascimento and Nascimento, *Quilombo*, 7–8.

Chapter 5

1. F. Sabino, "Semente de ódio," *Diário Carioca* of 16 July 1949; "Racismo, no Brasil!," *Quilombo*, May 1950, 5 (from *O Globo*, 13 April 1950). See also sociologist

Paulo Duarte's articles in *O Estado de São Paulo*, 16 and 17 April 1947, accusing black activist organizations of being aggressively antiwhite.

2. G. Freyre, "A atitude brasileira," *Quilombo*, December 1948, 8.

3. A. Nascimento, "Convite ao encontro," *Quilombo*, May 1950, 5 (from *A Folha do Rio*, 6 May 1950). See also A. de O. Camargo, "Diretrizes da Convenção do Negro Brasileiro," *Senzala*, January 1946, 11; and F. Lucrécio, "Partido político," *Senzala*, February 1946, 14.

4. Skidmore, *Politics in Brazil*, 192; Burns, *History of Brazil*, 396.

5. Hasenbalg, "Race and Socioeconomic Inequalities," 30–32.

6. Ibid., 30–31. See also Nelson do Valle Silva, "Updating the Cost," 43–44.

7. See, e.g., Hasenbalg, *Discriminação e desigualdades raciais*; Nelson do Valle Silva, "White-Nonwhite Income Differentials"; and Ianni, *Raças e classes sociais*.

8. R. J. Amaral, "Basta de explorações," *Alvorada*, October 1945, 1. See also unsigned, "Teatro Experimental do Negro," *Senzala*, January 1946, 26–27; unsigned, "Um fato digno de nota," *Novo Horizonte*, May 1946, 4; and unsigned, "Um ponto de vista," *Alvorada*, August 1947, 3.

9. R. J. Amaral, "Basta de explorações," *Alvorada*, October 1945, 1.

10. Unsigned, "Um ponto de vista," *Alvorada*, August 1947, 3. See also R. Magalhães Júnior, "Os negros brasileiros e as suas aspirações," *Senzala*, February 1946, 19; and W. Machado, "Desapareceu o vermelho da folhinha," *Novo Horizonte*, June 1947, 1.

11. J. C. Leite, "As duas etapas da liberdade," *Novo Horizonte*, November–December 1954, 1.

12. R. J. Amaral, "O negro não tem problemas?," *Alvorada*, September 1945, 1.

13. J. C. Leite, "Preconceito casa grande e senzala," *Alvorada*, March 1947, 1.

14. See, e.g., J. P. Teixeira, "Problemas específicos dos negros brasileiros," *Novo Horizonte*, September 1954, 5; O. Guaranha, "Clubes e negros," *Novo Horizonte*, November–December 1954, 2; unsigned, "Protesto da Assembléia contra a discriminação racial," *O Mutirão*, June 1958, 1; and L. C. S. Paiva, "Aquí é como nos EEUU, disse um funcionário," *Hífen*, February 1960, 1.

15. R. J. Amaral, "Tese errada," *Alvorada*, June 1947, 4.

16. Ibid.

17. Thales de Azevedo, *Les élites de couleur*, 93–105; Costa Pinto, *O negro*, part 2, chaps. 2 and 3.

18. A. Ramos in "Há vários problemas do negro no Brasil," *Senzala*, February 1946, 18; emphasis mine.

19. In one of its earliest uses, in 1918, the term referred to Japanese immigrants, though by the 1930s similar language was applied to other groups, like Assyrians and Jews. Lesser, *Negotiating National Identity*, 66–76, 93.

20. Unsigned, "Um fato digno de nota," *Novo Horizonte*, May 1946, 4. See also unsigned, "Um ponto de vista," *Alvorada*, August 1947, 3.

21. J. C. Leite, "Advertência do momento," *Alvorada*, November 1947, 1.

22. Unsigned [Leite?], "Estudos brasileiros sobre o negro," *Niger*, September 1960, 5.

23. R. J. Amaral, "O negro não tem problemas?," *Alvorada*, September 1945, 1; emphasis in original. See also J. C. Leite, "A incompreensão do negro," *Alvorada*,

December 1947, 3; and Amaral, "Aurora de compreensão," *Alvorada*, August 1947, 1. Elsewhere, Leite complained of black leaders who reduced the black problem to "an unfortunate academic chat." Leite, "Laços humanos," *Alvorada*, August 1947, 1.

24. Silva and Leite, *E disse*, 162.

25. Comité Universitário Pró-candidatura Geraldo Campos de Oliveira, "Contra o capitalismo escravizador," *Mundo Novo*, 23 September 1950, 3.

26. A. de Castro, "Um representante do negro no Legislativo bandeirante," *Mundo Novo*, 23 September 1950, 3. See also "Aos negros de São Paulo, ao povo em geral," *Mundo Novo*, 23 September 1950, 8.

27. Silva and Leite, *E disse*, 148.

28. L. Lobato, "Nossa apresentação," *Notícias de Ébano*, October 1957, 1.

29. Unsigned, "Linha de frente," *Alvorada*, April 1947, 4. See also A. Barbosa, "O elemento negro na terra do Tio Sam," *Novo Horizonte*, July 1946, 1.

30. On regional identity in both periods, see Weinstein, "Racializing Regional Difference"; and Weinstein, "Celebrating Modernity."

31. On immigrants, especially Italian, see *Diário de São Paulo*, 25 January 1954, caderno 2, 1–7; on Syrio-Lebanese migrants and immigration more broadly, see 9–10. One article in the *Estado de São Paulo* (11, 68), on religious festivities in the colonial period, made mention (deep in its text) of the participation of some slaves, mainly to discuss the prohibition of *sambas* and *batuques* on the grounds that they caused "disturbances and immoralities."

32. *Estado de São Paulo*, 25 January 1954, 80.

33. *Diário de São Paulo*, 25 January 1954, 5. On the marginalization of blacks and Indians in the iconography and discourse of the quadricentennial more broadly, see Weinstein, "Celebrating Modernity."

34. Silva and Leite, *E disse*, 163.

35. Ibid., 99. See also "Mãe Preta: De todos nós," *Folha da noite*, 28 June 2008.

36. Weinstein, "Celebrating Modernity," 19–22.

37. Silva and Leite, *E disse*, 99.

38. On the Clube 220, see Andrews, *Blacks and Whites*, 215; and Silva and Leite, *E disse*, 170. For examples of Penteado's relatively conservative discourse regarding the Mãe Preta, see Weinstein, "Celebrating Modernity," 19–22.

39. Proceedings of 24 August 1946, *Anais da Assembléia Constituinte* (1950): 410–13. It was not, however (as activists associated with the TEN later claimed), Silva's intervention that derailed Nogueira's proposal but rather the deeper conviction among many legislators that race prejudice was not an issue in Brazilian society. See Semog and Nascimento, *Abdias Nascimento*, 150; and Elisa Larkin Nascimento, *Pan-africanismo*, 190.

40. The discussion of Trinidade's life and work is from Moore, "Solano Trinidade"; and Malinoff, "Modern Afro-Brazilian Poetry."

41. See "Poesia negra," *Quilombo*, May 1949, 3; and "Teatro Folclórico Brasileiro," *Quilombo*, January 1950, 9, 12.

42. Excerpt from S. Trinidade, "Negros," cited in Malinoff, "Modern Afro-Brazilian Poetry," 53.

43. S. Trinidade, quoted in Moore, "Solano Trinidade," 234.

44. On the friendly rivalry between Trinidade and Nascimento over class- versus race-based politics, see Semog and Nascimento, *Abdias Nascimento*, 86–87; and Silva and Leite, *E disse*, 155–57.

45. A. Nascimento, "Espírito e fisionomia do Teatro Experimental do Negro," *Quilombo*, June 1949, 11.

46. P. Leal, "Teatro negro do Brasil," *Quilombo*, March–April 1950, 11.

47. A. Guerreiro Ramos, "Apresentação da negritude," *Quilombo*, June–July 1950, 11.

48. Unsigned [Nascimento?], "A Conferência Nacional do Negro," *Quilombo*, June 1949, 6–7.

49. A. Nascimento, "Espírito e fisionomia do Teatro Experimental do Negro," *Quilombo*, June 1949, 11.

50. Ibid.

51. A. Nascimento, "Nós," *Quilombo*, December 1948, 1.

52. A. Nascimento, "Convite ao encontro," *Quilombo*, February 1950, 3 (from *Folha do Rio*, 6 May 1950).

53. In March 1946, for instance, in an interview with Nascimento for the *Diário Trabalhista*, Guerreiro Ramos announced his belief that "men of color should never organize to combat racial prejudice"; quoted in Guimarães and Macedo, "*Diário Trabalhista*," 153.

54. Maio, "Uma polêmica esquecida." See also Maio, "A questão racial"; and Lucia Oliveira, *A sociologia*.

55. This view of blacks as the "people," and of racial problems as part of the broader problems of Brazil's mixed-race poor, appeared frequently in Nascimento's interviews with black intellectuals, students, and workers in Rio from 1946 to 1948; Guimarães and Macedo, "*Diário Trabalhista*."

56. See, for instance, *Quilombo*'s claim that in São Paulo, "a racial discrimination of the type present in the United States is taking shape." "Carta de um líder," May 1950, 3. Cf. Motta-Maués, "Quem somos nós?," 177. Raymundo Souza Dantas, a prominent black writer, voiced a similar view in interviews with Rio's *Diário Trabalhista* in the 1940s. Guimarães and Macedo, "*Diário Trabalhista*," 154. See also my discussion of this point in chapter 4.

57. On the Renascença, see Giacomini, *A alma da festa*. On similar clubs and carnival groups earlier in the century, see Leonardo Pereira, "E o Rio dançou."

58. For a transcript of, and commentary on, this interaction, see Abdias do Nascimento, *O negro revoltado* (1968), 153–59.

59. This was a particularly sensitive subject for Guerreiro Ramos, who, despite his sociological training and extensive publications, had not managed to secure a prestigious academic post and instead worked as a government bureaucrat. The TEN, in this context, provided a visible academic outlet for his work on race. Maio, "Uma polêmica esquecida."

60. Costa Pinto, *O negro*, 245–60.

61. Motta-Maués, "Quem somos nós?," 170; Maio, "Uma polêmica esquecida," 150.

62. A. Guerreiro Ramos, "O plágio," *O Jornal*, 17 January 1954, 1.

63. Costa Pinto, "Ciência social e ideologia racial: Esclarecendo intencionais obscuridades," *O Jornal*, 10 January 1954, 2. This interaction reshaped Guerreiro

Ramos's views of the sociology of race in Brazil. See his critique of Costa Pinto in Guerreiro Ramos, *Introdução crítica*, 210n19. For an in-depth look at this rivalry, and for an overview of Guerreiro Ramos's work in this period, see Maio, "Uma polêmica esquecida"; and Maio, "A questão racial." On black Cariocas' struggles to claim and protect rights to intellectual authorship in other contexts, see Hertzman, "Brazilian Counterweight"; and Hertzman, "Surveillance and Difference."

64. Nascimento recounts these events (and quotes Alves) in Abdias do Nascimento, *O negro revoltado* (1982), 61.

65. Guerreiro Ramos, *Introdução crítica*, 215. See also his article "Sociologia clínica de um baiano 'claro,'" in *O Jornal*, 27 December 1953; and Guerreiro Ramos, *O processo*.

66. A. Nascimento, "A sociologia desaculturada," *O Jornal*, 31 October 1954, 5; emphasis mine.

67. A. Nascimento, "Nós," *Quilombo*, December 1948, 1.

68. On *Présence Africaine*, see *Quilombo*, December 1948, 3; and June 1949, 2. On "Black Orpheus," see *Quilombo*, January 1950, 6–7. On the visit of Albert Camus, see *Quilombo*, January 1950, 11.

69. "Roteiro negro de Albert Camus no Rio," *Quilombo*, January 1950, 11.

70. A. Nascimento, "Espírito e fisionomia do Teatro Experimental do Negro," *Quilombo*, June 1949, 11.

71. A. Guerreiro Ramos, "Apresentação da negritude," *Quilombo*, June–July 1950, 11.

72. See Hermano Vianna, *Mystery of Samba*, chap. 7. Not surprisingly, Cendrars appears several times in *Quilombo* articles; the issue of May 1950 (p. 8) published the introduction to his famous *Anthologie de la poésie nègre et malgache*.

73. Nóbrega and Santos, *Mãe Senhora*, 14–16.

74. Lühning, *Verger/Bastide*, 13. For details of Verger's youth before arriving in Bahia, see Lühning, "Pierre Fatumbi Verger," esp. 316–24. On Verger's life and work, see Nóbrega and Echeverria, *Verger*.

75. See Lühning, *Verger/Bastide*; and Le Bouler, *Le pied à l'étrier*.

76. Lühning, "Pierre Fatumbi Verger," 319.

77. I expand on Verger's "outsider" status and his differences with other Brazilian and foreign scholars working on Afro-Bahia in Alberto, "Terms of Inclusion," 256–59, 271–73.

78. Lühning, "Pierre Fatumbi Verger," 320–21; Lühning, *Verger/Bastide*, 15.

79. Verger to Herskovits, 29 January 1950 (NU, MJH, Africana 6, 35/36, B50, F27.)

80. The *ataoya* or king of Oshogbo, Eastern Nigeria, was Christian, but his temporal power had its roots in a spiritual pact one of his ancestors made with Oxum, goddess of sweet waters and love. See Lühning, *Verger/Bastide*, 31, 98.

81. Verger to Herskovits, 22 July 1950 (NU, MJH, Africana 6, 35/36, B50, F27).

82. Hadji Adeyemi II, Alafin of Oyo, to Mãe Senhora, 14 August 1952 (FPV, unfiled); reprinted in Nóbrega and Santos, *Mãe Senhora*, 105.

83. See Lima, "Ainda sobre a nação de queto," 69, 76.

84. See Verger, *Orixás*, 30. An overview of these debates appears in Nóbrega and Santos, *Mãe Senhora*, 23–24.

85. Deoscóredes dos Santos, *História de um terreiro*, 19.

86. Nóbrega and Santos, *Mãe Senhora*, 25, 143; Deoscóredes dos Santos, *História de um terreiro*, 19–23. Commentators in the Bahian press covered the event with pride; see "Cinquentenário de Senhora" and "Bodas de ouro de Senhora," both in *A Tarde*, 3 October 1958.

87. "Escritores e livros," *Correio da Manhã*, 16 December 1958; "Senhora está de volta à Bahia," *Jornal do Brasil*, 16 December 1958; "Visitou o Rio, Senhora, uma autêntica rainha do Candomblé da Bahia," *Mês*, January 1959.

88. Nóbrega and Santos, *Mãe Senhora*, 118, 142.

89. On these exchanges, see Verger's letter to Senhora of 11 March 1966, and Senhora's to Verger of 7 July 1959 (FPV, unfiled); reprinted in ibid., 106–7. I am grateful to Angela Lühning for sharing these and other samples of their correspondence.

90. Verger to Herskovits, 29 January 1950 (NU, MJH, Africana 6, 35/36, B54, F41).

91. Verger to Herskovits, 22 July 1950 (NU, MJH, Africana 6, 35/36, B54, F41).

92. Lühning, "O diálogo transatlântico."

93. *Vamos cantar a Bahia*, transcripts, 15 and 22 December 1958 (FPV, unfiled). I am grateful to Angela Lühning for sharing these with me. She discusses these radio shows, and other aspects of Verger's "trans-Atlantic dialogue" through sound recordings, in Lühning, "O diálogo transatlântico." On Verger's use of a similarly ingenious method involving photography, see also Alberto, "Terms of Inclusion," 270.

94. For a critique of the "Herskovitsean" ideas of a "primordial" Africa that shaped pre-1950s anthropological studies of Afro-Bahia, see Matory, *Black Atlantic Religion*, 38–45.

95. Lühning, *Pierre Verger*, 42.

96. I am thinking here of the IBEAA (mentioned below) and the CEAA (see chap. 6).

97. See the copious correspondence between Silva and academic centers (primarily African-related) across Africa, Latin America, and Europe in 1959 and 1960 (Arquivo CEAO, Correspondência 1959, 1960).

98. Agostinho da Silva, "O nascimento do CEAO"; Agostinho, "Agostinho da Silva."

99. Silva, "Missão para a Bahia," *Diário de Notícias*, 2–3 October 1960.

100. On these voyages, see Freyre, *Aventura e rotina*; Freyre, *Um brasileiro*.

101. Agostinho, "Agostinho da Silva," 11–14.

102. Ibid.

103. Lühning, "Pierre Fatumbi Verger," 323; Bacelar, *A hierarquia das raças*, chap. 5.

104. V. C. Lima, "O ensino do iorubá na Universidade da Bahia," *Diário de Notícias*, 2–3 October 1960.

105. Risério, *Avant-garde*; Rubim, "Os primórdios."

106. Silva and Leite, *E disse*, 175.

107. Leite, "Mundo negro: O renascimento africano," *Niger*, July 1960, 2–3.

108. "O mundo aprende com os negros da Abissínia a fazer a verdadeira democracia," *Notícias de Ébano*, October 1957, 2; "O despertar da África," *Hífen*, July 1960, 1. See also, among many others, "Discriminação racial na África do Sul" and "A união sul-africana na assembléia da ONU," in *Mundo Novo*, September 1950; "Congo Francês, Katanga, e outros," "Brasil faz apêlo a Portugal: Angola," and "Nyerere quer ver Tanganika integrando uma Federação dos Estados Africanos," in *Hífen*, July 1960, September 1960, and January 1962, respectively; "Lumumba em preto e branco,"

"Líder africano prega o amor próprio," and "Libertação da Rodésia causará guerra na África," in *O Ébano*, March 1961.

109. Unsigned, "Congo: Quando a independência vier," *Hífen*, June 1960, 1; F. S. Piauí, "África Negra e colonialismo," *Hífen*, December 1960, 3; Tio Natalino, "Ronda mensal," *Hífen*, January 1962, 5.

110. Leite, "O Congo e nós," *Niger*, August 1960, 1.

111. Caption to a photo titled "O momento africano na história do mundo," in "Mundo negro," *Niger*, August 1960, 2–3.

112. Leite, "Mundo negro: O renascimento africano," *Niger*, July 1960, 2–3.

113. See, e.g., "Noite afro-brasileira," on the "ballet afro-brasileiro" and other "folkloric" acts, *Hífen*, September 1960, 5.

114. Silva and Leite, *E disse*, 178. The title of the Campinas newspaper *Hífen* (which published many articles on contemporary African developments) also seems to hint at this "hyphenated" Afro-Brazilian identity.

115. Saraiva, *O lugar da África*, 24–50. The pro-Africa minority included scholars who in the late 1950s and early 1960s wrote extensively on the potentials of Brazil's relations with the Afro-Asian world: Menezes, *Ásia, África*; Menezes, *O Brasil e o mundo*; Portella, *África*; Rodrigues, *Brasil e África*.

116. Saraiva, *O lugar da África*, esp. chaps. 3 and 4.

117. See, e.g., Itamaraty's *Relatório* 1961, 41–42.

118. Quadros, "Brazil's New Foreign Policy," 24.

119. Saraiva, *O lugar da África*, 91.

120. Portella, *África*, 87–92. For similar claims, see Menezes, *O Brasil e o mundo*, 12–13; and Rodrigues, *Brasil e África*, vol. 1, 117.

121. E. Portella, "O dilema cultural da África e a questão de Angola na ONU," *Caderno Econômico* 164 (1962): 58, quoted in Saraiva, *O lugar da África*, 92.

122. Portella, *África*, 87–92.

123. Quadros, "Brazil's New Foreign Policy," 24. A. J. B. de Menezes, for instance, referenced Brazil's "solução adequada de problemas raciais e sociais" as one of his nation's fundamental qualifications for adopting a position of leadership in Africa. Menezes, *O Brasil e o mundo*, 7. See also Rodrigues, *Brasil e África*, vol. 1, 105.

124. Saraiva, *O lugar da África*, 91.

125. José H. Rodrigues, quoted in ibid., 93. In a book that appeared just as this manuscript was going into production, Jerry Dávila adds new depth to our understanding of how Brazil's post-1961 African foreign policy reflected and reshaped contemporary ideas of Brazilian identity and racial democracy. See Dávila, *Hotel Trópico*.

126. This caused controversy in Brazilian diplomatic circles; historian José H. Rodrigues, for instance, accused Quadros of "reverse racism" in favoring Dantas. Saraiva, *O lugar da África*, 91.

127. Selcher, "Afro-Asian Dimension," 94, cited in Saraiva, *O lugar da África*, 90.

128. Saraiva, *O lugar da África*, 52.

129. "Bolsistas africanos aprenderão português em três meses para cursar as faculdades bahianas," *A Tarde*, [25] November 1961 (approximate date; undated clipping from FPV, folder: FGM [hereafter F: FGM]). See also "Estudantes africanos começam

a conhecer o Brasil pela Bahia," *Jornal da Bahia*, 17 December 1961; and "Primazia da UBa nas relações com África," *Jornal da Bahia*, 25 November 1961.

130. Agostinho da Silva, "O nascimento do CEAO," 5–8.

131. "Bolsistas africanos," *A Tarde*, [25] November 1961 (FPV, F: FGM).

132. "Life among the Grantees," *JB*, SEA, December 1962 (SC, MJH Papers, box 73, folder 728).

133. Articles on the CEAO's leading role in establishing cultural and academic contacts with Africa were frequent in the Bahian press of the early 1960s; indeed, two of the men in charge of the CEAO's publications and public relations areas were staff members of the *Jornal da Bahia* (*JB*, SEA, December 1962, 2). See, e.g., a series of clipped articles from FPV, F: FGM, apparently from 1961: "Brasil, Bahia e África," "CEAO no conselho de curadores do Instituto Afro-Asiático," and "Nossos bolsistas."

134. "Brasil, Bahia e África," [December 1961?] (FPV, F: FGM).

135. See, e.g., "African Diplomats Visit Salvador," *JB*, SEA, December 1962; and "Estudantes africanos começam a conhecer o Brasil pela Bahia," *Jornal da Bahia*, 17 December 1961. For more on this subject, see Alberto, "Terms of Inclusion," 302–37.

136. On Romana's visit, see Alberto, "Para Africano Ver."

137. Nóbrega and Santos, *Mãe Senhora*, 136, 142–43. The title was conceived of by writer Zora Seljan, wife of diplomat Antonio Olinto, and, like her husband, a devotee of Senhora's candomblé.

138. Deoscóredes dos Santos, *História de um terreiro*, 31.

Chapter 6

1. The discussion of politics in this section is drawn from Skidmore, *Politics of Military Rule*; and Skidmore, *Politics in Brazil*.

2. Silva and Leite, *E disse*, 168, 194.

3. Semog and Nascimento, *Abdias Nascimento*, 156.

4. Thales de Azevedo, *Democracia racial*, 53n27. See also Abdias do Nascimento, "O genocídio," 124–25.

5. Renato Ortiz, *Cultura brasileira*, 90–106; Guimarães, *Classes, raças e democracia*, 158.

6. Concerns about the accuracy of color categories may also have been a factor in this decision. Nobles, *Shades of Citizenship*, 110–13.

7. Hanchard, *Orpheus and Power*, 113–14; Kennedy, "Political Liberalization," 203.

8. Ministério do Exército, Gabinete do Ministro, to DOPS/Guanabara; "Show 'Brasil Export,'" 14 December 1971, DOPS; Secreto, 97 F456, APERJ. Many thanks to Victoria Langland for sharing this wonderful source.

9. For an account of this and other examples of censorship of dissenting views on race relations, see Skidmore, "Race and Class," 16; and Telles, *Race in Another America*, 40–42.

10. Semog and Nascimento, *Abdias Nascimento*, 164–65.

11. Saraiva, *O lugar da África*, 97–123.

12. Ibid., 125–77.

13. "Brasil & Cia.: Estamos fazendo a África," *Isto É*, 10 October 1979, 42–46.

14. Quoted in Saraiva, *O lugar da África*, 144. See also the Afro-Brazilian Chamber of Commerce's publication for this period, *Afro-Chamber*.

15. Saraiva, *O lugar da África*, 179–82; Dzidzienyo, "African Connection," 140; Shaffer, "What Will You Do?," 28.

16. Shaffer, "What Will You Do?," 30.

17. Ibid.; Dzidzienyo, "African Connection."

18. Saraiva, *O lugar da África*, 137–38.

19. See, e.g., "Brasil & Cia.: Estamos fazendo a África," *Isto É*, 10 October 1979, 42–46; "Gabriela, quem diria, acabou socialista," *Jornal do Brasil*, 8 May 1979.

20. See, e.g., his presentation of Bahia's Olga do Alaketo. Valladares, *Impact of African Culture*, 103–4. Valladares's text was published simultaneously in English, Portuguese, and French; I quote directly from the English.

21. Ibid., 39, 58, 83.

22. Renato Ortiz, *Cultura brasileira*, 96. On this "backward look," see Burns, *History of Brazil*, 474–75.

23. Valladares, "Casas de Cultura," *Cultura* 10 (April 1968): 58, cited in Renato Ortiz, *Cultura brasileira*, 100–101.

24. Valladares, *Impact of African Culture*, 108.

25. Ibid., 11, 15.

26. The letter appears in Abdias do Nascimento, "Sitiado em Lagos," 321–32.

27. The original paper was reprinted in the leftist magazine *Versus* (São Paulo) in three installments: November 1977, p. 40; December–January 1977–78, pp. 40–41; and February 1978, p. 41. For a similar contemporaneous critique, see Dzidzienyo, *Position of Blacks*.

28. At one point during the FESTAC, Nascimento suggested that Brazilian representatives educate themselves on racial discrimination by reading a series of contemporary black activist periodicals: *Tição* (Porto Alegre); *Jornegro* and *Cadernos Negros* (São Paulo); and *SINBA* and *Força Negra* (Rio de Janeiro). Abdias do Nascimento, "Sitiado em Lagos," 307.

29. Details about the CEAA in this paragraph are from my interview with José Maria Nunes Pereira on 21 February 2002, as well as from Helene Monteiro, "O ressurgimento," 49–56, and José Maria Nunes Pereira, "Os estudos africanos," 86–103.

30. Helene Monteiro, "O ressurgimento," 56–57.

31. Interviews with Amauri Pereira and Carlos Alberto Medeiros, in Alberti and Pereira, *Histórias do movimento negro*, 93–95, 88.

32. Skidmore, *Politics of Military Rule*.

33. Andrews, *Blacks and Whites*, 190–91.

34. Helene Monteiro, "O ressurgimento," 57–61; José Maria Nunes Pereira, "Os estudos africanos," 109, 122. On Fanon's influence on this generation of black activists, see interview with Pereira, in Alberti and Pereira, *Histórias do movimento negro*, 74–75.

35. Helene Monteiro, "O ressurgimento," 58.

36. Interview with Paulo Roberto dos Santos, in ibid., 60–61.

37. On SINBA, see interview with Yedo Ferreira, in Contins, *Lideranças negras*, 467. On the IPCN, see interview with Pereira, in Alberti and Pereira, *Histórias do movimento negro*, 196; and Helene Monteiro, "O ressurgimento," 85.

38. Interview with Pereira, in Alberti and Pereira, *Histórias do movimento negro*, 37–39. The "two-thirds" law was Vargas's law of December 1930 requiring all Brazilian industrial firms to employ Brazilian nationals as at least two-thirds of their total workforce.

39. Interview with Ferreira, in ibid., 136–37.

40. Interview with Pereira, in ibid., 139.

41. *SINBA* occasionally received articles from its "international contributor," Thierno Gueye (a Senegalese friend of the organization who traveled abroad frequently), or from other black activists, like Joel Rufino dos Santos or Léa Garcia.

42. Interview with Pereira, in Alberti and Pereira, *Histórias do movimento negro*, 128.

43. Araujo, *A utopia fragmentada*, 171.

44. "Comunicado," July 1977, 7; and "A volta," April 1979, 1. All articles cited in this section are from *SINBA*, unless otherwise noted.

45. "O que é a África?," July 1977, 5.

46. "Definição de termos," September 1980, 5. See also their critique of what passed for Afro-Brazilian culture in the FESTAC: "Quem deveria ter representado o Brasil no Festival de Arte Negra na Nigéria?," July 1977, 4.

47. "Movimento negro e o culturalismo," March 1980, 3; and "Por quê o Black-Rio incomoda?," July 1977, 6.

48. "Movimento negro e o culturalismo," March 1980, 3.

49. Ibid.

50. "O que é a África?," July 1977, 5.

51. "Movimento negro e o culturalismo," March 1980, 3. See also "Reflexão," March 1980, 4.

52. "O que o Brasil tem a ver com Idi Amin?," April 1979, 2.

53. Ibid.

54. "Apartheid é o regime racista da África do Sul," April 1979, 2.

55. "Depoimento de um líder estudantil de Soweto," July 1977, 1.

56. See "Comércio Brasil-África do Sul," "A pergunta que Helmut Schimidt não respondeu," "Irã, lição e exemplo," and "Imprensa Livre," April 1979, 2, 7.

57. "Afinal, quem tem razão?," April 1979, 4.

58. On discrimination on a range of fronts, see "O racismo nosso de cada dia," August 1979, 6; March 1980, 6; September 1980, 6; "Violência" and "Racismo e controle da natalidade," March 1980, 2, 5; "Lei Afonso Arinos," "A diretora que não sabia," and "Da olimpíada para a cadeia," September 1980, 6; and "Má companhia," April 1979, 6. For critiques of the hypocrisy of Brazilian racism, see "Definição de termos," March 1980, 3; and "O Hitler negro," April 1979, 6. On Freyre's ideas of racial harmony, see "Homenagem póstuma," March 1980, 8; "Descanse em paz," September 1980, 4; and "Comentário," September 1980, 4.

59. "Repressão e racismo," March 1980, 5. See also "Racismo do Brasil e da África do Sul," September 1980, 5.

60. "O Brasil e o apartheid: Exemplo de dois Estados voltados contra seus próprios povos," in "Seminário sobre o racismo e o apartheid na África austral," September 1980, 7. See also "Faz o que eu mando, não faz o que eu faço," March 1980, 7.

61. "Movimento Negro e consciência," April 1979, 3. See also, in the same issue, "Um negro após a ascensão," 4; and another installment of "Movimento Negro e consciência," August 1979, 3.

62. Semog and Nascimento, *Abdias Nascimento*, 164–65.

63. For an example of one prominent activist's transition from the Left to the independent black movement, see Gonzalez, "O movimento negro," 31–33, and interview with Gonzalez, in Pereira and Hollanda, *Patrulhas ideológicas*, 202–12.

64. "Movimento Negro, um movimento social," September 1980, 3. In March 1980, *SINBA* ran an article advocating black activists' distance from the process of party reformulation. Only the Partido dos Trabalhadores (Workers' Party) had even addressed the issue of race, the article argued; others either did not care about blacks or did not want to deal with "minority" questions. "Movimento negro e a reformulação partidária," March 1980, 1. See also Ferreira and Pereira, *O movimento negro*.

65. "Movimento Negro e Consciência," April 1979, 3.

66. Andrews, *Blacks and Whites*, 159–60.

67. "Item cor: Quem será contra?," August 1979, 4.

68. The headline for their September 1980 issue was "Censo 80: Exemplo de mistificação de um Estado racista." For more on the census campaign, and especially its articulation with other black activist groups in Rio de Janeiro and São Paulo, see Andrews, *Blacks and Whites*, 202; and Nobles, *Shades of Citizenship*, 115–19.

69. Telles, *Race in Another America*, 82. The survey yielded the following percentages among major color categories: white (*branco*), 41.9%; black (*preto* and *negro*), 7.6%; *pardo*, 7.6%; and *moreno*, 34.4%. Nobles, *Shades of Citizenship*, 113–14.

70. "Não basta apenas a inclusão do item COR," August 1979, 3.

71. "Definições de termos," April 1979, 3.

72. Nobles, *Shades of Citizenship*, 115–19.

73. Ibid., 105.

74. Helene Monteiro, "O ressurgimento," 84–85.

75. On Rio's political police, see Darién J. Davis, "Arquivos das Polícias"; and APERJ, *Os arquivos das polícias políticas*.

76. On the tendency of the secret police during the Estado Novo to read black activism as communism, see Carneiro and Kossoy, *A imprensa confiscada*, 54–55. See also chapter 3 in this book, n. 87.

77. One report, for instance, referred to the "black racist movement in Brazil." "Carlos Miguel Cabo Verde," 11 February 1977, DGIE 259, 46–40. (The citations for these APERJ files will follow the above format: subject, date, sector and folder number, and page numbers, which are in descending order in the original documents.) See also "Racismo negro," 18 May 1977, DGIE 258, 629–22; and "Racismo negro," 25 April 1977, DGIE 258, 632.

78. "Sociedade de Intercâmbio Brasil-África," 14 October 1977, DGIE 252, 160.

79. "Treinamento de guerrilheiros brasileiros em Angola," 18 October 1976, Comunismo 148, 233. See also a similar (earlier) investigation of Brazilian guerrilla

fighters training in Algiers and Cuba, allegedly making contact along the way with Cape Verde and Guinea-Bissau's PAIGC, Angola's MPLA, the Frente de Libertação of Portugal, and Algeria's El Fatah. "Grupo da Ilha," 3 April 1972, Secreto 104, 410.

80. "Centro de Informação e Documentação Anti-colonial (CIDAC): Portugal; Centro de Estudos Afro-Asiáticos; Referência: José Maria Nunes Pereira," DOPS 226, 69 (subpages A–O) and 386.

81. "Contatos PCB/FRELIMO," 11 June 1980, Comunismo 156, 319–18. See also "Frelimo—Moçambique—Portugal," Comunismo 159, 223.

82. For example, one "Pedido de busca," or search request, targeted a Seminar on Racism and Apartheid in Southern Africa, to take place in May 1980 (one of the planned lectures was "Brazil and Apartheid"). Police were instructed to gather the names of speakers and the subjects of their speeches, estimate the number of people at each event, and indicate who sponsored the seminar, as well as identify any known leftists, politicians, or clergymen present. "1º Seminário Sobre o Racismo e o Apartheid na África Austral," 20 May 1980, DGIE 291, 439, and 428. See also "'Moçambique: Primeira Machambas'—Livro de Propaganda," 20 July and 20 May 1977, DGIE 226-A, 34–23.

83. Gonzalez, "O movimento negro," 35–37.

84. Quoted in Helene Monteiro, "O ressurgimento," 97.

85. Interview with Pereira, in Alberti and Pereira, *Histórias do movimento negro*, 139–40; Helene Monteiro, "O ressurgimento," 84–86, 100–101.

86. "Quem somos?," *Boletim do IPCN*, June 1975, 1. All articles cited in this section are from the *Boletim do IPCN*, unless otherwise noted.

87. "O que queremos," June 1975, 1.

88. "Olorun Baba Min [*sic*] para a Nigéria," June 1975, 1.

89. B. do Nascimento, "Zumbi de N'Gola Djanga," July 1977, 1. Nascimento was also the founder of a smaller black student organization at the UFF, the Grupo de Trabalho André Rebouças. The Arquivo Nacional now holds her papers, including several GTAR publications (Fundo 2D, "Maria Beatriz do Nascimento"). Nascimento was murdered in Rio in 1995 while attempting to defend a friend from an armed man.

90. "Racismo Negro," 18 May 1977, DGIE 258, 629–22.

91. "O que queremos," June 1975, 1.

92. Ibid.

93. "O negro e a história," July 1976, 3.

94. B. do Nascimento, "Zumbi de N'Gola Djanga," July 1977, 1.

95. "O canto universal da negritude," July 1976, 5.

96. See Andrews, *Blacks and Whites*, 212–18.

97. "Racismo Negro," 18 May 1977, DGIE 258, 629–22.

98. On the Black Rio phenomenon, see Alberto, "When Rio Was *Black*"; McCann, "Black Pau"; Dunn, *Brutality Garden*, 177–87; and Hermano Vianna, *O mundo funk carioca*.

99. Lena Frias, "Black Rio: O orgulho (importado) de ser negro no Brasil," *Jornal do Brasil*, 17 July 1976; Tárik de Souza, "Soul: Sociologia e mercado," *Jornal do Brasil*, 27 August 1976; Tarlis Batista, "Os Blacks no embalo do soul," *Manchete*, 11 September 1976; Roberto M. Moura, "Carta aberta ao Black-Rio," *O Pasquim*, 2–8 September

1977. I develop the cultural politics of leftist nationalism further in Alberto, "When Rio Was *Black*," 18–20.

100. "Racismo," *O Globo*, 26 April 1977; Ibraim de Leve, "'Black Power' no Brasil," *O Globo*, 1 October 1977 (who explained that "no Brasil não existe racismo"); and Gilberto Freyre's article denouncing soul as separatist and un-Brazilian, "Atenção Brasileiros," *Diário de Pernambuco* (Recife), 15 May 1977. A secret police report noted the soul bands' "nomes . . . bombásticos," like Black Power, as it tried to discern whether the phenomenon constituted a political threat. "Black Rio," DGIE 252, 22 July 1976, 10.

101. "Black Rio," DGIE 252, 22 July 1976, 10.

102. Quoted in "Black Rio," *Um e Meio* (supplement of the *Jornal do Commercio*), 20–21 November 1977.

103. *Boletim do IPCN*, July 1976; Paulo Roberto dos Santos, quoted in Helene Monteiro, "O ressurgimento," 76.

104. The MAM at this time was a site of cultural innovation and opposition to the regime, also closely watched by the police for "subversive" activities held there. DGIE 252, 125–22, 30.

105. Paulo Roberto dos Santos, quoted in Helene Monteiro, "O ressurgimento," 83.

106. "Boletim do Instituto de Pesquisas das Culturas Negras," 9 January 1978, DGIE 252, 197.

107. From *Boletim do IPCN*, July 1977, 1; accompanying report "Boletim do Instituto de Pesquisas das Culturas Negras," 9 January 1978, DGIE 252, 197; *Boletim* comprises pages 196–89.

108. The list of organizations included local and national entities like the CEAA (Rio de Janeiro), the Afro-Brazilian Chamber of Commerce (São Paulo), and the carnival group Filhos de Gandhi (Salvador da Bahia). "Racismo Negro," 18 May 1977, DGIE 258, 629–22.

109. Ibid.

110. "Braço forte," from *Boletim do IPCN*, July 1977, 1, accompanying report "Boletim do Instituto de Pesquisas das Culturas Negras," 9 January 1978, DGIE 252, 197.

111. "Racismo Negro," 18 May 1977, DGIE 258, 629–22. I have found no evidence of funds from the soul dances being used to support the IPCN's activities.

112. Interview with Pereira, in Alberti and Pereira, *Histórias do movimento negro*, 141. Scholars sympathetic to civil rights struggles in the United States would later reverse the political valence of these different international affiliations, highlighting the soul phenomenon's embrace of a distinctly "black," U.S.-derived aesthetic as one of the most radical moments of racial consciousness in Brazil. See, e.g., Hanchard, *Orpheus and Power*, 111–19; and Mitchell, "Blacks and the *Abertura*." In these accounts, however, SINBA's overtures toward a politicized Africa are lost, especially in Hanchard's study, which sees SINBA as succumbing to "the path of unchartered culturalism" in its focus on Africa (88–90).

113. Interview with Pereira, in Alberti and Pereira, *Histórias do movimento negro*, 141.

114. "A volta," *SINBA*, April 1979, 1. The fact that the IPCN received funding from U.S. sources, whereas SINBA (proudly) did not, partly explains the first group's

greater security and longevity. See Hanchard, *Orpheus and Power*, 89; and Moutinho, "Negociando discursos," esp. chap. 1.

115. See, e.g., the IPCN's list of yearly activities in *Boletim do IPCN*, July 1976, 1; and Centro de Estudos Afro-Asiáticos, "CEAA: Cinco anos."

116. An IPCN *Boletim* for 1984 lists the previous year's committee of directors as composed of the two most prominent SINBA members: Amauri Mendes Pereira and Yedo Ferreira.

117. Caldwell, *Negras in Brazil*, chap. 6; Álvarez, *Engendering Democracy*, chap. 4.

118. Cited in Gonzalez, "O movimento negro."

119. Unsigned, "A omissão da mulher negra," *SINBA*, August 1979, 4.

120. Gonzalez, "O movimento negro," 34–35.

121. Interview with Pereira, in Alberti and Pereira, *Histórias do movimento negro*, 196.

122. Unsigned, "A omissão da mulher negra," *SINBA*, August 1979, 4; Léa Garcia, "Ação das mulheres negras," and Pedrina de Deus, "Mulher negra e as lutas feministas," *SINBA*, March 1980, 4.

123. "Comunicação mulheres," and L. Garcia, "Ação das mulheres negras," in *SINBA*, March 1980, 8, 4.

124. On these groups, including the Nzinga/Coletivo de Mulheres Negras (1983) in which Lélia Gonzalez participated, see Caldwell, *Negras in Brazil*, 157–61.

125. Interview with Gonzalez, in Pereira and Hollanda, *Patrulhas ideológicas*, 211.

126. In ibid.

127. Risério, "Carnaval," 90–93; Risério, *Carnaval ijexá*, 47–70; Daniel Crowley, *African Myth*, 20–21.

128. Risério, *Carnaval ijexá*, 24; Bairros, "Pecados no 'paraíso racial,'" 290–92.

129. Bairros, "Pecados no 'paraíso racial,'" 294, 305–6.

130. Risério, *Carnaval ijexá*, 27–37; Sansone, *Blackness without Ethnicity*, chap. 4.

131. Reggae also became very popular in Bahia beginning in the mid-1970s, thanks in great part to the recordings of Bahian artist Gilberto Gil. Dunn, *Brutality Garden*, 184–87.

132. Quoted in Risério, *Carnaval ijexá*, 38.

133. Interview with Vovô, in Alberti and Pereira, *Histórias do movimento negro*, 143–44.

134. See, e.g., "Bloco racista, nota destoante," *A Tarde*, 12 February 1975; reprinted in Jônatas da Silva, "História de lutas negras," 279.

135. Interview with Vovô, in Alberti and Pereira, *Histórias do movimento negro*, 144.

136. Risério, *Carnaval ijexá*, 40–43.

137. Ibid., 58.

138. On positive representations of the Mãe Preta in Candomblé, see Matory, *Black Atlantic Religion*, 200–203.

139. Eliézer Gómez Guimarães, "Senhora, Mãe Preta do Brasil e Iyanasô do Reino de Oyó, na Nigéria," *A Tarde*, 28 March 1970 (special supplement).

140. Agier, "As Mães Pretas."

141. Bule Bule and Onildo Barbosa, "Mãe Preta foi e é ama, mestra, e protetora," quoted in ibid., 198–200.

142. Interview with Vovô, in Alberti and Pereira, *Histórias do movimento negro*, 238.

143. On this dynamic, see Pinho, *Mama Africa*.

144. Andrews, *Blacks and Whites*, 191–92.

145. Interview with Cuti (Luiz Silva), in Alberti and Pereira, *Histórias do movimento negro*, 77.

146. See, e.g., "Imprensa x África," July 1978, 8; "Todos querem salvar a África: Por quê?," March 1978, 8; "Apartheid: Racismo e exploração," May 1978, 8, all in *Jornegro*.

147. "O sítio racista," *Jornegro*, no. 6 [no month], 1979, 15.

148. For instance, "Aqui ninguém tem nome," March 1978, 4–5; "Abolição?," May 1978, 6; "E a vida continua . . . ," July 1978, 2; "O asfalto e a favela," November 1978, 2; and "Alto falante de Campinas," no. 6 [no month], 1979, 4, all in *Jornegro*.

149. "James Brown," November 1978, 8; "E depois do Black Pau?," July 1978, 5; "Agora falando soul," May 1978, 1, 4–5; "Gilberto Gil," no. 7 [no month], 1979, all in *Jornegro*.

150. "Apresentação," *Cadernos Negros*, no. 1, 25 November 1978, cited in Gonzalez, "O movimento negro," 25. See also "África, poesia e vida," *Jornegro*, November 1978, 6.

151. Other important organizations at the time include the Clube Coimbra (with its publication, *Árvore das Palavras*) and the Grupo de Divulgação e Arte Negra (and its journal *GANA*). Their journals (which also included frequent articles on African politics and culture) were available at the time of my research in the extensive black press collection at the Centro de Estudos Afro-Asiáticos, Universidade Cândido Mendes, though this collection appears to have gone missing during the transfer of the CEAA's collections to the UCAM library. On the Clube Coimbra, see the interview with Flávio Jorge Rodrigues da Silva, in Alberti and Pereira, *Histórias do movimento negro*, 164–65.

152. See Hanchard, *Orpheus and Power*, 122–25.

153. "África," *Versus*, March 1979, 37.

154. Untitled, *Versus*, March–April 1978, 42.

155. Rio's Abdias do Nascimento is an obvious exception to this pattern, but his exile limited his ability to mentor young activists for much of the 1970s.

156. Silva and Leite, *E disse*, 168, 194.

157. Interview with Aristides Barbosa, in Barbosa, *Frente Negra Brasileira*, 27–29; Silva and Leite, *E disse*, 170–71.

158. Interviews with Ivair Alves dos Santos and Cuti, in Alberti and Pereira, *Histórias do movimento negro*, 90–91.

159. E. Oliveira e Oliveira, "Uma quinzena do negro," in Governo do Estado de São Paulo, Secretaria de Cultura, Ciência e Tecnologia, Pinacoteca do Estado, "Na Pinacoteca do Estado, 'A imprensa negra em São Paulo' (13 maio–26 junho 1977)" (exhibition booklet).

160. See, e.g., O. Camargo, "Pequeno mapa da poesia negra," July 1977, 31–33 (on poets Lino Guedes and Gervásio de Moraes); "Imprensa negra," August–September 1977, 33; "A Frente Negra Brasileira," February 1978, 40 (including an interview with Francisco Lucrécio), all in *Versus*.

161. Interview with Cuti, in Alberti and Pereira, *Histórias do movimento negro*, 91–92. The book is Silva and Leite, *E disse*.

162. For an overview of these projects, see Silva and Leite, *E disse*, 197.

163. Andrews, *Blacks and Whites*, 193.

164. Interview with Milton Barbosa, in Alberti and Pereira, *Histórias do movimento negro*, 150–51; Gonzalez, "Unified Black Movement," 123–25. On the emergence of the MNU, see also Hanchard, *Orpheus and Power*, 125–29; Andrews, *Blacks and Whites*, 193–94; Abdias do Nascimento and Elisa Larkin Nascimento, "Reflexões sobre o movimento negro"; and Elisa Larkin Nascimento, *Panafricanismo*, 215–18.

165. Interview with Pereira, in Alberti and Pereira, *Histórias do movimento negro*, 159; Andrews, *Blacks and Whites*, 194.

166. Cited in Alberti and Pereira, *Histórias do movimento negro*, 159–60.

167. Gonzalez, "Unified Black Movement," 125.

168. Ibid., 128–29.

169. See, e.g., interviews with Pereira and Flávio Jorge Rodrigues da Silva, in Alberti and Pereira, *Histórias do movimento negro*, 93–95, 98.

170. Andrews, *Blacks and Whites*, 215–16.

171. Ibid.

172. F. Penteado, Program of the 104th Anniversary of the Law of the Free Womb, cited in J. Minka and N. M. Pereira, "28 de setembro," *Versus*, September 1977, 28.

173. J. Minka and N. M. Pereira, "28 de setembro," *Versus*, September 1977, 28. See also the article by Hamilton Cardoso, editor of *Versus*'s "Afro-Latino-América" section, "Branco e sem mácula," *Isto É*, 26 September 1979.

174. Interview with Ivair Alves dos Santos, in Alberti and Pereira, *Histórias do movimento negro*, 201.

Epilogue

1. For an overview, see Mitchell, "Blacks and the *Abertura*"; Barcelos, "Struggling in Paradise"; Hanchard, *Orpheus and Power*; and Abdias do Nascimento and Elisa Larkin Nascimento, "Reflexões sobre o movimento negro."

2. Telles, *Race in Another America*, 50.

3. Ibid., 48–49; Andrews, *Blacks and Whites*, 204–7. On blacks in the Brazilian legislature, see Ollie Johnson, "Racial Representation."

4. Andrews, *Blacks and Whites*, 211–33; Hanchard, *Orpheus and Power*, 142–54.

5. This campaign received funding from the U.S.-based Ford Foundation. Nobles, *Shades of Citizenship*, 151. U.S. foundations' aid to black organizations in Brazil has provided more ammunition to those who see these groups as imitative or un-Brazilian. Andrews, *Blacks and Whites*, 495. For the latest version of this critique, and a lucid counterpoint, see Bourdieu and Wacquant, "On the Cunning of Imperialist Reason"; and Telles, "U.S. Foundations."

6. So will the 2010 census, according to "IBGE inicia contagem regressiva para o censo 2010": <www.ibge.gov.br/home/presidencia/noticias/noticia_visualiza.php?id_noticia=1602&id_pagina=1>, accessed 6 May 2010.

7. Despite the fact that the percentages of Brazilians identifying as *preto* or *branco* have decreased over time, *branco* remains the category chosen by the majority of

Brazilians (54% in the 2000 census), while those choosing *preto* are in the single digits (6.1% in 2000). Nobles, *Shades of Citizenship*, 160. (Figures for the 2000 census are from Telles, *Race in Another America*, 45.)

8. The percentages decreased from 5.9% in 1980 to 5% in 1991. Nobles, *Shades of Citizenship*, 160.

9. Telles, *Race in Another America*, 105.

10. Instituto de Pesquisa Econômica Aplicada website, "2010: Ano da maioria absoluta de negros," <www.ipea.gov.br/005/00502001.jsp?ttCD_CHAVE=374&bt Imprimir=SIM>, accessed 6 May 2010.

11. For overviews of affirmative action policies, see Telles, *Race in Another America*, 58–77; Sérgio da Silva Martins, Carlos Alberto Medeiros, and Elisa Larkin Nascimento, "Paving Paradise: The Road from 'Racial Democracy' to Affirmative Action in Brazil," *Journal of Black Studies* 34, no. 6 (2004): 787–816; Htun, "From 'Racial Democracy' to Affirmative Action"; Reichmann, *Race in Contemporary Brazil*; and Heringer, "Mapeamento de ações e discursos."

12. Telles, *Race in Another America*, 73–75.

13. For an example of this second viewpoint, see Fry et al., *Divisões perigosas*.

14. "Apresentação," in Nascimento and Nascimento, *Quilombo*. See chapter 4 in this book for discussion.

15. Sheriff, *Dreaming Equality*.

16. Telles, *Race in Another America*, 63–73.

BIBLIOGRAPHY

Archives and Periodicals Collections

Academia Brasileira de Letras, Biblioteca (Rio de Janeiro)
    Newspaper files by subject
Arquivo do Estado de São Paulo (São Paulo)
    Fundo Departamento Estadual de Ordem Política e Social
Arquivo Nacional (Rio de Janeiro)
    Papers of Maria Beatriz do Nascimento
    Photographic Collection of *Correio da Manhã*
Arquivo Público do Estado do Rio de Janeiro (Rio de Janeiro)
    Fundo Polícias Políticas do Rio de Janeiro (1975–82)
Assembléia Legislativa do Estado do Rio de Janeiro, Biblioteca (Rio de Janeiro)
Associação Brasileira de Imprensa, Biblioteca (Rio de Janeiro)
    Newspaper and periodical collections
Benson Latin American Collection, University of Texas (Austin)
Biblioteca Central dos Barris (Salvador da Bahia)
    Newspaper collections
Biblioteca Nacional (Rio de Janeiro)
    Jornais da raça negra, 1904–28/1935–53 (microfilm)
    Jornais da raça negra, 1928–63 (microfilm)
    Newspaper and periodical collections
Casa de Angola (Salvador da Bahia)
    Papers of the Associação Cultural Agostinho Neto (São Paulo)
Casa Ruy Barbosa, Biblioteca (Rio de Janeiro)
    Newspaper and periodical collections
Centro de Estudos Afro-Orientais, Universidade Federal da Bahia, Biblioteca and Arquivo (Salvador da Bahia)
    Newspaper files by subject
    Newsletters of the Centro, and Correspondence, 1959–65
Conjunto Universitário Cândido Mendes, Centro de Estudos Afro-Asiáticos (Rio de Janeiro)
    Coleção Imprensa Negra
    Newspaper files by subject
Fundação Gregório Mattos / Arquivo Municipal da Bahia (Salvador da Bahia)
    Newspaper files by subject
Fundação Jorge Amado, Biblioteca (Salvador da Bahia)
    Newspaper files by subject
Fundação Pierre Verger, Biblioteca and Arquivo (Salvador da Bahia)
    Correspondence, Documents, and Photographic Collections

Newspaper files by subject
Instituto Geográfico e Histórico da Bahia, Biblioteca and Arquivo (Salvador da Bahia)
Northwestern University Archives (Evanston, Ill.)
    Africana Manuscripts 6, Series 35/6
    Melville J. Herskovits (1895–1963) Papers, 1906–63
Palácio do Itamaraty, Arquivo Histórico and Biblioteca (Rio de Janeiro)
Princeton University, Firestone Library (Princeton, N.J.)
    The Black Press of Brazil (microfilm)
    Publications of the Centro de Estudos Afro-Orientais (microfilm)
Schomburg Center for Research in Black Culture (New York)
    Melville J. Herskovits Papers

Black Press

Note: Publications are listed in chronological order. Dates in parentheses indicate years for which issues have survived; complete periods of publication may have been longer.

O Baluarte (1903–4), Campinas

O Menelik (1915–17), São Paulo

A Rua (1916), São Paulo

O Xauter (1916), São Paulo

O Bandeirante (1918–19), São Paulo

O Alfinete (1918–21), São Paulo

A Liberdade (1919–20), São Paulo

A Sentinela (1920), São Paulo

O Kosmos (1922–25), São Paulo

O Elite (1923–24), São Paulo

O Getulino (1923–24, 1926), Campinas and São Paulo

O Clarim d'Alvorada (1924–32, 1940), São Paulo

Auriverde (1928), São Paulo

O Patrocínio (1928–30), Piracicaba

O Progresso (1928–32), São Paulo

A Chibata (1932), São Paulo

Brasil Novo (1933), São Paulo

Evolução (1933), São Paulo

A Voz da Raça (1933–37), São Paulo

Cultura (1934), São Paulo

Tribuna Negra (1935), São Paulo

O Clarim (1935), São Paulo

Alvorada (1945–48), São Paulo

O Novo Horizonte (1945–61), São Paulo

Senzala (1946), São Paulo

Quilombo (1948–50), Rio de Janeiro

Mundo Novo (1950), São Paulo

Redenção (1950), Rio de Janeiro

Himalaya ("A Voz do Negro," *A Voz da Negritude*) (1950–53), Rio de Janeiro

Cruzada Cultural (1950–60), São Paulo

Notícias de Ébano (1957), Santos

O Mutirão (1958), São Paulo

Hífen (1960–62), Campinas

Niger (1960), São Paulo

O Ébano (1961), São Paulo

Árvore das Palavras (1974–75), São Paulo

Boletim do IPCN (1975–77), Rio de Janeiro

Afro-Chamber (1976–84), São Paulo

Versus ("Afro-Latino-América") (1977–79), São Paulo

SINBA (1977–80), Rio de Janeiro

Jornegro (1978–80), São Paulo

GANA (1979–81), Araraquara

Boletim GTAR (1982–87), Rio de Janeiro

Other Periodicals

Correio da Manhã, Salvador da Bahia
Correio de São Paulo, São Paulo
Correio Paulistano, São Paulo
O Cruzeiro, Rio de Janeiro
Diário Carioca, Rio de Janeiro
Diário da Bahia, Salvador da Bahia
Diário de Notícias, Salvador da Bahia
Diário de Pernambuco, Recife
Diário de São Paulo, São Paulo
Diário Nacional, São Paulo
O Estado de São Paulo, São Paulo
A Folha da Manhã, São Paulo
A Folha do Rio, Rio de Janeiro
A Gazeta, São Paulo
O Globo, Rio de Janeiro
Isto É, São Paulo
O Jornal, Rio de Janeiro

Jornal da Bahia, Salvador da Bahia
Jornal da Bahia Tablóide, Salvador da Bahia
Jornal de São Paulo, São Paulo
Jornal do Brasil, Rio de Janeiro
Jornal do Commercio, Rio de Janeiro
A Luta, Rio de Janeiro
Manchete, Rio de Janeiro
Mês, Salvador da Bahia
A Noite, Rio de Janeiro
A Noite, Salvador da Bahia
A Notícia, Rio de Janeiro
O Paiz, Rio de Janeiro
O Pasquim, Rio de Janeiro
Pittsburgh Courier, Pittsburgh
A Tarde, Salvador da Bahia

Government Publications

Assembléia Constituinte dos Estados Unidos do Brasil. *Anais da Assembléia Constituinte*, vol. 9. Rio de Janeiro: Imprensa Nacional, 1948.

———. *Anais da Assembléia Constituinte*, vol. 18. Rio de Janeiro: Imprensa Nacional, 1949.

———. *Anais da Assembléia Constituinte*, vol. 22. Rio de Janeiro: Imprensa Nacional, 1950.

———. *Anais da Assembléia Constituinte*, vol. 23. Rio de Janeiro: Imprensa Nacional, 1950.

Brazil. *Relatório.* Ministério das Relações Exteriores. Brasília: Serviço de Publicações da Divisão de Documentação Diplomática, 1960–75.

Câmara dos Deputados dos Estados Unidos do Brasil. *Annaes da Câmara dos Deputados*, vol. 10. Rio de Janeiro: Imprensa Nacional, 1928.

———. *Annaes da Câmara dos Deputados*, vol. 12. Rio de Janeiro: Imprensa Nacional, 1929.

———. *Annaes da Câmara dos Deputados*, vol. 14. Rio de Janeiro: Imprensa Nacional, 1929.

Conselho Municipal do Rio de Janeiro. *Annaes do Conselho Municipal do Rio de Janeiro.* June–July 1926. Rio de Janeiro: Typographia do Jornal do Commercio, 1926.

Books and Articles

Abreu, Martha. "Mulatas, Crioulos, and Morenas: Racial Hierarchy, Gender Relations, and National Identity in Postabolition Popular Song (Southeastern

Brazil, 1890–1920)." In *Gender and Slave Emancipation in the Atlantic World*, edited by Pamela Scully and Diana Paton, 267–88. Durham, N.C.: Duke University Press, 2005.

Agier, Michel. "As Mães Pretas do Ilê Aiyê: Notas sobre o espaço mediano da cultura." *Afro-Ásia* 18 (1996): 189–203.

Agostinho, Pedro. "Agostinho da Silva: Pressupostos, concepção e ação de uma política externa do Brasil com relação à África." *Afro-Ásia* 16 (1995): 9–23.

Alberti, Verena, and Amilcar Araujo Pereira. *Histórias do movimento negro no Brasil: Depoimentos ao CPDOC*. Rio de Janeiro: Pallas; CPDOC-FGV, 2007.

Alberto, Paulina L. "Para Africano Ver: African-Bahian Exchanges in the Reinvention of Brazil's Racial Democracy, 1961–63." *Luso-Brazilian Review* 45, no. 1 (2008): 78–117.

———. "Terms of Inclusion: Black Activism and the Cultural Conditions for Citizenship in a Multi-Racial Brazil, 1920–1982." Ph.D. diss., University of Pennsylvania, 2005.

———. "When Rio Was *Black*: Soul Music, National Culture, and the Politics of Racial Comparison in 1970s Brazil." *Hispanic American Historical Review* 89, no. 1 (2009): 3–39.

Albuquerque, Wlamyra. "Esperanças de boaventuras: Construções da África e africanismos na Bahia (1887–1910)." *Estudos Afro-Asiáticos* 24, no. 2 (2002): 215–45.

———. "Santos, deuses e heróis nas ruas da Bahia: Identidade cultural na Primeira República." *Afro-Ásia* 18 (1996): 103–24.

Alencar, José de. *O guarani*. São Paulo: Cultrix, 1968.

Álvarez, Sonia. *Engendering Democracy in Brazil: Women's Movements in Transition Politics*. Princeton, N.J.: Princeton University Press, 1990.

Alves, Sebastião Rodrigues. "We Are All Equal before the Law." *Journal of Black Studies* 11, no. 2 (1980): 179–94.

Alves de Lima, J. C. *Recordações de homens e cousas do meu tempo*. Rio de Janeiro: Leite Ribeiro Freitas Bastos, Spicer, 1925.

Amaral, Raul Joviano. *Os pretos do Rosário de São Paulo: Subsídios históricos*. 2nd ed. São Paulo: J. Scortecci, 1991.

Andrade, Oswald de. *Obras completas*. Rio de Janeiro: Civilização Brasileira, 1972.

Andrews, George Reid. *Afro-Latin America, 1800–2000*. New York: Oxford University Press, 2004.

———. "Afro-Latin America: Five Questions." *Latin American and Caribbean Ethnic Studies* 4, no. 2 (2009): 191–210.

———. *Blacks and Whites in São Paulo, Brazil, 1888–1988*. Madison: University of Wisconsin Press, 1991.

———. "Brazilian Racial Democracy, 1900–90: An American Counterpoint." *Journal of Contemporary History* 31, no. 3 (1996): 483–507.

APERJ. *Os arquivos das polícias políticas: Reflexos de nossa história contemporânea*. Rio de Janeiro: Fundação de amparo à pesquisa do Estado do Rio de Janeiro, 1996.

Araujo, Maria Paula Nascimento. *A utopia fragmentada: As novas esquerdas no Brasil e no mundo na década de 1970*. Rio de Janeiro: FGV, 2000.

Arendt, Hannah. *The Origins of Totalitarianism*. New York: Harcourt, Brace and Co., 1951.

———. "'The Rights of Man': What Are They?" *Modern Review* 3 (1949): 24–37.

Azevedo, Celia Maria Marinho de. *Onda negra, medo branco: O negro no imaginário das elites—século XIX*. Rio de Janeiro: Paz e Terra, 1987.

Azevedo, Elciene. *Orfeu de carapinha: A trajetória de Luiz Gama na imperial cidade de São Paulo*. Campinas: UNICAMP, 1991.

Azevedo, Thales de. *Democracia racial: Ideologia e realidade*. Petrópolis: Vozes, 1975.

———. *Les élites de couleur dans une ville brésilienne*. Paris: UNESCO, 1953.

Bacelar, Jefferson. *A hierarquia das raças: Negros e brancos em Salvador*. Rio de Janeiro: Pallas, 2001.

Bairros, Luiza. "'Orfeu e Poder': Uma perspectiva afro-americana sobre a política racial no Brasil." *Afro-Ásia* 17 (1996): 173–86.

———. "Pecados no 'paraíso racial': O negro na força de trabalho da Bahia, 1950–80." In *Escravidão e invenção da liberdade*, edited by João José Reis, 289–323. São Paulo: Brasiliense/CNPq, 1988.

Bananére, Juó. *La divina increnca*. São Paulo: Editora 34, 2001.

Barbosa, Márcio, ed. *Frente Negra Brasileira: Depoimentos*. São Paulo: Quilombhoje, 1998.

Barcelos, Luiz Claudio. "Struggling in Paradise: Racial Mobilization and the Contemporary Black Movement in Brazil." In *Race in Contemporary Brazil: From Indifference to Inequality*, edited by Rebecca Reichmann, 155–66. University Park: Pennsylvania State University Press, 1999.

Barros, Orlando de. *Corações de chocolat: A história da Companhia Negra de Revistas (1926–27)*. Rio de Janeiro: Livre Expressão, 2005.

Bastide, Roger. "A imprensa negra no estado de São Paulo." In *O negro na imprensa e na literatura*, edited by José Marques de Melo, 50–78. São Paulo: Escola de Comunicações e Artes, 1972.

Bastide, Roger, and Florestan Fernandes. *Brancos e negros em São Paulo*. São Paulo: Companhia Editora Nacional, 1959.

———. *Relações raciais entre negros e brancos em São Paulo*. São Paulo: Anhembi, 1955.

Benchimol, Jaime Larry. *Pereira Passos—Um Haussmann tropical: A renovação urbana da cidade do Rio de Janeiro no início do século XX*. Rio de Janeiro: Secretaria Municipal de Cultura, Turismo e Esportes, 1990.

Benzaquen de Araújo, Ricardo. *Guerra e paz: "Casa-grande & senzala" e a obra de Gilberto Freyre*. Rio de Janeiro: Editora 34, 1994.

Bergad, Laird. *The Comparative Histories of Slavery in Brazil, Cuba, and the United States*. New York: Cambridge University Press, 2007.

Besse, Susan K. *Restructuring Patriarchy: The Modernization of Gender Inequality in Brazil, 1914–1940*. Chapel Hill: University of North Carolina Press, 1996.

Borges, Dain. *The Family in Bahia, Brazil, 1870–1945*. Stanford, Calif.: Stanford University Press, 1992.

———. "'Puffy, Ugly, Slothful and Inert': Degeneration in Brazilian Social Thought, 1880–1940." *Journal of Latin American Studies* 25 (1993): 235–56.

———. "The Recognition of Afro-Brazilian Symbols and Ideas, 1890–1940." *Luso-Brazilian Review* 32, no. 2 (1995): 59–78.

Bourdieu, Pierre, and Loïc Wacquant. "On the Cunning of Imperialist Reason." *Theory, Culture and Society* 16, no. 1 (1999): 41–58.

Boxer, C. R. *Race Relations in the Portuguese Colonial Empire, 1415–1825.* Oxford, U.K.: Clarendon, 1963.

Braga, Júlio. *Na gamela do feitiço: Repressão e resistência nos candomblés da Bahia.* Salvador: EDUFBA, 1995.

Burdick, John. "The Lost Constituency of Brazil's Black Movements." *Latin American Perspectives* 25, no. 1 (1998): 136–55.

Burns, E. Bradford. *A History of Brazil.* 3rd ed. New York: Columbia University Press, 1993.

Butler, Kim. "Africa in the Reinvention of Nineteenth-Century Afro-Bahian Identity." In *Rethinking the African Diaspora: The Making of a Black Atlantic World in the Bight of Benin and Brazil,* edited by Kristin Mann and Edna Bay, 135–54. New York: Frank Cass, 2001.

———. *Freedoms Given, Freedoms Won: Afro-Brazilians in Post-Abolition São Paulo and Salvador.* New Brunswick, N.J.: Rutgers University Press, 1998.

Caldwell, Kia Lilly. *Negras in Brazil: Re-envisioning Black Women, Citizenship, and the Politics of Identity.* New Brunswick, N.J.: Rutgers University Press, 2007.

Campos, Maria José. *Arthur Ramos: Luz e sombra na antropologia brasileira.* Rio de Janeiro: Biblioteca Nacional, 2003.

Capone, Stefania. *La quête de l'Afrique dans le candomblé: Pouvoir et tradition au Brésil.* Paris: Karthala, 1999.

Cardoso, Fernando Henrique, and Octávio Ianni. *Cor e mobilidade social em Florianópolis: Aspectos das relações entre negros e brancos numa comunidade do Brasil meridional.* São Paulo: Nacional, 1960.

Carneiro, Maria Luiza Tucci, and Boris Kossoy. *A imprensa confiscada pelo DEOPS, 1924–1954.* São Paulo: Ateliê, 2003.

Carvalho, José Murilo de. *Os bestializados: O Rio de Janeiro e a República que não foi.* São Paulo: Companhia das Letras, 1987.

———. *A formação das almas: O imaginário da república no Brasil.* São Paulo: Companhia das Letras, 2006.

Caulfield, Sueann. "Getting into Trouble: Dishonest Women, Modern Girls, and Women-Men in the Conceptual Language of *Vida Policial,* 1925–1927." *Signs: Journal of Women in Culture and Society* 19, no. 1 (1993): 146–76.

———. *In Defense of Honor: Sexual Morality, Modernity, and Nation in Early-Twentieth-Century Brazil.* Durham, N.C.: Duke University Press, 2000.

———. "Interracial Courtship in the Rio de Janeiro Courts." In *Race and Nation in Modern Latin America,* edited by Nancy P. Appelbaum, Anne S. Macpherson, and Karin Alejandra Rosemblatt, 170–86. Chapel Hill: University of North Carolina Press, 2003.

Centro de Estudos Afro-Asiáticos. "CEAA: Cinco anos de atividades." *Cadernos Cândido Mendes/Estudos Afro-Asiáticos* 1, no. 1 (1978): 62–68.

Chalhoub, Sidney. *Cidade febril: Cortiços e epidemias na corte imperial.* São Paulo: Companhia das Letras, 1996.

―――. "The Politics of Disease Control: Yellow Fever and Race in Nineteenth Century Rio de Janeiro." *Journal of Latin American Studies* 25 (1993): 441–63.

―――. *Trabalho, lar e botequim: O cotidiano dos trabalhadores no Rio de Janeiro da belle époque*. Campinas: Editora da UNICAMP, 2001.

―――. *Visões da liberdade: Uma história das últimas décadas da escravidão na corte*. 4th ed. São Paulo: Companhia das Letras, 2001.

Chasteen, John. *National Rhythms, African Roots: The Deep History of Latin American Popular Dance*. Albuquerque: University of New Mexico Press, 2004.

Conceição, Fernando. "Cultura como alienação: Poder e blocos afros na Bahia." Paper presented at the Terceiro Encontro de Estudos Multidisciplinares em Cultura, Faculdade de Comunicação, UFBa, Salvador da Bahia, Brasil, 23–25 May 2007.

Congresso Afro-Brasileiro. *Estudos afro-brasileiros: Trabalhos apresentados ao 1º congresso afro-brasileiro reunido no Recife em 1934*. Rio de Janeiro: Ariel, 1935.

―――. *O negro no Brasil: Trabalhos apresentados no 2º congresso afro-brasileiro (Bahia, 1937)*. Rio de Janeiro: Civilização Brasileira, 1940.

Conrad, Robert. *The Destruction of Brazilian Slavery, 1850–1888*. Berkeley: University of California Press, 1972.

Contins, Marcia. *Lideranças negras*. Rio de Janeiro: Aeroplano /FAPERJ, 2005.

Costa, Emília Viotti da. *The Brazilian Empire: Myths and Histories*. 2nd ed. Chapel Hill: University of North Carolina Press, 2000.

Costa Pinto, Luiz de Aguiar. *O negro no Rio de Janeiro: Relações de raça numa sociedade em mudança*. 2nd ed. Rio de Janeiro: Universidade Federal do Rio de Janeiro, 1998.

Coutinho, Eduardo. *Os cronistas de Momo: Imprensa e carnaval na Primeira República*. Rio de Janeiro: UFRJ, 2006.

Crowley, Daniel. *African Myth and Black Reality in Bahian Carnaval*. Los Angeles: Museum of Cultural History, UCLA, 1984.

Crowley, John. "The Politics of Belonging: Some Theoretical Considerations." In *The Politics of Belonging: Migrants and Minorities in Contemporary Europe*, edited by Andrew Geddes and Adrian Favell, 15–41. Aldershot, U.K.: Ashgate, 1999.

Cunha, Manuela Carneiro da. *Negros, estrangeiros: Os escravos libertos e sua volta à Africa*. São Paulo: Brasiliense, 1985.

―――. "Política indigenista no século XIX." In *História dos índios no Brasil*, edited by Manuela Carneiro da Cunha, 133–54. São Paulo: Companhia das Letras, 1992.

―――, ed. *História dos índios no Brasil*. São Paulo: Companhia das Letras, 1992.

Cunha, Olívia Maria Gomes da. *Intenção e gesto: Pessoa, cor e a produção cotidiana da (in)diferença no Rio de Janeiro*. Rio de Janeiro: Arquivo Nacional, 2002.

Daniel, G. Reginald. *Race and Multiraciality in Brazil and the United States: Converging Paths?* University Park: Pennsylvania State University Press, 2006.

Dantas, Beatriz Góis. *Vovó nagô e papai branco: Usos e abusos da África no Brasil*. Rio de Janeiro: Graal, 1988.

Dávila, Jerry. *Diploma of Whiteness: Race and Social Policy in Brazil, 1917–1945*. Durham, N.C.: Duke University Press, 2003.

―――. *Hotel Trópico: Brazil and the Challenge of African Decolonization, 1950–1980*. Durham, N.C.: Duke University Press, 2010.

Davis, Darién J. "The Arquivos das Polícias Politicais [*sic*] of the State of Rio de Janeiro." *Latin American Research Review* 31, no. 1 (1996): 99–104.

———. *Avoiding the Dark: Race and the Forging of National Culture in Modern Brazil.* Aldershot, U.K.: Ashgate, 1999.

Dean, Warren. *The Industrialization of São Paulo, 1880–1945.* Austin: University of Texas Press, 1969.

Degler, Carl. *Neither Black nor White: Slavery and Race Relations in Brazil and the United States.* New York: Macmillan, 1971.

de la Fuente, Alejandro. "Myths of Racial Democracy: Cuba, 1900–1912." *Latin American Research Review* 34, no. 3 (1999): 39–73.

———. *A Nation for All: Race, Inequality, and Politics in Twentieth-Century Cuba.* Chapel Hill: University of North Carolina Press, 2001.

Domingues, Petrônio J. *Uma história não contada: Negro, racismo, e branqueamento em São Paulo no pós-abolição.* São Paulo: SENAC, 2003.

———. *A nova abolição.* São Paulo: Selo Negro, 2008.

———. "Os 'Pérolas Negras': A participação do negro na revolução constitucionalista de 1932." *Afro-Ásia* 29–30 (2003): 199–245.

———. "Um 'templo de luz': Frente Negra Brasileira (1931–1937) e a questão da educação." *Revista Brasileira de Educação* 13, no. 39 (2008): 517–96.

Dunn, Christopher. *Brutality Garden: Tropicália and the Emergence of a Brazilian Counterculture.* Chapel Hill: University of North Carolina Press, 2001.

Dzidzienyo, Anani. "The African Connection and the Afro-Brazilian Condition." In *Race, Class, and Power in Brazil*, edited by Pierre-Michel Fontaine, 135–53. Los Angeles: Center for Afro-American Studies, UCLA, 1985.

———. *The Position of Blacks in Brazilian Society.* Minority Rights Group Reports. London: Minority Rights Group, 1971.

Ermakoff, George. *O negro na fotografia brasileira do século XIX.* Rio de Janeiro: G. Ermakoff, 2004.

Fausto, Boris. *A Concise History of Brazil.* Cambridge: Cambridge University Press, 1999.

———. *Crime e cotidiano: A criminalidade em São Paulo (1880–1924).* 2nd ed. São Paulo: Editora da USP, 2000.

———. "Imigração e participação política na primeira república: O caso de São Paulo." In *Imigração e política em São Paulo*, edited by Boris Fausto, Oswaldo Truzzi, Roberto Grün, and Célia Sakurai, 7–26. São Paulo: Editora Sumaré/ Fapesp, 1995.

———. *A Revolução de 1930: História e historiografia.* 16th ed. São Paulo: Companhia das Letras, 1997.

Fernandes, Florestan. *A integração do negro na sociedade de classes.* Vols. 1 and 2. São Paulo: Dominus, 1965.

———. *The Negro in Brazilian Society.* New York: Columbia University Press, 1969.

Ferrara, Miriam N. *A imprensa negra paulista, 1915–1963.* Antropologia. São Paulo: FFLCH-USP, 1986.

Ferreira, Yedo, and Amauri Mendes Pereira. *O movimento negro e as eleições.* Rio de Janeiro: Edições SINBA, 1983.

Ferrer, Ada. *Insurgent Cuba: Race, Nation, and Revolution, 1868–1898*. Chapel Hill: University of North Carolina Press, 1999.

Filha, Sofia Olszewski. *A fotografia e o negro na cidade do Salvador*. Salvador da Bahia: EGBA, 1989.

Filho, Alberto Heráclito Ferreira. "Desafricanizar as ruas: Elites letradas, mulheres pobres e cultura popular em Salvador, 1890–1937." *Afro-Ásia* 21–22 (1998–99): 239–56.

Fischer, Brodwyn. *A Poverty of Rights: Citizenship and Inequality in Twentieth-Century Rio de Janeiro*. Stanford, Calif.: Stanford University Press, 2008.

Fontaine, Pierre-Michel, ed. *Race, Class, and Power in Brazil*. Los Angeles: Center for African and African American Studies, UCLA, 1985.

French, John. "The Missteps of Anti-imperialist Reason: Bourdieu, Wacquant and Hanchard's *Orpheus and Power*." *Theory, Culture and Society* 17, no. 1 (2000): 107–28.

Freyre, Gilberto. "Acontece que são baianos." In *Bahia e baianos*, edited by Edson Nery da Fonseca, 91–134. Salvador da Bahia: Fundação das Artes/Empresa Gráfica da Bahia, 1990.

———. *Aventura e rotina: Sugestões de uma viagem à procura das constantes portuguêsas de caráter e ação*. Rio de Janeiro: J. Olympio, 1953.

———. *Um brasileiro em terras portuguêsas*. Rio de Janeiro: J. Olympio, 1953.

———. *Casa-grande e senzala: Introdução à história da sociedade patriarcal no Brasil*. Paris: ALLCA XX, 2002.

———. *The Masters and the Slaves*. New York: Knopf, 1946.

———. *Ordem e progresso*. Vol. 1. 3rd ed. Rio de Janeiro: José Olympio, 1974.

Fry, Peter. "Politics, Nationality, and the Meanings of 'Race' in Brazil." *Daedalus* 129, no. 2 (2000): 83–118.

———. "Por que o Brasil é diferente?" *Revista Brasileira de Ciências Sociais* 11, no. 31 (1996): 178–82.

———. "O que a cinderela negra tem a dizer sobre a 'política racial' no Brasil." *Revista USP* 28 (1995–96): 122–35.

Fry, Peter, Sérgio Carrara, and Ana Luiza Martins-Costa. "Negros e brancos no carnaval da Velha República." In *Escravidão e invenção da liberdade*, edited by João José Reis, 232–63. São Paulo: Editora Brasiliense/CNPq, 1988.

Fry, Peter, Yvonne Maggie, Marcos Chor Maio, Simone Monteiro, and Ricardo Ventura Santos, eds. *Divisões perigosas: Políticas raciais no Brasil contemporâneo*. Rio de Janeiro: Civilização Brasileira, 2007.

Giacomini, Sonia Maria. *A alma da festa: Família, etnicidade e projetos num clube social da zona Norte do Rio de Janeiro, o Renascença Clube*. Belo Horizonte: UFMG; Rio de Janeiro: IUPERJ, 2006.

Gomes, Angela de Castro. *A invenção do trabalhismo*. Rio de Janeiro: Dumará, 1994.

Gomes, Flávio. *Negros e política (1888–1937)*. Rio de Janeiro: Jorge Zahar, 2005.

Gomes, Tiago de Melo. *Um espelho no palco: Identidades sociais e massificação da cultura no teatro de revista dos anos 1920*. Campinas, S.P.: UNICAMP, 2004.

———. "Problemas no paraíso: Democracia racial brasileira frente à imigração afro-americana (1921)." *Estudos Afro-Asiáticos* 25, no. 2 (2003): 307–31.

Gomes, Tiago de Melo, and Micol Seigel. "Sabina's Oranges: The Colours of Cultural Politics in Rio de Janeiro, 1889–1930." *Journal of Latin American Cultural Studies* 11, no. 1 (2002): 5–28.

Gonzalez, Lélia. "O movimento negro na última década." In *Lugar de negro*, edited by Lélia Gonzalez and Carlos Hasenbalg, 9–66. Rio de Janeiro: Marco Zero, 1982.

———. "The Unified Black Movement: A New Stage in Black Political Mobilization." In *Race, Class, and Power in Brazil*, edited by Pierre-Michel Fontaine, 120–34. Los Angeles: Center for Afro-American Studies, UCLA, 1985.

Gould, Jeffrey. *To Die in This Way: Nicaraguan Indians and the Myth of Mestizaje, 1880–1965*. Durham, N.C.: Duke University Press, 1998.

Graden, Dale. "An Act 'Even of Public Security': Slave Resistance, Social Tensions, and the End of the International Slave Trade to Brazil, 1835–1856." *Hispanic American Historical Review* 76, no. 2 (1996): 249–82.

Graham, Richard. "Free African Brazilians and the State in Slavery Times." In *Racial Politics in Contemporary Brazil*, edited by Michael Hanchard, 30–58. Durham, N.C.: Duke University Press, 1999.

———. *Patronage and Politics in Nineteenth-Century Brazil*. Stanford, Calif.: Stanford University Press, 1990.

———, ed. *The Idea of Race in Latin America, 1870–1940*. Austin: University of Texas Press, 1990.

Graham, Sandra Lauderdale. *House and Street: The Domestic World of Servants and Masters in Nineteenth-Century Rio de Janeiro*. Cambridge: Cambridge University Press, 1988.

Grinberg, Keila. *O fiador dos brasileiros: Cidadania, escravidão e direito civil no tempo de Antonio Pereira Rebouças*. Rio de Janeiro: Civilização Brasileira, 2002.

———. *Liberata: A lei da ambigüidade—As ações de liberdade da Corte de Apelação do Rio de Janeiro no século XIX*. Rio de Janeiro: Relume Dumará, 1994.

Guerreiro Ramos, Alberto. *Introdução crítica à sociologia brasileira*. Rio de Janeiro: Editora UFRJ, 1995.

———. *O processo da sociologia no Brasil: Esquema de uma história de idéias*. Rio de Janeiro: n/a, 1953.

Guimarães, Antonio Sérgio Alfredo. "Africanism and Racial Democracy: The Correspondence between Herskovits and Arthur Ramos (1935–1949)." *Estudios Interdisciplinarios de América Latina y el Caribe* 19, no. 1 (2008): 53–79.

———. *Classes, raças e democracia*. São Paulo: Editora 34; Fundação de Apoio à Universidade de São Paulo, 2002.

Guimarães, Antonio Sérgio Alfredo, and Márcio Macedo. "*Diário Trabalhista* e democracia racial negra dos anos 1940." *Dados* 51, no. 1 (2008): 143–82.

Guran, Milton. *Agudás: Os brasileiros do Benim*. Rio de Janeiro: Nova Fronteira, 1999.

Haberly, David T. *Three Sad Races: Racial Identity and National Consciousness in Brazilian Literature*. Cambridge: Cambridge University Press, 1983.

Hahner, June. "Feminism, Women's Rights, and the Suffrage Movement in Brazil, 1850–1932." *Latin American Research Review* 15, no. 1 (1980): 65–111.

———. *Poverty and Politics: The Urban Poor in Brazil, 1870–1920*. Albuquerque: University of New Mexico Press, 1986.

Hanchard, Michael. *Orpheus and Power: The Movimento Negro of Rio de Janeiro and São Paulo, Brazil, 1945–1988*. Princeton, N.J.: Princeton University Press, 1994.

———. "Resposta a Luíza Bairros." *Afro-Ásia* 18 (1996): 227–34.

Harding, Rachel. *A Refuge in Thunder: Candomblé and Alternative Spaces of Blackness*. Bloomington: Indiana University Press, 2000.

Hasenbalg, Carlos. *Discriminação e desigualdades raciais no Brasil*. Rio de Janeiro: Graal, 1979.

———. "Race and Socioeconomic Inequalities in Brazil." In *Race, Class, and Power in Brazil*, edited by Pierre-Michel Fontaine, 25–41. Los Angeles: Center for African and African American Studies, UCLA, 1985.

Helg, Aline. *Our Rightful Share: The Afro-Cuban Struggle for Equality, 1886–1912*. Chapel Hill: University of North Carolina Press, 1995.

Hellwig, David, ed. *African-American Reflections on Brazil's Racial Paradise*. Philadelphia: Temple University Press, 1992.

Heringer, Rosana. "Mapeamento de açoes e discursos de combate às desigualdades raciais no Brasil." *Estudos Afro-Asiáticos* 23, no. 2 (2001): 291–334.

Herskovits, Melville. *The Myth of the Negro Past*. Boston: Beacon, 1958.

———. "The Social Organization of the Candomblé." In *The New World Negro*, edited by Francis Herskovits. Bloomington: Indiana University Press, 1969.

Hertzman, Marc A. "A Brazilian Counterweight: Music, Intellectual Property and the African Diaspora in Rio de Janeiro (1910s–1930s)." *Journal of Latin American Studies* 41, no. 4 (2009): 695–722.

———. "Celebration and Punishment: Making Samba, Race, and Intellectual Property in Brazil (Rio de Janeiro, 1880s–1970s)." Unpublished manuscript.

———. "Making Music and Masculinity in Vagrancy's Shadow: Race, Wealth, and *Malandragem* in Post-Abolition Rio de Janeiro." *Hispanic American Historical Review* 90, no. 4 (2010): 591–625.

———. "Surveillance and Difference: The Making of Samba, Race, and Nation in Brazil (1880s–1970s)." Ph.D. diss., University of Wisconsin, 2008.

Htun, Mala. "From 'Racial Democracy' to Affirmative Action: Changing State Policy on Race in Brazil." *Latin American Research Review* 39, no. 1 (2004): 60–98.

Ianni, Octávio. *Raças e classes sociais no Brasil*. Rio de Janeiro: Civilização Brasileira, 1972.

IBGE, ed. *Brasil: 500 anos de povoamento*. Rio de Janeiro: IBGE, 2000.

Joaquim, Maria Salete. *O papel da liderança religiosa feminina na construção da identidade negra*. Rio de Janeiro: Pallas/FAPESP, 2001.

Johnson, Ollie. "Racial Representation and Brazilian Politics: Black Members of the National Congress, 1983–1999." *Journal of Inter-American Studies and World Affairs* 40, no. 4 (1998): 97–118.

Johnson, Paul. *Secrets, Gossip, and Gods: The Transformation of Brazilian Candomblé*. Oxford: Oxford University Press, 2002.

Kannabiran, Kalpana, Ulrike Vieten, and Nira Yuval-Davis. "Introduction." *Patterns of Prejudice* 40, no. 3 (2006): 189–95.

———. *The Situated Politics of Belonging*. London: Sage, 2006.

Kennedy, James H. "Political Liberalization, Black Consciousness, and Recent Afro-Brazilian Literature." *Phylon* 47, no. 3 (1986): 199–209.

Kiddy, Elizabeth. *Blacks of the Rosary: Memory and History in Minas Gerais, Brazil.* University Park: Pennsylvania State University Press, 2005.

Kirkendall, Andrew. *Class Mates: Male Student Culture and the Making of a Political Class in Nineteenth-Century Brazil.* Lincoln: University of Nebraska Press, 2002.

Kössling, Karin S. "O discurso policial sobre o afro-descendente: Estigmas e estereótipos." *Revista histórica* 15 (2004): 4–10.

Kraay, Hendrik. "Between Brazil and Bahia: Celebrating Dois de Julho in Nineteenth-Century Salvador." *Journal of Latin American Studies* 31 (1999): 255–86.

Landes, Ruth. *The City of Women.* Albuquerque: University of New Mexico Press, 1994.

Laotan, A. B. *The Torch-Bearers, or Old Brazilian Colony in Lagos.* Lagos: Ife-Olu Printing Works, 1943.

Le Bouler, Jean-Pierre, ed. *Le pied à l'étrier: Correspondance échangée entre A. Métraux et Pierre Verger.* Paris: J. M. Place, 1993.

Lenharo, Alcir. *Sacralização da política.* Campinas: Editora da UNICAMP, 1986.

Lesser, Jeffrey. "Are African-Americans African or American? Brazilian Immigration Policy in the 1920s." *Review of Latin American Studies* 4, no. 1 (1991): 115–37.

———. "Immigration and Shifting Concepts of National Identity in Brazil during the Vargas Era." *Luso-Brazilian Review* 31, no. 2 (1994): 23–44.

———. *Negotiating National Identity: Immigrants, Minorities, and the Struggle for Ethnicity in Brazil.* Durham, N.C.: Duke University Press, 1999.

Levine, Robert. *Father of the Poor? Vargas and His Era.* Cambridge: Cambridge University Press, 1998.

———. "The First Afro-Brazilian Congress: Opportunities for the Study of Race in the Brazilian Northeast." *Race* 15, no. 2 (1973): 185–93.

———. "Some Views on Race and Immigration during the Old Republic." *Americas* 27, no. 4 (1971): 373–80.

———. *The Vargas Regime: The Critical Years, 1934–1938.* New York: Columbia University Press, 1970.

Lima, Vivaldo da Costa. "Ainda sobre a nação de queto." In *Faraimará, o caçador traz alegria: Mãe Stella, 60 anos de iniciação,* edited by Cléo Martins and Raul Lody. Rio de Janeiro: Pallas, 2000.

———. "O conceito de 'nação' nos candomblés da Bahia." *Afro-Ásia* 12 (1976): 65–90.

Love, Joseph. "Political Participation in Brazil, 1881–1969." *Luso-Brazilian Review* 7 (1970): 3–24.

———. *São Paulo in the Brazilian Federation.* Stanford, Calif.: Stanford University Press, 1980.

Lovell, Peggy, ed. *Desigualdade racial no Brasil contemporâneo.* Belo Horizonte: Universidade Federal de Minas Gerais/CEDEPLAR, 1991.

Lühning, Angela. "'Acabe com este santo, Pedrito vem aí . . .': Mito e realidade da perseguição policial ao candomblé baiano entre 1920 e 1942." *Revista USP* 28 (1995–96): 194–220.

―――. "O diálogo transatlântico como método de pesquisa de Pierre Fatumbi Verger." Paper presented at "The African Americas" conference, organized by the Latin American and Latino Studies Programs and cosponsored with the Center for Africana Studies Program, University of Pennsylvania (Philadelphia), 27-28 February 2003.

―――. "Pierre Fatumbi Verger e sua obra." *Afro-Ásia* 21-22 (1998/99): 315-64.

―――, ed. *Pierre Verger: Repórter fotográfico.* Rio de Janeiro: Bertrand Brasil, 2004.

―――, ed. *Verger/Bastide: Dimensões de uma amizade.* Rio de Janeiro: Bertrand Brasil, 2002.

Machado, Maria Helena. *O plano e o pânico: Os movimentos sociais na década da abolição.* Rio de Janeiro and São Paulo: Editora Universidade Federal do Rio de Janeiro/Editora da Universidade de São Paulo, 1994.

Maciel, Cléber da Silva. *Discriminações raciais: Negros em Campinas (1888-1921).* Campinas: UNICAMP, 1987.

Maio, Marcos Chor. "Uma polêmica esquecida: Costa Pinto, Guerreiro Ramos e o tema das relações raciais." *Dados* 40, no. 1 (1997): 127-62.

―――. "A questão racial no pensamento de Guerreiro Ramos." In *Raça, ciência e sociedade,* edited by Marcos Chor Maio and Ricardo Ventura Santos, 179-93. Rio de Janeiro: Fiocruz, 1996.

―――. "UNESCO and the Study of Race Relations in Brazil: Regional or National Issue?" *Latin American Research Review* 36 (2001): 118-36.

Malinoff, Jane. "Modern Afro-Brazilian Poetry." *Callaloo* 8/10 (1980): 43-61.

Mann, Kristin. *Slavery and the Birth of an African City: Lagos, 1760-1900.* Bloomington: Indiana University Press, 2007.

Manring, M. M. *Slave in a Box: The Strange Career of Aunt Jemima.* Charlottesville: University Press of Virginia, 1998.

Mariano, Júlio. "História da imprensa em Campinas." In *Monografia histórica do Município de Campinas,* edited by IBGE, 301-14. Rio de Janeiro: IBGE, 1952.

Martí, José. *Cuba, Nuestra América, los Estados Unidos.* Mexico City: Siglo Veintiuno, 1973.

Martínez-Echazábal, Lourdes. "Mestizaje and the Discourse of National/Cultural Identity in Latin America, 1845-1959." *Latin American Perspectives* 25, no. 3 (1998): 21-42.

Marx, Anthony. *Making Race and Nation: A Comparison of the United States, South Africa, and Brazil.* Cambridge: Cambridge University Press, 1998.

Matory, J. Lorand. *Black Atlantic Religion: Tradition, Transnationalism, and Matriarchy in the Afro-Brazilian Candomblé.* Princeton, N.J.: Princeton University Press, 2005.

Matta, Roberto da. "Notas sobre o racismo à brasileira." In *Multiculturalismo e racismo: Uma comparação Brasil–Estados Unidos,* edited by Jessé Souza, 69-74. Brasília: Paralelo, 1997.

Mattos, Hebe Maria. *Das cores do silêncio: Os significados da liberdade no sudeste escravista, Brasil, século XIX.* Rio de Janeiro: Arquivo Nacional, 1995.

Mattos, Hebe Maria, and Ana Lugão Rios. *Memórias do cativeiro: Família, trabalho e cidadania no pós-abolição.* Rio de Janeiro: Civilização Brasileira, 2005.

McCann, Bryan. "Black Pau: Uncovering the History of Brazilian Soul." In *Rockin' Las Américas*, edited by Deborah Pacini Hernández, Héctor Fernández L'Hoeste, and Eric Zolov, 68–90. Pittsburgh: University of Pittsburgh Press, 2004.

———. *Hello, Hello Brazil: Popular Music in the Making of Modern Brazil*. Durham, N.C.: Duke University Press, 2004.

McElya, Micki. *Clinging to Mammy: The Faithful Slave in Twentieth-Century America*. Cambridge: Harvard University Press, 2007.

McPhee, Kit. "'A New 13th of May': Afro-Brazilian Port Workers in Rio de Janeiro, Brazil, 1905–18." *Journal of Latin American Studies* 38 (2006): 149–77.

Meade, Teresa. *"Civilizing" Rio: Reform and Resistance in a Brazilian City, 1889–1930*. University Park: Pennsylvania State University Press, 1997.

Meade, Teresa, and Gregory Alonso Pirio. "In Search of the Afro-American 'Eldorado': Attempts by North American Blacks to Enter Brazil in the 1920s." *Luso-Brazilian Review* 25, no. 1 (1998): 85–110.

Menezes, Adolpho Justo Bezerra de. *Ásia, África e a política independente do Brasil*. Rio de Janeiro: Zahar, 1961.

———. *O Brasil e o mundo ásio-africano*. Rio de Janeiro: GRD, 1961.

Mitchell, Michael. "Blacks and the *Abertura Democrática*." In *Race, Class, and Power in Brazil*, edited by Pierre-Michel Fontaine, 95–119. Los Angeles: Center for Afro-American Studies, UCLA, 1985.

———. "Miguel Reale and the Impact of Conservative Modernization on Brazilian Race Relations." In *Racial Politics in Contemporary Brazil*, edited by Michael Hanchard, 116–37. Durham, N.C.: Duke University Press, 1999.

———. "Racial Consciousness and the Political Attitudes and Behavior of Blacks in São Paulo, Brazil." Ph.D. diss., Indiana University, 1977.

Monteiro, Helene. "O ressurgimento do movimento negro no Rio de Janeiro na década de 70." M.A. thesis, Universidade Federal do Rio de Janeiro, 1991.

Monteiro, John. "The Heathen Castes of Sixteenth-Century Portuguese America: Unity, Diversity, and the Invention of the Brazilian Indians." *HAHR* 80, no. 4 (2001): 697–720.

———. *Negros da terra: Índios e bandeirantes nas origens de São Paulo*. São Paulo: Companhia das Letras, 1995.

Moore, Zelbert L. "Solano Trinidade Remembered, 1908–1974." *Luso-Brazilian Review* 16, no. 2 (1979): 233–38.

Moraes, Evaristo de. *Brancos e negros: Nos Estados Unidos e no Brasil*. Rio de Janeiro: Miccolis, 1922.

Mota, Carlos Guilherme. *Ideologia da cultura brasileira, 1933–1974*. São Paulo: Ática, 1978.

Motta, Roberto. "Paradigms in the Study of Race Relations in Brazil." *International Sociology* 15, no. 4 (2000): 665–82.

Motta-Maués, Maria Angelica. "Quem somos nós? Anotações para um diálogo que não houve: Costa Pinto e a militância negra dos anos 50." In *Ideais de modernidade e sociologia no Brasil: Ensaios sobre Luiz de Aguiar Costa Pinto*, edited by Marcos Chor Maio and Glaucia Villas Bôas, 161–81. Porto Alegre: Universidade Federal do Rio Grande do Sul, 1999.

Moura, Carlos Eugênio Marcondes de. *A travessia da calunga grande: Três séculos de imagens sobre o negro no Brasil (1637–1899)*. São Paulo: EDUSP and Imprensa Oficial, 2000.

Moura, Roberto. *Tia Ciata e a pequena África no Rio de Janeiro*. Rio de Janeiro: FUNARTE, 1983.

Moutinho, Laura. "Negociando discursos: Análise das relações entre a Fundação Ford, os movimentos negros e a academia na década de 80." M.A. thesis, Universidade Federal do Rio de Janeiro, 1996.

Nabuco, Joaquim. *O abolicionismo*. London: Abraham Kingdon, 1883.

Nascimento, Abdias do. "O genocídio do negro brasileiro." In *O Brasil na mira do pan-africanismo*, edited by Abdias do Nascimento, 41–245. Salvador da Bahia: EDUFBA/CEAO, 2002.

———. *O negro revoltado*. Rio de Janeiro: Edições GRD, 1968.

———. *O negro revoltado*. Rio de Janeiro: Editora Nova Fronteira, 1982.

———. "Sitiado em Lagos." In *O Brasil na mira do pan-africanismo*, edited by Abdias do Nascimento, 247–338. Salvador da Bahia: EDUFBA/CEAO, 2002.

Nascimento, Abdias do, and Elisa Larkin Nascimento. "Reflexões sobre o movimento negro no Brasil, 1938–1997." In *Tirando a máscara: Ensaios sobre o racismo no Brasil*, edited by Antonio Sérgio Alfredo Guimarães and Lynn Huntley, 203–36. São Paulo: Editora Paz e Terra, 2000.

———, eds. *Quilombo: Vida, problemas e aspirações do negro* (edição fac-similar do jornal dirigido por Abdias do Nascimento, Rio de Janeiro, nos. 1–10, dezembro de 1948 a julho de 1950). São Paulo: Fundação de Apoio à Universidade de São Paulo, 2003.

Nascimento, Álvaro P. do. "Um reduto negro: Cor e cidadania na Armada (1870–1910)." In *Quase-cidadão: Histórias e antropologias da pós-emancipação no Brasil*, edited by Olívia Maria Gomes da Cunha and Flávio dos Santos Gomes, 283–314. Rio de Janeiro: Editora FGV, 2007.

Nascimento, Elisa Larkin. *Pan-africanismo na América do Sul: Emergência de uma rebelião negra*. Petrópolis: Vozes, 1981.

Needell, Jeffrey. "Identity, Race, Gender, and Modernity in the Origins of Gilberto Freyre's Oeuvre." *American Historical Review* 100, no. 1 (1995): 51–77.

———. "The *Revolta contra vacina* of 1904: The Revolt against 'Modernization' in Belle-Époque Rio de Janeiro." *Hispanic American Historical Review* 67, no. 2 (1987): 233–69.

———. *A Tropical Belle-Époque: Elite Culture and Society in Turn-of-the-Century Rio de Janeiro*. Cambridge: Cambridge University Press, 1987.

Nina Rodrigues, Raymundo. *Os africanos no Brasil*. São Paulo: Nacional, 1935.

———. *O animismo fetichista dos negros bahianos*. Rio de Janeiro: Civilização Brasileira, 1935.

Nishida, Mieko. *Slavery and Identity: Ethnicity, Gender, and Race in Salvador, Brazil, 1808–1888*. Bloomington: Indiana University Press, 2003.

Nobles, Melissa. *Shades of Citizenship: Race and the Census in Modern Politics*. Stanford, Calif.: Stanford University Press, 2000.

Nóbrega, Cida, and Regina Echeverria. *Verger: Um retrato em preto e branco*. Salvador da Bahia: Corrupio, 2002.

Nóbrega, Cida, and José Félix dos Santos. *Mãe Senhora: Saudade e memória.* Salvador: Corrupio, 2000.

Olinto, Antonio. *Brasileiros na África.* Rio de Janeiro: GRD, 1964.

Oliveira, André Côrtes de. "Quem é a 'gente negra nacional'? Frente Negra Brasileira e *A Voz da Raça* (1933–1937)." M.A. thesis, UNICAMP, 2006.

Oliveira, Lucia Lippi. *A sociologia do guerreiro.* Rio de Janeiro: Editora da UFRJ, 1995.

Oliveira, Maria Ines Côrtes de. "Quem eram os 'Negros da Guiné'? A origem dos africanos na Bahia." *Afro-Ásia* 19–20 (1997): 37–74.

Ortiz, Fernando. *Contrapunteo cubano del tabaco y el azúcar.* Caracas: Ayacucho, 1978.

Ortiz, Renato. *Cultura brasileira e identidade nacional.* São Paulo: Brasiliense, 1985.

Pereira, Carlos Alberto M., and Heloísa Buarque de Hollanda, eds. *Patrulhas ideológicas, marca reg.: Arte e engajamento em debate.* São Paulo: Brasiliense, 1980.

Pereira, José G. "São Benedito: A escola na construção da cidadania." In *Memórias da educação, Campinas (1850–1960),* edited by Terezinha Ribeiro do Nascimento, 275–310. Campinas: Editora da Unicamp, 1999.

Pereira, José Maria Nunes. "Os estudos africanos no Brasil e as relações com a África—um estudo de caso: O CEAA (1973–1986)." M.A. thesis, Universidade de São Paulo, 1991.

Pereira, Leonardo Affonso de Miranda. "E o Rio dançou. Identidades e tensões nos clubes recreativos." In *Carnavais e outras f(r)estas: Ensaios de história social da cultura,* edited by Maria Clementina Pereira Cunha, 419–44. Campinas: CECULT, 2002.

Perrone-Moisés, Beatriz. "Índios livres e índios escravos: Os princípios da legislação indigenista do período colonial (séculos XVI a XVIII)." In *História dos índios no Brasil,* edited by Manuela Carneiro da Cunha, 117–32. São Paulo: Companhia das Letras, 1992.

Pickering, Mary. "Angels and Demons in the Moral Vision of Auguste Comte." *Journal of Women's History* 8, no. 2 (1996): 10–40.

Pierson, Donald. *Negroes in Brazil: A Study of Race Contact in Bahia.* Chicago: University of Chicago Press, 1942.

Pinho, Patricia de Santana. *Mama Africa: Reinventing Blackness in Bahia.* Durham, N.C.: Duke University Press, 2010.

Pinto, Regina Pahim. "Movimento negro e etnicidade." *Estudos Afro-Asiáticos* 19 (1990): 109–24.

———. "O movimento negro em São Paulo: Luta e identidade." Ph.D. diss., Universidade de São Paulo, 1993.

Portella, Eduardo. *África: Colonos e cúmplices.* Rio de Janeiro: Prado, 1961.

Prandi, Reginaldo. *Os candomblés de São Paulo: A velha magia na metrópole nova.* São Paulo: Editora HUCITEC/Editora da USP, 1991.

Quadros, Jânio. "Brazil's New Foreign Policy." *Foreign Affairs* 40 (1961): 19–27.

Rama, Ángel. *The Lettered City.* Translated by John Chasteen. Durham, N.C.: Duke University Press, 1996.

Ramos, Arthur. *Aculturação negra no Brasil.* São Paulo: Nacional, 1942.

———. *As ciências sociais e os problemas de após-guerra.* Rio de Janeiro: Casa do Estudante do Brasil, 1944.

———. *Guerra e relações de raça*. Rio de Janeiro: Departamento Editorial da União Nacional dos Estudantes, 1943.

———. *O negro brasileiro*. São Paulo: Nacional, 1940.

———. *The Negro in Brazil*. Washington, D.C.: Associated Publishers, 1951.

Raphael, Alison. "Samba and Social Control: Popular Culture and Racial Democracy in Rio de Janeiro." Ph.D. diss., Columbia University, 1981.

Reichmann, Rebecca, ed. *Race in Contemporary Brazil: From Indifference to Inequality*. University Park: Pennsylvania State University Press, 1999.

Reis, Fidelis. *Paiz a organizar*. Rio de Janeiro: A. Gloria, 1924.

Reis, João José. "Candomblé in Nineteenth-Century Bahia: Priests, Followers, Clients." In *Rethinking the African Diaspora: The Making of a Black Atlantic World in the Bight of Benin and Brazil*, edited by Kristin Mann and Edna Bay, 116–34. New York: Frank Cass, 2001.

———. "Presença negra: Conflitos e encontros." In *Brasil: 500 anos de povoamento*, edited by IBGE, 80–99. Rio de Janeiro: IBGE, 2000.

———. *Slave Rebellion in Brazil*. Baltimore: Johns Hopkins University Press, 1985.

Risério, Antonio. *Avant-garde na Bahia*. São Paulo: Instituto Lina Bo e P.M. Bardi, 1995.

———. "Bahia com 'H.'" In *Escravidão e invenção da liberdade*, edited by João José Reis, 143–65. São Paulo: Brasiliense/CNPq, 1988.

———. "Carnaval: As cores da mudança." *Afro-Ásia* 16 (1995): 90–106.

———. *Carnaval ijexá*. Salvador da Bahia: Corrupio, 1981.

———. *Uma história da cidade da Bahia*. Rio de Janeiro: Versal, 2004.

———. *A utopia brasileira e os movimentos negros*. São Paulo: Editora 34, 2007.

Rodó, José Enrique. *Ariel*. Madrid: Cátedra, 2000.

Rodrigues, José Honório. *Brasil e África: Outro horizonte*. Rio de Janeiro: Civilização Brasileira, 1964.

Romo, Anadelia. "Rethinking Race and Culture in Brazil's First Afro-Brazilian Congress of 1934." *JLAS* 39 (2007): 31–54.

Rubim, Antonio Albino Canelas. "Os primórdios da universidade e a cultura na Bahia." In *A ousadia da criação: Universidade e cultura*, edited by Antonio Albino Canelas Rubim, 113–22. Salvador da Bahia: FACOM, 1999.

Russell-Wood, A. J. R. *The Black Man in Slavery and Freedom in Colonial Brazil*. London: Macmillan, 1982.

Sandroni, Carlos. *Feitiço decente: Transformações do samba no Rio de Janeiro, 1917–1933*. Rio de Janeiro: Jorge Zahar Editor/Editora UFRJ, 2001.

Sansone, Lívio. *Blackness without Ethnicity*. New York: Palgrave Macmillan, 2003.

Santos, Arlindo Veiga dos. *Idéias que marcham no silêncio*. São Paulo: Pátria-Nova, 1968.

———. *As raízes históricas do patrianovismo*. São Paulo: Pátria-Nova, 1946.

Santos, Deoscóredes Maximiliano dos. *História de um terreiro nagô*. São Paulo: Max Limonad, 1988.

Saraiva, José Flávio Sombra. *O lugar da África: A dimensão atlântica da política externa brasileira (de 1946 a nossos dias)*. Brasília: Editora Universidade de Brasília, 1996.

Schwarcz, Lilia Moritz. *The Emperor's Beard: Dom Pedro II and His Tropical Monarchy in Brazil.* Translated by John Gledson. New York: Hill and Wang, 2004.

———. *O espetáculo das raças: Cientistas, instituições, e questão racial no Brasil, 1870–1930.* São Paulo: Companhia das Letras, 1993.

Scott, Rebecca. "Brazil: Introduction." In *Societies after Slavery: A Select Annotated Bibliography of Printed Sources on Cuba, Brazil, British Colonial Africa, South Africa, and the British West Indies,* edited by Rebecca Scott, Thomas Holt, Frederick Cooper, and Aims McGuinness, 323–26. Pittsburgh: University of Pittsburgh Press, 2002.

———. *Degrees of Freedom: Louisiana and Cuba after Slavery.* Cambridge: Belknap/Harvard University Press, 2005.

———. "Public Rights, Social Equality, and the Conceptual Roots of the Plessy Challenge." *Michigan Law Review* 106, no. 5 (2008): 777–804.

Seigel, Micol. "The Point of Comparison: Transnational Racial Construction, Brazil and the United States, 1918–1933." Ph.D. diss., New York University, 2001.

———. *Uneven Encounters: Making Race and Nation in Brazil and the United States.* Durham, N.C.: Duke University Press, 2009.

Selcher, Wayne. "Afro-Asian Dimension of Brazilian Foreign Policy, 1956–1968." Ph.D. diss., University of Florida, 1970.

Semog, Éle, and Abdias do Nascimento. *Abdias Nascimento: O griot e as muralhas.* Rio de Janeiro: Pallas, 2006.

Serra, Ordep. *Águas do rei.* Petrópolis: Vozes, 1995.

Sevcenko, Nicolau. *Orfeu extático na metrópole: São Paulo, sociedade e cultura nos frementes anos 20.* São Paulo: Companhia das Letras, 1992.

Seyferth, Giralda. "Construindo a nação: Hierarquias raciais e o papel do racismo na política de imigração e colonização." In *Raça, ciência e sociedade,* edited by Marcos Chor Maio and Ricardo Ventura Santos, 41–58. Rio de Janeiro: Editora Fiocruz, 1996.

Shaffer, Kirwin. "What Will You Do to Become an Emerging World Power? Ethnic Manipulation in Brazil's Penetration of Africa." *International Third World Studies Journal and Review* 4, no. 1 (1992): 20–32.

Sheriff, Robin. *Dreaming Equality: Color, Race, and Racism in Urban Brazil.* New Brunswick, N.J.: Rutgers University Press, 2001.

Silva, Agostinho da. "O nascimento do CEAO." *Afro-Ásia* 16 (1995): 5–8.

Silva, Denise Ferreira da. "Facts of Blackness: Brazil Is Not (Quite) the United States . . . and Racial Politics in Brazil?" *Social Identities* 4, no. 2 (1998): 201–34.

Silva, Erminia. *Circo-teatro: Benjamim de Oliveira e a teatralidade circense no Brasil.* São Paulo: Altana, 2007.

Silva, Jônatas C. da. "História de lutas negras: Memórias do surgimento do movimento negro na Bahia." In *Escravidão e invenção da liberdade,* edited by João José Reis, 275–88. São Paulo: Brasiliense/CNPq, 1988.

Silva, Joselina da. "A União dos Homens de Cor: Aspectos do movimento negro dos anos 40 e 50." *Estudos Afro-Asiáticos* 25, no. 2 (2003): 215–35.

Silva, Luiz [Cuti], and José Correia Leite. *E disse o velho militante José Correia Leite.* São Paulo: Secretaria Municipal de Cultura, 1992.

Silva, Nelson do Valle. "Updating the Cost of Not Being White in Brazil." In *Race, Class, and Power in Brazil*, edited by Pierre-Michel Fontaine. Los Angeles: Center for Afro-American Studies, UCLA, 1985.

———. "White-Nonwhite Income Differentials: Brazil-1960." Ph.D. diss., University of Michigan, 1978.

Skidmore, Thomas E. "Bi-Racial U.S.A. vs. Multi-Racial Brazil: Is the Contrast Still Valid?" *Journal of Latin American Studies* 25 (1993): 373–86.

———. *Black into White: Race and Nationality in Brazilian Thought*. Durham, N.C.: Duke University Press, 1995.

———. *Brazil: Five Centuries of Change*. New York: Oxford University Press, 1999.

———. *Politics in Brazil, 1930–1964: An Experiment in Democracy*. Oxford: Oxford University Press, 1967.

———. *The Politics of Military Rule in Brazil, 1964–1985*. New York: Oxford University Press, 1988.

———. "Race and Class in Brazil: Historical Perspectives." In *Race, Class, and Power in Brazil*, edited by Pierre-Michel Fontaine, 11–24. Los Angeles: Center for Afro-American Studies, UCLA, 1985.

———. "Racial Ideas and Social Policy in Brazil, 1870–1940." In *The Idea of Race in Latin America, 1870–1940*, edited by Richard Graham, 7–36. Austin: University of Texas Press, 1990.

———. "Raízes de Gilberto Freyre." *Journal of Latin American Studies*, no. 34 (2002): 1–20.

Soares, Mariza de Carvalho. *Devotos da cor: Identidade étnica, religiosidade e escravidão no Rio de Janeiro, século XVIII*. Rio de Janeiro: Civilização Brasileira, 2000.

Sommer, Doris. *Foundational Fictions: The National Romances of Latin America*. Berkeley: University of California Press, 1991.

Stepan, Nancy. *The Hour of Eugenics: Race, Gender, and Nation in Latin America*. Ithaca, N.Y.: Cornell University Press, 1991.

Stocking, George E. *The Shaping of American Anthropology, 1883–1911: A Franz Boas Reader*. New York: Basic Books, 1974.

Telles, Edward. "Ethnic Boundaries and Political Mobilization among African Brazilians: Comparisons with the U.S. Case." In *Racial Politics in Contemporary Brazil*, edited by Michael Hanchard, 82–97. Durham, N.C.: Duke University Press, 1999.

———. *Race in Another America: The Significance of Skin Color in Brazil*. Princeton, N.J.: Princeton University Press, 2004.

———. "U.S. Foundations and Racial Reasoning in Brazil." *Theory, Culture and Society* 20, no. 4 (2003): 31–47.

Toplin, Robert B. *Freedom and Prejudice: The Legacy of Slavery in the USA and Brazil*. Westport, Conn.: Greenwood, 1981.

———. "Reinterpreting Comparative Race Relations: The United States and Brazil." *Journal of Black Studies* 2, no. 2 (1971): 135–56.

Turner, J. Michael. "Brown into Black: Changing Racial Attitudes of Afro-Brazilian University Students." In *Race, Class, and Power in Brazil*, edited by Pierre-Michel Fontaine, 73–94. Los Angeles: Center for Afro-American Studies, UCLA, 1985.

Twine, France W. *Racism in a Racial Democracy: The Maintenance of White Supremacy in Brazil*. New Brunswick, N.J.: Rutgers University Press, 1998.

Vainfas, Ronaldo. "História indígena: 500 anos de despovoamento." In *Brasil: 500 anos de povoamento*, edited by IBGE, 36–59. Rio de Janeiro: IBGE, 2000.

Valladares, Clarival do Prado. *The Impact of African Culture on Brazil (Brazilian Exhibition/II FESTAC/Lagos, Nigeria)*. Brasília: MRE/MEC, 1976.

Vasconcelos, José. *The Cosmic Race/La raza cósmica*. Translated by Didier T. Jaén. Pensamiento Mexicano. Los Angeles: Centro de Publicaciones, Department of Chicano Studies, California State University, 1979.

Velasco e Cruz, Maria Cecília. "Puzzling Out Slave Origins in Rio de Janeiro Port Unionism: The 1906 Strike and the Sociedade de Resistência dos Trabalhadores em Trapiche e Café." *Hispanic American Historical Review* 86, no. 2 (2006): 205–45.

Velho, Yvonne. *Guerra de orixá*. Rio de Janeiro: Zahar, 1975.

Verger, Pierre. *Fluxo e refluxo do tráfico de escravos entre o Golfo do Benin e a Bahia de Todos os Santos dos séculos XVII a XIX*. 3rd ed. São Paulo: Editora Corrupio, 1987.

———. *Orixás: Os deuses iorubás na África e no Novo Mundo*. Salvador da Bahia: Corrupio, 1981.

Vianna, F. J. Oliveira. *Evolução do povo brasileiro*. 2nd ed. São Paulo: Nacional, 1933.

Vianna, Hermano. *O mundo funk carioca*. Rio de Janeiro: Zahar, 1988.

———. *The Mystery of Samba: Popular Music and National Identity in Brazil*. Translated by John Chasteen. Chapel Hill: University of North Carolina Press, 1999.

Villas Bôas, Glaucia. "Passado arcaico, futuro moderno: A contribuição de L. A. Costa Pinto à sociologia das mudanças sociais." In *Ideais de modernidade e sociologia no Brasil: Ensaios sobre Luiz de Aguiar Costa Pinto*, edited by Marcos Chor Maio and Glaucia Villas Bôas, 51–59. Porto Alegre: Editora da Universidade Federal do Rio Grande do Sul, 1999.

von Martius, Karl Friedrich Philipp. "How the History of Brazil Should Be Written." In *Perspectives on Brazilian History*, edited by E. Bradford Burns, 21–41. New York: Columbia University Press, 1967.

Wade, Peter. *Blackness and Race Mixture: The Dynamics of Racial Identity in Colombia*. Baltimore: Johns Hopkins University Press, 1993.

———. "Images of Latin American Mestizaje and the Politics of Comparison." *Bulletin of Latin American Research* 23, no. 3 (2004): 355–66.

———. *Race and Ethnicity in Latin America*. London: Pluto Press, 1997.

Wagley, Charles. *Race and Class in Rural Brazil*. Paris: UNESCO, 1952.

Warren, Jonathan. *Racial Revolutions: Antiracism and Indian Resurgence in Brazil*. Durham, N.C.: Duke University Press, 2001.

Weinstein, Barbara. "Celebrating Modernity: São Paulo's Quadricentennial and the Historical Construction of Regional Identity." Paper presented at the David Rockefeller Center for Latin American Studies Colloquium, Harvard University, 8 May 2002.

———. "Erecting and Erasing Boundaries: Can We Combine the 'Indo' and the 'Afro' in Latin American Studies?" *Estudios Interdisciplinarios de América Latina y el Caribe* 19, no. 1 (2007).

———. *For Social Peace in Brazil: Industrialists and the Remaking of the Working Class in São Paulo, 1920–1964*. Chapel Hill: University of North Carolina Press, 1996.

———. "Racializing Regional Difference: São Paulo versus Brazil, 1932." In *Race and Nation in Modern Latin America*, edited by Nancy P. Appelbaum, Anne S. Macpherson, and Karin Alejandra Rosemblatt, 237–62. Chapel Hill: University of North Carolina Press, 2003.

Wexler, Laura. *Tender Violence: Domestic Visions in an Age of U.S. Imperialism*. Chapel Hill: University of North Carolina Press, 2000.

Williams, Daryle. *Culture Wars in Brazil: The First Vargas Regime, 1930–1945*. Durham, N.C.: Duke University Press, 2001.

Winant, Howard. *Racial Conditions: Politics, Theory, Comparisons*. Minneapolis: University of Minnesota Press, 1994.

———. "Racial Democracy and Racial Identity." In *Racial Politics in Contemporary Brazil*, edited by Michael Hanchard, 98–115. Durham, N.C.: Duke University Press, 1999.

Wolfe, Joel. "'Father of the Poor' or 'Mother of the Rich'? Getúlio Vargas, Industrial Workers, and Constructions of Class, Gender, and Populism in São Paulo, 1930–1954." *Radical History Review* 58 (1994): 80–111.

Wright, Winthrop. *Café con Leche: Race, Class, and National Image in Venezuela*. Austin: University of Texas Press, 1990.

Xavier, Giovana. "'Leitoras': Gênero, raça, imagem e discurso em *O Menelick* (São Paulo, 1915–1916)." Paper presented at the Tenth International Congress of the Brazilian Studies Association, 22–24 July 2010.

Yuval-Davis, Nira. "Belonging and the Politics of Belonging." *Patterns of Prejudice* 40, no. 3 (2006): 197–214.

Zeuske, Michael. "Two Stories of Gender and Slave Emancipation in Cienfuegos and Santa Clara, Central Cuba: A Microhistorical Approach to the Atlantic World." In *Gender and Slave Emancipation in the Atlantic World*, edited by Pamela Scully and Diana Paton, 181–98. Durham, N.C.: Duke University Press, 2005.

and, 11–12, 14–15, 16, 179, 181, 193–94, 220, 255–56, 295, 300; racial discrimination and, 13, 15, 173, 175, 177, 178, 291, 332 (n. 53), 333 (n. 73), 345 (nn. 27–28); racial discrimination and, approach to vs. Paulistas, 214, 215–16, 220, 340 (nn. 53, 55); racial harmony and, 17, 198; "right to Rights" and, 171–72, 185; social science and race and, 190, 191, 193, 216, 219–20; TEN and, 164–65, 171, 175, 213, 214, 215, 218, 221, 249, 255, 332 (n. 53)

Nascimento, Beatriz do, 257, 272, 273–74, 277, 279, 348 (n. 89)

Nascimento, Deocleciano, 35, 37, 64, 140

National. See Nacional

Navarro, Saul de, 89–90

Negreiros, Aristides, 176–77

Negreiros, Carlos, 272

Negritude, 221–22, 239

Négritude, 220–21

Negro: defined, 22; early uses of term, 6, 44, 46, 47, 48, 308 (n. 25); identifying openly as, 21, 30, 50, 81, 87, 143, 284, 285; proud use of term, 102, 119, 138, 144–45, 147, 148; as unified racial category, 94, 95, 111, 169, 208, 268, 276, 298, 352 (n. 5); use of term in Rio, 162, 196; use of term in Salvador da Bahia, 145; use of term in São Paulo, 18, 57–58, 67, 85, 95, 119, 161, 162, 169, 208; use of term in São Paulo black press, 30, 42, 46, 47, 48, 52, 53, 54–55, 56, 68, 91–92, 236. See also Racial terminology

Negroes in Brazil (Pierson), 182

Negro no Rio de Janeiro (Costa Pinto), 218

Negro World, 140, 146, 188

Neto, Antonio Agostinho, 259, 287

Neto, H. M. Coelho, 91

Niger, 234, 235, 236

Nigeria, 240–41, 251, 273; Candomblé and, 123, 124, 225, 228, 231, 232, 233, 242, 341 (n. 80); FESTAC II and, 14–15, 252–53, 254, 255–56, 269, 300, 302, 345 (nn. 27–28)

Nina Rodrigues, Raymundo, 121, 124, 182, 184, 187, 188, 219

Nkrumah, Kwame, 239, 259

Nogueira, Hamilton, 174, 175, 176, 177, 211, 212, 215, 333 (n. 75), 339 (n. 39)

Nossa Senhora do Rosário dos Homens Pretos, 210, 293

Notícia: Mãe Preta campaign and, 72, 76, 78–79, 91, 93, 113, 114, 145, 315 (n. 4); people of color and, 82–84, 87, 88, 318 (n. 66)

Notícias de Ébano, 235

Novo Horizonte (*New Horizon*), 165, 167, 168, 170, 180, 205, 289; Africa, ties with and, 187–88, 189, 190; founding of, 151, 157; Mãe Preta figure and, 186–87; social science and race and, 184, 337 (n. 141)

Ojelabi, Maria, 228

Olinto, Antonio, 241–42, 344 (n. 137)

Oliveira, Augusto, 35, 38, 42

Oliveira, Eduardo de Oliveira e, 287, 289, 290

Oliveira, Euclydes, 57, 62, 68, 325 (n. 85)

Oliveira, Francisco José de, 24, 26, 27, 29, 30, 33, 38

Oliveira, Geraldo Campos de, 157, 165, 166, 176, 207

Oliveira Vianna, Francisco José de, 27, 49

Olorum Baba Mim, 262, 272

O'Neill, Eugene, 164, 213

Orixás, 118

Orlando, Alberto, 89, 130, 133

Ortiz, Fernando, 78

Ortiz, Renato, 253

Osório, Joaquim, 43, 44

Oxum, 225, 341 (n. 80)

Oyo, 225–27

Paiz, 48, 75

Palmares, 68, 89, 137, 140, 273–74

Pan-Africanism, 65, 104, 109, 132, 140–41, 142, 149, 236, 259

Pardos, 6, 8, 11, 22, 30, 48, 57. See also Racial terminology; Rio de Janeiro; Salvador da Bahia; São Paulo

Paris, 71

Partido Social Democrático (PSD, Social Democratic Party), 154

Partido Trabalhista Brasileiro (PTB, Brazilian Labor Party), 168, 173, 175, 199, 333 (n. 74)

Patrianovismo, 132

Patrocínio, José do, 9, 67, 85, 137, 155

Paulistanos (from city of São Paulo): African culture and, rejection of, 58, 65, 103, 107, 139–40, 141–42, 149–50, 187, 188, 189, 208, 220, 234; black associations of, 34–35; black employment, 32, 35; black writers, 24, 306 (n. 1); European immigrants as, 63

Paulistas (from state of São Paulo): black writers among, 24, 36–37, 38–39, 187, 306 (n. 1); educated men of color among, 31, 39–40, 310 (n. 64); population of, whites vs. people of color, 28, 307–8 (n. 19); resistance to Vargas regime, 116, 127–28, 138, 208

Pedro I (emperor of Brazil), 7

Pedro II (emperor of Brazil), 7, 96, 320 (n. 101)

Peixoto, Afrânio, 49–50

Penna, Belisário, 99

Penteado Júnior, Frederico, 209, 210, 211, 294

Pereira, Amauri Mendes, 257–58, 260, 261, 262, 263, 278, 279, 292, 350 (n. 116)

Pereira, José Maria Nunes, 257, 270

Pereira, Miguel, 99

Pereira, Neusa, 288

Pereira Passos, Francisco, 71, 159

Pernambuco, 2, 42, 112, 113, 212

Picchia, Paulo Menotti del, 103, 104, 107

Pierson, Donald, 124–25, 182, 183, 191

Pinacoteca do Estado de São Paulo (state art museum), 290

Pinto, Barreto, 175

Pinto, Louis Inácio, 242

Pires, Jurandir, 211

Pittsburgh Courier, 175

Portella, Eduardo, 238–39

Portinari, Cândido, 209

Portugal, 143, 179; African colonialism and, 230, 233, 237, 238, 246, 251, 252, 257, 270, 287, 295

Portuguese in Brazil, 9, 11, 22, 39, 61–62, 134, 274; Brazilian independence and, 7, 78, 96, 303 (n. 9); as immigrants, 25, 86; slavery and, 6–7, 11, 24, 306 (n. 3)

Prandi, Reginaldo, 142

Présence Africaine, 221

Prestes, Júlio, 93

Pretos, 22. *See also* Racial terminology; Rio de Janeiro; Salvador da Bahia; São Paulo

Progresso, 97, 130; Africa, ties with and, 104, 234, 236; black activism in First Republic and, 105–6, 128, 327 (n. 117); Vargas regime and, 128, 129

Protectora, 47, 312 (n. 90), 313 (n. 114)

Quadros, Jânio, 200, 201, 209, 248; Brazilian foreign policy and Africa and, 237–40, 243, 251, 256, 343 (n. 126)

Querino, Manoel, 147

Quilombo, 165–66, 170, 176; Africanness of Brazilian culture and, 189, 190–91, 197, 220, 341 (n. 72); *negritude* and, 220–21, 239; party politics and, 168, 331 (n. 51), 332 (n. 52); racial democracy and, 180, 194; racial discrimination and, 175, 214, 215, 340 (n. 56); social science and race and, 184, 215; TEN and, 164, 171, 213, 214, 215, 220

Quilombo (samba school), 262

Race and Class in Rural Brazil (Wagley), 224

Race relations, 16, 18, 21; social science research and, 12, 13, 152, 181–93, 203, 204, 217–20, 224, 250, 304 (n. 22), 305 (n. 30), 312 (n. 96)

Racial democracy: Africa, ties with and, 201, 233–36, 239, 241, 242, 287–89, 351 (n. 151); appearance of term, 21, 178–79, 335 (n. 96); failure of, 178, 204, 211, 258, 276, 291; ideal of, 179–81, 298, 301; military dictatorship and, 15, 244, 245–46,

248, 250, 280; "myth" of, 13–14, 15, 16, 17, 49, 193–96, 246, 254–56, 264, 268, 277, 294, 295–96, 297, 300–301; racial equality and, 42, 177, 179, 194, 197, 202, 203, 296; racial harmony and, 5, 153, 178, 182, 183, 184, 212, 300–301; racial mixture and, 16, 179, 194, 220, 305 (n. 36); after World War II, 11–12, 152

Racial discrimination: affirmative action and, 21, 172, 211–12, 298–99, 305 (n. 36); black activism after 1964 and, 15, 247, 289, 291–94, 297–98; call for end of, Second Republic, 152, 156–57, 172, 173–75, 176–78, 179, 198, 200–202, 211–12, 333 (nn. 73–75), 334 (nn. 86, 88); class and, 183, 204, 206–7, 212, 213, 330–31 (n. 33), 332 (n. 53), 336 (n. 110); middle-class men of color and, 20, 21, 23, 29–30, 31, 35–37, 38, 46, 47–48, 52–57, 67–68, 309 (n. 45); military dictatorship and, 249–50, 258, 264, 345 (nn. 27–28); purported absence of extreme, 12–13; reverse discrimination and, 202, 343 (n. 126); in Rio de Janeiro, 85, 86, 158–59, 160, 174, 175–76, 177, 207, 318 (n. 58); in Salvador da Bahia, 282, 283–84; in São Paulo, 131, 150, 158, 162, 163, 177, 201–7, 214, 217, 290–92, 340 (n. 56); in São Paulo, early twentieth century, 18, 23–24, 29–30, 31, 54–57, 68, 84, 85, 89, 99, 120, 318 (n. 58); TEN's approach to fighting, 175, 214, 215–17, 219–20, 339 (n. 39), 340 (nn. 53, 59). *See also* South Africa; United States

Racial equality, 179, 194, 202, 311 (n. 73); democracy and, 25, 42, 151, 156–57, 170, 172, 175, 177, 178, 296; middle-class men of color and, 53, 54; racial harmony and, 3–5, 197; slavery having prevented, 201, 203, 336 (n. 110)

Racial fusion, 109, 305 (n. 36); black Brazilian thinkers and, 51, 102; Mãe Preta figure and, 94, 101–3, 104, 108, 115, 145; "one race" perspective and, 45, 62, 94, 115, 242; racial harmony and, 9, 12, 24, 44–45, 49–50, 54, 62, 275–76;

"two race" perspective and, 19, 102, 145, 242. See also *Mestiçagem*; Racial mixture of Brazil

Racial harmony: black Brazilian thinkers and, 8, 9–10, 11–12, 24, 48–49; black Brazilian thinkers refuting existence of, 13–14, 15, 17, 198; dictatorship and, 249–50, 254–55, 256, 294, 295; erasure of black race through assimilation and, 9, 42, 45, 48–50; in Latin America, 16–17; military dictatorship and, 15, 245; and national identity, 10–11, 15, 112–15; origins of idea of, 5–9, 202–3; racial democracy and, 5, 153, 178, 182, 183, 184, 212, 300–301; racial equality and, 3–5, 197; racial fusion and, 9, 12, 24, 44–45, 49–50, 51, 54, 62, 94; racial mixture and, 11, 114, 115, 230, 275; social scientific research and, 181–82, 183–84; "two race" perspective and, 138, 207–8, 222, 266, 267, 291; "whitening ideal" and, 27, 42, 49–50, 51, 62, 114. *See also* Fraternity ideal

Racial inclusion, 151, 246, 300; lack of, in First Republic, 20–21, 24, 25, 44, 45, 63

Racial inclusiveness, 10, 14, 17, 71, 254, 295–96, 302

Racial mixture of Brazil: after abolition of slavery, 3, 8, 10; Africanness of Brazilian culture and, 112–16, 230, 254, 255, 262, 281; black Brazilian thinkers and, 17–18, 51, 52; degeneration and, 26–27; denying blacks racial identification, 14, 15, 16; Mãe Preta figure as symbol of, 78, 79, 80, 81, 101–3, 108; military dictatorship and, 275–76; national identity and, 70, 71, 78–79, 122, 127, 128, 138; other Latin American countries and, 77–78; purported absence of extreme discrimination and, 12–13; racial democracy and, 16, 179, 194, 220, 305 (n. 36); racial harmony and, 11, 114, 115, 230, 275; "two race" perspective and, 18, 19, 102, 104, 108, 148, 149; "whitening ideal" and, 10, 27, 79, 305 (n. 27). See also *Mestiçagem*;

—black activism in: after 1964, 19, 247, 249, 256–81, 282, 287, 289, 291, 292, 349 (n. 108), 351 (n. 155); after 1985, 297, 298; during Estado Novo, 163–64; during First Republic, 46, 50–51, 82–83, 85–86, 317–18 (n. 53), 318 (n. 63); during Second Republic, 151, 155, 172, 173, 197–98, 204, 211–23, 330–31 (n. 33), 333 (n. 73), 340 (nn. 53, 55–56)

—black press of: activism, Second Republic, 165–66, 168, 170, 175–77, 194, 207; Africa, debate about ties with, 198, 220–22, 261–69, 271; lack of, 18, 19–20, 84–85, 87, 317–18 (n. 53); racial democracy and, 179, 180–81; racial discrimination and, 174, 175–76, 207; social science and race and, 181, 184, 189–91, 193, 221.

—mainstream newspapers of, 88, 224, 271; black organizations perceived as racist and, 196; black writers and, 18–19, 69, 173, 215–16; carnival and, 85, 317 (n. 45); immigration debates and, 48, 50; Mãe Preta figure and, 74, 75, 80, 82, 83, 87, 91. See also *Notícia*
See also Teatro Experimental do Negro; União dos Homens de Cor

Rio Grande do Sul, 43, 130, 159, 160
Rocha Miranda, Edgard da, 175
Rodrigues, Liberato José, 82
Roquette-Pinto, Edgard, 78

Salazar, Antonio de Oliveira, 143, 230, 251
Salvador da Bahia, 2, 20, 99, 140, 236; African cultural traditions and, 19, 111, 113, 116, 117, 118, 119–27, 145, 184, 231–33, 241, 243–44, 285; Afro-Brazilian Congresses and, 125, 188, 191; Afro-Brazilian religions and, 111, 118–19, 120–21, 145, 190, 199; "Afro" carnival groups of, 283, 284–87, 291; anthropology and, 113, 116, 119, 121–22, 124–25, 147, 153; anti-African sentiment in, 19, 118, 120, 121, 122, 145, 314 (n. 122), 323 (nn. 32, 39); black activism in, 19, 147, 148–50, 198–99, 247, 281–87, 291,

293, 349 (n. 108); *blocos afro* and, 283, 284–87, 291; carnival in, 118, 224–25, 247, 282–83, 284–87, 291, 323 (n. 32); Catholic black Brazilians of, 143, 147; Centro de Estudos Afro-Orientais and, 229–32, 240–41, 242, 344 (n. 133); containing essence of Brazilianness, 113, 116, 121–22; Frente Negra Brasileira and, 130, 143, 146–49; Mãe Preta figure and, 143–44, 145–46, 147, 243, 285–86, 328 (n. 127); mainstream newspapers of, 122, 144–45, 146, 314 (n. 122), 323 (n. 32); majority black population and, 5, 19, 111, 119, 148, 198, 216; *pretos* and *pardos* of, 19, 119–20, 144–45, 147, 148, 282–84; race relations and social science and, 182, 183, 201, 224; racial mixture and, 5, 111–12, 307–8 (n. 19); slavery and, 7, 19, 117–18, 119, 121, 122; soul and funk music and, 284, 350 (n. 131); Vargas regime and, 112, 116, 121, 199. *See also* Candomblé; Yoruba culture

Samba, 86–87, 114–16, 128, 161, 213, 217, 221, 262, 276, 322 (n. 15)
Santana, Joaquim Guaraná de, 133, 139
Santos, 2, 136, 146, 187, 207
Santos, Antonio Carlos dos. *See* Vovô
Santos, Arlindo J. Veiga dos, 290, 326 (n. 88); African culture, rejection of by, 103, 107, 139–40, 141; Centro Cívico Palmares and, 89, 95; *Clarim d'Alvorada* and, 35, 95, 99–100, 132; communism and, 134, 325–26 (n. 86); Congress of Black Youth and, 95, 99; Frente Negra Brasileira and, 35, 109, 129–30, 131, 132–33, 134–36, 137, 138, 139, 146, 165; increasing conservatism of, 109, 132–36, 139–40, 325 (n. 79), 326 (n. 91); racial activism of, 99–100, 103, 105, 138–39, 147, 149
Santos, Deoscóredes M. dos, 227
Santos, Eugenia Anna dos. *See* Mãe Aninha
Santos, Isaltino Veiga dos, 89, 131, 132, 134, 136, 146, 147, 160, 165, 325–26 (n. 86)

Santos, José Olympio dos, 82

Santos, Marcos Rodrigues dos, 146, 147

Santos, Paulo Roberto dos, 268, 271, 276

Santos, Suzete P. dos, 279, 280

São Paulo: Africa, non-acceptance of and, 58, 65, 103, 107, 139–40, 141, 149–50, 208, 220, 234; African cultural traditions, acceptance of, 292–93; Afro-Brazilian religions and, 142, 189, 327–28 (n. 121); Bexiga neighborhood, 59, 287; Black Brazilian National Convention and, 164, 172, 173, 186, 205; black Brazilian thinkers of, 19, 78, 152–53, 154; black lay brotherhoods of, 88, 210, 293, 319 (n. 70); call for confederation of black organizations in, 94–95, 99; Candomblé and, 142, 189, 293; celebration of 400th anniversary of founding, 208–9, 210; Centro Cívico Palmares, 89, 91, 92, 94, 95, 129, 130, 131, 146; Civil Guard, 31, 89, 131; colonial period of, 18, 39, 208–9, 339 (n. 31); communism and, 134, 136, 137, 325–26 (n. 86), 326 (n. 102); conservative black Catholics of, 99, 132, 141; constitutionalist uprising, 116, 127–28, 133, 138, 208, 209; elite of, 25, 28, 86, 110, 208; European immigrants in, 18, 23, 24, 28, 29, 56–64, 84–85, 86, 99, 100, 128, 162, 209; Federação dos Homens de Cor, 84, 87, 317 (n. 50), 318 (n. 65); mainstream newspapers, 33, 37, 54, 55, 63, 69, 73, 92–93, 100–101, 132, 173, 208, 209, 310 (n. 54), 320 (n. 90); middle-class men of color in, 23–24, 30–40, 87, 90, 308 (n. 29), 309 (n. 38); population of, whites vs. people of color, 28–29, 31, 111, 119, 157, 160, 208, 307–8 (n. 19); *pretos* and *pardos* of, 28, 29–30, 31, 47, 54–57, 58, 84–85, 111, 119, 157–58, 161, 290, 307–8 (n. 19), 329 (n. 17); racial discrimination and, 131, 150, 158, 162, 163, 177, 201–7, 214, 217, 290–92, 294, 340 (n. 56); racial discrimination and, early twentieth century, 18, 23–24, 29–30, 31, 54–57, 68, 84, 85, 89, 99, 120, 318 (n. 58); racial

mixture and, 5, 10, 28, 111–12, 222; Second Republic and, 289; segregation and, 31, 131, 158; slavery and, 7, 23, 28, 208, 209, 303 (n. 8), 339 (n. 31); state vs. city of, 2, 24, 28, 306 (n. 1); Syrio-Lebanese community of, 105–6, 107, 128, 209, 322 (n. 131); Vargas regime and, 110, 111–12, 116, 127–30, 133, 142, 163, 208; "whitening ideal" and, 23, 128, 137–38, 209; "whitening" of, 28–29, 70, 71, 100

—black activism in: after 1964, 246–47, 249, 274, 281, 287–94, 349 (n. 108), 351 (n. 151); during Estado Novo, 155–56, 157, 163, 164; during Second Republic, 156–57, 161, 162, 164, 165, 166, 167, 172, 173, 192, 197–98, 201–11, 213; through Frente Negra Brasileira, 111, 129, 130–33, 134, 135–38, 139–41, 143, 146, 147, 149, 162, 163, 216

—black press of, 19, 20; activism, after 1964, 287–90; activism, First Republic, 30, 45–64, 67–68, 84–85, 89–101, 105–9, 311 (n. 81), 312 (nn. 99–100), 313 (n. 101), 317 (n. 52); activism, Second Republic, 151, 157, 164–65, 166, 168–72, 176–77, 211; Africa, First Republic debate about ties with, 64–67, 104–5, 321 (n. 126); Africa, Second Republic debate about ties with, 188–90, 198, 208, 234–36; Africa, 1930s debate about ties with, 139–41, 142, 149, 327 (nn. 116–17, 119–20); Africa, 1960s and 70s debate about ties with, 263, 281, 288–89; African Americans, news about, 46, 48, 208, 311–12 (n. 85), 312 (n. 90), 336–37 (n. 131); Africanness of Brazilian culture and, 86, 87, 94, 128, 137, 141–42, 327–28 (n. 121); call for confederation of black organizations, 94–95, 99; coverage of people of color abroad, 46, 66, 311–12 (n. 85), 336–37 (n. 131); emergence of, early twentieth century, 18, 24, 29, 34–40; European immigrants, debate over in, 56–57, 59–64, 99–100, 109, 110, 129, 132, 133–34, 135–36, 309

38, 98, 186, 308 (n. 29), 310 (nn. 56, 58); cross-racial sexual intimacies and, 6–7, 11, 76, 80, 90, 113, 255; suffrage, 131, 153, 325 (n. 69). *See also* Candomblé; Wet-nurses of African descent

Worker's Party, 299

World Conference on Racism (2001), 301–2

World War I, 77, 83

World War II, 151, 153, 164, 182

Wretched of the Earth (Fanon), 259, 287

Xangô, 225, 226

Yoruba culture, 117, 263, 293; African contact and, 224, 225, 226–27, 236; anthropology and, 121, 122, 124; Candomblé ritual and, 119, 123–24, 125, 126, 127; FESTAC II and, 252, 253; Ilê Aiyê carnival group and, 284, 285; superiority and purity of, 123, 127; teaching of, 231, 232

Zumbi, 137, 140, 273, 274

FSC
www.fsc.org

MIX
Paper from
responsible sources
FSC® C013483